INN SPOTS

*By
Nancy and
Richard Woodworth*

& MID-ATLANTIC NEW YORK/VA.
SPECIAL PLACES

*A guide to
where to go,
stay, eat and
enjoy in 32
of the region's
choicest areas.*

Wood Pond Press
West Hartford, Conn.

The authors have personally visited the places included in this book. They make their recommendations based on their experiences and findings, and there is no solicitation or charge for inclusion.

Prices, hours and menu offerings at inns and restaurants change seasonally and with business conditions. Readers should call or write ahead to avoid disappointment. The prices and hours reported in this book were correct at presstime and are subject, of course, to change. They are offered as a relative guide to what to expect. Rates quoted for inns are for peak periods; weekdays and off-season periods may be lower. They are for bed and breakfast, unless otherwise specified (MAP, Modified American Plan, breakfast and dinner; EP, European Plan, no meals).

The authors welcome readers' reactions and suggestions.

Cover Design by Bob Smith the Artsmith.

Cover Photo by Nancy Woodworth: Cape May porches from The Mainstay Inn, Cape May, N.J.

Graphics by Jay Woodworth

Contents

Introduction

This is yet another inn book. But it's far more than that, too.

We enjoy reading all the others, but they rarely tell us what we *really* want to know, such as where to get a good meal and what there is to do. And the inns often are not grouped by location, so you don't get a feeling for what the area is like. We've found that out by talking with innkeepers, reading all the local guides and brochures, visiting tourist bureaus and Chambers of Commerce, and poring through the local newspapers.

That's what we now share with you. We start not with the inn but with the area (of course, the existence of inns or lack thereof helped determine the areas to be included). We sought out 32 extra-special areas, some of them the Mid-Atlantic's best-known and some not widely known at all.

Then we toured each area, visiting the inns, the restaurants and the attractions, as well as drawing on our experiences and memories of more than 35 years of living in and vacationing in New York and the Mid-Atlantic. We *worked* these areas as roving journalists, always seeking out the best and most interesing. We also *lived* them – staying in, eating in, and experiencing as many places as time and budget would allow.

The result is this book, a comprehensive yet selective compendium of what we found to be the best and most interesting places to stay, eat and enjoy in these 32 special areas.

The book reflects our tastes. We want creature comforts like private bathrooms and comfortable reading areas in our rooms; we like to meet other inn guests, but we also value our privacy. We seek interesing and creative food and pleasant settings for our meals. We enjoy unusual, enlightening things to do and places to see. We expect to receive value for money and time spent.

While touring the past year to research this book as well as the fourth edition of its companion, *Inn Spots & Special Places in New England,* we were surprised by how many innkeepers said we were among the few guidebook writers who ever visited their facility and did not simply expect them to fill out a form and forward it with a considerable fee.

We also were struck – as we have been while preparing our other books – by how times and places change. In general, inns and B&Bs seem to be a newer, more contemporary phenomenon in the Mid-Atlantic region than in New England. Some of the inns and restaurants that were "in" a decade or so ago have faded, their places taken by any number of newcomers not yet widely known. We're fortunate that our newspaper training and tight deadlines make this book as up-to-date as its 1995 publication date.

Yes, the schedule is hectic and we do keep busy on these, our working vacations that everyone thinks must be glamorous and nothing but fun. One of us says she never again wants to get up in the middle of the night having forgotten where the bathroom is. The other doesn't care if he never eats another truffle.

Nonetheless, it's rewarding to discover a little-known inn, to savor a great meal, to enjoy a choice musuem, to poke through an unusual store and to meet so many interesting people along the way.

That's what this book is all about. We hope that you will enjoy its findings as much as we did the finding.

Nancy and Richard Woodworth

About the Authors

Nancy Webster Woodworth began her travel and dining experiences in her native Montreal and as a waitress in summer resorts across Canada during her McGill University years. She worked in London and hitchhiked through Europe on $3 a day before her marriage to Richard Woodworth, whom she met while skiing at Mont Tremblant. They lived for the first ten years of their marriage in upstate New York and became familiar with the Mid-Atlantic during trips to visit his brother in Baltimore and his parents in Lynchburg and Smith Mountain Lake, Va. She started writing her "Roaming the Restaurants" column for the West Hartford (Conn.) News in 1972. That led to half of the book, *Daytripping & Dining in Southern New England,* written in collaboration with Betsy Wittemann in 1978. She since has co-authored *Inn Spots & Special Places in New England, Weekending in New England, Getaways for Gourmets in the Northeast, Waterside Escapes in the Northeast,* and *The Restaurants of New England.* She and her husband have two grown sons and live in West Hartford.

Richard Woodworth has been an inveterate traveler since his youth in suburban Syracuse, N.Y., where his birthday outings often involved train trips with friends for the day to nearby Utica or Rochester. After graduation from Middlebury College, he was a reporter for newspapers in Syracuse, Jamestown, Geneva and Rochester before moving to Connecticut to become editor of the West Hartford News and eventually executive editor of Imprint Newspapers. With his wife and their sons, he has traveled to the four corners of this country, Canada and portions of Europe, writing their findings for newspapers and magazines. With his wife, he has co-authored three editions *of Inn Spots & Special Places in New England* and *Getaways for Gourmets in the Northeast,* as well as *The Restaurants of New England.* Between travels and duties as publisher of Wood Pond Press, he tries to find time to weed the garden in summer and ski in the winter.

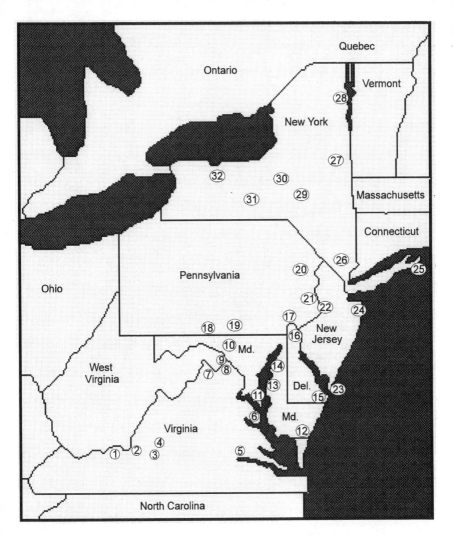

1. Hot Springs
2. Staunton
3. Charlottesville
4. Orange
5. James River
6. Northern Neck
7. Washington
8. Loudoun County
9. Harpers Ferry
10. Frederick
11. Solomons
12. Snow Hill/Berlin
13. St. Michaels
14. Chestertown
15. Lewes
16. New Castle
17. Chadds Ford
18. Gettysburg
19. Lancaster County
20. Canadensis
21. Bucks County
22. Lambertville
23. Cape May
24. Spring Lake
25. East Hampton
26. Cold Spring
27. Saratoga Springs
28. Westport/Essex
29. Cooperstown
30. Cazenovia
31. Ithaca
32. Canandaigua

Championship golf courses are among attractions at The Homestead.

Hot Springs, Va.
The Lure of the Baths

Since the days of Washington and Jefferson, the warm medicinal springs that emanate from the valleys of the Allegheny Highlands have lured the nation's elite. Their curative powers and social importance are legendary, having spawned two of America's world-class resorts, The Homestead at Hot Springs and The Greenbrier in White Sulphur Springs, W.Va.

This remarkably scenic area tucked between mountain ridges along the Virginia-West Virginia border offers much for today's visitor. You can soak in the "baths" in the same structures that Thomas Jefferson and Mrs. Robert E. Lee did. You can revel in contemporary spa treatments that would do California proud. You can play golf on some of the world's most challenging and scenic courses. You can partake of the good life at the Homestead and the Greenbrier.

You also can bask in one of the most picturesque, unspoiled regions we know. Verdant mountains, idyllic valleys, backroads hamlets, untrafficked byways and an exhilarating climate are the draws. Ninety percent of Bath County – so named because its warm waters reminded the earliest settlers of those in Bath, England – is forested. And half of that is part of the George Washington National Forest. The entire county has neither an incorporated town nor a traffic light. About the only signs of commercialism – and they're a lovely, colorful touch – are the trademark wildlife mailboxes donated to every Bath County homeowner by the local Bacova Guild Factory. The guild exports them to paying, fashionable boxholders across the country.

What this area offers are endless tranquility and rural pleasures, from walks to waterfalls. Its mountain air yields cool, restorative summer days and nights, as well as

1

long springtimes and spectacular autumns (the fall foliage outshines even the showy redbud and dogwood that light up the hillsides in spring). Small inns and B&Bs contrast nicely in scale and price with the grand resorts, and their guests can take advantage of Homestead and Greenbrier facilities.

Even those ensconced at one of the resorts (and paying dearly for the privilege) should get out and about to enjoy fully a region of uncommon beauty. If you're staying at The Homestead, visit The Greenbrier for lunch, or vice-versa. Stay at one of the smaller inns or B&Bs and the money you save will allow you to do both.

Some people do energetic things, like hiking, fishing and golfing. Others never get beyond the front veranda or backyard hammock.

Inn Spots

The Homestead, Hot Springs 24445. (703) 839-1766 or (800) 838-1766.

The Homestead and Hot Springs have been synonymous, ever since the first hotel was built around the hot springs in 1766. In fact, The Homestead *is* Hot Springs, its presence dominating the small community in every respect. The hotel exudes tradition and grandeur, Southern style.

Although the Homestead was becoming a tad frayed at the edges, change happily is at hand. After a decade of losing money and reportedly near bankruptcy in late 1993, the oldest family-run resort in the world entered into a joint venture with the Dallas-based Club Resorts Inc., one of the nation's leading owner/operators of golf and conference resorts. The result was a new management team and $7 million of renovations in the first year alone. An investment of nearly $25 million more was planned over the next four years to "restore this grand dame of American resorts to the splendid glory it has boasted for more than 200 years," in the words of new president Gary K. Rosenberg. Club Resorts, which is known for its turnaround of North Carolina's Pinehurst golf resort, is to assume sole ownership by 1999.

The Homestead's setting is stupendous. The landmark hotel tower is the only real break in 15,000 privately owned acres of Allegheny Mountains and valleys. The 521 rooms, most in low-rise wings, look out onto hillsides and golf fairways. Most are spacious and have all the amenities. Our parlor suite at the far end of what the staff calls "the older and more elegant" West Wing had a loveseat and two side chairs, a writing desk, a console TV, a kingsize bed, no fewer than four telephones and a full-length, screened veranda big enough to seat a party of twenty. Extra touches included European percale sheets, good reading lights, maid service twice daily, a walk-in closet that lighted up automatically and nightly turndown service with chocolates on the pillows.

Such amenities as turndown service were a holdover of the days when old-name families like the Vanderbilts arrived with their trunks for the summer. Turndown and bedtime chocolates are available only upon request now as the new management concentrates on things that are more important to today's visitor. Explains Gary Rosenberg: "We're positioning The Homestead as a 4½-star property as opposed to a five-star property because that's what the guest wants."

Today's guests are still greeted in the majestic Great Hall, where af-

ternoon tea is accompanied by live music and guests mingle at all hours in a living-room setting. They play tennis on fifteen courts, swim in three pools, bowl on eight lanes, dance during dinner and take in a movie in the theater afterward. In winter, they ski at the South's first ski area.

As he has since 1962, European executive chef Albert Schnarwyler oversees the production of 3,000 meals a day in a variety of venues (see Dining Spots).

The original hot springs are incorporated into The Homestead's European-style spa, built in 1892 and undergoing a state-of-the-art renovation in 1995 and 1996. Their 104-degree waters provide a variety of treatments from $15 for a mineral tub bath to $25 for a combination bath. The Homestead also operates the original baths at Warm Springs.

An even greater attraction is the golf on three championship eighteen-hole courses (see Diversions).

The new look at The Homestead was becoming evident at our 1994 visit, and both guests and staff were decidedly upbeat. The entire East Wing with 86 guest rooms was being refurbished, the hotel's main floor received new carpeting (long a sticky point with the AAA rating inspectors who awarded The Homestead four diamonds as opposed to the coveted five), the dining room was upgraded and acquired a handsome new wine room with a signature stained-glass window, and major improvements were made to the golf facilities. Landscapers have added thousands of flowers to the grounds. The Casino, located between the spa building and hotel, was converted into a sports shop and a casual, indoor/outdoor grill. The old Tower Lounge was transformed into a richly paneled library and museum, where longtime resort publicist John M. Gazzola Jr. – known to generations of Homesteaders – has put together quite a collection of Homestead photos and memorabilia.

As Johnny gave us yet another tour, guests and staff alike constantly interrupted him to say hello. The Homestead's warm and personal tradition continues.

Doubles, $245 to $320, EP; $335 to $410, MAP.

The Greenbrier, White Sulphur Springs, W.Va. 24986. (304) 536-1110 or (800) 624-6070.

If the Homestead is the grand dame of genteel Southern tradition, The Greenbrier just across the West Virginia border is the vivacious debutante – or maybe post-debutante, for surely this five-star, five-diamond resort has come of age. The Greenbrier is new money rather than old, corporate-owned rather than family-run (as The Homestead had been until lately), glittering and eye-popping. Where it lacks the scenic setting of The Homestead, it compensates with spectacular landscaping and flowers. Splashes of vivid colors and chintzes in the Dorothy Draper style make the interiors of its Virginia counterpart look a bit drab. Its three eighteen-hole golf courses are not quite so highly rated as The Homestead's, but the new Spa, Mineral Baths and Salon building is state-of-the-art. In fact, everything at The Greenbrier is up to date and spiffy, and not in any under-stated way.

Horses await at The Greenbrier entrance.

Here you'll ogle an indoor pool to end all pools with a billowing white sailcloth above, peach-hued walls and wicker furniture all around. Pause at the bar for "healthy-living drinks" made of whole fruit. The black and white marble floors of the Georgian lobby reflect the sunlight from sixteen-foot windows and french doors dressed in the brilliant florals that made Draper and protégé Carleton Varney, who decorated The Greenbrier, famous. The entry lobby gives way to a succession of smaller lobbies and living rooms, each a study in interior design. From wallpaper to china, Draper's signature rhododendrons accent the columned dining room (see Dining Spots). Crystal chandeliers contrast with pecky wood walls and are a sight to behold in the Old White Club, the deluxe lounge named for the former hotel on the site, called the Old White. Draper's Cafe serves informal meals of cutting-edge cuisine. Such grandeur prompted columnist Elsa Maxwell to write, upon the hotel's reopening after service as a military hospital in World War II: "The Greenbrier is perhaps the most beautiful hotel in the world."

The public spaces tend to overshadow the 650 guest rooms, including 49 suites and 69 cottages, all decorated in the Dorothy Draper style and no two exactly alike. Draperies and wallpapers are color-coordinated and the refreshment center in each room matches the furniture. Our room, more spacious than most we saw, was most comfortable and provided every amenity but was not as superlative as the public facilities. We admit we did not visit the fourteen-room Presidential Suite that covers two floors.

Always upgrading, The Greenbrier now offers LaVarenne at The Greenbrier, bringing in its French founder to supplement the original resort cooking school founded in 1977. The adjacent Greenbrier Clinic performs complete health diagnostic evaluations. The Gallery of Shops on the lower level includes some of the fanciest we've seen, and makes you wonder how they manage to stay open with only a limited, though captive, audience.

A veteran staff of 1,600 (average tenure: thirteen years) caters to the needs of guests, who number no more than 1,400 at a time. The clientele here appears to be as rich as the facility, but as hotel historian Robert Conte pointed out during a tour, guests "stay as long as the money holds out – it used to be weeks, and now it's usually days."

Doubles, $396 to $496, MAP.

The Inn at Gristmill Square, Box 359, Warm Springs 24484. (703) 839-2231.

This good-looking complex of guest rooms, recreation facilities, a store and a restaurant resembles a small village and, indeed, is the biggest enterprise in the dear little hamlet of Warm Springs (population, 250, and every building redone in the last few years, according to innkeeper Janice McWilliams). Former owners of a ski lodge in Vermont, the McWilliams family took over this going concern in 1981 and have continued to expand.

Sixteen guest rooms are scattered in four 19th-century buildings around an old gristmill that now houses a good restaurant (see Dining Spots). Rooms vary widely in size and decor. Each has antique furnishings, TVs, refrigerators, hair dryers and phones, and half have fireplaces. One is called the Silo for obvious reasons, and the Tower Apartment has a round living room and a fantastic tin chandelier. New in the Blacksmith Shop containing the inn's office are a Loft Room with kingsize bed and deck and the Spring Suite with a living room, a jacuzzi tub and a queensize bed in the bedroom, which opens to a private patio beside babbling Warm Spring Run. We liked the Board Room, cozy and dark in barnwood with two double beds and a clawfoot tub. Others are partial to the extravagant Singapore Room and its two-part bathroom, one part being a tub in a niche behind a screen.

A country flavor prevails in the adjacent Miller's House, which offers two rooms

Meadow Lane Lodge is centerpiece of a rural, sixteen-acre farm estate.

and two suites. Four smaller rooms are across the street in the Steel House, close to the pool, a small sauna and three tennis courts. One hundred miles of walking and riding trails surround the property.

In the morning, Mrs. McWilliams delivers a picnic basket to each room. It contains juice, coffee and breads, plus the day's Richmond Times-Dispatch.

Doubles, $80 to $95 B&B, $155 to $165 MAP.

Meadow Lane Lodge, Star Route A, Box 110, Warm Springs 24484. (703) 839-5959.

The rural tranquility that is this area's main allure is perhaps nowhere more alluring than at Meadow Lane Lodge. Retired gentleman-farmer Philip Hirsh and his wife Catherine offer nine rooms with private baths in their lodge and two cottages on a 1,600-acre estate complete with fishing streams, fields and woods. A big white barn is full of exotic animals, from peacocks to nubian goats.

Set well back from Route 39 at the end of a long driveway, the accommodations are spacious and luxurious in a country-manor kind of way. Fireplaces at either end, antiques, sofas and a big table full of magazines attract guests to the lodge's long common room. The lodge offers a kingsize suite, an upstairs suite with sitting area and a screened porch and, most in demand, a small room with a corner porch affording the best view. The Snuggery, with a loveseat and TV tucked beneath the eaves, attests to the owner's knack for architectural design. Furnishings are a mix of items from the Hirshes' travels. He is the third generation of a thoroughbred horse-breeding family (his father was the author of Yale's "Boola Boola"), and when here in summer he and his wife occupy the main house next to a swimming pool (available to guests by invitation).

Near the lodge, Craig's Cottage contains a suite with a small kitchen and living room, plus a fireplaced room with a kingsize bed and a bay window. The Car Barn has two more contemporary bedrooms sharing a living room.

Resident innkeepers Cheryl and Steve Hooley manage the place for owner Hirsch, who now is fully retired. A true Southerner, he trained the breakfast chef to continue the tradition. Expect things like curried scrambled eggs, sweet pea omelets, creamed turkey and chicken, batter bread and fried grits, many of the ingredients coming from the farm. The meal is taken in a sunny breakfast room at tables set with floral mats.

Outside are a tennis court, a croquet court, the owners' pool, fifteen miles of walking trails and the Jackson River, two private miles of which pass through the property. You can swim there, fish or go canoeing. A favorite spot is a wooden deck, built atop a cliff overlooking a slough and the river bottom below. Guests take cocktails and even picnic suppers here to watch the beaver, deer, herons, ospreys and such. Few can resist stopping in the barn to check out Harvey the donkey, Mrs. Hirsh's favorite, who bunks with Nelson the horse. You'll hear guinea hens squawking and geese honking. Peacocks and Japanese silkies, a type of chicken with black skin and white feathers, parade about.

The Hirshs conceived, built and operated the Inn at Gristmill Square in Warm Springs before selling it in 1981 to concentrate on their home property. They retain two cottages for guests in Warm Springs.

Doubles, $115; suites, $125; cottages, $145.

King's Victorian Inn, Route 220, Hot Springs 24445. (703) 839-3134.

Atop a sloping lawn, this turreted Victorian house with a wraparound veranda overlooks the Homestead golf course. Inside, all is crisp and country elegant, with none of the clutter and darkness often associated with the period. "I like it light and airy," explains ex-Richmonder Liz King, innkeeper with her husband Richard, who is with the U.S. Postal Service in Staunton.

They have decorated six guest rooms, four with private baths, in traditional Williamsburg colors against a backdrop of reproduction antiques. A solid mahogany Charleston rice bed graces one room with two sitting areas, one in a sunny alcove over the living room, and a bath with a double vanity and colored soaps arrayed in a wicker basket. Another room, pretty in teal and rose, has a step-up bed and a wicker sitting area. A third room, done in lilacs and pinks, shares a bath with the Victorian Room, which contains a porch-like nook, a fireplace and a sitting area with a double bed. Two bedrooms on the third floor share a bath and a sitting area beneath a colorful glass ceiling.

The Kings offer cottage accommodations in an adjacent former ice house. It comes with a deck, an efficiency kitchen, a sofa and TV, plus an upstairs bedroom with a queen bed and a shower bath. In 1995, they acquired a duplex cottage next to the Homestead's Cascades Inn and were in the process of refurbishing to add more guest accommodations. Each side of the duplex contains two bedrooms, a kitchen and living area and a porch.

Public areas in the main inn include a second-floor garden room with wicker and TV, a smashing living room with a mauve carpet, two enormous sectional sofas dressed in a yellow floral print and a card table in a sun room alcove, and an elegant parlor with a white sofa, two rose wing chairs and an oriental rug. A raised fireplace with three stained-glass windows above, silver service on the sideboard and an 18th-century reproduction Chippendale table and chairs enhance the dining room. A piano is tucked in a hallway alcove beneath the stairway.

A full breakfast might include sausage and eggs with homefries, fried apples and coffee cake. Afternoon refreshments include tea, crackers and cheese.

Doubles, $85 to $95; cottage, $110; two-bedroom cottages, $140.

Guests at King's Victorian Inn enjoy turrets and wraparound porch.

Vine Cottage Inn, Route 220, Box 918, Hot Springs 24445. (703) 839-2422 or (800) 666-8463.

"We're the next best thing to the Homestead," says Wendell Lucas of his B&B just a stone's throw away. Most of the resort facilities are available to his guests on a fee basis, as they are to Homestead guests who are not on package plans. Here you can pay for golf, horseback riding, bowling, the spa and meals and enjoy the Homestead experience at a fraction of the price.

In 1984, Wendell and his wife Pat purchased the house, which had been a lodging facility since 1905. Both valley natives, they returned after service with the Air Force in Europe and four years with Westinghouse in Saudi Arabia to give their teenage daughters a home base. They added their personal touches, adapting "late Victorian to country comfortable," in Wendell's words. There's a big TV in the comfy sitting room full of books. At the other side of the entry is a large, fireplaced dining room in red and blue with bentwood chairs at tables topped with quilted mats.

Upstairs are nine guest rooms with private baths, plus a bunkroom for families and two dormitory rooms. One of the dorm rooms has five beds done up in blue for men and the other has four beds in pink for women. Biggest rooms are on the third floor, where the Red Room sports a colorful quilt on a queensize bed and the Honeymoon/Anniversary Room on the end has a kingsize bed covered in lace, framed anniversary cards, wedding photos of the hosts and a statue of a kissing couple.

The Lucases are famous for their homemade sticky buns, a favorite at breakfast, which also includes cereals and fruits. Full breakfasts can be arranged and are popular with ski groups, who also can be served dinner.

Doubles, $55 to $85; dormitory rooms, $25 per bed.

Hidden Valley Bed & Breakfast, Hidden Valley Road, Warm Springs 24484. (703) 839-3178.

Hidden in the back of beyond beside the Jackson River, three roundabout miles west of Warm Springs, is this many-dimensioned treasure that was the setting in 1992 for the movie "Sommersby." Hidden Valley is at once a small and historically true antebellum B&B, an ongoing archaeological dig, a teaching site, and a wilderness mecca for hikers and trout fishermen. It's also quite a story.

The story begins more than 9,000 years ago with the Indians; the resident archaeologist and college students have catalogued thousands of artifacts from the area. Fast forward to 1848 when Bath County Judge James Warwick began construction of Warwickton, one of the finest Greek Revival mansions in western Virginia. After being a hunt club, a school and a hay barn, it eventually fell into disrepair. Fast forward to 1965, when the George Washington National Forest acquired the 6,400-acre tract for recreational purposes but had no use for the mansion, which is listed on the National Register of Historical Places. Enter Pam and Ron Stidham from Ohio, who had fallen in love with the place in 1978. "I wanted a brick house with a babbling brook and Ron wanted a house in the mountains with solitude," recalls Pam. "We got the best of both worlds here."

They also got more than they bargained for. It took years of pleading and bureaucratic maneuvering for the Stidhams to persuade the U.S. Forest Service to lease them the house and issue a special-use permit to run a B&B. The unprecedented agreement allowed the Stidhams to operate a commercial venture for 30 years in return for restoring the structure and opening it to the public for tours. They moved in 1990 into a house "in dire need of massive restoration."

Some of the restoration coincided with the filming of "Sommersby," which required an antebellum mansion and a 360-degree panorama without a sign of modern civilization. The moviemakers built a set of eighteen structures (only two of which are left), but also delayed the Stidhams' plans for opening. They could do no restoration work during the six months of production, and then spent months returning the mansion to the condition it was in before the film crews arrived. Meticulous to a fault, Pam stripped off nine coats of paint that a set artist had applied to one fireplace mantel for a faded marble look because it was not the color used when the house was built. Her work was continually interrupted by sightseers who stopped to visit the interpretive center in the new, film-built summer kitchen and to visit the mansion (tours by appointment, $4).

"People said we were crazy," Pam recalled, "but all this work was worth it. You just sit out on one of the porches and you'll realize it." Pam and Ron, who works full-time for the Virginia Department of Corrections, opened their B&B in mid-1993. They offer three spacious, antiques-filled bedrooms, served by three private baths in a special bath and laundry wing. They also offer fine formal furnishings and antiques collected over 25 years and displayed in "a house that tells a story as it unfolds," according to Pam. Guests enjoy a Music Room and a high Victorian parlor, which holds an 1844 square grand piano. A formal dining room is the setting for a full breakfast, including fresh fruit, banana or zucchini bread and perhaps a five-cheese egg strata. There are a couple of porches and a gazebo for taking in the utter stillness and marvel of it all. "When you enter the valley," as Pam says, "you leave the world behind."

There's really no choice. Hidden Valley is not just a B&B. It's a way of life.
Doubles, $79 to $85. No smoking. No credit cards.

The Anderson Cottage, Old Germantown Road, Box 176, Warm Springs 24484. (703) 839-2975.

A two-story-high, wraparound veranda distinguishes this rambling house whose

Hidden Valley Bed & Breakfast provides historic plantation experience.

original four rooms were an 18th-century tavern. It then was a girls' school and an inn, and now is a private home-turned-B&B with two houses joined together. Jean Randolph Bruns, whose family has owned it since the 1870s, often is asked to open it for tours for Homestead guests.

She offers a first-floor suite with a queensize bed, well-worn oriental rugs, a huge fireplaced parlor and the only modern bath in the house. Upstairs is a second suite with a queen bed, a parlor with a twin bed and a wicker sitting area, and a clawfoot tub. A bedroom with a queensize bed comes with private bath. A large end room with beamed ceilings, working fireplace and a double and a single bed has a shared bath. A fifth large bedroom is seldom rented – "it's my museum room and pulls everything together on my historical tours," says Jean. With exposed chestnut log walls, it contains a little desk from the time it was a school, old textbooks and a museum-quality quilt of home-spun, hand-stitched French fabric on the double bed. Out back is an 1820s brick kitchen cottage with two bedrooms and a fireplaced kitchen-dining room.

Guests pick out a mug from a huge collection and help themselves to coffee in the country kitchen, the only room in the house without a fireplace because it started as a porch. Breakfast, taken at a long table in the dining room, might include sausage, cheese strata and apples baked with brown sugar. The guest parlor opens onto the veranda, where church pews and rockers overlook two pleasant acres. The stream out back flows from the warm springs pools and is so tepid that "my grandchildren think all mountain streams must be warm," Jean reports.

Doubles, $60 to $110. No smoking. Closed December to early March.

Hummingbird Inn, Wood Lane, Box 147, Goshen 24439. (703) 997-9065 or (800) 397-3214.

Their children grown, Diana and Jeremy Robinson decided to chuck their high-pressure careers in 1993 for a lifestyle change in the Shenandoah Valley. Jerry had been an editor-in-chief and book publisher in New York and British-born Diana had been a registered nurse when they met up with the aborted Rose Hummingbird Inn, which had variously been an inn, boarding house or a residence since 1853. They set out to upgrade guest rooms, add more rooms and serve meals of distinction in a destination inn just west of Goshen Pass, a spectacular gorge favored by fishermen, hikers and picnickers.

Nearly a dozen hummingbird feeders surround the unusual fourteen-room Victorian Carpenter Gothic villa located along a residential street. The birds are on view from

Hummingbird Inn occupies unusual Victorian Carpenter Gothic villa.

the front-corner solarium as well as the two-story verandas that wrap around part of the main structure built in 1853. Guests also enjoy an elegant, chandeliered parlor with a fireplace and a rustic, paneled and beamed den with a fireplace, located in a section of the house dating to 1780.

The Robinsons started with four bedrooms with private baths, each equipped with ceiling fans, natural-fiber linens, down comforters, fine antiques and handsome scatter rugs on the polished wood floors. The Eleanor Room appears much as it did when Eleanor Roosevelt slept here in 1935; its antique bird's-eye maple bedroom set includes a unique serpentine-front dresser, vanity and chaise lounge. Deciding to stick with the names of presidents or their wives, the Robinsons created the Franklin Room with a queensize, rice-carved four-poster canopy bed and a mahogany Empire chest. Another serpentine-front oak dresser graces the Abigail Room with its queensize brass bed. In early 1995, Jeremy applied his construction talents to installing a gas fireplace and a jacuzzi in the largest Martha Room with a corner sitting area. He also was creating another bedroom with private bath on the main floor, and hoped to have a sixth ready later in the year. Plans called for four more deluxe bedrooms with fireplaces, jacuzzis and kitchenettes on the second floor of the old barn that was once the Goshen livery.

Guests are welcomed with tea and English shortbread, served on antique Meissen china in the parlor. By reservation, Diana cooks a four-course dinner ($27.50 prix-fixe, with complimentary wine). A typical meal includes potato and roasted garlic soup with orange-pepper puree, a mixed salad dressed with raspberry vinaigrette and a choice of two main courses, always filet mignon and perhaps salmon en croûte, chicken with porcini mushrooms or smoked rabbit on linguini carbonara. Dessert could be a lemon tart or chocolate mousse terrine.

Breakfasts are bountiful. Start with fresh fruit or fruit compote, homemade muffins, raisin scones and rose-geranium bread. The main course could be omelets, cornmeal pancakes or french toast baked in honey and cinnamon, with bacon, ham or sausage. Jerry, a connoisseur of such things, grinds and blends his own coffee.

Doubles, $70 to $95. No smoking.

Three Hills, Box 9, Warm Springs 24484. (703) 839-5381.

Built in 1913 as a residence by early feminist novelist Mary Johnston, this is a stunner – a large mansion occupying a hilltop site with a wondrous view of the Warm Springs Gap and the Alleghenies beyond. It's also shrouded in mystery, as far as the community is concerned.

The novelist and her sisters operated the mansion as an inn, and a subsequent owner turned it into apartments. In 1984, a German woman purchased it and spent millions restoring it to its former status as an inn, which never measured up to its potential. She finally sold it in 1994 to Charlene and Doug Fike from Indiana and Joy and Doug Adams from Ohio, principals with two other couples. All are longtime friends, parents of young children and members of Mennonite or Brethren churches.

The Fikes and the Adamses moved to Three Hills and planned to build homes on the 38-acre property. They also built a fitness center with an outdoor hot tub and a small conference center. Charlene wanted to continue her career of leading training sessions for small businesses and Doug, as executive director of a Mennonite organization, planned retreats for clergymen of various faiths. "We were both on the road traveling in separate directions and decided it was time for a change," Charlene said. "We wanted to pick a spot where instead of us going out all the time, people would come to us."

A more beautiful spot is hard to imagine. And the religious connection is mere coincidence, the Fikes stressed. They set to work renovating and redecorating the entire inn, a task they expected to complete by the spring of 1995. After that, they planned to serve dinners to inn guests and the public, as had their predecessors.

The new owners inherited most of the heavy, European-style furnishings in the rambling main house and four older cottages. They lightened up the decor and modernized some of the bathrooms. The twelve guest rooms in the main house still show their apartment heritage. They range from "hotel rooms" with double and twin beds to one-bedroom junior suites with separate living room or kitchen to full master suites with one or two bedrooms, living room with fireplace and a kitchen (only six rooms do not have kitchens). All have private baths and color TV. The second-floor Birch Suite in front includes a formal living room with fireplace, kingsize bed, a huge mirrored armoire and a deck on the roof. The rear Dogwood junior suite, with a kingsize bed and twin sleeper sofas in the living room, overlooks the English boxwood garden.

A full breakfast is served in the dining room. Fresh fruit and muffins precede a main courses of fruit crêpes, puffed apple pancakes, stuffed french toast or individual omelets. Afternoon tea is served on weekends.

Families with children are welcome, and the inn's new brochure promotes Three Hills as an environmentally conscious "green inn."

Doubles, $65 to $95; suites and cottages, $110 to $145.

Dining Spots

The Greenbrier, White Sulphur Springs, W.Va. (304) 536-1110.

The dining experience at The Greenbrier is as extravagant as everything else about this world-class resort. Most guests take dinner in the handsome **Main Dining Room,** a long space notable for enormous artworks on its pink walls, crystal chandeliers and arched windows onto the gardens. It's nicely broken up by columns, dividers and a

Contemporary cuisine is offered in Main Dining Room at The Greenbrier.

center platform where a pianist and violinist entertain nightly. Vichyssoise and a famous dessert of peaches and cream are traditional favorites. Everything is prepared from scratch by the 120 chefs, many of whom received their training through The Greenbrier's Culinary Apprentice Program instituted in 1957 to ensure the resort an ample supply of quality chefs. The short MAP menu changes daily and is contemporary as can be. Start perhaps with corn and oyster chowder or an appetizer of blackened quail with grilled marinated vegetables and orzo pesto, and a spinach and arugula salad with marinated tomatoes and black olives. Main courses range from smoked arctic char with saffron seafood risotto to grilled veal filet with crayfish and lentil chili to roast leg of lamb with roasted garlic spoonbread. Dinner nightly by reservation, 7 to 9.

Want a different experience? Head for the dark and masculine **Tavern Room,** where a $31.50 supplement brings a five-course dinner beneath silver domes. Cooking is at open rotisseries and the cuisine is contemporary, as in an appetizer of honey-smoked breast of pheasant with marinated peppers and warm cilantro potato salad or an entrée of charbroiled veal T-bone steak with morel cream sauce and a roasted barley pilaf.

Colorful in rose, white wicker and chintz, **Draper's Cafe** serves à la carte breakfast and lunch. For a mid-day treat, one of us enjoyed black bean soup topped artistically with jalapeño pepper and sour cream ($3) and a cobb salad ($9.75) that unfortunately was tossed instead of composed in the traditional style. The other had an excellent seared salmon steak with green and red tomato salsa, sweet California mustard and salad greens ($11.50) and the specialty dessert, a Greenbrier peach on rum-raisin ice cream topped with blackberry sauce ($5.25). Breakfast, 7 to 11:30; lunch, 11:30 to 6.

The elaborate Sunday buffet jazz brunch ($25.25) is a popular tradition at **The Greenbrier Golf Club Dining Room,** where lunch entrées are priced in the $10 to $15 range and a five-course dinner is $29.50 extra for registered guests, $75 for the public. Lunch on the Porch, 11:30 to 2:30; Sunday brunch, 11:30 to 3; dinner, 7 to 10.

Food and drinks also are available in the **Ryder Cup Grille Room,** the **Old White Club** and the **Rhododendron Pool Lounge.**

The Homestead, Hot Springs. (703) 839-1766.

"You eat at The Greenbrier and you dine at The Homestead," we were advised by several of the latter's admirers – and they are legion.

The Main Dining Room is an L-shaped, football field-size expanse of the old school (lately enhanced with french doors and greenery to serve as room partitions). At dinner, a band was playing for dancing as we gazed out at a sea of white tables and hovering staff. The dinner menu, somewhat pedestrian and passé at our first visit, has been elevated with the elimination of such traditional fixtures as tomato juice, vichyssoise and omelets. Now, along with the tried and true, the night's menu (available prix-fixe to the public for $36) might yield innovations like an appetizer of carpaccio of pork with dill-mustard sauce, a salad of belgian endive on mesclun with herbed cheese and taro root chips, and a main course of grilled ginger-marinated sea scallops, shrimp and swordfish with Turkish saffron rice and wilted spinach.

We were well satisfied with appetizers of smoked salmon and supreme of lump crabmeat and shrimp, and watercress salads on radicchio with jicama julienne. One of us had roast prime tenderloin with armagnac sauce, green peppercorns and grapes, served on a small plate with ratatouille and macaire potato. The other chose saltimbocca, accompanied by side plates of belgian endive au parmesan and puree of carrots. For dessert we tried good homemade cappuccino ice cream served over crushed ice in a silver bowl and a crème de menthe parfait like those we remember from ancient days.

The pride of The Homestead is **The Grille,** a handsome room with huge windows onto the golf course, where we had a delicious breakfast buffet the next day. From the table with a fantastic array of fresh fruits (including gigantic strawberries, mangoes and kumquats) to the hot dishes of creamed beef, broiled fish, eggs and grits, it was a Southern treat to be remembered. Nothing exotic, mind you, except for some of the fruits, but wholesome and old-fashioned. We found the dinner menu here more interesting than that of the dining room, and the former surcharge for MAP guests has been eliminated. Dinner entrées for the public are priced from $16.50 for grilled tropical marinated paillard of chicken with black bean salsa, steamed rice and fried plantains to $29.50 for dover sole sautéed in olive oil with garlic and lemon zest. Dinner is served here Tuesday-Saturday from 7 to 10, April-October.

Light fare is available seasonally in the casual new indoor-outdoor 19th-hole grill at the old Casino. Golfers are partial to eating in the **Cascades Club Restaurant** or the **Lower Cascades Clubhouse Restaurant.** The Homestead also operates **Cafe Albert** and **Sam Snead's Tavern** (see below), which are popular with the public as well.

The Homestead's new management has changed hours of operations of most of its restaurants, especially early in the week and in the off-season, according to the number of guests. Visitors are advised to call ahead for specific hours.

The Waterwheel Restaurant, The Inn at Gristmill Square, Warm Springs. (703) 839-2231.

Fed by Warm Spring Run, the old waterwheel rotates constantly outside this 1900 gristmill, now transformed into an appealing restaurant with barnwood walls, beamed ceilings and ladderback chairs at tables on different levels. Gears and cogs of the gristmill are still in evidence, but free-standing candles, fresh flowers, linens and service plates emblazoned with a waterwheel logo create an elegant ambiance. Off to one side is a small, ten-seat neighborhood tavern called the Simon Kenton Pub.

One unique touch: there's no wine list. Instead, diners descend to a wine cellar to pick their choice from bins of bottles. The hazard is that in winter, the cellar occasionally gets so chilly that the red wines have to be warmed before serving.

Innkeeper Janice McWilliams's son Bruce oversees the dining operation, which is highly regarded. Among appetizers ($4.50 to $7.75), we liked the mountain trout smoked over hickory chips and the country pâté of sausage, chicken livers and pork tenderloin blended with brandy and spices and served with the house chutney. Entrées run from $18.25 for broiled trout with herb butter to $22.50 for tournedos au poivre. Our choices were tenderloin en croûte and New York sirloin with horseradish butter, each accompanied by a sprig of plain steamed broccoli and nothing else. Profiteroles, cheesecake, zabaglione, bourbon pie and walnut torte were dessert choices.

Dinner nightly, 6 to 9 or 10; Sunday brunch, 11 to 2. Closed Monday in winter.

Sam Snead's Tavern, Main Street, Hot Springs. (703) 839-7666 or 839-1776.

Located in an historic bank building in the center of town, this was renovated by golfer Sam Snead in 1980. Its symmetry and weathered gray barnwood exterior give it a distinct Wild West look. Golf memorabilia is at the entry, naturally, and wines are stored in the original bank vault. Staff clad in Sam Snead golf shirts serve patrons in a small, paneled dining room with green leather booths and chairs, known as the "lunch room," or the larger dining area in the tavern with a fireplace and a dance floor. A large porch on the second story is favored for outdoor dining in season.

The menu takes a golf theme, from chip shots for starters to the 19th hole for beverages. Lunch entrées are priced from $5.75 to $9.50. Dinner items run from $12.50 for pan-fried Allegheny mountain trout with pecan crust to $21.95 for T-bone steak or surf and turf. Start with Buffalo wings, crabmeat chimichanga or a Gulf Coast shrimp cocktail. Finish with berry shortcake, ice-cream pie or rainbow sherbet.

Lunch, Thursday-Sunday 11 to 4; dinner, Thursday-Sunday 5 to 10. Hours vary.

Cafe Albert, Cottage Row, The Homestead, Hot Springs. (703) 839-7777.

Light, casual fare is offered inside and out at this appealing cafe in the Homestead's quaint Cottage Row of shops and services. Jaunty umbrellaed tables on an outdoor deck provided the setting for our lunch of cold Virginia apple soup, a delectable croissant of turkey and spinach leaves ($7.25) and a good potato salad, and a tropical chicken salad sandwich on rye ($5.75). Excellent chocolates, honey cookies and bread fresh from the Homestead's 19th-century ovens can be purchased along with meats, cheeses and other specialty items. Desserts range from pastries to sundaes.

Open daily in summer, 9 a.m. to 8 p.m. Hours vary.

Diversions

The Springs. As did their forefathers, today's visitors can take part in the ritual of the baths. The Homestead's **Warm Springs Pools** remain as they were upon opening, the men's pool in 1761 and the ladies' pool in 1836. Thomas Jefferson took the waters here for his health. He is credited with designing the octagonal bathhouse that surrounds the men's pool, which has been in continuous use longer than any of its kind in the country. The crude device that lowered the ailing widow of Robert E. Lee into the restorative waters is still on view in the circular women's bathhouse. The waters, a constant 98 degrees, contain a greater variety of minerals than others in the valley. Visitors pay $6 for a towel, a very basic changing room and an hour's communal soak (in the nude for men) in a six-foot-deep pool that's 40 feet across and so clear that you can distinguish the stones on the bottom. The water has a gentle fizz of tickling bubbles. Bathers lie back against steps or float along ropes, but "this is not for swimming, it's for bathing," Steve the attendant advised at the men's bath. Shirdell Pryor, the women's attendant, makes the brightly colored calico bathing shifts trimmed with rick rack during the winter when the pools are closed. Women can bring a bathing suit, wear one of

Footpath leads to men's octagonal bathhouse at Warm Springs Pools.

the shifts or bathe as the men do. Springs open Tuesday-Saturday 10:30 to 5, Sunday 1 to 5, mid-April through October; $6 per session. The **Hot Springs** at The Homestead are warmer, averaging 104 degrees. Attendants in the bathhouse built in 1892 use a variety of springs and follow practices of old European spas in offering mineral baths, sauna, steam room and massage at various prices year-round.

The Spa. The Greenbrier's $7 million Spa, Mineral Baths and Salon occupies a full wing of the legendary resort begun 217 years ago because of its healing waters. This is another of the few American spas to follow the European treatment of using fresh, natural mineral waters. The spa's bath facilities include walk-in whirlpool baths, Swiss showers, Scotch spray, steam, sauna and therapy rooms for massage and body wraps. Eighteen treatments are available, varying from 30 to 90 minutes in length. We tried the basic Greenbrier treatment ($60). The hour-long assault and battery of aching showers and massages combined with relaxing baths and body wraps left one of us so relaxed he literally could not walk his normal double-time pace back to the room. It took an hour's nap to revive him for dinner.

Golf. World-renowned for golf, The Homestead and The Greenbrier each boast three eighteen-hole championship courses, and The Homestead's new management is putting even greater emphasis on golf (a new teaching facility, and the highly respected Golf Advantage School, developed at sister-resort Pinehurst, was added for 1995). Built in 1892, the first tee of the Homestead Golf Course is the oldest in continuous use in the country. The Homestead's Cascades course, known for its tight fairways and undulating greens, is considered the most testing mountain course in North America. Slammin' Sam Snead, who grew up here (his father worked in the resort's powerhouse) and went on to become the winningest golf pro in the country, rates the Cascades "the finest course in the South." He often plays the local courses and shows up at Sam Snead's Tavern. The original, year-round Homestead layout is a short course with few hazards, ideal for those who enjoy leisurely golf in a beautiful setting. The Lower Cascades Course, designed by Robert Trent Jones and the longest of the three, is noted for long tees, large well-trapped greens and water hazards. Also the sites of many tournaments, the Greenbrier courses aren't quite as challenging as The Homestead's in general. The Lakeside Course is open year-round, and all courses begin and end at the Golf Club House. Green fees at The Homestead range from $60 for the Homestead and Lower Cascades courses to $85 for the Cascades. Green fees at the Greenbrier are $85 for guests, $175 for the public.

Garth Newel Music Center, Route 220, Hot Springs, 839-5018. The hillside estate of a former dean of the Yale School of Fine Arts is a destination for chamber music lovers. It's been called the Marlboro of the South. Summer weekend concerts feature the Garth Newel Chamber Players and guest artists Saturdays at 4 and Sundays at 3, early July through Labor Day; tickets, $12. The architecture and acoustics of air-conditioned Herter Hall are perfect for chamber music, and the mountain setting is unsurpassed. In the spring and fall, center directors Arlene and Luca DiCecco, who double as violinist and cellist with the Chamber Players, offer special Garth Newel holiday weekends. Up to twenty guests enjoy overnight accommodations and gourmet meals, wine and nightly concerts.

George Washington National Forest. About half of Bath County lies in the George Washington National Forest, which encompasses numerous recreation areas, trails and campgrounds. Surrounded by the national forest, **Lake Moomaw** extends twelve miles along the Jackson River and offers boating, swimming and fishing.

Shopping. The **Palm Beach Corridor** shops on the main floor of The Homestead are elegant and pricey, as you'd expect. Outside in the **Cottage Row,** shopping is slightly more down to earth. We particularly liked the gifts at **The Captain's Cabin,** the interesting jackets made of old quilts and the fabric plant sculptures at **Quilts Unlimited** and the toys at **The Things Papa Brings.** Hunting and fishing equipment is featured at **The Outpost,** whose young owners also run the newish **Bear Paw Bookstore** at The Homestead. The artworks, ceramics and kitchen ware at the **Gallery of Hot Springs** and the variety of items at **The Gift Caboose** along the old railroad platform are highlights in the center of Hot Springs. **The Country Store** at the Inn at Gristmill Square in Warm Springs offers local crafts.

The **Greenbrier Creative Arts Colony** is in a group of cottages known as Alabama Row at the Greenbrier. Craftsmen are among those who work and sell their wares here. The extravagant corridor of shops at The Greenbrier includes **The Candy Maker,** where the resort's famous chocolates are made by hand; the **Greenbrier Shop,** purveying Greenbrier signature merchandise, including the rhododendron-patterned china; **the Best of West Virginia Shop,** showcasing handiwork of local artisans, and the **Greenbrier Gourmet,** one of the best kitchen shops we've seen.

Extra-Special _____

Bacova Guild, Main Street, Hot Springs. (703) 839-2105.

The mailboxes with wildlife scenes that the Bacova Guild gives to every household in the county are made at the factory in the charming company town of Bacova, a few miles west of Warm Springs. The BA stands for Bath, CO for county and VA for Virginia. The owner of the entire town of 45 cottages, grocery and company commissary teamed up with local wildlife artist Grace Gilmore to laminate her works around objects such as mailboxes, service trays, ice buckets and such. The distinctive birds, deer and the like on pale yellow backgrounds are prized everywhere and available at the Guild's factory-outlet showroom in downtown Hot Springs, which also sells clothing and gifts for the sporting life. The mailboxes, which retail for $65 to $95, are the biggest seller. The guild does a large mail-order business.

16

Dogwoods are in bloom along brick sidewalks in front of Woodrow Wilson Birthplace.

Staunton, Va.

A Frontier Town Grown Up

The first thing you should know about Staunton is that its name is pronounced STAN-ton. The second is that this is Virginia's oldest town west of the Blue Ridge Mountains and was part of America's first western frontier. The third is that it is the Queen City of the Shenandoah Valley, a showcase for architecture and the arts.

Founded in 1732, just a decade later than Richmond, Staunton was settled by the first wave of immigrants heading west from the thirteen original colonies into Appalachia and beyond. Its boom days lasted from the Civil War past the turn of the century. Lately, its downtown has been held up as an example of historic rejuvenation.

Staunton is what you might call a frontier town grown up.

Thanks to local architect T.J. Collins, who designed or remodeled more than 200 local buildings between 1891 and 1911, Staunton has an architectural importance far greater than its population of 25,000 would indicate. It contains no fewer than five historic districts. One is the wharf area – a wharf without water, incidentally – where the coming of the railroad produced the largest collection of Victorian warehouses still standing in Virginia. The wharf area is now the centerpiece of a downtown revitalization known for dining spots, shopping and lodging.

A city of hills that some think give it a European look, Staunton is wonderfully focused for the visitor. Most attractions are within walking distance of the tight little downtown, which, as local innkeeper Michael Organ likes to say, embraces "ten delicious dining experiences within ten blocks, all in historic buildings."

Old buildings thrive in new incarnations. The Belle Grae Inn, offering both guest rooms and dining, grew up around a Victorian mansion. The Frederick House harbors lodging in five restored townhouses. An old grain mill is now the Mill Street Grill.

McCormick's restaurant grew out of the old YMCA. Part of the train station houses The Pullman Cafe and a Victorian ice-cream parlor and another part the Depot Grille. The old American Hotel beside the station was slated by developer Victor Meinert for restoration as an inn.

Staunton's best-known attraction is the Woodrow Wilson Birthplace, lately expanded with the addition of a full-fledged museum. Up and coming is the new Museum of American Frontier Culture, a state-backed museum of living history showing early farm life. The Statler Brothers Complex is of interest to fans of the red-white-and-blue country singers who for 25 years favored their hometown with a Happy Birthday USA celebration every July 4. Some fine little shops and unusual garden enterprises are scattered around the countryside.

Staunton is surrounded by schools: Mary Baldwin College, Stuart Hall prep, the College of the Holy Child Jesus for students from Spain. And it is surrounded by scenery: the Blue Ridge Mountains, the Appalachian foothills and Shenandoah National Park. It makes a good base for exploring a compact area bounded by historic Lexington, Charlottesville, Hot Springs and the Skyline Drive.

This old frontier town has matured well, indeed.

Inn Spots

Sampson-Eagon House, 238 East Beverley St., Staunton 24401. (703) 886-8200 or (800) 597-9722.

Some B&Bs seem to have everything going for them, and this is one. Restorationist Frank Mattingly and his wife Laura, business dropouts from the Washington area, renovated the 1840 house into a deluxe B&B that won the Historic Staunton Foundation's annual Preservation Award in 1992. A marker relates that the house is on the site of a blacksmith shop in which the first United Methodist Church was organized in 1797 and from which the fashionable Gospel Hill area derived its name. The house is "an absolute textbook of architectural styles," says Laura, including Empire, Greek Revival, Egyptian Revival, Colonial Revival and Victorian.

The main floor contains one guest room, a guest living room and a center dining room, plus a side porch with a two-seater swing overlooking the garden. They and the upstairs rooms showcase the couple's various collections. "We had a small antiques business and our dream was to have a place to show our collections," explains Laura. They range from antique delft to horse brasses.

Each of the five guest rooms is large enough for a queensize canopied bed with down pillows, reading chairs, a desk, TV/VCR and private bath. We liked the Eagon master suite with a sleeping porch outfitted in wicker and balloon curtains, and an immense T.J. Collins-designed bathroom. The designer sheets were neatly folded back on a diagonal atop the bed covers. Rooms are decorated to perfection and with great attention to detail — from flashlights to hand-held mirrors, from albums of local restaurant menus to bottles of mineral water in each room. A guest refrigerator hidden off the second-floor hallway holds juices, mixers, ice and wine glasses. A pail at the foot of the stairway is full of candies, and gourmet chocolates are put out at nightly turndown.

A full breakfast is served on Royal

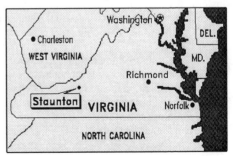

Sampson-Eagon House won Staunton preservation award.

Doulton china in the formal dining room. Ours started with fresh raspberries and blueberries with lemon yogurt made by Frank, along with homemade breads, including cranberry, apple and Laura's favorite bourbon-pecan. The pièce de résistance was Laura's specialty grand marnier soufflé pancakes with ham and grand marnier-strawberry and orange syrups. Eggs benedict and pecan belgian waffles are other favorites. After breakfast, Frank, an avid Staunton booster and Virginia B&B leader, will supply you with enough ideas to keep you busy around here for a week.

Doubles, $75; suites, $90.

Frederick House, 18 East Frederick St., Staunton 24401. (703) 885-4220 or (800) 334-5575.

Six suites and eight rooms varying in size from small to vast are offered in five side-by-side townhouses restored by Joe Harman, one of the few Staunton natives we encountered on our rounds here. The ex-Washington banker came home to purchase a jewelry store and to save from demolition a cluster of empty buildings. He and wife Evy turned them into a small hotel at the edge of downtown, a task that took ten years to complete. "We've taken this little corner and made it nice," says Joe in an understatement masking the massive effort and expense that have gone into the undertaking. Theirs is a comfortable refuge of uncommon appeal and value.

Because of the buildings' heritage and layout, rooms vary widely. They range from a second-floor suite reached by a graceful, curved stairway and containing a large living room and two bedrooms to a walkout English basement bedroom with a queensize bed and a sitting area with floral sprigged wallpaper. Works of Virginia artists, American antiques, ceiling fans, good reading lamps, phones, TVs and terrycloth robes are in each room. All have modern baths. Most rooms have private entrances, and guests are not likely to run into each other except on the nicely landscaped cobblestone terrace, an outdoor gathering spot, or in the spacious tea room below, where breakfast is served by the hands-on innkeepers, who live upstairs.

As classical music played, we enjoyed a breakfast of orange juice, grapefruit and a choice of ham and cheese quiche or egg casserole with whole wheat toast. Upon request, Joe Harman played tapes of the Statler Brothers country singers, hometown boys who made good.

Guests have access to the indoor swimming pool and gym in the Town Center Athletic Club next door.

Doubles, $65 to $95.

The Belle Grae Inn, 515 West Frederick St., Staunton 24401. (703) 886-5151.

The first of Staunton's innkeepers, Michael Organ started in 1983 with a rambling 1873 Victorian mansion. He now has nineteen rooms and suites in six restored houses encompassing nearly an entire block west of downtown. "You can tell our matriculations by our restorations – 1983, '85, '87, '89, '91 and '93," says he. "That also tells where our heads were."

The main red brick house harbors a good restaurant (see Dining Spots), a parlor and a garden room with chess and backgammon games on the first floor, plus eight guest rooms of varying size with antique beds and private baths. A rocking horse is in one, a wicker seating area in another and armoires are in most. Choicer accommodations appealing to business types are found in the Townhouse, the Bungalow, the former gift shop, the Bishop's House and the Jefferson House. The last is a two-story duplex, where four suites are outfitted with sitting areas, wet bars, TVs, phones and queensize four-poster beds. Gilchrist & Soames toiletries and decanters of sherry abound. The various buildings and a new conference center in a cottage are joined by pathways and boardwalks across a pleasant garden terrace.

Breakfast involves what Michael calls "innkeeper's fare," anything from french toast to steak and eggs and perhaps including roast pork with cheese soufflé.

The inn derives its name from two nearby mountains, Betsy Belle and Mary Grae, named by Scotch-Irish settlers for landmarks in Scotland.

Doubles, $69 to $115; suites, $119 to 139.

Kenwood, 235 East Beverley St., Staunton 24401. (703) 886-0524.

Located next door to the Woodrow Wilson Birthplace, this four-room B&B has a pleasant rear screened porch looking across the Wilson gardens, a restoration project of the Garden Club of Virginia. Kenwood owners Liz and Ed Kennedy fixed up their back terrace to match.

The Kennedys were visiting friends in Staunton when they saw this turn-of-the-century Colonial Revival house for sale in 1987 and bought it. Renovations took more than two years, Liz wallpapering every square inch of the house herself and Ed commuting from his banking job in Boston.

The main floor with eleven-foot ceilings contains a gracious parlor, a formal dining room in deep rose and wedgwood blue illuminated by a crystal chandelier, and a great library. It has floor-to-ceiling bookcases stocked with books and magazines, a large TV and a Boston Celtics banner that Ed puts over the beds of visiting New Englanders.

Crystal door knobs, original brass locks and pulls on the windows, ceiling fans, fancy wallpapers and antiques enhance the upstairs rooms, two with private baths and two sharing. Here again are displays of magazines waiting to be pored over. Three rooms contain queensize beds. One that shares a bath has a double and a twin bed and is used with its opposite number by families.

The Kennedys serve a substantial breakfast of fresh fruit, homemade muffins and a main dish like a sausage and cheese soufflé or pancakes on prized china and silver.

Doubles, $60 to $70.

Thornrose House at Gypsy Hill faces 300-acre municipal park.

Thornrose House at Gypsy Hill, 531 Thornrose Ave., Staunton 24401. (703) 885-7026 or (800) 861-4338.

The previous owners got this "B&B in the English manner" off to a good start. But it has come of age with considerable sophistication under new owners Suzanne and Otis Huston, who were widely traveled during his career as an executive with du Pont.

They lightened up the decor with lace curtains and good-looking fabrics, added two bedrooms (making a total of five, all with private baths), restored the masterful gardens surrounding a brick terrace and a couple of pergolas, and imbued the place with their enthusiasm and hospitality. Although some rooms are on the small side, not so is the master bedroom, with two twins joined together as a kingsize bed and windows on three sides. Suzanne's favorite is the rear Yorkshire Room with a clawfoot tub, overlooking the gardens.

The Hustons continued the tradition of British tea, served in season on the inviting veranda or beneath the pergolas by the gardens. On cooler days it's taken in the living room, where a gas fireplace, grand piano and a TV are among the amenities. Breakfast, served in a cozy dining room, might feature mushroom and cheese omelets, banana-pecan pancakes or oat whole-grain waffles with apples along with choice of juices and, at our visit, cantaloupe with blueberries. Otis makes his own muesli, for which guests frequently ask the recipe.

Besides enjoying the Hustons' gorgeous property, guests only have to cross the street for golf, tennis, swimming and walking in the 300-acre Gypsy Hill Park.

Doubles, $55 to $75.

Ashton Country House, 1205 Middlebrook Road, Staunton 24401. (703) 885-7819 or (800) 296-7819.

Though less than a five-minute drive from downtown, this Greek Revival brick house beside Lewis Creek seems out in the middle of nowhere. Sheila Kennedy and Stanley Polanski opened their B&B in 1990 on 24 hilly acres of pastureland that include two goats, thirteen cats and a neighbor's cattle.

This is no farmhouse operation, however. Inside all is sophisticated in five guest rooms with private baths, a living room with a grand piano, a dining room with two lace-covered tables, an upstairs porch furnished in wicker and a rear veranda where afternoon tea is served.

Sheila is a sixth-grade teacher, which accounts for the fact the B&B is open only weekends, holidays and in summer. Stan, a computer programmer by day, is a professional pianist at night. He's usually around on weekends to play some Gershwin or Porter at teatime and, always, during breakfast. Sheila loves to cook and entertain, serving guests Stan's specially blended coffee, a fruit compote in a silver goblet and perhaps a baked egg dish with Idaho home fries and bacon or sausage.

Comfortable bedrooms have an elegant mix of decor. They range from the Audubon Room with a four-poster bed and bird wallpaper in the bathroom to the master bedroom suite with a step-up queensize Charleston rice four-poster bed, two wing chairs and shelves of books in shallow open closets. Less formal is the secluded Cottage Bedroom off the rear porch with a five-piece matched faux woodgrain bedroom set.

The place is named for the ash trees that shade the front lawn. All are on view from rockers on a pillared porch that, in Sheila's words, beckon guests "into a time warp, to lie back and mellow out."

Doubles, $70 to $80. Open weekends, holidays and summer. No smoking.

The Iris Inn, 191Chinquapin Drive, Waynesboro 22980. (703) 943-1991.

Stands of iris line the wide, curving driveway leading up to this stunning structure on a forested, 21-acre hillside overlooking the western mountains. The irises reflect one of the themes that Iris Karl, innkeeper with her husband Wayne, have executed throughout their very personalized inn.

Be advised that this is very different from the "old" inns with which Virginia is well endowed. The Karls looked at scores of potential properties to restore as a B&B when Wayne retired from the Federal Aviation Agency. "He was an engineer and always saw the things that were falling down," says Iris. "One day he said, 'why don't we build?' We started looking for land and never looked back."

They found a secluded hilltop high above an I-64 interchange just southeast of Waynesboro, the sister city of Staunton in Augusta County. An architect designed a sprawling, two-story inn with seven guest rooms and suites off two 92-foot-long porches running the width of the structure, a lookout tower above a whirlpool spa and a soaring, 28-foot-high great room enhanced with a large and realistic wall mural of a woodland scene.

"You don't have to be in an old, historic building to succeed in this business," Iris contends. Thanks to a receptive business clientele (one du Pont Co. executive stayed for five months, and a du Pont physician books here two nights every week), the inn enjoys unusually high occupancy year-round. "People like a place that's new, spacious and comfortable," says Iris.

Our quarters were in the Bird Room, the last available that evening. A kingsize bed, modern bathroom, refrigerator-wet bar and TV blended nicely with the bird theme, which included pictures of birds, birds on the wallpaper border, birds pictured along the tiled bath, a bird in a nest resting on the sink and a melange of bird feeders outside. Other rooms are larger; some have day beds and jacuzzi tubs. Iris has decorated all to the nth degree in accordance with their names, from Deer to Hawk's Nest. The Woodland Forest even adds a Secret World for little children, an attic alcove with a single bed and a teddy bear's picnic.

Breakfast is an event in the Great Hall, alongside the remarkable wall mural. At our visit, a plate of fresh fruit preceded a choice of light, heart-shaped belgian waffles or

Breakfast is taken beside remarkable wall mural in Great Hall at The Iris Inn.

eggs any style with sausages. Banana bread, good bran muffins and bird-shaped rolls accompanied. The treats began with a glass of milk and homemade chocolate-chip cookies from a bottomless jar the evening before. They culminated with a loaf of "road bread," wrapped in saran with a plastic knife, and a hug from Iris upon departure.

Doubles, $75 to $95. No smoking.

Dining Spots

Belle Grae Inn, 515 West Frederick St., Staunton. (703) 886-5151.

Occupying the front portion of the main floor of this expanding inn are three elegant Victorian dining rooms plus a veranda and a garden terrace, as well as an art deco bistro for lighter dining and entertainment.

We dined in front of a fireplace amidst tables dressed in white and pink with blue china and glassware and an assortment of family keepsakes and heirlooms. Tables are well spaced and some seating is on couches. The short, contemporary menu might list such entrées ($13.95 to $19.50) as oven-roasted salmon with plums and merlot, roast pork loin with granny smith apples and figs, medallions of beef with grilled oyster mushrooms and hickory sage butter, and Chincoteague crab cakes with puree of sweet red pepper and herb mayonnaise, a seasonal treat that we had enjoyed earlier here at lunch (since discontinued). Tasty appetizers included ale-battered soft-shell crab with smoked tomato butter and roast quail with leek stuffing and corn vinaigrette. The basket of "bubble bread," spicy with caraway, was so good we readily accepted a refill. That meant we had to forego such desserts as almond-amaretto torte, chocolate-mocha crepe and chocolate mousse pie.

"Fun dining" is offered in the airy bistro, billed as Staunton's only indoor-outdoor cafe, with lots of glass. The menu is very limited (chef's salad, cheeseburger, a couple of sandwiches, chicken stir-fry with rice pilaf) but pleasantly priced. Everything is under $7.95 except for the medallions of beef $10.95), served with béarnaise sauce on an English muffin with potato and vegetable.

The ham, broccoli and cheese quiche that we also enjoyed at lunch is a staple on the Sunday brunch menu, which incorporates much of the bistro menu with things like eggs benedict and fettuccine with basil pesto.

Dinner nightly, 6 to 9; Sunday brunch, 10 to 2.

Mill Street Grill, 1 Mill St., Staunton. (703) 886-0656.

If this restaurant in the first Wharf Historic District building to be restored looks a bit like a gallery, thank the former owner whose wife also used to own the interesting art gallery upstairs.

Six panels of stained glass are a focal point of the decor of the old White Star Mills flour mill. Done by a local couple, they depict the journey of wheat from the harvesting to the baking of bread. There's much to look at on several levels with exposed beams and thick fieldstone walls: paintings and collages, old light fixtures, etched glass and copper rails.

Tablecloths and candlelight are the setting for dinner. The specialty here is ribs, slow-cooked baby back ribs and beef ribs in the Midwest style. A barbecue platter yielding samples of both costs $9.95. One well-traveled innkeeper calls them the best ribs she's ever had. She says the rest of the food has zip as well. The menu is priced from $8.95 for raspberry chicken or chicken, shrimp and andouille sausage creole to $13.95 for a large filet mignon sautéed in peppercorn cream sauce. Grilled mahi-mahi, charbroiled yellowfin tuna, crab cakes and pastas are among the offerings. Appetizers run to steam spiced shrimp, Buffalo wings, potato skins and chicken nachos. Bourbon pecan and key lime pies are among desserts.

Dinner nightly, 4 to 10 or midnight. Closed January.

The Depot Grille, 42 Middlebrook Ave., Staunton. (703) 885-7332.

Immensely popular is this steak and seafood house opened in part of the old C&0 facility, called Staunton Station. It's one of the few complete train complexes in the country and lately rejuvenated by transplanted Atlanta developer Victor Meinert. By complete we mean an operating passenger terminal with a couple of new eateries. Also a stunning curved outdoor concourse that's the scene of a series of free outdoor Shakin' at the Station concerts every other Friday evening in summer. Plus a free-standing signal tower, a freight depot, and three cabooses and three baggage cars that have been turned into antiques shops and boutiques.

The old terminal houses the **Whistlestop Soda Shop,** with an extraordinary 1880s ice-cream parlor and pharmacy interior for which Vic Meinert outbid the Smithsonian. Ice-cream treats are featured beneath four massive bronze and stained-glass chandeliers salvaged from the old Milwaukee train station. Occupying part of the station concourse is the **Pullman Cafe,** where we admired the ornate bar with swinging doors as we lunched on a crab cake sandwich and the offerings from a help-yourself salad bar that was more interesting than most.

The depot restaurant contains a 50-foot-long, 19th-century oak bar that Meinert purchased from an old New York hotel and believes to be the longest in the country. It also has a solarium with windows opening onto the outdoors and a vast dining room displaying railroad memorabilia and lit by oil lanterns even at noon. There's an old shoeshine chair at the door.

The all-day menu appeals to all tastes, and the seafood and nightly specials come highly recommended. We hear good things about the backfin crab cakes ($11.95), the black angus sirloin steak ($24.95 for two) and the grilled shrimp and feta pizza. The

Stained-glass panels on wall are focal point of Mill Street Grill.

prices certainly are right: $7.95 for cajun or mesquite-grilled chicken and nothing over $13.95 except the steak for two. Salad and two choices of fries, applesauce, cole slaw, steamed vegetables, rice or new potatoes come with.

Open daily, 11 to midnight.

L'Italia Restaurant, 23 East Beverley St., Staunton. (703) 885-0102.

The site of the much-acclaimed 23 Beverley restaurant was reopened in late 1994 by an Italian family from Harrisonburg, who have the well-established L'Italia Restaurant there. Such was the stature of their predecessors that they maintained the 23 Beverley logo in the front window beneath their own name. They retained the elegant decor and even the china, and filled the recessed niches in the walls with paintings by art students from James Madison University. They offered an extensive Italian menu for lunch and dinner, and early reviews were quite good.

The menu, more Sicilian than northern Italian, is a far cry from the 23 Beverley glory days. For dinner (mostly $9.95 to $11.95), expect nine variations of chicken (from cacciatore to marsala to piccata), nine of veal (from parmigiana to saltimbocca), nine seafood (from conch marinara to shrimp fra diavolo) and sixteen pastas (from manicotti to fettuccine alfredo with shrimp).

The appetizers are predictable, too, although the low prices may not be. How about antipasto salad for two for $4.90? Ditto for desserts, from spumoni and cannoli to grasshopper pie and tirami su. A few Virginia wines are on the short, primarily Italian wine list, priced from $9 to $30.

Many of the same dishes turn up at lunch time, when you can order anything from an Italian hoagie ($3.95) to calamari marinara ($8.75).

Lunch, Monday-Saturday 11 to 3:30; dinner, Monday-Saturday from 3:30.

J. Rugle's Warehouse, 18 Byers St., Staunton. (703) 886-4399.

Gourmet pizzas and pastas are the specialties at this informal downtown restaurant in a restored warehouse with a large bar area, an upstairs dining room and, in season, a popular sidewalk cafe. The restaurant is part of developer Vic Meinert's group of restorations, which also includes the Depot Grille and the Pullman Cafe.

The specialty pizzas come in various sizes and with a variety of toppings, so in effect you create your own. Or you can choose one of the "history-making combinations:" spinach and artichoke hearts, cajun chicken or white cheese and pesto ($9.95 to $12.95).

There's more. Entrées, served with house or caesar salad, are mostly $9.95 or $10.95 for things like steamed crab legs, blackjack chicken (flamed with Jack Daniels), chicken pesto, steak kabobs and New York strip steak. A shrimp and steak combination tops off the menu at $13.95. There also are sandwiches and appetizers, from potato skins to nachos to mozzarella sticks.

Homemade desserts range from snicker bar pie and fried ice cream to tirami su. Cappuccino, lattes and Italian wines also are featured.

Dinner nightly, 5 to midnight.

McCormick's Pub & Restaurant, 41 North Augusta St. at Towne Centre, Staunton. (703) 885-3111.

Another downtown restoration houses this busy establishment in the building's former lobby. This was the old YMCA, funded by the Cyrus McCormick family (of reaper fame), who lived nearby. Walnut lumber cut from the McCormick homestead created the lavish mantelpieces, woodwork, doors, the curved bar (originally a clerk's counter) and the tall, built-in case clock still ticking after seven decades. Beyond the large pub is a fireplaced dining room with white linens, high-back chairs and crystal chandeliers.

The dinner menu is short and to the point. It features a dozen pasta dishes, from shrimp and crab alfredo to blackened chicken with rotini to scallops and feta with penne, nicely priced from $5.50 to $10.95. Prime rib is the specialty, available in three cuts for $8.25 to $12.95. The remaining dishes are also priced out of the past: crab cake, Jamaican jerk chicken and Kentucky bourbon strip steak in the $6.25 to $8.50 range, and only filet mignon going for $11.95 (with backfin crab and béarnaise sauce, for $14.50). There are numerous salads, appetizers and sandwiches available for those with lighter appetites — or budgets.

After dinner, you might adjourn to **McCormick's Cabaret** for a country music revue or dinner theater run in conjunction with ShenanArts.

Lunch, Monday-Friday 11:30 to 5; dinner nightly, 5 to midnight, weekends to 1.

The Beverley Restaurant, 12 East Beverley St., Staunton. (703) 886-4317.

For local color and Southern home-style cooking, head for this landmark storefront run since 1960 by Janet and Paul Thomas. The action starts at 6 a.m. with breakfast for the delivery folks; the crowd then shifts to blue-collar workers, followed by bank presidents. Retirees come in at mid-morning to catch up on the latest gossip before the lunch crowd takes over.

Except for the four stained-glass windows depicting items from the menu, decor is predictable: six high booths, glass tables and bric-a-brac on the walls. But it's camaraderie and food you're after, perhaps a ham and cheese omelet ($3.45) or golden hotcakes ($1.90) for breakfast, or a special of meatloaf with two vegetables, rolls and butter for lunch, $2.95. Sandwiches start at $2.25 for egg salad ("fresh and made to order.") The hot roast beef smothered in brown gravy and served with mashed potatoes is the old standby at $3.25. A club sandwich tops the list at $3.90.

Come in for old-fashioned English tea (a buffet table contains everything from chicken and cucumber sandwiches to trifle and pound cake), served Wednesday and Friday from 3 to 5, or an early supper of baked Virginia ham, veal cutlet, ribeye steak or hot roast beef, $3.50 to $6.

Open Monday-Friday, 6 a.m. to 7 p.m., Saturday to 5.

Rowe's Family Restaurant, Route 250 at I-81, Staunton. (703) 886-1833.

Another local institution since 1947, this is an enormous red wood house conveniently situated beside the interchange of two interstate highways. It's a destination for travelers and national food writers.

Clippings about founder Mildred Craft Rowe are at the entry and her cookbook ($8.95), preserves, barbecue sauce and pastries are for sale at the counter. Son Michael says she still comes in four days a week "and quickly knows if anything is wrong."

More than 230 patrons can be seated in two large rooms. The basic menu is supplemented by white-card specials changing daily – minced pork barbecue dinner ($6.95) and golden fried wing dings ($4.50) at our visit. Most of the other offerings are $4.25 to $5.25 for the likes of fried fillet of flounder, grilled liver, baked pork tenderloin with gravy and a hamburger that comes on a wooden plank, with a choice of vegetables and salad. All the homemade breads, biscuits, muffins, cookies and pies are baked daily to Mrs. Rowe's specifications. They are available for purchase from the cashier.

Open daily, 6:30 a.m. to 9 p.m. in summer, to 8 in winter; Sundays, 7 a.m. to 8 p.m.

The Pampered Palate, 26-28 East Beverley St., Staunton. (703) 886-9463.

The old Atlantic Lunch hot-dog stand has been transformed into this sprightly deli and gourmet food and wine shop. John and Marian Miskell offer dining upstairs in a tearoom atmosphere (seven tables and a high chair) and downstairs in an ice-cream parlor setting.

Sandwiches with local names are "the Palate's pride." We liked the New Theater (vegetables, mushrooms and havarti, $2.95) and the Statler (a quartet of meats and cheeses, $3.95). Both were stuffed in pita bread. A few salads, quiche, pampered potatoes, cheese boards, bagels and sweets round out the fare. Everything's available to take out.

Open Monday-Saturday 9 to 5:30, Sunday 11 to 2:30. No smoking.

Diversions

Historic Walking Tours. The Historic Staunton Foundation, founded in 1971 to promote preservation over demolition, has concentrated its efforts in the downtown and adjacent residential areas. That makes it easy to view the results on foot. Indeed, as county tourism coordinator Sergei Troubetzkoy noted, visitors can arrive at the restored railroad station by Amtrak, walk to lodging and restaurants, and never need a car – a rarity for a small town these days. The foundation's walking tour map and brochure focuses on 59 sites of outstanding architectural or historical merit in the Downtown, Wharf Area, Newtown, Gospel Hill and North End. Many sites were designed or remodeled around the turn of the century by local architect T.J. Collins, whose son continued the tradition. Visitors accustomed to Virginia's formal Jeffersonian brick styles will be struck by Staunton's exuberance, the result of one family having a major impact on the design of a community.

Woodrow Wilson Birthplace, 24 North Coalter St., Staunton, 885-0897. The Presbyterian manse in which America's 28th president was born in 1856 is a registered National Historic Landmark. On guided tours every half hour, visitors see the room where he was born, the crib in which he slept and the chair in which his mother rocked him. The tour and furnishings feature the way of life of Stauntonians in the 1850s –

"the way they would have lived as a Southern family," according to our guide. You see twelve rooms containing many items that belonged to the Wilson family. The rear balcony affords a view of the historic gardens restored by the Garden Club of Virginia, the cream-colored buildings of Mary Baldwin College and the downtown. "Now you're part of the family," says the guide at tour's end. "You get to leave by the back door."

Before the tour, browse through the **Woodrow Wilson Museum,** the only museum in the country spanning Wilson's entire life. Seven galleries cover everything from his parentage to his funeral. The re-creation of his Princeton University study contains his old Hammond typewriter. Other galleries trace his economic and social reforms, the tumultuous war years, and his search for peace and a new world order. The well-spaced displays are tasteful, significant and not at all overwhelming. A highlight is his beloved 1919 Pierce-Arrow White House limousine, donated by his widow to be shown in his hometown in a large garage beside the museum. An attractive gift shop adjoins the garden. Open daily 9 to 5. Adults, $6.

Statler Brothers Complex, 501 Thornrose Ave., Staunton, 885-7297. Opposite Gypsy Hill Park is this renovated school building, now the corporate headquarters of the Statler Brothers country singers, all of whom reside in the area. Still on view is the gymnasium stage where the brothers won their first talent show in 1955. Hallway cases sparkle with Grammys and records. One tour a day is given Monday-Friday at 2. Souvenir shop hours are weekdays, 10:30 to 3:30.

P. Buckley Moss Museum, 2150 Rosser Ave., Waynesboro, 949-6473. On a hill-top overlooking Waynesboro, the stately brick Moravian mansion that celebrated art-ist Pat Moss designed herself in 1989 showcases many of her works. She still paints at her home and barn two miles to the south, her studio since the early 1960s, although her official residence now is in St. Petersburg, Fla. Three floors of the mansion trace her evolution from her Pennsylvania childhood through her time as a children's de-signer in the New York garment district to the height of her "Valley style." Her fame has spread mainly since the mid-1980s through the marketing efforts of her husband-manager, Malcolm Henderson. Most of the art here reflects the Amish and Mennonite "Plain People" in local and Pennsylvania scenes; exceptions like one of sailing on Tampa Bay and a Washington mountain landscape come as surprises. Her watercolors and original prints in the large shop start at $30 and go way up. An oil of Sedona in the Gallery/Studio was listed at $48,000. Open Monday-Saturday 10 to 6, Sunday 12:30 to 5:30. Free.

André Viette Farm and Nursery, Route 608, Fishersville, 943-2315. In early spring, the rolling countryside here is ablaze with tulips. The spectacular perennial gardens continue with poppies, peonies, iris and, their real claim to fame, lilies. André Viette's fame, spread through his national gardening radio program, draws people from afar to his garden center and flower clinics.

Shopping. As you walk around downtown, you'll surely be struck by the interesting plants and gardens that are the work of a fulltime city horticulturist. **The Emporium** at 101 East Beverley St. stocks nice pottery, baskets, windsocks, unusual birdhouses, silk flowers, stuffed animals and the like. **Turtle Lane** at 10 East Beverley is filled to the brim with appealing gifts. We liked the jewelry from exotic places at **Silver Lin-ings,** 16 West Beverley. **Honeysuckle Hill** offers antiques and collectibles. The **Wharf Gallery** in the restored White Star Mills has an exciting collection of arts and crafts by Virginia artisans, plus a new third-floor gallery containing studios for working artists. **Depot Antiques** carries interesting folk art, primitives and Shenandoah Valley furni-ture; we were struck by the rustic twig chair with a birdhouse on top for $150. **Rails,** owned by the folks from the Belle Grae Inn, stocks casual clothing, home accessories and gifts from around the world. Quite a sight is the old automobile showroom now

Rear of Woodrow Wilson Birthplace yields view of restored gardens.

housing **Bruce Elder Antique and Classic Automobiles;** it has an elevator to transport cars to all three floors. **The Virginia Made Shop** at Exit 222 from I-81 is full of local items. If you'd like a peanut basket – with peanut soup, peanut butter and an assortment of peanuts – this is the place. The new Staunton-Augusta Farmers' Market quickly became a Saturday fixture; all participants are required to produce what they sell.

Shops in Stuarts Draft. Amid rolling suburbia part way between Staunton and Charlottesville is this growing community populated mostly by Mennonites and known for four unusual shops. You can almost inhale the calories at **Kinsinger's Bakery,** where a Mennonite family bakes Monday-Wednesday and sells its goods in a small shop Thursday-Saturday 9 to 5. Hymns play in the background as shoppers peruse the shelves of apple butter and blackberry jam, angel food cakes with strawberry toppings, Amish oatmeal cookies and other delectables "like Grandma used to make." Half a mile away in the lower floor of a brick ranch house is **The Cheese Shop,** where bearded Mennonites purvey bulk goods at good prices, several kinds of cheeses, natural foods and more. While one of us picked up some low-fat Colby for the cooler, the other ogled the fantastic birdhouses out back. Also worth a stop is **The Candy Shop,** featuring a complete line of Hershey products. Some – including Reese's Pieces, Whatchamacallits and Bar None – are made here in the area. The newest attraction is **Milmont Greenhouses,** which started as a Mennonite housewife's hobby and has grown into a thriving year-round enterprise.

Side Trips. Don't miss the jaunt about eighteen miles south of Staunton to the hilly, rural Raphine area. Here, almost side by side, are two must stops:

Buffalo Springs Herb Farm, Route 606, Raphine, 348-1083. Former florists from northern Virginia restored a 1793 brick and stone homestead and a big red barn beside a rushing creek, a grand space that lent itself to workshops, drying and demonstration areas and an exceptional shop. Don Haynie and Thom Hamlin offer herbal products, dried flowers and designs, garden books, herb plants in season, nature trails, an arbor garden and herbal happenings, from workshops to picnics to an herbal dinner followed

29

by Broadway show tunes. Their 170-acre educational farm is so scenic that it's been a setting for weddings. Open April through Dec. 18, Thursday-Saturday 10 to 5 and Sunday 1 to 5 (no Sundays June-August).

Wade's Mill, Route 816, Raphine, 348-1400. This neat place is one of the few operating gristmills actually producing flour as a business in this country. The miller and his wife are Jim and Georgie Young, ex-Washington bureaucrats who bought the circa 1750 mill in 1991. Now Jim grinds a couple of thousand pounds of flour exclusively on mill stones each week. They also sell fresh breads and muffins in the fall, run cooking classes and occasional brunches in their renovated farmhouse, and give tours and demonstrations in their mill, which is powered by a 21-foot water wheel fed by the nearby stream. Georgie's shop features local pottery and baskets, buckwheat pancake mixes and apple syrup, and a cook's corner with everything you need to cook and bake with flour. Open same hours as Buffalo Springs Herb Farm.

Nearby along Route 606 is **Rockbridge Vineyard,** a new winery in a gravel-floored barn, where founder Shepherd Rouse produces some award-winning chardonnays, rieslings and pinot noirs. Open Thursday-Sunday 11 to 5, May-October.

The Cyrus McCormick Farm, Route 606, Steele's Tavern, 377-2255. Cross a little creek from the wayside parking lot at Walnut Grove Farm to the old gristmill, powered by water from a mill pond, and the blacksmith shop. This simple little farm smithy was the birthplace in 1831 of the first mechanical reaper, a horse-drawn harvesting machine. Young Cyrus McCormick's invention ushered in the age of farm mechanization and hastened the westward expansion of the United States. The story unfolds in a simple museum above the blacksmith shop, where facsimiles of early reapers are on display. Open daily, 8:30 to 5.

Extra-Special

Museum of American Frontier Culture, Route 250 at I-81 Exit 222, Staunton. (703) 332-7850.

Curiously juxtaposed next to the interchange of two interstate highways, this outdoor, living-history museum opened in 1990 to interpret the American frontier. This is not the frontier of the Wild West, but rather of America's first frontier – the Shenandoah Valley. The state-owned tract has four reconstructed farmsteads, three of which are from European nations (England, Northern Ireland and Germany) that the pioneers left behind. They are authentic reconstructions of historical working farms from each country, and costumed interpreters demonstrate daily life to visitors. The fourth and largest farm is the American synthesis, reflecting the melding of European influences. You might see a carpenter making pegs for the German barn, a pig-calling contest at the English farm, rare Kerry cattle, wonderful fencing in different styles and even stray farm cats. It's a special place for the young and the young at heart. The contemporary visitor center and the sounds of interstate traffic are in marked contrast to the farmsteads from the 18th and 19th centuries. Open daily, 9 to 5, winter to 4. Adults, $7.

30

Thomas Jefferson's Monticello lures visitors to Charlottesville.

Charlottesville, Va.

Jefferson's Lively Mountain Eden

History. Mountain vistas. A lively university town. Vineyards and wineries.

These are among the assets that draw visitors to Charlottesville, the Piedmont area favored by Thomas Jefferson. He built Monticello, his "little mountain" home, in the rolling countryside he later described as "the Eden of America." It overlooks the Blue Ridge Mountains, the town and the University of Virginia, which he founded.

Jefferson also persuaded his friend and fellow president, James Monroe, to build a home nearby. Another colleague, James Madison, lived two dozen miles to the north in Orange.

Jefferson's influence is everywhere obvious in the Charlottesville area. The University of Virginia that he designed is the region's major presence. Thousands of tourists are directed to Monticello from a large new visitor information center at the foot of its access road. A dozen or more small wineries fulfill the hopes of Jefferson, a wine connoisseur and would-be grape grower.

The Blue Ridge Mountains to the west are a spectacular backdrop for a prosperous university town tugged between tradition and change. The visitor to Charlottesville detects few Southern accents, testimony to the influx of outsiders and their amalgamation into a sophisticated, academic culture. The city is rife with dining, lodging, shopping and cultural opportunities.

Traditionalists lament some of the changes. They contend that Charlottesville (now with a metropolitan population of 115,000) isn't the nice little place it used to be. Rush-hour gridlock stalls traffic on the expressways, and shopping malls have sprung up on farmlands. But this is urban sprawl with a difference: highways and commerce co-exist with antebellum plantations and an amazing number of palatial new homes, each with sizable property and a view of the surrounding Blue Ridge.

Sir Bernard Ashley chose the Charlottesville area as the site for his third and largest country-house hotel. He was struck by the beauty and heritage of the town and countryside. "It's not just a modern, thrown-up town," he said. "It has heart."

31

Inn Spots

The route numbers used for addresses here, as elsewhere in Virginia, are rural postal routes, not highways.

Clifton – The Country Inn, Route 13, Box 26, Charlottesville 22901. (804) 971-1800.

Superlatives and Clifton go hand-in-hand. But for a gracious plantation built by Thomas Mann Randolph, who married Thomas Jefferson's daughter Martha and was an early governor of Virginia, this inn is surprisingly unpretentious. A hilltop away from Monticello on a cliff by the Rivanna River, it has fourteen spacious rooms and suites, each with wood-burning fireplace and private bath. The 45 acres of verdant grounds off Route 729 in rural Shadwell harbor a croquet pitch, a hard-surface tennis court, a fabulous new swimming pool with terraced waterfall and lots of loungers amid the landscaping, an outdoor spa heated year-round, a 26-acre private lake, walking trails and wildlife, plus a couple of resident sheep.

"We want to the atmosphere to be relaxed and casual, yet elegant," says Craig Hartman, hands-on innkeeper for owner T. Mitchell Willey, the Alexandria attorney who bought Clifton in 1984 and turned it into one of our favorite inns anywhere. "We don't want to lose the quaint, Jeffersonian feeling."

That is not to say rustic. Clifton is anything but. The six guest rooms in the main house offer lots of space and border on the majestic. Among their various accoutrements are antique beds with canopies built into the high ceilings and draped at the corners, cedar closets and comfortable sitting areas or rooms. One has a sunken bath beside which "Mrs. Wood," a nude sculpture, reclines. Our quarters in the cathedral-ceilinged carriage house included an expansive living room with a fireplace and french windows on both sides opening to let the breeze flow through, and a loft with a queensize bed. Two guest rooms on the lower floor of the carriage house also have full-length windows across the back. They and two large rooms fashioned from Randolph's old law office share a garden courtyard and a number of historic fixtures from the recently dismantled Meriwether Lewis home in Charlottesville. Our latest stay was in one of the three new rooms in the secluded Livery. It came with a queensize bedroom, full bath with separate shower and a sunken sun room with sofabed and fireplace, and opened onto a patio and garden sloping toward the lake, shielded from view in summer by the woods all around.

Guests enjoy the run of the inn's main floor. There are a formal living room, a country library, a paneled dining room, a garden room and a rear dining porch, created by enclosing the old veranda. Access extends even to the kitchen, where guests help themselves to the treats in a big cookie jar as well as wine, beer and such. We felt quite at ease poking around the refrigerator and consuming part of a pint of sherbet upon our

return from a dessert-less dinner at our first visit.

Afternoon tea is put out in the garden room. At our latest visit, the copious spread teamed hot tea, herbed cranberry punch and lemonade with luscious canapés of goat cheese, scones and rich chocolate cake.

Breakfast is served on white linens and Villeroy & Boch china at five tables in the dining room or, our

Clifton occupies mansion built by Thomas Jefferson's son-in-law.

choice on a lovely summer morning, at individual tables on the rear dining porch. A fruit smoothie (orange, pineapple and banana juice) and apple-bran muffins began one repast; a platter of fresh fruit and apple coffee cake the next. The main dish at our latest visit was spectacular: poached eggs on a toasted croissant topped with a sauce of potage lyonnaise, tomatoes and chèvre. "I made it up in my head last night," sous chef Ron Miller said when we asked the ingredients.

That didn't particularly surprise us, given the quality of dinner the preceding evening. Ron had proved a worthy substitute for chef-innkeeper Craig, who had greeted us upon arrival and helped get our luggage to the room, but was taking a night off from the kitchen. Both Craig and Ron trained at the Culinary Institute of America, and Craig was a guest chef at the James Beard House in New York City in 1993. He and his wife Donna moved here in 1992 after cooking at Pinehurst and running a pastry shop and deli in Nag's Head, N.C.

Our dinner began with tomato bisque with grilled cornbread and crème fraîche and a salad of baby organic greens with Iron Rod chèvre and red grape dressing. A very tart raspberry ice, served in a brandy snifter, cleared the palate for an exceptional breast of duck with mulberry demi-glace, basmati rice and a julienne of carrots and haricots verts. Dessert following such a superb feast was hardly an anti-climax: dark chocolate pots de crème with miniature torte cookies.

The prix-fixe dinner, with a choice of two entrées, is $38 for five courses on weekdays and $48 for six courses on weekends, when there is live music by a pianist. Dinner is open to the public by reservation. The chef appears near the end of the cocktail hour in the living room to describe the treats to come.

Doubles, $185 to $225. Dinner nightly by reservation, 7:30. No smoking.

Keswick Hall, 701 Country Club Dr., Keswick 22947. (804) 979-3440 or (800) 274-5391.

"Absolutely spectacular" was the advance billing for this 48-room country-house hotel developed by Sir Bernard Ashley of Laura Ashley fame. It's the jewel in the crown of his Ashley House triumvirate, which began in 1987 with the acquisition of Llangoed Hall in Wales and continued in 1990 with the purchase of the Inn at Perry Cabin (which see) in St. Michaels, Md. Also in 1990, Ashley House acquired the bankrupt Keswick property, 600 acres of rolling countryside east of Charlottesville next to Shadwell, first owned by Thomas Jefferson's father. It set out to make this the largest Ashley hotel and the first to include a private golf club and a development of 100 homes in the $1 million price range.

The $40 million rejuvenation of the Keswick estate, which was basically completed by 1994, was executed in the traditional Ashley idiom, a personalized mix of old and new. First, the existing eighteen-hole golf course, designed by Arnold Palmer, was reopened and a posh pavilion built with fitness facilities to serve as a clubhouse. Next, a residence, the $1.5 million Keswick House, was built to showcase the private residential development. Finally, a 40-room wing was added to the original Italianate-style Villa Crawford, built in 1912 and serving as the original clubhouse. It became the hotel and restaurant.

"In the hotel," envisioned Sir Bernard, or "B.A." as his staff fondly calls him, "I want to wear what I like and sleep when I like. And if there are to be excitements, let them arrive at the dining table or on the golf course." The place could be intimidating, but this is not his intent, according to Anne E. Hooff, marketing director. "The idea is to escape. Comfort is the key, not elegance. He wants you to feel that this is his home and that you are his guest."

Our room with its pewter kingsize bed was large and assuredly comfortable, one of eleven "studios" – ranking in price behind four suites and ahead of twenty-one state rooms and twelve house rooms. All are furnished in a mix of European antiques and appointments from the Laura Ashley collection, and no two are alike. Every decision down to the selection of dessert spoons for the dining room awaited Sir Bernard's final approval, although the execution was left to son Nick and a decorator from Bethesda, Md.

Most accommodations have king or queen beds, but a few have twins or doubles. Each has a different armoire, a writing desk and an old reproduction radio. A handful of bathrooms possess oversize jetted tubs with separate showers.

More showy are the public rooms: the Great Hall in which arriving guests are greeted by a staff member, the comfortable Morning Room (a study in off-white), the main Drawing Room outfitted with furniture from Sir Bernard's former house in Brussels (and a number of his personal family photos here and there), a snooker room with a billiards table and a beautiful fireplace, and the large Crawford Lounge at the foot of a majestic staircase. Downstairs is a board room with state-of-the-art audio-visual equipment and antique trains perched on a high shelf. After a tour, we toddled down the path to the Keswick Club Pavilion for a swim in solitary splendor in an indoor-outdoor pool about three feet deep. Overnight guests are granted access to the pool, tennis courts, spa, sauna and steam rooms. Golf costs $85 a round.

Meals are served in three serene dining rooms, dressed in light pastels with white tablecloths and striped and patterned upholstered chairs. Before joining Keswick, chef Richard William Smith worked with the Ashley interests at Llangoed Hall in Wales and ran a country-house hotel with his wife in Great Britain.

Dinner is prix-fixe, $55 for five courses, offered in two variations: chef's choice, which changes nightly, and à la carte, with five selections for each course, changing seasonally. We went with the latter, one of us sampling the salmon argenteuil with asparagus and a sauce of roma tomatoes and basil, followed by grilled turbot on an exquisite sauce with broccoli. Dessert was pear sorbet served with wafer-thin crystallized

Keswick Hall (left) overlooks Keswick Club and golf course.

slices of pear. The other enjoyed the bouillabaisse terrine in aspic, braised monkfish and shrimp with salsa and baby bok choy, and a stellar iced lemon soufflé with berries. A pink champagne sorbet was served between courses. A $20 bottle of Groth sauvignon blanc accompanied an impeccably presented, memorable meal.

Breakfast the next morning was another culinary treat. It began with unlimited fresh orange juice and an iced pineapple surprise that was like a sorbet. A basket of croissants, blueberry muffins and Virginia ham biscuits preceded the main dishes, a tomato and cheese frittata with hash browns and a platter of fresh fruits with fruit compotes. We liked the sound of the English mixed grill with eggs, tomatoes, blood sausage, mushrooms and the like.

Lunch is available prix-fixe, $21 to $25 for two courses (appetizer and entrée, or entrée and dessert), with three or four selections for each course. An extravagant Sunday brunch is served for $25. The Pavilion clubhouse serves three meals a day.

Lunch, Monday-Saturday noon to 2:30; dinner nightly, 6 to 10; Sunday brunch, 11:30 to 2:30.

Doubles, $195 to $495; suites, $545 to $645.

The Inn at Monticello, Route 19, Box 112, Charlottesville 22902. (804) 979-3593.

Nestled at the foot of Monticello Mountain on spacious dogwood-dotted lawns beside quiet Route 20 is this small country manor house, which dates to 1850 but does not seem that old in its new incarnation. It was converted in 1989 into a comfortable, welcoming and non-smoking B&B by Midwesterners Carol and Larry Engel.

The Engels offer five guest rooms with private baths, each decorated in a different period with antiques and reproductions. Cotton sheets and down comforters are on every bed. Our quarters on the first floor, fashioned from the former dining room, had a high, step-up queensize bed and a private screened porch. Another favorite is the second-floor Victorian room boasting Carol's first antique purchase, a carved walnut Eastlake bedstead, and an antique mantel over the working fireplace. A loveseat slants across a corner. Guests in the other upstairs front bedroom can look out to adjacent Willow Lake, a pond with catfish and snapping turtles, at the edge of the property. Another main-floor bedroom has an arched canopy queen bed.

Homemade chocolate-chip and oatmeal cookies, tea, beer and Virginia wines and other beverages are offered in the long, comfortable common room outfitted with Virginiana. Breakfast is taken in the large country kitchen. Carol is known for her orange yogurt and banana-walnut pancakes. We were treated to a delectable crabmeat quiche and raspberry muffins along with fresh orange juice, bananas and strawberries, and hazelnut-flavored coffee.

The Engels, assisted by a resident innkeeper, furnish helpful handwritten directions to their favorite restaurants.

Doubles, $110 to $140. No smoking.

Silver Thatch Inn, 3001 Hollymead Drive, Charlottesville 22901. (804) 978-4686.

A New England look and air pervade this rambling white clapboard house, built by Hessian soldiers who were imprisoned on the site during the Revolutionary War. The original 1780 log house now is a small common room. Later owners expanded so that the inn backing up to a residential subdivision has seven guest rooms with private baths, a cozy bar and three dining rooms (see Dining Spots).

New innkeepers Rita and Vince Scoffone from Arlington "took over a going concern" and only had to remodel three bathrooms. The guest rooms, all named after presidents, remain the same. Watermelon stenciling, wooden slices of watermelon and a watermelon wreath grace the bright and airy James Madison Room, a Federal period room upstairs in the main house with pencil-post queensize canopy bed, working fireplace and square bathtub. A brick patio and a sitting area are available for guests who stay in the four rooms in the adjacent cottage. The burled wood armoire in the George Washington Room is so tall that the ceiling had to be cut back for it to fit. Less formal is the Tyler Room with country pine furniture, deep mulberry walls, an old quilt and a fireplace. Country pine also is used in the upstairs Harrison Room, which has an antique iron double bed and a strawberry motif.

Coconut-granola-honey or chocolate-chip cookies are placed at bedside at night. Breakfast in a cheery sun room is continental-plus, from melons, berries and muffins to cereals and what our informant described as the best granola ever.

Guests have access to the tennis courts and pool of the adjacent Hollymead neighborhood association.

Doubles, $110 to $125. No smoking.

200 South Street, 200 South St., Charlottesville 22901. (804) 979-0200.

Two side-by-side houses at the edge of downtown were a shambles when a team of investors acquired them in 1986. After $1.5 million worth of renovations and at least that much in antique furnishings, they were opened as a suave in-town B&B in the Charleston and Savannah idiom. Most downtown restaurants are within walking distance.

Seventeen rooms and three suites are handsomely outfitted with 18th- and 19th-century antiques from England and Belgium. Most have queensize canopy or four-poster beds and sitting areas, and a few add fireplaces and whirlpool baths.

At our visit, a scrapbook in each room detailed the furnishings, most of which were for sale. In our first-floor front room, we were informed about the Georgian mahogany armoire circa 1800, the mahogany bow front chest of drawers (1815 and apparently having been sold, the more ornate replacement not being described), and eight other prized pieces, down to the Seljuk rug and brass candlesticks on the mantel. A clock-radio and a telephone were concessions to the times, and a TV set was available beneath the eaves in a small third-floor lounge. The room was extra-comfortable and, given its proximity to the street, surprisingly quiet.

Afternoon tea, wine and cheese are set out in the main inn's library, chock full of local reading material. The library also has three scrapbooks portraying the inn's restoration plus more descriptions of all the antiques in living color. A buffet breakfast is served here and on the side veranda and a tranquil terrace courtyard. On a warm morning on the veranda, we were blessed with a breeze along with fresh orange juice, cut-up fruit, cereal, molasses muffins and blueberry cake. A bag of potpourri was an unexpected going-away gift.

Doubles, $90 to $150; suites, $170.

Chester, Route 4, Box 57, Scottsville 24590. (804) 286-3960.

Fifty varieties of trees and shrubs surround this choice property twenty miles south of Charlottesville. Outgoing innkeepers Richard Shaffer and Gordon Anderson like to point out each one, from English boxwood to a 150-year-old white pine. "That's a female holly and in November you can't see the tree for the berries," said Dick as we ogled the gigantic tree, reputed to be the largest in Albemarle County. "And that's a rare tulip poplar."

The trees on seven landscaped acres surround a large Greek Revival home built in 1847 by a retired landscape architect from Chester, England, who left his legacy all around. The interior is decidedly homey. Witness the parlor, called "the doggie room," in honor of the partners' ten award-winning borzoi (Russian wolfhounds) raised in a kennel out back. Dog figurines are on display here and throughout the house. So are open containers of cigarettes, ready for the smoking.

The ex-New Yorkers who opened their retirement retreat as a B&B in 1985 are known for their optional dinner parties – lively, informal affairs that start at 8 o'clock around a Hepplewhite-style mahogany table for fourteen in the dining room. The $24-per-person pricetag includes four courses and all the wine you want. You might start with steamed artichokes and go on to breast of chicken in cream sauce with Chinese snow peas and carrots with dill. An endive salad with a soy dressing and caraway seeds cleanses the palate for dessert, a pear poached in wine, stuffed with ice cream and covered with chocolate sauce. Dick sits at one end of the table and Gordon at the other, playing the perfect hosts and hopping up to clear one course and bring on the next.

A party atmosphere prevails, as one guest learned the night before our visit. She arrived late as the hosts were enjoying dinner with two houseguests. "We gave her dessert and coffee and sat up til 1 drinking port," Dick recounted the next day, looking none the worse for wear. He'd been up at 6:45 to prepare a breakfast of honeydew melon, "my version of Swedish popover pancakes," bacon and fried apples garnished with fresh strawberries. The recipe for pancakes, as well as others of their favorites, are reprinted in a booklet created by friends as a Christmas present for the innkeepers, who now share copies with B&B guests.

Five bedrooms are outfitted with antiques, oriental rugs, artworks and other paraphernalia the partners have gathered on their travels or at auctions. The nicest is the corner room on the main floor, the only one with a private bath and boasting windows on three sides. It and three others have woodburning fireplaces. Two upstairs rooms – one a suite with a sitting room and a queensize four-poster have pedestal sinks and share a bath (the bathrobes in the closets are color-coordinated with each room). Guests in another larger room with twin beds face a bit of a hike through the library and past the laundry room to a bath shared with a small room in the rear. The library and laundry are worth noting. Guests are welcome to use both (how we constant travelers wish more inns offered access to laundry facilities), and the library contains a TV and many classical records.

Doubles, $65 to $100.

High Meadows, Route 4, Box 6, Scottsville 24590. (804) 286-2218 or (800) 232-1832.

The sign out front dates High Meadows twice, 1832 and 1882, to reflect an oddball, two-in-one house. But that's only the half of it. It seems that in 1882, this was a house divided. A new owner wanted to raze the brick Federal structure in back so as not to block the view of his Italianate-Victorian white stucco villa going up in front. His wife and children said no way. What to do with the back porch already built, facing the old house rather than the countryside? He turned it into a longitudinal breezeway and two-story hall connecting the two structures. Thus were preserved two very different modes of architecture and lifestyles in one unusual dwelling.

The two modes are everywhere in whimsical contrast, from the clutter of the Patrick Henry Parlor and the historic aura of the brick-floored downstairs breakfast room to the main-floor Fairview guest room in the Victorian section with a clawfoot tub at the edge of the room facing the fireplace or, a floor below, the paneled Meadow View bedroom with a whirlpool tub, queen bed and a foldout murphy bed. The Fairview is a trove of Victoriana with swaths of netting crisscrossing the queensize blanket-roll rope bed and a bay window overlooking the azalea garden; the Meadow View is barely a cut above a basement den. Possibly more conventional is the Surveyor's Suite on the main floor of the Federal structure. It has an ornate fireplaced sitting room with heartpine floors and the original nine-over-nine window, plus a bath with clawfoot tub and a queensize brass bed in a room with windows on three sides off a porch. All told, there are five bedrooms and two suites, plus a small two-room carriage house with queen and double beds and a TV. The last overlooks the inn's antique rose garden, which contains 40 kinds of roses, some supposedly from pre-Roman days.

Each room contains a bound memorabilia book detailing guest information, photos on the restoration and verses about the room. Each also has a crystal decanter of port, and homemade cookies and fruit are set out in a parlor. Besides three common rooms, the inn has four porches to view 23 acres of gardens, woods and vineyards (the pinot noir grapes are sold to Jefferson Vineyards). Billed as a vineyard inn, High Meadows is the only one in Virginia that combines a place on the National Register of Historic Homes with a new viticultural happening.

In 1992, High Meadows acquired a newer, 1907 private home a four-minute walk down the north meadow and added four more guest rooms with private baths, all but one with decks or porches and fireplaces. This is called the Mountain Sunset Inn to differentiate it from the main Vineyard Inn, but both go under the original High Meadows umbrella.

Owners Peter Sushka and Mary Jae Abbitt live on the property, although she works at a brokerage in Richmond during the week. Peter or his two resident innkeepers prepare a six-course dinner on Saturday, available by reservation for $40 per person in two lower-level dining rooms. A bistro dinner is offered Thursday, Friday and Sunday for $40 to $60 a couple, including wine. Other nights you can get a European evening basket of hot and cold foods ($50 for two with wine). Peter might prepare chicken chablis on puff pastry, beef bourguignonne or lasagna with a couple of salads, fresh fruit and dessert. He puts it in a big picnic hamper with flowers and silver, a bottle of Jefferson or Burnley wine and a book of poetry and sends guests "out to the fields or the gazebo for a romantic dinner."

The dinner option follows a wine-tasting of Virginia vintages at 6:45 in the Grand Hall or the West Terrace. A full breakfast the next morning might involve fresh orange juice and muffins, a main dish ranging from shirred eggs with turkey to various stratas, followed by a fruit dish, perhaps pear and currant crisps or a compote with yogurt.

Doubles, $95 to $145; suites, $120 to $155; carriage house, $140. Add $80 MAP for Saturday stays. Two-night minimum most weekends. No smoking.

The 1817 Antique Inn, 1211 West Main St., Charlottesville. (804) 979-7353.

Owner Candace DeLoach Wilson is an antiques dealer, and all the furnishings in the B&B she opened in 1993 beside her DeLoach Antiques Shop are for sale. The two adjoining townhouses were built by one of Thomas Jefferson's master craftsmen, an Irishman who was the principal carpenter for Monticello and for the Rotunda at the University of Virginia, a few blocks away.

A Georgian who met her engineer-husband Jon while she was an interior designer in New York, Candace has imbued her B&B with a spirit as eclectic as the decor. The living room is appointed with American Empire chests, Venetian tables, Biedermeier chairs, a large zebra-skin rug and a bowl of M&Ms. Upstairs are four bedrooms with private baths. Miss Olive's Room in the rear has a kingsize bed, a marble bathroom with shower and a sitting area. The Mattie Carrington Suite in front has a kingsize bed in the large main room with a sitting area, French antiques and a glass chandelier, plus a canopied double bed in the small room beyond. One bedroom in the interior has no windows whatsoever (it's air-conditioned, our guide pointed out).

The Wilsons live next door and turn over B&B operations to a manager, Vickie Gresge, who also runs the **Tea Room Cafe** on the site with her husband Mark. The cafe occupies a sun porch and dining room. Vickie serves a continental breakfast of fresh fruit, granola and homemade muffins (fancy egg dishes with grits, sausage gravy and biscuits are added on weekends). Exotic sandwiches, salads, desserts and teas (a different flavor daily) are offered Monday-Friday from 11 to 3. The Gresges also serve dinner upon request.

Doubles, $89 to $129; suite, $179.

Dining Spots

Metropolitain, 119 West Main St., Charlottesville. (804) 977-1043.

This unlikely looking place that emerged in 1991 from the Fat City Diner provided one of our best meals in a long time. We say unlikely because the decor is somewhat lacking: uncomfortable booths and small black tables, mini-jukeboxes that put you at the mercy of everyone else's musical tastes, circular mirrors, whirring fans and a generally deco, diner feeling.

Great food emanates from the grill and deep fryer installed up front by owners Vincent Derquenne, a young Frenchman, and partner Tim Burgess. They teamed up at their own place after a stint at The Galerie, which until it closed in 1991 was generally considered the area's best restaurant.

Good sliced bread, a plain salad of Boston lettuce with a mustardy vinaigrette and a simple muscadet from a wide-ranging wine list were mere preambles to the triumphs that were ahead. Among entrées ($15.50 to $20.50), a paillard of plate-cooked (and barely cooked) salmon with basil puree, diced tomatoes and shoestring vegetables was a masterpiece, magnificently presented on an oversize plate speckled with parsley flakes. Equally presented was the grilled pork loin with spring onion puree, absolutely delicious fried cilantro wontons and cabbage slaw, the dish so ample that even two of us could not finish it.

We had to save room for dessert. Good thing, because the champagne granité with fresh citrus and mint goes down as one of the most refreshing finales we've had. A close runnerup was the grilled banana bread with homemade honey vanilla ice cream and warm praline sauce. The description hardly does justice to the presentation, again on oversize plates <197> one with a rainbow of strawberries, peaches and grapefruit; the other surrounded by squiggles of caramel and powdered sugar.

The two young innovators are equally at home with starters ($4.50 to $7.50). How could one choose among ravioli of lamb with arugula and chèvre, shrimp cakes in a sweet potato basket with Thai sauce, blackened tuna sashimi with creamy daikon carrot salad, or grilled rabbit livers with warm black-eyed peas and bacon dressing? Every menu gets more interesting, and dinner has become such a successful production that the weekday lunches have been terminated.

Now if only these guys would enhance the atmosphere to match their food.

Dinner, Monday-Saturday 5:30 to 10.

Cafe Bocce, 330 Valley St. (Route 20 South), Scottsville. (804) 286-4422.

All the foodies in Charlottesville have been heading down to Scottsville lately to try this little pizzeria gone upscale. We joined them one day for lunch and found a long and narrow storefront with brick walls, a crowd seated on mismatched, ice-cream-parlor chairs at small marble tables, 1940s music playing in the background, a black wood banquette along one wall and a black and white tiled-look linoleum floor.

We also found some remarkably good tastes: a cup of spicy gazpacho (as good as we make at home and garnished by a sprig of mint), a hearty BLT on Tuscan bread ($4) and an unforgettable grilled flank steak sandwich with herbed cheese, caramelized onions and sliced tomatoes ($5.25). Both sandwiches were of the knife and fork variety and each came with a zippy new-potato salad nested in a leaf of raddichio. We were so sated we couldn't even think of trying the blueberry tart, the charlotte mousse or the lemon chiffon cake offered for dessert.

We did manage to traipse through the warren of tiny kitchens to find self-taught chef Annamaria Taylor, an architect by training. She and her husband renovated the place themselves and opened a pizzeria in 1993. "This fulfills my need for creativity," Annamaria said of her transition from pizzas and calzones to more exciting fare.

Besides the former, the dinner menu offers a handful of items ($12 to $20) like grilled swordfish with a mango and papaya salsa served with saffron rice, osso buco served over orzo and parslied rack of lamb with a garlic confit. Tempting starters include minted spinach and sweet pea soup, a salad of sautéed corn and mushrooms over arugula, a classic housemade gravlax, potato cakes with sour cream and caviar, and a signature bruschetta with grilled fresh mozzarella and sliced tomatoes.

At our visit, Annamaria was planning to add a patio and bocce court beside her herb garden out back.

Lunch, Tuesday-Saturday 11 to 3; dinner, Tuesday-Saturday 5 to 9, Sunday 3 to 9. Also closed Tuesday in summer. Beer and wine license. No smoking. No credit cards.

Silver Thatch Inn, 3001 Hollymead Drive, Charlottesville. (804) 978-4686.

The restaurant here, always highly regarded locally, is said to be better than ever under new owners Rita and Vince Scoffone and chef Gordon Carlson, who trained at the Inn at Little Washington. The two-level main dining room is pretty and pristine with large spindle-back windsor chairs at well-spaced tables draped in white linens. A quilt hangs on one wall, baskets hang from an old ladder, and Villeroy & Boch china graces the tables. Windows look onto lawns and gardens. A smaller English dining room is pretty in green and rust, and diners in the sun room almost feel they're outside.

Silver Thatch Inn is known for fine dining and lodging.

The complex dinner fare, described by Rita as "beautiful modern American," changes every six to eight weeks. Typical among the eight main courses ($19 to $24) are a sesame sauté of soft-shell crabs served over coriander perfumed rice, grilled local rabbit rubbed with pickling spices with an ancho chile succotash, grilled smoked turkey medallions with a kahlua-soaked dried berry compote and hazelnut-hominy madeleines, and roast loin of veal with a blackberry-balsamic vinegar sauce and roasted pepper polenta. The day's catch might be grilled salmon crusted with roasted pecans and spices, splashed with a mango-papaya vinaigrette flavored with cardamom and cayenne pepper, and served over baby greens with fresh mulberries and flower petals.

Appetizers intrigue, perhaps carpaccio of salmon with a black radish salad or chilled, blanched asparagus with a wild rice and spicy peanut salad on a raspberry-peach coulis. Desserts follow suit: perhaps maple-pecan cheesecake with maple cream and white chocolate maple sauce, chocolate-caramel-almond mousse cake and honey-almond tarts with honey crème anglaise and fresh mulberries.

The wine list, honored by Wine Spectator magazine, features Virginia wines at the low end of the price spectrum. Guests like to pause before or after dinner in the dark and comfy bar.

Dinner, Tuesday-Saturday 5:30 to 9. No smoking.

Memory and Company, 213 Second St. S.W., Charlottesville. (804) 296-3539.
We tried three times to eat at this lovely old townhouse across from the 200 South Street inn. The first time its 45 seats were fully booked. The second time owners Ann Memory and her husband Hans had closed for a few days to recover from the University of Virginia graduation weekend. They did show us around, however, and gave us a sample of one of their splendiferous desserts – homemade coffee ice cream laced with rum on chocolate meringues. Yum! The third time we succeeded, only this time the couple were away on vacation and our experience suffered as a result. And the last time, surprise! The Memorys were only a memory, having sold the restaurant that evolved from the cooking school Ann started here in 1981.

The memory continues, however. New chef-owner John Corbett worked with Ann

Memory for several months before he took over in 1994. He retained the same style and concept. But with fourteen years' experience in California, the native Philadelphian added California and Southwest influences to the country French and Italian fare.

One reason Memory and Company has been so popular is the price. A mere $25 brings a prix-fixe dinner of several courses. Starting with an amuse-bouche of basil pesto savory cheesecake, you might choose among cream of shiitake mushroom soup, house-smoked salmon with sweet mustard sauce or a terrine of eggplant, sweet red peppers and chèvre with a parsley sauce. There are usually three entrées: maybe red snapper in parchment with tomatoes and crème fraîche, local braised rabbit with homemade fettuccine or angus beef tenderloin with red onions caramelized in madeira. A salad of baby greens follows the main course. The dessert choice could be lemon meringue pie, cheesecake with a raspberry and strawberry puree or homemade chocolate ice cream.

John bought Hans's extraordinary wine inventory, which has awards from Wine Spectator. With more than 1,250 bottles, about 100 in the $25 range, Memory and Company attracts serious oenophiles.

Dining takes place in a front room with starched cloths, heavy silver and jam jars filled with fresh flowers, a larger rear dining room where you may view the open kitchen or a back patio beside the herb garden.

Dinner, Tuesday-Saturday 6 to 9.

Duner's, Route 250, Ivy. (804) 293-8352.

From the outside it looks like a roadhouse, but locals as well as itinerant chefs on their nights off pack the place for some of the area's most inventive fare. Beyond a main room with booths and tables overshadowed by a brass canopy-topped bar lies a porch, dressed up with brick walls, patterned wallpaper above wainscoting and seven white-clothed tables with oil lamps and flowers in bud vases.

The water comes in beer mugs. The noise level is high, and so is the lighting. No matter. The food is good to excellent, especially the dozen or more nightly specials that supplement a fairly pedestrian menu. For starters ($4.95 to $7.95), how about grilled duck and spinach salad tossed with pinenuts and a peach-cherry dressing or poached calamari in coconut milk and Moroccan spices? The latter dish came spiced with lots of coriander and a soupy broth that was great for dipping the accompanying monkey bread.

Among entrées ($12.95 to $17.95), we felt the somewhat dry crab cakes cried out for a sauce. "No sauce," the waitress advised; "needs sauce," we insisted. The kitchen obliged with an interesting chile tartar sauce that filled the bill. The veal sweetbreads with shiitake mushrooms and cream sauce were heavenly, though a minimal portion. A zesty salad with Greek olives and red onions accompanied. One of us would have liked to splurge for the night's "entrée salad" of Louisiana oysters with greens tossed in caesar dressing for an extra $12.95. Ginger pound cake with local mulberries, strawberries and raspberries and a peach and pistachio crumb tart were satisfying endings.

A local Montdomaine chardonnay ($19) was a good choice from an extensive wine list, which contained a front page of specials under $20. A restaurant since the 1950s, Duner's was named for a former owner, a Turk whose wife bought it for him as a toy. It was about to close in the late 1980s, when former manager Robert Caldwell took over and saved the day. "It's a crazy place," our waitress acknowledged, "but a lot of good chefs have come through here."

Dinner nightly, 5 to 10; brunch, Saturday and Sunday 10 to 3.

Award-winning wine collection is displayed in dining room at Memory and Company.

C&O Restaurant, 515 East Water St., Charlottesville. (804) 971-7044.

"The least prepossessing fine restaurant in America," the Washington Post calls it. A Travel-Holiday writer considers it the homeliest and "best restaurant in America." National food writers wax rhapsodic about the food, if not the atmosphere.

The local consensus seems to be that the C&O is resting on its laurels. Certainly our experience in the smoke-filled downstairs Bistro did not measure up, nor did that of fellow inn guests who termed their meal all but inedible. Another countered that her dinner was one of the best she'd had, a claim echoed by others at our most recent visit.

The contradictions emanate from a small brick building – identified by an old-fashioned Pepsi sign – across from the old Chesapeake & Ohio Railroad station. Upstairs is high-style dining for 30 patrons in a simple room with high windows, pale yellow walls, high-back chairs and little to distract from the food. The short menu changes daily, is written entirely in French, and is served at two seatings, generally 6:30 and 9:30 – "to give you time to enjoy the five courses," we were informed. Dining at 9:30 on a Monday night seemed preposterous, and we were told that hours could be more flexible on slow evenings.

Downstairs is a dark, noisy and claustrophobic little bistro with a long bar where smokers seem to gather. The bar is cheek to jowl with nine white-linened tables for two amid brick and barnwood walls, considerable bric-a-brac and illumination from three wagon-wheel chandeliers with every other bare light bulb off. The same kitchen serves both dining rooms, so this is considered a good value. David Simpson, owner since 1991 and the chef before that, now does the baking.

Our bistro meal began with generous drinks and a decent artichoke pâté ($5) with good French bread. Disappointment began with the wine list, an extraordinarily expensive affair starting at about $25 and with many in the hundreds. It's a list shared with the upstairs, but quite inappropriate for bistro fare. We liked the steak chinois (flank steak) sliced with tamari and ginger cream sauce, but found the chicken breast with eggplant-avocado salsa bland beyond redemption. The small plates were overcrowded with new potatoes, tomatoes, carrots and onions. We passed up dessert, but heard that the crème caramel was perfect.

The chef was off and the upstairs unexpectedly closed that night, we were informed afterward. Otherwise, a typical upstairs menu lists soup (cream of asparagus, $6.50), half a dozen appetizers ($6.50 to $8) like crab croquette and timbale of sweetbreads, an equal number of main courses ($18 to $27) from salmon en papillote to rack of lamb with pesto, salad or cheese, and seven desserts ($6 to $6.75), from coupe maison and seasonal sorbets to baba au rhum. The downstairs menu is a bit lengthier, although they quickly run out of some items, and less pricey (entrées, $7.50 to $15; desserts, $3 to $3.75).

Dining room, Monday-Saturday 6:30 to 9:30. Bistro, lunch, Monday-Friday 11:30 to 3; dinner nightly, 5:30 to 11.

Brasa, 215 West Water St., Charlottesville. (804) 296-4343.

This striking new downtown restaurant and tapas bar with a Mediterranean theme obviously cost a bundle. It's colorful as can be, from the geranium-bedecked front courtyard for outdoor dining to the vivid colors and wrought-iron accents beneath a high black ceiling inside. Wines are stored in a big copper tub at the prominent tapas bar. The restaurant's name is taken from the embers of the wood-fired brick oven, a focal point of the open kitchen up front.

Although obviously popular with the young crowd, the consensus was that the food fails to measure up to the million-dollar setting. Eight tapas are offered, from $3 for roasted marinated olives to $5.75 for spicy sizzling shrimp. We liked the sound of one involving wood-roasted yukon gold potatoes and salt cod brandade with mint-caper vinaigrette. Otherwise, most of the action — at least on the culinary side — is in eight pastas and entrées ($9.50 to $18.50). Some of the more interesting were toasted angel-hair pasta in a spicy saffron broth with shrimp, scallops, peas and toasted almonds; wood-roasted salmon with flageolet beans and grilled asparagus; crispy duck, catalan style, and grilled loin lamb chops with couscous, tapenade and grilled celery.

Desserts were different: citrus-almond cake with hot lime sauce, crema catalan with espresso biscotti, navel oranges marinated in vanilla bean and cointreau syrup, and a serpentine of phyllo with pistachios, dates, currants and cardamom-honey sauce.

The lunch menu looks interesting as well, though we're told it also reads better than it tastes. Tapas are served on the terrace all day.

Lunch, Monday-Friday 11:30 to 2; dinner nightly, 5:30 to 10.

Starr Hill Cafe, 320 West Main St., Charlottesville. (804) 295-4456.

Formerly the home of the authentic Le Snail restaurant, this refurbished newcomer in a cream-colored house with blue trim still looks like it would be at home in a village in France. Here, it is an unexpected sight, tucked between commercial enterprises just west of the downtown pedestrian mall.

Chef-owner Sheila Hauser Joss returned to the Starr Hill neighborhood in Charlottesville in 1994 after ten years in the kitchen of the Hays-Adams Hotel in Washington, D.C. Like her French predecessors, she lives upstairs. Her place is authentic and her two cozy dining rooms and little bar have been brightened up with fresh paint and the changing works of local artists. A single rose from her garden in back graces each table.

Her regionally inspired menu, short and to the point, has been well received by the local food cognoscenti. Expect main courses ($14.50 to $18) like chicken basted in maple syrup and beer with barley and wilted arugula, orange-crusted sole on steamed spinach, marinated lamb with broiled eggplant and hominy, seared beef tenderloin

Artworks grace walls in rear dining area at Brasa.

with roasted garlic, and roasted pork chop with crisp Virginia ham, sage popover and vanilla sweet potato. Bay scallops with applewood-smoked bacon and a salad of warm shiitake mushrooms, pecans and dried cherries over mixed greens are among the starters. The desserts change daily.

Virginia selections are featured on the well-chosen wine list, pleasantly priced with most in the teens and a few French vintages for big spenders.

Dinner, Tuesday-Saturday 6 to 10; Sunday brunch, 10 to 3.

Southern Culture, 633 West Main St., Charlottesville. (804) 979-1990.

Porch chairs and loungers are grouped beside the planters inside the entry to this quirky looking cafe and restaurant that proved so popular that it expanded into the adjacent hair salon after its first two years. The decor in three dining rooms is 1950s kitsch style. The chef describes the food as Gulf Coast cuisine with an islands theme.

That translates to dinner entrées like pasta jambalaya, grilled tuna steak with lime-cilantro butter, chicken mexicali and roast jamaican jerked pork tenderloin with mango. Things get really interesting with the specials: perhaps grilled swordfish with roasted yellow pepper and crab salsa, perch wrapped in collard greens with mango, bacon and fresh herbs, alligator jambalaya and pan-seared venison chop with barbecue sauce and corn relish. The prices for all this are astonishing, only $7.95 to $13.95. So even the college students who frequent the place can afford an appetizer, perhaps a crab and pepper quesadilla or mushrooms with Virginia trout caviar and crème fraîche. Not to mention desserts like Georgia peach cobbler, chocolate-raspberry cheesecake, la habana banana custard or a Tennessee trifle.

The drink specials are amazing, perhaps a black seal rum and ginger beer ("dark and stormy") or a cajun martini. Stop here also for one of the fancy egg dishes with grits and biscuits for Sunday brunch.

Dinner nightly, 5 to 10:30; Sunday brunch, 11 to 2:30.

Ivy Inn, 2244 Old Ivy Road, Charlottesville. (804) 977-1222.

Sedate types have traditionally gravitated to the outskirts of town and this lovely old red brick dwelling built around 1800. It houses a long-playing, intimate restaurant with a series of small dining rooms upstairs and down. Lately the bar area has been expanded toward a large tent-covered patio to provide a more open feeling.

The short contemporary menu ranges from $14.50 for poissin stuffed with duck and rabbit sausages to $25.95 for rum-glazed rack of lamb. We can vouch for the Jack Daniels shrimp, served in a cream sauce over angel-hair pasta – a nice lunch portion for $11.95 – and the Caribbean chicken breast with tropical fruit salsa. Less successful were a luncheon order of limp mushrooms stuffed with sundried tomatoes and ricotta cheese and a not-very-exciting caesar salad. The day's specials of chicken caesar salad and salmon on salad greens might have been better.

Hazelnut-cappuccino torte, bourbon-pecan pie, apple-walnut cream cheese pie and key lime cheesecake are among the luscious desserts.

Lunch, Monday-Friday 11 to 2; dinner nightly, 5 to 10; Sunday brunch, 11 to 3.

Kafkafé, 20 Elliewood Ave., Charlottesville. (804) 296-1175.

Only in a bustling university area would you expect to find a fledgling coffeehouse/ wine bar/bookstore/cafe like this. With atmosphere in spades, and good food, to boot.

It takes its name from Franz Kafka, some of whose works are in the cluttered bookstore upstairs. A hot spot among University of Virginia professors and medical personnel from the University Hospital, it's also a favorite of many of the town's more creative chefs. Here, in a spare and casual setting made up of book shelves and wine racks plus shady outdoor patios and porches, you can sip cappuccino or beaujolais, munch on a bagel with smoked salmon or eggs Kafkafé (poached and served with crab cakes), lunch on a warm duck salad, listen to jazz and browse through hard-to-find cooking, New Age and travel books.

The food is as innovative as the concept, especially at dinner time. Look for things like pasta with spinach, garlic, crushed red pepper flakes and pinenuts or Jamaican jerked chicken served over jasmine rice ($6.95 to $16.95). Grazers are in their element, enjoying food for thought as well as for the tummy.

Lunch, Monday-Saturday 11:30 to 3 or 4; dinner, Monday-Saturday 5 to 10 or 11.

Tastings, Market and Fifth Streets, Charlottesville. (804) 293-3663.

Another tasty entry on the Charlottesville eating scene, this American grill and wine bar is an adjunct to a wine shop in the Downtown Parking Garage. It claims to be the only such combination of its kind on the East Coast, and boasts a wine list as big as its shop. Unlike many Virginia restaurants that do not segregate smokers, this is a totally non-smoking restaurant. The changing menu features items from a wood grill.

Dinner might include such treats as chef William Curtis's secret crabmeat casserole, $5.95 as an appetizer and $16.95 as an entrée. Grilled salmon with béarnaise sauce, grilled loin lamb chops and roasted tawny duck with spicy orange glaze are among the possibilities, $15.95 to $19.95. Desserts could be caramel apple tart, Vermont maple cream flan and chocolate mousse with sundried cherries. Or you could order a late-harvest riesling or port for what Tastings calls "dessert in a glass."

Meals are taken in an informal room at tables made from the tops of wine crates, or at stools at a bar in the wine shop. A real plus is that the entire 1,000-bottle inventory is available for a $5 corkage fee, meaning splurgers can sample a $40 burgundy for a bargain $45.

More than 120 wines are available by the glass or half-glass, some as part of a sampling of three.

Lunch, Monday-Friday 11:30 to 2:30; dinner, Tuesday-Saturday 6 to 10. No smoking.

Historic Michie Tavern houses a museum and a restaurant featuring Southern cooking.

The Hardware Store, 316 East Main St., Charlottesville. (804) 977-1518.

You have to see this to believe it <197> a warren of boutiques, a gallery promenade and, in the far end of the block-long Grand Old Hardware Store Building, a long and narrow restaurant that looks, well, like a hardware store. Hardware paraphernalia figures prominently in the decor, which is a mix of booths, tables and stools at a counter, plus a loft dining area. Owners Stan and Marilyn Epstein have managed to turn it into an historical attraction, celebrating its centennial in 1995.

The ten-page "menu catalogue" is into all kinds of things by the numbers, some 285 at last count. You name it, they've got it, from quiche, crêpes, sandwiches and tortilla salads to shrimp provençal with pasta (the most expensive item at $13.95) and sundaes. Few can resist at least a nibble of a dessert from the pâtisserie.

Open daily except Sunday from 10 for lunch, dinner and snacks.

Extra-Special

Historic Michie Tavern, Route 53, Charlottesville. (804) 977-1234.

Southern cooking is featured in the 200-year-old converted slave house called The Ordinary beneath one of Virginia's oldest homesteads.

And it's like no "Southern" cooking we've had. That is, it's — dare we say? — tasty and not cooked to smithereens. Food with a bit of a kick is how we'd describe it. You stand in a cafeteria line, help yourself to the unchanging buffet, and sit at communal tables in the old log-walled tavern or at picnic tables in an enclosed garden courtyard. You'll probably have a bigger meal than you want at midday, for a hefty $9.25 pricetag, plus $1 each for beverage and dessert.

The fried chicken was moist and tender, the black-eyed peas and cole slaw fine, the stewed tomatoes interesting and the green beans, which we often find inedible in the South, had a nice herb flavor. Good biscuits and cornbread came with, and the apple cobbler was far better than institutional fare. Ice water and a half bottle of Autumn Hill chardonnay were served in tin cups. Waitresses in Colonial costume refilled plates with items of the diner's choice.

Before or after, you can tour the tavern-museum, which has a large collection of pre-Revolutionary furniture and artifacts. The Meadow Run Grist Mill, a separate building down a steep hill, contains the good **General Store** and the small **Virginia Wine Museum.**

Lunch daily, 11:30 to 3. Museum and store, daily 9 to 5.

Diversions

The new Thomas Jefferson Visitors Center is located off I-64 at Exit 121 along Route 20 south, near the entry road to Monticello. It houses one of the more helpful local information centers we've seen, plus the Thomas Jefferson at Monticello Exhibition and a museum shop. The center offers a combination ticket for tours of Monticello, Ash Lawn-Highland and Historic Michie Tavern Museum for $17.

Monticello, Route 53, Charlottesville, 984-98222. Starting in 1768, Thomas Jefferson designed and built his showplace hilltop home over 40 years, transforming his "essay on architecture" into an amalgam of Italian villas, Rome's Pantheon and a townhouse he observed in Paris while he was there as U.S. ambassador. Now as then, it is the area's chief attraction, having been saved by a private foundation in 1924. It draws more than 550,000 visitors a year who wait in line up to three hours for the privilege. Go early or late, and you may have only a twenty-minute wait, as we did, from the time you board a bus at the shuttle station until the lineup outside the rear of the house is shepherded inside, 25 at a time.

The 35-minute guided tour of the main floor is an unfolding revelation of Jefferson's inventive mind: a calendar clock in the entry "museum," automatic sliding doors, an upside-down mirror, a revolving bookstand, a contraption that made copies of everything he wrote, a rotating pole to hold clothes, and dumbwaiters for wine at either end of the fireplace in the dining room.

Although ahead of his time with skylights and such, his was a house better suited to a bachelor than a family, one of us thought. The tour ends somewhat abruptly outside. Visitors are left to troop on their own around lavish gardens and through the basement passageway past the kitchen to the household service dependencies built into the hillside.

We particularly liked the optional half-mile walk back down to the shuttle station, past flourishing vegetable gardens (said to include nineteen varieties of peas, Jefferson's favorite, all staked on branches and ready to pick at our mid-May visit). Pause at the family graveyard, where Jefferson's obelisk notes his fathering of the University of Virginia and his authorship of the Declaration of Independence and the Statute of Virginia for Religious Freedom, but makes no mention of his presidency. One family gravestone was as recent as 1988.

Back at the shuttle station, visit the **Thomas Jefferson Center for Historic Plants;** plants and seeds are available for purchase at a shop beneath a tent. The primitive **Little Mountain Luncheonette** serves a nice variety of sandwiches and salads in the $3 to $4.50 range. Top them off with Virginia apple cider.

Open daily, March-October 8 to 5, rest of year 9 to 4:30. Adults, $8.

Ash Lawn-Highland, Route 795, Charlottesville, 293-9539. The charming home of President James Monroe is dwarfed by its better-known neighbor, Monticello, whose gift shop is visible two miles away up a path from the front door. Thomas Jefferson

Docent demonstrates spinning wheel at Ash Lawn-Highland.

persuaded Monroe to move to Highland to "create a society to our taste." Monroe's "cabin castle" is very different from Monticello, however. The squawks of resident peacocks could be heard (and their plumes seen) as our small group was led on a guided tour that was both more informative and more personal than the one at Monticello. This was a more lived-in and livable house than Jefferson's, and locals advise seeing it before Monticello, which they consider so novel and different. Monroe was forced to sell the house because of financial difficulties in 1826. It was bequeathed by one of its subsequent owners in 1974 to the College of William and Mary, which has just completed a major restoration. The tour ends when the guide turns you over to an "herb lady" for a five-minute talk on plants and herbs (we enjoyed her chat about nosegays). You can stay on to enjoy "lunch on the first lady's lawn." The new **Kortright Cafe,** honoring Monroe's wife, features foods from the Monroe table (from baked ham sandwich to a pâté plate ($3.50 to $6), served with a cloth in a picnic basket to enjoy on the grounds. Open daily, March-October 9 to 6, rest of year 10 to 5. Adults, $6.

University of Virginia. This prestigious university of 17,000 students was founded in 1819 by Thomas Jefferson, who designed its buildings, planned the curriculum and was its guiding spirit as "a hobby of his old age," according to our guide. Its heart remains the "academical village" along the Lawn, focusing on the Rotunda – a design rated by the American Institute of Architects as the outstanding achievement in American architecture. Free hourly guided tours show visitors the finer points of the Rotunda, a masterpiece patterned after the Roman Pantheon. Our tour was led by a most informative graduate student in English. We peeked into some of the 52 rooms occupied by students as well as two-story faculty pavilions along the Lawn and overheard one guide telling prospective students that these fireplaced rooms are the most coveted housing for seniors who have distinguished themselves on campus, offering heat but no lavatories. Piped up one prospect's mother: "It's an 'honor' to live in rooms with-

without bathrooms?" Deadpanned the guide: "Yes, they have heat." Walk the magnificent campus, see Room 13 where Edgar Allan Poe resided (a raven is on his desk and there's a recorded commentary) and admire the gardens framed by serpentine walls throughout the academical village.

Wineries. Thomas Jefferson failed in his effort to cultivate grapes for wines at Monticello, but he would be proud of what has been accomplished in Virginia in re-

Wines and view at Oakencroft Vineyuard.

cent years. Charlottesville bills itself as the winemaking capital of Virginia, claiming five wineries in Albemarle County and a dozen more in the surrounding area. The most impressive here is **Oakencroft Vineyard & Winery,** whose colorful red-barn winery occupies a stunning site between a farm pond and mountains in estate country just northwest of town. Owner Felicia Warburg Rogan started with a self-taught female winemaker, giving hers the distinction for nearly a decade as the only winery in America to be run by two women. Lately, current winemaker Shepherd Rouse was spending part of his time at his fledgling Rockbridge Vineyard in Raphine. Gabriele Rausse, described as "the sage of Virginia wines," is the legend behind **Jefferson Vineyards** (formerly Simeon Vineyards**),** just up the road from Monticello. You can sample quite a variety (from sauvignon blanc to chardonnay to merlot to a rare pinot grigio, $8 to $18) in the new tasting room with out-

door deck. Jefferson wines also are available at the affiliated **Simeon Farm Store,** where you can pick up a cream cheese and olive or chicken sandwich or a baguette and cheese for a picnic between Monticello and Ash Lawn.

The Downtown Mall. Charlottesville's historic district, especially the Courthouse area and Market Street, surrounds its downtown pedestrian shopping mall. Main Street and its cross streets have been closed to vehicular traffic. The result is a pleasant, tree-shaded brick walkway interspersed with planters, benches, whimsical cut-out figures, sidewalk cafes and frequent directory signs as in enclosed shopping malls. Good for browsing are such shops as **Palais Royal** (French linens for bed, bath and table), the **Pewter Corner, The Coffee Exchange, Windsworth Kites, Spirit Vision Art Gallery** and **Artworks,** for contemporary crafts.

More Shopping. College types gravitate to **The Corner,** an area of shops and restaurants centered along West Main Street between 14th Street and Elliewood Avenue. Upscale shops are concentrated at **Barracks Road Shopping Center,** where you'll find **Laura Ashley** and **Talbots** as well as such local prizes as the **Happy Cook** kitchen shop, the extraordinary **Plow and Hearth** and **Nature by Design** stores and the **Virginia Shop** with everything from Smithfield hams to Williamsburg candles. **HotCakes** is a nifty bakery, cafe and gourmet-to-go shop here.

If you love browsing through unusual grocery stores as much as one of us does, don't miss **Foods of all Nations** at 2121 Ivy Road. Everything Indian, Mexican and Indonesian, for example, is here. So is a huge selection of wines, takeout salads and sandwiches for picnics. If we lived in Charlottesville, we'd be here every week.

Crowd gathers at Montpelier for annual Steeplechase races in November.

Orange County, Va.
On the Trail to Discovery

Few people outside central Virginia have heard of Orange County, much less been there.

Its county seat, Orange (population 2,700), is "still a sleepy little Southern town," in the words of local restaurateur John Bass. Its landed gentry maintains a lower profile than that of its neighbors to the south in Albemarle County surrounding Charlottesville. "People come here from urban centers to escape to the country," says local booster Donna Bedwell. One writer even wrote a piece in a Charlottesville magazine about taking a country weekend respite in Orange from the stresses of Charlottesville.

But this dormant, unspoiled, scenic countryside that spawned presidents James Madison and Zachary Taylor is taking on a new role. Mrs. Bedwell, the former county tourism director, became the first marketing director for Montpelier, the lifelong home of James Madison, now undergoing a major restoration. She was hired to double its annual attendance in a year to 80,000. With that increase will come an inevitable in-

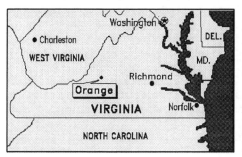

flux of tourism accompaniments along Route 20, the Constitution Trail (so named for the number of homes of presidents and governors along its path) that meanders through the heart of the county.

The horsey set of northern Virginia hunt country is moving toward Orange. The area is the center of the state's winemaking industry, Orange having more acres in grape production than any other Virginia county. B&Bs are emerging to supplement the more established inns. The area "is beginning to be discovered," says Suzie Blanchard, a former Chicagoan whose market research led her to this part of Virginia to establish the new Inn at Meander Plantation.

Meanwhile, it retains the sense of history and unspoiled countryside of old Virginia, suspended in a time warp against the encroaching pincers of Charlottesville to the south, Fredericksburg to the east and Washington to the north. The picturesque charms of the rolling Piedmont, the wineries, the emerging Montpelier, a couple of museums, the Civil War battlefields – all make an interesting destination for those who cherish peace and quiet.

Inn Spots

The Hidden Inn, 249 Caroline St., Orange 22960. (703) 672-3625 or (800) 841-1253.

Hidden down a hillside beneath Route 15, this century-old Victorian inn offers tranquility on five wooded acres deeded from the forebears of Zachary Taylor. It also has some of the fanciest guest rooms around.

Ray Lonick, innkeeper with his wife Barbara, greets guests with his own map and suggestions for touring and shows off his back yard containing "just about every tree that grows in Virginia." The Lonicks – he an early-retired Xerox sales executive from New Jersey – acquired the inn in 1987 and totally redecorated, adding Barbara's samplers, her mother's quilts, family photos and their homemade bath salts and cinnamon soaps. They offer five-course dinners by reservation, have compiled a cookbook, and have added two deluxe suites in outbuildings and three guest rooms in an adjacent house.

Rooms now total ten, all with private baths and period furnishings and some with jacuzzi tubs and fireplaces. Our expansive quarters in the Verandah Room, upstairs and to the rear, included a queensize pencil-post bed with a fishnet canopy and ruffly pillows, a chaise lounge, an enormous bathroom with windows on two sides and, crowning touch, a private balcony with wicker furniture for viewing the back yard. Also special is the upstairs suite in the carriage house, dark and masculine with a rooftop balcony, jacuzzi, and paisley sheets and pillowcases matching the bathroom wallpaper. A new treat is the garden cottage, pink and flowery with a skylight in the ceiling, a queensize four-poster, TV, jacuzzi and rear deck.

The Lonicks provide candlelight picnics and bubble bath in the rooms of late-arriving guests on Fridays and for those on romantic getaway packages. The optional five-course dinner, priced at $29, is served to house guests by reservation Tuesday-Saturday, though somewhat irregularly. The night we stayed turned out to be Barbara's birthday, and it was her turn for an evening out at Prospect Hill (see Dining Spots).

Ordinarily, dinner here begins with a wine reception featuring area vintages in the living room. Ray and daughter Chrys escort guests to tables in the dining room and serve the meal prepared by Barbara. Typical fare includes artichokes romano, asparagus soup, hearts of palm salad, filet of beef with chasseur sauce or chicken with mushrooms in puff pastry, and cheesecake or white chocolate mousse pie.

Ray takes over at breakfast. While Barbara served, he cooked our french toast made with thick homemade bread and sausage following openers of peach-orange juice, cut-up grapefruit and carrot muffins. Orange-granola pancakes and cheese eggs with ham and biscuits are other favorites.

Doubles, $79 to $129; larger jacuzzi rooms with porches, $139 to $159. Two-night minimum on weekends. No smoking.

Dogwoods and azaleas provide springtime welcome to The Hidden Inn.

The Inn at Meander Plantation, James Madison Highway (Route 15), Route 5, Box 460, Locust Dale 22948. (703) 672-4912.

"It's a real treat to be in a house where so many historical figures have tread the floors." So says Suzie Blanchard, co-innkeeper with her husband Bob of the Inn at Meander Plantation. They know. Their stately Colonial manor house with six pillars in front was built in 1766 by Henry Fry Sr., whose close friend, Thomas Jefferson, often stopped here on his way to and from Monticello. A print of the first official map of Virginia, as surveyed and drawn by the fathers of both Fry and Jefferson, hangs on their living room wall. And Robert E. Lee rested in the shade of a sycamore on Meander land while a blacksmith shod his horse and Confederate troops crossed the Robinson River en route to the Civil War Battle of Cedar Run.

Today, guests who stay at this new five-room inn can tread in the same footsteps. They are greeted in a reception room behind the pillared portico that's large enough to hold a grand piano. They gather in the sunken living room, long and comfortable, and on the rear porches of the L-shaped house. They stay in one of the five bedrooms, one of them a two-room suite. All have private baths and queensize four-poster beds and are elegantly furnished to the period with lacy pillows, down comforters, wing chairs, armoires and oriental rugs on the polished heartpine floors. The suite and a downstairs room both open onto the rear porches. The adjacent groom's cottage holds a sitting room with a sofabed, a queensize bedroom and a kitchenette. A deluxe two-room suite was planned in the former summer kitchen, and more guest rooms are envisioned in the former kennels. A TV and game room was in the works in an out-building.

Guests also enjoy some fairly exotic meals whipped up by Suzie, a food writer for Pioneer Press newspapers in suburban Chicago. The former publisher there, Suzanne Thomas, shares innkeeping duties here with the Blanchards.

Breakfast, as delivered by these two articulate women, is a convivial affair in the formal dining room. You might start with fresh fruit (a seasonal favorite is sautéed orange slices and cranberries), a choice of juices and a spicy upside-down sausage cornbread. Next come scrambled eggs flavored with herbs from the garden and baked hash browns. Sour cream coffee cake, poppyseed bread or croissants might accompany. Others of Suzie's specialties include wild rice and walnut pancakes, spinach strata, crab or asparagus quiche and grits.

Dinner is offered by reservation for $32.50 a person, BYOB. A typical meal might be spicy shrimp with homemade rémoulade sauce, crab bisque or cream of broccoli soup, a salad of baby greens with grilled portobello mushrooms, and a main course of grilled game hen with soy-pineapple marinade, accompanied by green beans with red pepper slices and garlic. Dessert could be a fresh strawberry tart.

Adjourn to one of the white rockers on the expansive back porches to survey the scene. The 80-acre property contains formal boxwood gardens, a portion of the Robinson River and pastures for seventeen resident horses.

Doubles, $95 to $130; suites, $155 to $175.

The Shadows, 14291 Constitution Hwy., Orange 22960. (703) 672-5057.

"I target the child in every adult," says Barbara Loffredo, who goes so far as to put rubber duckies in the bathrooms so you can play in the tub. Ex-New Yorkers Barbara, a legal secretary, and husband Pat, one of New York's finest, fell in love with the area, bought the 1913 stone craftsman's cottage and opened in 1987 as a B&B. "Our debut was the Christmas tour," recalled Barbara, "and 320 people came through."

The house is up a long and winding drive through many trees (hence the name Shadows). The Loffredos have added lush cutting gardens of flowers and herbs to the side around a gazebo. As you tour the grounds you might be accompanied by the couple's dog, James Madison, found at – you guessed it – Montpelier.

With Stickley furniture and a staircase that architects make a special trip to see, the downstairs common areas are charming. Lots of antiques and pieces the couple have collected decorate the four upstairs bedrooms, all with private baths. We like best the Rose Room, which has a huge private veranda overlooking the lawns and the Loffredos' goat, Nanny, grazing near the barn (guests feed her flowers and dog food to gain her affection). The Blue Room has a cedar-lined bathroom and a queensize walnut bed pre-dating the Civil War. The smaller Peach Room with a king bed of burled walnut is particularly pretty, and the Victoria Room is full of ruffles.

Also on the property are two outbuildings converted into sleeping quarters. The Cottage has a separate sitting room with wicker furniture and its own deck. The Rocking Horse Cabin, also with two rooms and a porch, is all natural wood on the inside and decorated with country crafts. There's an array of rocking horses, and the horse motif extends from the cover on the kleenex box to the toilet lid.

Pat is in charge of the wonderful breakfasts served on fine crystal and china: maybe a fruit course like poached pears in grand marnier cream or a big bowl of local strawberries. Stuffed french toast with cream cheese sauce and a dish of sautéed apples that comes out like a soufflé is a favorite. The ham, cheese and egg bake uses local eggs, their yolks so yellow they make the orange juice look pale, Pat says. Barbara calls his buttermilk biscuits the best around.

From refreshments like hot spiced cider or iced tea upon arrival to a homemade sachet when you leave, you'll be treated with TLC and a lot of mothering at the Shadows.

Doubles, $80 to $95; cottages, $100 and $110.

Sleepy Hollow Farm, 16280 Blue Ridge Tpke. (Route 231), Gordonsville 22942. (703) 832-5555 or (800) 215-4804.

Nestled in a hollow off Route 231, Orange County's prettiest byway, Sleepy Hollow is a paradise of sorts. Beverley Allison, innkeeper with her daughter Dorsey, moved to the house as a bride in 1950 and calls it "a poor man's Montpelier, a humble little frontier house in the midst of all the estates." Expanded over the years, the house is beautifully but comfortably furnished and has a lived-in feeling. It is surrounded by

Main house at Sleepy Hollow Farm is surrounded by lawns, woods and pastures.

lawns, woods and pastures. In front is a farm pond beside a gazebo, a dock that says "swim at your own risk" and, at our visit, a bunch of ducklings scurrying after their mother.

Beverley, an ABC News journalist turned Episcopal missionary, calls hers an organic house that's still growing and evolving. The process continued with the conversion of a TV room into a sixth guest room with a queen bed, fireplace and jacuzzi and the enclosing of the adjoining terrace for a new TV room. The jacuzzi is "bowing to the trend," Beverley acknowledges, "even though this is a place for people not to lie in a bathtub but to go birding, to discover the wildlife, to smell the flowers."

Guests have plenty of space to spread out in a cozy living room, a beamed dining room and what used to be a country porch, now expanded into an enormous sun room with a showpiece dollhouse (Beverley provides a less precious one for the kiddies to play with). This is the setting for a breakfast of fruit compote, farm-fresh eggs (from Dorsey's chickens) or pancakes, and extra-good coffee because the water comes from a deep spring on the property.

Accommodations include a main-floor master bedroom with a queensize canopy four-poster, dressing room, full bath and a stunning handpainted chest from the Orient. Others are an upstairs room with a large bathroom overlooking the pond and a small bedroom known as the Ghost Room, though the ghost has not been seen since the house was blessed. What's called the children's suite has two rooms connected by a bath. Just outside is the Chestnut Cottage made up of two suites: the kitchen house, which obviously has a kitchen, and the older and smaller slave house. Each has a deck, a fireplaced sitting room with a pullout sofa and a bedroom and bath upstairs. For 1995, Beverley was planning a two-story addition to the kitchen house to include a washer, dryer and a whirlpool tub off the bathroom.

Baskets of fruit and Virginia peanuts are in the rooms. Beverley serves refreshments, from tea to local wine, upon guests' arrival.

Doubles, $65 to $95; new suite, $125.

Willow Grove Inn, 14079 Plantation Way, Orange 22960. (703) 672-5982 or (800) 949-1778.

Perched on a hillside with 37 acres, this Federal and Classic Revival plantation home commands attention. You can see it as you approach along Route 15 from the south, and the number of cars in the parking lot attests to the popularity of its restaurant (see Dining Spots).

Like many houses of its size, Willow Grove had fallen on hard times when it was purchased in 1987 by Angela and Richard Mulloy to operate as a restaurant and inn. They're proud that the woodworking in the original 1778 portion was done by the artisans who crafted Montpelier, and that the brick portion was built in 1820 to Thomas Jefferson's design by workmen who had just finished his University of Virginia campus. The Mulloys are restoring the Victorian gardens and primping the sloping lawns with their stately magnolias, English boxwood and the willows for which the place was named.

Seven guest rooms with private baths on the second and third floors are named for Virginia presidents born along the Constitution Trail and decorated to the appropriate period. The Wilson suite with a turn-of-the-century motif contrasts with the mid-18th-century Harrison Room, which has what Angela calls a sailboat's bathroom with a toilet beyond the step-through shower. Rooms are handsomely furnished, contain beds with triple sheeting and down pillows, and possess such amenities as Saratoga water and a large basket of assorted toiletries, many of them Neutrogena. A hearty breakfast of fresh fruit with scrambled eggs, frittatas or french toast is served in the front tavern room, full of hunting prints and atmosphere.

Doubles, $95 to $155. No credit cards.

The Holladay House, 155 West Main St., Orange 22960. (703) 672-4893.

This in-town, Federal-style brick house dating to 1830 offers six guest rooms with private baths and, a treat for some, breakfast in your room. "My grandfather bought this place in 1899," says genial host Pete Holladay, "and some of the family have been here ever since." His father was raised in the house and, though Pete and his wife had long talked of doing a B&B, it wasn't until 1989 when their kids were through college that they opened. He'd been in charge of food and housing services at private schools for 30 years, so considered this a logical move.

Since his wife teaches school, most of the innkeeping chores fall upon him. He prepares a full breakfast, heavy on fruits, fresh breads, perhaps scones with eggs or baked eggs with tomatoes and popovers, biscuits, peach puffs or apple muffins that were voted the best in Virginia by the state B&B association. He serves the meal in guests' rooms, anytime between 6 and noon, saying that's the way people want it. A lovely formal dining room is put into use if groups want to eat together.

Each bedroom is furnished with family pieces, including armoires, sleigh beds and four-posters, as well as a table and chairs for breakfast service. A ground-level suite contains a small sitting room, a large bedroom and a bath with a whirlpool tub and walk-in shower. It can be rented in conjunction with an existing ground-floor bedroom with kitchenette and bath. In late 1994, the Holladays opened a new recreation/game room on the ground floor. Guests also enjoy a side porch and two outdoor decks.

Doubles, $95 to $120; suite, $185.

Prospect Hill Plantation Inn, Route 3, Box 430, Trevilians 23093. (703) 967-0844 or (800) 277-0844.

Although often thought of in connection with Charlottesville, which is fifteen miles to the west, this renowned inn is quite close to Orange, and is often recommended by Orange innkeepers for its dining.

Out in the middle of nowhere, the place is idyllic: a thirteen-room country inn and restaurant (see Dining Spots) on a 40-acre wheat plantation dating to 1732. The hand-

Prospect Hill Plantation Inn offers rooms in dependencies as well as in main house.

some, pale yellow main house is the oldest continually occupied frame plantation manor in Virginia and comes complete with the original dependencies, all transformed into deluxe lodgings tucked away in the trees. All but one room have fireplaces and about half have double jacuzzis. Afternoon tea, a fixed-price candlelight dinner and breakfast in bed are included in the tariff. A basket of fresh fruit, a box of raisins, homemade cookies and half a bottle of red wine are in each room.

The five guest rooms in the manor house vary in size from servant quarters to the Overton. The latter is dark, quiet and rich in blue with a high queensize four-poster bed, sitting area and a balcony overlooking the back lawn. Most coveted are the eight rooms and suites in dependencies on either side of the manor house. They are cherished for their privacy as well as their comforts. The original summer kitchen is dark and historic and offers a double jacuzzi. The carriage house contains two expansive suites with sitting areas. The walls of the boys' cabin, oldest on the property (1699), are exposed logs, reminding one of us of summer camp long ago. Overlooking the inn's swimming pool, it has a large cedar bathroom (nothing like the shower houses of summer camp) and a double jacuzzi.

A country breakfast, perhaps fresh fruit compote and a cream cheese and herb omelet with bacon, toast and muffins, is served in guests' bedrooms or the dining room.

Innkeepers Bill and Mireille Sheehan, who converted the plantation into an inn in 1977, have turned day-to-day operations over to their son Michael and his wife Laura.

Doubles, $210 to $270, MAP; suites, $280 to $310, MAP.

Dining Spots

Willow Grove Inn, 14079 Plantation Hwy., Orange. (703) 672-5982.

The rural setting is tough to beat and the dining rooms are as luxurious as can be. Dining is in three venues. The Library is a comfortable room dressed in white with different floral china at each table (as is the case throughout the inn). The larger and more formal Dolley Madison Room has a crystal chandelier, Queen Anne chairs and deep rose swags over the windows. The ground-floor Clark's Tavern sports a new bar of heartpine, hand-hewn beams and assorted antique china on the tables. Service was leisurely at lunch (no longer served), when we sampled a mesquite chicken salad and poached salmon with a cucumber salad. We also enjoyed the inn's specialty, Willow pie, a decadent concoction with chocolate chips, walnuts and bourbon in a puff pastry shell topped with real whipped cream.

The chef changes the short dinner menu weekly. Typical main courses ($19.50 to $22.95) are cornmeal-crusted local trout with Virginia ham and black walnuts, grilled swordfish with sundried tomato and cilantro butter, napoleon of grapevine-smoked chicken breast with forest mushrooms and grilled beef tenderloin with bourbon sauce. Starters could be wild watercress vichyssoise, baked walnut-crusted goat cheese with field greens and raspberry-walnut vinaigrette, and tomatillo and country sausage tart with a toasted cornmeal crust. For dessert, how about bourbon-walnut-chocolate pie, fruit cobbler or frozen white chocolate mousse with praline sauce?

A vocalist and pianist may entertain on weekend evenings, and live jazz is played at brunch.

Dinner, Thursday-Saturday from 6, Sunday from 4; Sunday brunch, 11:30 to 3. No credit cards.

Prospect Hill, Route 613 off Route 250, Trevilians. (703) 967-0844.

Dining is an event at this plantation inn, so secluded that it feels it must offer dinner to house guests who have nowhere else to eat, but so special that it draws outsiders from Orange, Charlottesville and beyond.

Executive chef Michael Sheehan changes the menu for the set (no choice), five-course meal nightly. Guests are invited into the manor house half an hour before the appointed dinner hour to help themselves to complimentary wine and cider in the entry hall, relax by a fireplace in the parlor or stroll the grounds. When the innkeeper rings the dinner bell, everyone is seated at a private table – in the front dining room, the Rose Room or the Conservatory. The innkeepers introduce themselves to the diners in each room, describe what they are about to be served, offer a grace and the meal begins.

Although we're partial to the Conservatory with its summery wrought-iron chairs and view onto the back lawns, we think each room is pretty as a picture. Tables are set with cut glass, fine china, heavy silver (including three forks) and a vase of alstroemeria. The French cooking reflects Mireille Sheehan's background in Provence.

A typical meal ($40 to $50, including pre-dinner wine or cider) could be cream of leek and potato soup, house salad tossed with vinaigrette, and châteaubriand in puff pastry with white wine and mushroom sauce. An orange cream mousse served over ladyfingers and sprinkled with grand marnier might conclude. There's an excellent wine list, and a nightly special is offered for under $20 a bottle.

Dinner nightly by reservation, Sunday-Thursday at 7, Friday and Saturday at 8.

The Gourmet, 182 Byrd St., Orange. (703) 672-3514.

Arrive at this highly rated spot and you might think you've got the wrong place, for it isn't terribly attractive and doesn't even look like a restaurant. But go inside for what everyone locally says is the most consistent food in town. Gourmet it really isn't, but good it is.

We barely made it in time for "lunch on the porch," which isn't really a porch but an L-shaped room with a bar. And the menu wasn't at all what we'd envisioned from the name. But we were very satisfied with the ham quiche and salad ($5.25) and the sea-

Dining rooms at Willow Grove Inn feature crystal chandeliers and swag draperies.

food special, a just-in soft-shell crab perfectly sautéed, with cole slaw and carrots ($7.95). (Lunch since has been discontinued, but the porch serves light fare from 4 p.m. on.) We enjoyed chatting with the chef, John Bass, and the solicitous waitress, Mary, who kept refilling our iced-tea glasses and who has been with the restaurant since it opened in 1978.

Afterward, Mary proudly gave a tour, showing a fairly large rear dining room looking outside onto a little fenced-in garden containing a small Japanese cherry tree. "We have white tablecloths and napkins on the weekends," said she. And the local art on the walls is for sale. Another interior dining room is on view through windows from the "porch," and there's a sitting room for those waiting for tables.

The dinner menu is a mix of continental and Southern favorites. You could start with crudités with dip, country ham biscuits, pâté maison or baked brie with sliced almonds. Try the French onion or potato-leek soup if you're really hungry before digging into coq au vin, broiled scampi with garlic butter, New York strip steak, country ham steak with redeye gravy, calves liver with onions or, the house specialty, fried oysters. Entrées are priced from $12.50 to $19.50, except $22 for veal medallions with mushroom cream sauce. Soup, salad, vegetable, potato and spoon bread or rice come with. For dessert, sample the almond cheesecake or pecan pie.

Everything is made on the premises, which, we guess, is why they call it gourmet. The short, all-Virginia wine list is priced in the teens.

Dinner, Tuesday-Saturday from 5; light fare on porch, from 4.

Toliver House, 209 North Main St., Gordonsville. (703) 832-3485.
This Victorian house converted into a restaurant underwent major changes and expansion in 1994. Owner Mike DeCanio brought in two friends from the Midwest as partners, chef Gary Johnson and manager Jim Reber. They closed for six months to add a screened dining porch, a new kitchen and a new lounge as well as to redecorate

existing dining areas in the front parlor, dining room and paneled library. The result is a spiffy, white and green decor that varies from room to room with more seating for dining on the porch and in the lounge. The new chef added excitement to the cuisine.

White tablecloths, colored overcloths and candlelight are the backdrop for an extensive menu with an emphasis on fresh seafood and down-home Southern cooking. Dinner entrées are priced from $11.95 for grilled pork tenderloin cutlets to $18.95 for filet mignon or charbroiled porterhouse steak. The specialty is crab cakes, available as an appetizer or a main course. Other favorites are broiled jumbo shrimp stuffed with lobster filling, grilled swordfish or halibut, and a fried oyster sandwich is a luncheon standout. Popular starters include Brunswick stew, french onion soup with madeira and gruyère, smoked salmon and shrimp cocktail. The dessert tray might hold pumpkin or brandy-alexander cheesecake, coconut-carrot cake and sweet potato-pecan pie.

Chef Johnson added international or ethnic fare on Thursday nights, the themes changing monthly and planned a year in advance. Oktoberfest brought German food; November, Colonial American; December, international Christmases, and February, Asian.

Tinted photos of Gordonsville and area are displayed in the new Nathaniel Gordon lounge, named for the town's founder and featuring an oak bar custom-made by a cabinetmaker from Charlottesville. The lounge, where the dining tables are topped with cloths and kerosene lamps, is the only room in which smoking is allowed. The restaurant serves wines from Virginia exclusively.

Lunch, Tuesday-Saturday 11:30 to 2:30; dinner, Thursday-Sunday 5:30 to 9; Sunday brunch, 10:30 to 2:30. Closed first two weeks in January.

Firehouse Cafe & Market, 137 West Main St., Orange. (703) 672-9001.

The old firehouse with its high ceilings, tall front windows and abundant greenery provides lots of atmosphere for this new cafe and market. It serves breakfast, lunch and deli takeout fare, and offers light meals and a house band on Friday nights, when local yuppies have made it the place to be and people are apt to end up dancing in the streets.

Things were quieter at our lunchtime visit, when we enjoyed a cup of gazpacho, a pasta salad, and a vidalia onion quiche with house salad. Specials were cold curried broccoli and cold zucchini soups, minted fruit salad and chocolate-almond torte. The menu is limited, but you'll find nachos, a burrito plate, deli sandwiches and desserts, and everything is under $5.95.

Nothing is over $4 at breakfast, when you can order french toast with fried apples and sausage or a breakfast burrito with home fries or grits.

Open Monday-Thursday 7 to 4, Friday to 11 p.m., Saturday 9 to 4.

Firehouse Cafe is local hot spot.

Wayland's, 322 Madison Road, Orange. (703) 672-3203.

This is the well-regarded successor to the old Horsefeathers restaurant, a vast place fashioned from a horse barn. New owners Tony and Debbie Wayland have given fresh life to the place, where tables and booths are in former horse stalls and farm implements hang from the barnwood walls. Live bands play on weekends in the large bar and lounge in back, fortunately well separated from the more sedate dining room.

The thing to order here is the specialty prime rib, available in three sizes. Also recommended are the six chicken dishes, but you'll find a variety of entrées from fried fish fingers, steamed shrimp and snow crab legs to beef tips on rice and lasagna, priced generally from $8.95 to $14.95. Appetizers run to nachos, potato skins, mozzarella sticks and Buffalo wings; most make up part of a $6.50 sampler platter for two. Sandwiches and light fare also are available at night, as well as for lunch.

Desserts include strawberry shortcake, hot fudge sundae and Mississippi mud pie.

Lunch, Monday-Friday 11:30 to 2; dinner, Monday-Saturday 5 to 10, Sunday to 9.

Charley's, 377 Madison Road, Orange. (703) 672-9012.

Only in a small town like Orange would a family restaurant and pizza parlor be one of the favored dining spots, and Charley's – though not to sophisticates' tastes – is locally popular. Tucked into the Orange Village Shopping Center, it is attractive on two levels in pink and gray. The focal point in back is a salad bar, "all the soup and salad you can eat" for $4.45.

The rest of the extensive menu is standard family fare, from four kinds of omelets and eight burgers to lasagna, chicken cacciatore and veal parmigiana with spaghetti. One might wish that Greek chef-owner Charles Kambanelios would offer more Greek fare. Gyros, souvlaki, Greek salad, shish kabob and baklava are about it, although he does incorporate stuffed grape leaves into the salad bar.

Lunch and dinner daily, 11 to 9 or 10.

Mario's, 269 Madison Road, Orange. ((703) 672-3344.

A chef from Sicily is plying his trade at this modest new eatery, "home of the authentic pizza and real Italian cuisine." He's so proud of his pizzas that he challenged Pizza Hut to a head-to-head competition at the Orange County Fair in 1994 (we didn't hear the results, but we certainly can guess). "There's a big difference between the big chains and the independent pizzeria and you can taste that difference right here," he advertises.

Neapolitan, Sicilian and white pizzas, strombolis and calzones are among the offerings on the enormous menu, priced by size from $5.25 to $11.95. Also available are pastas, chicken and veal dishes (we hear great things about the veal marsala, $7.95), hot subs, hoagies and spinach calzones that are said to be out of this world. There are a few beers and wines to go with.

Open daily, 11 to 11 or midnight.

Happy Garden, 130 East Main St., Orange. (703) 672-1044.

There don't seem to be many takers for Chinese food in downtown Orange, based on our visits when this newcomer's short-lived predecessor was all but empty. But city folks from Washington rate the place highly, and we certainly liked our chicken with garlic sauce ($7.25), hot and spicy, and an $8.50 dish called "mish mosh" that brought roast pork, chicken and shrimp stir-fried with vegetables on a nest of pan-fried egg noodles. The wide noodles with two sauces that preceded were extra good; the tea that followed, rather strange. We passed on the honey-banana ice cream in favor of rainbow sherbet.

A sea of white-linened booths and tables with accents of pink and black and small globes on the walls, the place is fairly large and brightly illuminated. "Sizzling Triple

Barboursville Ruins area is backdrop for winery and, in summer, Shakespeare plays.

Delight" ($10.95), sliced beef, chicken and shrimp sautéed with Chinese greens on a sizzling hot platter, is one of the new owner's specialties.

Lunch daily, 11 to 3; dinner, 3 to 10 or 11.

Diversions

Montpelier, Route 20, Montpelier Station, 672-2728. A Johnny-come-lately as tourist attractions go, the home of President James Madison was opened for public tours in 1987 by the National Trust for Historic Preservation. It's very much a restoration in progress, so don't expect to find a furnished home as at nearby Monticello or Ash Lawn. Do expect to see what was — and will be again when finished — a showplace renowned for entertaining. Started as an eight-room house, it was expanded over the years to the point that when the National Trust inherited it from Marion du Pont Scott, it was a 55-room mansion that the du Pont heiress had made into a hunt-country mecca. Since 1934, it's been the site of the Montpelier Steeplechase races, staged annually on the first Saturday in November. The trust is restoring the house to show both the Madison and du Pont influences. A bus shuttles visitors from the excellent gift shop called the **Montpelier Supply Co.** up a pretty hillside drive to the imposing home, somewhat the worse for years of neglect. Interior highlights include the Corning Glass fireplace with enormous mirror above in "La Modern" Red Room, all art-decoed up by Marion du Pont, the horsewoman. The du Ponts' Adams Room is the most "furnished" room with a rare Persian carpet, reproduction Steinway piano and gilt ceiling; another part of the house will show how the Madisons lived. Visitors can amble through the reconstructed double-tiered gardens, quite a sight against a forested hillside backdrop, and follow a tree walk brochure that points out 40 trees from across the world. The shuttle bus traverses a portion of the 2,700-acre estate, which has 100 other structures including houses, a bowling alley and stables, plus race courses, thoroughbred horses and working farmlands leased to tenants. On the way out, notice the Montpelier station built in 1910 at the entrance to the estate. It seems William du Pont wanted the train to stop there; the railroad wouldn't allow it without a station, so he built one. Although the train no longer stops, the station lives on as a post office. And Montpelier lives on as a social center for the county, hosting wine festivals, the county fair and such — preserving what marketing director Donna Bedwell calls "not only the architecture but the cultural heritage of the area." Open daily, 10 to 4. Adults, $6.

James Madison Museum, 129 Caroline St., Orange, 672-1776. This small down-town museum is an excellent complement to Montpelier, showing possessions of the president and his wife Dolley, furnishings from Montpelier, presidential correspondence and books from his library. Downstairs is a fine Hall of Agriculture exhibit in tribute to Madison's farming techniques. Open Monday-Friday 9 to 4, weekends 1 to 4; closed weekends in winter. Adults, $3.

Exchange Hotel Civil War Historic Museum, 400 South Main St., Gordonsville, 832-2944. Built as a railroad hotel in 1860, this handsome Greek Revival was transformed into a military hospital during the Civil War and later abandoned. A forward-looking group of women formed an historical society to buy it in the 1970s for $14,000; it was recently appraised at $340,000. It's furnished to illustrate both its hotel and hospital functions and has quite a collection of Civil War memorabilia, from weapons and uniforms to medical artifacts and surgeons' implements used in the very room in which they are displayed. Tour guide Walter Jennings treats this as if it were his home and is full of enthusiasm and minutia. Open mid-March through December, Tuesday-Saturday 10 to 4; also Sundays in summer, 12:30 to 4:30. Adults, $3.50.

Barboursville Vineyards and Ruins, 17655 Winery Road (Route 777), Barboursville, 832-3824. Virginia winemaking started here in 1976, nearly two centuries after pioneering vintner Thomas Jefferson's vineyards of European stock were blighted. The Zonin family from Italy were the first in the state to plant viniferas successfully and have many awards to show for them. Specializing in premium wines, winemaker-manager Luca Paschina offers an excellent chardonnay for $9.99 and limited releases of pinot noir ($10.99) and merlot ($11.99) in an impressive tasting room with a Mediterranean facade. Visitors get to sample at least four of the fifteen wines. Seventy-five scenic acres are under grape cultivation and more than 10,000 cases are produced annually. Nearby on the property are the **Barboursville Ruins,** the Jefferson-designed home of Gov. James Barbour, which was destroyed by fire in 1884. Open to public view behind dense shrubbery, the shell of the mansion is remarkably close to two handsome outbuildings, joined into one and lived in today as the primary residence of the estate. Ruins on view, Monday-Saturday 10 to 4:30, check in at winery office. Winery: tastings, Monday-Saturday 10 to 5; tours, Saturday 10 to 4.

Shakespeare at the Ruins, Barboursville, 832-5355 or (800) 768-4172. The Barboursville Ruins are a spectacular backdrop for the annual Shakespeare at the Ruins each August. The Four County Players, Central Virginia's longest-running community theater, stages one of its year's five productions on the grounds of the mansion, combining Renaissance costumes and music with a Shakespearean play ("As You Like It," on four weekends in 1994). A catered buffet dinner ($15) and wines are available from the winery for a picnic before the show. Curtain, Thursday-Saturday at 8, Sunday at 5. Tickets, $12.

Burnley Vineyards, Route 641, Barboursville, 832-2828. Chardonnay and cabernet were the first two wines issued in 1984 by this small winery. Winemaker Lee Reeder said only twenty percent of their visitors liked them, the rest preferring sweeter wines, so he obliged and Burnley now produces 4,000 cases a year of riesling and blends as well as limited amounts of cabernet and chardonnay. Lee serves visitors in a large skylit tasting room, and his parents take in overnight guests at the **House in the Vineyard,** a two-bedroom house with full kitchen, living room and deck for $125 a night,

$600 a week. Tours and tastings, March-December, Thursday-Monday 11 to 5, weekends only in winter.

Horton Vineyards & Winery, 6399 Spottswood Trail (Route 29), Gordonsville, 832-7440. Although it has been growing grapes behind the Hidden Inn in Orange and producing wines in connection with Montdomaine Cellars south of Charlottesville, in 1994 Horton Vineyards was building a large new underground winery topped by a sales room looking rather like a French château. Dennis and Sharon Horton, who have produced a number of award-winners, were earning acclaim for their new Horton norton ($12). An oak-aged wine patterned after the 19th-century Monticello Wine Co.'s original claret, it incorporates red hybrid norton grapes propagated in Thomas Jefferson days. Horton has committed to other French Rhone-type grapes (the Horton viognier won six gold medals in national wine competitions). Wine writers consider the Horton cabernet franc one of the better reds produced in Virginia. With the winery scheduled for completion in 1995, tours and tastings were to be offered daily, 10 to 5.

Shopping. Downtown Orange was getting a shot in the arm with the conversion in 1995 of its old railroad depot into a transportation center, visitor center and food court with a park beside. New stores were already opening, among them **Wisdom-Good,** an eclectic gift shop run by airline stewardess Claudia Wisdom-Good, who crosses the country on buying trips and turns up interesting finds. We liked the wares at the **Country Mouse,** 143 East Church St., where several rooms are filled with baskets, baby and bath things, hats, herbs, spices, organic foods, garden items and great jewelry, especially that depicting animals. The large **Somerset Shop** in Somerset, two miles south of Montpelier, is fun to browse through and has every kind of country gift, handcrafted item and accessory you could imagine. Adjacent is the new **Somerset Print Shop,** an excellent gallery specializing in upscale watercolors, mostly pastoral scenes from the English countryside. We love the paintings of the Blue Ridge Mountains by Frederick D. Nichols, but they are out of our price range. See them at **Beth Gallery & Press,** Route 678 in Barboursville. Appointments are advised.

Extra-Special

Ed Jaffe Gallery, 108 West Main St., Orange. (703) 672-2400.

This 5,000-square-foot studio and gallery — "unlike any other north or south of Manhattan," according to its creator — opened in a former five-and-dime store in downtown Orange in June 1994. Sculptor Jaffe had tired of the way traditional galleries showed his sculptures for twenty years on the East and West coasts. As the middleman, "the gallery tends to put up a wall between the artist and the collector," Ed said. He liked having collectors visit his farmhouse-studio in southern Vermont, discovering "a bond that comes from direct contact." He also didn't care for the way the galleries handled pieces that were as dear to him as family members, so he "pulled all my babies home" and decided to open his own gallery. The question was where. He didn't want to return to New York City, where he'd worked as a professional photographer, and a Vermont mountain top was not the place to reach a broad market. His search took five years; the change took five months. The center of his universe is now downtown Orange, which he calls the heart of the nation's North-South corridor. He converted part of the store into a studio and his living quarters, and the rest was like a museum in need of a few more exhibits. The entire space is devoted to the works of one man, mostly sculptures but some paintings. They carry pricetags from $300 to $15,000. The three pieces he sold on opening night helped pay for his move. Open Tuesday-Sunday 1 to 5 and by appointment.

Original family is still in residence on Shirley Plantation complex beside James River.

James River Plantation Country, Va.
Where Time Is On Hold

Plantation Country. The name evokes images of early aristocracy, vast tracts of farmlands, lazing riverboats, manor homes, belles in hoop skirts and gentlemen attired for the hunt.

What could be more Southern? And where – with the possible exception of Natchez – is that Southern lifestyle more in evidence today than along the James River in Virginia's Tidewater? Its way of life has been established since the area was settled during the first westward expansion of English-speaking America in the early 1600s and the James became the highway to inland commerce.

Close by Virginia's busy Historic Triangle (Williamsburg, Jamestown and Yorktown), plantation country goes its own way just inland along the James. Time has been put on hold in this rare Southern oasis where American history officially began.

About a dozen plantations of note still thrive, and half are open to the public. Miles of fields, farmlands and forests give way to the occasional river vista in this far-flung, sparsely populated stretch along both sides of the river.

There are no cities. Indeed, Charles City County, home of most of the great plantations on the river's sylvan north side, is really a county without a city. Charles City, a one-horse hamlet with little more than a courthouse and a school, stands in stark contrast to its neighbor to the east, touristy Williamsburg.

Upriver and across the James is Hopewell, America's busiest port during the War Between the States. A visit to Grant's Headquarters at City Point is a welcome contrast to plantation tours. As the region's nearest urban link, Hopewell offers overnight accommodations, riverfront restaurants, and antiques and collectible shops.

Down river on the south side are two relatively undiscovered prizes. Surry, population 300, is the center of peanut country and a lazy Southern hamlet, if ever there was one. Smithfield, population 4,100, is a 1750s river town that produces the world's most famous ham. It's the epitome of Tidewater and the center of the aptly named Isle of Wight County.

Only at the far ends of Plantation Country does one sense a few urban encroachments from Williamsburg, Norfolk and Richmond. Otherwise, all is peaceful and quiet at the plantations as the Harrisons, the Tylers, the Carters and the rest go about their business. They reflect to this day the web of kinship that has linked Virginia aristocracy from the beginning.

Inn Spots

Several plantations take in overnight guests, and a few B&Bs have sprung up on the south side of the river. More traditional and more numerous accommodations are available in Williamsburg and Hopewell.

Edgewood Plantation, Route 2, Box 490, Charles City 23030. (804) 829-2962 or (800) 269-3343.

When in Plantation Country, why not stay in a plantation, even if it is not a typical manor house and is relatively small in comparison? Don't stay here, mind you, if you want to be in the thick of Williamsburg activities, don't care for antiques, dislike clutter and want a large bathroom.

Prepare to be overwhelmed. Dot and Julian Boulware have assembled a collection to end all collections at their ten-year-old B&B. They created it from an ugly duckling of an 1849 Gothic Revival that no one else wanted across from, and once part of, the

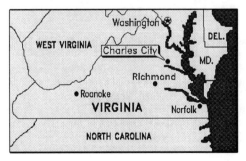

Berkeley Plantation. Dot, a Richmonder who has an eye for displaying things stylishly, has furnished the place with "a little bit of everything" – and lots of it. She must have thousands of dolls, books, buggies, dollhouses, hat boxes, hats and antiques and they are everywhere. At our July visit, she still had some of her eighteen Christmas trees up and lit.

Bedroom at Edgewood Plantation holds canopied bed, loveseat and perambulator.

A gorgeous spiral staircase, its banister draped in lace, pink satin, baby's breath and evergreen branches, winds to the second floor. Here off a central hall are four bedrooms, all with private baths and at least fourteen pillows on each bed.

"Each room is a fascination," says Dot. "You may not have TV but you sure have entertainment." Roses abound, for the inn caters to romance. "This is a lady's house," explains Dot. "The men ask, 'where do we sleep?'" That's no idle question. Although the beds are high and comfy, Dot must remove all those pillows and layers of antique coverings at night. Empty your pockets before retiring and you could lose their contents in all the collections, for there's not an uncovered space to be found. If you head for the bathroom in the dark of night, you might mistake a headless mannequin costumed in white for the resident ghost and land, as one of us nearly did, in a waiting perambulator. Showering the next morning in what must be the world's smallest bathroom was a feat. The bathrooms aren't big, Dot concedes, but contain "everything you need to have."

On the third floor is a sitting area, set with a teddy bears' tea party, between two bedrooms that share a bath.

Upstairs in the old slave quarters behind the house are two more rooms, one a honeymoon suite called Prissy's Quarters. Grapevines strung with dried flowers festoon the pencil-post queen bed and the quilt is patched with hearts. The country decor is simpler than in the main house, and amenities include a small kitchen and a sitting area with TV.

What next? "I'm not finished yet," said Dot as she talked of more rooms in a 1725 grist mill built by Benjamin Harrison at the side of the property. Julian had just completed planting a large, symmetrical boxwood garden with gravel walks lined in brick, a trickling fountain and a tiered terrace descending to a pond.

Already, Edgewood offers a swimming pool and hot tub, a side patio, a front veranda, a 38-foot-long living room full of Victoriana, a formal dining room and a country kitchen so cluttered it's a wonder that breakfast can be prepared. But prepared it is, and served by candlelight at a long, lace-covered table in the dining room. At our visit, orange juice in a pewter cup and fresh berries and other fruit in a pewter dish preceded delicious thick french toast with cinnamon and powdered sugar. The hostess sits with her guests and keeps up a running commentary on all the fascinations of her place.

The house is open daily except Monday for tours ($6, including second-floor bedrooms), led by Dot in Victorian costume. She also serves lunch and tea by appointment ($20 to $30) in the downstairs tavern and tea room. Her gift and antiques shop in a front room is as chock full as the rest of the house.

Doubles, $118 to $178.

Piney Grove at Southall's Plantation, 16920 Southall Plantation Lane, Charles City 23030. (804) 829-2480.

Out in the middle of nowhere is this delightful restoration, not really a plantation home of the dimensions considered hereabouts but a remarkably historic and appealing place nonetheless. Restorationists Joan and Joseph Gordineer of Williamsburg first purchased a general store and residence that had begun life in 1800 as a log corncrib. With their son Brian, whose graduate thesis focused on tourism in the James River Plantation Country, they opened a B&B with one room in the main house that's as atmospheric as can be. In 1989, they moved a modest Greek Revival plantation house from Ladysmith to a site behind the main house. It backs up to woods and a farm corral, and faces gardens, loblolly pines and an open shed housing Joseph's collection of old cars. At its side is a gazebo next to an idyllic, hidden swimming pool surrounded by lounge chairs. The Gordineers now offer four guest rooms with private baths and considerable comfort.

Brian and his father did the restoration of the Ladysmith house themselves. The son's artistry is evident in the stenciling and in the ongoing mural of Greek buildings working its way around the walls of both floors of the center hall. The four rooms on either side of the hall, upstairs and down, have been granted extra space, thanks to a rear addition that holds the bathrooms. Each high-ceilinged room has a fireplace and comes with a double bed (two also have a twin), loveseats, wing chairs and/or rockers, mini-refrigerator and coffeemaker. One is a two-bedroom suite suitable for three people.

A decanter of apple brandy is in the hall, and mint juleps or hot toddies are served upon arrival. A farm bell is rung ten minutes before breakfast is ready in the main house. It's served at three tables in the parlor/library of the oldest, log-walled section. The fare includes juice, fresh fruit, Virginia ham or sausage, homemade breads and one of six casseroles made from fresh eggs. Afterward, adjourn to the neatest little screened porch, snug with two wicker chairs facing a wicker loveseat and screened from the odd passing vehicle by a boxwood hedge, or linger by the fire in the formal parlor with its rich blue walls, wood moldings and stenciling. Rows of rose of sharon trees, hibiscus gardens, pear and plum trees, trellised grapes and raspberries, a corral holding ducks, geese, sheep and a goat, and the swimming pool offer plenty of diversion. A nature trail leads through the woods to a ravine with springs and a swimming hole.

Doubles, $125 to $140; suite, $150. No smoking.

North Bend Plantation B&B, 12200 Weyanoke Road, Charles City 23030. (804) 829-5176.

This unpretentious, 1819 Greek Revival house at the end of a long road harbors a lot of history. Owner George Copland is a great-great grandson of Edmund Ruffin, the Southerner who fired the first shot of the Civil War. Union General Sheridan used the

Horses graze outside Piney Grove at Southall's Plantation.

house as his headquarters. And the owner still farms the plantation, when he's not busy with his four-room B&B.

George and his wife, Ridgley, a family nurse practitioner, offer four large guest rooms, all with private baths. Each is furnished with family antiques and collectibles in the spare Federal style. The rear Magnolia Room overlooking the swimming pool has a private bath, a canopied queensize rice bed and a connecting bedroom in the maid's quarters. The Sheridan Room features a canopied step-up queen tester bed bearing a gunshot wound from the Civil War and covered by a floral comforter. Also here are a velvet settee, a rocker and the general's Civil War desk containing special orders from New York. The Rose Room, also with a queen canopy bed and a chaise lounge, has a more feminine look with dolls and pillows. The newest Federal Room contains an 1850 sleigh bed, a rich patterned gold loveseat and a cast-iron bath.

Guests watch passing deer in the fields and listen to chattering birds from an enclosed upstairs sun porch outfitted in wicker. Downstairs are a double parlor, a dining room with an old billiards table with a marble base at one end and a homey kitchen where most guests prefer to eat as George whips up his specialty waffles. Eggs with sausages and biscuits are another breakfast favorite.

Doubles, $95 to $120.

Seward House Inn, 193 Colonial Trail East (Route 10), Box 352, Surry 23883. (804) 294-3810.

British-born Cynthia Erskine was picking pole beans and cucumbers in her backyard garden at our first visit. She led us in the back way past the kitchen, the dining room and the living room, where a TV shared space at the time with a sewing machine "because we're still making curtains."

The B&B was opened in 1990 by Cynthia and a Norfolk friend, Jacqueline Bayer. It is homey and welcoming, from the pictures of Jackie's children in the front hall to the jars of basil jelly that Cynthia makes and gives to guests. The sewing machine is long gone, but there's now a piano in the hall.

The four guest quarters are furnished with mementos of three generations of their families, including handcarved beds, old toys, bits of needlework, a handcarved trunk, and prints of Andrew Wyeth and Maxfield Parrish. The front corner downstairs room has a private bath. A bathroom with a clawfoot tub serves two upstairs bedrooms, one with a queensize bed. The other has twin beds, a teddybear on a trunk and a fireplace mantel bearing a miniature sewing machine and toy soldiers. A small guest cottage at the side is called the Surgery; this is the office in which Jackie's great uncle used to practice medicine. It now offers a full bath, a queensize bedroom and a living room with a rattan loveseat and chair.

Although almost in the center of town (what there is of it), the inn is surrounded by fields of soybeans and corn. Guests enjoy a front veranda and a trellised side deck overlooking the tranquil scene, including a small fish pond. Sherry and a jigsaw puzzle are at the ready in the living room of what Cynthia calls "a family-friendly house."

For breakfast, "we do things family style, and lots of it." That might involve an omelet with slivered carrots, onions, bacon, sausage and two kinds of cheese, with a side of country ham from the nearby Edwards Virginia Ham Shoppe. Or the main course could be waffles containing pecans picked from trees outside. Spicy sausage gravy over biscuits has been a hit lately. Overnight guests may use the hosts' barbecue grills for dining al fresco or have dinner prepared by reservation. The tab averages $12 for something like organically grown salad with homemade dressing, biscuits, French bread, pasta with garden vegetables, fruit and cheeses.

Besides the basil jelly, Cynthia puts up wild blackberry jam and sent us on our way with a small jar. It sure did liven up our toast while it lasted.

Doubles, $55 to 65; cottage, $75.

Smithfield Station, 415 South Church St., Smithfield 23430. (804) 357-7700.

New in 1986 and with water on three sides, this was designed by a local business-man/sailor to look like a Victorian Coast Guard station. Its busy marina and restaurant (see Dining Spots) draw crowds, but overnight guests can be above the hubbub in fifteen guest rooms on the second and third floors.

In contemporary motel style, they are attractive with pine furnishings, kingsize or two double beds, a table with two chairs and waterfowl pictures on the walls. By far the most appealing are those overlooking the Pagan River and Cypress Creek across deep rear balconies running the length of the building. Our balcony would have gotten a workout except that we were there during weather so torrid that we couldn't venture outside our air-conditioned room even after the sun had gone down.

A continental breakfast is served buffet-style on weekdays in one of the dining rooms. Juices, fruit, danish and homemade rolls filled with Smithfield ham are the fare.

In 1994, owners Ronald and Christina Pack added a boardwalk with gazebos and an outdoor bar and grill. They were building a lighthouse for use as a deluxe honeymoon suite and a conference center, surrounded by water. It was to have a giant whirlpool tub and a circular staircase to the top of the lighthouse for the best view in Smithfield. A swimming pool was in the works for 1995.

Doubles, $59 to $89.

Isle of Wight Inn, 1607 South Church St., Smithfield 23430. (804) 357-3176 or (800) 357-3245.

Its location among relatively new buildings along a commercial strip at the southern entrance to town surprises. Which came first – the inn or the strip? The latter, appar-ently, for this was built as an office building and renovated a few years ago into a twelve-room inn and antiques shop.

Seward House Inn and adjacent cottage offer four guest rooms.

The residential exterior masks its origin, and inside all is dark and antiquey. The parlor is part of the antiques shop, which specializes in period furniture and old clocks. Off the parlor is a dining room, where clocks tick away as guests help themselves to a continental breakfast of fruit, danish and Smithfield ham biscuits.

The first and second floors contain a variety of guest rooms, each with private bath, TV and telephone. Four are large suites with private entrances, two with jacuzzis. One we saw had a huge corner fireplace, a canopied step-up queensize four-poster and a double jacuzzi with tall candles beside a mirrored wall in the bathroom. A large efficiency on the lower level is decorated in country style.

Doubles, $59; suites, $99.

Four Square Plantation, 13357 Four Square Road, Smithfield 23430. (804) 365-0749.

Amelia and Roger Healey moved in 1994 from a small B&B in Wrightsville, Pa., to a larger and older home built in 1807 as the centerpiece of a 23-acre plantation. Here, in a house listed on the National Register and declared a Virginia Landmark Property, they offer three large bedrooms with fireplaces and private baths.

A Pennsylvania quilt graces the kingsize poster bed in the Thomas Room, comfortable with thick carpeting and two armchairs. A secluded bedroom in the rear of the house is nineteen feet square and furnished in the Empire style with a queen bed and large walnut armoire.

European and American antiques enhance the public rooms. A Spanish portable writing desk dating to the 1600s takes center stage in the parlor. The dining room holds a French trestle table from a monastery, dating to the 1500s and the oldest piece in the house. Quite a collection of French tinkers' miniatures (copper pots and pans) adorn one wall.

Amelia serves a full breakfast — a Southwest omelet with Virginia ham and banana bread the day of our visit. Fruit compote, lemon-poppyseed muffins and blueberry pancakes were on the docket the next day.

Doubles, $65.

Dining Spots

Indian Fields Tavern, Route 5, Charles City. (804) 829-5004.

In an area of few people (other than plantation-goers, most of whom don't spend the night), a local young man who grew up on one of the biggest plantations is making a go of it with a most appealing restaurant. In 1988, Archer H. Ruffin Jr., a relative of the family that owns nearby Evelynton Plantation, turned a ramshackle, century-old farmhouse into a bustling eatery accommodating 90 patrons in four dining rooms upstairs and down, plus 30 more on screened porches. The name derives from the surrounding fields, which natives were farming when the first English settlers arrived in Virginia.

Archer's mother and his sister-in-law helped with the decor. They went with an early tavern look and a burgundy, green and beige color scheme. Bare hardwood floors, windsor chairs and well-spaced tables topped with burgundy cloths, votive candles and bud vases bearing large lilies set the stage for an ambitious dinner menu, which changes frequently.

For starters, we sampled the night's gazpacho and the huge Indian Fields garden salad with dijon vinaigrette as we munched on homemade sweet Sally Lunn bread. Other possibilities were baked camembert wrapped with currants in puff pastry and a plate of smoked bluefish pâté and Irish oak-smoked salmon with toasted French bread. Among entrées ($13.95 to $21.95), we liked the soft-shell crabs served with a spicy pecan butter, carrots and yellow squash. Also excellent was the mixed grill of lamb, quail and Surry sausage with a brandied pear demi-glace, accompanied by broiled potatoes and haricots verts.

The wine list is short and reasonably priced. Desserts are to groan over, particularly if you're into cakes. The raspberry cheesecake was extra-good.

New chefs Mark and Debbie Hallett, a husband and wife team from Boston, have added a few New England touches to the contemporary regional cuisine. The mixed grill, happily still on the menu, is also available at lunch and brunch. Recent dinner choices included a jambalaya of seafood and prosciutto on fresh pasta with a corn and roasted jalapeño cake, roasted pork tenderloin on a white bean and sundried tomato salad, applewood-smoked duck breast with a sundried cranberry salsa, and grilled venison tenderloin wrapped in smoked bacon and served with a wild blueberry vinaigrette.

Indian Fields also serves interesting fare in the $5.50 to $11.95 range for lunch and Sunday brunch. The throngs pouring in for weekday lunch at our latest visit attested to the success and drawing power of a restaurant way off the beaten path.

Lunch daily, 11 to 4; dinner, 5 to 10; Sunday brunch, 11 to 4.

Coach House Tavern, Berkeley Plantation, Route 5, Charles City. (804) 829-6003.

Once the place where Benjamin Harrison garaged his coaches, this small outbuilding at Berkeley Plantation has been transformed into a thing of beauty for special-occasion dining. With white cloths and fanned napkins, large tables on two levels look through french doors onto an expanse of lovely gardens.

Votive candles flicker on wall sconces among dark beams and posts at night, when the room is positively magical. Dinner is leisurely and the table is yours for the evening. The concise menu changes nightly. Entrées (generally $16.95 to $22.95) might include poached salmon in saffron tomato broth with littleneck clams, sautéed veal scaloppine with sundried tomato ragout, and grilled lamb chop with truffled jus. Start

Archer H. Ruffin Jr. turned ramshackle farmhouse into Indian Fields Tavern.

with chilled gazpacho with sea scallops, Chesapeake crab cakes with pommery cocktail sauce or penne pasta tossed with sundried tomatoes and roasted elephant garlic. A separate menu offers light fare in the $7.25 to $9.95 range, including salmagundi, billed as a Colonial chef's salad, and grilled chicken breast on tossed greens with mushrooms and parmesan cheese.

At lunch ($5.50 to $8.95), waitresses in Colonial dresses pour non-stop iced tea. Between plantation tours we enjoyed a crab cake sandwich and a seafood salad in a halved avocado. Pretty as a picture, the latter was garnished with an abundance of fresh fruit, from strawberries to kiwi to honeydew. It came with potato salad and cold roasted peppers. The crab sandwich arrived on thick toasted bread described as "baked bass." Was it Sally Lunn bread? "No, suh, it's fresh baked bah-us." For dessert, owner Sally Capp's famous rum cake lived up to its billing. Surrounded by blueberries, raspberries and strawberries and resting on crème anglaise, it was one of the best cakes we've tasted.

Lunch daily, 11 to 3; dinner, 6 to 9 (closed occasionally if too few reservations); Sunday, 11 to 4.

David's White House Restaurant, 3560 Courthouse Road, Providence Forge. (804) 966-9700.

The original chef and partner from Indian Fields, David Napier, opened his own restaurant in 1994 to good reviews. The setting is a turn-of-the-century house built by the town miller in the center of historic Providence Forge. Well-spaced tables in four dining rooms are dressed with white cloths and fresh flowers. David set out to offer "fine dining in plantation style" with an added embellishment: the food at this White House "could easily by served at any state dinner held at the one in Washington."

The regional food press seems to agree. David has earned considerable acclaim for dinner appetizers ($4 to $5.50) like sherried crab, seafood seviche and hunter's sausage, patties of venison, duck, quail and tenderloin seasoned with sage and fennel seed

New boardwalk leads past raw bar and grill toward Smithfield Station.

and topped with veal glaze. His Big Daddy seafood gumbo blends shrimp, okra and garlic with French bread croutons.

Main courses are priced from $9.95 for baked Virginia ham with bourbon-glazed apples to $16 for a sampler plate of three house favorites: sautéed oysters topped with Smithfield ham, filet mignon with a red wine and roquefort glaze, and slow-roasted baby back ribs. Crab cakes with caper mayonnaise and grilled duck breast with fried grits are other standouts.

Lunch, Tuesday-Saturday 11 to 4; dinner, Tuesday-Saturday 5 to 10; Sunday, brunch 11 to 4, dinner, 4 to 10.

Smithfield Station, 415 South Church St., Smithfield. (804) 357-7700.

Nicely nautical to go with its setting, the main floor of this contemporary hotel-marina-restaurant has four dining areas including a lounge, plus a solarium and a waterside deck, and seats up to 150. Burgundy napkins and votive candles top formica tables edged in wood.

The extensive menu (dinner entrées, $9.95 to $17.95) has something for everyone, from chicken stuffed with Smithfield ham, swiss cheese and roasted peanuts to beef teriyaki. Seafood is king here, along with ham. It comes as seafood rarebit, fried catfish, crab imperial, surf and turf (crabcakes and Smithfield ham), and what have you. We can vouch for the sampler of Smithfield ham ($4.50 as an appetizer, served with crackers), the Station pasta combining shrimp, smoked salmon and Smithfield ham chunks over spinach fettuccine, and seafood norfolk, accompanied by yellow squash parmesan. A peachberry sundae, marinated in triple sec and served over vanilla ice cream, made a refreshing ending.

A Smithfield ham platter, served with fried apples and vegetable of the day, is a favorite at lunch for $7.95.

Outside on the new boardwalk along the Pagan River bridge, the **Boardwalk Raw Bar & Grill** serves Wednesday-Saturday from 4 to 10 or 11, Sunday from 1 to 10.

Lunch, Monday-Saturday 11 to 4, Sunday noon to 4; dinner nightly from 4.

The Surrey House, Routes 10 and 31, Surry. (804) 294-3389.

Predictable Southern cooking is served up with lots of local color at this oldtimer in the heart of peanut country. New owner Michael Stevens from Newport News expanded the menu, but retained the old favorites rendered by longtime owner Helen Gwaltney Lenox. Even though it now serves Williamsburg wines, iced tea with frequent refills remains the beverage of choice at noon or night.

At lunchtime, one of us sampled a cup of peanut soup ($1), a creamy chicken broth with spices and crunchy peanuts, and a club sandwich ($5.25) like those we remember from thirty years ago, overflowing with Edwards ham, bacon, turkey, cheese, lettuce and tomato. The other went for the surf and turf ($8.95), a midday whopper of Edwards ham with a crab cake, plus a trip to the salad bar, an apple fritter, hushpuppies and rolls. Four kinds of sauces in a pewter relish tray accompanied.

Those in the mood can sample the famous Surrey House peanut butter board ($3.50). This do-it-yourself affair involves slices of white and brown bread, a jar of peanut butter, down-home honey, a rasher of bacon, raisins, jelly, a whole ripe banana, apple wedges and cheese, served up on a Surry County pine cutting board.

Ham comes any number of ways, from eggs benedict at breakfast ($6.95) to a dinner special with fried oysters ($16.75). The all-day menu also offers local seafood, fried chicken, delmonico steak and roast turkey. Prices run from $4.95 for ham croquettes to $14.95 for a combination seafood dinner.

The paneled dining room is down-home homey, with booths, banquettes and a hodge-podge of art on the walls. Waitresses in vaguely Colonial ankle-length dresses with puffed sleeves provide quick service. The Carriage Room is more formal with white and blue tablecloths.

Breakfast daily, 6:30 to noon; lunch and dinner, 11 to 9.

Dockside, 700 Jordan Point Road, Hopewell. (804) 541-2600.

One of the few places around here to eat beside the water, this has a large deck and an open, circular dining room with a cathedral-type ceiling and picture windows onto one of the widest sections of the James River. Located just south of the Benjamin Harrison Memorial Bridge linking the two sides of the river and plantation country, it makes a good stop between tours for lunch. At night, it's the best place for sunset viewing, and a cooling breeze comes off the water.

We found lunch service on a slow day to be lackadaisical, however. The she-crab soup with a small Greek salad was unremarkable, and the $4.95 club sandwich pedestrian. The dinner menu looked a bit more interesting, especially specials like blackened tuna with mild chiffonade, Cajun mahi-mahi with scallops and broiled salmon with dill butter. The regular dinner menu runs from $8.95 for marinated chicken to $17.95 for a broiled seafood platter.

Lunch, Monday-Friday 11:30 to 3; dinner nightly, 5 to 10; Sunday brunch, 11:30 to 2:30.

The Backfin Seafood Restaurant, 1193 Jamestown Road, Williamsburg. (804) 220-2249.

Folks in Surry swear by this modest eatery, a twenty-minute ferry ride across the James River and five miles from the Jamestown ferry landing. This is not a tourist restaurant, our informants insisted — just a great place for seafood, nicely served by a young staff. "Neither we nor our guests have ever been disappointed," advised these helpful innkeepers, whose recommendations we trust.

The dinner menu ($7.95 to $11.95) is basic, from fried catfish and fried oysters to the specialty crab cakes, soft-shell crab and a broiled or fried seafood platter. Each comes with fries, baked potato or herbed rice, cole slaw and hushpuppies. Start with steamed crabs or oysters on the half shell (a dozen of the latter cost only $6.95). Various salads including backfin crab, chicken caesar and Greek are available for $4.95. Fried chicken, barbecue platter and New York strip steak also are available.

At lunch, come for a crab cake sandwich ($4.50) or a soft crab sea basket, at $5.95 the priciest of eight seafood baskets served with fries, cole slaw and hushpuppies.

Backfin crab fans are in their element. With a pitcher of draft beer or a carafe of chablis, you can enjoy to your heart's content.

Lunch, Monday-Saturday 11 to 3; dinner, Monday-Saturday 4:30 to 9.

Diversions

Most visitors come here to see the plantations (only a few of which are open to the public). Be advised that there also are a couple of historic towns, a marvelous state park with a model farm, peanut farms, purveyors of Smithfield hams, and more peanut, tobacco, soybean and cotton fields than we ever thought we'd see.

Plantations. Of the dozen or so landmark plantations, some like **Brandon, Westover** and **Sherwood Forest** are open to the public only by appointment and during Historic Garden Week. Others like **Weston** and **Appomattox Plantation** are off the beaten path in Hopewell. Still others like **Bacon's Castle** and **Smith's Fort** are undergoing restoration, and **Chippokes** was inexplicably closed when we were there. Those plantations that are open help support their upkeep by charging for tours. Our favorites:

Shirley Plantation, Route 5, Charles City, 829-5121. Started in 1613, the home of ten generations of Hills and Carters (and the mother of Robert E. Lee) is perfectly poised with a long view up the James River. Its dependencies form the only Queen Anne forecourt in America, and here you may encounter the Carter pets at play. We found this to be the most personal of plantations, the only one in its original condition and the only one with direct descendants of the original family still in residence. Charles Hill Carter Jr., the county supervisor and handyman about Shirley, lives upstairs with his wife, who runs the gift shop, and two sons who eventually will take over Shirley but who had just opened a clay shooting course at our visit. Guided tours run continuously and there are no roped-off areas. You'll learn the intriguing story behind the family portraits done by an itinerant painter, see dates etched in the dining-room window by ladies testing the quality of their diamond rings, spot two spigots beside the dining-room fireplace for cleaning dishes, and marvel at a unique free-standing square staircase with no visible support in the foyer. The family's silver, coats of arms and other heirlooms are out for all to see. Open daily, 9 to 5. Adults, $6.

Evelynton, Route 5, Charles City, 829-5075. An air of modern luxury pervades Evelynton, to our minds the most appealing and livable of plantations. It's on a shady, tiered lawn overlooking Herring Creek. The impressive Georgian Revival manor house was built in 1936 on property purchased in 1847 by Edmund Ruffin Jr., the states' rights activist and agricultural reformer who fired the first shot in the Civil War at Fort Sumter. The war came to Evelynton when Union General George McClellan occupied the area, burning the original house belonging to the Southern martyr. Today, rope hammocks and two Adirondack chairs flank a cannon and a plaque commemorating the Battle of Evelynton Heights. Ruffin's great-grandson built the showplace home that stands today as testimony to the good life. A guide points out the Chippendale necessary chair in the front bedroom, a sunken family garden room glamorous in brick and chintz, the carved moldings along the ceilings, the formal dining room with an 18th-century Heppelwhite curved buffet, and recent portraits of the four offspring of Saunders Ruffin, current occupant. Portions of three movies were filmed here. The canopied rear terrace was added lately as a setting for weddings and corporate parties. Open daily, 9 to 5. Adults, $6.

Berkeley Plantation, Route 5, Charles City, 829-6018. The most obviously commercial of the plantations, this is known for its firsts. It was the site of the first official Thanksgiving in 1619. It was the birthplace of Benjamin Harrison (signer of the Declaration of Independence) and of William Henry Harrison, ninth U.S. president, and

Bacon's Castle is oldest documented brick house in English North America.

the ancestral home of 23rd president Benjamin Harrison. And "Taps" was composed here in 1862. Following a slide show, costumed guides shepherd visitors through the main floor of the 1726 house, admonishing them not to touch or lean on the furniture. Exceptional Heppelwhite, Chippendale and Louis pieces abound. Octogenarian owner Mac Jamieson rides around on a golf cart to oversee the magnificent gardens; often mistaken as a groundskeeper, he loves to talk with those who approach. He leases the Coach House out as a restaurant (see Dining Spots). Open daily, 8 to 5. Adults, $8.

Bacon's Castle, Route 617, Surry, 357-5976. The oldest documented brick house in English North America (1665) holds particular fascination. The high Jacobean-style structure is in the process of restoration, which gives insights into construction techniques as well as history spanning three centuries. A ten-minute audio-visual presentation precedes an informative 45-minute guided tour. Visitors see graffiti on a wall (one child's scrawl dated 1886 says "this day I am sick"), a love letter written in glass, a 1710 one-hand clock and a room full of artifacts acquired in archaeological digs on the property, from clay marbles to egg shells. Outside, what was thought to be a 19th-century garden turned out to be a Renaissance-style English garden from the 17th century. Uncovered in 1985, it prompted the New York Times to declare it the "earliest, largest, best-preserved and most sophisticated garden that has come to light in North America." The resident gardener likes to show off its prizes. Open Tuesday-Saturday 10 to 4, Sunday noon to 4. Adults, $4.

Smithfield. Known for its hams, the hog capital of the world also is a case study of an early river port. Some say Smithfield's collection of 60-plus historic houses represents the best selection in Tidewater because it spans both 18th and 19th centuries. The Chamber of Commerce's walking-tour map notes a blend of more than 60 Colonial, Federal, Georgian and Victorian structures side by side – including Victorian Row, which would do Cape May proud. We chanced upon Hayden's Lane, a brick walkway beneath a canopy of flowering crape myrtle trees leading to Hayden Hall. Check out the old-time country store complete with early postal boxes, pot-bellied stove and revolving stools in the Barlow Gallery at the **Isle of Wight County Mu-**

seum, housed in two bank buildings. At **Joyner of Smithfield's** downtown retail shop, you can sample and purchase a variety of Smithfield hams, their pungently salty and smoky taste distinctive partly because the hogs are raised on local peanuts. The shop also features peanuts. The interesting **Collage Studio and Gallery** is ensconced in one of the five Victorian Row houses. Twenty-three dealers show their wares in the new **Smithfield Antiques Center** co-op.

Surry. Named for the English county of Surrey, this was the home of some of the first black settlers in America. Today, peanuts rule (the little Smithfield-Surry phone book carries two pages of listings for peanut products in its yellow pages). The annual Pork, Peanut & Pine Festival draws thousands on a mid-July weekend to **Chippokes Plantation State Park,** the oldest continuously farmed property in the country. Besides swimming, picnicking and hiking, the park offers an 1854 mansion with formal gardens, a visitor center with windows onto the James River, and a model farm and forestry museum illustrating agricultural life as it was in Colonial times. The farm tour alone is worth the trip. The **Surry-Jamestown Ferry,** one of Virginia's last, links the two sides of Plantation Country; the round trip costs pedestrians 30 cents. In town, tours of the smokehouse are offered hourly on the half hour at **Edwards Virginia Ham Shoppe,** where you can snack on such local specialties as ham rolls, sausage sandwiches, peanut soup and Brunswick stew.

Hopewell. The area's biggest city has bounced back, sort of. Although its City Point section was founded in 1613 as the second English settlement in America, Hopewell was developed only in this century when the E.I. du Pont de Nemours Co. built a major munitions center during World War I and the population peaked at 40,000. Following the war, the center closed and the population dropped to 2,000. Hopewell is a city of contrasts, where visitors can see an assemblage of 1920s Sears, Roebuck mail-order houses on a driving tour and, a few blocks away, visit the 18th-century plantation house, **Weston.** Across town, the City Point national historic district juts into the James River. This is where Ulysses S. Grant set up his Union headquarters in Virginia during the Civil War and directed the siege of Petersburg. His headquarters cabin, the nerve center for the entire Union war effort, is part of the **Appomattox Manor** plantation and national park.

Extra-Special

St. Luke's Church, 14477 Benns Church Blvd., off Route 10, Smithfield. (804) 357-3367.

Hidden English-style in the middle of a forested cemetery beside a creek, this is America's only original Gothic church and its oldest English-speaking church (1632). Its original traceried windows, stepped gables and buttresses are unique in American architecture. A guide points out the stained-glass window commemorating Pocohontas, the first convert in Virginia to the gospel. The pews were put together with wooden pegs on a raised platform to keep the feet warm. The triple-decker pulpit bearing the rector's hour glass is topped by a sounding board that served as an amplifier. A spectacular 1665 English organ has wood pipes in the shape of a three-dimensional hallway. The church's construction at a time when the Indians were still hostile explains the recessed doorway; "they would trip or hit their heads if they ran too fast, giving time for the men in the back of the church to get their guns," the guide said. Today the Anglican church is used once a year for a non-denominational service. Outside the Old Brick, as this precious church is called, the setting is shady and tranquil, like that of an English churchyard. There are benches, a bowl and a sundial, and graves of the locally ubiquitous Jordan family. Open daily except Monday, 9:30 to 5; donation.

All is tranquil in inlet scene typical of Virginia's Northern Neck.

The Northern Neck, Va.
Tidewater's Bypassed Treasure

A National Park Service film calls this "The Athens of the New World." Historians consider it "the Cradle of the Nation." George Washington described it as "the Garden of Virginia."

High praise for an area that many people outside Virginia have never heard of. Known as the Northern Neck, Tidewater's treasure is a peninsula wedged between the Potomac and Rappahannock rivers on the western shore of the Chesapeake Bay.

Locals would scoff at the "Athens" title, knowing how relatively impoverished and how off the beaten path the area is today. They know that the 20th century favored Williamsburg and Norfolk to the south and Richmond and Fredericksburg to the west. The Neck was left to languish in nostalgia, its watermen fishing for a livelihood and its planters harvesting their crops. No town of size or reputation developed, with the possible exceptions of Reedville – which the unique menhaden fishing industry once made the richest per capita in the country – or Irvington, to which the posh Tides Inn lures golfers, yachtsmen and retirees.

"We're really undiscovered, and the people who have discovered us don't tell anybody," says Francene Barber, former head of the Northern Neck Travel Council. "We're unspoiled, mostly local people and the offspring of local people." The folks are so friendly that motorists quickly pick up what part-time resident Roger Mudd described in an article as the Northern Neck wave – two fingers lifted off the steering wheel. No one locks houses or cars except in July, according to local lore, and then simply to avoid receiving unwanted zucchinis.

Only lately have newcomers – mostly retirees from Richmond, Norfolk and northern Virginia – created something of a confrontation between new and old. The "come heres" savor the slower lifestyle but lament the lack of amenities. The "from heres" welcome the economic shot in the arm but worry, probably unnecessarily, that the Neck will become one elongated suburb of Washington and Virginia Beach.

The area's first tourist actually was Capt. John Smith, whom Pocohontas saved from the Indians in 1607. "Heaven and earth never agreed better to frame a place for man's habitation," said he. Three of the nation's first five presidents agreed, and one of the four counties that make up the Neck produced more American statesmen than any other.

Now, some people come here to see ancient churches, George Washington's birth-place and the Stratford Hall childhood home of Robert E. Lee. Others are drawn by the mysterious, often hidden presence of water. The bay, rivers and wide creeks offer miles of uncharted shoreline, and almost every road ends at the water.

Here, more than in most places, travelers must detour from the main highway to discover the joys of picturesque inlets and historic sites at the end of nowhere. "History abounds and water surrounds," the local Travel Council proclaims. But the visitor must seek them out.

Most sightseeing attractions are at the more primitive top end of the neck, while most inns and restaurants are at the more affluent southern end or across the Rappahannock on the Middle Peninsula. State Route 3 is the main highway running up the center of the neck. Creeks and rivers rambling hither and yon often make road access roundabout and time-consuming.

Inn Spots

The Tides Inn, Irvington 22480. (804) 438-5000 or (800) 843-3746.

For nearly 50 years this waterside golfing resort has been attracting the Cadillac set, who return year after year to enjoy what the Stephens family calls "the company of the finest people in the world, your genteel fellow guests." Now run by grandson Lee Stephens (his uncle oversees the equally resorty but less aristocratic Tides Lodge across Carters Creek), this is a bastion of elegance and service. The entire staff exudes friendliness and the inn increasingly is taking an active role in the surrounding community.

The wonderfully landscaped, waterside setting on a narrow peninsula jutting into Carters Creek as it empties into the two-mile-wide Rappahannock is unsurpassed. Many of the 110 elegant, hotel-style rooms in connecting tiered, three-story lodges take full advantage, especially those with balconies in the newer Garden House extension. Positively idyllic are the twenty rooms and semi-suites in the Lancaster and Windsor houses. Here the floral comforters match the draperies and valances, the TVs are hidden in armoires or behind shutters in the walls, the bath/dressing rooms are extra-large and outfitted with Smith & Vandiver toiletries, and the beds are kingsize or two doubles

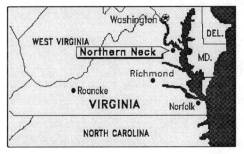

and "triple-sheeted for comfort." The private balconies are of the "wow" variety. Any business transacted in the Lancaster's picture-windowed meeting room must play second fiddle to the view. Standard and even superior rooms in the main lodge are smaller and may appear dated; we'd save our shekels for a splurge in the Lancaster or Windsor houses.

Rates include two or three meals

Coach house flanks main inn at Linden House.

daily. Lunch is also served aboard the yacht Miss Ann, at the Summer House by the beach or at the golf course. Dinner is formal (jackets required) in two adjoining dining rooms, all windows onto the water (prix-fixe meals are available here to the public, $10 for lunch and $35 for dinner). Oriental rugs grace the floors and crystal chandeliers the ceilings of the public rooms. Along a hallway is a tony shop, its display windows beckoning to passersby. But nothing competes with the view of the water through floor-to-ceiling windows as the bellman opens the doors at the port cochère.

Luxuries include a heated saltwater pool beside a sandy river beach at the tip of the peninsula, the inn's cruising yachts, four tennis courts, a fitness and health facility, and the beautiful grounds, dotted with seats here and there. The crowning touch is 45 holes of golf, including the inn's nearby Golden Eagle Golf Course, ranked among the top three courses in Virginia.

The resort has more than two staff members for each room and claims an employee turnover rate of less than ten percent annually. With three generations of Stephenses involved in the operation, little wonder it's known for its family-like atmosphere.

Doubles, $244 to $286, MAP; semi-suites, $306 to $326; suites, $476 to $688. Closed January to mid-March.

Linden House, Route 17, Box 23, Champlain 22438. (804) 443-1170 or (800) 622-1202.

Horses and cows graze in the pastures beside this restored planters' home, set well back from the highway on 200-plus acres northwest of Tappahannock. "You want to see a bull so spoiled he eats apples right out of my hand?" asks innkeeper Sandra Pounsberry. And she proceeds to feed the critter apples that she picks from a tree just beyond his reach, while his companions settle for fallen apples on the ground.

Sandra and Ken Pounsberry from Maryland's Prince Georges County bought the 1750 house, which had not been lived in for 25 years, and set about restoring it into a comfortable B&B. They offer five bedrooms in the main house, plus two larger rooms and a suite in the coach house they built next door. All are nicely appointed with country furnishings and antiques, and Bibles are on display in each. Queensize beds, fireplaces and sitting areas, one with an oversize chair and a half with matching ottoman, are features of the spacious second-floor Robert E. Lee and Jefferson Davis rooms, which share a large bathroom with a double jacuzzi and steam shower (another bathroom was in the works here for 1995). A very narrow staircase tiptoes to the third floor, site of the Linden Room with a cannonball queen and a single bed and Miss K's Room, so named "because our daughter Kelly moved out and we took back her room," notes Sandra. It's hidden away in the eaves without even a window, but equipped with a night light "or people might never wake up in the morning."

Rooms in the adjacent coach house come with queensize beds and private baths. The ground floor is devoted to the Carriage Suite, with wicker seating in front of a working fireplace, TV, refrigerator and enormous bathroom with corner shower and space earmarked for a jacuzzi. It opens onto a covered front porch with brick floor and an antique sleigh for a seat. Two rooms upstairs share a little rear balcony.

Back in the main house are a variety of handsome common areas. The "receiving room" almost looks like a museum piece with antique furnishings and a spinning wheel in the corner. More livable is the rear family room, where guests can watch TV in front of shelves holding the hosts' collections of depression glass and beer steins. A side smoking porch overlooks the herb garden, while the wicker-filled back porch enjoys a view of the yard, woods and gazebo. Still another arched nook under the front porch entry holds blue wrought-iron chairs for an intimate tête-à-tête. Inside, the white textured walls are striking with restful pale blue doors and trim on the main floor, celery green trim on the second floor, pink trim on the third and yellow trim on the ground floor. The latter floor holds a large dining room with tables for sixteen and a country kitchen. Here is where Sandra, a caterer, serves a hearty breakfast. The plantation special consists of half a belgian waffle and an omelet incorporating green peppers, onions, cheese, tomatoes and ham, plus bacon and sausage. A plate of fried green tomatoes or fried corn might accompany. A fresh fruit plate and juice precede.

Sandra's cooking talents also are displayed at dinner, served by reservation to ten or more. The night before our visit she served caesar salad, New York strip steak, baked potatoes, green beans amandine and peach cobbler with ice cream for $16.95, BYOB. Maryland crab cakes and breast of chicken are other main-course possibilities.

Doubles, $55 to $85; suite, $135.

Cedar Grove, Route 1, Box 2535, Reedville 22539. (804) 453-3915.

One of the more appealing rooms we have stayed in was at this light and airy, Colonial Revival B&B overlooking the Chesapeake Bay from the affluent peninsular hamlet of Fleeton. It's the Lighthouse Suite, with a nifty bay-window seat outfitted in chintz, from which you can view the Great Wicomico River as it enters the bay. That is if you're not already ensconced on the spacious rear porch, up a couple of stairs from the room and screened to the floor on three sides. With its white wicker furniture it's a perfect spot in which to enjoy the breeze as you look through the thoughtfully provided binoculars at the nearby light, the wildlife and the broad sweep of the bay south toward Norfolk beyond a tennis court, a field and a little beach. Ceiling fans whirring on the porch and over the queensize bed kept the room cool enough that we could sleep without air-conditioning on a hot summer night.

Two smaller front bedrooms have private baths outside their rooms. The Rose Room is done with roses, from the rug to the wreath, and the Front Room is dainty in wicker.

Sue and Bob Tipton, early retirees from IBM in Poughkeepsie, N.Y., opened in 1990 and furnished their 1913 house in a light, uncluttered style. Victorian Eastlake pieces dignify the comfortable living room. Guests also enjoy a sun room with a TV.

Breakfast to the strains of classical music (we enjoyed "Spring" from Vivaldi's Four Seasons) is served beneath a crystal chandelier in the formal dining room, handsome in pale green and rose. Sue, who took courses at the Culinary Institute of America in Hyde Park, offers a choice of juices served in her grandmother's dainty glass mugs,

Grounds of Cedar Grove B&B back up to Chesapeake Bay.

fresh fruit like the bursting-with-flavor local cantaloupe topped with yogurt sauce and blackberries, and an entrée like an Italian vegetable omelet with rashers of bacon. Remarkably good blueberry muffins made with oatmeal and lemon zest might accompany. Poached pears with melba sauce, peach french toast, vegetable frittata, banana buttermilk griddle cakes and crab omelets are other possibilities.

The Tiptons offer beverages in the evening and cream sherry at bedside.

Doubles, $60; suite, $80.

Elizabeth House, Main Street, Box 163, Reedville 22539. (804) 453-7016.

A grand wraparound veranda, open in front and screened at the side, enhances this sea captain's house built in 1895. Take note of all the original carved oak in the entry hall, ornamented with carved ribbons, bells, bows on the banister posts and shells on the doors.

Besides a living room and dining room, guests have use of an upstairs garden room with TV and phone. Owner Beth Arbogast, a Northern Virginia transplant, likes her two front guest rooms the best. The Fern Room in green and white has a queen bed, a chaise lounge in a circular window and a private porch. The Strawberry Room has twin wicker beds joined as a king. The two rooms share a hall bath with a clawfoot soaking tub. The Bluebird Room with a bay-window alcove, a queen bed and Waverly floral accents comes with a private bath. So does a small first-floor room with a double bed topped by a hand-crocheted spread.

The entire third floor is a suite with a large and sunny sitting room dressed in wicker and aqua; it has a sleep sofa, a game table and a wet bar with complimentary champagne. Off to one side is a smaller room with a draped queensize bed. On the other is a large bathroom with a double jacuzzi flanked by candles and a stuffed parrot.

Most rooms in the house have water views of Cockrells Creek, to which the large rear lawn backs up (it's deep enough for swimming and boating). The best views are obtained from a waterside guest cottage, which contains a living room with TV and a bedroom with an antique double bed.

In the screened veranda or formal dining room, a resident manager serves a breakfast of juice, fresh fruit and a main course like eggs, french toast or waffles, with sausage and bacon. Wine, cheese and crackers are offered in the evening.

Doubles, $65 to $75; cottage, $85; suite, $110. Closed January and February. No smoking.

The Inn at Levelfields, Route 3, Box 216, Lancaster 22503. (804) 435-6887 or (800) 238-5578.

Warren and Doris Sadler – he from Chicago and she from Memphis – were the first of the Northern Neck's latter-day innkeepers. They acquired their antebellum manor house set well back from Route 3 in 1984 and turned it into an inn with a small, part-time restaurant.

The main floor has two formal dining rooms (where the inn serves dinner to a minimum of eight people and caters private parties), a kitchen through which overnight guests often enter the inn, and a homey common room doubling as an office that guests share with the innkeepers and their two large and loving brown labrador retrievers. Out back is a fenced-in swimming pool. The rest of the 54 acres left from the original 1,200-acre Dunaway plantation involves crops and forests.

Upstairs off a wide central hallway are four lofty corner bedrooms, each with fireplace and private bath and done in bright Colonial colors. One is in olive green with a bathroom all in pink. Another is yellow and a third is painted barn red. Our room, in blue and white with a high-rise four-poster king bed, was charmingly quirky. It was big enough to rattle around in, but had only one easy chair (one of us had to bring over a desk-type chair from a far corner as we read before dinner). After dinner, we crouched through the bottom of a half door in the bathroom to get to our private balcony, with a view out the long driveway. It's the spot to listen to the loudest tree frogs around as you watch the stars sparkling in a pitch-black sky. The next morning one of us showered beneath an eight-foot-high spigot, which was like standing outside in a drizzle. The other enjoyed the extra-long bathtub.

Doris cooks and Warren serves breakfast in the hushed front dining room. Fresh orange juice, succulent local cantaloupes, coffee cake and eggs any style with crisp bacon, sliced local tomatoes and English muffins were the fare at our visit.

Doubles, $85.

Atherston Hall, 250 Prince George St., Box 757, Urbanna 23175. (804) 758-2809.

The innkeeper here is an antiques dealer, and her calling shows. Phyllis G. Hall furnishes her 1880 house with a changing collection of Virginia and Southern antiques. They're most noticeable in the front of the house, from the cozy parlor with TV to the dining room with a stunning display case, transformed from a closet, illuminating a collection of oriental china. Upstairs are two front bedrooms, one holding a general's high-poster double bed from Kentucky and the other with two twin beds. These rooms share a bath, but are seldom rented simultaneously.

In a new addition off the summer kitchen at the rear of the house are two more bedrooms with private baths and queensize beds. An oriental soapstone screen sets off the loveseat in one, while a Victorian settee is upholstered in plaid wool in the other. The fabrics here are in some of Phyllis's favorite dark colors, but the walls are painted in light tones.

Guests enjoy a full breakfast, often eggs benedict, with fried apples, fruit compote and blueberry muffins. They also enjoy a side porch and brick patio enhanced by wicker furniture, pots of prolific flowers and quite a collection of birdhouses for sale.

Doubles, $65 to 75.

Elizabeth House B&B occupies sea captain's home built in 1895.

Hewick Plantation, Route 602, Box 82, Urbanna 23175. (804) 758-4214.
Dating to 1678 and occupied by ninth-generation descendants of its original owner, this place is historic from the state marker along the highway to the primitive stone-slab steps at the front door. Overnight guests may not find all the creature comforts. What they will find is authenticity.
Californians Helen and Ed Battleson bought the house 1987 from a very distant cousin. Ed and the cousin are related to original owner Christopher Robinson, a member of the House of Burgesses and a founding trustee of the College of William & Mary (whose archaeology department has been conducting an ongoing dig here since 1989). "You can see the history of this building from the colors of its brick facade," says Ed, pointing out a second story that was added and windows that were bricked in at the side of the house. "The B&B idea sort of evolved," he said. The Battlesons had no plans other than the restoration of the house. "It took seven years to complete the restoration. Now we're starting the second time around with the finishing touches."
The Battlesons live in the back of the house with their daughters and turn over the front to overnight guests in two large bedrooms. One bedroom with attached bath has two double beds on opposite sides of the room, two chairs, Wedgwood blue walls with stenciling and the only TV in the house. We were assigned to the other, a vast affair with a private bath in the hall and no fewer than six beds – two twins on opposite walls with trundles underneath, a canopied double bed tucked in a corner and an antique crib/day bed – enough variety to sleep several generations. There were oriental rugs in the bathroom, custom-made soap embossed with the name Hewick, an attic fan in the bedroom window for cooling, dainty pink swags over the windows and two chairs. What there weren't were shades on the windows or lights properly positioned to read by. Nor were there reading lights in the dark formal parlor, its elegant furniture grouped in the center of the room (curiously, the large dining room was much better lit, and floor lamps were lighted beside armchairs in two corners). Fortunately, the weather was good, so we read until dusk on lawn chairs beneath towering trees on the front lawn.

Hewick Plantation, dating to 1678, is occupied by descendants of orginal owner.

The setting was utterly serene. We managed to exert ourselves long enough to walk through the side yard to the family cemetery and a look at the aging tombstones. The only sounds around the house, set back a third of a mile from the highway and surrounded by 66 acres of woods and farmland, emanated from a rooster who did his thing periodically all night. A couple of enormous pecan trees yield 200 pounds of pecans annually. Helen puts them to use in the coffee cake that's the centerpiece of her continental breakfasts.

In the future, the Battlesons envision a gazebo for their long front yard and perhaps some Williamsburg-type cottages to be erected on 26 building sites the archeological dig has uncovered out back. Meanwhile, Helen and daughters don period costumes for house tours by appointment ($6). The experience of staying here, while somewhat primitive on the surface, grows on you.

Doubles, $80 to $100.

The Gables Bed & Breakfast Inn, Main Street, Box 148, Reedville 22539. (804) 453-5209.

"There's something about this house that begs to be shared with the public,' says Barbara Clark. So share she does, with an avowed "sense of noblesse oblige." Overnight guests in two bedrooms face enough ultra-Victorian common areas and exotica to qualify the place as a museum. "If we had a sign out front," says Barbara, who does not advertise and has no inn brochure, "I'd be answering the doorbell all day to give tours."

Built in 1909 by a sea captain who also was one of Reedville's menhaden industry titans, the Queen Anne Victorian has eight sides and eight gables, configured on the points of a compass rose. The mast of the captain's schooner, built into the center of the top floors, supports the roof and the ship-like appointments within. The house is an architectural treasure, from its exterior walls of custom-made pressed bricks speckled with steel to the slabs of marble on the floors and the glazed brick in the kitchen, baths and entry way. Barbara and her husband Norman, a dentist with the Public Health Service, bought the Gables as a potential retirement home in 1982. While he practices in Maryland during the week, she holds down the fort here, "singlehandedly stripping all the paint from the woodwork" and collecting curiosities ever since.

For Barbara, who's addicted to her house and its history, the B&B is almost an after-thought. She's like a museum docent as she guides visitors through the guest rooms, one with a bedroom set from Wales and the other with an ornate antique walnut bed and well-worn Orientals. She's more interested in showing the master bath across the hall from the first bedroom. It's huge, with chandeliers, glazed brick walls, marble floors, a clawfoot tub and a corner shower. Guests in the other bedroom use a private bath tucked into a gable on the third floor. And that third floor is like none we ever saw – a huge open sitting room punctuated with gables in the corners. The ship's mast extends through its center (and up to the fourth-floor crow's nest). A munitions cabinet at the head of the stairs displays assorted memorabilia. Two leather sofas form a seating area beneath a window, and a third leather sofa faces a TV set in one gable.

Although the third floor is most unusual, rooms on the main floor are no slouches. A dark double parlor is outfitted with Victorian museum-piece furnishings and gilt-edged mirrors. A lace-clothed table in the dining room rests beneath an ornate, pink-glassed chandelier from Vienna, and Barbara may rummage through sideboard drawers filled not with dinnerware but papers to shed more light on the subject at hand. At either end of the second floor are sun rooms, one in the rear for the morning with a spectacular view onto Cockrells Creek and the Chesapeake Bay and the other in front for the afternoon sun and the sunset. A screened veranda wraps around three sides of the main floor.

Apple fritters are Barbara's breakfast specialty, light and fluffy and served with sausage or bacon. Fresh fruit or grapefruit meringue precede. Soufflés and rum french toast are other possibilities.

Doubles, $65 to $70.

The Inn at Montross, Courthouse Square, Montross 22520. (804) 493-9097 or (800) 321-0979.

The only inn in the top half of the Northern Neck, this has been around since 1683 and feels it. Innkeepers Eileen and Michael Longman from Baltimore upgraded con-siderably the abandoned building they acquired in 1985. They put out a sign saying "We're here. Nothing working except us." Some 55 gallons of paint and 98 rolls of wallpaper later, they opened to the public.

"We're trying to be a European-style inn in the manner of Michael's background," says Elaine, referring to her British husband, whom she met on an inn-going trip to Ireland. That translates into a full dining room (see Dining Spots), a dark living room with a cozy bar and a downstairs "ordinary" that Michael has converted into The Wine Seller, a retail wine and gift shop offering more than 200 wines.

The narrow entry hall is a jumble of stairs, a reception desk, the workings of an intricate sound system and possibly the largest collection of classical and jazz records and tapes on the Northern Neck. "Michael's a music freak and I married this system," says Elaine, rolling her eyes at its complexities. She adds that golden retrievers Sybil and Basil, who are usually underfoot in the front parlor, are her assistants. Michael's collection of British cartoonist Searle's original lithographs is of great interest.

Upstairs is another common room with a TV, lots of magazines and a guest refrig-erator. The six guest rooms are named after the original justices of Westmoreland County, who served in the courthouse across the street. Rooms vary in size and decor, but all have four-poster beds, private baths, television, telephones and in-room coffee.

We liked the Justice Washington Room, the biggest room, with a Charleston rice four-poster, two chairs and a sofa at the foot of the bed, an antique bureau with two mirrors, and interesting art. A small flask of brandy and two snifters on a tray with chocolate truffles are in each room. Ashtrays everywhere, from bedrooms to common rooms, encourage smoking, a fact duly noted in the inn's brochure.

A continental breakfast buffet with fruit, cereals, pastries and excellent croissants is served on the sun porch in the morning.

Doubles, $65 to $75; weekends, $115 to $125, MAP.

Dining Spots

The River Cafe, Windmill Point Road, White Stone. (804) 435-0113.

No fewer than four sets of local innkeepers were eating here, unbeknownst ahead of time to us or to each other, the Wednesday night we first were here. So you know this has to be good and a local favorite. The fact that a number of stylish, power types from Washington seemed to make up the rest of the clientele – and that owner-host Jim McDaniel table-hopped back and forth with them all – added to the "in" feeling.

The cognoscenti swear by the food, the nicely priced and interesting wine list and the conviviality of intimate tables and an everyone-knows-everyone-else atmosphere. We were surprised that the River Cafe was nowhere near a river, that the interior of the roadhouse was nondescript except for some nautical art and charts and a wine bottle on each glass-topped table, and that the assorted crackers were wrapped in cellophane.

No matter. The food *was* good, from the basket of French bread that finally arrived with the entrées to the raspberry bourbon fudge pie for dessert. David McDaniel, a Culinary Institute of America graduate who has succeeded his mother as chef, prepares a sophisticated menu that's changed daily. Prices range from $13.95 for grilled tuna with béarnaise butter to $19.95 for rack of lamb with mint sauce or sautéed venison with red wine sauce. David also added pasta dishes like sundried tomato fettuccine with sautéed lobster medallions and saffron butter, and lemon-basil fusilli with smoked Norwegian salmon and parmesan cream. We sampled an excellent chargrilled seafood kabob that included a couple of large chunks of lobster, and a tasty broiled salmon with creamy basil sauce. Portions were generous to huge, and accompanied by zucchini and a nice rice pilaf. Good salads with creamy Italian or raspberry-poppyseed vinaigrette preceded. We overheard Jim advising one couple to ask for a plate of his "half-million-dollar tomatoes." We asked, too, and were rewarded with a few slices of the first of the season – juicy, tender beauties grown, he said, on property worth a half million dollars.

With his son fully involved in the restaurant, Jim turned his attention in late 1994 to opening an upscale grocery store, the **River Market**, in White Stone. It features choice meats, seafood, organic vegetables and specialty food lines.

Lunch, Tuesday-Friday 11:30 to 2; dinner, Tuesday-Saturday 5 to 9, Sunday noon to 9.

The Crab Shack at Rappahannock Seafood, Route 672, Kilmarnock. (804) 435-1605.

Here's the kind of place we'd hoped to find all across the Neck: A sprightly solarium with a handful of tables covered with red and white checked cloths, fresh food from the adjacent seafood market, picnic tables outside by the water and a grand view of Indian Creek and the Chesapeake Bay. Although when we first met this place it was called the Rappahannock Cafe and was open only for lunch, at our latest visit it also was serving dinner three nights a week as The Crab Shack.

First, let's cover lunch. Ice water came in paper cups with a slice of lemon – now that's class – as we sampled very spicy peel-and-eat shrimp said to be mildly seasoned ($6.50) and a crabmeat salad with a side of cole slaw and potato salad ($5.95). Calistoga lime mineral water was a good accompaniment, and the short wine list was prepared by someone in the know. The fare runs from a hot dog ($1.25) to seafood salad or crab louis (both $6.95).

We liked our lunch so much that we returned to the seafood market the next day to acquire crab cakes and fresh crabmeat to take home, and to add our suggestion that they ought to serve dinner.

In 1994, the suggestion had become reality. The cafe in a section of the seafood market and its former gift shop had been transformed into the high-style Crab Shack. Some shack, this, with dark green walls trimmed in white, a thatched "hood" over the bar, brightly patterned fish cloths and fresh flowers in Perrier bottles on the tables, and potted palms and hanging plants all around. Before sunset, ducks waddled up to the windows, as if looking for handouts, as we shared a dinner appetizer of fabulous crabmeat nachos ($5.50). The house raspberry vinaigrette dressed good little salads that come with each entrée. Choices ranged from $8.95 for fried chicken to $15.95 for filet mignon with lump crabmeat. We were pleased with the plate of crab cakes and the seafood platter that teamed a crab cake and soft-shell crab with flounder, trout, shrimp and a side of rice. The key lime pie was excellent, and two peppermints came with the bill.

So successful proved the cafe and Crab Shack that owner Martha McLaughlin planned a similar, bigger installation at Smith Seafood & Deli in Reedville. Here she was envisioning a building at water's edge — with a screened porch literally over the water — for possible opening in 1995 .

Lunch daily, 11 to 3; dinner, Friday-Sunday, 5 to 9. Closed in winter.

The Northside Grille, Route 3. Kilmarnock. (804) 435-3100.

This popular new restaurant in a commercial strip north of town was converted from a Dairy Queen, we're told. You certainly would never know it, given the sprightly green and white decor, the planked wood ceiling, the natural wood booths with green tables set inside, and all the hanging plants. Owner Mike Robertson, a town councilman and building contractor, tried to create an "urban environment." What he got was a suburban fern bar, very popular with all ages if the noon-hour crowd was any indication the summer weekday we were there.

The all-day menu is heavy on burgers (six), sandwiches, salads, omelets and appetizers, most of the last of the potato skins and Buffalo wings variety. The dinner section adds three chicken dishes, crab cakes, shrimp stir-fry, shrimp scampi, fried shrimp, beef and shrimp kabob, delmonico steak and filet mignon, $8.95 to $14.95. The presentations are straightforward, but considered very good. Sutter Home white zin heads the short wine selection, pleasantly priced from $11.95 to $15.95. Desserts run from apple dumpling to bread pudding to hot fudge sundae.

Lunch and dinner daily, from 11 a.m.

The Inn at Montross, Courthouse Square, Montross. (804) 493-9097.

A first-class, reasonably priced European/continental restaurant was owner Michael Longman's aim. And chef Loren Mitchell, who trained at Colonial Williamsburg, obliged. Besides making a name for the inn at dinner, the two team up for periodic wine-tasting dinners, seven-course affairs pairing Virginia wines with some of Loren's more creative efforts.

Considerable artistry goes into the regular fare. Piping-hot sourdough bread was

Lodging, dining and a tavern are offered at The Inn at Montross.

served as we nursed a bottle of the house chardonnay, one of four private labels bottled for the inn by Virginia's Misty Mountain Vineyards. Dinner started with a nicely presented appetizer of gravlax served with red caviar in spears of endive ($6.95) and the house salad ($3.50) tossed with a mustardy vinaigrette in an unusual ceramic, skillet-shaped dish. Entrées ($14.95 to $24.95) range from crab croquettes to rack of lamb. We liked the chicken roulade, stuffed with spinach and red bell peppers and accompanied by roasted garlic cloves, and a house specialty, breast of duck with lingonberry sauce. A good Ingleside Plantation pinot noir accompanied. Interesting vegetables, stylishly served, included a zucchini flan with swiss and parmesan cheese, baby carrots, sweet and sour cabbage with balsamic vinegar, and roasted potatoes or wild rice.

From a dessert list that included a strawberry tart with grand marnier cream came an intense raspberry sorbet and praline ice cream in a tuile basket. The bill was gilded with petits fours.

Dinner is served in three main-floor dining rooms seating a total of 60. On the same floor is a pub/lounge that Michael likens to those of the English countryside.

Dinner nightly, 5:30 to 8:30 or 9; Sunday brunch, noon to 3.

Awful Arthur's Seafood Company, 210 Oyster Road, Urbanna. (804) 758-0758.
The latest of the Awful Arthur group (others in Richmond and Charlottesville), this is owner Arthur Webb's favorite. He likes Urbanna so much he's living here, and has opened Awfully Sweet and Tex-Urbanna Barbecue offshoots up Virginia Street.

Here, he's taken over the glamorous Windows on Urbanna Creek restaurant vacated by famed chef Jimmy Snead, who moved on to culinary fame with the Frog and the Redneck in Richmond. On a spit of land jutting into Urbanna Creek, with the wide Rappahannock beyond, the restaurant occupies the second floor of a circular structure. Full-length windows look onto the water beyond a wraparound, canopied deck.

The place is noisy and casual, with oil cloths on the tables and yachting banners overhead. The young serving staff was picked, no doubt, because they looked so good in short shorts. We sampled a few oysters from the prominent raw bar before digging into the rest of the fare, which was basic and predictable. Among main courses ($9.95 to $13.95) with an emphasis on things grilled or blackened, we chose grilled scallops and fried oysters. Both came with good tossed salads, heavily battered hushpuppies and surprisingly limp fries.

Not in the mood for one of the heavy desserts, we were kindly directed by our short-shorts waitress up the street to Awfully Sweet for some ice cream. Unbeknownst to her and us, however, the place had closed an hour earlier.

Open daily from 11; dinner from 5.

Windmill Point Resort, Route 695, Windmill Point. (804) 435-1186.

New owners have taken over this 63-unit motor inn and conference center, blessed with a yachty location where the Rappahannock meets the Chesapeake. The complex has seen better days (a sign at the lobby entry warned of broken glass at one visit), but the restaurant was receiving good reports.

A Key West deco look is the aim in the pink and aqua dining room. Portholes look onto a porch with full-length windows onto the marina, which harbors some spectacular yachts. There's a huge brick fireplace, plants are covered with white lights, and rattan chairs with upholstered seats face up to polyurethane tables topped with fishy paper placemats.

The dinner menu has something for everyone, from quite a selection of mostly exotic pizzas ($9.95 to $12.95, served with a tossed salad and bread sticks) to filet mignon for $17.95. We were satisfied with the crab cakes, sautéed and served with a

Porthole view at Windmill Point Resort.

red pepper sauce, and the seafood medley over angel-hair pasta. From the mostly home-made desserts listed on the menu, we shared a refreshing "sobert," which tasted better than it was spelled, even though it wasn't homemade.

Lunch daily, 11 to 3; dinner, 6 to 9; Sunday brunch.

Lancaster Tavern, Route 3, Lancaster. (804) 462-5941.

Ann Parsons runs this old Southern-style dining room in her house dating to 1790. There's no menu and no liquor. Folks dine communally at one of four oilcloth-covered tables and take pot luck.

When we stopped by, Ann was preparing chicken and dumplings and pot roast for the evening's dinner. Among her other offerings that night was Colonial gazpacho, so called "because we're serving it in Lancaster County." The night's salads were lemon cream congealed salad and apple sauce. Veggies were green beans, whipped squash and broccoli casserole. A yellow cake with coconut cream frosting concluded.

Ann says she can seat 30 people at once "if they're on good speaking terms." Meals are served family-style, all you can eat for $5 at lunch, $8 at dinner.

Lunch that day was stuffed shells with three kinds of cheese, accompanied by beans, squash, cole slaw, cucumbers and gazpacho. The place is highly rated for home cooking and local color.

Lunch, Wednesday-Sunday 11 to 2; dinner, Wednesday-Sunday 5 to 8.

Horn Harbor House, Great Wicomoco Campground and Marina, Burgess. (804) 453-3351.

This oldtimer, part of a campground and marina overlooking the Great Wicomoco River, is favored by locals, who wait up to two hours for a table on weekend nights. The wait is made more pleasant by drinks served at wood-slat benches and tables outside near the water.

Inside, the decor is nautical around tables set with banquet chairs, paper mats, artificial flowers, oil lanterns and baskets of crackers. Seafood specialties are mostly fried, but you can order seafood norfolk style or au gratin. Otherwise the menu lists Italian selections (two spaghettis and shrimp parmesan), beef and fowl. They're priced from $6.95 for fried chicken to $13.95 for broiled seafood platter, except for lobster tails and a fancy seafood platter. The food is considered mediocre, but after two hours of waiting and drinking, who notices?

Dinner nightly except Tuesday, 5 to 9 or 10; weekends in spring and fall; closed in winter. No credit cards.

White Stone Wine & Cheese Co., Route 3, White Stone. (804) 435-2000.

This is a good place to pick up a sandwich for a picnic or to eat at one of the tables here. Specialties are grilled chicken salad and apple-walnut tuna salad. Sandwiches ($2.75 to $4.95) include one of brie and prosciutto. A fajita chicken pita pizza with iced tea was going for $4.95 at our latest visit. You also can get applewood-smoked Virginia trout, chili, Maryland crab soup, and key lime or snickers pie. Sticky buns on Saturday are special. Of course, there's a good selection of cheese, and the wine selection is the best on the Neck.

Open Monday-Saturday, 10 to 5.

Diversions

History and water are the main attractions here and they pop up in unexpected places. Head down almost any side road and you'll likely see an historic marker, an old church, cornfields, a hodgepodge of houses with perhaps a manor in between and, eventually,

George Washington Birthplace is a little-known treasure on the Northern Neck.

Great Hall at Stratford Hall Plantation is considered one of most beautiful rooms in America.

water – in the form of creek, river, bay, inlet or what have you. The water here often seems elusive, but it's all around.

Stratford Hall Plantation, Route 214, Stratford, 493-8038. The birthplace of Robert E. Lee in 1807 was built about 1738 by Thomas Lee, a distant relative. Thomas, president of the Council of Virginia, was father of the only two brothers to sign the Declaration of Independence, Richard Henry and Francis Lightfoot. The H-shaped brick manor house, situated high above the Potomac, is one of the largest private dwellings of the Colonial period open to visitors. Costumed guides show the house, usually starting in various bedrooms, a school room and a winter kitchen on the ground floor. The grander rooms are upstairs, including the 29-foot-square Great Hall, supposedly one of the most beautiful rooms in America. Everyone enjoys seeing Robert E. Lee's cradle in his mother's room. After touring the house, visitors wander around the various gardens and dependencies, including the kitchen, where ginger cookies and cider are served. Usually one can drive to the bluffs for a good view of the Potomac, seven miles wide here, but at our visit the road was closed after a storm had turned it to mud. Also on the property is a restaurant in a log cabin, with a large screened porch overlooking a forested ravine where we felt as if we were eating in the treetops. The Plantation luncheon for $7.95 included Virginia ham or southern fried chicken, candied sweet potatoes, cole slaw, hot biscuits and preserves and beverage (and everyone seems to drink iced tea). Of course, you can get the ubiquitous ham biscuits and crab cakes. Lunch is served from early March through October, daily 11:30 to 3. Plantation open daily, 9 to 4:30. Adults, $7.

George Washington Birthplace National Monument, Route 204, Washington's Birthplace, 224-1732. A 51-foot-tall granite obelisk rises unexpectedly at the end of a country byway. The miniature Washington monument is appropriate but somehow startlingly out of character at the restoration of George Washington's birthplace and memorial house, the re-creation of the site as it was in the early 1700s. It was on this point overlooking Popes Creek and the Potomac River that the president spent the first three years of his life, and he returned here frequently as a teenager. Destroyed by fire in 1779 while Washington was leading the Continental Army, the house was rebuilt in 1930 as a memorial. It's a lovely, livable house, made even more appealing by its tranquil surroundings. Costumed docents spin wool in the hallway, make candles outside and cook waffles in the kitchen house. The 200 or 300 visitors a day to what one docent called "the government's best-kept secret" enter through a modern visitor center, see a fourteen-minute film and walk to the restoration site for a tour. Then they're on their own for a look at the farmlands, the family burial ground and a picnic area. There's even a beach, where one can frequently find shark's teeth washed up from the river bottom. Open daily, 9 to 5. Adults, $1.

Mary Ball Washington Museum and Library, Route 3, Lancaster, 462-7280. This historic complex including an old jail and an old clerk's office in the center of tiny Lancaster honors "the mother of the father of our country." The museum is of less general interest than, say, the George Washington Birthplace or Stratford Hall. But genealogists come from across the world to trace the lineage of early Virginians from documents dating to 1651. Open Tuesday-Friday 9 to 5, Saturday 10 to 3. Donation.

Westmoreland State Park, Route 347, Montross. Situated on cliffs overlooking the Potomac between the birthplaces of Washington and Lee is one of the more attractive state parks we've seen and one of the few with a visitor center. Miles of wooded trails draw hikers. A sand beach is popular with sunbathers (the swimming is better in the adjacent pool, we're advised). Paddleboats are available for exploring the Potomac. There are campgrounds and cabins for overnighters. Open year-round. Admission, $1 per car.

Ingleside Plantation Vineyards, Oak Grove, 224-8687. The plantation house here designates one of Virginia's larger and more enterprising wineries as a registered National Historic Place. It's owned by the Carl Flemer family, whose 2,500-acre plantation embraces three manor homes, the East Coast's biggest wholesale nursery and 45 acres of vineyards planted with fifteen varietals. The modern winery produces 15,000 cases annually under the direction of Belgian winemaker Jacques Recht, who paused here with his wife on a round-the-world sailing expedition and stayed. Jacques is in considerable demand as a consultant, but oversees production of some fine chardonnays, cabernet sauvignons and a limited-edition pinot noir. His sparkling wine was voted one of the top ten in the country. A large tasting room offers samples of up to a dozen offerings, priced from $6 to $17. There are tours, a good gift shop, historic artifacts and a video presentation. Open daily 10 to 5, Sunday noon to 5.

Reedville Fishermen's Museum, Main Street, Reedville, 453-5371. The trash fish, menhaden, was money in the bank to Reedville, which at the turn of the century was purported to be the richest town per capita in the country. Oils of the menhaden are used today for paints, cosmetics and soaps, and Reedville is the home of Ampro Fisheries and of Zapata Haynie Corp., the largest fish oil producer in the United States. The quaint Victorian hamlet – a long one-street National Historic District without so much as a general store – is considered the charter fishing capital of the country and sponsors an annual bluefish derby in June in which 2,000 fishermen compete for $75,000 in prize money. The little William Walker House was opened in 1990 as a museum to detail the menhaden industry. Out back along the banks of Cockrells Creek, a new museum structure enlarged the exhibition space in 1995. The original museum was converted into a typical waterman's home of the late 19th century. Open Monday-Friday 2 to 4, Saturday and Sunday 1 to 5; weekends only in winter. Adults, $2.

Driving Tours. Pick up a detailed Northern Neck map to find your way along back roads to favorite spots. They include **Fleeton,** a summer colony built by prosperous

Reedville fishermen to escape the smell of menhaden; **Kinsale,** described to us as a New England-type harbor town, but that's stretching it; **Sharps,** a one-street Victorian village centered by a big Presbyterian church; **Weems,** a beachy-looking summer colony on the way up, and **Irvington,** where some of the yachts are as expensive as the homes along Carter's Creek. Two free state-run **ferries** make a couple of the trips shorter on either side of the Neck. The Sunnybank ferry has a more picturesque crossing than the Merry Point. Each takes two vehicles at a time and, supposedly, you honk your horn if the ferry is waiting on the opposite shore.

Near Irvington, historic **Christ Church,** the only virtually unchanged Colonial church in America, was built in 1734 by Robert "King" Carter, the agent for the English proprietor of the Northern Neck, whose descendants included eight governors of Virginia, two presidents and something like 250 Carter listings in the local telephone directory. Cruciform in design, it has a rare three-decker pulpit that is still used for services in summer. While Christ Church is exquisite in its awesome perfection, **St. Mary's White Chapel** near Lively is charming in its simplicity. Dating to 1669, it contains the oldest altar boards in Virginia – three tablets reciting the Lord's Prayer, the Ten Commandments and the Apostles Creed. Churchwomen did the spectacular needlework for the curved kneeling pads at the altar.

Shopping. You're not going to go crazy shopping in this area, but there are little antiques stores dotted here and there, and a few local artisans. A tree is dedicated to John dos Passos in front of **Company's Coming** at 40 Irvington Road, Kilmarnock, which stocks kitchenware and a good selection of paper plates and napkins. In White Stone, **Mary Anne & Co**. has lots of the kinds of things you wish you could gussy up your porch or patio with. Irvington is home to a few nifty stores like **The Dandelion** and **The Bay Window** for the local gentry. A lobster trap hangs from the ceiling at **Wood-A-Drift Artifacts Shop** in Irvington, chock full of decoys, shells, lamps, nautical gifts, books, paintings and more. Artist-owner Graham Bruce stocks unusual items like a crab shell transformed into a Santa for the Christmas tree and walking sticks with white pine duck heads on top.

Every time we went by **Artisans of the Tidewater** in Lancaster it was closed, but we peeked in the windows and saw some wonderful pottery, pictures, baskets and the like. The **Barn Shop at Mary Young's Herbs,** Route 202, Hague, offers perfectly beautiful wreaths, dried flowers, potpourri, herbal gifts and more. Fresh-picked or pick-your-own fruits are the theme and peach melba sundaes a specialty at **Westmoreland Berry Farm and Orchard,** Route 637, Oak Grove. **The Corner Store** at Routes 3 and 214 in Lerty, near Stratford, has gifts, antiques and a farm market, as well as a little craft shop featuring weathervanes.

Extra-Special

Nadji Nook, 303 Queen St., Tappahannock. (804) 443-3298.

Just across a bridge from the Northern Neck is the antiquey town of Tappahannock, which boasts an appealing riverfront historic district and St. Margaret's School, an Episcopal boarding school for girls. The star among antiques shops is this glittering emporium, where old saws and a railroad lantern hanging from the ceiling are overshadowed by a fourteen-tiered chandelier. A born collector, late owner Jackie Allen Fisher was known to dicker, but not much, as antiquers sought her one-of-a-kind prizes. Her husband Randolph continues the tradition. You might find a rare music box for $8,750 or a restored carousel horse for $9,500. We picked up a couple of odd salt and pepper shakers for a gift for considerably less. Open Monday-Thursday 10 to 5, Friday and Saturday to 6, Sunday 1 to 6.

Washington, Va.
The Place That an Inn Built

After seventeen-year-old surveyor George Washington laid out its streets in 1749, this was to become the oldest of 28 towns named for the father of our country and the only one so designated before he became president. Not until rather lately has this still somnolent place been lifted from obscurity by an unlikely source, a restaurant and inn playfully called The Inn at Little Washington.

This was "almost a ghost town," in the words of Patrick O'Connell. He teamed with Reinhardt Lynch to convert what once was a garage at the main crossroads into a restaurant in 1978. Rave reviews quickly attracted the movers and shakers from big Washington, along with food and lodging cognoscenti from around the world. Because their clientele complained of the late-night drive back to the other Washington, the restaurant eventually added bedrooms and suites to become a full-service inn. Not an ordinary inn, mind you, but a pricey paragon that has been exalted to incredible heights. It is the only establishment ever to capture five-star awards for both dining and lodging from the Mobil Travel Guide and the first inn to receive five-diamond awards for both food and lodging from the American Automobile Association.

Its accolades – and the adulation of the nation's elite – have put on the map, for better or worse, the two-bit hamlet in which it resides. But, its press to the contrary, this is no one-inn nor one-restaurant town. Others have popped up in the inn's footsteps.

Happily, success has not spoiled little Washington. The entire village is designated an historic district and remains unscathed by development.

Washington is the county seat of Rappahannock County, though you'd scarcely know it from the unassuming government buildings a block off Main Street. With 6,000 people, Rappahannock is the second smallest of Virginia's counties. It's a relic of the past, situated between prosperous hunt country to the east and the bucolic Blue Ridge Mountains to the west, a detour off the main road and not really on the way to anywhere else.

The village's estimated population of 232 ranks it as the county's largest, ahead of Sperryville and Flint Hill. The mountainous county has more cows than people and more apple trees than cows. There are no traffic lights (only a couple of flashers), no supermarkets or chain stores. It is a spectacularly scenic place, yet tranquil and gentle. A few good shops, wineries and outdoor activities, plus the area's cachet, make it a destination for weekenders (almost everything is closed early in the week).

It's a diverse area because it is home to the poorest of the poor as well as the richest of the rich. Sometimes it's hard to tell which is which because almost everybody drives

a pickup truck – except for those visitors, most in luxury cars, whose destination is the Inn at Little Washington.

Note: A new telephone area code (540) was scheduled to take effect in July 1995 for this area. Until then, the 703 area code was to remain in effect. Also, under the new 911 calling system, all street addresses were to be changed in 1995.

Exotic plants are featured in inner courtyard at The Inn at Little Washington.

Inn Spots

The Inn at Little Washington paved the way, but others have followed — and are much in demand as lodging alternatives for visitors who don't wish to pay top dollar. They are worthy on their own, banding together in a county B&B guild and offering a Moveable Feast that has diverted some of the publicity from "the inn," as it's called locally. (The event, staged periodically in the off-season, includes an overnight stay and a progressive dinner with a different course at each B&B). Like the inn, some of the B&Bs carry surcharges for weekends and the month of October. Although 75 percent of their business at certain times comes as a result of overflow from the inn, each is increasingly able to stand on its own.

The Inn at Little Washington, Middle and Main Streets, Washington 22747. (540) 675-3800.

There's no sign to detract from its aura of exclusivity. Only by the process of elimination does the visitor determine that the unremarkable, three-story white building at what passes for the village crossroads is, indeed, the vaunted Inn at Little Washington. Depending on the time of day, the handful of fancy cars parked in pickup territory might give it away. But lace curtains on the windows and a closed entry thwart the gaze of curious passersby.

This is an inn turned inward unto itself, as one might find in a large city. From the inn's perspective, the village is not particularly compelling, and those with the wherewithal to spend a night or two here seem to want to screen themselves from the outside. Owners Patrick O'Connell and Reinhardt Lynch provide a cocoon of luxury patterned after an English manor home. Everything has been draped, flounced and swagged by a London stage-set designer who, curiously, never saw the place until she attended the grand-opening party. Her elaborate conceptual drawings of each room hang in the hallways.

The restoration of the two-story lobby alone cost more than the original building; its gilt ceiling is decorated with a collage of 500 hand-drawn blocks that resemble stained glass. Surely the inn's reported $2 million renovation tab does not include the furnishings. Otherwise, the reports of bedspreads costing $10,000 are apocryphal.

The banister leading upstairs to a second-floor lobby favored by overnight guests for tea or cocktails is wrapped in velvet. The ten rooms here are designated standard (one, $365); intermediate (three, $425); superior (four, $495), and suites (two, $615). An additional intermediate room and suite in the inn's new guest house above the Rare Finds gift shop down the street are described by its proprietor as "just as nice if not nicer" in comparison with the main accommodations. All are decorated to the nth, up to the wallpapered ceilings and down to the oriental rugs on the floors. Each has a bathroom with countertops of Greek marble, heated towel racks, a shoe polisher and Gilbert & Soames toiletries. There are terrycloth robes, padded and removable coat hangers, a telephone but no TV or radio, lush beds draped within an inch of their lives, and double doors at the entry to eliminate hallway noise. All have a cozy chair with a hassock and a throw on top. Some have window seats and others have private balconies. Those looking onto the garden courtyard appeal more than those facing the street. Each is furnished with antiques and custom-made contemporary pieces, and "Mr. O'Connell is always on the lookout for new things," our guide offered. A staff of about 60 attends to every detail.

Two duplex suites, furnished and decorated similarly except for their color schemes, crown the inn's third floor. In the more striking of the two, an arched doorway leads to a sitting area with a velour sofa/banquette a dozen feet long, all draped in mulberry and awash with pillows. Walls are a soft sponged peach and oriental throw rugs cover the oatmeal-colored carpeting. A side balcony overlooks the garden. A wet bar and a stereo system separate the sitting room from the bathroom. The latter contains a jacuzzi in a window alcove, a double sink, a dressing area with a built-in seat, a toilet and bidet behind one door and, behind another door, a shower stall for two with English hinged glass doors. One entire wall is mirrored. Upstairs in a loft is the bedroom with another balcony, from which you can see most of the village. Layered fabrics like those used in the sitting area decorate the kingsize bed. A stunning canopy is painted on the ceiling that slopes to the floor below.

Fresh flowers furnished by the inn's fulltime gardener (often supplemented by orchids grown for the inn by a nearby purveyor) greet guests. Bottles of mineral water await. Tea and a fruit and cookie tray are served in the room at check-in.

Colorful gardens welcome guests to Bleu Rock Inn.

The patio beside an exotic garden incorporating oriental and native Virginia plants is a favorite spot for breakfast. Fresh fruits, juices and homemade breads and pastries like applesauce-walnut croissants are included in the rates. A hot breakfast that brings the acclaimed pan-fried rainbow trout or eggs scrambled with Scottish smoked salmon and cream cheese costs an extra $12 per person.

Is a stay here worth the expense? Perhaps, for those who aspire to the ultimate in decor and service, though some might find the cocoon claustrophobic. Perhaps the five-star difference is one that must be experienced rather than merely looked at. The cache of glowing press reprints in the lobby and the flyer headlined "Avalanche of Awards Hits Inn at Little Washington" surely must dispel any doubts.

Doubles, $365 to $495; suites, $515 and $615.

Bleu Rock Inn, Route 211, Route 1, Box 555, Washington 22747. (540) 987-3190.

Morning may be the best part of the experience here, say staff and guests at this deluxe inn, a pretender to the Inn at Little Washington's throne. That's because of the lavish breakfasts served in a matchless setting: in a dining room beside the garden or on a rear terrace overlooking a Napa Valley-ish vista toward a pond, vineyards and the Blue Ridge Mountains.

The dominant inn cannot match the newcomer's complimentary breakfast, scenery or value. Consider the morning repast, which changes daily: perhaps grand marnier french toast, shrimp and tomato omelet, poached eggs with smoked salmon or omelets with shiitake mushrooms, chives and local goat cheese. Little drop biscuits, carrot and poppyseed muffins and blueberry and cinnamon rolls with three homemade preserves might accompany. "We try to do something extra," says chef Dan Cornish in a reference to the lack of a full breakfast included in the rates at the other inn.

The Bleu Rock, which serves mighty good meals (see Dining Spots), also offers a spectacular, rural setting on 80 acres. It was opened in a converted farmhouse a few miles southwest of the village in 1990 by brothers Bernard and Jean Campagne, who operate La Bergerie Restaurant in Alexandria and are tinkering with this as a place to which they will retire.

The five unpretentious guest rooms with private baths are pristinely elegant (but why the small, stand-up balconies without chairs?). All upstairs rooms have queensize beds. The largest is outfitted in peach and moss green colors with draped lace curtains.

A nearby room, much smaller, is done in blues and yellows. Another room in deep blue has a dark blue comforter adorned with tulips. The shower curtains in most bathrooms match the bed covers. Fresh flowers, a hair dryer and fancy Kingsbridge toiletries, and pretty dried wreaths and potpourri are hallmarks. Fruit baskets and candies are placed in each room. A downstairs room in blue-green and deep rose offers two double iron and brass beds and a large bath tiled in pink.

An attractive and spacious sitting room, quite elaborately furnished, harbors books and games and a fireplace. Out in front of the restored white stucco farmhouse with a tin roof and blue accents are colorful gardens and a trickling fountain. And in back, well away from Route 211, are the pond, vineyards and mountains, with plenty of seating to take it all in.

Doubles, $150.

Sycamore Hill House & Gardens, Route 1, Box 978, Washington 22747. (540) 675-3046.

Off by itself on 52 acres at the end of a mile-long driveway up Menefee Mountain, this is one of the few contemporary B&Bs in all Virginia. "No dolls, ducks or bunnies here," says Kerri Wagner, innkeeper with her husband Stephen. Just tasteful furnishings, exquisite flowers and plants, original artworks, three comfortable rooms with private baths, gourmet food and a view that won't quit.

Kerri, a former lobbyist in the other Washington, and Steve, a well-known illustrator, spotted a for-sale sign on a Sunday drive in 1987. "We came back as a lark, saw the house and had to have it," says Kerri. "Steve's job was portable and mine was not, so that was the impetus for the B&B." They opened on New Year's Day in 1988, having decided the house was so big and the location so special that they ought to share it.

And share they do. Kerri greets summertime guests with homemade cookies and iced tea on the 65-foot wraparound veranda, where Amish bentwood rockers take in a 180-degree panorama of the Blue Ridge Mountains across Kerri's prized gardens. The originals of Steve's illustrations for Time-Life Books (and others) enhance each room. His illustration of the inn on a winter night with deer in the snow and a zillion stars is magical. It hangs in the master bedroom, where we awoke in a waist-high four-poster queen bed to a mist-shrouded vista that looked like an oriental landscape. No fewer than four arrangements of garden flowers decorated our bedroom, dressing room and the bathroom with its double sinks. A decanter of after-dinner brandy had provided a nightcap beneath the stars on the veranda the night before.

Though the master bedroom is the biggest and has the best view, the other choices are no slouches. A closet that once blocked the view in the Peach Room has been opened up; wicker chairs and built-in shelves full of books and lush African violets have been added on either side of the new window. White wicker furniture gives the smaller Wicker Room its name; its bath across the hall was Kerri's rejuvenation project one recent winter.

All three rooms have sitting/reading areas. But most guests prefer to relax in the airy living room with its circular wall of glass and accents of plants or on the veranda beyond.

That is, when they're not enjoying the grounds. The massed floral plantings are spectacular, wildlife and birds are abundant, and Kerri's vegetables and herbs are much in demand at local restaurants.

The glass table in the open dining room is covered with a pink cloth for breakfast. Classical music played as we enjoyed orange-pineapple juice, slices of melon and strawberries with ham, and Kerri's special apple puff, almost like a soufflé and served

Sycamore Hill House & Gardens, as portrayed by illustrator-innkeeper Stephen Wagner.

in a quiche dish. Other entrées could be steak and eggs, light-as-a-feather angel pancakes and sometimes a shrimp soufflé.

Good as they are, the breakfasts here necessarily play second fiddle to the setting. Not to mention the views.

Doubles, $100 to $140. Two-night minimum on holiday weekends and during October. No smoking.

Blue Knoll Farm, Route 676, Route 1, Box 141, Castleton 22716. (540) 937-5234.

If the Wagners provide a mountaintop setting and contemporary elegance at Sycamore Hill, Mary and Gil Carlson offer serenity and a spirit of whimsy in their restored Virginia farmhouse on five rural acres in the middle of nowhere.

This is now home for the Carlsons, who had moved twenty times in as many years during his service as a Navy submarine officer. Retired in Annapolis and "always wanting to do the B&B thing," they jumped at the chance to purchase a ready-made B&B in tiny Castleton, barely a dot on the map some ten roundabout miles east of little Washington. Gil built a double garage with a workshop and office that his wife calls "The Taj Garage" and set to work constructing a sundeck on the side of the house and a double-sider Victorian glider for the lawn.

The Carlsons offer four guest rooms with private baths and king or queen beds. They range from Rebecca's Room, full of dolls and a dollhouse, with an old quilt behind the bed and the bath across the hall, to the master bedroom with an elaborate antique bed headboard and Ralph Lauren comforter, lacy curtains and a jacuzzi. The Meadowview Room with a kingsize bed at the back of the house is for those who cherish privacy. Our choice was the fireplaced main-floor Library, where a queensize brass bed shared quarters with shelves of books and an old desk bearing all the requisite accessories. "We've tried to make it fun," Mary advised as we remarked on the rooster-related pottery, "because this is not a really elegant house."

Guests spread out beside a wood stove in the front parlor, over afternoon refreshments at the breakfast table and on two great porches, one facing a farm pond. The latter porch was where we greeted the day over a masterful breakfast, punctuated by the mooing of nearby cows and the quacking of baby ducks. Mary's specialties include a prosciutto-provolone-basil breakfast strata and pineapple upside-down french toast. A lavish fresh fruit platter, lemon poppyseed breads and key lime or peach bran muffins might accompany. Fine china and linens, silver, fresh flowers and flickering candles transformed an ordinary picnic table into an entrancing setting.

Doubles, $95 to $125. Two-night minimum on holiday weekends and during October. No smoking.

Sunset Hills Farm, Route 1, Box 562, Washington 22747. (540) 987-8804 or (800) 980-2580.

The front doorbell chimes out a ragtime melody in this architect-designed, stone house in the Frank Lloyd Wright tradition high up Jenkins Mountain. Betty and Leon Hutcheson moved here in 1978 from Alexandria after their four offspring had left for college. They were responsible for bringing the principals of Bleu Rock Inn to a site below theirs along Route 211. In 1993, they started taking in overnight guests in their showplace of a house.

For starters, the Hutchesons offer three bedrooms, each with private marble bath and TV and furnished in traditional style. Two in the rear come with queensize beds and fieldstone walls made of stones from the property. The extra-large Gazebo Room has a kingsize poster bed, a sitting area with TV and a bath with jacuzzi tub, twin vanities and a wall mural of belgian horses painted by Betty and a friend. It has direct access to a large side deck, full of heavy Adirondack-style chairs and tables and prolific flowers, leading to a screened gazebo. Both are great spots for enjoying the farm gardens, the horses grazing near the sunken pond in front, and the Blue Ridge vistas. Guests also enjoy a huge, circular, open living/dining room with a table for six looking somewhat lonely in the center. Here or in the gazebo is where Betty serves a full breakfast. Expect fresh fruit (the couple pick their own berries and peaches), juice, and perhaps pancakes or an egg casserole with blueberry muffins. Beverages come from an espresso-cappuccino machine. Afternoon treats include lemonade, iced tea and cakes. Bedrooms are stocked with soft drinks and fresh fruits.

The Hutchesons, who live in a separate section of the house, have plans for three more guest rooms and a library. Meanwhile, they oversee production of brandied peaches, fruit butters, other fruit products and gift baskets at their mountaintop Sunset Hills farm store and Christmas shop in a barn near their house.

Doubles, $145; suite, $195. No smoking.

Fairlea Farm Bed & Breakfast, Mount Salem Avenue, Washington 22747. (540) 675-3679.

For an edge-of-town residence, this fieldstone manor house has a remarkable setting. It's surrounded by a 40-acre sheep and cattle farm and yields 180-degree vistas. "You really feel like you're in the country," says Susan Longyear, who with husband Walter moved here from Falls Church and opened their home as a B&B after raising a family. The property was the old county fairgrounds, and a shed near the backyard gazebo and shady flagstone terrace was once a concession stand.

Few would guess its background, for today all is quite elegant and comfortable, from the lovely living room with fireplace and oriental rugs to the four guest quarters with queensize beds and private baths. The Magnolia Room, so named because it looks onto a couple of magnolia trees, is the main-floor master bedroom with a sofa, bathroom with double vanity, and a collection of miniature mirrors (53 at last count) on one wall. Upstairs, the Meadow Room has a brass bed, while the Rose Room over-

Blue Knoll Farm offers tranquility on five rural acres.

looking the rose garden contains a canopy bed. A suite in the walkout basement is fashioned from a paneled family room; it has a four-poster bed, a sofabed, a stone fireplace, TV and kitchenette.

Fresh fruit and flowers are in each room, and ice water accompanies nightly turndown. A sumptuous breakfast is served at guests' convenience. Expect things like strawberry-rhubarb compote, apple puff, egg casserole, crêpes with local fruit, homemade breads and muffins.

Doubles, $75 to $105; suite, $125.

Caledonia Farm, Route 1, Box 2080, Flint Hill 22627. (540) 675-3693 or (800) 262-1812.

"I've been to 262 B&Bs in North America and we do it differently from any other," says broadcaster-turned-innkeeper Phil Irwin. And loquacious Phil, who was the Breakfast Show host on the Voice of America, is quick to tell you how he does it.

"We produce a custom breakfast on demand," says he. That means a choice of menu, from smoked salmon on a bagel with neufchatel cheese to eggs benedict, following Eastern Shore melon, juices and cereal. Aspenglow sparkling cider in a champagne glass opens the presentation; a hot apple strudel concludes. Breakfast is served at hourly intervals "because of our shared-bath situation." Which is fine if you get your hour of choice, but it's first come, first served, and no deviations are tolerated. You arrive late for breakfast and you may go hungry; you arrive late at night and your reservation may not be honored. Phil does things his way.

He really gets going as he leads guests on a tour of part of the 183-year-old stone house after sharing a glass of wine or beer in the late afternoon in a gorgeous front gathering room. Here you'll find exposed beams, a great stone fireplace, paneled window wells and cross-and-bible doors – some are "architectural impurities," Phil points out. Up a very steep staircase is a landing with seating to enjoy the mountain view and two guest rooms sharing a bath (lately, Phil has been trying to rent them as a suite). One has a double bed with old pine furniture and a fireplace; the other a single and a double. Both have oriental scatter rugs on wood floors, electric candles in the windows and "the thirstiest towels and the best foam mattresses money can buy." Phil assures, "you will have the best sleep you ever had." An oversize lantern, robes, a lighted makeup mirror and extra pillows and blankets in the closets are extra touches of hospitality that, Phil says, make his B&B unique.

Beyond a winter kitchen with a cooking fireplace is the Summer Cottage, billed as a honeymoon suite. It's connected to the main house by a breezeway with garden chairs. A huge spinning wheel rests in front of an enormous stone fireplace. A kitchenette offers a wet bar, mini-refrigerator and a microwave. Upstairs is a pretty bedroom with four-poster double bed, two armchairs and a full bath. "People often check in here and we never see them again," says Phil.

Those who are seen may enjoy three porches, stroll around the 52-acre working cattle farm crisscrossed by nearly a mile of stone fences, borrow bicycles, play badminton or climb the 3,000-foot mountain upon which the Skyline Drive passes behind the house.

Doubles, $80; suite, $140; 50 percent surcharge if only staying Saturday; two-night minimum, holidays and October. No smoking.

Heritage House, Main Street, Washington 22747. (540) 675-3207.

Gray with black shutters and two-story-high pillars, this attractive B&B is the village's closest in proximity to the Inn at Little Washington, a block's walk for dinner. The former owners' old Country Heritage shop next door accounts for the name.

Broadcaster Frank Scott, a former NBC vice president, and his wife Jean offer four guest rooms, all with private baths. Because of their years of world travel, the Scotts changed to "a more international decor." A Black Forest cuckoo clock, a Spanish ship model and drinking steins from Bavaria are on display in the public rooms.

A ground-floor corner space called the Lace Room fully lives up to its name; frillier and lacier than ever, it has a kingsize bed outfitted in white and draped with lace. Upstairs are three guest rooms. The Victorian Suite with queen bed and authentic Polish village art has a slanted, creaky sun porch with wicker furniture and wild pink walls. The Amish Room is furnished in the simple Amish style with an antique double bed and rag dolls. David Winter cottages cover the mantel in the British Room, with antique double bed, loveseat and much Dickens memorabilia.

Breakfast, served in the dining room, might be a soufflé, spicy shirred eggs or strata. Homemade fruit breads and fresh fruit accompany.

The Scotts were considering converting the Earth Gallery rock shop alongside their inn into a guest cottage.

Doubles, $95 to $125. No smoking.

The Foster-Harris House, Main Street, Box 333, Washington 22747. (540) 675-3757 or (800) 666-0153.

The area's first B&B to emerge in 1984 in the shadow of the Inn at Little Washington, this was acquired in 1992 by Phyllis Marriott, a former caterer and delicatessen owner from big Washington. She's known for her sumptuous breakfasts. Juice, fruit, muffins and tea breads precede such treats as egg, spinach and mushroom strata; a potato, cheese and egg casserole, or Southwest-style poached eggs with breakfast meats. In the afternoon, tea or lemonade and cookies may be taken in the parlor, on the front porch or beneath an old plum tree.

Between meals, Phyllis tends the country-style perennial gardens that border her turn-of-the-century house. She also has improved the room configuration and enhanced the decor. All four bedrooms now offer private baths and all but one of the beds is queensize. Her favorite is the side Garden Room, cool and serene and reminiscent of spring year-round. A new sun room with wicker chairs connects the Mountain View's bedroom and its bathroom containing a whirlpool tub for two. Another mini sun room with a table for two adjoins the rear Meadow View Room, where a duvet covers the step-up Eastlake bed. Folk art is the theme in the cozy Americana Room, which has a double bed and excellent examples of faux painting in the full bathroom.

Doubles, $95 to $135. No smoking.

Gay Street Inn, Gay Street, Box 237, Washington 22747. (540) 675-3288.

This restored 1860 white pebbledash farmhouse at the end of Gay Street features three spacious guest rooms with private baths and antique double beds. Originally from Nantucket, Donna Kevis is innkeeper with her husband Robin, a carpenter, whose handiwork shows in the stacked bathrooms he added for two guest rooms as well as the soaring addition that serves as family quarters.

The darkish bedrooms are decorated with large patterned wallpapers and furnishings of the period. One downstairs has a canopy bed and a chair and a rocker beside the working fireplace. The chaise in Clyde's Room, which Donna named for her brother-in-law, was a wedding gift supposedly acquired at a Kennedy tag sale in Hyannis Port.

For some years, breakfast has been served buffet style at tray tables in the Mount Vernon living room, so named because her mother-in-law's Mount Vernon prints are hung on the walls. The meal involves juice, fresh fruit, homemade buttermilk muffins or coffee cake and perhaps french toast or a one-egg soufflé with vegetables. In 1995, the Kevises were planning to build a breakfast conservatory off a brick terrace in the back. Theirs is one of the few area B&Bs that accepts children and pets.

Doubles, $95 to $110.

Dining Spots

The Inn at Little Washington, Middle and Main Streets, Washington. (540) 675-3800.

The restaurant here preceded the inn, Patrick O'Connell and Reinhardt Lynch having decided to settle down in one spot rather than expand the thriving catering business they had started in Virginia hunt country. With a teenaged kitchen helper as the only staff, they opened their dining room in a former garage on a January weekend in 1978. Seventy patrons showed up and the next weekend, a Washington Star reviewer visited and proclaimed it the best eatery within 150 miles of D.C. Since then, gourmands from across the world have joined the powers-that-be from that other Washington in seeking one of the 75 seats in culinary euphoria.

Few are disappointed, but count us among them. We were unfortunate enough to encounter five-star lapses and gaffes in service along with five-star triumphs in food and surroundings.

First it should be noted what the inn is not. It is not particularly intimidating nor pretentious, unless you balk at a waiter refolding your napkin when you leave the table for the restroom. It is not unpopular; witness the need for reservations weeks in advance for weekends and the denial of up to 3,000 requests for dinner on a Saturday night. It is not inexpensive; meals are prix-fixe, $78 on weekdays, $88 on Fridays and $98 on Saturdays. It is also not uniformly perfect, as its reputation would have it.

The main dining room and the smaller Terrace Room and Garden Room, both facing the inner courtyard, are as elegant as the rest of the inn. Peach-colored taffeta lampshades hanging over most tables in the main room are the decorative hallmark; the lamps cast a glamorous glow over patrons and more light over-all than one would expect. A ceramic swan holds a mass of flowers in the center of the rich but subdued room. More splashy is the Terrace Room, where a wall of banquettes faces the garden beneath fans whirring and fabric billowing from the ceiling. This was where the co-proprietor was ensconced the night we dined. Except for an occasional walk-around the main dining room, he was not keeping his proverbial eye on the happenings — at least at our table — that evening.

Chef Patrick's menu blends classic French and new American creativity into what he calls "cuisine of the territory." The menu is relatively simple and straightforward, eschewing European terminology to the point that grilled poussin is described parenthetically as "young succulent chicken."

The food is anything but simple, however. Dinner begins with a couple of items not on the menu — in our case, a delicate puff pastry of leeks and a canapé with foie gras, one for each person, plus a demitasse of chilled vichyssoise accented with sorrel. A basket of rolls and breads accompanied. We gladly would have tried any of the ten first-course selections. Eventually we settled on a stupendous (and famous) sauté of New York State foie gras with smoked goose breast and local ham on a vinaigrette of black-eyed peas and a dish called salmon four ways, which turned up in three rosettes and three puffs with an excellent dill-mustard sauce.

The first sign that something was amiss was a half-hour delay between appetizers and our between-course selections of a mixed green salad and a grapefruit-tarragon sorbet. Another half hour ensued before the arrival of our main courses, grilled rack of lamb and a sauté of veal sweetbreads. "Here's your lobster," the waitress said to the lamb-orderer, who was nursing a $36 bottle of Stag's Leap merlot, one of the least expensive wines on an extraordinary list. Informed that we had not ordered lobster, she whisked both plates back to the kitchen. The original waiter in the team that served many tables returned five minutes later and asked how the lamb was to have been cooked. The order was re-taken without fanfare or apology. Five or so minutes later the waitress arrived with another salad and another sorbet without explanation; when asked what was going on, she replied "we thought you might be hungry." Fifteen minutes later the ordered main courses came with a perfunctory apology. Elapsed time between appetizer and entrée: more than an hour.

Only as he later cleared the main courses did the waiter offer to make amends: a complimentary after-dinner drink to follow dessert. Besides the chosen seven deadly sins (a sampler of the inn's remarkable offerings on a plate painted with strokes of chocolate and fruit sauces) and a trio of nut tarts with caramel ice cream, he also presented a complimentary "white chocolate mousse in bed between dark silky sheets." And the house chardonnay that began our meal more than three hours earlier turned out to be on the house.

Other service faults and the main-course fiasco made our dinner memorable in a way we'd rather forget. From all we've heard, however, the five-star gaffe was anything but the norm.

Dinner by reservation, 6 to 9:30, Saturday 5:30 to 10:30, Sunday 4 to 9:30. Closed Tuesday except in May and October.

Bleu Rock Inn, Route 211, Washington. (540) 987-3190.

This newcomer with a misleadingly pretentious name (why not just "Blue?") aspires to the heights set by the Inn at Little Washington. We think it succeeds in food and service — at about a third of the cost — and its location is unsurpassed. Set against a backdrop of vineyards and mountains, it looks like an inn out of California wine country, with a French provincial accent.

Dining is in three simple but elegant rooms seating a total of 75, plus a spectacular rear terrace. One small room is striking for elaborately painted wall panels that remind

Blue Ridge Mountains are backdrop for dining terrace at Bleu Rock Inn.

one of Versailles. In the main dining room, tapestry chairs, white cloths over burgundy and pink, fanned napkins standing tall in wine glasses, white china, heavy cutlery, little lalique-style lamps and fresh flowers create an elegant backdrop for the food.

Owners Bernard and Jean Campagne, who also run La Bergerie Restaurant in Alexandria, assign cooking duties to chef Dan Cornish, a Culinary Institute of America graduate who worked in Washington. D.C. The menu changes seasonally, but we wouldn't tamper with anything we tried. Among starters ($6.50 to $9.50) were an eggplant and goat cheese terrine with artichoke, tomato and zucchini, small but ever so good, and confit of duckling with orange onion marmalade and grilled radicchio. Fabulous rolls that turned out to be onion poppyseed with finely chopped sage accompanied.

Main courses run from $15.95 for breast of duckling and leg confit with braised red cabbage and black currant glaze to $21.95 for pecan-crusted loin of lamb with minted couscous and puree of fresh beet. The chicken fricassee with glazed apples, shiitake mushrooms and spaetzle we tried here was one of the best chicken dishes we've had; it was accompanied by an out-of-this-world Shenandoah cider sauce. Grilled shrimp paired zucchini and julienned vegetables in a tomato sauce over angel-hair pasta, all mounded in the shape of a lobster.

Dessert could have been an anti-climax, but not here. We sampled a peach shortbread tart with cassis sauce, and a terrine of three sorbets. The latter brought passion fruit, black currant and coconut on a plate painted with a mosaic of sauces, plus two ginger-molasses cookies.

An excellent Virginia chardonnay (Naked Mountain, $23) accompanied from a choice, fairly priced wine list. (Nearby Oasis Vineyard makes wines from the inn's grapes under the Bleu Rock Vineyard label.) Service throughout was excellent, by waitresses so unobtrusive you hardly realized they were there. And the bill for near-perfection came to $86 for two, about one-third as much as we were to spend the next night at the other inn in little Washington.

Next time we'd ask for a table on the rear terrace, for dinner or Sunday brunch. The interesting brunch menu ($4.95 to $13.50) ranges from cinnamon-spiced apricot pancakes to sautéed shrimp with smoked cheddar grits and caramelized onions.

Dinner, Tuesday-Sunday 5:30 to 9; Sunday brunch, 11 to 3.

Four & Twenty Blackbirds, Routes 522 and 647, Flint Hill. (540) 675-1111.

Two alumni of the Inn at Little Washington opened this urbane little place in an old general store in 1990. Chef Heidi Morf, who was dessert chef at the inn, and Vinnie DeLuise, a former waiter there, have generated an avid following who appreciate the creativity, the informality and the prices. It's the place to which local gourmands return time and again.

Lunch is certainly a treat, taken in the upstairs dining room that has a bit of a tearoomish atmosphere by day. The chintz draped around the windows matches the chair seats, walls are pale peach above the chair rail and deep green below, and the woodwork is deep purple. It's all quite colorful and casual. Lace paper mats on wood tables and booths by day give way to linens at night, when the room turns glamorous. A downstairs room with a stone bar and red trim is more rustic.

Every one of the ten lunch choices ($5.25 to $6.50) appealed, from Italian chicken salad sandwich with sundried tomatoes and basil on oat bread to an acclaimed crab cake sandwich, from an oriental noodle and vegetable salad with peanut-basil dressing and ginger biscuit to the hot diggity dogs with Blackbird baked beans that we saw the owners sampling at the end of the meal. We found the local applewood-smoked trout with curried lentil salad and melon slices tasty and the marinated garden tomatoes and basil on an English muffin topped with prosciutto and melted mozzarella most satisfying. The glutton among us devoured an enormous almond shortcake with local peaches and plums, piled high with whipped cream, for a mere $2.75.

On another occasion, dinner by candlelight with live guitar music was even more delectable. Unusual hot bread sticks, curled up at the end like a fiddlehead fern, tasted of fennel and hot chilies. Among appetizers in the $5 range were a great California sushi roll with crabmeat and avocado and an assertive tart bearing smoked peppers, caramelized vidalia onions and maytag blue cheese. A small salad of assorted greens with a lovely dijon vinaigrette prepared the palate for the main courses ($13.50 to $18.50). One of us had sautéed soft-shell crabs atop a shrimp jambalaya with hush puppies. The other tried the grilled rockfish with the best sundried tomato aïoli ever and orange couscous, garnished with tiny johnny jumpups. Sweet endings were strawberry shortcake on heart-shaped biscuits with homemade lemon ice cream and a fresh plum, nectarine and almond tart with Rappahannock raspberry sauce.

These are the stuff of which culinary dreams are made, at prices that won't break the bank. A good little wine list is priced in the teens and twenties.

Lunch, Wednesday-Saturday 11:30 to 2; dinner, Wednesday-Saturday 5:30 to 9; Sunday brunch, 10 to 2.

The Flint Hill Public House, Route 522, Flint Hill. (540) 675-1700.

High atop a broad lawn, this majestic old structure built in 1899 served as a grade school for most of its years. Lately it has been a restaurant with a variety of dining options, including a great outdoor deck lined with impatiens and overlooking prolific gardens.

Conrad and Robin Koneczny offer white-tablecloth dining on weekends in the First Colony Room, where the walls are lined with ticking antique clocks. Less formal and used regularly is the Public Room with high black ceiling, paneled bar, stained glass accents and old English pub tables. Rattan chairs and benches are at wood tables in the rear parlor, which opens onto the aforementioned deck for a view of Robin's gardening skills.

Outspoken Conrad, a European of the old school, oversees the far-flung dining operation with the aid of a chef. The regional/continental dinner menu differs slightly from weekday to weekend, mainly in terms of price and aspirations. Expect main dishes

($12.95 to $18.75) like grilled yellowfin tuna with lemon caviar sauce, grilled mountain trout with lemon-caper-pinenut sauce, chicken boursin, grilled pork medallions on a roasted red pepper coulis with spicy black beans, and filet mignon wrapped in smoked bacon with green peppercorn sauce. Starters range from vegetable strudel with potato-leek sauce to cajun chicken breast with spicy black beans. Dessert could be raspberry torte, carrot cake or key lime pie.

The extensive lunch menu is priced from $3.95 to $7.75 (for a crab cake sandwich with smoked tomato mayonnaise). Conrad is particularly proud of his wine list and his quarterly vintner dinners.

Upstairs are two spacious, high-ceilinged guest rooms with queensize beds and private baths, renting for $95.

Lunch, Monday-Saturday 11:30 to 2:30 or 3:30; dinner, Monday-Saturday 5:30 to 9 or 9:30; Sunday, brunch 11 to 3, dinner 5 to 8.

The Appetite Repair Shop, Main Street, Sperryville. (540) 987-9533.

The young waitresses wear T-shirts labeled "service technician" and there's much memorabilia from auto repair shops and gasoline stations all around. Owners Cindy and Gregg Gillies have spent a lot of time around auto shops, so the theme seemed a natural.

Their vast space is mainly kitchen fronted by a counter, where you place your order for burgers, sandwiches, "fluids" and accompaniments from the "parts department." But there are unexpected surprises like fresh flowers atop some of the bare wood tables and a pastry case that includes blackberry cobbler and red raspberry pie. There's even a summer music series with live entertainment here on Sunday evenings from 6 to 8.

We did a test drive on a couple of sandwiches, the grilled chicken with lettuce and tomato ($4.15) and the pulled pork barbecue topped with cheese and bacon ($4.25). Served with cole slaw and the best fried potato wedges, both proved quite satisfactory. Other sandwiches were priced from $1.50 for grilled cheese or a hot dog to $4.90 for the "luxury model" Italian chicken fillet with provolone, sautéed onions and peppers. Dinner specials add things like pizzas, liver and onions, baked chicken, deep-fried catfish and steak, from $4.50 to $8.50.

Noticing the slogan "appetite repair at a price that's fair," we had to ask the owner if this was a takeoff on a famous nearby restaurant that was born in a garage. "No, I didn't know that," came the laconic answer. "We started in Madison County."

Open Monday-Wednesday 8 to 4; Thursday-Sunday 8 to 8.

Diversions

The Blue Ridge Mountains, Skyline Drive and Shenandoah National Park bestow on this area a spectacular backdrop, plus scenic drives and hiking trails. Old Rag Mountain is a hiking favorite. Drive the Skyline Drive for awesome scenery — and perhaps lunch on top of the world at Skyland Lodge.

Walking Tour of Washington. The Rappahannock Historical Society sells a pamphlet-size treatise billed as a walking tour along the quiet, tree-shaded streets of "the first Washington of them all." There's no map, and the text is for the truly interested. The Washington Business Council provides a more readily available free map, geared to commercial interests. Others will be satisfied with a leisurely stroll along Main and Gay and their connecting side streets, stopping to see whatever charms them. This really is a small rural village; that's the beauty of it. There are a few county and municipal buildings, a couple of churches and three log houses. Note the neat old printing press outside the door of the Rappahannock News building. **First Washington's Mu-**

seum, run privately and commercially by its creator, Ruby Jenkins, is an 18th-century tavern and schoolhouse all aclutter with historic and local memorabilia. **The Theatre at Washington** stages movies, recitals and other events, usually one night a weekend.

Driving Tours. The most rewarding way to sense the area's tranquility and beauty is to drive along any of the back roads (obtain a county map to avoid getting lost). You can bicycle if you bring your own, but this is winding, hilly territory, not for the faint of heart. Some of our favorite rural byways are Route 628 between Washington and Flint Hill, Route 729 between Flint Hill and Ben Venue and beyond to Laurel Mills or Viewtown (really!), and Routes 635, 688 and 726 in the winery country around Hume, Linden and Markham. You'll stumble onto surprises like the 1842 **Leeds Church** and its big parish house, manse and graveyard out in the countryside south of Markham. In foliage season, these are the best ways to beat the bumper-to-bumper traffic of leaf-peepers on main Route 211.

Wineries. Three nearby wineries are blessed with gorgeous locations like those of the Napa Valley. They appeal to those who enjoy scenery as well as good wines.

Oasis Vineyard, Route 635, Hume, 635-7627, is one of Virginia's oldest and largest wineries. "We learned as we went and made every mistake," said Corinne Salahi, a Belgian married to an American, of the vineyard she and husband Dirgham established in 1975. They're best known for their champagnes ($16), which amount to one-third of their 12,000-case production a year; their chardonnays ($9) are also prize-winners. Visitors tour a large downstairs facility boasting oak barrels for chardonnay and concrete holding tanks from Italy. They sample wines upstairs on wine-barrel seats around tables facing the Blue Ridge.

Naked Mountain Vineyard & Winery, Route 688, Markham, 364-1609. Up a mountain and down a hairpin driveway lies this prize, nestled between hills and producing Virginia's most-honored chardonnay. Sold here for a bargain $11, it's so esteemed that it's one of only two East Coast wines served at Domaine Chandon's restaurant in California wine country. Not bad for what had been a hobby for amateur winemakers Bob and Phoebe Harper. Most of their 3,000 cases a year are chardonnay; a few rieslings, sauvignons and clarets also are produced. The cathedral-ceilinged tasting room overlooks a close-in vista that has been described as the most picturesque of any East Coast winery.

Linden Vineyards & Orchards, Route 638, Linden, 364-1997. On a hilltop facing east, this versatile winery yields quite a view and makes the most of it with an outdoor deck and picnic tables scattered about. All the better to enjoy a lunch pairing goat cheese, smoked trout mousse, pâtés and baguettes with a good bottle of chardonnay ($12) or a dry seyval ($10), all available on premises. More Virginia wineries should do this, for owners Jim and Peggy Law have plenty of takers. The operation has grown rapidly since their 1988 opening. The Laws produce a good late-harvest vidal dessert wine that won the 1994 Virginia Governor's Cup as the best in Virginia. They offer pick-your-own fruits, including apples and blueberries. They also stage vintner dinners, barrel tastings and jazz days, and produce a snappy-looking little newsletter-magazine.

Shopping. Washington has a few excellent galleries and antiques shops, most open only weekends or by appointment. An exception is the **Rush River Gallery,** an excellent arts and crafts gallery featuring 85 area artisans, which is open seven days a week in relocated quarters along Main Street. Here you'll find a treasury of corn-husk dolls, woven throws, decoys, blankets, stained glass, materials for patchwork, cards with the illustrations of innkeeper Steven Wagner and the wonderful local photos of Gene Taylor. Downstairs is **Rush River Bottom** with books, gifts, gourmet foods and toys. **Cabin Fever Books** has expanded its selection with a move from its atmospheric

19th-century cabin into the old Rush River Gallery space on Gay Street. Nearby is the showroom of master cabinetmaker **Peter Kramer;** his stunning furniture is much prized locally. In front is wife Elaine Kramer's **Talk of the Town,** a wonderful small shop with suave cards, jewelry, T-shirts, accessories, garden implements and such. Jeannie Redfield offers authentic native American arts and crafts, including some lovely jewelry at her new **Red Fields** shop. **Rare Finds** is an antiques, gift and accessory shop, every bit as eclectic as the room and suite offered upstairs by the expanding Inn at Little Washington.

Sperryville harbors a few good shops, among them **The Church Mouse** gift shop and gallery in a converted country church, **Southern Drawl Artworks** and **Faith Mountain Company,** a two-story ramble of rooms full of dolls, prints, clothing, specialty foods and garden accessories, plus an outlet room in back.

Extra-Special

Laurel Mills Store, Route 618, Castleton. (540) 937-3015.

The one-horse hamlet of Laurel Mills, population 15 (as tabulated on her fingers by Mary Frances Fannon, one of the fifteen), is the unlikely home of a general store, gallery and antiques shop. And Mrs. Fannon, whose husband is a prosperous oil dealer in big Washington, is the unlikely proprietress. When the store, dating to 1877, was about to be converted into apartments, she bought the place and "thought I'd have all this time to sit behind the counter and read books, as the former employees did." Not at all. She stocks the shelves, makes sandwiches, lends books, mans the cash register and probably pumps gasoline, all the while chatting amiably with farmers, truckers and politicians who make the front porch their own and fill their coolers with water from the spring at the side. Mrs. Fannon has since branched out, restoring the stone cellar into an antiques shop and gallery called **Down Under Laurel Mills Store.** Here she showcases country antiques and one-of-a-kind pieces from area artisans and furniture-makers — an upscale adjunct to a down-home country store.

Mary Frances Fannon runs Laurel Mills Store, gallery and antiques shop.

Loudoun County, Va.

Heart of Hunt Country

Less than 40 miles from the Washington Monument and the halls of Congress lies hunt country and some of America's most hallowed ground. The transition from the nation's capital to the horse and hunt capital to the west occurs rather suddenly around Leesburg in eastern Loudoun County. Left behind are Interstate 66, Washington Dulles International Airport and all the trappings of galloping suburbia. Ahead, the farms and pastures of horse country undulate toward the Blue Ridge Mountains.

It's a curious juxtaposition, this feeling of being so near, yet so far – so close to Washington, yet so far removed in body and spirit. The juxtaposition is most striking in Leesburg, the commercial seat of Loudoun County, where the timbered cottage holding the Loudoun Museum's gift shop backs up to a municipal ramp parking garage in the center of town. On the outskirts, the congestion of residential subdivisions, highways and strip shopping centers yields abruptly to the tranquility of plantation estates, dirt roads and country stores.

If bustling Leesburg reflects Loudoun's commercial and historic interests, tony Middleburg represents the equine theme so imbued in the fabric of the region. In prime horse and foxhunt country, some of the horses live better than ordinary Americans, as the well-heeled farms around Upperville and Waterford attest. The retailing emphasis (Dominion Saddlery, the Madison Street Saddlery and The Tack Box Saddlery) and shop names (The Finicky Filly, the Upper Crust) tell the story. The Middleburg Police Department sports a red fox on its insignia. The paintings hung in homes, restaurants, inns and banks adhere to the theme.

Middleburg is the home of The Chronicle of the Horse, the weekly hunt newsmagazine. Leesburg is headquarters of the Masters of Foxhounds Association, the Morven Park Equine Medical Center and the U.S. Combined Training Association. The fact that one of the nation's richest counties declines to pave many of its roads is not a sign of impoverishment – it's better for the horses that way. Horses and horse people are everywhere. That does not mean the casual visitor is likely to see a foxhunt, however. The hundred or so members of each of the dozen hunt clubs in the area usually ride with the hounds three times a week from fall through spring, but their territories are out of the public eye. More visible are the point-to-point races, steeplechase meets and polo games staged weekends in spring and fall.

Its proximity to Washington and its affluent lifestyle draw the rich and famous. The Roman Catholic church in Middleburg was built in 1963 for President John F. Kennedy; his family rented the Glen Ora estate locally and Jacqueline Onassis rode with the

Piedmont Fox Hounds and Orange County hunts until just months before her death in 1994. Writer Russell Baker, actor Robert Duvall, philanthropist Paul Mellon, Sen. John Warner and Washington business magnates Donald Graham and Jack Kent Cooke have homes here.

Spectacularly scenic is this rolling, manicured and serenely undeveloped landscape, crisscrossed

Hounds lead foxhunters in front of Morven Park mansion in Leesburg.

with the pristine fences and corrals of horse country. It seems more English than England, in the words of one resident Brit, and not just in terms of topography. Loudoun retains its early hamlets, settled variously by Quakers, Scots and Germans. There's no more picturesque a Cotswolds hamlet than tiny Waterford, the entire village a designated National Historic Landmark and preserved as a community of a century ago.

Waterford, Lincoln, Aldie, Philomont, Lucketts, Upperville — these are the quiet places that add dimension to the Loudoun sheen forged by Leesburg and Middleburg. Some of the historic inns that housed the Lees and Washingtons have been upstaged by a flurry of small and promising newcomers. One plantation owned by descendants of America's first organized hunt takes in overnight guests, and another B&B owned by foxhunters caters to equestrians.

The aura of history and the mystique of foxhunting are palpable here. Plantation houses and museums, good restaurants, wineries, shops and recreation facilities help make Loudoun County uncommonly popular with visitors, especially on weekends. This is, after all, a place for escape. And Washington, eminently escapable, is so near yet so far.

Note: A new telephone area code (540) was scheduled to take effect in July 1995 for most of Loudoun County except for Leesburg, which continues as 703. The entire county was to remain in the 703 area code until July 1995.

The Ashby Inn & Restaurant are headquartered in this white brick house built in 1829.

Inn Spots

The Ashby Inn & Restaurant, Route 1, Box 2A, Paris 22130. (540) 592-3900.

When John and Roma Sherman purchased in 1984 the property that started this fine inn, it was an old farmhouse with one bathroom. Ten years later, they have an acclaimed restaurant, six guest rooms in the inn and four going on eight deluxe suites in buildings nearby. Theirs is a class act all the way.

The tiny town of Paris and its quiet main street, fortuitously bypassed by busy Route 50, are the setting for the whitewashed brick main inn, built in 1829. Its restaurant draws folks from Washington and beyond, and its four newer suites in the old schoolhouse – 60 paces, as the inn brochure says, down the street – draw from everywhere.

Two upstairs and two down, the suites are of the same configuration but each is painted in a different glowing color, one a dazzling pumpkin gold and ours a restful deep red. The upper rooms come with a cathedral ceiling and a high round window over the door to their own porch, through which we found it entrancing to watch the passing clouds. They could not be more comfortable with queensize canopy bed, fireplace, small TV, telephone, a cushioned window seat, a two-part bathroom with steeping tub and many amenities, including coffee service, and two wing chairs placed strategically in front of the fireplace. We even found a copy of "Middlemarch" in the bookshelf. Biggest treat of all is the covered porch, where we lounged in Adirondack chairs and watched black angus cows roam up and down the hill in back – a truly pastoral scene. The roar from the trucks on the Route 50 bypass was the only flaw in paradise.

Four more deluxe, even larger rooms plus a common/meeting room were in the works in 1995 in an old house behind the schoolhouse. The six rooms the Shermans started with are upstairs in the main inn. Four have private baths. Two "dormer" rooms on the third floor share a full bath and separate water closet; each has its own sink. The grand Fan Room, with palladian window in back and a fan bed handmade by a friend of the Shermans, has its own entrance and balcony. All are handsomely furnished with antiques, oriental rugs and hunting prints.

114

A small front common room in the inn is available to overnight guests and to those coming in for dinner. Adirondack chairs dot the spacious lawns behind the inn, and the lavish gardens are a joy to behold.

Breakfast involves a choice of juices, muffins, eggs any style, pancakes, homefries, breakfast meats and grilled tomatoes. We particularly enjoyed the tomatoes alongside fat, juicy sausages.

British-born Roma, who hunts with the Blue Ridge Hunt and can tell the guest all about foxhunting, handles the breakfast detail. Husband John, an ex-journalist and Congressional speech writer, is ever present at dinnertime, keeping the four dining rooms running smoothly. He became enamored with food and restaurants during his Army days in France and, despite a high-profile Washington career that caused him to commute until lately, "always knew I eventually wanted to do this." He and Roma do it very well indeed.

Doubles, $90 to $150; suites, $175.

Poor House Farm, Poor House Lane (Route 756), Route 1, Box 218, Round Hill 22141. (540) 554-2511.

"If you have to end up in the Poor House, this is the one." So reads one of the adulatory notes in the guest book in the Cook House Cottage, a deluxe retreat fashioned from the cook house at what was first a plantation and later served as the Loudoun County home for the indigent.

Fred and Dottie Mace, transplants from Machias in the easternmost reaches of Down East Maine, bought the circa 1814 property in 1987, spent four years renovating the cottage and main house, and were on their way to producing some of the most appealing and comfortable B&B accommodations in Loudoun County.

This really is out in the country, an utterly quiet twelve acres reached by dirt roads. About the only "traffic" comes from the horses and hounds of the prestigious Piedmont Fox Hounds hunt club, which passes out front in its thrice-weekly rituals with occasional guests like the late Jacqueline Onassis.

The Maces started with a guest room and a small suite in the main house, both stylishly decorated and designed for comfort, and the romantic brick Cook House Cottage. The latter has an open living room with sofabed and armchair facing a small TV and a huge fireplace, a kitchen and dining area, and a second floor with a queensize pencil-post bed and a clawfoot tub in the bath.

In the works for 1995 were two more fireplaced rooms in a former slave cottage, a two-level suite with a fireplace in the patent house, and a third bedroom in the main house, all with private baths. The Maces were expanding the main house to the rear, adding a new kitchen and freeing up space for a library and a cozy sitting room. That's in addition to the existing living room/dining area, a suave space where gorgeous china collections are displayed in cabinets on either side of the fireplace.

A full breakfast is served in the dining area or, our choice, on the wicker-filled side veranda overlooking the plantation outbuildings, rolling farmlands and a farm pond. Amid an abundance of flowering plants, Villeroy & Boch china and fine crystal, we feasted on bowls of perfect fresh fruit (raspberries, blueberries, grapes and sliced peaches), homemade scones and a feather-light quiche with ham, onions, vegetables and cheese. Another of Dottie's favorites is stuffed french toast with cream cheese.

Birds twittered and flitted in and out of a birdhouse dubbed "Nest and Breakfast" as we took in the tranquil scene from a chintz-covered wicker swing. Fred told of plans to acquire a couple of horses to provide cart rides for guests. Who wouldn't think, this is the life?

Doubles, $85 to $95; suites, $125 to $140. No smoking.

115

The Norris House Inn, 108 Loudoun St. S.W., Leesburg 22075. (703) 777-1806 or (800) 644-1806.

Elegant common rooms, a long side veranda, award-winning gardens and grounds, and an adjacent tea room are among the attributes of this handsome, three-story brick Federal residence built in 1806 at the edge of downtown Leesburg. Californians Pam and Don McMurray, former traveling business executives, searched the country before settling on Leesburg and the house owned by the Norris family, builders responsible for many of Loudoun County's better houses.

With painstaking renovation and attention to detail, they have imbued the property with taste and charm. Guests enjoy a main-floor library with built-in cherry woodwork, a formal living room with windows onto the side veranda (a particularly photogenic scene), and a formal dining room graced with sterling silver, crystal and antique Royal Doulton china. Especially enjoyable in the urban Leesburg setting is the spacious side yard with prolific gardens, an old magnolia tree and a 65-foot-tall black walnut tree, the biggest in Loudoun County. Take it all in from the wicker furniture on the side veranda, screened from the street by shrubbery and the living-room wing, where afternoon libations include wine from nearby Tarara Vineyard.

When it's time to retire, settle into one of six upstairs guest rooms, three with working fireplaces. We enjoyed the Norris Room, "which fulfills most guests' fantasies," in Pam's words. It is pretty in pink, blue and white, with a lacy canopy queensize bed, a plethora of pillows, beautiful sheets and towels, and a Victorian settee. It comes with a fireplace and a refrigerator stocked with Evian water and soft drinks outside the door. The second floor also contains three other bedrooms, one done with a hunt country look and another in English garden decor. All four share two commodious bathrooms. Two smaller rooms on the third floor also share a bath. Potpourri is in all the rooms, and you're apt to find handmade and handpainted chocolates on your pillow when the beds are turned down at night.

Pam serves a breakfast to remember. We liked the oven-baked pancakes, really more like crêpes, filled with fresh berries and served with Smithfield ham sausage patties. A frittata with red, yellow and green peppers, zucchini and roma tomatoes was on tap the next day. These are accompanied by fresh fruit and a special blend of coffee.

The McMurrays recently acquired the oldest stone building in Leesburg next door. They leased it to Sandy Ruefer, who operates it on weekends as **The Stone House Tea Room.** Here you can order cream tea, light tea or full tea ($5 to $12.50), complete with tasty treats like minced ham and pineapple sandwiches, mini-quiches, chocolate zucchini cake and lemon curd tartlets. The goodies are served at calico-clothed tables in two atmospheric rooms, one in which Henry Clay inscribed his name on the wall for posterity. Sandy also makes and sells tea cozies and gift baskets wrapped with ivy ribbons.

You just know the energetic McMurrays aren't finished with the Norris House complex. They already manage and lease out six nearby rooms on weekends, and had their sights on adjacent properties for more accommodations and landscaping. The finicky guest hardly minds the absence of private baths or the lack of a parking area. You simply stash your vehicle a block away in the municipal parking garage and, trite as the saying is, step back in time, elegantly and with style.

Doubles, $90 to $145. No smoking.

The Longbarn, 37129 Adams Green Lane, Middleburg 22117. (540) 687-4137.

A renovated century-old barn imparts Italian country-style elegance, thanks to Chiara Langley from Bologna, whose sister runs an inn in Italy. Chiara decided to do the same in Hunt Country in 1994 after moving from San Francisco with her American husband

Veranda overlooks lawn at Norris House.　　Breakfast on veranda at Poor House Farm.

Roland, a high-powered Washington business executive. "I fell in love with this house," she explains. "You can see why."

Hidden back in woods and gardens behind a farm pond, The Longbarn is the epitome of a country-elegant retreat. It takes a good imagination to visualize this architect-designed restoration as a barn, despite the abundant barn wood and a loft above the glamorous, soaring living room, with two separate sitting areas below. "This house just keeps going on and on," says Chiara as she shows the "dinette" used for breakfast beside her large kitchen at one end of the structure and the Garden Room guest quarters at the other end. Here you'll find a queensize bed dressed with a floral quilt and a down comforter, with matching pillows and fabric draped behind the bed.

Head upstairs to a loft dining area so big that the Langleys can entertain 40 for a Thanksgiving buffet dinner. It's warmed by a museum-quality art collection and terra cotta sculptures by Italian sculptor Don Gianni Gilli, whom Chiara enticed to Middleburg in 1994 to create similar works for St. Stephen the Martyr Church, built three decades earlier for the Kennedys. Off the loft is an expansive deck facing gardens, gazebo and pond. Beyond is the Blue Room, named for its blue metal bed, again with private bath. Adjacent is a third guest room that's sometimes pressed into use, when it's not serving as the hostess's laboratory (she used to work as a scientist). You get the idea that Chiara will do more with the house, which has five bedrooms and five bathrooms. At our visit, a scant three months after opening, she was talking of starting a small restaurant in the former milking barn out back, "but I'm going to move slowly."

That's the way to go, given the serene setting and the classical music that plays throughout the house. Chiara serves a lavish continental breakfast – from cereal to croissants, "everything but eggs." She has been known to give complimentary facials to guests, and sometimes a friend presents piano concerts in the great room. "We do enjoy this house," she says. "It's like living inside a violin, with all this wood paneling. It's such a joy to be here."

Doubles, $100. No smoking.

Brookside Bed and Breakfast, off Route 723, Millwood 22646. (540) 837-1780.

Take the 1782 Nathaniel Burwell House, a beige and brown clapboard structure on six shady acres beside a working grist mill-turned-museum. Add antiques dealers Gary and Carol Konkel as energetic innkeepers. Infuse with period furnishings and TLC. Season with time, and you have a recipe for a successful B&B. The Konkels, who started with three rooms in 1986, were planning to open a small restaurant in the main house and were adding more guest rooms in outbuildings in 1995.

Theirs is one of the more comfortable old houses we've encountered. The common and guest rooms are spacious, each bedroom with private bath, working fireplace, queensize canopy bed and a sitting area with wing chairs. "Everything slants," Carol noted as she pointed to the sloping floors that convey a sense of antiquity. The couple salvaged an old newspaper from Civil War days stuffed in a rat hole in a wall when they were renovating a bathroom, They made use of a step-up, 18th-century cupboard bed with one side open to the room; snug and cozy, it's difficult to get in and out of but even more difficult to make, says Carol. Yet antiquity need not mean rusticity. Witness the feather beds so plump they look pregnant, the down comforters and the fireplaces that are for fires rather than show. Gilbert & Soames toiletries, fresh fruit and a decanter of sherry are in each room. Old boots adorn a fireplace mantel and birds turn up on the pattern of a rug.

At one edge of the property is a red toll house that has been converted into a cottage with fireplaced living room, kitchen and queensize feather bed. At our visit, the Konkels were planning four more rooms in the former miller's house. They were installing a commercial kitchen in the main house to be able to serve dinners to house guests. Meanwhile, they plied overnighters with lavish breakfasts, served at individual tables in the dining room. The fare could be stuffed french toast with caramelized strawberry preserves, eggs florentine with Virginia ham, or cornmeal and buckwheat pancakes, made with flour ground at the working Burwell-Morgan Grist Mill beside their property.

The Konkels specialize in American country furnishings in their antiques shop at the rear of the property. A bicycle route that meanders through the nearby countryside begins at the grist mill at the entrance to their property.

Doubles, $95 to $125. No smoking.

The Pink House, Main Street, Waterford 22190. (540) 882-3453.

The National Historic Landmark Village of Waterford, as British as they come on this side of the Atlantic, is an appropriate home for The Pink House. It, too, is as British as they come, thanks to English-born owner Marie Anderson and her husband Chuck. Marie, a garden designer and travel packager-planner for those heading to the British Isles, has made the house a reflection of her homeland.

From the main intersection in this postcard hamlet out of the Cotswolds, you step directly into the fireplaced parlor and dining room on the ground floor of the three-story pink structure dating to 1790. The furnishings are Edwardian, and a converted 19th-century wardrobe is now the "music cabinet" with a stereo system.

Music is important in this household, you realize on the second floor, where the main guest quarters is a suite to end all suites. The front section is a sitting room with fireplace, its sofa and chairs clad in white. It opens into what was the family music room, with a grand piano and a stunning wall-length mural of the Metropolitan Opera House. This one is unique, done by a local artist who peopled it with Waterford folks. You could dawdle for hours as Marie points out the local butcher, who is conducting the orchestra, and the Anderson family, including their three daughters, a beagle and an Irish wolfhound, occupying their favorite corner box in the mezzanine. "This was

Towering trees surround 1782 house that's now Brookside Bed and Breakfast.

our stage," Marie recalls of family gatherings around the piano, "and the mural was our audience."

Beyond the music room, in the original kitchen banked against the hillside, is a bed chamber with a queensize Italian mahogany bed and a bathroom containing a whirlpool tub. The room is warmed by a French stove inside the old beehive oven. Just outside is a picturesque terrace with a grape arbor, perfect for relaxing and admiring Marie's lavish side gardens, stretching from street level up nearly an acre of hillside. You'd think you were part of the Cotswolds countryside rather than right in the heart of town.

This is the setting for a hearty English breakfast. The day of our visit it included cantaloupe rounds with mint, fried eggs (obtained from a nearby farm), bacon, corn fritters, grilled tomatoes, crumpets and homemade plum jam. Other treats could be puff pastry shells stuffed with crabmeat, served with sautéed apples and onions, flapjacks or Chuck's specialty, cheese grit soufflé.

A second suite is available on the third floor. It involves a huge bathroom, a bedroom and a sitting room furnished in Lincoln-era Victoriana.

Doubles, $95.

Dandongreen Manor, off Snickersville Turnpike (Route 734), Route 2, Box 172, Purcellsville 22132. (540) 338-4202 or (800) 278-4333.

The Fairfax Hunt starts on the front lawn of this fifteen-acre farm surrounded by large horse farms and foxhunting properties. Dannielle and Donald Edlund like it that way, since they're foxhunters in the heart of foxhunting paradise. Their children grown, they moved cross-country from southern California with four horses, four dalmatians and a cat when Don was transferred East in 1990. They took up residence in a spacious Colonial-style home, joined the Loudoun Hunt and found their California foxhunting friends descending for visits. "I was just playing hostess without getting paid and said, 'whoa,'" recalls Dannielle. She decided to run a B&B in their home and a stable in partnership with a friend, and began catering to those who share their interest in horses.

The house is notable for a foxy two-story living room surrounded by a loft, a Civil War library, a cozy den with TV and a dining room that's the setting for gourmet breakfasts (and occasional hunt breakfasts for the Fairfax Hunt). A 65-foot porch across the front of the house looks onto grazing pastures, rolling hills and, front and center, a gazebo topped by a homemade fox weathervane and containing a large jacuzzi in which to soak aching bones.

Trains, dalmations, hats and literature are among the collections in the cozy Civil War Library off the airy, expansive living room. The library adjoins the Civil War Room, producing a main-floor guest suite whose queensize bed is draped with a feather-bed topper.

Upstairs is Aunt Violet's Room, a riot of blue and green reflecting Dannielle's passion for violets, down to the violets painted on the toilet seat. It comes with two double beds and a small sitting room. Victorian furnishings, hand-embroidered flowers, and heirloom silks and laces surround the queen bed in the Silks & Laces Room, where four different fabrics are swagged above the window. Its bathroom may be shared with an adjacent room with twin beds.

Although the three main bedrooms have private baths, matching bathrobes and slippers are provided in each for trips out to the jacuzzi.

Breakfast, a gala affair, starts with a fruit sorbet, made with berries and bounty gathered from the farm. Blended coffees and homemade breads and biscuits accompany. The main event could be french toast incorporating walnuts, apples, cream cheese and caramel sauce; chicken fritters with mashed potatoes; savory pancakes with basil, parmesan and onions, or venison steak with lemon-basil sauce.

Dovetailing with their equestrian interests, the Edlunds rent horses, arrange horseback rides, play host to foxhunters and take guests "hilltopping" to glimpse a hunt, if there's not already one in their front yard.

Doubles, $90 to $150. No smoking.

Welbourne, Welbourne Road, Middleburg 22117. (540) 687-3201.

No inn property in the area better reflects the past than Welbourne, a time warp and truly a special place. It's not for everyone, but comes highly recommended by authorities ranging from Gourmet magazine to innkeeper John Sherman of the Ashby Inn, who advised that if he had to choose one place to spend an evening, it would be here.

Welbourne, a circa-1775 working plantation, is hardly your typical inn. It's a living museum, occupied by the seventh generation of the family of Col. Richard Dulany. He was the Civil War general who in 1840 founded the country's first horse show and hunt club, the Piedmont Fox Hounds. His great-great-grandson, Nathaniel Morison, a Piedmont board member, lives here today with his wife and children.

"I'm the host, not the innkeeper," advises Nat, who is proud that Welbourne has no brochure. To keep the place going, the family started taking in paying guests "by introduction" in the 1930s; the Morisons continue by word of mouth. "I call the experience faded elegance," says Nat, who fortuitously happened to arrive home in his pickup truck as we stopped by. "If you want interesting history and something real, it's here. If you want TVs and jacuzzis, it's not for you."

"Something real" pervades the entire 550-acre plantation in the heart of prime Middleburg hunt country, reached by the dirt road named Welbourne, County Route 743.

The front foyer opens on one side into two living rooms, placed end to end and flanked by a great back porch. The other side opens into the library, where you can spot the date 1862 inscribed in a window and where some of the family's vast collection of miniature giraffes is housed along with such treasures as a sword from the Civil War and Stonewall Jackson's gloves. The library opens into a bedroom of majestic proportions, outfitted in vaguely oriental style with a canopy bed, clawfoot tub, a Tiffany set on the desk and a tray of bottled waters and mixers on a sideboard. F. Scott Fitzgerald and Thomas Wolfe stayed here, and you can, too, for $80 a night. A friend

Welbourne is living museum of antebellum plantation life.

made a plaque to designate this as the Jeb Stuart Room, Nat says in his typical droll style, "but we never used it." So what do they call it? "The End Room."

Upstairs is the Over the Parlor Room, with two twin beds, and another room with two twins joined as a king. In back is the Over the Gun Room, Sherry Morison's favorite, because it gets lots of light. A settee and a window seat take advantage of the view through the vine-covered windows.

The five main guest rooms in the house plus two cottages have private baths; four smaller bedrooms share baths and are used for overflow. All come with family memorabilia reflecting a way of life. "I tell people it's like visiting Grandma's house as a child," says Nat. Most reply that theirs didn't have a house like this.

The household staff, who are like family, help oversee the place while Sherry is at work as a real-estate agent and while Nat is taking care of the 65 "retired" horses he boards here for owners who want them to live out their days with grace. The Morisons and staff serve a grand southern breakfast amid much silver and china in the dining room, where the table is set for ten to fourteen. Bacon, eggs, sausage, grits and fried tomatoes are the usual fare, with pancakes reserved for Sundays.

When we'd arrived, Nat had said he has five friendly hound dogs "you have to climb over to get inside," which we did. As we eventually drove away, we happened to look in the back seat of our car. There was Danny the hound, who had jumped in an open window, settled down for a nap and refused to budge. Nat's teenaged son Joshua had to be summoned to get Danny out.

Doubles, $80; cottages, $90; small rooms, $60.

Cornerstone Bed & Breakfast, Routes 9 and 662, Route 1, Box 82-C, Paeonian Springs 22129. (540) 882-3722.

Molly and Dick Cunningham purchased this homey 1745 farmhouse from Arthur Godfrey's widow, raised their family and started taking in guests in 1989. They were following a precedent set by previous owners who ran first an 18th-century ordinary and later a 19th-century rail-stop guest house. The house occupies a hilltop spread between Leesburg and Waterford, near the Paeonian springs that attracted escapees from the cities in Victorian times.

This is a very much lived-in house, from the expansive front porch with its wicker glider and lineup of mountain bikes ready for the borrowing, to the rear sun room overlooking the pool. Guests also use a formal double parlor with sitting and dining areas, graced with handsome oriental rugs and bouquets of flowers that the Cunninghams, avid gardeners, grow on their property.

Upstairs are two guest rooms with private baths, furnished with antiques and family heirlooms. One in the rear has a queensize bed. The one in front contains a poster bed.

Breakfast could be "about anything," Molly says. Favorites are eggs benedict with asparagus from the garden, corn fritters and blueberry pancakes. Occasionally, the couple serve a Southern breakfast with grits and country ham. The tomato juice is homemade.

Doubles, $80.

Little River Inn, Route 50, Box 116, Aldie 22001. (703) 327-6742.

One of the area's earlier B&Bs, this was established by antiques dealer Tucker Withers, who had moved his shop here from Bethesda, Md. He bought his great-uncle's house for the first six rooms of his B&B in 1982. He later added the 1790 patent house and 1810 log cabin across the driveway and the newer Hill House west of the main house, and now offers twelve historic rooms, six with private baths.

Aldie is built around a restored grist mill on the Little River. With his antiques shop and other interests in the hamlet, Tucker seems to be Aldie's chief landholder as well as its main persona. Breakfasts here are legendary as he spins tall tales and local recollections while a varied repast is served. The fare includes juices and fruit, homemade poppyseed muffins or banana bread, cereals, and main dishes like dutch apple baby, local sausages with eggs, baked french toast and pancakes. The meal is taken in a dining area beside the kitchen in the main house, at tables scattered through two atmospheric main-floor common rooms, out back at wrought-iron tables on the flagstone patio or in guest quarters in the outbuildings.

The bedrooms are furnished authentically and rather sparsely with double or twin beds, antique chests and bureaus, quilts, and hooked or braided rugs. One coveted room has a loveseat and a working fireplace, but shares a bath with two other bedrooms on the second floor. Other chairs in the bedrooms we saw were wood and not the kind you'd feel comfortable sitting in for long. Some would not be happy with the noise from traffic lumbering along busy U.S. Route 50 just outside. Quieter and more spacious are some rooms in the outbuildings.

Doubles, $80 to $145.

The Red Fox Inn, 2 East Washington St., Box 385, Middleburg 22117. (703) 687-6301 or (800) 223-1728.

A handsome four-story stone structure dating to 1728, this represents many people's vision of a large but quaint old inn from days of yore. Billed as America's oldest original inn, it's cloaked in all the appropriate honors, from AAA four-diamond ratings to Travel/Holiday dining awards. Lately it seems to be resting on its laurels – or is it simply too big for its breeches? We found the welcome to be lacking, service indifferent, management not on hand and the guest rooms lackluster and overpriced.

The Red Fox advertises 23 "romantic accommodations" with private baths in the original inn and three nearby buildings. We were given keys to two "typical" rooms up steep stairs on the third floor. The spacious Bridal Suite had the requisite kingsize

Beamed tavern is cozy spot for dining at The Asbhy Inn & Restaurant.

canopy bed, a parlor with a sofa, two wing chairs and a huge built-in armoire, hooked rugs on wide-board floors, two TV sets and two telephones. Another kingsize bed graced the corner Martha Washington Room. Its two wing chairs were spaced twelve feet apart on either side of a bureau, facing the bed and not the TV set. The beds were covered with white chenille spreads that looked like Bates, the bathtubs were equipped with hand-held showers, the toiletries consisted of a Gilbert & Soames shoeshine cloth and sewing kit and a plain bar of Camay soap, and the welcoming touch was two bottles of local Meredyth wines in each room, "available for consumption or to take home, $16." An order form outlined fairly basic choices for a continental breakfast, to be delivered to the room at a specified time in the morning for $1 service charge per person. The front desk, which gave our queries short shrift, assured that what we saw was representative of the inn. Given the absence of personal touches and the prices charged, we would hope that the newer rooms in the Stray Fox Inn annex on a side street behind the inn might be more inviting.

Doubles, $135 to $155; suites, $155 to $225.

Dining Spots

The Ashby Inn & Restaurant, Paris. (540) 592-3900.

If the name Paris brings culinary bliss to mind, the Ashby Inn at the crossroads of this rural town obliges. Innkeepers John and Roma Sherman have created a restaurant of distinction with an unpretentious atmosphere and friendly, flawless service.

About 80 diners are accommodated in four small rooms, ranging from a cozy tavern to a room with high booths and small engraved plaques bearing names of friends and regulars, of which the Ashby seems to have many. A thunderstorm had rendered the handsome, wisteria-covered side courtyard out of commission the night we dined, but the sun porch dressed in white (the Ashby's favorite "color") proved as radiant as a bride. Rotating artworks by a Leesburg artist who paints in Provençe provide color throughout and sell briskly.

The waitress fulfilled a complicated dinner order without taking notes, as did inn-keeper John at breakfast the next day. Great starters on the menu that changes nightly were a chilled carrot puree soup, artistically decorated with citrus crème fraîche, and a caesar salad with grated parmigiano-reggiano and unusual polenta croutons. The eight main dishes are priced from $13.50 for spinach tagliatelle pasta with goat cheese and roasted peppers to $22 for a chipotle-marinated veal chop with roasted corn sauce, potato pancake and swiss chard. We liked the Atlantic tuna sautéed with extra-virgin olive oil and white beans and the crab cakes (an Ashby Inn classic of 100 percent pure lump crabmeat with a bit of tarragon, moist and tasty as could be), accompanied by sides of potato ribbons and fresh spinach. Zesty grapefruit sorbet was a refreshing dessert from a choice that included crème brûlée, strawberry shortcake with biscuits and bittersweet chocolate torte with chocolate ganache and crème anglaise.

John has lovingly prepared a select wine list, whose spirit and underlying philoso-phy as described in the introduction are to be applauded. Though there are plenty of choices for a splurge, we felt quite comfortable ordering one of his recommended specials, a Honig sauvignon blanc for $16.50.

The Shermans are a major presence at Sunday brunch (a local institution), cooking omelets and carving ham at the buffet table set up in the sun porch.

Dinner, Wednesday-Saturday 6 to 9; Sunday brunch, noon to 2:30.

The Lightfoot Cafe, 3 West Market St., Leesburg. (703) 771-2233.

This with-it establishment of recent vintage is billed as a progressive American bistro in the heart of old-town Leesburg. It takes its name from Francis Lightfoot Lee, a signer of the Declaration of Independence and a member of the Virginia family for which the town was named. Sisters Carrie and Ingrid Gustavson feature food that is "gently prepared, graciously served and sensibly priced."

Visitors are greeted at a small service-reception bar in the main-floor entry. They are led past an impressive wine rack at the head of the stairs into a long, narrow, second-floor dining area with close-together tables covered with butcher paper and white cloths. Votive candles provide most of the illumination. At night, we found the lighting so dim it was difficult to take in the decor – dark print wallpaper above wainscoting, large French prints on the walls and tall windows – let alone read the menu.

The dinner fare falls into two categories: soups, salads and small plates, and large plates. One of us made a satisfying meal out of three of the former. The Lightfoot plate yielded a standout herbed feta cheese dip plus hummus and a tuna and calamata olive spread, served with herbed pita chips and toasted baguette slices. The salad of cafe greens was tossed with soybean sprouts and oven-roasted walnuts. A couple of mini shrimp and crab cakes were fired by a Thai red curry sauce. Large plates were priced from $12.95 for padre island chicken with black beans, rice, and cucumber and green chile salsa to $16.95 for grilled lamb salad on a bed of spring greens tossed with everything from asparagus and roasted cumin potatoes to anchovies, wild mushrooms and garlic aioli. The pasta de la casa ($14.95), also an innovative melange, was hearty and tasty: chipotle fettuccine with shrimp, swiss chard, oyster mushrooms, tomatoes and prosciutto tossed with roasted garlic, extra-virgin olive oil and romano cheese. Desserts ranged from fresh berries to bread pudding, mocha ya-ya and shoofly pie.

Lunch, Tuesday-Saturday 11:30 to 2:30; dinner, Tuesday-Saturday 5:30 to 10 or 11, Sunday 11 to 9.

Tuscany Inn, 101 South Madison St., Middleburg. (540) 687-6456.

The 1790 Wright house, the second oldest home in Middleburg, is the setting for some of the best food in the area. Gino Ballarin tired of the New York City scene,

Formal table settings lend sophisticated air to Tuscany Inn.

where he catered to the rich and famous as maître-d' and general manager of the famed 21Club. He opened a Tuscan/Northern Italian restaurant in partnership with Michel Golden, an area woman who knows the territory, and began catering to the rich and famous here.

The Tuesday night we dined they were busy sheltering a reclusive heiress from an Italian countess who wanted to get to know her. Several other local moguls were on scene and the rest, we were told, recently had been or were about to be. The layout in four small, homey rooms inside or at tables on the side lawn is such that celebrities can be spaced apart and out of the way, and no one seems to take much notice anyway. Suave host Gino has been known to return to the kitchen when oldtimers ask for such 21 Club treats as senegalese soup, chicken hash or burgers. Otherwise he leaves the cooking to capable chef Christopher Elcavage, who joined Gino when he returned to the helm here in 1994 after a brief period in which the year-old venture had suffered in the hands of a management company.

Well-spaced tables dressed with white cloths and red clay service plates present a sophisticated yet informal setting like that in rural Tuscany. The menu is short but sweet. We were impressed with the chef's splendid tomato-basil soup and a classic caesar salad, an ample portion made exactly the way it's supposed to be. Among main courses ($14.50 to $20.50), the chicken scaloppine with garlic, olive oil and lemon and the scampi with shrimp, garlic and roma tomatoes over angel-hair pasta held particular appeal. We also heard good things about the pork loin sautéed with apples and whiskey and the salmon with black olives and sundried tomatoes. Good breads came with. And desserts included a stellar tartuffo and tirami su.

Upstairs are three bedrooms, one with king bed and private bath across the hall and two sharing a hall bath. Continental breakfast is put out in the hall, there being no common room here. Rates are $110 to $125. Gino also puts up overflow in three rooms of a friend's plantation west of town.

Lunch, Tuesday-Sunday 11:30 or noon to 2:30; dinner, Tuesday-Sunday 5:30 to 8:30 or 9:30.

Chamblin Mill, Route 611, Middleburg. (540) 338-3509.

As he says, "this is a labor of love." Ed and Sandy McGushin certainly don't need to open their 1792 home to throw dinner parties for perfect strangers. But Ed, the senior vice president of a computer software company, loves to cook and "started catering for money" fifteen years ago. Now he and Sandy, their son Brian and a couple of servers present festive dinners for groups of six or more on weekends in their stately home of seven years.

Dinner here is, literally, a party in a private home. The McGushins seat ten to twelve at a large table in their formal dining room, the core room of what had been a working grist mill. Another 24 can be accommodated in the great room, where our party gathered for a pre-dinner glass of champagne with hostess Sandy, who talked about the house and her husband's cooking interests. "We want to do the perfect evening," she said.

The six-course meal is $75 per person, including two kinds of wine, tax and gratuity. A little souvenir card with the night's menu is at each seat in the dining room, and the chef emerges from the kitchen to greet his guests and describe in some detail the treats to come.

Our dinner got off to an auspicious start with a super Mediterranean lobster cocktail touched with fresh ginger, minted cold sweet pea soup, ravioli filled with house-smoked salmon on a lobster sauce, and a summer salad (with real tomatoes and shallot vinaigrette). Some of us hardly had room left for the main course, tea-marinated duck breast with duck cracklings and apple-raisin chutney. Sandy's chocolate swirl cheesecake was the grand finale.

Other meals follow a similar pattern, with main courses varying from medallions of venison to blanquette of veal to lamb shanks milanese. The room is lit entirely by candles and oil lamps, as Sandy seeks to recreate the experience of dining 200 years ago. Afterward, the McGushins, who seem to have as much fun as their guests, are apt to offer a snifter of cognac and adjourn to the back patio or the billiards room to keep the party going.

Although corporate groups and local residents were the main takers of their unusual dining experience in the beginning, the McGushins were working on packages with nearby innkeepers to broaden their clientele and provide a special treat for visitors to the area. One inn might send six guests who are traveling together, or three inns could furnish one couple each. If you're traveling solo, the likelihood is iffy, but worth asking about.

Dinner for six or more by reservation, Friday and Saturday (and occasionally other evenings).

Tuscarora Mill, 203 Harrison St., Leesburg. (703) 771-9300.

This establishment – popularly dubbed Tuskie's but far more sophisticated than that sounds – was a working grain mill until 1985. Then it was moved a couple of blocks to form part of the restored Market Station shopping and business complex, which also includes a freight depot and station master's house, an 18th-century mill from Pennsylvania and a log cabin from West Virginia. The second-floor restaurant still holds many mill artifacts and equipment. Built into the floor is an old-fashioned scale that used to weigh bags of grain and now is occasionally tested by curious diners. Quilted wall hangings are spotlit on the soaring barnwood walls, and purple lacquered chairs and colorful patterned tablecloths provide plenty of color in the main bar and restaurant. Hanging plants and Victorian street lamp standards make the adjacent garden room, with walls of windows bridging the shopping complex below, a pleasant setting.

Hanging plants and Victorian lamps enhance garden room at Tuscarora Mill.

The menu covers are as artistic as the presentation of the fare described inside. At lunch, we were impressed by the gazpacho filled with crisp vegetables and topped with a bit of salmon and crabmeat, and a Thai chicken salad ($6.95). Not so impressive was the wonderful sounding asparagus and crab salad marinated in tequila, lime and cilantro – great tasting but a niggardly portion for $7.95. Only a second helping of crispy rolls with herb butter and an order of frozen lemon mousse with strawberries and golden raspberries separated one of us from starvation.

The dinner menu incorporates many of the lunchtime appetizers and entrées ($13.50 to $19.95), with half available as small plates. Expect things like sesame-roasted salmon with ginger relish, grilled Brazilian pork chops with black beans and plantains, grilled tuna steak on three-tomato salsa with jalapeño-lime butter, and grilled filet mignon with caramelized shallots and scalloped potatoes. All are available for lunch, but we would rather have those and such noontime specials as rack of lamb with mashed potatoes for dinner.

Tuskie's wine selections earned the Wine Spectator award of excellence. Interesting imported beers are on tap, available by the pint or glass.

Lunch and dinner daily, 11:30 to 9:30 or 10, Sunday from noon.

Traditions of Leesburg, 19 East Market St., Leesburg. (703) 771-8000.
A bullet hole from Civil War days remains in the front door of this handsome new restaurant occupying what had been a private residence since 1758. Owner Elaine Barnes, who started with a jewelry store next door, gave it its name because "this is a traditional town. The people who grew up here tend to stay here, which is nice because most places are so transient."

Four small dining rooms on the main floor are nicely appointed with sleek black chairs, cream-clothed tables topped with peach fanned napkins, cream-colored walls with brick-red trim and interesting window treatments. An expansive rear deck provides outdoor dining in season.

The extensive American-continental menu maintains the traditional theme. Expect starters like escargots, clams casino, oysters rockefeller and hearts of palm salad. Main courses ($12.95 to $25.95) are all listed as Traditions specialties (a bit of hyperbole for a year-old establishment). They run from chicken nory (with smoked salmon and cherry wine sauce) to steak diane and veal oscar. Southern tastes are served by dishes like scallops norfolk and salmon topped with crab imperial and béarnaise sauce.

The upstairs lunch menu becomes the dinner menu in the cozy downstairs tavern.

Lunch, Monday-Friday 11:30 to 2:30, weekends from noon; dinner nightly, 5 to 9, tavern to 10.

Fiddler's Green, Loudoun and Stuart Streets, The Plains. (540) 253-7022.

Hunt country foodies trek the back roads to this rambling establishment, perhaps the most visible landmark in The Plains. Beyond an unusually attractive trellised patio – a great spot for lunch or dinner – lies a rambling barn of a structure. It holds a lounge in front and an airy, two-story-high rear dining room, where tall windows display the outdoors and a stuffed giraffe in the corner surveys the scene. The decor here is country-stylish in peach and gray, with copper cooking pans hanging on walls and beams, an assortment of upholstered booths and round Shaker-style tables, and colorful, mismatched service plates at each setting.

The short, interesting menu is printed daily. For dinner, look for starters like chilled avocado soup with smoked tomato salsa, smoked trout crostinis with pommery mustard and horseradish, and carpaccio of beef with arugula and parmesan. Caesar salad with grilled shrimp and grilled salmon salad with french beans are listed under light fare. The eight entrées ($11.50 to $17) run from fettuccine with wild mushrooms, parmesan and cream to stuffed quail with country sausage and roasted shallots. Swordfish with sundried tomato butter,

Rear dining room at Fiddler's Green.

sausage and breast of duck with bordelaise sauce, and strip steak with herbed butter are other possibilities. For dessert, how about sour-cream cheesecake with strawberries, plum and apple crisp with ice cream, lemon chiffon pie with blueberries or tirami su with Bailey's Irish Cream and dark chocolate?

Many of the same items turn up on the appealing little lunch menu.

Lunch, Tuesday-Saturday 11:30 to 2; dinner, Tuesday-Sunday 6 to 9; pub menu, Thursday-Saturday 9:30 to 11; Sunday brunch.

Back Street Cafe, 4 East Federal St., Middleburg. (540) 687-3122.

Some locals think this small Italian restaurant and catering establishment of ten years' vintage is the best place to eat in town.

Certainly its front patio is one of the more jaunty settings, and its salad bar is one of the better we've seen.It's so good, in fact, that one of us decided to go with the consensus and made a fine lunch of the all-you-can-eat salad bar for $4.95. He got two hefty platefuls of mesclun, spinach and radicchio with a variety of accompaniments, plus such extras as tuna, curried chicken, three-bean and pasta salads. The other was satisfied with a cup of chilled cucumber soup and a toasted BLT with cheese.

Pastas are featured at dinner, nicely priced from $9.95 to $14.95 (for tagliatelle verdi with shrimp, mushrooms and gorgonzola). The night's specials ($13.95 to $17.95) could be chicken al forno, grilled swordfish with a salsa of sweet bell pepper, avocado, tomato and mango, and strip steak with wild mushroom sauce. Steamed mussels, pizzas and crostini with crab and artichoke are among appetizers and light fare.

All this is served in a simple setting of close-together tables covered with green cloths or print mats, bentwood chairs and lots of ivy painted on the walls.

Lunch, Monday-Saturday noon to 3; dinner, 5 to 9 or 10. Closed Sunday.

Candelora's, Route 287 and Church Street, Lovettsville. (540) 822-5705.

"A taste of Italy in the country" is how chef-owner Frederick Petrello bills his new restaurant transformed from the old Lovettsville Village Inn in northern Loudoun County. We call it true, from the basket of garlic at the entry to the wonderful pasta sauce that went home that night for dinner.

Opera music played as we lunched on a crock of gazpacho, the assorted antipasti and a chicken parmesan sandwich with pomodoro sauce and homemade mozzarella cheese in a Tuscan roll, followed by a dish of lemon sorbet. The food took precedence over the setting, country fresh but spare with rush-seat chairs at well-spaced tables beneath a vaulted ceiling. The front deck and rear solarium seemed more appealing.

Reasonably priced pastas ($7.95 to $9.95) and a short list of entrées ($10.95 to $13.95) comprise the dinner menu. Look for such specialties as chicken marsala, lamb sausage over polenta, veal saltimbocca and veal sautéed with sundried tomatoes and served on a bed of greens. We had a long drive home, and were grateful for a sampling of prepared treats from the takeout shop. The shrimp tagliatelle and the fusilli topped with grilled chicken, pinenuts and goat cheese made a nifty dinner that evening.

Lunch daily, 11 to 3; dinner nightly, from 5.

Mosby's Tavern, 2 West Marshall St., Middleburg. (540) 687-5282.

"D.C.-type bar food" is how one innkeeper describes this "loud and rocking" barn of a pub with an outdoor patio, a claustrophobic small dining room and an attached banquet facility, all run by the Red Fox Inn. The bar was full of young people the weekday late afternoon we stopped by, and large family groups spanning several generations already were arriving for early dinner.

The huge menu offers six grilled chicken dishes, pot roast, meat loaf, crab cakes, london broil and porterhouse steak from $9.95 to $16.95. Tex-Mex fare, sandwiches and burgers are considerably cheaper.

More sedate types, tourists and big spenders gravitate to the downstairs dining rooms, full of atmosphere, in the main **Red Fox Inn.** Crab dishes are featured, as in appetizers of crab and artichoke casserole, crab cocktail or black bean cakes on corn and crabmeat salsa, and an offering of crab cakes among main courses ($18.50 to $21.95). The cooks stay au courant with things like whole rainbow trout with spinach, grapes, pinenuts and tomato chutney and grilled lamb chops with coriander sauce.

Tavern open daily from 11 a.m.; champagne brunch on weekends.

Diversions

Horses and foxhunting are the chief draws in this area. Unless you have local connections or book with knowledgeable (and well located) innkeepers, you're not likely

National Trust operates Oatlands as an appealing house museum.

to see – let alone participate in – a foxhunt, which is a private affair for members and invited (paying) guests. But you may hear or catch a glimpse of one of the area's dozen hunts in pursuit of their quarry, generally three days a week from September to March. You're more apt to catch the equine flavor at one of the horse shows, polo matches or the point-to-point or steeplechase events, scheduled for weekends in spring and fall.

Quaint Hamlets and Scenic Drives. From uppercrust and horsey Upperville to antiquey Millbrook to the German enclave of Lovettsville, quaint hamlets abound. Perhaps the most quaint is Waterford (see Extra-Special). To best appreciate the area, shun the main highways and get off the beaten path, which is easily done only if you have a good county road map. Having toured most of the area, we're partial to Routes 662 and 665 out of Waterford, Route 734 (the Snickersville Turnpike) from Aldie to Bluemont, Route 709 (the Zulla Road past huge horse estates south of Middleburg), Route 626 (the Halfway Road) south of Middleburg, and particularly Route 626 (the Pot House Road) north of Middleburg past the Glenwood Racetrack, through forested hill and dale to the fabled and surprisingly remote Foxcroft School for young ladies.

Morven Park, Old Waterford Road, Leesburg, (703) 777-2414. Turkey buzzards haunt the fences and two black lion sculptures guard the pillared portico of Morven Park, the stately home of Virginia reform governor Westmoreland Davis, whose widow gave the entire 1,500-acre estate in trust to the public in his memory. The mansion, left as it was and decorated to the hilt in a Renaissance theme, is truly a museum. Four Brabant tapestries – said to be in better condition than those in the Vatican – hang in the front foyer, vying for attention with graceful cherubs over the doorway. Those into showy European decor will enjoy the guided, hour-long tour of the mansion's sixteen restored rooms, rich with Tiffany silver in the formal Jacobean dining room, Hudson River School paintings in the informal dining room, and a Hapsbourg crown mirror in the ladies' drawing room. Those into foxhunting will enjoy the twenty-minute film and the memorabilia in the **Museum of Hounds and Hunting,** which occupies the north wing of the mansion (the fabulously wealthy Govenor Davis was master of the Loudoun Hunt). Others like the **Carriage Museum,** built around the 100-vehicle col-

130

lection donated by a Warrenton woman and on rotating display in the old coach house. It includes everything from a charcoal-burning fire pumper and a ladies' phaeton to surreys and a funeral hearse. The magnificent grounds are known for rare specimen trees, including the oldest small-leaf linden on the East Coast, and the Marguerite Davis Boxwood Gardens. The Morven Park Steeplechase Races are held here in mid-October. Nearby is the Morven Park Equestrian Center. Open Tuesday-Sunday noon to 5, April-October. Adults, $4.

Oatlands, Route 15, Leesburg, (703) 777-3174. The 1813 plantation house built by a descendant of Virginia's famed Robert "King" Carter is better known and has a higher profile than Morven Park, thanks to its operation by the National Trust for Historic Preservation. It was purchased in 1903 by William Corcoran Eustis (of the Washington banking and Corcoran Gallery family), and Mrs. Eustis used it as her English-style country house during the summer and foxhunting seasons until her death in 1964. Their daughters, who live nearby at Little Oatlands and Oatlands Hamlet, left the house and the 261-acre estate to the National Trust. Unlike Morven Park, this is a livable house rather than a museum, and visitors feel as if "the family has just stepped out for a spell," in the words of our tour guide. You'll see George Washington's dessert service displayed in the formal dining room and William Eustis's foxhunting garb in his dressing room. Four acres of formal, terraced gardens are open to visitors, as is the carriage house visitor center and gift shop. Open Tuesday-Saturday 10 to 4:30, Sunday 1 to 4:30, April-December. Adults, $5.

Tarara Vineyard & Winery, 13648 Tarara Lane, Leesburg, (703) 771-7100. This happening place is the "retirement project" of Margaret and Whitie Hubert, he a developer and contractor in Gaithersburg, Md. They bought a 475-acre corn and soybean farm along the banks of the Potomac River near Lucketts in 1985 and planted more than a hundred acres of grapes, fruit trees and nursery stock. They named it Tarara, Margaret explains, after the river flooded the year they bought the place. "We felt we'd landed and come to rest like Noah's Ark at Ararat up here on this cliff – but we didn't like the rat at the end of Ararat, so we spelled it backward." The centerpiece is the winery and wine cave blasted out of a rocky cliff 30 feet deep, beneath their showplace of a house. The spacious tasting and sales rooms are full of interesting touches, like the acrylic jewelry and baskets of artist-daughter Karen Hubert of Alexandria and the mixed-media artworks of daughter Martha Hubert, whose designs adorn the winery labels. Tarara sells its fruits to the public (we sampled a couple of delicious blackberries prior to the official pick-your-own weekend following our visit) and sponsors special events from wine dinners to grapevine decorating workshops to pig roasts to picnics to pony rides – all designed to bring people to the winery. Its barrel-fermented chardonnay ($11.99) and reserve cabernet ($15.99) are highly rated, but we and others are partial to the unique non-vintage charval ($6.99), a sprightly blend of chardonnay and seyval blanc. Tarara plans to quadruple the winery's size. Look for it to become one of the largest and best in Virginia. Open Thursday-Monday, 11 to 5; weekends only in January and February.

Piedmont Vineyards & Winery, Route 626, Middleburg, (540) 687-5528. Virginia's first commercial vinifera vineyard was established by Mrs. Thomas Furness in 1973 on 37 acres of a pre-Revolutionary farm called Waverly. Her daughter, Elizabeth Worrall, has made a name among connoisseurs for the boutique winery, producing 5,500 cases a year of some of the best white wines in Virginia. The small flagstone-floored tasting room, quite appealing with wicker furniture, is rather like a Southern veranda, and the shady picnic grounds beside a pond are enchanting. Wines are priced from $7 to $15 (for the award-winning reserve chardonnay). Open daily, 10 to 5.

Hiking and Bicycling. The **Chesapeake & Ohio** and **Washington & Old Domin-**

ion trails are ten-foot-wide pathways much loved by joggers, bikers, walkers and horseback riders. The towpath in the C&O Canal National Historical Park is part of a trail system stretching from Cumberland, Md., along the Potomac River to Georgetown. The blacktop path of the former W&OD Railroad runs from Purcellville, just west of Leesburg, to Alexandria. Together they attract more than one million users annually.

Shopping. Leesburg is the commercial hub of Loudoun County, although most of its major and basic businesses have moved to strip plazas south and east of town. The Old Town downtown section is of interest for establishments like **Leesburg Vintner,** which serves up great deli sandwiches along with wines and beverages; the **Kitchen Shop, Queen of Hearts Collectibles** with collector dolls and **Yesterday's Memories** (with a native American and New Age theme). **Loudoun Western Wear** is almost a department store of clothing and accessories. The feline-lover among us had a field day at **Classy Cat Gifts.** Stores come and go in Leesburg's restored **Market Station** at the edge of downtown. We admired the fine gifts with a Virginia theme at **The Cornerstone,** where we were attracted by a sculptured bird feeder out front and tasted samples of wild blackberry jelly and pumpkin butter.

Tiny Middleburg is perhaps of more appeal to visiting shoppers. Its quaint, tree-lined downtown is chock-a-block full of stylish stores, many with an equine theme. Established in 1956, **The Fun Shop** with the strange name is a mini-department store in a warren of rooms, stocking everything from table linens and clothing to toys, books, lamp shades and notions (it even offers a toll-free 800 phone number for customers from afar). Also quite big and au courant is **Gourmet Kitchen Plus,** a dream store for those interested in culinary matters. The **Irish Crystal Company** is the first store in Virginia to carry the fine Tyrone Crystal and, unlike most shops of its ilk, the owner urges visitors to touch the merchandise. **The Finicky Filly** offers wonderful women's wear; it's the female counterpart to venerable horseman Tully Rector's men's store. He also offers a "painting of your horse" as one of the services of **The Shaggy Ram,** specialist in country antiques, hunt items and English imports. **The Papery** is a good paper and gift shop. Pick up a croissant or a sandwich at **The Upper Crust,** an excellent bakery.

Extra-Special

Waterford. Every state should have a Waterford, but precious few do. Reminiscent of the British Cotswolds, this treasured community of a few hundred souls is no longer an endangered species, having been saved by the Waterford Foundation, which celebrated its 50th anniversary in 1993. The must-see town, settled by Quakers in 1733, is one of the few communities totally encompassed on the National Register of Historic Places. Waterford's Quakers and thriving free black community supported the Union in the Civil War, when it was harassed both by Union forces because of its location and by Confederate forces because of its beliefs. Today, Waterford's buildings and rolling fields, wedged into a fold between hills, look much as they did a century ago. As you drive through on High Street (Route 662 northwest of Leesburg), don't make the mistake of thinking the town consists of a few nice houses, the Catoctin Presbyterian and Waterford Baptist churches and the red-brick Loudoun Mutual Insurance Co. Instead, head west down one of the side streets to Second and Main streets. Here you'll find a remarkable variety of log, stone and brick houses, the Pink House B&B, the Peaceable Kingdom gift shop, the Waterford Forge, the mapmaker-historian and who knows what all. On a weekday you're likely to have the place to yourself. But come the first weekend of October, thousands are drawn here for the Waterford Foundation's annual house tour and crafts exhibit, one of the nation's best juried shows.

Potomac and Shenandoah rivers converge at Harpers Ferry.

Harpers Ferry, W.Va.
Worth the Voyage

The view of the convergence of the Potomac and Shenandoah rivers here is "one of the most stupendous scenes in nature – worth a voyage across the Atlantic."

So said Thomas Jefferson back in 1783. The view of Harpers Ferry continues to astound travelers, especially those emerging from the Baltimore-Washington megalopolis and suddenly confronting a different vista: one of rivers slicing between mountains, endless greenery and a rugged aspect all around.

Harpers Ferry, a boomtown that died after the Civil War, remains much the way it was during the days of John Brown's infamous raid. An old, hilly, European-looking town that never ceases to amaze, it's the start and the heart of this area known locally as West Virginia's Eastern Panhandle.

Beyond lies busy Charles Town, the Jefferson County seat where John Brown was tried and hanged. Young surveyor George Washington purchased his first land and settled members of his family here in 1748. More Washingtons lived here and more Washingtons are buried in the Zion Episcopal Church graveyard here than anywhere in the country. Today, it has more traffic lights than any small town we know of.

Make a triangle – that's the route the roads seem to take – from Harpers Ferry to Charles Town around to Shepherdstown, West Virginia's oldest town. It's across the Potomac from Sharpsburg, Md., and the bloody Antietam National Battlefield (see Frederick chapter). A quaint college town, Shepherdstown has retained the charm that bustling Charles Town seems to have lost.

This area is paradise for mountain climbers, hikers along the old Chesapeake & Ohio Canal towpath, Civil War buffs and the rest of us. Country inns and B&Bs arrived here late (about 1985), but seem to be making up for lost time. Zoning precludes their presence in most of Harpers Ferry, the soul of the area.

The National Park Service has restored Harpers Ferry's lower town, which serves as a national model of historic preservation and draws more than a million visitors annually. Despite all the people, the view and the surroundings are just as Thomas Jefferson said they were.

Inn Spots

Except for the ancient Hilltop House, something of a time capsule that is appropriate for Harpers Ferry, accommodations here are generally limited to B&Bs of no more than two guest rooms. There is a new Comfort Inn, but that's uptown in Bolivar. Country inns and B&Bs prevail in Charles Town and Sheperdstown, each about six miles away as the crow flies. Rates quoted are for weekends; in almost every case, weekday rates are lower. Some inns add surcharges for use of credit cards.

The View, Ridge Street, Box 286, Harpers Ferry 25425. (304) 535-2688.

The name says it all. Or does it? Certainly the view is the first thing you will notice upon arriving at what looks to be a small ranch house on a residential street along a bluff in the upper town. The front door opens onto a wide, deep view from five levels of a contemporary house onto a spectacular Potomac River mountain scene.

Indiana natives Etta Mae and Bill Hannon moved from Virginia's Fairfax County in 1988 to open their new residence as a B&B. They offer one room with kingsize bed and shower and a two-bedroom suite. Both are furnished with a mix of old and new that reflects a contemporary house, rather than one of history. Since it's a house rather than a museum, children, pets and even smoking are permitted.

Entry is on the second level (a loft above the Hannons' quarters is the top). This is the dining room, which overlooks a sunken living room on the third level with soaring ceiling, dramatic windows and sectional seating. Here, beside a rare paulownia tree, is one of three wide decks upon which to take in the view. Underneath the second-level kitchen is the king bedroom on the fourth level. Beneath the living room on the fifth level are the two-bedroom suite and a rec room-style common area with a wood stove, TV, VCR and a jacuzzi beside the window. Outside is a brick patio with more views onto the river.

The Hannons furnish sodas, peanuts and such in the common room. Quite a continental-breakfast spread is served in the attractive dining room: fresh orange juice, plates with up to a dozen kinds of fresh fruit and three kinds of breads, including raspberry muffins and cinnamon rolls. Coffee is poured from a silver pot.

Doubles, $75.

Ranson-Armory House, 690 Washington St., Harpers Ferry 25425. (304) 535-2142.

A good-looking 1830 house, its original portion one room deep, was turned into a B&B in 1990 by John and Dorothy Hughes, he a retired teacher from Silver Spring, Md. They offer two guest rooms with private hall baths. The room to the rear, with a view of Maryland Heights, has windows in four directions because of the one-room-deep layout. An antique quilt covers its double bed. A smaller front room, with windows on two sides, looks toward Loudoun Heights.

A stained-glass front door opens onto a big front porch full of rockers, well screened from the street by shade trees. Guests also relax in the parlor and on a flagstone terrace beside the lovely rear gardens. Breakfast is served in an interesting-looking dining room with a fan-shaped window and

Wide front porch leads into Ranson-Armory House.

balloon curtains. Dorothy's mainstay is stuffed french toast ricotta, accompanied by warmed maple syrup, grits or home fries and sausage. Other possibilities are an egg casserole or individual soufflés.

Doubles, $70 to $75. No smoking.

Lee-Stonewall Inn, 1145 Washington St., Harpers Ferry 25425. (304) 535-2532.

Opened in 1990, this is the most historic of Harpers Ferry's B&Bs. The Georgian-Federal brick structure dates to 1795 and is on the National Register. It takes its name from builder Richard B. Lee and Stonewall Jackson, who is believed to have occupied it briefly during the Civil War.

Gary and Regina Sharp, he a school guidance counselor in Virginia's Loudoun County and she a teacher at Jefferson County High School in Charles Town, offer two guest accommodations with private baths. One on the second floor has a queen canopy bed, an antique rocking chair, an old fainting couch and stenciling around the chair rail. On the third floor is a two-bedroom suite, also decorated in Colonial style with antique brass and high-back oak beds.

Guests relax on the back porch or on lawn chairs in the front or back yard, beneath a fragrant weeping myrtle imported from England and as old as the house. They are offered sherry or brandy by the fireplace in the French-style living room, which has interesting tapestry window treatments. A hearty country breakfast, served fireside in the dining room, might start with chilled peach soup pureed with cream cheese or, in cool weather, baked apples. House specialties are eggs benedict, eggs annapoli (with crabmeat) and lemon-anise waffles.

Because they are located just across the town line in Bolivar and are not subject to Harpers Ferry's zoning regulations, the Sharps were thinking of adding two more rooms with private baths.

Doubles, $80.

Harpers Ferry Guest House, 800 Washington St., Box 1079, Harpers Ferry 25425. (304) 535-6955.

This B&B looks and smells new. And it is. Al and Allison Alsdorf obtained photos of the original Victorian house on the property, which had burned ten years earlier, and rebuilt it to look much the same.

They offer three bedrooms with private bath. One on the main floor is designed for the handicapped. Allison was still in the process of furnishing and decorating two upstairs bedrooms, where quilts top the poster reproduction beds made in nearby Berkeley County. Alison is particularly proud of her West Virginia kitchen, built by a retired industrial-arts teacher and his wife.

The adjacent dining room is the setting for some grand breakfasts. Al cooks omelets and Allison prepares cornmeal or blueberry waffles to accompany juice, fruit and banana or lemon-poppyseed muffins.

Because of its newness, rooms in this house seem bigger than in the average Victorian. There's a large living room with TV. "Guests can be as private or as much a part of the house as they wish," says Alison.

The Alsdorfs moved in 1993 from New Paltz, N.Y., when Al was transferred to Gaithersburg, Md. He likes trains and, when he came across the railroad bridge, Harpers Ferry reminded him of home.

Doubles, $75.

Hillbrook Inn on Bullskin Run, Summit Point Road, Route 2, Box 152, Charles Town 25414. (304) 725-4223.

This beauty of a Tudor mansion on seven levels and seventeen rural acres is an anomaly. It has earned national awards and magazine coverage, and yet is little known within the area and its brochures are not available through visitor centers. Perhaps that's because innkeeper Gretchen Carroll is out to attract an upscale clientele that appreciates a richly furnished house in the English country style and prix-fixe gourmet dinners and is willing to pay for the privilege.

Only one room wide and in places only one room high, the stuccoed house of thirteen gables, timbered walls, windows with more than 2,000 panes of glass and an unmistakable English look tiptoes up a hillside. That makes things mighty interesting, inside and out.

Start in the living room, twenty feet high, with tall mullioned windows on two sides. It contains a battery of art objects, elegant furnishings and oriental rugs characteristic of the entire manor. Fireplaces on either end of the room add warmth in winter. Above the living room is the large Bamford Suite with fireplace and porch, a queen bed in the corner and an old Vuitton steamer trunk for a luggage rack. The suite and the Cottage, reached by a private entrance and known as the room of the nine oriental rugs, command top dollar. The Cottage offers a queen bed, a glass-front Swiss wood-burning stove, a red velvet loveseat and two side chairs, two balconies, and a deep red and blue paisley decor.

Other rooms include Locke's Nest, entered high above the living room and harboring two beds with thick brass headboards that are polished every other week. The tub and the toilet retain the colors of what had been an all-purple bathroom. Two smaller rooms with antique double beds, the Lookout and the Point, are tucked into the eaves. Sloping walls create odd angles and spaces in the former, windows look out in three directions, and a Thai spirit house intricately carved in teak sits atop an ancient English oak table. A six-foot-long tunnel leads to the Point, which reflects the innkeeper's passion for oriental rugs, rich but dark fabrics and upholstery, and fine paintings.

The public spaces are sights to behold, especially the dining room that is higher than

Rear porch and yard are good for gatherings at The Gilbert House.

it is wide, where a seven-course dinner is served at 8 o'clock (see Dining Spots). There's a library full of interesting books. A smashing tavern with a box-beam ceiling, a grand piano and lots of wing chairs has been created from a three-car garage. The breakfast porch off the dining room overlooks gorgeous back lawns, an old boxwood grove, a tall willow tree and a duck pond. A full country breakfast features pecan pancakes with ginger butter, and french toast tatiana, served with warm cranberry-orange syrup and sour cream. The inn has started serving lunch by reservation, and English teas are offered Sunday afternoons in winter at $20 a head.

Fresh flowers and a small box of Lake Champlain Chocolates from Vermont are in each room. The guest book is full of raves, the theme being "a special, magical place." And the owner plans to add a new building in the woods with suites and decks. She wants to make Hillbrook one of the most spectacular inns in the nation, assistant inn-keeper Nadia Hill advised. She was off to a good start.

Doubles, weekends $330 to $380, MAP; weekdays $240, MAP.

The Gilbert House, Box 1104, Charles Town 25414. (304) 725-0637.

Smack up against the street in the quaint historic district of Middleway, this grand stone house with bright red shutters harbors much antiquity. It dates to 1760, making it one of the older places to stay in the area. It's big enough to house the palatial furnishings, some of them with ties to European greats, of well-traveled owner Bernie Heiler and his late wife Jean.

He's continuing the tradition launched by Jamaica-born Jean, one of the first female graduates of Harvard Business School, who was president of a Washington investment management firm when she "started dreaming of green grass. I couldn't work. We bought this house, began restoring it and I had to be here." Isolation wasn't for her, however. "I decided to open a B&B for people to come and be my company." That was in 1985, when Hillbrook and the Thomas Shepherd Inn in Shepherdstown also opened. Until her untimely death, she ran the B&B while Bernie, who is from Winnipeg, commuted to D.C. twice a week for his work as a petroleum engineer and to shop for all the goodies that the couple plied guests with. Now Bernie opens the B&B principally on weekends, but makes himself available for weekday guests.

The L-shaped house offers three guest rooms, each with private bath. Two more at the rear of the house were in the planning stage. Romantics go for the Polk Suite, where "Pokey" graffiti on the wall was written by former owners who were close friends of Martin Van Buren, a visitor, and "poked" fun at his rival. The sitting room is partitioned by a wall against a frilly queen bed that looks built-in; actually the bed was made to fit the space. The third-floor Remington Room has a vaulted ceiling, a high 18th-century rope bed and an old English marble washstand. We found the mid-priced Van Buren Room to be the size of a suite, with a good sitting area, a large fireplace, an English armoire and a queensize bed that had just changed its top from summer feminine to fall masculine colors that day and sported wildly patterned sheets. Exotica in the bathroom included Jamaican facial tonic, Tahitian shower gel, bath salts and more.

Fresh flowers, seltzer, candy and fruit as well as countless antiques enhance all three rooms. But the real prizes are in the parlor and dining room: two ornate mirrors purchased from the Hapsburgs' Schoenberg Palace in Vienna, a painting and a settee that belonged to Marie Antoinette, four throne chairs (one that belonged to Henry IV of France), a game table intricate with mother of pearl, a Sheraton sideboard, a Robert Adam china cabinet, a Chippendale hall table, a Louis XVI clock and more.

Breakfast in the antiques-filled dining room is a treat. When we were there, grapefruit juice, an apple turnover and oatmeal with apples and raisins preceded the pièce de résistance, french toast to be topped with a choice of eight or nine fresh fruits from a platter and whipped cream with an orange liqueur. The smoked pork chop that accompanied was too much to finish.

Doubles, $100 to $140.

The Cottonwood Inn, Route 2, Box 61-S, Charles Town 25414. (304) 725-3371.

Black and white cows from the farm up the road were lying in the shade beside Bull Skin Run as we approached this 200-year-old farmhouse off Kabletown Road out in the countryside east of town. Eleanor and Colin Simpson had raised nine children here and the time came to decide whether to keep the house or sell it. They kept it, opening as a B&B in 1986.

Seven rooms with private baths vary widely. Some, up an original staircase so creaky that the Simpsons surely knew what time their teenagers were getting home at night, are cozy and historic with clawfoot tubs, old beds and fireplaces. Others up narrow stairs in an older section are carpeted; one with a kingsize bed, a day bed and a full bath is cheery with white walls and no clutter. A 1988 addition holds modern rooms that almost look motel-like in their newness. All rooms have television, four-poster beds, sitting areas and air-conditioning. Both the guest rooms and common rooms are designed for comfort. There's a large, beautiful living room with a library at the far end. Its floral blue carpet picks up the pale yellow and apricot colors on the walls. Windsor chairs are at four tables in the beamed dining room, site of a huge brick fireplace with a raised hearth and butter molds hanging along a beam.

Breakfast the next day was to be french toast "with as many fruits as I can find to top it off," said Eleanor. The weekend would bring pecan griddle cakes with sausage one day, quiche lorraine with one of Colin's grilled pork chops the next. Afternoon tea is taken on Adirondack chairs on the front lawn, looking toward those cows lazing beside the creek.

Doubles, $95 to $105.

Washington House Inn, 216 South George St., Charles Town 25414. (304) 725-7923 or (800) 297-6957.

Opened in 1990, this fine example of late Victorian architecture offers six rooms

New and old merge nicely at rural Cottonwood Inn.

with private baths, a turret and a wraparound veranda dressed in wicker. New owners Mel and Nina Vogel, who moved with two teenagers from suburban Washington, have added handmade quilts crafted by a distant relative from Charleston, and other family heirlooms.

Unusual corner fireplaces – two of seven in the three-story house – back up to each other in the pink and maroon parlor and the pink lace-clothed dining room. Ensconced in the turret, the parlor is the place for games like backgammon and cribbage. The dining room is the setting for Nina's breakfasts, whose cooking interests were inspired by her parents' restaurant in Ohio. Expect fresh fruit, gourmet coffees and a main dish like sausage and eggs or cinnamon raisin french toast stuffed with cream cheese.

The upstairs foyer contains a sitting area with TV. The Lavender Room in the turret and the Rose Room next door are decorated in pale colors, as are the third-floor Turret Room and the Dormer Room. More vivid is the Green Room, done in hunter green with a four-poster bed, desk and two side chairs. All rooms are simply but nicely furnished, some with fireplaces and casablanca paddle fans. The modern baths have pedestal sinks and showers.

Fresh fruit, homemade cookies and tea or coffee are offered in the afternoon.

Doubles, $95. No smoking.

The Carriage Inn, 417 East Washington St., Charles Town 25414. (304) 728-8003.

Costumes of a Victorian-era maid and butler are displayed on the coat rack in the entry at this B&B, built in the early 1800s and hidden behind huge shade trees on the town's main street. Innkeepers Virginia and Bob Kaetzel offer five guest rooms, all with full private baths and all quite different.

Bob, a contractor, is credited with devising the sunken private baths found in former stairwells to the rear of the house. He also made the beds by hand. Named for the color of their wallpaper, all rooms have queen canopy beds and four have fireplaces; some have day beds or a velvet loveseat with two side chairs, and one has its own enclosed porch with TV and refrigerator. You'd never know the Lavender Room on the third floor was once the attic; it has a four-poster bed, a sitting room with a daybed and a settee, and a Franklin stove.

Guests enjoy a heavily shaded front veranda with a swing and a deep back yard. Breakfast on china and crystal at three lace-covered tables in the dining room brings fresh fruit like pears with mandarin oranges and cinnamon french toast topped with pineapple, strawberries, kiwi and whipped cream, plus eggs and sausage. Afternoon tea or wine are available in the drawing room, which has twelve-foot-high ceilings, a piano and TV. A resident manager is in charge while the hosts are at work.

Doubles, $95.

Thomas Shepherd Inn, German and Duke Streets, Box 1162, Shepherdstown 25443. (304) 876-3715.

A very Colonial but comfortable feeling pervades this cream-colored brick Federal house at the main intersection in Shepherdstown, West Virginia's oldest town. The warmth comes from Margaret Perry, the hospitable hostess known for caring touches and gourmet meals.

The inn, opened in 1985, has a rich, formal living room furnished with wing chairs, oriental scatter rugs and decanters of sherry at the ready and two dining rooms, the better to serve people at different times. Another favorite gathering space is the upstairs library, with a small TV and a stash of material on the area. Off it is a porch with rockers and lots of plants overlooking the rear garden.

There are six guest rooms, all with private baths. We liked Room 6 in back looking out over the garden; it comes with a canopied bed, a full bath and a loveseat. Other rooms vary: one is rather small with a double bed, another has a double and a twin, and still another a sleigh bed. A front corner room offers a partially canopied bed, two upholstered chairs and a large full bath with big, thirsty towels. At our latest visit, Margaret was hoping to add a deluxe room with kingsize bed, fireplace and jacuzzi in a little black and white striped log cabin up the street.

Breakfasts here are special. "There's not a morning I don't get up and can't wait to get to the kitchen," says Margaret. The meal might begin with chilled orange-blueberry soup garnished with crème fraîche or a nectarine poached with ginger. Baked eggs florentine, omelets with asparagus and mushrooms, sour cream pancakes with home-made sage sausages or bread pudding with raspberry sauce follow. Herbed basmati rice with soy sauce and garnishes like nasturtiums, pansies and calendulas from her gardens could accompany. Margaret, whose love for cooking is exceeded only by her hospitality, plies arriving guests with cookies and sherry and will fix dinner for guests by prior arrangement. She has been known to make little gifts of soaps and bags of potpourri for departing guests.

Doubles, $95 to $125; two-night minimum on weekends. No smoking.

Bavarian Inn and Lodge, Route 1, Box 30, Shepherdstown 25443. (304) 876-2551.

This was the area's first, starting as a restaurant in 1962 and adding lodging in chalet-style buildings overlooking the Potomac River in 1981 and a conference center in 1994.

Though the restaurant remains the priority of Munich-born owner Erwin Asam and his English wife Carol, their overnight accommodations are attractive as well. Four Bavarian-style, beamed chalets bear exterior murals of mountains and castles. They contain 39 well-appointed rooms with queensize four-poster beds (mostly canopied), sitting areas with TV, many with sleeper sofas, and private balconies high above the Potomac. Twenty-six have gas fireplaces and eighteen offer jacuzzi baths.

From our balcony we could watch canoeists below on the river and rabbits scurrying along the hillside and hear lovely bird calls at both dusk and sunrise. Only the

Tudor-style Hillbrook Inn on Bullskin Run offers luxury lodging and dining.

noise of traffic from the nearby Route 480 bridge pierced the tranquility. Inside our spacious, stucco-walled room in white and light brown were a couple of welcoming apples, two wing chairs and an archway to the entry and the bath, which included a dressing room with extra vanity and an assortment of Lord & Mayfair amenities. Our chalet building had nine units, three on each floor.

Nearing completion at our 1994 visit were 30 more rooms, nine with fireplaces and jacuzzis, plus a conference and exercise facility in a new building located between the chalets and Route 480.

There also are three guest rooms in the main greystone inn and restaurant, uphill from the chalets. Twelve acres of nicely landscaped grounds include a secluded swimming pool. Breakfast is available at hotel prices in the restaurant.

Doubles, $90 to $145, EP.

Dining Spots

Hillbrook Inn on Bullskin Run, Summit Point Road (Route 13), Charles Town. (304) 725-4223.

We don't know whether the setting or the food is more the attraction here. It could be both, but who knows? Only the flush tend to eat here because of the pricing structure, which commands a hefty $60 for a prix-fixe dinner on weekdays, $68 on weekends (the price includes French and California table wines poured throughout the meal). Innkeeper Gretchen Carroll says the experience is designed to be relaxed and unpretentious, rather like a dinner party in a private home.

The dining room in this stunning Tudor mansion is taller than it is wide or long, which makes for an interesting sense of space. A brass chandelier comprised of old oil lamps casts soft shadows over a handful of tables showing the patina of old wood and set with brass service plates. Flickering candles in hurricane chimneys are reflected in the silver and crystal and in a brass teapot collection on the buffet, and the gold print on the wallpaper shimmers by candlelight. The adjacent breakfast porch, used for dinner overflow, overlooks the rear lawns and gardens that are spotlit at night.

141

Executive chef Christine Hale, a Pittsburgh Culinary Institute graduate who trained in France, oversees the prix-fixe, single-choice menu. The seven-course dinner is served at a single seating at 8 o'clock. It might start with white button mushrooms in a garden herb marinade, curried onion soup and penne with a tomato-caper sauce. The main event could be grilled marlin with tarragon butter, teamed with jasmine rice, sautéed squash with thyme, pernod cucumbers and oil-roasted green beans. A salad of red leaf lettuce with avocado and mango follows. The meal concludes with smoked havarti cheese with bremner wafers, honeydew melon and red grapes, and a dessert like poached pears with caramelized pecans, chocolate ganache and strawberry coulis.

A prix-fixe lunch ($20) offering a sampling of the inn's specialties is served by reservation on the enclosed dining porch or on the garden terrace.

Meals by reservation only. Lunch daily, noon to 2; dinner, nightly at 8. No smoking.

Bavarian Inn, Route 480, Shepherdstown. (304) 876-2551.

This well-known dining room attracts diners from near and far. It's not the kind of place to which we were attracted for a Saturday lunch – we stopped, looked at the menu, saw all the staff and customers in dressy attire and decided to go on to a more casual place where we could eat outside. But it fit the bill perfectly for dinner at another visit.

The main dining room in the living room of the original greystone mansion resembles the interior of a Bavarian lodge with paneled walls, beamed ceiling, deer-antler chandeliers, a deer head over the huge stone fireplace and racks with displays of Bavarian china and beer steins. We preferred the pleasant, glassed-in terrace dining area with windows onto the gardens.

The extensive dinner menu covers all the bases, including Bavarian, continental, American, cold platters and "lean and healthy." Entrées start at $10.50 for the last; otherwise they run from $12.75 for shepherds pie, kassler rippchen or schweinbraten to $18.75 for filet mignon, except $38 for rack of lamb or châteaubriand for two.

When in Bavaria, do as...and one of us did. Wiener schnitzel ($15.75) with red

cabbage and pan-fried potatoes with caraway seeds was the real thing. The other sampled the grilled medallions of pork tenderloin with red cabbage and green beans, which was unmemorable. Good German bread arrived as we sat down. A small slab of the chef's mellow veal, liver and duck pâté ($5.50) with all the trimmings and house salads tided us over until the entrées came. A Bavarian nut ball – vanilla ice cream rolled in peanuts and topped with chocolate sauce and coconut flakes – was not cold enough but quite good.

Bavarian Inn chalet viewed from restaurant.

There are interesting, reasonably priced international coffees and after-dinner drinks. You might want to adjourn downstairs to the Rathskellar, a very alpine place that wraps around the bar and offers weekend entertainment.

Lunch daily, Monday-Saturday 11:30 to 2:30; dinner, 5 to 10, Sunday noon to 9.

Yellow Brick Bank, 201 West German St., Shepherdstown. (304) 876-2208.

Bright red apples hang from ficus trees in this colorful – make that flamboyant – restaurant inside an old yellow brick bank. A more casual room done up in white

Yellow Brick Bank restaurant is colorful inside and out.

wicker contains the bar. In the main dining room, huge old posters decorate the pink walls, the chairs are pink and mauve, and the high coffered ceiling is edged in handpainted blue clouds. Little stained-glass lamps and pink vases with red roses topped the tables at our visit.

At lunch, one of us enjoyed a bowl of sweet corn and jalapeño chowder ($3.50), loaded with chopped ham and tomatoes and packing a spicy wallop, and an appetizer of shiitake mushrooms on lemon thyme toast ($5). The other chose pesto pasta with chopped tomatoes ($8.95), served in a big bowl with French bread alongside. The interesting Italian/international menu listed few luncheon salads and sandwiches, concentrating instead on appetizers and pastas priced in the $9 to $10 range. Pan-seared bluefish coated with brandied black pepper, linguini with caramelized vidalia onions and shallots, and fettuccine alfredo with fresh raspberries were the day's specials. We had no room left for desserts, among them lemon cheesecake with caramelized mascarpone, Mexican chocolate bread pudding with crème fraîche, coffee ice cream with kahlua and coconut and a hot fudge sundae. On weekends, there are two sampler plates of four desserts each for $6.

The luncheon menu is served day and night (except Saturday night) in the Wicker Room with the bar. Otherwise, the dinner menu goes from $9 for pastas to $17 for tuna grilled with tamari and freshly ground horseradish. Grilled pork loin with black bean fritters and hot fruit salsa, raspberry chicken and london broil are among the choices. The cooking here is assertive, to go along with the eclectic atmosphere.

Upstairs are three rooms in a little-known B&B called The Little Inn, which appears to function as an afterthought.

Lunch, Monday-Saturday 11:30 to 4:30; dinner from 5; Sunday brunch, 11 to 4.

Charles Washington Inn, 210 West Liberty St., Charles Town. (304) 725-1030.
The oldest home in Charles Town on property purchased from Charles Washington (for whom the town was named), this was known as the Tiffin House for most of its 203 years. New owners gave it a facelift and a new name, and expanded the dining capacity. Meals are served in three small fireplaced rooms, a casual one on the main

floor and two fancier rooms upstairs, decorated in what co-owner Pam Jones calls "Colonial romantic" style. There are also a bar and a trellised outdoor patio.

Crab cakes and veal dishes are the specialties, but the blackboard menu changes daily. For dinner ($12.95 to $16.95), you might find cajun scallops, salmon with hollandaise sauce, blackened redfish with toasted garlic, shrimp scampi, chicken marsala, veal sorrentino or française, and prime rib. Start with stuffed mushroom caps, mussels provençal or escargots. Finish with coconut cake, fresh strawberries or chocolate pâté with raspberry sauce.

Lunch, 11:30 to 4; dinner nightly, 5 to 9 or 10.

Shu Chen, 100 West Washington St., Charles Town. (304) 728-0033.

The biggest, and usually the busiest, restaurant in town is this Chinese establishment in the historic Charles Washington Hall, the old marketplace and town meeting hall front and center on the main street. The outside looks historic; the inside is a cross between European and Oriental in rich reds and blacks.

The menu is fairly standard Chinese, with many chicken, seafood and beef dishes in the $6.25 to $9.25 range. The hot orange beef, the crispy prawns with walnuts and the lobster szechuan are among specialties, and Peking duck can be ordered for $15.95 for two. We liked the lemon chicken, the mandarin combination of shrimp, beef and chicken stir-fried with snow peas, broccoli and bamboo shoots, the dumplings and cold noodles with sesame sauce that we ordered to take out for a candlelight dinner in the back yard at our inn in Middleway.

Lunch daily, 11:30 to 2:30; dinner, 5 to 9:30.

The Iron Rail Inn & Cellar Pub, 124 East Washington St., Charles Town. (304) 725-0052.

A Tiffany-style lamp hanging on the porch over the front door attests to the age of this beige brick Federal-style building with a turret, built around 1810. There's an aquarium in the front foyer, beneath a ceiling covered in floral fabric. The main floor holds three high-ceilinged dining rooms with old high-back chairs at wood tables. Downstairs is owner George Quinn's Cellar Pub, three rooms with stone walls and one with a billiards table.

"Fine international dining" is the hallmark. The dinner menu ($13.95 to $18.95) embraces four veal and three chicken dishes in the continental idiom, plus cajun steak, prime rib, steak au poivre and seafood specials. All come with fresh bread, vegetable and a choice of potato, fettuccine or rice. Stuffed mushrooms and escargots in puff pastry are favorite appetizers. Desserts are homemade cakes and pies.

The appetizers and salads turn up on the lunch and pub menu, which also features sandwiches and light fare, most under $5.

Lunch, Monday-Saturday 11:30 to 2; dinner, 5 to 9 or 9:30; pub, Monday-Saturday 11:30 to 10.

The Anvil Restaurant, 1270 Washington St., Harpers Ferry. (304) 535-2582.

This oldtimer in the uptown Bolivar section packs in the tourists in a pub out front, a big early American dining room to the rear and an outdoor patio beyond. Although the dining room and patio were empty at our visit, there was a waiting line for lunch in the crowded pub and we couldn't wait.

Too bad, for this is considered the best place to eat in town. The menu is traditional continental-Italian. Seafood linguini en papillote is the house specialty. Blackboard specials at our visit were baked potato soup, chicken roulade and blackened grouper. Other entrées priced in the teens include crab cakes, stuffed or broiled flounder, salmon en croûte, chicken parmigiana, veal cordon bleu and filet mignon. They are served with a choice of two of the following: cole slaw, applesauce, cottage cheese, tossed salad, vegetable of the day, rice pilaf, baked potato or french fries.

Starters include clam chowder, crab soup, cheese sticks, shrimp cocktail and egg rolls. Among desserts are cheese cake, carrot cake and midnight chocolate cake.

Open daily except Monday, 11 to 9 or 10.

Hilltop House, Ridge Street, Harpers Ferry. (304) 535-2132 or (800) 338-8319.

This is a hotel and conference center of the old school (very old, built in 1888 and apparently not changed much since). Its location just above the lower town makes it popular with old-timers and diners who like the view of the confluence of the Potomac and Shenandoah rivers. There are a veranda and telescopes to take it all in.

The pub and the side dining room really get the views of the Potomac. Most of the seating is in a main dining room beyond the buffet tables and away from the windows.

Folks come out of the woodwork for the weekend buffets: $13.95 on Friday and Saturday nights for everything from seafood newburg and steamed spiced shrimp to fried chicken, top round of beef, hushpuppies, apple fritters, biscuits and desserts. The Sunday dinner buffet ($12.95) adds chicken and dumplings and hot ham with pine-apple sauce to the fried chicken and beef selections. The rest of the week the menu is à la carte and a little more varied, from wiener schnitzel to New York strip steak.

The hotel has 73 guest rooms. Most are old-fashioned rooms upstairs on the second and third floors with private baths and a few with TVs. Rooms in the motel-style annex are seven years old.

Open daily, noon to 8, weekends to 9.

Diversions

Harpers Ferry National Historic Park, 535-6029. The immensely picturesque area that Thomas Jefferson said was "worth a voyage across the Atlantic" to see is seen today by more than one million visitors annually, yet remains little changed from the 19th century. From an information center west of town (parking, $3 individual, $5 per carload), buses shuttle visitors every five minutes into the historic lower town, which is blissfully tranquil because vehicular traffic is light.

The town of Harpers Ferry boomed after it was designated a federal armory and arsenal, manufacturing many of the munitions used in the War of 1812 and the Civil War. The buildings were the targets of abolitionist John Brown's raid, aimed at arming the slaves for insurrection. The town of 3,000 declined rapidly because of destruction wrought by the Civil War and repeated flooding. It was a sleepy little hamlet when taken over by the National Park Service in 1944 and restored in what has since become a national model for historic park preservation.

The park's four themes are industry, John Brown's raid on the arsenal, the Civil War and black history. The last is represented by Storer College, a normal school for the education of freed blacks that started in an abandoned armory dwelling in the upper town. Park employees in period clothing present living-history programs and guided tours in the streets and restored buildings during summer and on certain weekends in spring and fall.

Most of the sites are clustered along Shenandoah Street in Lower Town. The old Stage Coach Inn is now the Harpers Ferry Historical Association's excellent book-store and an information center. The Master Armorer's House is a museum on gunmaking. Stop at the old dry goods store, where the 1850s price list puts neckties at 35 cents each. John Brown's Fort is the old armory firehouse where he and his follow-

Shenandoah Street retains feeling of yesteryear in Harpers Ferry's Lower Town.

ers were captured. Other attractions include the Blacksmith Shop, Provost Office, John Brown Museum, Whitehall Tavern and a confectionery.

From the lower town, the town marches in European fashion up a steep hill without a 20th-century intrusion. The **Stone Steps** – we counted 56 of them – begin a trail to the upper town. A sign says the trail takes 45 minutes and is steep at the start, but the views of rivers, bridges, lower town and surrounding heights "are well worth it." First comes the 1775 **Harper House,** built by the town's founder, now restored as an 1850s tenant house to represent the crowded conditions and lack of housing in the town's industrial heyday. Opposite are spring houses and root cellars, small caves carved into the shale cliffside. Next is St. Peter's Roman Catholic Church, an 1833 stone church and a commanding presence, but difficult to reach by car for Sunday Masses. Beyond are the ruins of St. John's Episcopal Church and **Jefferson Rock,** vantage point for the "stupendous" view.

Hiking. The **Appalachian Trail** crosses the Potomac on the same railroad-pedestrian bridge that tourists use to get near the railroad tunnel and onto the Chesapeake & Ohio Canal towpath. Favorite hikes are to Maryland Heights and Overlook Cliffs, a four-mile round trip that rewards the hardy with the view of Harpers Ferry that is the trademark of the area. Other trails lead to Virginius Island, Jefferson Rock, Loudoun Heights and Bolivar Heights.

Other Towns. Charles Town, the busy county seat, does not have much to commend it to visitors unless they are Washington family buffs or racetrack fans. A Washington descendant still lives in Harewood, the 1770 home of Samuel Washington, but all six Washington family homes are privately owned and not opened to the public. Satisfy yourself with the collections at the Jefferson County Museum. Thoroughbred racing is featured at the Charles Town Races and sports car racing at the Summit Point Raceway. More to our liking is quaint **Shepherdstown,** endowed with street after street of historic homes, some good shopping and the campus of Shepherd College. Current and foreign films are shown in the Old Opera House, and the Contemporary American Theater Festival presents four new plays each July at Shepherd College.

The Chesapeake & Ohio Canal. With 74 lift locks and designation as a national

146

historic park, the C&O Canal stretches 185 miles from the heights of Cumberland, Md., to Rock Creek in Georgetown. The towpath along the Maryland side is immensely popular with joggers, walkers and cyclists because it's so level, and nowhere more so than in the Sharpsburg-Harpers Ferry area, where it incorporates six miles of the Appalachian Trail. Here a stone and dirt path follows the Potomac beneath a canopy of trees. Particularly interesting is the 3.5-mile stretch south of Shepherdstown to Antietam Creek, where you'll see the Antietam Viaduct, Lock No. 38 and the sites of two bloody Civil War battles along Antietam Creek. Park rangers lead periodic tours to various locks, aqueducts and even caves. Information is available at park headquarters in the impressive **Ferry Hill Place,** an 1813 plantation manor above the Potomac off Route 34 opposite the Bavarian Inn in Shepherdstown.

Shopping. We weren't particularly impressed with a lot of the shops in Harpers Ferry, most of them geared to tourists and the better ones tucked away out of sight. But there are exceptions like the handcrafted stoneware and porcelain at **Westwinds Potters,** the wonderful scenes of Harpers Ferry along with Carmel Foret Creations and watercolors at **The Studio,** and the new **Elegant Country Flowers & Antiques. Grape Expectations** offers "something grape for everyone," especially West Virginia wines, picnic baskets, glassware and ceramics. We like the jewelry at **The Spy Mountain Jewelry Company and Clothing Boutique,** the handicrafts at **Sleepy Hollow Creations** and the collectibles at **Stone House Antiques.** Almost every other building along High Street seems to be a snacky cafe, ice cream or coffee shop; their names (The Garden of Food, Oriental Xpress Cafe, the Coffee Mill) indicate what they are about.

In Shepherdstown, **Sanguine Gryphon** offers super gifts and pottery among its contemporary handicrafts – brightly colored fishes, painted tiles, boats of different woods, jewelry and folk art all caught our attention. **Practically Yours** has unique handcrafted gifts, from pottery to windsocks, and herbs and related products are stocked at **Open Hearth Herbs & Gifts. Village Green** is a trove of gifts and decorative accessories. **Keith H. Knost** specializes in fine gifts and interiors of the kind to appeal to guests at the Homestead and the Greenbrier, where it also has shops. For a snack, stop at **Ye Olde Sweet Shoppe,** a bakery that makes everything it sells, specializes in whole-grain European breads with no sugar or additives, and the coffee is 35 cents if you bring your own cup (otherwise, 45 and 80 cents). **The Old Pharmacy Cafe & Soda Fountain** is recommended for snacks, lunch and light supper. Reunion restaurant offers burgers, chili, soups and club sandwiches in the $3 to $5 range. Besides coffee and candles, the **German Street Coffee & Candlery** offers oil lamps, glassware and garden accents.

Extra-Special

Blue Ridge Outlet Center, 315 West Stephen Street, Martinsburg. (304) 263-7467 or (800) 445-3993.

It's not as big as the Reading outlet centers nor as new as Potomac Mills. It's a destination for bargain-seekers and usually a side trip for visitors to Harpers Ferry, however. The first outlets opened in 1984 in Martinsburg's old woolen mills and numbered 60 stores in four buildings at last count. The shopping setting is newer and nicer than those of older outlets; there's even a mall-type atrium in the Dunn Building. The stores are mostly fashion-oriented (Evan Picone, Jonathan Logan, Etienne Aigner, J.Crew and Britches). Three relatively trendy restaurants raise fast food to new heights: Judy's, the American Deli and the Clock Cafe. Open daily and Thursday-Saturday nights.

Stately architectural styles prevail in downtown Frederick historic district.

Frederick, Md.
'So Proudly We Hail'

"Our town has been here since 1745 and is still thriving on the same streets," said the woman at Frederick's visitor center. You can feel its longevity as you view the 18th- and 19th-century structures throughout the city's 33-block historic district. You can sense its prosperity in its downtown, enlivened by restaurants, boutiques and galleries.

And you can empathize with its new slogan, "So Proudly We Hail," borrowed quite appropriately from the anthem written by native son Francis Scott Key. Here's a town that possesses a strong sense of identity, as reflected in its slick monthly city magazine called, simply, Frederick.

This area is "heaven in Maryland for yuppies," extolled a state tourism promoter. They come here to go antiquing, tour the battlefields, enjoy the restaurants and walk the sidewalks tread earlier by George Washington, Abraham Lincoln, the Marquis de Lafayette, Stonewall Jackson and Barbara Fritchie.

Barbara Fritchie? She's the Civil War heroine who challenged rebel troops to target her rather than the Union flag she was waving as they marched the city's streets. "Shoot if you must this old gray head, but spare this country's flag," she pleaded, her defiance immortalized by poet John Greenleaf Whittier.

Whittier's tale of "the clustered spires of Frederick" comes alive as the visitor explores the sights, an experience made much more worthwhile by the guided walking tours offered weekends and holidays. Court House Square was the scene of the first official repudiation of the British Stamp Act in 1765, ten years before the Boston Tea Party. A century later, Frederick was a town divided by the War Between the States, its sympathies lying both north and south. Churches and public buildings became hospitals for the wounded from nearby Antietam, site of the bloodiest battle on American soil.

The local battle of Monocacy is credited with saving Washington, D.C., from destruction. Frederick itself was spared, after Confederate General Jubal Early occupied the town briefly and levied a $200,000 ransom for its salvation – an amount borrowed from local banks and finally repaid in 1951. Thus the city is a model of original architecture – "almost as fine as Williamsburg, and not reconstructed," in the words of our tour guide. Even the new downtown parking garages blend into the historic scene.

Steeped though it is in the past, Frederick wears well its latter-day theme as "Cinderella City." Its proximity to the Baltimore-Washington megalopolis has turned it into the fastest growing city in Maryland, an up-to-date community of 40,000 with a vision and a sense of place tied to its past.

Tourism is said to be the area's second largest industry. Many are attracted by Newmarket, a one-street town called the antiques capital of Maryland, just east of the city. Others head west to Antietam, the graveyard of the Civil War. At the center of it all is Frederick, a delightful blend of old and new.

Inn Spots

Tyler-Spite House, 112 West Church St., Frederick 21701. (301) 831-4455 or (800) 417-3264.

History was made here in 1814 when Dr. John Tyler, who performed the nation's first cataract surgery, built this classic three-story Federal mansion to prevent the city from extending Record Street through to the National Pike. The foundation was constructed literally overnight out of spite: hence the name.

New owners Bill and Andrea Myer worked quickly, too, opening Frederick's first downtown B&B in 1990 and adding the adjacent **Lane House** a year later. Bill, a retired Montgomery County school administrator, oversees the operation while his wife handles her court-stenographer business based in Gaithersburg.

A beauty of a place is this, boasting thirteen-foot-high ceilings and full of priceless antiques. It's blessed with a lush rear garden courtyard and the only swimming pool in downtown Frederick. The Philippine mahogany desk upon which guests register in the main hall was used by Gen. Douglas MacArthur to sign the peace treaty in Manila. The mirror in the hall is tall enough that Abe Lincoln is believed to have used it to adjust his hat during his Frederick visit. The chandeliers are reproductions from the Tryon Palace in New Bern, N.C. The stunning oriental screen in the library is a reproduction of the 14th-century "The Last Emperor." The Music Room harbors a Packard Victorian pump organ, a 1914 Ludwig grand piano, a victrola and a tiny child's piano, a Christmas present for the Myers' young daughter, Annalee. Most of the eight working fireplaces sport imported carved marble mantels. Next door in the Lane House are

crystal doorknobs, Chinese Chippendale beds and an 1820 chandelier of Waterford glass.

"Once guests get here, a private bath is not an issue," Bill says. We had booked a room and simply assumed we had a private bath, mention of which is carefully avoided in the inn's literature. It turned out we did get a private bath, since the house was not full, but otherwise three of the five rooms in the Tyler-Spite share baths. Only the honeymoon suite among the four Lane House rooms has its own facilities.

Guest rooms are commodious, most with queensize canopy beds and too many prized furnishings to enumerate. We were assigned originally to Bill's favorite Charles Parsons Room, third-floor front. It shares with the Barbara Fritchie Room a large carpeted hall bath, big enough to include a sitting area. The room comes with a queensize sleigh bed and a cane and rattan side chair made in the Philippines. The dresser was made of shipping cartons, the lamps are old sake bottles and a Japanese chest serves as a coffee table. We decided instead to settle in the Hood Room of what was then a two-bedroom suite, with an adjoining bath in between and a quieter, rear location overlooking the garden. (It since has been rechristened the Mosby Suite, the second bedroom having been turned into a living room with queensize sofa bed and the bath having been rehabbed with a whirlpool tub and a "rainforest" shower.)

Decanters of cream sherry are in every room, supplementing the exceptional teatime spread –at our visit, lemonade, tea, wine, watermelon slices, cookies, an extravagant strawberry cake, cheese and crackers. Sometimes there are tea sandwiches. Breakfast is a gustatory treat as well, served on the patio or, with some pomp and circumstance, in the large and formal dining room graced by fancy wallpaper and a Chippendale screen in the corner. Juice and fresh fruits precede such main dishes as Roosevelt eggs scrambled with cream cheese, baked apple dumplings, creamed chipped beef or, at our visit, airy belgian waffles topped with fresh peaches and whipped cream.

The 1820 Lane House has a parlor and dining room with fourteen-foot ceilings, matching fireplaces and a bible door unique to the area in between. Its guests also enjoy an enclosed rear porch with a tin roof, sofas and a TV, a sleek black and white kitchen, and an outside deck on two levels surrounding a giant swamp magnolia tree.

An evening horse-drawn carriage ride through the historic district to a downtown restaurant of the guest's choice is offered on weekends.

Doubles, $120; suites, $175. No smoking.

Turning Point Inn, 3406 Urbana Pike, Frederick 21701. (301) 874-2421.

Set well back from the road on four nicely landscaped acres in the center of suburban Urbana, this Edwardian estate home with Georgian features is a full-service country inn known for its dining (see Dining Spots).

A gracious parlor is pretty in rose, pink and teal. It offers striped sofas, antique furniture, built-in bookshelves and a table with family pictures of innkeeper Charlie Seymour and his young son Tom as well as his mother and stepfather, Ellie and Bernie Droneburg, who founded the inn in 1985. The parlor separates the main dining rooms from the entry hall and a couple of small dining rooms on the other side.

Upstairs are five spacious guest rooms "out of the pages of House Beautiful," according to Charlie. All have private baths. The six-windowed Green Room contains two four-poster double beds and two upholstered chairs in a moss green decor. Steps are provided to climb into the queensize four-poster in the Blue Room. Fan windows overlook the countryside from two dormer rooms on the third floor, furnished in country style. The king-bedded room here has a whirlpool tub.

New and proving extremely popular are suites with TVs in outbuildings behind the inn. The three-level cottage contains a living room with wet bar and small refrigerator, a bathtub with jets on the mid level, and a kingsize bed and formal country decor upstairs. Furnished in what the staff calls "country quaint" style is the spacious Dairy House room with kingsize bed, wing chairs and a recliner.

A basket of fruit and a full country breakfast are included in the rates. The latter starts with assorted fresh fruit, juice and Swiss breakfast cereal. Then comes a choice

Tyler-Spite House backs up to garden courtyard and swimming pool.

of six entrées, from eggs creole or benedict to corned beef hash with eggs. Last but not least are the breakfast meats, including spicy andouille and sometimes wild boar sausage.

Doubles, $85; suites, $125 and $150.

Stone Manor, 5820 Carroll Boyer Road, Middletown 21769. (301) 473-5454.

Elegant suites of uncommon spaciousness, a fine dining experience and a rural location as part of a 114-acre working farm. These are among the attributes that distinguish this new country inn in the rolling hills southwest of Frederick.

The majestic, eighteen-room farmhouse dates to the late 1700s, with additions built in 1830 and the 1970s. "It was always a private residence and we want to keep that feeling," said Judith Harne, general manager and one of the five local business investors who bought it in 1991 to run as a B&B and restaurant (see Dining Spots).

They maintain the feeling of a country home – albeit one of considerable means – very nicely. The five suites are spaced well apart throughout the structure. Each is stylishly furnished with antiques and comes with extravagant bath facilities and tables for "in-suite dining" (used for breakfast and special-occasion dinners). Three have private porches and two have working fireplaces.

Largest and most formal is the second-floor Gardenia Suite with working fireplaces in both the living room and bedroom, a queensize rice-carved four-poster bed, crown molding around the ceiling, and unusual window treatments in which swags and sheers are pulled to one side. The canopied queen bed in the main-floor Hibiscus Suite is draped entirely in white. Vintage clothing and toys, including a pair of old figure skates, are hung instead of artworks in the main-floor Trillium Suite, charming for its Shaker-style poster bed and colorful antique quilt and quilted pillows.

But it is the bath facilities that command most attention. The Gardenia comes with a whirlpool bath for two, a separate shower, a double vanity and the thickest carpet

151

imaginable. The Thistle, the smallest, has a double whirlpool bath in a corner of the bedroom, opposite the poster bed and not far from the dining table. And the Laurel Suite in the oldest section of the original farmhouse masks well its antiquity with a jetted shower spraying from six directions, a room with pedestal sink, toilet and bidet, and another vanity beside the oversize whirlpool, in which the waters are illuminated from below like a swimming pool.

Guests are welcomed with a plate of fruits and cheeses, delivered to the sitting areas of their rooms. In the morning, continental breakfast is served on the formal dining table in the room. The fare consists of juice, fruit, yogurt and breads.

There are lots of good magazines for perusing in the library at the top of the stairway. Outside are gardens, a pond, a stream and working farmlands and forests, from which deer might emerge to feed at the pear trees or drink from the fountain.

Doubles, $125 to $250.

Middle Plantation Inn, 9549 Liberty Road, Frederick 21701. (301) 898-7128.

The "rustic bed and breakfast" description on its brochure best describes this place ten minutes east of town in Mount Pleasant. Or does it? Fronting on a suburban highway amid tract homes, it's really much more.

Shirley and Dwight Mullican tore down his grandfather's farmhouse on 26 acres and rebuilt in 1989 from the ground up, using logs, beams and floors from the original house. "So it looks old," says Shirley, "but has all the modern conveniences."

Guests enter through a rear keeping room, cozy with a tall corner stone fireplace, a skylight and built-in stained-glass windows separating it from the Mullicans' quarters on the main floor. Upstairs are three guest rooms with private baths, each bearing novel touches but contemporary amenities like plush carpeting and hidden TVs. Dwight's elaborate hand stenciling graces the Victorian Room, which contains a carved walnut bed, a Victorian loveseat and side chair. There's a modern shower stall beside the clawfoot tub. Old hunting prints and white pine country furniture are in the Hunt Room, where the TV is hidden in the corner washstand and an old icebox with a shelf is for storing clothes. The rear Plantation Room has more stenciling, a tester canopy bed and the original poplar floor.

The most private lodging is in the Log Room with its own entrance at one side of the house, finished inside and out with logs. A colorful quilt brightens the blue iron bed, the TV is found in a dry sink, a harness holds the mirror and a pottery bowl serves as the washstand. Mints and vases of fresh flowers are in each room.

Breakfast in the keeping room is continental-plus, involving juice, fresh fruit, homemade breads and muffins, pastries and cheese.

Doubles, $85. No smoking.

Spring Bank, 7945 Worman's Mill Road, Frederick 21701. (301) 694-0440 or (800) 400-4667.

This is out in the country, on ten acres sandwiched between two busy highways. The brick building with verandas and cupolas built in 1880 as a country house shows its age.

Beverly and Ray Compton became only the third owners of the house when they acquired it in 1980 and started taking in guests, restoring as they went along. Because it is listed on the National Register, restoration is minimal and the Comptons maintain it as it was. All beds are double and only one of five guest rooms has a private bath; the others share two old tiled baths. Despite ongoing and painstaking restoration, some of the original frescoed ceilings and deep plaster moldings have become frayed in the rooms and dark, narrow corridors.

Deluxe Gardenia Suite is ready for guests at Stone Manor.

Rooms are furnished in dark and heavy Victorian style, with velvet chairs, armoires, carved headboards and inside shutters on the windows. A sleigh bed is smack in the middle of one room beneath a silver chandelier. A rear room with a lace canopy bed and black leather loveseat, chair and rocker has direct access to the upstairs side veranda.

Well-worn orientals lead into a parlor outfitted with a velvet sofa and chairs and one of three large bow windows that brighten the house. A library has TV and leather chairs, and there's a pipe organ inside the front door. A continental breakfast of fresh fruits and warm pastries is served on trays in the rooms, or buffet-style in the parlor if there's a full house.

Doubles, $75 to $90.

Strawberry Inn, 17 Main St., New Market 21774. (301) 865-3318.

Innkeepers Jane and Ed Rossig used to go antiquing in New Market and then have dinner at the famed Mealey's restaurant, like thousands before and after them. They bought their 1837 farmhouse in the center of town in 1973 for retirement from New Jersey. "We started restoring it and the mayor said, 'why don't you open a place to stay in this little town?'" recalls Jane. They gutted the building and reopened as a guest house, which took off immediately. "We didn't feel right sending people off without even a cup of coffee," says Jane. But four years passed before they added the breakfast part of their B&B.

The oldest B&B in Frederick County has weathered well as the Rossigs have moved into semi-retirement. They now offer five guest rooms with private baths, all furnished in Victoriana. One on the first floor with twin beds has its own side porch. The large upstairs rooms contain queen or two double beds, and one has a sitting room with a Victorian loveseat overlooking the rear garden. Common areas include a living room,

153

a small front porch with rockers up against the sidewalk, a formal dining room with individual tables and a lovely grapevine-covered back porch. A continental-plus breakfast of fruit, cereal and homemade muffins, banana bread or soda bread is served in the dining room or on the porch.

Wild strawberries still grow along Strawberry Alley beside the house, from which the inn derives its name. The long back yard includes a gazebo, a distant patio where tomatoes grow beside park benches and a log house containing Rossig's Art & Framing gallery and the owners' quarters.

Doubles, $75 to $95. No credit cards.

National Pike Inn, 9-11 West Main St., New Market 21774. (301) 865-5055.

Almost next door to the Strawberry Inn and across the street from Mealey's restaurant, this five-year-old B&B offers five rooms, three with private baths. The brown brick Federal house with a distinctive widow's watch atop is named for the nation's first federally funded highway. The house was built in three stages from 1796, accounting for the fact the upstairs bedrooms are on different levels. Owners Tom and Terry Rimel have furnished them in a mix of Federal and Victorian decors.

An oriental rug covers the original wide-plank floor in the attractive parlor, fashioned from two rooms and containing an organ. A full breakfast, perhaps pancakes or eggs, is served at a lace-covered table in the dining room or on a pleasant side courtyard, furnished with a table and lounge chairs and surrounded by azalea gardens, sculptured bird bath and fountain.

Two windsor chairs, a rocker and a queensize brass bed are in the red and white rear bedroom. Toward the front and up a bit from the smallish Oak Room are the Victorian Room, where a floral comforter on the spindle bed matches the draperies, and the Canopy Room with, of course, a canopy bed and a loveseat. Floral print fabrics cover the queensize bed and facing daybed and match the curtains in the newest room, lately vacated by one of the Rimel sons. Two mints are at each bedside.

Doubles, $75 to $125.

Antietam Overlook Farm, Porterstown Road, Keedysville 21756. (301) 432-4200 or (800) 878-4241.

From the large rear porch, guests can see the Antietam National Battlefield, the town of Sharpsburg and mountains in four states. The view isn't all they get at one of the more comfortably elegant new B&Bs we've seen in a long time. They get five

Private porches are among amenities at elegant Antietam Overlook Farm.

154

Wide wraparound veranda is a feature for guests at Inn at Antietam.

queen-bedded suites, each with gas-burning fireplace, its own screened porch and a tub surrounded by plants; a plush common room that's made for conversation in front of a huge fireplace; a table of cordials from which to help themselves after dinner, and a "groaning plate" of a country breakfast.

"I didn't think I was the only person in the world who likes a porch and a bubble bath," Barbara Dreisch said after opening her B&B with husband John. They added a contemporary wing to their existing 19th-century-style farmhouse on 95 acres and let the fun begin.

"Country but state of the art" is how Barbara describes it. The suites are carpeted, the fireplaces are operated by remote-control from the beds, the individual porches have two comfy chairs, the open steeping tubs fairly cry out for a bubble bath and there are sit-down showers in the bathrooms, where a basket of extras includes shaving cream, hair dryer and curling iron.

If you can tear yourself away from your own little heaven, you'll find a small kitchen area with welcoming wine or lemonade and an instant hot-water tap for tea or hot chocolate. Beyond is the Country Room, a vast sitting room with dining area paneled, like the rest of the house, in rough barnwood. Off this is the big rear porch with four-state view. The dining area is where John provides the "groaning plate" in the morning, perhaps pancakes with honey, muesli, hot homemade applesauce, bacon and homemade sausage balls, pitchers of orange juice and carafes of coffee. The day before our visit he served English broil with mushrooms and tomatoes and french toast made with thick raisin bread, coffee creamer and amaretto.

The house sits by itself atop a ridge in the middle of nowhere. The Dreisches give directions via a roundabout route so guests don't pass the shanties of hillbilly country that lie close to this fantasyland. The direct route from Sharpsburg is much shorter.

Doubles, $103 to $148. No smoking.

Inn at Antietam, 220 East Main St., Box 119, Sharpsburg 21782. (301) 432-6601.
A sign over the clawfoot tub in the rustic Smoke House suite here says "showers are for the strivers of the world." When guests see that, says innkeeper Betty Fairbourn, "they're content with the tub." And why not? The suite has a fireplace, a loft bed, a wet bar, barnwood walls, oriental rugs on the floors and a sofabed in the sitting room.

Betty and Cal Fairbourn, GMAC transfers who moved here from Salt Lake City,

155

took over a 1908 farmhouse that was "not as old as we'd like it to be." They've made do quite nicely, furnishing in country and Victorian styles with goods acquired from area estate sales. They offer four rooms that are more like suites with sitting areas and private baths. Each is decorated gracefully and without clutter.

Guests enjoy a slate-floor solarium at the entry, a formal parlor and a front veranda that wraps around the house to an attractive rear patio. Breakfast is served at a long table in the formal dining room beside an ornate glass china cabinet. Juice, melon, waffles with local strawberries and bacon were the fare at our visit. Blueberry pancakes, egg dishes and blintzes might be available other days. Afternoon tea, snacks and homemade cookies are offered on the patio with a view of the Blue Ridge Mountains.

Doubles, $105; two-night minimum on weekends.

Piper House B&B, Route 65, Sharpsburg 21782. (301) 797-1862.

Most people who stay here are serious Civil War buffs, say innkeepers Regina and Lou Clark. That's understandable, for this is the mid-19th-century log and frame farmhouse that Confederate General James Longstreet claimed as his headquarters during the bloodiest single day of the Civil War. The house evokes haunting memories, situated as it is, surrounded by the Antietam National Battlefield and just down the road from the park entrance.

The Clarks saved the B&B in 1994. Its former principals, Hagerstown residents whose occupation is restoring old buildings, had decided to give up their long-term lease from the National Park Service. When word got out among Civil War buffs regarding the planned closing of the house, protests came from all over the country. The Clarks learned about it, visited the property and quickly negotiated a new long-term lease. Of the potential lessees, "we were the only married couple who wanted to live on-site," Regina said. They moved in and found it "simply wonderful to live in an historic home on federal property."

They share their small treasure with overnight guests in three bedrooms with private baths. Each is simply but attractively furnished to the Civil War period. The Clarks have tried to make the rooms more comfortable, and their live-in presence adds a dimension heretofore lacking. There are a couple of small downstairs parlors and an upstairs sitting room and rear screened porch. Regina serves guests a continental-plus breakfast of juice, fruit compote, cereals, muffins, breads and pastries at a long table in the kitchen.

The old slave house, smoke house and stone root cellar out front add to the Civil War ambiance here.

Doubles, $89.

Dining Spots

Stone Manor, 5820 Carroll Boyer Road, Middletown. (301) 473-5454.

For some of the most pure, exciting food in the area, drive fifteen minutes or so into the countryside southwest of town to this restored restaurant and country inn. It's in an impressive fieldstone manor house, and the experience is likened to that of dining in a private home – which it was, for its first 200 years.

Five local business investors have turned it into a refined restaurant of distinction. Dining is in the main beamed and stone dining room with an enormous fieldstone fireplace and damask-covered tables seating a total of 25 to 30, in a private room set for ten or twelve, or in the gracious living room, where lace mats top the fine polished tables.

Impressive fieldstone structure is home to Stone Manor, country inn and restaurant.

Periodic cooking demonstrations, a remarkably extensive wine cellar and special wine dinners attest to the fact that this is a restaurant that takes food and drink seriously. Chefs John Walla and Ann Donahue grow many of their own vegetables and herbs and acquire others from nearby purveyors.

The menu is prix-fixe, $45 for four courses with two or three choices in each course, or $55 for a pre-selected seven-course dinner. Add $20 or $25 respectively for wines with each course.

A typical meal might start with an amuse-gueule, warm avocado soup with truffled parsley oil and gulf shrimp, seared sea scallops with puree of snow peas and carrot threads and a ragout of Pennsylvania escargots with local shiitakes in puff pastry. An intermezzo sorbet (and perhaps an adjournment for a short walk in the gardens) precedes the main course, which could be roasted pheasant with wild rice cake. For the grand finale, you might find a chocolate mousse torte drizzled with white chocolate.

Other main courses in this talented kitchen's repertoire could be papillote of Pacific halibut with lobster medallions and gulf shrimp with organic basil, summer squash and baby carrots; herbed roast chicken stuffed with shiitakes and sundried tomatoes, or pan-grilled filet of beef with potato pancakes and green peppercorn sauce.

Brunch and lunch are offered in three courses for $25. Expect treats like a gratin of blue crab with creamed corn and crispy leeks, a frittata of curried sea scallops and sweet peppers, and black raspberry ice cream with a pineapple compote.

Because this is a favorite place for private functions and because of its out-of-the-way location, meals are served by reservation only and the schedule may vary.

Lunch, Tuesday-Saturday 11 to 2; Sunday brunch, 11 to 3; dinner, Tuesday-Saturday 6 to 9, Sunday 3 to 6.

Tauraso's, 6 East St. at Everedy Square, Frederick. (301) 663-6600.
This is quite an establishment, from the old Jaguar sometimes parked in front of the entry to a sleek dining room to the enormous, high-ceilinged **Victor's Saloon & Raw Bar** in the original Victor's Home Remedies patent medicine business that paved the

way for the old Everedy factory. The Jaguar is "our mascot – I drive it every day," said Dr. Nicola Tauraso, a physician who opened the restaurant in 1987 for his son Michael, a talented chef not long out of Rhode Island's Johnson & Wales culinary program. "This is the toughest business I've been in," says Nick, who's been involved in his share. The place seats 300 and is open every day except Christmas.

Although there's considerable show, the food is taken seriously here. We've seldom been served a better pasta dish than the luncheon special of linguini with seared grouper fillet, marinated green olives, roasted garlic and white wine ($7.95), accompanied by a dish of grated parmesan cheese. We also liked the homemade seafood sausage with pepper and olive compote ($5.25) and the focaccia seasoned with sage, oregano and garlic. The cappuccino, dusted with fresh nutmeg and served like most drinks here in glass mugs, arrived with an amaretto cookie. All this was delivered by a tuxedoed staff at white wrought-iron tables on a large outdoor courtyard under a red, black and white canopy, beside a trickling fountain.

The soaring interior dining room is just as dramatic. Its high black ceiling contrasts with exposed ducts painted pinkish-mauve. The black marbled tables bear huge white service plates emblazoned with the Tauraso logo. An extensive list of daily specials supplements an ambitious menu. Dinner prices range from $7.95 for one of the eight pasta dishes to $23.95 for rack of lamb with mushrooms and port wine. Your only difficulty may be settling on a choice among entrée salads and light fare (chicken caesar salad, salad of duck confit) and gourmet pizzas fresh from the wood-fired oven, and specials like peppered tuna with braised vegetable ragout and sundried tomatoes or grilled rockfish with tomato-basil vinaigrette.

Bananas foster, chocolate mousse, blueberry cobbler, cannoli and Italian ice creams are possible dessert selections. A staggering wine list has great range in both price and origin and is computerized for changes every week.

Open daily, 11 to 11.

The Province Restaurant, 131 North Market St., Frederick. (301) 663-1441.

Billed as a bistro-style restaurant, this is not French as its name might suggest, but creative American and international, in the words of co-owner Nancy Floria. It takes its name from the 1767 deed to the property, when the area was known as the Province

Michael and Nicola Tauraso have made Tauraso's a busy and versatile establishment.

Snowshoe chairs and handmade quilts are decorative hallmarks of The Province Restaurant.

of Maryland. The brick walls of the first building on the site form the central part of the restaurant, which is cozy and historic in the front and middle, and opens onto an airy garden room addition in back.

The last is a stunning space for lunch, overlooking a flower and herb garden eked out between downtown buildings. New Age music plays against a backdrop of brick floors, comfortable snowshoe chairs and handmade quilts on the walls. Here we enjoyed chilled peach soup, a seafood pasta salad, a brie and almond pâté and a Greek salad. An orange mousse cake from a dessert tray bearing at least nine yummy desserts was a light and refreshing ending.

At night, prix-fixe dinners including salad, entrée and dessert range from $13.95 to $17.95 on weekdays. The full menu also is available and is offered on weekends. It's priced from $12.95 for tortellini with sweet Italian sausage or Southwestern grilled chicken to $18.95 for porterhouse steak. The house-made pâté, hummus and pita, antipasto plate, spanakopita and crab imperial in potato shells lend an international flavor to the appetizers.

Desserts range from hazelnut cream cake to derby pie to Washington apple cake. They are made daily at the Bake Shop at **Province II,** a caterer, baker and sandwich maker at 12 East Patrick St.

Lunch, Monday-Friday 11:30 to 3; dinner, Tuesday-Saturday 5:30 to 9 or 10; Saturday brunch, 11:30 to 3; Sunday, brunch 11 to 3:30, dinner 4 to 8.

The Brown Pelican, 5 East Church St., Frederick. (301) 695-5833.

Pelicans are the theme of this elegant basement restaurant in a downtown building. They appear on drawings and paintings on the walls, in an etched-glass partition separating the bar from the dining room, and atop the oversize parchment menu that arrives rolled up like a scroll and refuses to lie flat. The atmosphere is serene: white-linened tables, captain's chairs, fieldstone walls and beamed ceilings.

Scallops scampi and crab norfolk might supplement the nearly two dozen entrées on the continental dinner menu, which seldom changes and appeals to traditionalists. Priced from $12.95 to $18.95, it includes walnut bourbon chicken, shrimp Louisiana, lobster savannah, roast duckling with orange or green peppercorn sauce, mixed grill (filet, pork chop and German sausage) and New York strip steak. Appetizers cover all the bases from marinated herring and shrimp cocktail to baked brie and escargots. Six pasta dishes and caesar salad are listed under appetizers for two or more.

Some of the dinner entrées and pastas turn up on the lunch menu ($7.50 to $9.95). Interesting salads and sandwiches also are available.

Lunch, Monday-Friday 11:30 to 3; dinner nightly, 5 to 9:30 or 10.

Turning Point Inn, 3406 Urbana Pike, Frederick. (301) 874-2421.

For a special-occasion meal out in the country, this glamorous spot is where many locals go. The view of the surrounding landscape from the large garden-style dining room through floor-to-ceiling windows is lovely. Rose tablecloths, rattan chairs and vases of alstroemeria add to the setting. Two small, formal dining rooms are located on the other side of the entry.

Dinner entrées are priced from $13.95 for chicken dijon to $19.95 for twin tournedos with roquefort sauce. Choices include pan-seared Atlantic salmon with chive butter sauce, shrimp and scallops sauté, pecan-crusted rainbow trout sautéed with sage and prosciutto, roasted duck with raspberry sauce, grilled pork loin with roasted corn, black beans and tasso ham, and rack of lamb with rosemary, roasted garlic and pan-seared spinach. Nightly specials could be shrimp creole, chardonnay-steamed halibut and soft-shell crabs meunière.

Popular starters are lobster stew, caesar salad and country pâté with cornichons. Or you could opt for a white pizza with fontina and herbs. Homemade desserts include Kentucky derby pie, apple crisp, applesauce cake with caramel sauce, citrus cake with strawberry sauce and raspberry bread pudding.

The lunch menu features things like smoked turkey club sandwich, seafood salad melt, crab cake sandwich, grilled salmon fillet, and potato and leek pancake with smoked salmon, red onion, dill and sour cream.

Lunch, Tuesday-Friday 11:30 to 2; dinner, Tuesday-Saturday 5 or 5:30 to 9 or 9:30; Sunday, brunch 11:30 to 2, dinner 4 to 8:30. No smoking.

Bushwaller's Market Street Saloon, 209 North Market St., Frederick. (301) 694-5697.

There's quite a history attached to this atmospheric establishment, all spelled out in detail on the back of the menu. Started as a house, it became a drug store, dry goods store and liquor store before the Bushwaller brothers converted it into a seafood saloon. Photos, clippings and such on the brick walls are family artifacts and make for interesting perusal for those who get there early or during off-hours. Tables are dressed in mint green and white, there's a pressed-tin ceiling, and beer, ale and stout are dispensed from a long, old exposed-wood bar.

The attention to detail extends to the food, this offering some of the more interesting seafood fare among many mid-level downtown restaurants. At dinner, how about grilled yellowfin tuna with soy and ginger, crab imperial or shrimp, crab and lobster sauté? There are showy veal, beef and chicken dishes as well, on a menu priced from $9.95 to $14.95 (for steak diane or flounder stuffed with crab imperial). Sautéed alligator tail and crab-stuffed mushrooms are among appetizers. Salads, light fare, sandwiches and raw-bar items also are available. Death by chocolate cake, strawberry parfait and mile-high mud pie are desserts of choice.

The wine list is nothing to write home about, but most of the patrons seem to be into piña coladas or beer, anyway. Live bands play here on weekends.

Lunch daily, 11:30 to 5; dinner, 5 to 9 or 10.

160

Fieldstone walls and beamed ceilings are backdrop for dining at The Brown Pelican.

DiFrancesco's, 26 North Market St., Frederick. (301) 695-5499.

A beamed ceiling, arches and hanging brass lamps lend a country Italian look to this local favorite. There's lots to look at, from the brick bar to the alcoves and niches filled with pottery and the pottery jugs filled with carnations on each white-clothed table.

Paul DiFrancesco's highly regarded homemade pastas are featured, $4.50 to $5.95 for lunch and $10.95 to $11.95 at dinner. Fettuccine with prosciutto and peas, fettuccine with smoked salmon, linguini calabrese, lasagna and cannelloni are a few of the choices. Entrées run from $11.50 for chicken cacciatore to $18.95 for surf and turf (filet mignon and grilled shrimp with pesto sauce). Five veal dishes are offered, as are mixed grills and filet mignon ($16.95) from the wood grill. Some regulars say they've never ordered anything but the manicotti, the the best around. Among appetizers are fried mozzarella and fried calamari. Assorted pastries make up the dessert tray. The short but serviceable wine list is priced mainly in the teens.

Lunch, Tuesday-Friday 11:30 to 3; dinner nightly, 5 to 10; Sunday brunch, 11 to 3.

Alpenhof Restaurant, 137 North Market St., Frederick. (301) 662-2866.

The Starving Artist Cafe gave way to this Swiss-German restaurant specializing in the cuisine of Anneliese Kalman, who hails from the German-speaking section of Switzerland. She and husband Alex and their offspring have fashioned a cheery atmosphere in peach and green with floral tablecloths and fresh flowers. Swiss cowbells and banners from the different cantons hang from the ceiling, and huge photos of Switzerland adorn the walls.

The menu is predictable, except perhaps for the low prices. Dinner entrées run from $9.95 for grilled chicken through geschnetzeltes and schnitzels in the mid-teens to $16.95 for delmonico steak with roesti potatoes. A plate of smoked pork loin with assorted sausages, sauerkraut and parsley potatoes can be had for $12.50; goulash and chicken viennese are $10.95. Good German bread accompanies. Start with pickled herring or cheese tartlets. Finish with black forest cake or strudel. Nurse a German beer or a Swiss wine. You couldn't do better in the Old Country.

Lunch, Tuesday-Saturday 11:30 to 3; dinner, 5 to 10, Sunday noon to 8. Closed Monday.

161

Cafe Kyoko, 10 East Patrick St., Frederick. (301) 695-9656.

Upstairs over Province II is this intriguing Japanese-Thai combination, a branch of Restaurant Kyoko in Washington, D.C. The high-ceilinged room could be any restaurant in Frederick, except for a couple of fancy chandeliers and some hanging lanterns on the landing and, of course, an authentic sushi bar. The third floor has a dining room with cushions on the floor.

The menu pairs Japanese tempura, teriyaki, sukiyaki and such side by side with Thai standards like goong-pad and seafood pattaya, at prices from $8.95 to $13.95. The sushi choices are extensive, and Japanese and Indian beers are on tap.

Lunch, Monday-Friday 11:30 to 2; dinner, Monday-Saturday 5:30 to 9 or 10.

The Orchard Restaurant, 48 East Patrick St., Frederick. (301) 663-4912.

There are more ethnic and seafood restaurants in downtown Frederick, but how about a change of pace? This vegetarian-oriented establishment fills the bill with two upstairs dining rooms crisp in cream and butcher-block with teal and mauve accents.

Salads, sandwiches and other vegetarian fare are supplemented by stir-fries and steamed dinners to appeal to most persuasions. Try them Japanese, Chinese, Indian, European, Indonesian or Creole style, with tofu, chicken or shrimp. They're priced at $4.50 to $5.95 for lunch, $7 to $10 at night. Dinner entrées ($10 to $13.50) might be honey-mustard chicken, shrimp scampi or seafood linguini putanesca. Lunchtime specials at our visit were Southwest corn chowder, an omelet with brie and black pepper, soft-shell crab sandwich and falafel with tahini sauce.

Open Tuesday-Saturday, lunch 11:30 to 2:30, dinner 5 to 9.

Mealey's Restaurant, 8 Main St., New Market. (301) 865-5488.

Dating to 1793, this old hotel turned into a dining institution is, as its name might imply, a place for a good meal. After a kitchen fire, owners Jose and Pat Salaverri rebuilt, to the approval of their large and loyal following. The main beamed dining room is dark, authentic and almost too atmospheric for words. Check out the vintage Wurlitzer jukebox near the entry in the bar.

The menu stresses seafood, from broiled scallops to shrimp stuffed with crab imperial, shrimp scampi and crab cakes. Other entrées are priced from $9.95 for half a fried spring chicken to $15.95 for lamb loin chops or filet mignon. Crab bisque, baked escargots and smoked baby trout are among appetizers. Favored desserts are homemade cheesecake with raspberry sauce and bread pudding with bourbon sauce. Maryland selections are featured on the wine list.

Lunch, Friday and Saturday 11:30 to 2:30; dinner, Tuesday-Saturday 5 to 9, Sunday noon to 8.

Diversions

Historic Frederick. The historic district embraces 33 blocks of central Frederick, but the important structures are concentrated along eight short blocks of downtown. The downtown Visitor Center offers a map for a short walking tour, but its 90-minute guided walking tour given weekends and holidays at 1:30 is well worth the $4.50 tab. Many of the fascinating sights (and insights) we were told about aren't detailed in the written tour. Among these are the unique top hats atop dormer windows, the cast-iron dog stolen by Confederate soldiers desperate for bullets and later returned and resting today in front of Dr. John Tyler's Home and the unbelievably realistic murals painted on downtown store walls under the city's Angels in the Architecture program. You see the law offices of Roger Brooke Taney and Francis Scott Key (famous brothers-in-

Antietam was scene of bloodiest one-day battle of Civil War.

law, one a Supreme Court justice known for the Dred Scott Decision and the other the author of the National Anthem) opposite City Hall and Court House Square. Other tour highlights: the oldest consecrated Catholic church in the country, the oldest ginkgo tree in the country across from the synagogue, the Barbara Fritchie House and Museum (open Thursday-Monday or by appointment, $2), the home of the first president of the Continental Congress, the Historical Society of Frederick County (same hours and price as Fritchie House, but free to walking-tour participants) and stately townhouses, mansions and public buildings shaded by trees and parks. Of particular interest are the stained-glass windows in All Saints Episcopal Church, one side of which is original Tiffany glass, beneath a ceiling that is a replica of Noah's Ark.

Carroll Creek Park. A new promenade and linear corridor, the result of a flood-control project, stretch nearly a mile and a half through the city's heart. Benches, fountains, plantings, wood sculptures and a bridge with trompe-l'oeil stone walls are among diversions for passersby. The first **Frederick Festival of the Arts** was a huge success here in 1994, and more activities and commercial and office developments were in the works along the creek banks. Already, an old mill has been turned into the **Delaplaine Visual Arts Center** at 40 South Carroll St. and the **Frederick Brewing Company** started brewing Blue Ridge beers and ales and giving weekend tastings and tours at its microbrewery at 103 South Carroll St.

War Memorabilia. Frederick, a city where families and friends were divided by the War Between the States, is a center for devotees of the Civil War. It's centrally located between Gettysburg, Antietam and Harpers Ferry, among the more significant sites. More than 500 Confederate soldiers are buried in the city's vast **Mount Olivet Cemetery.** The Revolutionary War **Hessian Barracks,** the only surviving structures of the Civil War hospital complex here, are nearby. The National Civil War Medical Museum was scheduled to open in 1995 on West Patrick Street. A new visitor center serves visitors at **Monocacy National Battlefield,** where Confederate General Jubal Early's advance on Washington was delayed long enough to allow Union reinforcements to enter and save the city.

Antietam National Battlefield. This battlefield is another story. One of America's best preserved (and least crowded) battlefields, it was the site of the bloodiest battle in U.S. history. More than 23,000 men on both sides were killed or wounded on Robert

E. Lee's first invasion of the north on Sept. 17, 1862. Antietam Creek "actually ran red that day," we were told by our Frederick walking-tour guide. Pause at the visitor center to view the award-winning, 26-minute movie, "Antietam Visit." It's gripping, grisly and melancholy. An eight-mile-long tour road allows visitors to drive past important sites and more than 350 monuments, tablets, markers and cannons. Adults, $1.

Antiquing in Newmarket. Just off the interstate, this little one-street town crossed by alleys is heaven for antiquers. The village that originally served as a stopover for travelers on the National Pike between Baltimore and Frederick has staked its reputation on being a destination for those with a serious interest in antiques. More than 30 shops are tucked in and behind houses in a half-mile stretch. There's not a souvenir shop or boutique in sight, and the Newmarket General Store and Kitchen is a chapter from the past. Most shops are open only the latter half of the week or on weekends.

Shopping. Frederick's downtown has never been lost, and even retained a local department store into the early 1990s. Although boutiques and crafts shops have sprouted up, it still has a barber shop located on the main street, where the window was filled with old glass milk bottles and seven men were waiting on a Tuesday morning for the three chairs. And people are apt to say hello; even the policeman bade us good morning and the meter maid awarded us a reprieve with a courtesy parking ticket. The owners of the **Museum Shop,** well-known for restoring museum paintings, moved from Washington to Frederick to open a gallery of exotic works, including a line of cards and plates with animal prints; Frederick proved so responsive that they moved to larger quarters on North Market Street. **That Pottery Place** has lovely pottery. **Fredericktowne Jewelry & Leather Co.** is fun to browse through. Pick up a cinnamon-sugar pretzel or a pretzel pizza at **C.K.'s Pretzel Works** or hand-dipped chocolates from **The Candy Kitchen,** dispensing candy the old-fashioned way for 48 years.

There's another concentration of shops, some of them hard to find or get to, at the restored **Everedy Square & Shab Row** east of downtown. Wonderful specialty foods, chocolates and Maryland wines are among the offerings at **The Frederick Basket Company. The Kitchen Witch** stocks every gadget known to woman and quite a selection of Junior League cookbooks. **Flights of Fancy** is a colorful place on several levels with a New Age atmosphere, handmade items, educational toys and our favorite Salt Marsh Pottery from Massachusetts. **Highland Fling** is full of Scottish things, and **Misty Isles Irish Imports** speaks for itself.

Extra-Special

Lilypons Water Gardens, 6800 Lilypons Road, Buckeystown. (301) 874-5133.

If you've ever been interested in water gardening, and even if you haven't, you should drive out to this fascinating aquatic farm and shop (incidentally named for Lily Pons, the opera star) eight miles south of Frederick. Here are 300 acres of tranquility, with pond after pond containing lilies and lotus with names like queen of whites, glorisa, rosy morn, floating heart and pink sensation. Holding tanks in back of the shop contain koi, the colorful Japanese carp (some as expensive as $250), comets, calico fantails and the like. The shop carries everything one needs to start a water garden, from books to filters, pumps and pool de-icers. Lectures and demonstrations are offered from spring to fall. The annual Lotus Blossom Festival occurs around the middle of July when the lotus begin to bloom, and the Koi Festival takes place in early September. Any time, you can take a picnic, stroll around the ponds, and dream of your own lagoon-shaped pool with the underground lights, the fan fountain and the black Japanese snails, tadpoles and clams to help keep it all clean. Open daily 10 to 5, March-October.

Solomons, Md.
The Ultimate Watering Place

Barely a mile long, this strip of watery real estate conjures up many an image in the minds of Marylanders. They think of the shore, boating, bugeyes, crabbing, watermen, the Patuxent River and the Chesapeake Bay.

They also think of a village bustling with belated tourism development – a far cry from its earlier description as a typical coastal fishing village.

Typical it is not, this narrow peninsula jutting from the foot of the graceful Governor Thomas Johnson bridge that arches over the Patuxent widewaters as they empty into the bay. Airplanes soar overhead from the Patuxent Naval Air Station across the river. More boats seem to jockey for position in Solomons' deep-water harbor than in Annapolis. And more visitors from nearby cities descend during a summer weekend on what one booster calls "this sleepy little town" than it can possibly absorb.

Think of Ocean City – without the beaches and the high-rises – and you may get the picture. Life, though hectic on weekends, is quieter here along the bay and Maryland's western shore.

View from Calvert Marine Museum store.

Solomon's Island was named in 1870 for Isaac Solomon, who established the area's first oyster-packing facilities. The island part of the name was quickly dropped by the post office and Solomons really looks more like a peninsula than an island. It grew as a waterfront community, with a fishing fleet of more than 500 vessels, most built locally. More bugeyes – large, decked-over sailing canoes – were built here than in any bay community. Solomons gave birth to racing yachts of international fame. The maritime tradition continues today at the Calvert Marine Museum and the Chesapeake Biological Laboratory.

As with other resort communities of its ilk, this one is ever-changing. There were virtually no places to stay until a Holiday Inn opened in the mid-1980s. Today, Solomons has five bed-and-breakfast facilities offering a total of two dozen rooms. There are at

least a hundred times that many restaurant seats. "I've been here since 1977 and have seen a lot of coming and going," says shopkeeper Joann Kersey of all the changes.

What doesn't change is the inherent Solomons appeal – its watery aspects, the sailing, the charter fishing, the maritime museum and the natural attractions of a special watering place.

165

Inn Spots

Back Creek Inn, Calvert and A Streets, Box 520, Solomons 20688. (410) 326-2022.

Location, location, location. The Back Creek Inn has it, plus tranquility, beauty, artistry and sophistication. Artist Carol Pennock and gardener Lin Cochran offer seven elegant guest accommodations in a century-old waterman's house, a new addition and a great little cottage.

The pair were living in the area while their husbands were on military duty at Patuxent when the fledgling inn property became available. "It was love at first sight," Carol recalls. How could it be otherwise?

The house is a couple of blocks off the island's main street in a residential section along the waterfront. Thick foliage blocks the front entrance; a gnarled paper mulberry tree along the side path makes you duck or go around. The verdant side lawn slopes gently to the deep waters of wide Back Creek. In the midst of lavish English-style gardens is a hot tub with a patio beside and a view of all the waterway goings-on.

Guests are welcomed with iced tea in big blue glasses bearing the inn's logo. It's served in a comfy, contemporary, brick-floored common room with floor-to-ceiling windows on two sides to bring the outdoor garden in. Beyond are an open kitchen and a stenciled dining room where four tables are set for breakfast. Lyn's beautiful herbal wreaths and Carol's paintings enhance both common and guest rooms. The art of the latter, who works in a variety of media, is so striking that we had to buy a couple of her small renderings of oysters and clams.

Off the dining room on the main floor is a room with a brass double bed and private bath. Upstairs are three rooms with doubles or a king bed and shared baths. All are nicely decorated with frilly curtains, an abundance of pillows and quilts made by Carol's sister-in-law.

Two suites are in the addition that also serves as a studio and living quarters for the innkeepers. Both suites have sitting areas, TV sets and oversize beds; one faces the vegetable-herb garden and the other the hot tub. But we'd splurge again to stay in the cozy, peaked-ceilinged cottage, with a queensize bed, a bathroom in shades of mauve, TV, fireplace and an idyllic screened porch from which to view the water and gardens.

Breakfast was a treat, even though an overnight rain had made things too wet for the usual service outside on the patio when we were there. Juice, coffee and fancy breads awaited on side tables in the dining room as Carol took orders for her "Back Creek Bennies Our Way," superb eggs benedict with a sweet tang (ask her what the mystery ingredient is). These came garnished with fresh fruit, including kiwis and figs. Other choices might be a ham and cheese omelet, waffles topped with warm fruit compote or crab quiche – "when we have time to pick our own crabs off the pier," Carol advises. Sunday often brings a buffet with two different casseroles.

Doubles, $65 to $75; suites, $100; cottage, $125. Open February to mid-December. No smoking. No credit cards.

By-the-Bay Bed & Breakfast, 14374 Calvert St., Box 504, Solomons 20688. (410) 326-3428.

Owners Joan and Tom Hogenson spent six years renovating their Victorian house beside Back Creek before opening as a B&B in 1988. They stripped and refinished all the stained-pine woodwork. They painted the exterior a striking mulberry rose color with pink trim. She did the stenciling and he the stained glass in the front door and living room. Victoriana is the rule here – fairly dark in the living room and quite light and airy in the guest rooms.

Innkeepers Lin Cochran and Carol Pennock are ready for breakfast at Back Creek Inn.

The three bedrooms possess what Joan calls "an old-time flavor with modern comforts," such as private baths, queensize beds and TV sets. A main-floor bedroom off the dining room has a private entrance, a potbelly stove and a small refrigerator. It opens to an adjacent sitting room for optional use as a suite. Upstairs is a rear room with a step-up iron bed and plants in the windows. The front room has a recliner chair and a rocker. You'll find decorative touches like two old irons, but little of the clutter that fussies-up some other Victorian inns.

A full breakfast is served at a lace-draped table beneath an elaborate old chandelier in the dining room. Fresh fruit or baked apples, Tom's muffins, hot or cold cereal and omelets, french toast or strata could be the fare. The Hogensons offer a deep-water dock, a swing on the wraparound veranda, a rear patio, lovely rear gardens with statue and fountain, and a screened-in sitting room and terrace down by the water.

Doubles, $75; suite, $90. No credit cards. No smoking. Two-night minimum on weekends.

Davis House, 125 Charles St., Box 759, Solomons 20688. (410) 326-4811.
A turn-of-the-century Victorian house on a rise overlooking water on three sides,

this reflects the international style and tastes of Finnish-born Runa Howley and her husband Jack. Furnishings from across the world enhance the wicker library accented by lovely oriental screens, a formal dining room with lace curtains and oriental rugs, and a more formal living room in which a decanter of sherry tops a huge coffee table. Runa wishes she'd bought more of the unusual high-back canvas chairs that guests admire on the side veranda; "I could have sold a hundred of them by now," she says.

Four of six guest rooms on the second floor come with private baths. All have queen or twin beds that can be made up into kings and are nicely done in soft colors. Two afford good water views, one in the turret from windows on three sides. The ultimate for views, however, is the huge third-floor suite richly paneled in pine, segmented into separate areas by sloping ceilings with skylights. Big windows front and side frame water scenes, enjoyed from built-in lounging sofas or a modern white chair with otto-man and binoculars at the ready. Beige and blue carpeting provides a plush backdrop for the kingsize bed, a kitchenette and dining area.

There's no need to cook, however, for the Howleys offer a hearty breakfast. In-cluded are juices, fresh fruit and a choice of two main courses, perhaps pancakes with sausages or eggs benedict. Crab deviled eggs and hash made with ham, broccoli, pota-toes, green pepper and basil are other favorites.

While his parents were abroad for a two-year stint with the Agency for International Development in Budapest, Hungary, the inn was being run by newlyweds Julie and Mark Howley.

Doubles, $65 to $85; suite, $125. Two-night minimum on weekends. Smoking re-stricted.

Webster House, 14364 Sedwick Ave., Box 1607, Solomons 20688. (410) 326-0454.

Running a B&B was "an afterthought" for Peter and Barbara Prentice, who had envisioned opening a place for retreats for clergymen. "We were riding our bicycles and wondering where we'd live when we saw the old Webster house," reports Bar-bara. They demolished and rebuilt the house, designing it to look old in front. "We felt we were giving a new house a history."

Peter, a Navy physician, and Barbara opened their new/old house as a B&B in 1993. With their kids gone, Barbara said, "I missed having people around." The prime ac-commodations are out back in The Haven, upstairs over a detached garage, where a private deck overlooks the long back yard and catches a glimpse of the broad waters in Back Creek. Here you'll find a queensize bed, private bath, a little kitchen with a dining table and cable TV.

Two large bedrooms on the front of the second floor in the main house share a hall bath (plus a half bath on the main floor) and also share a third-floor common room with TV, videos and exercise equipment. The bright and airy Lydia Beekman Room, named for Peter's grandmother, has a queensize English oak bedstead, lacy curtains on the windows and a loveseat with a Scrabble game at the ready. The Vanderpoel Room, stately in green, contains a cherry four-poster queen bed and two armchairs.

The Webster House brochure advertises "a homey Christian atmosphere," although we did not find it obvious. Artist Carol Pennock from the nearby Back Creek Inn stenciled the grape pattern around the entry; Barbara made the china dolls that line the window seat. She got Amish carpenters to build the built-in shelves in the dining room. A rear family room opens into the country kitchen. Here is where Barbara pre-pares a full breakfast – a fruit cup followed perhaps by puff pancakes with strawber-ries, waffles, or eggs benedict with asparagus or zucchini. The meal is often taken on the rear porch beside the patio and gardens.

Solomons waterfront and soaring bridge are on view from suite at Davis House.

Iced tea and shortbread are served in the afternoon. In the evening, Barbara puts out candles so guests can soak in the outdoor spa by candlelight.

Doubles, $70; The Haven, $85. No credit cards. Two-night minimum on weekends.

Adina's Guest House, 14236 South Solomons Island Road, Solomons 20688. (410) 326-4895.

A wide front porch with comfortable lounge chairs faces the Patuxent River and the soaring Governor Thomas Johnson Bridge across a cornfield at this B&B, which opened in 1993. Inside are a large living room with dining area, five bedrooms and the quarters of owners Adelaida and Glen Papure, who have done considerable renovations to the house. The expense was such that both had to resume fulltime jobs and, while officially open year-round, they tend to concentrate on weekends.

The Papures offer four guest rooms with queensize beds and cable TV. Two on the main floor have private baths, while two upstairs share a bath. Opening of a third upstairs room awaited the completion of a second bathroom. The rooms have a variety of beds from sleigh to four-poster and are furnished with a few antique pieces in country style.

The Papures prepare a hearty breakfast of the guest's choice, including scrambled eggs with bacon, omelets or french toast, with fresh fruits and homemade muffins. Guests can make requests and "if I have it in my kitchen, I'll make it," says Adelaida.

The couple commute 90 minutes each way to their daytime jobs in Washington, D.C. Who said running a B&B in your spare time is easy?

Doubles, $65 to $80. No smoking.

Holiday Inn, Routes 2 and 4, Box 1099, Solomons 20688. (410) 326-6311.

This is not your typical Holiday Inn, and local tourism boosters claim it qualifies as a real inn rather than a formula motel. It's built around a big swimming pool and a lagoon, and certainly is big. A 150-room wing added in 1991 gives it a total of 326

169

rooms and the air of a resort and conference center. Unfortunately, most rooms lack direct access to the water, although a few suites have balconies, and outside doors of some rooms on the main floor open onto the grounds. Otherwise, rooms go off central corridors in two wings on four floors and could be anywhere.

Everything about the facility, including the attractive restaurant and lounge, makes it a better bet than the nearby Comfort Inn, the town's only other large lodging facility. We generally like Comfort Inns, but found the one at the Beacon Marina here to be a depressing exception as rock music blared across the swimming pool area and our room off a second-floor corridor offered a mere glimpse of the water and no access to the outside. And the $73 room tab put it right up there with the Holiday Inn, without its amenities. That's one of the hazards of visiting a town that lacks sufficient numbers of accommodations for busy periods.

Doubles, $76 to $87; suites, $95 to $160.

Dining Spots

Dry Dock Restaurant, C Street at Back Creek, Solomons. (410) 326-4817.

Part of the impressive Zahniser's Sailing Center, Dry Dock is upstairs over a small bathhouse with great views of the harbor. Innovative fresh seasonal cuisine is featured on the blackboard menu, which changes daily, and the food is considered the best in Solomons.

Decor is simple and nautical, with eight bare wood tables bearing paper napkins, pepper grinders and candles in globes. A lineup of signal flags frames large windows overlooking the busy waterfront. We watched with fascination the parade of boats finishing the weekly Wednesday night race. Racers accounted for much of the activity in the noisy bar, which is cheek to jowl with the tables in the small, L-shaped room.

Dinner began with a complimentary wooden board bearing Wispride cheese spread and assorted crackers. We liked the oyster stew ($3) better than the highly touted spinach salad with fruit and nuts ($5.25).

Good main courses were lightly breaded oysters and grilled tuna with tomato-basil salsa (both $16.95). They came with rice, broccoli and an abundance of non-edible garnishes. Prices ranged from $14.95 for barbecued chicken kabobs to $20.95 for surf and turf (prime rib and soft-shell crab). Other possibilities were blackened mahi-mahi, rosemary and garlic monkfish, pesto sea scallops, spiced squid platter, calamari and shrimp pasta and prime rib. Desserts included key lime pie, bourbon pecan pie and a number of chocolate extravagances.

Light dining is available at the outdoor bar beside the sailing center's pool in summer. The menu includes chef's salad, veggie pita, nachos and a few sandwiches (ham, turkey, BLT and variations thereof), $3.50 to $5.25. Muffins and bagels are available on weekends for breakfast.

Dinner, Monday-Thursday 6 to 9, Friday and Saturday, 5:30 to 9:30; Sunday, brunch 10 to 1:30, dinner 5:30 to 8:30. Closed two weeks in winter.

Lighthouse Inn, Patuxent Avenue, Solomons. (410) 326-2444.

The bar here is in a skipjack, the Spirit of Solomons, custom-built in the restaurant. It's a conversation piece at a contemporary, high-ceilinged establishment with huge windows onto the harbor and an outdoor deck that takes full advantage of its waterside location.

The chef's cuisine has won awards for the restaurant, which was built in 1986. Seafood takes precedence on the menu, which is priced from $13.45 for grilled herbed chicken with basil pesto to $19.95 for a mariner's platter of grilled swordfish paired

Diners at window tables at Dry Dock Restaurant enjoy view of harbor scene.

with sea scallops. Scallops with mushrooms, crab in the usual guises, baked stuffed shrimp, lobster supreme and filet mignon are favorites; flounder renaissance and snapper royale could be specials. Start with scallops wrapped in bacon, stuffed mushrooms or escargots. A good wine list with labels is priced from $15 to $55.

Interior dining is on two levels on the main floor and on a spacious mezzanine. Oil lamps cast shadows on each shiny wood table. Sandwiches and light fare are served outside at the Quarter Deck, a separate entity run by the same enterprise.

Lunch, weekends noon to 4, April-October; dinner nightly, 5 to 9.

Main Street Grill, Avondale Center, 14350 Solomons Island Road, Solomons. (410) 326-3877.

This is the full-service successor to the auspicious little Brick Oven, a gourmet bakery and deli that opened in a good-looking, contemporary retail complex built by Skip and Ellen Zahniser of the marina family. The Zahnisers thought the town needed another decent, casual restaurant serving dinner, and this grill that retains much of its bakery-deli origin is the happy result.

The sleek gray decor is minimal. Cane chairs are at butcherblock tables topped with gray inlays. The menu offers design-your-own pizzas ($5.95) and half a dozen dinner entrées ($7.50 to $12.95), from pasta primavera (available with chicken or shrimp) to chicken fajitas to blackened tuna steak to New York strip steak. The rest of the all-day menu adds appetizers, sandwiches (many of them grilled) and salads (the grilled chicken Key West salad for $6.95 sounds interesting).

Folks still come from all over for the cakes and bakery products, among them Bavarian chocolate pie, lemon mousse pie, rocky road fudge pie and key lime pie. Frozen margaritas are the specialty of the bar. The weekend breakfast fare also appeals.

Open Monday, 11 to 5, Tuesday-Friday 11 to 8 or 9, Saturday 9 to 9 and Sunday 8 to 8.

Harbour Island, Harbor Island Marina, Solomons. (410) 326-9522.

Two Greek brothers who had a restaurant in the Washington suburb of Potomac run this venture with upper and lower outdoor decks. Chef Napoleon Zaharopolos upgraded the menu and acceded to customer requests for more Greek food, including moussaka and a souvlaki platter.

Otherwise, the menu by the numbers offers a little of everything, from sole amandine and seafood norfolk to veal marsala, veal parmigiana and filet mignon. Two house specialties are listed: broiled flounder topped with sautéed shrimp, clams and mushrooms and a seafood and artichokes concoction over linguini. Dinner prices range from $11.95 to $19.95. Light fare and salads also are available.

The location is one of the best on Solomons, on a point with a commanding vista of the harbor. From the trellised upper deck, water is visible on three sides.

Lunch daily, 11 to 4; dinner, 4 to 10. Closed Monday-Wednesday in winter.

Solomons Pier, Route 2, Solomons. (410) 326-2424.

My goodness, what a location – out on a pier in the Patuxent River. And goodness, what a shambles was our dinner on a Saturday night. Upon reserving, we asked for and were assigned a window table in the main dining room with water on three sides. But all the windows were ringed with lights, which only distracted from the view. The crab cakes ($15.50) and soft-shell crab ($14.95) were fine – how could they be otherwise in crab country? But they came with mediocre salads and baked potatoes wrapped in foil. From a limited wine list that inexplicably contained more reds than whites, we nursed a Robert Mondavi fumé blanc and watched all the activity – singles imbibing on the waterside patio outside our window and an obnoxious guy trying to pick up any of the three women at a nearby table. Our young waiter, a real pro, had to deal with both the crowd and the trouble.

Too late (like after the music started blasting our eardrums) did we learn that the Pier turns into a disco shortly after 8 on busy nights and weekends. You must eat early here – say at Sunday brunch, which we understand is quite good, or at lunch or a late-afternoon dinner. The menu is priced from $12.95 for flounder with shrimp sauce to $19.95 for a broiled platter of shrimp, scallops, flounder and seafood imperial. Prime rib and twin filet mignons are the only non-seafood items.

The $9.95 brunch buffet includes made-to-order omelets, a belgian waffle bar, flounder thermidor and complimentary bloody marys or champagne with your meal.

Lunch daily, 11 to 4; dinner from 4; Sunday brunch, 9:30 to 1:15.

Baltimore Seafood Company, Dowell Road Extension, Dowell. (410) 326-0200.

This jaunty newcomer opened to high expectations in 1994 on the second-floor of a new brick boathouse building in the Calvert Marina, just across the harbor from Solomons. The L-shaped room is done up in Ramada Inn-style rose and green, with votive candles on the tables, lighthouse prints on the brick walls and windows onto the Floating Theater moored in the water outside.

The place looked more promising than was its delivery, according to early reports. At our visit shortly after opening, it offered nearly two dozen dinner entrées, from $8.95 for fried clams to $22.95 for a Chesapeake Bay platter. The predictable spiced shrimp, snow crab clusters, fried oysters and crab cakes were augmented by broiled snapper, salmon fillet and catch of the day. Chicken and steaks were available for non-seafood eaters. Appetizers ran the gamut from clams casino, catfish fingers and hot crab dip with crackers to chicken wings and potato skins.

Lunch daily, 11 to 4:30; dinner, 4:30 to 9 or 10.

The Naughty Gull, Spring Cove Marina, Solomons. (410) 326-4855.

The view is everything from this nautical restaurant and pub, centered by a large bar

Soaring windows overlook harbor from dining rooms at Lighthouse Inn.

in the middle, with tables on several levels. Alas, there's no deck for outdoor dining beside the water, but we lucked into the next best thing, one of the few window tables. The lunch menu yielded a soft-shell crab sandwich ($7.95) and an enormous, gloppy platter of aztec nachos, accompanied by plenty of guacamole, sour cream and hot salsa on the side.

Come nightfall, a varied menu is priced from $10.95 for fish and chips to $18.95 for filet mignon. Crab imperial, a crab cake platter, three shrimp dishes and prime rib are among the possibilities. Dessert could be carrot cake, cheesecake or chocolate cake.

Open daily from 11; Sunday champagne brunch, 10 to 2.

Diversions

Solomons boasts an impressive new **Riverwalk,** a sixteen-foot-wide boardwalk stretching a third of a mile along the bulkhead of the Patuxent River. There are benches as well as a pavilion and an amphitheater, which were christened in 1994 with a wildly successful July Fourth concert that ranged from gospel singers to a twelve-piece band. Area residents also were banding together to convert an old Navy barge, now docked in Solomons, into the James Adams Floating Theatre, named after a showboat that brought live entertainment to ports along the Chesapeake Bay and its tributaries in the first half of this century.

Sailing, boating and charter fishing are the big attractions. They are offered through various marinas, which seem to be the second most prevalent business activity here after restaurants. Hour-long cruises around Solomons Inner Harbor are offered by the 1899 log-built bugeye William B. Tennison, the oldest passenger-carrying vessel on the Chesapeake Bay. They're scheduled to leave at 2 p.m. Wednesday-Sunday, May-October, from the Calvert Marine Museum, but often depart early, as we found to our chagrin upon arrival one afternoon at 1:56.

173

Calvert Marine Museum, Route 2, Solomons, 326-2042. Started in the old school building, this growing museum specializes in local maritime history, the paleontology of the nearby Calvert Cliffs and the estuarine life of the tidal Patuxent River and adjacent waters. Its impressive exhibition building, dedicated in 1989, has extensive exhibits on the Patuxent, including 500 photographs, scale models and artifacts. Among them are a 28-foot-long, three-log canoe and an underwater mine and torpedo from World War II testing in the river. A new permanent exhibit on the river and its life features seventeen aquariums, live otters and a touch tank for children. A hall of fossils from the Calvert Cliffs was in the works. Fascinating to visit is the Drum Point Lighthouse, which dominates the waterfront and is one of three remaining cottage-type lights from the bay. Fifteen visitors get to go inside on guided tours given hourly. Varied watercraft are on display in the small craft building or are afloat in the boat basin. Half a mile south of the main museum complex is the J.C. Lore Oyster House, which traces the region's commercial seafood industry and portrays the area's traditions of boatbuilding. Nautical and local items of interest are sold in the excellent Museum Store. Open daily 10 to 5. Adults, $4.

Annmarie Garden on St. John, off Dowell Road, Solomons. Accented with contemporary sculptures, 30 acres of forests and gardens along St. John Creek were in the early developmental stage in 1994. Walkways in the woods take visitors past juried sculptures set in garden "rooms" cut out of the forest; a sculpture of an oyster tonger had just been dedicated as the focal point at our visit. One local artist predicted the sculpture garden would ultimately rival the famous Brookgreen Gardens of South Carolina. The late Francis Koenig, who had donated the land and named it for his ailing wife, envisioned it as "a contemplative and creative place" for the public to commune amid floral and fauna. All kinds of visual and performing artists made the garden rooms come alive at the September Artsfest in 1994. Initially open weekends, May-October.

Calvert Cliffs State Park, Routes 2 and 4, Lusby. Nearly 30 miles of cliffs along the Chesapeake Bay's western shore north of Solomons hold one of the world's richest concentrations of fossil whales among more than 600 species of fossils up to seventeen million years old. A lengthy hike through the 1,460-acre wooded park takes visitors to the cliffs, some of which have been closed to fossiling lately. Open March-October.

Jefferson Patterson Park and Museum, St. Leonard, 586-0050. Pre-historic and Colonial sites, nature and archaeology trails, farm exhibits and a visitor center with exhibits on history and nature are featured in this 512-acre preserve on the banks of the Patuxent River. Wagon tours are offered weekends in summer. Open Wednesday-Sunday 10 to 5, mid-April to mid-October.

Battle Creek Cypress Swamp, Route 506, Prince Frederick. The northernmost natural stand of bald cypress trees distinguishes this 100-acre nature sanctuary. An elevated boardwalk covers a quarter mile of the swamp, now home to white-tailed deer, muskrats and other wildlife. The mysteries of the swamp are examined more closely in presentations at the nature center. Open Tuesday-Saturday 10 to 5, Sunday 1 to 5; closes at 4:30, October-March.

Point Lookout State Park, Route 5, St. Mary's County. The southernmost point in Maryland is at the tip of a 580-acre peninsula at the confluence of the Potomac River and the Chesapeake Bay. The park is so large and so far from the mainstream that it's almost always uncrowded. Attractions include miles of beaches on both river and bay, a fishing pier jutting 700 feet into the bay, a lighthouse, a swimming beach, a Civil War museum and a Confederate cemetery. The Confederate Monument here is the only federal monument dedicated to those who died for the rebel cause. We liked the park's seclusion and the broad view across to the Northern Neck of Virginia. Open daily, sunrise to sunset.

Shopping. Ensconced in a structure built right over the water along the boardwalk is **The Sandpiper,** a gift shop adjacent to the town dock, which also rents bicycles and sells ice cream. We picked up some clever Christmas cards from owner Joann Kersey's excellent selection, plus more from her other shop at the Holiday Inn. Handpainted clothing, T-shirts, jewelry, resortwear and gifts are featured at **Solomons Style.** Thousands of used and rare books are available **at Lazy Moon Book Shop,** where the owner is as interesting as his stock. Hoping to set a standard for future commercial development of Solomons, Ellen and Skip Zahniser of sailing-center fame erected Avondale Center, a retail and professional complex along the main street. Among its treasures are **Fine Things,** whimsically stocked with one-of-a-kind shell items, pottery, cut crystal, accessories and such, in exquisite taste. If we'd had a spare $155 we might have emerged with a gold-shell wreath. But it was on to **Solomons Mines,** where we ogled all the gems and jewelry, and the increasingly well-known **Carmen's Gallery,** which displayed appealing artworks.

Extra-Special

Historic St. Mary's City, Route 5, St. Mary's City. (410) 862-0990. Founded in 1634 by Catholic pilgrims, this National Historic Landmark was the fourth permanent settlement in British North America and served as the Colonial capital of Maryland until 1695. The abandonment of the town and the subsequent shift to agriculture was an archaeological blessing, for most of the 17th-century town was preserved under the plowed soils, awaiting excavation. A low-key, outdoor living-history museum opened on the site in 1984, and work continues to uncover and restore the nation's only Colonial capital still undisturbed by development or erosion. Four main exhibit areas include the Visitor Center with an archaeology exhibit hall, a tobacco plantation, the Chancellor's Point Natural History Area (site of a Chesapeake Indian Lifeways Center) and the Governor's Field. We found the last to be of most interest. You can walk

out on a dock in the St. Mary's River to board the square-rigged replica of a ship that brought the first settlers from England, hear your footsteps echo as you explore the reconstructed State House of 1676 and stop for a lunch featuring traditional Colonial dishes and regional seafood specialties in the $5 to $10 range at Farthing's Ordinary. The remains of the first Catholic chapel in the Chapel Field, whose excavation is in progress, marks the birthplace of the Roman Catholic church in America. The old town – what little there is of it – blends nicely into the waterfront campus of St. Mary's College, a liberal arts college of 1,500 students. Open April-November, Wednesday-Sunday 10 to 5. Adults, $5.

State House at Historic St. Mary's City.

Tillie the Tug takes passengers for leisurely cruise along Pocomoke River.

Snow Hill/Berlin, Md.
300 Years Along the River

Like a waterway in the bayous of Louisiana, the Pocomoke River lazes through the flatlands and forests of Maryland's Lower Eastern Shore. Stands of bald cypress trees define its path. Bald eagles, osprey, egrets and other wildlife populate its shores. The river – deep, languorous, mysterious and hauntingly beautiful – is Maryland's first to be designated "wild and scenic."

Such is the watery backdrop for little-known Snow Hill, founded by English colonists in 1642 and billed today as "the undiscovered treasure of the Eastern Shore." The county-seat town of 2,200 is not really on the way to anywhere. It claims more than 100 homes that are at least 100 years old, a way of life that's 40 years behind the times and almost no downtown at all. The big social events are church suppers and monthly dances in summer under the stars beside the river.

Snow Hill's counterpoint in the path of non-discovery is Berlin, an old-fashioned town of 2,600 about fifteen miles to the northeast. The old houses here are not as

compelling as the rejuvenated Victorian storefronts up against brick sidewalks on a maze of downtown streets. Berlin languished in the shadow of Ocean City until the late 1980s, when ten hometown boosters bought and renovated the Atlantic Hotel to wide acclaim. Now Berlin, pronounced BUR-lin by most natives, has a first-class restaurant, a restored theater, a working downtown, a dozen antiques shops and enough gawkers on weekends to qualify as the newly discovered "jewel of the Eastern Shore."

The attractions of Snow Hill, Berlin and environs are diverse: the Assateague Island National Seashore, canoeing on the Pocomoke, riverside parks, the site of a vanished 19th-century industrial village called Furnace Town. The coastal habitat and temperate climate produce the best bird-watching opportunities in Maryland.

Three centuries of history converge in Snow Hill. Its Presbyterian church is the first of the American denomination. All Hallows Episcopal Church, a brick antique surrounded by gravestones in the center of town, displays a bible and bell presented to the community by Queen Anne. Chain stores and fast-food outlets are noticeably missing here and in Berlin. The two small towns live up to their theme, "where the good life still lives on."

Inn Spots

The River House Inn, 201 East Market St., Snow Hill 21863. (410) 632-2722.

A two-acre, 700-foot-deep lawn slopes down to the Pocomoke River behind this 1850 Victorian beauty, blessed with a wraparound veranda in front and screened porches upstairs and down in the rear. Larry and Susanne Knudsen from Ohio bought the residence in 1991 and turned it into an elegant B&B with an expanding guest complex.

Besides the porches, they offer a bevy of attractive, comfortable public rooms on two sides of a green center hallway: a parlor with TV, a rosy red sitting and game room, a formal dining room and a breakfast room with draperies puddled on the floor. The breakfast room, which would be a fairly formal dining room in anyone else's lexicon, was the site for an impressive feast of orange juice, cantaloupe, blueberry muffins and a cheese omelet with bacon or sausage, toast or English muffins.

In the morning the Baltimore Sun was at our door outside the East Room, outfitted in Sheraton furniture with plush carpeting, fancy floral wallpaper coordinated with the

River House Inn occupies ornate 1850 Victorian beauty on two-acre lawn.

curtains, and a high-ceilinged bathroom with windows. Three of the four guest rooms in the main house have fireplaces; all have queensize beds and private baths, one down the hall. The decor is French in the rear River Room and American Chippendale in the West Room. A third-floor suite with a wicker sitting area is done up in pastel pink and green in American country style.

Guests like to gather on the upstairs back porch full of wicker or its downstairs companion, smashingly appointed in tropical colors with bamboo-rattan furniture. The black decorative wrought iron on the front veranda could be straight out of New Orleans. Matching the wrought iron are the Knudsens' two friendly big black poodles, Bonnie and Belle, who love to go for romps down by the river.

Dinner for house guests is available upon request. A prix-fixe dinner is $30, including wine. The meal might start with scallops seviche or crabmeat gratin and a salad. Barbecued steaks or salmon could be followed by frozen yogurt with fresh berries and homemade chocolate sauce.

Since our initial visit, the River House has added three guest rooms in the Little House, an 1834 Tidewater Colonial cottage a few steps from the main house. A small suite occupies the second floor. The main floor holds two bedrooms with private baths and a screened porch. The newest addition is a separate River Cottage, complete with antique king bed, mini-refrigerator, radio and a neat wicker porch looking onto the lovely lawn with its Adirondack chairs and hammocks.

The Knudsens have put in water gardens and walkways to supplement the lavish landscaping behind the main house. For 1995, they acquired a 26-foot pontoon boat to offer guests tours and picnics on the upper river. They also were looking to add a swimming pool. "Our objective is to make a home where guests feel comfortable," said Larry. It is a goal they have already realized.

Doubles, $90 to $110; cottage $130. No smoking.

Chaunceford Hall, 209 West Federal St., Snow Hill 21863. (410) 632-2231.

Museum-quality furnishings – many of them made by the owner – are the hallmark of this refined B&B opened in 1986. Michael Driscoll lavishes as much attention on his custom furniture-making hobby that blossomed into a business as he and his wife Thelma devote to their dinner parties for guests.

The narrow, deep brick Greek Revival mansion dating to 1759 was built by Robert Morris, financier of the Revolution. Its three sections include the original house, a ballroom that's now the kitchen and a middle section joining the two. Beyond that kitchen, for which Michael made all the cabinets, is a stunning new five-sided, high-ceilinged solarium shaded by the second biggest walnut tree in Maryland. Wine and hors d'oeuvre are offered here in the late afternoon, overlooking a brick patio with a 32-foot-long lap pool beneath a fiberglass roof.

Breakfast is served in an impressive dining room graced by Michael's sideboard and round tables in the Queen Anne style. Fresh fruit (strawberries, kiwi and bananas when we were there), apple-raisin muffins and eggs any style with sausage, bacon and potatoes O'Brien could be the fare.

The five guest rooms bear English names starting with the letter "C." All have working fireplaces (the house has a total of ten), private baths, wing chairs, oriental rugs and canopied beds. All but one of the beds is queensize and all were made by Michael. Largest is the rear Carrington Suite with a loveseat and wing chair, a leather chair and rocker, and an extra twin bed. We're partial to the Chadwick, which has one of the two full baths as well as a crystal chandelier. The Chanceford Room on the main floor has the other full bath, a highboy, dark wainscoting and molding and a fancy medallion in the ceiling.

Elegant Greek Revival mansion dating to 1759 takes in guests as Chaunceford Hall.

Elaborate dinners are served to overnight guests by arrangement, one couple an evening. These are not to be taken lightly. "It takes us all day to get ready and takes them all evening to eat," says Michael. The $110-per-couple tab includes a bottle of champagne, shrimp cocktail and a main course such as lobster newburg, filet mignon, stuffed flounder or quail. Raspberry cheesecake with pecans and cocoa on a pecan-chocolate graham cracker crust could be the finale.

Doubles, $110 to $130.

Merry Sherwood Plantation, 8909 Worcester Hwy., Berlin 21811. (410) 641-2112 or (800) 660-0358.

Is this a museum or a B&B? The painstaking restoration and the priceless furnishings that owner Kirk Burbage lavished on this grand antebellum beauty hint of the former, as does the sign "no guided tours today." But the run-of-the-house welcome for overnight guests and the energy of resident innkeeper Todd Durand attest to the latter.

The Victorian showcase is a place where architectural historians, antiques enthusiasts and those into Victoriana are in their element. True, the place has its incongruities. Built in classic Italianate style, it also has Greek Revival and Gothic influences. The long main parlor (once a ballroom) holds both a grand piano and a square Victorian piano, while a pipe organ awaits in the front sitting room. The honeymoon suite comes with a marble bath and jacuzzi, yet the sunken bedroom with carved Victorian walnut double bed is the smallest in the house, and as for "suite," there's a little sitting room with uncomfortable chairs made for viewing rather than sitting. The other seven corner bedrooms on the second and third floors, all but two with private baths, seem quite spacious, particularly those with high ceilings on the second floor. The bathrooms are wallpapered and have marble floors and showers. The bedrooms are painted in lighter colors to set off the dark wood flooring. Most beds are dwarfed by heavy, ornate headboards and footers of solid walnut; "these beds need a lot of dusting," the chambermaid volunteered. On the nightstands are mints and Bibles. Fine oriental runners lead to the fourth-floor widow's walk, all windows with another Bible under the only seat.

Extravagant oriental rugs and carpets are particularly notable in the main ballroom/ parlor, full of maroon velvet sofas and settees. In the center of this expanse is a marble table topped by an enormous artificial floral arrangement in a three-foot-tall sterling silver vase imported from Germany, one of three in existence (and the owner claims two). The main-floor rooms are lit by no fewer than five huge brass chandeliers; a particularly striking one hangs over the table in the dining room. The house was in restoration for two years prior to its opening in 1993. The plaster walls, the loblolly pine flooring and a few of the furnishings are original. Kirk brought in the rest of the furniture, some of which had been in storage at his family's funeral home, oldest in Maryland, and had come from the area's finest estates.

"This is not a museum," innkeeper Todd stresses. "We want guests to play the pianos and read the books in the library." Tea and cookies are served in the afternoon. Next day in the great, dark dining room, guests sit down to a breakfast of apple pancakes, belgian waffles or egg casserole, served on fine china.

Although the owner has no plans for expansion ("this is a hobby for him," says Todd), he intended to enhance the eighteen-acre property with a formal rose garden and a stocked pond.

Doubles, $125; suite, $150.

Atlantic Hotel, 2 North Main St., Berlin 21811. (410) 641-3589 or (800) 814-7672.

Built in 1894 and once the pride of what was the commercial capital of the Eastern Shore, this had seen better days before ten local partners got together to buy the building. Each put up $150,000 for its painstaking restoration in 1988. The hotel is now best known for its restaurant (see Dining Spots), but the upstairs lodging facility is no slouch.

The sixteen guest rooms on the second and third floors are the height of colorful Victoriana. Some are quite small, while others are large enough for two beds. All have private baths with clawfoot tubs and Gilbert & Soames toiletries. Beds come with dark and heavy wood headboards. The rooms we saw possessed wild floral carpets, Victorian lamps, mirrored armoires, fringed curtains and fishnet canopies. Decorated by one investor's wife who is an art teacher at Salisbury State College, each is distinctive for its antique furniture, window treatment and artworks. Telephones and clock radios are contemporary conveniences, and TV is available on request.

On the second floor is a small lounge for guests. A table contains a bowl of fruit, a scrapbook of area attractions and a photo album tracing the hotel's two years of restoration. A stark rear porch with a not particularly appealing view offers a couple of wicker chairs and rockers. More to guests' liking are the new sidewalk cafe and the lineup of rockers on the wide front veranda facing the goings-on in the heart of the rejuvenated downtown. Ditto for the large Victorian bar and lounge on the main floor, where the prevailing sedateness is enlivened by weekend singalongs.

Rates include a country breakfast with fresh fruit, cereal, scrambled eggs and pastries.

Doubles, $75 to $135. No smoking.

The Garden and the Sea Inn, Route 710, Box 275, New Church, Va. 23415. (804) 824-0672 or (800) 824-0672.

For some time a restaurant of distinction (see Dining Spots), this out-of-the-way prize near the Maryland-Virginia line is now an overnight destination as well. New owners Sara and Tom Baker from the Shenandoah Valley inherited a going concern when they bought the property in 1994. They offer two bedrooms above the showy Victorian restaurant and three rooms, one a suite, in the oldest house in New Church,

Major restoration preceded opening of Merry Sherwood Plantation as a B&B.

which was moved to the rear of the property in 1992. A handsome brick patio and rose garden with fountain and walkways connect the two.

Our quarters in the Vaucluse Room at the rear of the new Garden House could not have been nicer. The kingsize bed, loveseat, chair and desk were pretty in French wicker. The green wood floor was partly covered by a large oriental rug, while the pale green walls were accented by green floral print wallpaper trim along the ceiling. The floral print theme extended to the wallpaper and the cover of the Kleenex box in the bathroom, which was equipped with twin wash basins and a jacuzzi tub beneath a skylight. We shared a screened side porch outfitted in green wicker with occupants of the adjacent room, and never did see the honeymooners in the suite upstairs. The Garden House offered plenty of common space: a living room formal in swags and florals, a dining area and kitchenette with a refrigerator in which to stash your own goodies, and a front porch. Sherry, chocolate and fruit were at the ready.

Two more guest rooms of French country sophistication are in the main Victorian House. You might find a dressing table draped in paisley fabric, lace and ribbons, rugs patterned with flowers, painted furniture, porcelain doorknobs painted with flowers, and squares of colored glass around the windows. The Chantilly Room has a wicker queensize sleigh bed and the Giverny Room a headboard draped in lace. The modern bathrooms here include bidets.

A continental-plus breakfast is served in the sun-porch section of the dining room. Ours included mixed berries and fruit, choice of cereals and granola, and melt-in-the-mouth croissants and blueberry muffins.

Doubles, $110; suite, $155. Open April-November.

Holland House, 5 Bay St., Berlin 21811. (410) 641-1956.

A turn-of-the-century physician's residence at the edge of downtown was turned into the area's first B&B in 1986 by Jim and Jan Quick, he a chef at the Dunes Manor Hotel in Ocean City and she a dental hygienist. Five guest rooms, all with private

181

baths and four with queensize beds, are decorated simply with early American furnishings. Three are on the main floor, where a plaque designates the site of the former doctor's office and maternity ward. A new family suite with connecting bath combines a bedroom with a queen bed with a room with a double bed.

Breakfast is served on striking octagonal china plates in a pink dining room, decorated to match Jan's collection of pink depression glassware on the side shelves. The fare could be whatever Jim feels like preparing: perhaps blueberry pancakes, french toast or crêpes accompanied by fresh fruit and muffins.

Guests enjoy a comfortable living room, a paneled TV room, a wicker-filled front porch and a rear patio. They also have access to a picnic table and a basement refrigerator.

Doubles, $78; suite, $95 for four.

Snow Hill Inn, 104 East Market St., Snow Hill 21863. (410) 632-2102.

Acclaimed lately for its restaurant (see Dining Spots), this house dating to 1790 offers three guest rooms, one with in-room bath and two with private baths down the hall. A fourth room formerly used as a bedroom was turned into a much-needed upstairs common room by Jim and Kathy Washington, innkeepers since 1991. They also converted a downstairs bedroom into a cocktail lounge.

Though their main thrust is the dining experience, they have upgraded the homey bedrooms, two of which have working fireplaces. The Barrister Room features a double bed with a quilt, and a Victorian settee on the original 1790 floor. The Wicker Room has a queensize and a day bed.

Breakfast is continental-plus: juice and fruit, raisin bread or pumpkin muffins, quiche, cereal and cheese.

Doubles, $50 to $75.

Dining Spots

The Atlantic Hotel, 2 North Main St., Berlin. (410) 641-3589.

The local investors who renovated this "jewel of the Eastern Shore" knew what they wanted: a fine, special-occasion dining room. They searched the nation for their first chef, who rewarded their trust with culinary honors (the Atlantic quickly became one of six four-star restaurants in Maryland as determined by the Baltimore Sun). In 1994, they looked closer to home for Thomas Murray, a 26-year-old Berlin native who had been a waiter at the hotel before heading off for culinary training at Johnson & Wales University in Rhode Island and working in restaurant kitchens in New Orleans and Washington, D.C. He was adding cajun and Southern touches to the hotel's new French menu.

The 60-seat dining room is pretty in a hotel kind of way. Balloon curtains around tall etched-glass windows match the walls papered in deep rose, teal and dark blue. High-back upholstered chairs are at well-spaced tables topped with white linens.

We were seated for the acclaimed Sunday brunch in a more intimate, narrow side room to distance ourselves from the live jazz that was to follow. The $13.95 tab yielded orange juice (alas, it was not fresh-squeezed as the menu had promised), blueberry muffins, choice of entrée, coffee and a platter of sweet treats, from sticky buns to shortbread cookies to petits fours. The kitchen redeemed itself for the orange juice lapse with shrimp Americaine and tomato concasse in an herbed crêpe as well as poached eggs Chesapeake, served on an artichoke bottom, surrounded by lump crab and topped with a delicate hollandaise sauce. The latter was accompanied by good potato pancakes and garnished with a wedge of watermelon topped with a strawberry.

Victorian downtown Berlin is on view from veranda of restored Atlantic Hotel.

The short, changing dinner menu is priced from $21.95 for grilled duck breast with peach chutney to $28.95 for lobster sauté and rack of lamb with goat cheese, the last a house specialty. Salmon stuffed with spinach and oysters in puff pastry, grilled veal chop puttanesca and tournedos au poivre are other choices. Start with snapper soup, coconut shrimp, grilled quail or seafood sausage ($5.25 to $12.95). Finish with a selection from the dessert tray: perhaps Bailey's Irish Cream cheesecake, lemon-lime curd cheeesecake, chocolate-raspberry ganache cake or homemade ice cream. The Wine Spectator award-winning wine list is on the expensive side.

Interesting, less pricey fare is offered day and night in **Drummer's Cafe,** the Victorian lounge with a new sidewalk cafe that's stylish with wicker furniture and petunias in planters. How about a blackened chicken salad, a flank steak sandwich, a lamb shish kabob or a basil pizza with roma tomatoes and provolone cheese ($5.95 to $14.95)?

Lunch daily in cafe, all-day menu from noon to 9 or 10; dinner nightly, 6 to 9 or 10; Sunday brunch, 11 to 2.

The Garden and the Sea Inn, Route 710, New Church, Va. (804) 824-0672.

The polished restaurant here made quite a name for itself under the previous innkeepers, she in the kitchen and he out front. The roles were reversed when it was purchased in 1994 by Tom and Sara Baker. Tom, a Culinary Institute-trained chef who had been at the Waterwheel restaurant at the Inn at Grist Mill in Warm Springs, is in the kitchen and Sara oversees the front of the house. Both carry out their duties with aplomb.

The sophisticated dining room is pretty with pale peach walls, dusky pink pillars and trim, and remarkable window treatments. China in the delicate "Plantation Blossom" pattern, pink-stemmed glassware and shell-patterned silver are as refined as the service.

Diners order à la carte or from a couple of prix-fixe menus, four courses for $24.25

183

or $31.25. One of us tried the lower-priced prix-fixe option, which produced a thick and tasty corn and crab chowder, a good salad of romaine lettuce with caesar dressing, and a superior breast of chicken dressed with pecans and dijon cream, served with slivered carrots and wild rice. The other ordered the sliced pork loin sautéed with backfin crabmeat and served with béarnaise sauce from six à la carte options ($14.75 to $22.50). Good rolls with two kinds of butter (one of them herbed) and a $20 bottle of our favorite Sanford sauvignon blanc from California (rarely seen on the East Coast) accompanied. Peach melba and crème brûlée were worthy endings to a memorable meal.

Visiting musicians perform during the inn's chamber music dinners, scheduled one Sunday each month with seatings at 1 and 5.

Dinner nightly in summer, 6 to 9; Thursday-Sunday in off-season. Open April-November.

Snow Hill Inn, 104 East Market St., Snow Hill. (410) 632-2102.

When Jim and Kathy Washington took over this restaurant in 1991, it had nowhere to go but up. And up it went, to the point where we heard nothing but raves. Jim mans the kitchen, while Kathy presides over the front of the house. This includes an airy dining room in the rear and a more intimate front room colorful with stained glass and a decor of hunter green with red accents. There are also a new lounge and a shady rear patio for dining al fresco.

Dinner selections include choice of tossed or spinach salad and homemade herbed bread or muffins, served with butter wrapped in aluminum foil – who said this was sophisticated dining? But it sure is affordable. We ordered a carafe of the house Sebastiani chardonnay ($9). The waitress filled our glasses to the brim as we dug into salads dressed with parmesan pepper and honey dijon. Main courses were the locally ubiquitous crab imperial and crab cakes, accompanied by red potatoes and mixed squash. We had no room for dessert, a choice of carrot cake or cheese-cake. Entrées are priced from $9.95 for seafood pasta or chicken marsala to $15.95 for a dish called Snow on the Hills, twin petite filets topped with imperial crab. Prime rib is far and away the most requested choice, according to Jim.

Dining room at Snow Hill Inn.

The restaurant also is popular for lunch. Among the options are crab quiche, chicken caesar salad, sandwiches, pasta and shrimp scampi, with most items priced below $5.

Lunch, Monday-Friday 11 to 2; dinner, Wednesday-Saturday 5:30 to 9, Sunday 4 to 8.

Evelyn's Village Inn, 104 West Green St., Snow Hill. (410) 632-1282.

For local color, you can't beat Evelyn's – a local institution where the judges and lawyers go for coffee and assorted characters and codgers hang out at all hours. So it comes as little surprise to learn that the Rotary Club meets here on Wednesday nights.

Summery decor is backdrop for prix-fixe dinners at The Garden and the Sea Inn.

The draw is not the round tables, the side counter or the fluorescent lights. Rather it's the clientele and the food, which is good, plentiful and downright cheap. Those in the know say that Evelyn prepares the best fried chicken in Worcester County; ditto for her fried oysters.

For breakfast, come here for scrapple and eggs. For lunch: a grilled cheese or toasted crab cake sandwich ($1.25 to $3.50). The steak sandwich costs a mere $2.50.

Dinner platters run from $5.50 to $9. The latter is for a seafood platter – crab cake, oysters, shrimp, clam strips and fish with cole slaw and french fries. Shrimp, baked ham, crab cakes and those acclaimed fried oysters and fried chicken dishes are also on the typewritten menu. Coffee and iced tea are included with dinner. Desserts cost an extra $1.

Owner Evelyn Allen is winding down her hours, leaving the cooking chores in the capable hands of her daughter, Ernestine Bailey. But Evelyn still comes in a couple of days a week, much to the relief of her loyal following.

Open Monday-Friday, 8:30 to 7; Saturday, 12:30 to 8.

The Judges Bench, 200 West Green St., Snow Hill. (410) 632-0034.
"A courtly place to dine" is how this new restaurant advertises itself, adding "A good place to raise your spirits after your day in court." Why, we can only surmise, for the hostess viewed us skeptically, glowered as we looked around for a few moments and refused to let us take a menu.

We did note that atmosphere seemed to be haute tea room and the fare was typically Southern. Dinner prices range from $5.95 for grilled ham steak to $11.95 for stuffed flounder. We understand that they serve good soups and salads, and that there's live entertainment on Friday and Saturday nights.

Open, daily 6 to midnight.

Globe Cafe & Deli, 12 Broad St., Berlin. (410) 641-0784.
Just what the visiting lunch-goer ordered is served up at the deli counter adjacent to the Duck Soup Bookstore. Large, healthful sandwiches, bagels, soups, salads and quiche are ordered at the counter and delivered to tables scattered around the main-floor cor-

ridor outside the entry to the little Globe Theater. We liked the Globe sandwich (combining havarti, tomato, avocado, sprouts, cucumber and mayo on seven-grain bread for $3.25) and the chunky chicken salad sandwich called a chico ($3.50). Those and a couple of cafe lattes ($2) sent us happily on our way.

Open Monday-Saturday 10 to 6, Sunday 11 to 5.

Diversions

The **Pocomoke River** is the area's principal attraction and defines its character. You can view it from two riverside parks, Byrd and Sturgis, in Snow Hill and from Milburn and Shad landings in Pocomoke River State Park. Otherwise, it's pretty much hidden from public view as it winds like a tropical jungle stream past thick forests and an occasional farm. The tidal river is the deepest (up to 45 feet) for its width in the United States.

The best way to experience the river is by canoe. The **Pocomoke River Canoe Co.** at the Route 12 drawbridge in Snow Hill rents canoes for $5 an hour and $30 a day. Groups can rent a pontoon boat for $65 for two hours. The less adventurous can settle for a tour on **Tillie the Tug,** an open tugboat that carries 22 passengers downriver from Snow Hill to Shad Landing and back. We saw lots of lily pads, duck blinds and stumps of bald cypress trees, but found the boat too low to see much – not that there was all that much to see. The odd bird and passing speedboat helped while the hour away. We got the distinct impression that life in the Snow Hill area moves just as slowly as Tillie the Tug and the Pocomoke River. Cruises available mid-June through Labor Day and fall weekends. Adults, $6.

Birdwatching. More than 350 species have been sighted in Worcester County from the Assateague coastline across the Pocomoke Forest and down the Pocomoke River. They are detailed in two lengthy brochures furnished by the country tourism office at 105 Pearl St., Snow Hill.

Historic Walking Tours. Maps for self-guided walking tours are available both for Berlin and Snow Hill. We like the shops and harmonious row of brick Victorian storefronts along Main Street in Berlin. The houses and the mix are more illustrious in Snow Hill, where most of the sights are concentrated along Market and Federal streets. Especially noteworthy are All Hallows Episcopal Church, established in 1692 and occupying its present structure since 1756, and nearby Makemie United Presbyterian Church, whose Gothic Revival facade hides the fact it was established in 1683 and is considered the birthplace of American Presbyterianism. The town's three inns were among the houses opened for tours on Snow Hill's annual Heritage Weekend when we were there.

Viewtrail 100. About 100 miles of contiguous scenic bicycle trails along secondary roads are marked by Viewtrail logos and outlined on a map available through the County Extension Service.

Julia A. Purnell Museum, 208 West Market St., Snow Hill, 632-0515. A former Catholic church houses local memorabilia involving Julia Purnell, a seamstress and storekeeper who lived here 100 years and took up folk art after breaking her hip at age 85. Because of her age and her penchant for relating stories of Snow Hill, her son opened a museum in her honor in 1942 and people flocked to see her and her creations before her death a year later. A few of her hundreds of needlework pictures are on display, but most of the space now operated by the town is devoted to a step-in boardwalk, a Colonial cupboard, the Purnell general store, a toy shop and Mrs. Purnell's sewing room. Open April-October, weekdays 10 to 4, weekends 1 to 4. Adults, $1.50.

Globe Theatre, 12 Broad St., Berlin, 641-0784. The old theater in the center of

Berlin has been restored and revived, encompassing a cafe, a book and gift shop and an art gallery. At the rear is a small theater of about four dozen seats, which started showing movies in 1989 "after a twenty-year intermission." It now schedules live musical entertainment of increasing distinction on many weekends. A wildfowl carving display and an exhibit of heritage boats occupied part of the old stage of this eclectic building at one of our visits. The Balcony Gallery shows interesting works of local guild members and guests.

Shopping. Most of the area's shopping opportunities are in Berlin, and those primarily involve antiques. They have names like **Cozy Corner Antiques, Victorian Charm,** the **Brass Box,** which had quite a collection of brass candlesticks, and **The Last Straw,** with lots of wicker things. You could pick up a prom gown for $5 or $10 at the **Church Mouse Thrift Shop,** operated by St. Paul's Episcopal Church.

Until now, the best part of Snow Hill's downtown has been the little triangular park, lushly dotted with flowers, at Green and Washington streets. **The Green Street Shop** offers antiques and collectibles on a limited basis Thursday-Saturday. The **W.W. Pusey & Sons Country Store** is a relic featuring gifts and practical stuff from boots to bird seed. Change is in store for the downtown area. For 1995, the old Mason Opera House was being converted into an antiques emporium on the main floor. The old Cannery beside the river was slated to become a crab house with additional antiques and craft shops later in the year.

Extra-Special

Furnace Town, Old Furnace Road, Snow Hill. (410) 632-2032.

Rarely can you see the remains of a 19th-century industrial village, least of all one that rose like a phoenix and thrived briefly on the gathering and smelting of bog iron ore. A short-lived boomtown of 300 people produced iron here in the 1830s, floating it on barges down Nassawango Creek to the Pocomoke River and the Chesapeake Bay. Almost as rapidly as it emerged it failed and became a ghost town. The Furnace Town museum shows the gathering of bog ore, archeological relics, a model of the mansion house and a loom, plus Snow Hill newspaper pages of the time citing the collective debt to "those enterprising strangers who have erected an iron furnace in our county" and the sudden notice of a sale involving 7,000 acres "embracing immense beds of iron ore." Visitors can tour an old print shop, peer into the Old Nazareth Church, inspect the crumbling Nassawango Iron Furnace, watch a craftsman making brooms in the broom house and a smithy at work in the blacksmith shop, and ascend the reproduction charging ramp for a four-story-high view of the countryside. Markers show foundations of long-lost buildings. We enjoyed the mile-long Nature Conservancy trail along a curved boardwalk through the adjacent, bayou-like swamp forest. We passed the stumps and "knees" of one of the northernmost bands of bald cypress trees, whose needles hang like grass clippings on trees below, and saw what remained of the twenty-foot-wide shipping canal. At appropriate times of the year you may see American holly and sweet gum trees, muscadet grape vines and fifteen varieties of orchids.

Open April-October, daily 11 to 5. Adults, $3.

Fogg Cove and Miles River are on view from rear grounds of The Inn at Perry Cabin.

St. Michaels, Md.
Waterfront Living in Style

Along the languorous shores of the Miles River, not far off the Chesapeake Bay, the historic town of St. Michaels has turned waterfront living into high style. The Eastern Shore's most upscale address is a mecca for visitors and second-home owners, some of whom eventually become year-round residents.

Tucked off the beaten path down a peninsula heading toward the bay, St. Michaels has long been known by yachtsmen and by affluent retirees who settled here for watery pleasures and a slower pace not far from the big cities. But it has really been discovered only in the last decade or so. Large new inns have emerged, trendy restaurants and shops have opened, and waterfront properties now sell at a premium.

Today's St. Michaels, still small and rather self-consciously quaint, is a far cry from that of a generation ago – before the Bay Bridge opened up the Eastern Shore to outlanders, before James Michener wrote *Chesapeake* in a rented house along the Miles River, and before the Chesapeake Bay Maritime Museum evolved into a major tourist attraction.

The first settlers in 1632 called its landlocked harbor "Shipping Creek," an apt reference for a place that would become a busy trading and shipbuilding center. Around the first Episcopal Church, named for St. Michael the Archangel, developed the town that took its name.

During the War of 1812, St. Michaels staged the first blackout in recorded history. British warships gathered on the Miles River to shell this coveted target. Townspeople darkened their homes and hung lanterns in the treetops to trick the invaders into aiming high. When the shelling ceased, the ploy had worked; only the now-famous Cannonball House was hit. St. Michaels had earned a place in history as the town that fooled the British.

Now the year-round population of 1,500 is easily matched by visiting yachtsmen and landlubbers on summer weekends, and by even more decoy collectors and duck hunters in fall. A few skeptics pass off St. Michaels as something of a stage set – mainly fronts and no backs, at least along Talbot Street, the only thoroughfare. They obviously have missed the side streets, the boatyards, the undulating waterfront and the surrounding countryside that better reflect the old St. Michaels, one of America's earliest port towns.

Inn Spots

The Inn at Perry Cabin, 308 Watkins Lane, St. Michaels 21663. (410) 745-2200 or (800) 722-2949.

The first American innkeeping venture of Sir Bernard Ashley, widower of Laura Ashley, this is like no other inn on the Mid-Atlantic coast. With beautiful grounds, an idyllic waterfront location, sumptuous accommodations and a first-class restaurant (see Dining Spots), it's luxury to the max.

Many millions were spent redoing it for a 1990 reopening, even after multi-million-dollar refurbishings by previous owners of what started as a cabin for Commodore Oliver Perry ("we have met the enemy and they are ours") following the War of 1812. Still more millions went into a wing that more than doubled the inn's size in 1991.

Touring the inn on two occasions, we were stunned by the stripes, flowers, flounces, ruffles, fancy window treatments, beautiful colors, wallpaper, borders and painted furniture. Here is decoration to the nth degree.

From the dining room to the lounges to the bedrooms, all is plush, plush, plush. Stressing service, Sir Bernard is quoted as saying his philosophy is to welcome guests as he would to one of his homes. Each of the 41 rooms and suites is elegantly furnished in antiques, offset by what the promotion material calls "understated, classic Laura Ashley fabrics and wallpapers." Understated? Laura Ashley – in more guises than we'd ever hoped to see – is splashed everywhere. On our tour of all the rooms, we got Laura Ashleyed out.

Admittedly, if you were staying in only one room, you would not find it overkill. You would likely find a four-poster bed topped by a draped corona, a wicker sitting area in a corner sun porch, a huge armoire imported from England, splashy colors, and a spacious bathroom with a striped ceiling and that most British of luxuries, a heated towel rack. Plus, of course, television, telephones, air-conditioning, coffee-table books and magazines, terrycloth robes, fresh fruit and mineral water. In Room 5, you would sleep in Sir Bernard's unique kingsize four-poster from his home in Bermuda. In Room 16, you would raise the curtains by remote control onto soaring windows yielding the inn's best water view. A couple of prized two-story suites have living rooms on one floor, bedrooms on the next and jacuzzi bathtubs. They share a balcony overlooking the river and harbor.

Rates include a full breakfast. The meal is served in the yellow-hued breakfast room with its willowware collection displayed in a glass case. There are three lounges, all filled with lovely antiques and spectacular flower arrangements. French doors lead to a brick terrace, where comfortable chairs invite sitting and looking at the water. House guests may take tea here – a proper British one with little tea sandwiches, scones and sweets. The new wing adds an hibiscus-filled conservatory, where two model planes are suspended under the skylight, and a billiards room described as "a meeting room in disguise." An indoor swimming pool and exercise facility are the newest attractions.

There's not even a check-in counter in the understated little reception area, where someone spots visitors through one-way glass doors and asks them to have a seat. The guest book at the concierge's desk is filled with superlatives, most relating to special occasions. "Perfection personified," one guest summed up.

Doubles, $175 to $395; suites, $475 to $525.

St. Michaels Harbour Inn & Marina, 101 North Harbor Road, St. Michaels 21663. (410) 745-9001 or (800) 955-9001.

Opened in 1986, this contemporary structure commands a prime location at the head of the busy St. Michaels harbor.

The L-shaped, three-story structure has 46 guest rooms, 32 of them two-room suites facing the water. Each has a living room with a sofabed, desk, television and kitchenette with a sink and refrigerator, and a bedroom with two queensize beds, remote-control TV and a large bathroom with double vanities and thick towels. French doors lead from each room onto a private terrace or balcony with good-looking chairs and a table overlooking the harbor. One of us thought it quite a luxury to be able to watch her show of choice on the bedroom TV while her spouse was glued to a baseball game (this was playoff time) in the living room. Smaller quarters on the third floor have rooms with one queen bed; some have kitchenettes.

The pleasant **Lighthouse Restaurant** serves three meals a day (see Dining Spots). At breakfast, we enjoyed a stack of apple-pecan pancakes while watching the harbor activity.

A small outdoor pool beside the harbor is flanked by a jacuzzi and a bar for beverages and snacks. Overnight docking slips are available for 60 boats. There's a **Ship's**

Black Walnut Point Inn complex spreads over 57 acres on point at end of peninsula.

190

Lawn of The Inn at Perry Cabin faces Fogg Cove and St. Michaels waterfront.

Store, and an aqua center offers canoes, sailboats and pedal boats for adventuring around the harbor.

Doubles, $169 to $189; suites, $259 to $349. Two-night minimum on weekends, May-October.

Black Walnut Point Inn, Box 308, Tilghman Island 21671. (410) 886-2452.

This 57-acre portion of paradise at the end of Tilghman Island is surrounded by water on three sides. A gate blocks the entrance to the dirt road leading past a wildlife preserve and landscaped lawns to the secluded complex on a point between the widewaters of the Choptank River and the Chesapeake Bay. Once here, you're rather isolated, so it's understandable that this once was the summer retreat for the Soviet embassy. The state acquired the property in 1986 and ultimately leased it to Tom and Brenda Ward to run as a B&B.

In the charming main house, part of which predates the Civil War, they offer four guest rooms with private baths. The Bay Room, with double poster bed and a twin bed, has a beamed ceiling and windows on three sides. Overlooking the pool is the Tilghman Room, totally refurbished and now with a queensize bed. We stayed first in the Choptank Cottage, which has a spacious bedroom, tiny sitting room and screened porch, With waves lapping at the rocky shore outside, it's just like the summer cottage of our dreams. Other cottages raise the total number of bedrooms to eight. The two sections of the Riverside Cottage in which we stayed at our last visit were being re-modeled and reconfigured in 1995 to offer french doors facing the water. The large Cove Cottage with kitchen and living room was next on the list for renovations.

The main house has a parlor with TV, VCR, games and grand piano, a chandeliered dining room and a summery sun porch with rattan furniture. Wine glasses and an ice machine are available in a room off the kitchen, where guests may help themselves to

191

lemonade, iced tea, soft drinks or wine from the refrigerator. In the morning, Brenda serves a continental-plus breakfast with choice of juice, fresh fruit, cereal and home-made muffins.

Outside are a jacuzzi beside a delightful freeform swimming pool, with roses bloom-ing all around, plus a lighted tennis court, a swing, rope hammocks and seemingly endless lawns. Once you stretch out in a hammock by the bay, perhaps watching one of the resident great blue herons, you won't want to get up. Tom may be persuaded to pilot guests around the island on a champagne tour in his speedy commercial fishing boat.

The Wards are outgoing hosts and energetic innkeepers. Their very special place has a casual, laid-back feeling in keeping with the St. Michaels of yesteryear.

Doubles, $110 to $120; cottage rooms and suites, $120 to $140. Smoking restricted. Open weekends only in January and February.

Chesapeake Wood Duck Inn, Gibsontown Road, Box 202, Tilghman Island 21671. (410) 886-2070 or (800) 956-2070.

Stephanie Feith was feeding ducks at the back door as we arrived. "We started with two and now have twelve," she said of the flock that has made the grounds of the inn their second home since she and David opened in 1993. "Now all we need is a pond for the ducks and a gazebo for watching them," she said.

The pond and the gazebo were in the planning stage for the long back yard leading to Dogwood Harbor, home of the last remaining working skipjack fleet in the country. You get the idea that they will soon be reality, given the speed with which the couple turned the 1890 boarding house and sometime bordello into an elegant six-room B&B. Both corporate dropouts from Atlanta, the Feiths scoured the country for the perfect B&B site and a simpler lifestyle. They found it on Tilghman Island.

Now ex-executive David is a part-time working waterman, picking up substantial pin money to support the couple's penchant for dining out several nights a week. Cooking gourmet breakfasts, he goes all-out – arising at 5 a.m. to start prepping and baking fresh muffins from scratch, and you can taste the difference. Stephanie has turned her talents to interior decorating and dispensing Southern hospitality, which sounds trite but ends up true.

About those breakfasts. We started with a dish of cantaloupe, blueberries and kiwi and a glass of orange juice before digging in to some melt-in-your-mouth lemon-poppyseed muffins. The best was yet to come: an original that Dave calls a Tilghman omelet puff. Filled with cheddar and mozzarella cheeses, capers, tarragon and sundried tomatoes, it's wrapped in smoked ham and puff-pastry dough, then baked and topped with key lime-mustard sauce and raspberry puree, and served with fresh asparagus spears. Unforgettable! Sherried crab quiche, a crab pie that could well be a luncheon dish, and banana-stuffed french toast topped with cinnamon and roasted pecans are other specialties. Lately, Dave has added such side dishes as Spanish mackerel and crostini wrapped in bacon with caramelized brown sugar and mild chile pepper. Re-freshments later in the day include 24-hour coffee and tea service, wine, soft drinks and sherry – the former available in the kitchen and guest refrigerator and the latter in a decanter in the hallway.

Stephanie has furnished the house in what she calls a "traditional/eclectic" style that's most comfortable except, perhaps, for the small antique double beds that she was hoping gradually to replace with queensize beds. Each air-conditioned bedroom comes with private bath, assorted comforters, good artworks, savvy window treat-ments and fine antique furnishings. There are unexpected touches like a foxhunter's hat on the dresser in the Rutledge Room, which is handsome in deep blues and reds

Porches of Kemp Building yield views of bay and main house at Wades Point Inn.

and paisleys, and a stunning Victorian stained-glass piece hanging in the window of the Magnolia Room, which is light and airy in shades of peach and green. Occupants of rooms facing the water in the back of the house are apt to hear the local watermen leaving Dogwood Harbor before dawn to start their day's rounds (David may be among them, if his breakfast prepping is under control).

Interesting artworks – including a display of oyster plates – grace the walls of the kitchen, living room, dining room and sun room. Over the dining table is an antique chandelier that has followed the Feiths around from its original home in Charleston. There's plenty of space to spread out on the screened porch, the rear patio and soon, no doubt, in the gazebo beside the pond-to-be.

Doubles, $115 to $125.

Wades Point Inn on the Bay, Wades Point Road, Box 7, St. Michaels 21663. (410) 745-2500.

Very Southern looking, this imposing white brick plantation-style home at the end of a long lane is surrounded by unusually attractive grounds and backs up to the Chesapeake Bay about five miles west of St. Michaels on the way to Tilghman Island. The original house was built in 1819 by Baltimore shipwright Thomas Kemp. A summer wing was added in 1890 and it has operated as a guest house in the old Bay tradition ever since.

"We've been updating but want it to stay comfy and homey," said innkeeper Betsy Feiler, who's owned the inn with husband John since 1984. Their prime accommodations are in the new Mildred T. Kemp Building, which has twelve hotel-style rooms with modern baths, some with kitchenette facilities to encourage families and all but two with waterfront balconies that you may never want to leave. Each is furnished traditionally and individually with down comforters, plush carpeting and interesting window treatments, with Bibles on the night stands, and TVs noticeably missing.

The main house has fourteen guest rooms, two with private baths and several more with wash basin in the rooms. Most rooms here are interestingly if sparely furnished,

Front porch of Victoriana Inn faces broad lawn leading to harbor.

and the annex that Betsy once candidly described as a "sophisticated Girl Scout house" is now called "a country farmhouse." The summer wing is what you'd expect to find around Tidewater: rooms with high ceilings (and windows) open off the long corridor, the entrance to each containing a screen door inside the regular door, which guests tend to leave open for cross-ventilation on summer nights.

Guests enter a new reception area in the original summer kitchen. The main parlor is furnished with two sofas, a piano, a tapestry over the fireplace and more books than a Southern gentleman could possibly have read. These rooms give little inkling of the astonishing Bay Room in back – a huge sun room like none we've seen, a veritable sea of white wicker furniture with columns and arches, a fireplace, bleached floors topped with colorful patterned rugs and windows on all sides onto the water. Here is where guests linger over a continental breakfast of fruit salad, juice, cereal, muffins and french rolls or relax with a book and watch the boats go by. If you can stir yourself from the Bay Room or one of the hammocks and chairs spread out on the shady grounds beside the water, saunter along the special nature trail that curves along the shoreline and traverses the interior of the property. Be on the lookout for deer, a rabbit, red fox, terrapin, bald eagle, great blue heron, osprey and more. The prolific flower gardens in front of the Kemp House are worth a close look, too.

Doubles, $75 to $125, $125 to $175 in Kemp Building. Two-night minimum stay on weekends and holidays. Closed January and February. No smoking.

Victoriana Inn, 205 Cherry St., Box 449, St. Michaels 21663. (410) 745-3368.

All is frilly and lacy at this inn that lives up to its name. Converting a private residence built in 1883 and facing the harbor, Janet Bernstein opened her elegant little gem in 1988. She resides on the premises and generally is more in evidence than are other innkeepers in town.

Tiny sachets are on the beds, candies of the season are at bedside and fresh flowers are in the five air-conditioned guest rooms. Other thoughtful touches are embroidered pillows, toiletries and velvety towels folded up in baskets. The most coveted room is one on the main floor with a canopied four-poster bed, fireplace and the only private bath. Three of the four rooms on the second floor have in-room sinks but all share two baths. Beds vary from twins/king to queensize four-poster.

A collection of glass animals adorns the parlor mantel, and there's a sensational oriental piece in the upstairs hall. Victorian antiques, samplers and dolls are all around.

A sun room facing the waterfront contains a TV and VCR. A front porch in gray and white wicker overlooks lovely flower gardens, one of the biggest magnolia trees we ever saw, a little fish pond where Janet's pet frog hangs out and, of course, the boats in the harbor. Chairs are scattered about the lawns, and the setting is quite idyllic.

Breakfast is sumptuous: fresh fruit and juice, perhaps corned beef hash or eggs benedict, and at least two homemade breads.

Doubles, $95 to $135.

The Inn at Christmas Farm, 8873 Tilghman Island Road (Route 33), Wittman 21676. (410) 745-5312 or 820-7125.

For a change of pace, stay overnight in a church. Not any church, mind you, but a little dollhouse of a chapel that David and Beatrice Lee moved to the side of their circa-1800 farmhouse about seven miles southwest of St. Michaels. The 1893 Methodist church belonged to their housekeeper's congregation down the road, but was available when it merged with another.

"We moved it, rebuilt it and renovated it to the Victorian period," said David. They converted the interior into two bright and airy, high-ceilinged suites. Each has a wet bar and refrigerator, a kingsize black iron canopy bed topped with frilly coverings, and double sinks in the bathrooms. The front Bell Tower Suite, entered through the double doors of the belfry, enjoys a brick patio running the width of the building. At the other end of the structure is the Gabriel Suite, whose french doors open onto a large, raised deck. Relax on the wrought-iron furniture on patio or deck, watch the goats, hear the farm sounds and look across the fields to the new farm pond with a dock for swimming and sunning and the distant waters of Cummings Creek. Here's contentment.

There's more. The Lees offer a suite with a kingsize bed, sitting room and a wood stove on the first floor of their main house. Another suite called Christmas Cottage was transformed from a little waterman's house they moved to the property and at-

Rural chapel has bneen converted into two suites at The Inn at Christmas farm.

tached to the side of their house. It comes with a private entrance, a sitting room with a two-person jacuzzi at the far end and, upstairs, a kingsize bedroom and bathroom. The private courtyard here looks onto a cove where peacocks spend a lot of time.

Now semi-retired in Beaufort, S.C., the Lees hired a French woman, France Goupil, as resident innkeeper to run the place full time. She serves a full breakfast featuring French-Canadian recipes in the sun room of the farmhouse. Her specialty is french toast stuffed with cream cheese and almonds and served with real maple syrup. Turkey bacon, fruit, fresh orange juice and gourmet coffee accompany.

Suites, $135.

The Parsonage Inn, 210 North Talbot St., St. Michaels 21663. (410) 745-5519.

Its entry tower topped by a steeple and flanked by two-story octagonal sections with paneled chimneys, this is one of the more architecturally striking structures along the main street. Check the unusual brick facade with its many inlay patterns and the Victorian gingerbread trim over the porches.

The house, built in 1883, was extensively renovated from a Methodist church parsonage in 1985. Five bedrooms were fashioned from the parsonage and three with separate entrances were added motel-style at the rear. All have private baths with Victorian pedestal wash basins and brass fixtures. They have king or queensize beds, plush carpeting and thick towels, Queen Anne-style furniture and Laura Ashley linens and accessories. Three possess working fireplaces, the two most appealing open onto an upstairs deck and two have television.

Oriental rugs and fine Victorian furniture enhance the cozy fireplaced parlor and a large formal dining room, where freshly ground coffee, fruit, cereal and muffins are served by resident managers for owner Willard Workman. Outdoors is a nicely landscaped patio with wicker furniture.

Doubles, $110 to $130. No smoking.

Kemp House Inn, 412 South Talbot St., Box 638, St. Michaels 21663. (410) 745-2243.

This three-story clapboard house was the first B&B to open in St. Michaels (in 1982), and it's said that Gen. Robert E. Lee was a guest here long before that. Built in 1805, it has six guest rooms, two on each floor, plus a cottage with cathedral ceiling and full bath out back. It suffers from a lack of common facilities other than a rocker-lined front porch and a nice back yard.

Period furnishings, wingback chairs and Queen Anne tables are in each room, which have antique four-poster rope beds with trundle beds beneath, patchwork quilts and down pillows. Four rooms have washstands and W/C, others washstand only, and guests share shower rooms on the second floor. Four also have working fireplaces, which are lit on cool nights. Candles, low-light sconces and old-fashioned nightshirts create "an ambiance of romantic 19th-century life," according to owner-innkeepers Steve and Diane Cooper.

Continental breakfast with hot pastries is taken on trays in the room or outside on the porch or lawn in summer.

Doubles, $65 to $105.

Dining Spots

208 Talbot, 208 North Talbot St., St. Michaels. (410) 745-3838.

Since its opening in 1990 in a mid-19th-century house, this has become the area's hottest and best-regarded restaurant. A lounge with a marble bar leads into a serene

Bricks and sconces create sophisticated setting for dining at 208 Talbot.

main dining room and three smaller rooms, one a garden room with floral paintings on the white brick walls. Decor is crisp in teal green and white, and the staff is informed and suave.

Culinary Institute-trained chef Paul Milne was featured on the 1993 television series, Great Chefs of the East. He and partner Candace Chiaruttini present here what they call casual gourmet dining . Others call it quite sophisticated. Among dinner entrées ($18.50 to $22.50) might be seared yellowfin tuna with charred onions and burgundy butter sauce, potato-crusted red snapper with tomato coulis, grilled pork loin with braised cabbage and sweet potato napoleon, and grilled ribeye steak with wild mushrooms, crispy onions and homemade worcestershire sauce.

Start with a napoleon of smoked salmon with crispy wontons and wasabi sauce, rum-glazed grilled quail with a salad of frisée, grapes, almonds and bacon, or house-smoked local bluefish with a blue corn tortilla, guacamole and chipotle sauce. Candace makes the delectable desserts, perhaps lemon tart, apple spice cake with warm caramel sauce, tirami su or assorted ice creams.

The lunch menu is short but sweet, the five entrées likely ranging from $7.50 for grilled chicken salad with oriental dressing and five different greens to $12.50 for grilled salmon with olive oil. The grilled salmon and capellini pasta tossed with clams, scallops and tomato sauce also are featured at brunch.

Lunch in season, Wednesday-Friday noon to 2; dinner, Tuesday-Saturday 5 to 10; Sunday, brunch 10 to 2, dinner 5 to 9.

The Inn at Perry Cabin, Watkins Lane, St. Michaels. (410) 745-2200.

The dining room setting is as perfect as the rest of the first Ashley House venture in the United States. We cannot vouch for the food, because when we stopped for a summer lunch, one look at the prices was enough to scare us off. This is a place for high-rollers at leisure, not working stiffs.

The peak-ceilinged dining room is a panoply of rose, green and white chintz. Tables,

Dining room at The Inn at Perry Cabin is dressed in Laura Ashley fabrics.

skirted to the floor and dressed to the hilt, are flanked by chairs upholstered in a burgundy fabric. Expansive windows and french doors look out onto a terrace and treed lawns leading to Fogg Cove.

Dinner guests have cocktails and complimentary hors d'oeuvre in a parlor-lounge, where they study the menu and place their order. Chef Mark Salter presents a complicated, four-course menu (prix-fixe, $55) that embraces the latest culinary trends and ingredients. One side of the menu changes nightly and the other seasonally. Diners are ushered to their table when the first course is ready. That could be a cream of sweet corn soup with crab cake and chopped chives, a smoked salmon truffle and spinach pasta terrine with a lemon water dressing, a duck spring roll with housemade plum chutney and lentils, and fillet of trout topped with salmon mousse and served with sea scallops, sautéed bok choy and a tomato and citrus nage. A sorbet, perhaps cranberry and hazelnut, clears the palate for the main course. Choices at our visit included seared fillet of tuna with foie gras on a pea and coriander puree, open ravioli of lobster with a creamy mustard sauce, seared medallions of monkfish and jumbo shrimp on a tomato and pepper fondue, roasted cornish hen with savoy cabbage served on truffled couscous, roast veal tenderloin on crushed black olive potatoes with a ribbon of vegetables and caramelized shallots, and honey-glazed lamb shank with a sundried tomato sauce. A choice wine list is priced from the mid-$20s up; many wines are available by the glass. The signature dessert is a trio of chocolate extravaganzas. Others include a lemon and poppyseed soufflé with strawberry sorbet, white chocolate crème brûlée with kirsch-flavored cherries, and summer pudding with devon clotted cream.

About that lunch menu. The meal is available prix-fixe in four options (from $16.50 for two courses to $26.50 for three courses, including a glass of wine). The main-course choices run from a turkey club sandwich with prosciutto to smoked swordfish with haricots verts, sautéed arugula and a cantaloupe relish.

Lunch daily, noon to 2:30; dinner nightly, 6 to 9:30. No smoking.

Bay Hundred Restaurant, Route 33 at Knapps Narrows, Tilghman Island. (410) 886-2622.

Don't be deceived by this small gray waterfront building sporting a funky lounge with jukebox and video games. Some of the area's most interesting food emanates from the kitchen of chef-owner Donelda Monahan and is served in a pleasant dining porch beside the water. The decor of sleek black upholstered chairs, mint green linens, fresh flowers and votive candles is quite elegant. Accents are assorted glass jars and bottles containing flowers, tools on the walls and other knickknacks given to Donelda and husband Jamie by a supportive community.

Donelda is into all-natural ingredients and healthy food, which is not surprising when you learn that she hails from Tacoma, Wash. She's also into garnishing her plates with many herbs and even a pansy. Our latest dinner here started with a crispy tuna tempura, wonderful with the wasabi sauce. Other appetizer possibilities ($4.95 to $6.95) include vegetable spring rolls, sushi, cajun coconut shrimp, and a tasty mix of smoked salmon and marinated scallops with oranges, red onion and watercress.

Window table at Bay Hundred Restaurant.

Entrées run from $12.95 for the signature zuni stew (a bean, rice, cheese and vegetable concoction inspired by the Pueblo Indians) to $18.95 for New York strip steak smothered with onions. We loved the backfin crab with prosciutto and spinach in a brandy cream sauce, served over fettuccine, and the grilled shrimp flavored with hoisin and oriental chile sauce and served over sesame noodles. An earlier dinner produced a special of soft-shell crabs with green beans plus shrimp sautéed with zucchini, peas and tomatoes in a creamy basil-parmesan sauce and served over fettuccine. Salads of wild greens or the original house version come with. The house dressing – a mayonnaise base with curry, thyme, onion and vinegar – is so popular it's for sale by the pint.

A dense and delectable grand marnier pudding is the signature dessert, for which Bon Appetit magazine requested the recipe. The wine list, heavy on California vintages, is one of the area's best.

Many of the nighttime treats are available also for lunch. Most choices are in the $6.95 to $9.95 range.

The view of the passing boats and the colorful lights from the drawbridge help make this place special. It's like dining along the Intra-Coastal Waterway.

Open daily, 11:30 to 9:30.

Town Dock Restaurant, 125 Mulberry St., St. Michaels. (410) 745-5577.

The waterfront setting at this huge establishment is one of the town's best. The food was on its way to measuring up after the Town Dock was purchased in 1994 by Michael Rork, who had made quite a name for himself as executive chef at Baltimore's fancy Harbor Court Hotel. With his wife and three children, he sought a more rural location in which to run his own business. The locals were agog with the prospect, and Michael was up to his ears in the long process of converting a touristy, 400-seat restaurant into "an upscale but casual dining destination."

The short daily specials menu was where the action was in his first summer. Instead of twenty servings of each, he had to think in terms of a hundred. Typical were grilled salmon topped with roasted leeks and peppers, soft-shell crabs with a tomato-herb cream sauce, grilled shrimp served over saffron orzo, and grilled duck breast with dried cherries and fresh currants. These were the standouts on a seafood-oriented menu priced from $12.95 for deep-fried shrimp to $22 for Brazilian lobster tail stuffed with crab imperial.

The pedestrian lunch menu that had bored us previously was being spiced up with specials like grilled chicken caesar salad, avocado stuffed with crabmeat served on field greens, and a sandwich of grilled tenderloin medallions with caramelized onions on sourdough bread ($7.95 to $9.95). Desserts in the lighted pastry display case that Michael inherited near the entry included peanut-butter cheesecake, french silk pie and chocolate-raspberry torte.

In the winter, Michael planned to bring in visiting chefs from Baltimore for special ethnic weeks. For the summer of 1995, he hoped to have ready an elegant upstairs dining room with an open grill kitchen. That would be the showcase for the grilled specialties of his contemporary regional cuisine; he thought he might call it Michael's on the Miles. He brought two cooks and a general manager with him from Baltimore, so you knew the place was in good hands.

Lunch daily, 11:30 to 4; dinner, 4 to 10. Closed Monday and Tuesday in winter.

Lighthouse Restaurant, St. Michaels Harbour Inn and Marina, 101 North Harbor Road, St. Michaels. (410) 745-5102.

Talented local chef Carl Langkammerer left the Bakery restaurant in 1994 to do his creative thing in the second-floor waterfront restaurant at the Harbour Inn. The contemporary, nicely angled dining room here is decked out in mauve cloths, fanned napkins and blond wood chairs. It commands a great sunset view over the harbor.

Carl is known for his ways with crab, from soups of cream of crab and crab vegetable through an appetizer of backfin terrine with mushroom duxelles, served on a country biscuit, to main courses of pan-seared crab cakes, soft-shell crabs, shrimp and backfin baked in a lemon-garlic sauce, and handmade tortellini stuffed with crabmeat, spinach and ricotta cheese in a tomato-basil sauce. Even the surf and turf here involves crab, pairing a crab cake with an herb-crusted lamb chop. Other entrées ($13.95 to $19.95) could be grilled salmon served on a ginger and spring onion sauce, California chicken with spinach and sundried tomatoes, and grilled black angus sirloin steak.

The Sunday champagne brunch buffet is a hot item with anyone who wants to eat beside the water.

Lunch daily, 11 to 2; dinner, 5 to 10; Sunday brunch, 10:30 to 2.

Morsels, 205 North Talbot St., St. Michaels. (410) 745-2911.

Creative casual dining is the billing for this expanding place that started as a gourmet-to-go shop. New owners Danny and Becky Ness sold their interest in Bandaloops, which they likened to a bigger version of Morsels in the Federal Hill section of Baltimore, to live on a sailboat. Now they do the cooking here for a casual dining room on the main floor, for a handful of outdoor tables on the side alley and for a new upstairs area with 22 seats at tables and bar stools (the last expansion allowed them to obtain a full liquor license).

The menu, supplemented by blackboard specials, changes monthly. Expect main courses ($11.95 to $19.95) like sautéed shrimp served on curried orange rice, grilled swordfish topped with pesto and served on peach chutney, basque seafood pasta, grilled lamb with smoked tomato-pepper coulis and grilled filet mignon with horseradish-

Famous chef and harbor view draw diners to Town Dock Restaurant.

caper sauce. There also are a few appetizers like smoked bluefish pâté and light fare, including pizzas and smoked turkey quesadilla. Desserts could be key lime pie, Sicilian cassata, chocolate mousse pie and tirami su.

At lunch time, look for things like grilled fish, chicken boursin and oriental shrimp salad. Huevos rancheros and crab omelet are favorites at Sunday breakfast.

Lunch daily, 11 to 3; dinner nightly, 5:30 to 9 or 10; Sunday breakfast, 8:30 to noon.

The Tilghman Island Inn, Coopertown Road, Tilghman Island. (410) 886-2141.

The food quality is on the rise in this inn's pleasant, white-linened dining room done up in rose and green, with works by local artists on the barnwood walls. There's a good view of boats and, around the corner and beyond the jaunty outdoor deck, a glimpse of the Chesapeake Bay.

At one summer night's dinner, we started with zesty black-eyed pea cakes served with tomato salsa and a crab bisque so thick that a spoon could stand up in it. The crab imperial and the grilled soft-shell crabs were excellent. The dinner menu was priced from $14.95 for pork tenderloin with dried cranberries, currants and pistachios in madeira sauce to $21 for veal chop in a spicy mustard crust with apple-brandy demi glaze. Choices included oysters Choptank (with julienne of country ham and spinach with champagne sauce in puff pastry), shrimp and sausage gumbo, stuffed quail with spicy grits soufflé, and rack of lamb with minted cabernet sauce. Homemade ginger-pear ice cream made an excellent ending.

Dinner nightly, 6 to 9:30 or 10; closed Monday and Tuesday in off-season. Sunday jazz brunch buffet, noon to 3.

Diversions

Chesapeake Bay Maritime Museum, Navy Point, 745-2916. Built on mounds of crushed oyster shells, this growing museum founded in 1965 is the town's major tourist attraction. Its focal point is the 1879 Hooper Strait Lighthouse, one of only three cottage-type lighthouses remaining on the bay. You learn what a lightkeeper's life was like and pass some interesting exhibits of fog signals, lamps and lenses as you climb to the top level for a bird's-eye view of the St. Michaels harbor. The Waterfowling Building contains an extensive collection of decoys, guns and mounted waterfowl. The museum has the largest floating fleet of historic Chesapeake Bay boats in existence, including a skipjack, log canoe, oyster boat and crab dredger. They're maintained in a traditional working boat shop, where you get to see craftsmen at work and view a small display of primitive boat-building tools. Other attractions include the Small Boat Exhibit Shed, a bell tower, a Victorian bandstand where concerts are staged in summer and a museum shop. A Watermen's Village was being developed to show life in a typical bay settlement of a century ago. Open daily in summer, 9 to 6; rest of year, 10 to 4; January-March, weekends only. Adults, $6.

St. Michaels Walking Tour. A self-guided walking tour with a map is provided by the St. Mary's Square Museum and the St. Michaels Business Association. It covers the meandering waterfront, including the footbridge from Cherry Street to Navy Point (one wishes there were more footbridges to get from point to point), the Talbot Street business section and St. Mary's Square, an unusual town green laid out away from the main street and apt to be missed unless you seek it out. The map identifies 23 historic houses (none open to the public), churches and sites. We found equally interesting things along the way.

Shopping. Shopping is a big draw along narrow Talbot Street in St. Michaels. **Chesapeake Trading Company,** a bookstore and gift shop, is where you stop for espresso or great cold drinks as you browse among the collection of hats, jewelry and paperbacks. Owner Linda Boatner stocks all the right things and displays them right. At the quirky **Connoisseur Shop** in the Town Hall Mall, Louise Clifford sells everything from cookbooks to soup mixes. Those of us who like food spicy enough to bring tears to the eyes are in seventh heaven at **Flamingo Flats.** This little shop must have every hot, spicy sauce or relish ever bottled – more than 2,600, including many from the Caribbean. **Bags Aloft** stocks all kinds of bags from laundry to lunch. **Paper Moon** offers interesting imported costume jewelry, contemporary American Indian silver jewelry, unusual picture frames and carved animals. Resort-type clothes are found at **Shaw Bay Classics** and **Chesapeake Bay Outfitters,** while the **Broken Rudder** carries nice sportswear with a Chesapeake accent. Room after room of wicker, brass, lamps, shades, baskets, kitchen gadgets, lucite items and, of course, lots of pottery are the attraction at **St. Michaels Pottery.** A resident decoy carver works at **The Calico Gallery,** which has a large selection of local art posters. **Woodworks, Etc.** stocks a fine selection of decoys and at the **Blue Swan,** we liked the nautical Christmas ornaments. **Celebrate Maryland!** has more Maryland gifts and souvenirs than we ever imagined there were, most not schlocky and quite useful.

Extra-Special _____

Patriot Cruise, Navy Point, St. Michaels. (410) 745-3100.

Since most of its meandering shoreline is very private and far from view, the best way to see and savor this part of the Eastern Shore is by boat. David Etzel provides a leisurely 90-minute cruise up the Miles River on a two-deck boat carrying 180 passengers. He advised beforehand that he points out "birds, houses, duck blinds, whatever I see." We saw the Mystic Clipper in the distance, various kinds of bulkheading to prevent shore erosion, several osprey nests on channel markers, the ruins of St. John's Chapel, and some mighty impressive plantations and contemporary homes. We learned that James Michener wrote *Chesapeake* in a rented house along the river. Our only regret was that the boat didn't go closer to the sights the guide or the taped narration were pointing out on the eleven-mile round trip. Cruises mid-April to mid-November, daily at 11, 1 and 3 (minimum fifteen persons). Adults, $7.50.

Stately homes along Chestertown's Water Street back up to Chester River.

Chestertown, Md.
A Town that Has It All

The impression one gets upon entering Chestertown over the U.S. Route 213 bridge is unforgettable. Across the wide Chester River are grand brick mansions along the shore. In the center of town are great churches, squares and parks with monuments, the county courthouse, a couple of inns and suave stores. The streets in the nicely symmetrical downtown grid are lined with historic homes and townhouses, many dating to the 18th century.

Here's the perfect small town, you think – close to the water, with ties to the past, obviously prosperous, a manageable size, good quality of life. The first impression is not erroneous. Subsequent forays in and around the Eastern Shore town of 4,000 and conversations with its residents confirm that this is one great place to live, as well as to visit.

Local boosters are proud that Chestertown was rated in a national survey as the tenth favorite historic place in America. The lure is more than the fact that this small town claims the second largest district of restored 18th-century homes in Maryland, however.

Life is slower here, Chestertown lying well off the beaten path. As the county seat of Kent County, Maryland's smallest, it exudes an air of self-sufficiency and a sense of place that evades towns twice its size. The park fountain works, the clock tower is

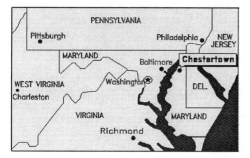

illuminated at night, tiny white lights twinkle in a downtown alleyway. Galleries, boutiques and shops, all owner-operated, purvey wares normally associated with metropolitan areas. Creative chefs have settled here to instill their culinary marks.

The good life is enhanced by the cultural offerings of Washington College, the nation's tenth oldest and the only one that George Washington allowed to use his name (he served as a trustee and received an honorary degree).

Not far away are attractions as diverse as the oldest Episcopal church in Maryland, the best bathing beach on the Chesapeake Bay at Betterton, a hokey but bustling auction house and Rock Hall, a once-sleepy fishing community that's become a happening place lately.

Who would challenge the claim that here is a small town that has it all?

Inn Spots

Brampton, 25227 Chestertown Road, Chestertown 21620. (410) 778-1860.

The thoughtful comments in the guest books in each room testify glowingly that innkeepers Michael and Danielle Hanscom do things right. Theirs is one of the more comfortable and elegant B&Bs in which we've stayed.

On 35 acres about a mile out High Street (Route 20) south of town, the imposing three-story brick Italianate Greek Revival commands a hilltop set back from the road. Two gliders swing toward each other and an array of wicker chairs from either end of the pillared front veranda.

Inside the 1860 house, listed on the National Register, are a majestic living room with twelve-foot ceilings, high bookshelves and gray leather couches facing each other across an oriental rug next to the fireplace; a brick and paneled guest parlor and TV room (TVs also are available in guest rooms); a fireplaced dining room with peach draperies matching the wallpaper and four tables beneath a crystal chandelier, and solid walnut baseboards and doors that never suffered the humiliation of paint. What restoration needed to be done was ably handled during the six months prior to their 1987 opening by Mike, who had restored Victorian homes in San Francisco.

Danielle, a former flight attendant with Swissair, oversaw the decorating. The eight air-conditioned guest rooms and suites are classics. Each has a private bath and a queen or twin beds that can be put together as a king, and six have fireplaces or Franklin stoves. They are tastefully decorated with period and reproduction antiques, many of them from Switzerland. Rooms are perfect down to the smallest details: plump pillows, duvet comforters, thick towels, night lights in the bathrooms, brass shoe horns on the closet doors. The bowl on our dresser in the Blue Room matched the blue and white wallpaper; a bird and butterfly from the stunning wallpaper pattern in the bathroom had been painstakingly cut out and pasted on the vanity. Most of the paintings in the house were done by Danielle's grandfather, an artist in Switzerland.

All rooms, with the exception of the Mezzanine Suite that is more cozy, are unusually airy and spacious. Even the two guest rooms on the third floor are surprisingly high-ceilinged and big for their location, each measuring twenty by twenty feet. Choice new accommodations include the Fairy Hill Suite with a ground-floor sitting room and an upstairs bedroom notable for a Swiss cherry armoire and an antique chimney cupboard, and the renovated 19th-century Smoke House, now a high-ceilinged, beamed bedroom with couch, fireplace and an 1860 walnut armoire. At our latest visit, Mike was converting a rear outbuilding into two large guest rooms with fireplaces and jacuzzi baths, to be ready in early 1995.

The Hanscoms, who live with their young daughters in an outbuilding on the property, offer afternoon refreshments and wine or sherry in the evening. Breakfast in their beautiful dining room starts with orange juice, fresh fruit and sticky buns. Our entrée was a delicate puffed pancake with a fresh plum sauce. Others could be french toast, blueberry pancakes, waffles or sausage, and cheese and green pepper quiche.

Doubles, $90 to $125; suites, $110 to $150.

Italianate Greek Revival house has been converted into Brampton, an elegant B&B.

Great Oak Manor, 10568 Cliff Road, Chestertown 21620. (410) 778-5943.

Majestic. How better to describe this red-brick Georgian manor house grandly situated on twelve acres overlooking the Chesapeake Bay? Written descriptions, even photos, fail to convey fully the understated elegance and the alluring appeal of this winning B&B, as transformed by energetic new owners Don and Dianne Cantor from California. They took over in 1993 from an absentee owner who owned eight area lodging facilities and quickly invested a quarter million dollars in refurbishing and upgrading what had been a tired, rather cold facility that catered to functions.

"What really attracted us was the large common rooms," said Don. "Our guests don't feel like they're intruding on the owners' quarters." The 25-room mansion, built in 1938 by an heir to the W.R. Grace shipping fortune, has regal public rooms, eleven guest rooms and plenty of space left over for the Cantor family at one end.

Guests enter a great hall worthy of the name, with a graceful spiral staircase on one side. Intricate carvings over the doorways announce each room's use (a rising sun over the entrance, a crab over the dining rooms). On the left are a formal living room, a rich-looking library with shelves of books, hunting prints and a huge oriental rug, and a side porch full of wicker and wisteria stenciling. On the right are the dining room and the Gun Room, dark and masculine with guns behind leaded glass doors, plush leather sofas and chairs, a TV/VCR and a small help-yourself bar hidden in a space beneath the spiral staircase. One of Dianne's stained-glass creations, a colorful parrot, stands sentry in a window. Outside, a broad, tree-shaded lawn leads to a bluff above the bay, where a screened gazebo and a deck with rocking chairs await.

The bedrooms vary in size and decor. Each comes with full bath, kingsize bed, a sitting area with comfortable chairs, and bottles of Perrier and Evian water. Several have fireplaces and bay views. An artist hand-painted whimsical touches here and there: a squirrel on a desk in one room, an extra window on the wall of another. Even the third-floor rooms convey an unusual sense of space with their high vaulted ceilings. The Cantors provide a TV in the one room that lacks a view.

205

A continental-plus breakfast is served at individual tables amid lots of silver and china in the dining room. The fare includes fresh fruit, cereals, bagels and Dianne's special peach-pecan muffins. The Cantors are hands-on innkeepers whose innkeeping savvy shows.

Doubles, $80 to $135; suites, $180. Smoking restricted.

The Imperial Hotel, 208 High St., Chestertown 21620. (410) 778-5000.

Built as a hotel in 1903, the Imperial had been converted to apartments and shops before it was grandly restored into a small, urbane lodging establishment and restaurant by ex-Washingtonians Carla and Albert Massoni. New innkeepers Barbara and Bob Lavelle from suburban Philadelphia took over in 1994 and applied the icing to the cake.

The hotel's eleven guest rooms on the second and third floors are decorated to the Victorian hilt with original art and period furnishings. All have private baths with heated towel racks and Gilchrist & Soames toiletries. Armoires conceal TV sets and antique potty cupboards hide the telephones. Bold wallpapers, wild borders, ornate lamps, floral carpeting, coordinated fabrics, lace curtains and heavy draperies are the rule. Rooms vary widely in size. Some are rather small, but we found the third-floor suite big enough for a cocktail party, what with a living room that is total Victoriana, a bedroom with kingsize bed, a mini-kitchen and a porch the size of a volleyball court across the front of the hotel.

Some think the best room in the house is No. 206 mid-week, when rates are discounted. It's located in the front corner across from the guest parlor and beside the common second-floor porch, which don't get much use during the week. There also are two more accommodations in the rear carriage house. A favorite is the spacious, country-style suite, a welcome break from the pervading high Victorian decor and good for families. It has a beamed cathedral ceiling, a skylit bathroom and a full kitchen.

The hotel has an award-winning restaurant (see Dining Spots) and a handsome little cocktail lounge with a new fireplace. A rear parking lot has been transformed into a landscaped courtyard for lunch, lounging and Friday evening jazz concerts. The newest addition is the Cellar Coffee Bar & Bakery (serving Starbucks coffee) on the lower floor.

A complimentary continental breakfast of juice and large, flaky croissants and other pastries is served in the Hubbard Room.

Doubles, $125; suites, $200 to $300.

Moonlight Bay Inn, 6002 Lawton Ave., Rock Hall 21661. (410) 639-2660.

Guests at this new B&B in a residential section along the Chesapeake Bay enjoy one of the more appealing water settings of any inn anywhere. A screened gazebo, garden chairs scattered about the large lawn and a wicker-filled porch take full advantage. As the sun sets over little Swan Island, yellow lights outline docks in the foreground, white lights twinkle on the Bay Bridge in the distance and the glow of Baltimore to the west lights up the evening sky. The feeling is nothing short of magical.

So it may be difficult to comprehend why innkeeper Dorothy Santangelo "cried for two weeks" after her husband Bob bought the place in 1992. "I thought I'd be at Great Oak Manor or Tara," said she. "I wanted a B&B and he wanted a marina." What they got initially was a fantastic marina location and an abandoned house that had successively been a post office, a restaurant and a boarding house. They razed all but the front of the house and, after fifteen months of rebuilding and renovations, opened in late 1993 with five handsome bedrooms, all with private baths and caring touches, from clock radios to diaries for guest comments.

Abandoned house has been restored and rebuilt to take in guests as Moonlight Bay Inn.

The largest room is on the main floor off a spacious living room. It comes with a sitting room, canopy queensize bed and windows onto the water. Even more windows onto the water were evident in our upstairs corner room, comfortable with kingsize bed, a large and elegant bathroom, and an antique rocker beside a chair with a rush seat. If you're so inclined, says Dorothy, you can lie in bed here or in the adjacent room and "watch the boats pass outside." The adjacent room is large and lovely in white and blue, the patterned fabrics here matching some of the miniature vases displayed on a shelf on the wall. A cozy side room that's summery in white lace and wicker, with accents of pink, "is every woman's dream," says Dorothy. Each room contains a decanter of sherry, fancy window treatments and a framed wall hanging called "Inn Reminders," in which the usual guest instructions are rendered in poetry. The inn has been lovingly furnished by Dorothy. The decorating is quite remarkable, given that she did it herself and is legally blind.

She's also quite the cook, as evidenced at breakfast in the dining room overlooking a showy English garden. Waffles in many forms are her specialty. We enjoyed belgian waffles after preliminaries of orange juice, a fruit cup with bananas and strawberries, and two kinds of muffins. English tea is served in the late afternoon.

Doubles, $99 to $109.

The Inn at Mitchell House, 8796 Maryland Pkwy., Chestertown 21620. (410) 778-6500.

A long driveway leads, plantation-like, to this lovely old manor house seven miles west of Chestertown in the Tolchester section near Chesapeake Bay. The ten-acre property beside Stoneybrook Pond was part of a 1,000-acre working plantation. The manor, built in 1743 and expanded in 1825, is still fit for the landed gentry.

Jim Stone, a Washington native who summered here, his wife Tracy and their youngsters share the expansive house with guests in six rooms and suites, all with private baths. They serve sumptuous breakfasts and offer weekend dinners to guests and the public.

Theirs is very much a family home, reflecting heirlooms and mementos from both sides of the family as well as the telltale signs of their youngsters. Jim acquired the eagle over the entrance from the cornerstone of a building in Baltimore. In one of the two parlors on the left is a portrait of Sir Peter Parker, a British commander who was wounded near here in the War of 1812 and was brought to the Mitchell House for aid; the portrait was found by coincidence many years later by Tracy's father. A signed Tiffany lamp graces the square baby piano converted into a desk. Family portraits cover a square grand piano, and a watercolor of Tracy and their youngsters hangs on one wall. Who can help but be fascinated by the lineup of framed White House Christmas cards dating from Tracy's years at the White House when she handled President Reagan's mail? The side-by-side parlors are attractive in pale yellow and deep green decor.

Art works from Jim's grandmother, who started painting oils at age 60, enhance the Joseph Mitchell Room, the largest bedroom with a queensize canopy bed, a fireplace and a sitting area with sofabed. The large Ringgold Room has a queensize bed, a loveseat and a fireplace. On their way to other bedrooms, guests pass a refrigerator stocked with complimentary sodas and beer and a hallway decorated with flapper dresses and hats that belonged to Jim's great aunt. A king-bedded hideaway is up steep stairs in the beamed attic.

A country breakfast is served at five tables in the high-ceilinged dining room, where the floor is brick and plates and artifacts dot the walls. The main course might be french toast, omelets, featherbed eggs, peach-raspberry coffee cake – "everything you can think of that's bad for you I do," says Tracy.

The Stones also offer dinners on Friday and Saturday nights by reservation, a single seating for up to sixteen people at 7 o'clock. A classical guitarist plays as guests sip a complimentary rum cocktail. The $26 to $29 tab includes hors d'oeuvre and wine with the meal. You might start with steamed shrimp or cold soup and salad, move on to grilled tuna with mustard sauce or pork tenderloin with blackberry sauce, and finish with homemade apple pie (with apples from the couple's orchard), chocolate mousse or ice cream pecan ball with homemade hot fudge.

Outside, guests enjoy a screened porch containing a 1956 jukebox with old records that belonged to Tracy's father. The porch overlooks the pond, which you can traverse by means of two bridges. Jim put in the raised herb and flower garden, terraced gardens and a fish pond beside the old smokehouse.

Doubles, $75 to $100.

The Inn at Osprey, Route 20, Rock Hall, 21661. (410) 639-2194.

Philadelphia Main Line investors who like to sail built this yacht club, marina, inn, restaurant and bar from scratch in 1993 along a section of Swan Creek known as "The Haven," an inlet from the nearby Chesapeake Bay. The place looks and feels new, although it was scrupulously designed with the Williamsburg look and actually patterned after the Coke-Garrett House, the mayor's house in Williamsburg, Va. It's all rather slick for Rock Hall.

Stuck on a rather barren landscape that first strikes visitors as mainly sailing masts and parking areas, the endeavor suffers from a split personality. Overnight guests "register" at a second-story office that also serves the marina or, after hours, in the main-floor restaurant. The seven bedrooms are on two floors of the main house. All equipped with modern baths, they are true to the Williamsburg look, from paint colors to wide-plank floors, and feature "showcase furnishings and gallery art throughout," according to the slick inn brochure. Amenities are "the finest that can be found, from our 250-count pima cotton sheets to our authentic oriental rugs," adds inn manager Susannah

The Inn at Mitchell House is situated beside Stoneybrook Pond.

Ford. We found the Windigo room fairly spacious but rather spartan, with queensize poster bed, a windsor chair at a writing desk, nautical and bird prints on the white walls, swagged curtains matching the pillows and the skirt on the night stand, and a couple of oriental scatter rugs on the bare floors. Coat hooks along one wall are pressed into service in lieu of a closet. Less chilly and more comfortable was the Carina room, equipped with two twin beds and a small TV between the sofabed and a wing chair. A third-floor landing area, described as a common room, holds two wing chairs and a TV set. Two water-view rooms, one with jacuzzi and the other with a fireplace, also have TV, but the jacuzzi room "can be noisy due to the restaurant," the inn literature advises.

A complimentary continental breakfast is served in the restaurant's Hunt Room. There's a nature trail along the woods in back of the inn, but the chief asset here may be the large, club-like swimming pool and deck area with bathhouse.

Doubles, $110 to $150.

The White Swan Tavern, 231 High St., Chestertown 21620. (410) 778-2300.

Stay here if you're into history. The White Swan, dating to 1733, is full of it. Its restoration began in 1978 with an archeological dig and produced a "museum" room of the old bar, showing artifacts in a lighted display window.

Despite its lavish refurbishing, the place conveys a rather impersonal and commercial feeling. The hired innkeepers, who live off-premises, may or may not answer the locked front door. Afternoon tea is served by the fireplace in a chandeliered tea room for $2, with a plate of sweets available for $1.50. An article on the tavern's restoration is sold for $1. Occupants of the Sterling Suite find the bow window like that of a storefront, which it once was; though it's partially screened, one nevertheless feels on view to the street here.

Eighteenth-century period furnishings dignify the main-floor common rooms. An austere front parlor is set up as a game room. A more welcoming rear parlor, dressed in yellow floral chintz, contains a TV. All six guest rooms have private baths and at least an extra twin bed for additional guests. Various passages lead to the rooms, which range from the small Thomas Peacock with a lace canopy double bed and a twin under the eaves to the large T.W. Eliason Suite, with a twin bed in the entry, a kingsize bed with imposing wood headboard in the main room and a Victorian sitting room beyond.

A favorite is the John Lovegrove Kitchen, a one-room dwelling that was the first building on the lot. It has a brick floor, dark beamed ceiling, twin beds and an old dining-room table in front of the enormous cooking fireplace. The room exudes atmosphere, but the fireplace (like those in other bedrooms) is not functional and the chairs aren't really comfortable for sitting.

Guests are served a continental breakfast at the time specified on a "breakfast preference card." The fare is "changing," but the innkeeper on duty at our visit would not be specific. It comes with a fruit basket and the morning paper.

Doubles, $100 to $130; suites, $140 to $150. No credit cards.

Widow's Walk Inn, 402 High St., Chestertown 21620. (410) 778-6455 or 778-6864.

Raising six children was "our introduction to running a bed and breakfast," friendly Joanne Toft says of the good-looking, pale yellow establishment with burgundy trim to which they moved from Bucks County after husband Don retired. The children and grandchildren return upon occasion, which accounts for all the teddybears around. The Tofts aim to make guests feel as if "they're coming to grandmother's home."

This grandmother's home is a mix of antiques and family treasures, decorated to the Victorian period but not at all fussy. Guests gather in a comfortable living room, a dining room with one long table for breakfast, a front porch with a swing and a couple of rockers, a screened side porch and a brick patio.

The Maryland Suite, downstairs left, has a queensize bed, a wicker sitting area, full bath, TV and pink carpeting. Blue scatter rugs top the original pine floors in three upstairs rooms and a suite, which offer double, twin or kingsize beds. The suite and another room here have private baths and two share.

The Tofts serve wine or herbed iced tea, cheese and crackers in the late afternoon. Continental breakfast the next morning might involve fresh cantaloupe with strawberries, juice and blueberry-walnut muffins.

Doubles, $85 to $110. No smoking.

Lauretum Inn, 954 High St., Chestertown 21620. (410) 778-3236 or (800) 742-3236.

A long winding lane leads up a knoll just south of town to an exotic Queen Anne Victorian house of unusual character, full of wonders and eccentricities.

Remarkable windows range from sixteen panes over four to 42 over four. The fireplace in one parlor is draped in Waverly fabric because there's no mantel. There's a wedding cake medallion in the ceiling plaster. Pocket windows rise into the ceiling so you can walk through them onto the veranda, as at Monticello. The hall floor combines striped walnut with white ash. A larger, comfortable living room contains a piano and TV. A guest kitchen is available off the dining room, where a continental breakfast of homemade breads, toast and danish is served. Afternoon refreshments also are available.

The second floor has three guest accommodations, one in the Peach Room with a queensize bed and a stained-glass sixteen-over-four-pane window and private bath. Two end rooms combine as a suite and share a hall bath. The third floor contains a secluded bedroom with private bath and a two-bedroom suite, one with a queen bed in what was the classroom for a private school and an outer room with a double bed.

The house was built by U.S. Sen. George Vickers, who cast the deciding vote to overturn impeachment charges against Andrew Johnson from his sickbed at Lauretum, the Latin name for plantation. Many local notables, including Wilbur Ross Hubbard, owner of the landmark riverfront mansion Wide Hall and a descendant of the builder

Lauretum Inn is full of architectural eccentricities and unusual character.

of the Imperial Hotel, attended classes at the private school here. The house remained in the Vickers family until 1986, when it was converted into a B&B.

Innkeepers Peg and Bill Sites bought the inn in late 1991. He commutes weekends from Philadelphia, where he's in administration at Temple University. Peg enjoys being "back home" in the town where her mother was born. Running a B&B is a natural for Peg, who raised sixteen children and once owned a pretzel factory. Now, besides her B&B guests, she caters to 58 grandchildren, "each one cuter than the last."

Doubles, $65 to $85; suite, $95 to $105.

Huntingfield Manor, 4928 Eastern Neck Road, Rock Hall 21661. (410) 639-7779 or (800) 720-8788.

Built in 1950, this was another of the area hostelries owned by an absentee investors and, like Great Oak Manor, it was sold in 1992 to live-in innkeepers who began a long upgrading process. It still retains much of its hunting-lodge atmosphere, however.

Set equidistant from the road and the bay on 70 acres, the house is on the flight path for Canada geese and is surrounded by cornfields ("part of its charm," says owner George Starken, a retired missile engineer who assists his wife Bernadine). It's also 136 feet long and one room wide, with 61 windows and three staircases serving separate sections of the house.

Much of the main floor is devoted to a dining room, a reading room and the Red Room, a long and comfy room with TV and fireplace, which takes its name from the prevailing color of the leather window seat, swag curtains and oriental rugs. Beyond is the big, three-sided screened porch.

Five bedrooms with private baths are located in separate sections of the house. The New Yarmouth Room is billed as the New England room, with twin beds joined as a king between a vaulted ceiling. Other rooms also have twins beds joined as kingsize, but readily split for the bicycle and hunting groups that are frequent visitors. Rooms are outfitted functionally but simply. A separate cottage also is available.

Breakfast is continental, with a selection of fruits, cereals and three kinds of baked goods, from white or dark breads to sweet sticky rolls.

Doubles, $75 to $95; cottage, $115.

Porches mark facade of Imperial Hotel.

Clubby dining room at Imperial Hotel.

Dining Spots

The Imperial Hotel, 208 High St., Chestertown. (410) 778-5000.

Two opulent, intimate dining rooms, one on either side of the main corridor are the setting for some of the area's finest meals. The smaller room is dark and clubby in hunter green and Stuart tartan plaid, while the larger is light and feminine in shades of claret and celadon. Victorian round-back chairs are at tables draped in white damask with little fringed silver lamps on top. Meals are served on white china so as not to distract from the attractively presented food.

Master of the kitchen is Rodney Scruggs, executive chef, assisted by his wife Lisa, who was trained by the White House pastry chef. The Zagat survey of Washington-Baltimore restaurants rates the Imperial among the tops in the area for food.

We certainly were impressed with our dinner. It began with a complimentary cheese straw. Starters were a rich cream of wild mushroom soup with port and chives and a wondrous plate of smoked shrimp, mussels and bay scallops with a cucumber and dill cream. Next time we'd like to try the Louisiana crayfish and rabbit sausage tartlet with grilled leeks and smoked tomato coulis and the warm jalapeño corn muffin with lump crabmeat and cilantro butter sauce.

Among entrées ($16.25 to $23.50), our party sampled the sautéed lump crab cakes, grilled fillet of snapper with sundried tomatoes, grilled scallops with fresh tarragon and fennel and grilled New Zealand rack of lamb with artichokes, calamata olives and pinenuts, all superb. The pan-seared Atlantic salmon with a tropical fruit relish over wilted greens and the grilled filet mignon with a vidalia onion compound butter and cabernet-tarragon sauce were winners at another visit.

Pastry chef Lisa's desserts are the recipients of much acclaim. Her signature chocolate praline triangle with grand marnier sauce is heavenly. Ditto for the apple-ginger custard torte with caramel sauce, the white chocolate raspberry cheesecake with a raspberry coulis and the chocolate-espresso torte with a vanilla bean anglaise.

At lunchtime, when prices are considerably lower ($5.75 to $8), you might try pizza with grilled duck sausage, roasted vegetables and two cheeses or grilled chicken salad with roasted corn, black beans, peppers and a cumin vinaigrette.

On Friday evenings in summer, light fare is served as top artists present live jazz in the hotel's garden courtyard.

The Imperial Wine Society sponsors periodic wine-tasting dinners and publishes an informative wine newsletter. The wine list earns an Award of Excellence from Wine Spectator magazine. Wines from the hotel's **Wine Alley** and Lisa's delectable pastries are featured along with Starbuck's coffees in the hotel's popular new **Cellar Coffee Bar & Bakery.**

Lunch, Tuesday-Saturday 11:45 to 2; dinner, Tuesday-Saturday 5 to 8 or 9; Sunday brunch (September-May), 11:45 to 2.

Ironstone Cafe, 236 Cannon St., Chestertown. (410) 778-0188.

Ironstone china from her father's collection made both an appropriate name and a decorative theme for this highly rated cafe run by Barbara Silcox and Kevin McKinney. The L-shaped dining room occupies an old carriage shop and glass company, which accounts for the garage door at the rear.

Kevin, the executive chef, turned over kitchen duties in 1994 to chef Paul Strickland as he and Barbara prepared to open another restaurant in the Kennedyville Inn, eight miles north of Chestertown in Kennedyville. They planned more casual, rustic food than at the Ironstone, with Kevin based at the Kennedyville site and Barbara floating back and forth.

The menu here changes every couple of months, but the food remains consistently among the best in the area. Expect such dinner entrées ($15 to $20) as sautéed sea scallops and shrimp with catalan romesco sauce and capellini, sautéed veal sweetbreads, grilled duck breast with orange-cardamom glaze and grilled filet of beef sauced with gorgonzola cheese and port wine. The appetizers are oriented toward seafood: lump crab flan with sea scallops and warm tomato vinaigrette, seared salmon with Asian cabbage and orange-fermented black bean sauce, and seafood salad of shrimp, littleneck clams, bay scallops and calamari with roasted garlic vinaigrette.

For a late-summer lunch, the choices were as appealing as the prices ($5.50 to $7.50). They ranged from Santa Fe and Mediterranean salads to a sliced flank steak sandwich with roasted onions and a potato boat filled with pork and green chilies and baked with jack cheese. We enjoyed the smoked mussel and roasted tomato quiche, served with a

Ironstone china on shelf is decorative focal point at Ironstone Cafe.

green salad, and a cup of cream of celery soup with a caesar salad bearing a warm seafood terrine. Wonderful homemade bread accompanied, and the oversize glasses of iced tea were refilled frequently.

Barbara calls herself the "dessert slave," responsible for such treats as peach cobbler, apple-cranberry angel food cake with chocolate sauce, crème brûlée, fruit pies and homemade ice creams. Most of the selections on the short but serviceable wine list are priced around $20 or less.

Lunch, Tuesday-Saturday 11:30 to 2; dinner, Tuesday-Saturday 5:30 to 9.

Bay Wolf, Rock Hall Avenue (Route 20), Rock Hall. (410) 778-6855.

A European-trained chef was in the kitchen at this pleasant new restaurant, which succeeded the late Lewis's Rainbow's End in 1994 and looks a bit church-like with stained-glass windows (the site used to be a funeral home). Robyn and Wolfgang Wendt lightened up the decor in three dining rooms and added a bit of a nautical motif – the latter a natural for these avid sportsmen who moved East to pursue their sailing dreams from Winter Park, Colo., where they met at a ski lodge. Robyn, a well-traveled New Zealander, handled the front of the house, while her German-born husband tended to the kitchen. Local seafood was the forte, along with homemade soups, fresh breads and dessert pastries.

The main dining room is a mix of booths and tables, their tops covered with maroon-over-white cloths and white butcher paper, with crayons provided in a glass for doodling. The crayons indicate a light approach at what was becoming a local gathering place, and the food was highly rated.

Our dinner happily met our expectations. Over a $16 bottle of Raymond sauvignon blanc from an affordable, well-chosen wine list, we sampled a couple of potstickers (pork and vegetable dumplings with teriyaki dipping sauce), excellent house salads enhanced with toasted walnuts, and three kinds of rolls (poppyseed, sesame and plain), marred only by the foil-wrapped pads of butter. Main courses ($12.95 to $18.50) were an excellent breast of chicken with artichoke hearts and a couple of sautéed soft-shell crabs. Each was accompanied by an impressive array of sautéed vegetables, including snap peas, squash, broccoli and onions. A fruit trifle that included kiwis and mandarin oranges showed the kitchen's sure hand with desserts, which come so highly rated that the menu advises "Life is short. Eat dessert first."

Monday night is Wurst Night at Bay Wolf, and German specialties win plaudits from receptive locals. They're missing from the short regular menu, which clings to the traditional with items like grilled swordfish, blackened ribeye steak, grilled filet of beef and a trio of pasta dishes.

Robyn and Wolfgang received an offer they could not refuse and sold unexpectedly in late 1994. The new owner planned to keep their tradition going, and the Wendts were looking to open an inn and restaurant in the area.

Dinner nightly, 5 to 9 or later. No smoking.

The Inn at Osprey, 20786 Rock Hall Ave., Rock Hall. (410) 639-2194.

The handsome restaurant at this luxury new inn opened in 1994 and, although the original chef left and the serving hours were sharply curtailed, the assistant chef's food received high marks. White linens cover the well-spaced tables in the L-shaped dining room, which wraps around a small, historic-looking bar. A formal Colonial Williamsburg look is conveyed by french doors and tall, many-paned windows, a large fireplace, and white walls with Williamsburg blue trim.

The short dinner menu changes weekly and bears a contemporary Mediterranean touch. Among starters ($6 to $7.50), we heard raves for the Maryland crab soup, the

Chesapeake Flyer provides backdrop for diners on deck at Waterman's Crab House.

beef carpaccio with salsa and extra-virgin olive oil, and the sautéed crab cakes served atop spinach, onions and bacon. Main courses ($16.95 to $21) include such winners as sautéed oysters with prosciutto and pistachio nuts in a cream sauce, served over linguini and "a masterpiece," according to our informant, and flank steak stroganoff over penne pasta. Other possibilities at our visit included baked rockfish topped with a rockfish mousse, served over sautéed spinach and red onions; garlicky pork medallions atop black-eyed peas with a pear-mint chutney, and sautéed duck breast on a mix of scallions, basmati and wild rice with broccoli and pecan butter.

The wine list, priced from $18 to $32, spotlights boutique California wineries. Although the restaurant initially opened for breakfast and lunch six days a week, service was quickly curtailed to dinner only.

Dinner, Thursday-Monday 6 to 9. Closed January-March. No smoking.

Waterman's Crab House Restaurant, Sharp Street Wharf, Rock Hall. (410) 639-2261.

The best waterfront location of any area restaurant is the draw of this oldtimer, which sprawls across a pier beside the landing for the Chesapeake Flyer, the catamaran passenger ferry that makes 75-minute trips to Annapolis and Baltimore.

You can see the ferry and lots of other marina activity from the heavy six-sided picnic tables shaded by jaunty umbrellas on the pier, from another section with picnic tables under a vast canopy or from interior dining rooms that seat a total of 400.

On a sunny summer's day, we were quite happy with a cold beer and a frozen tequila sunrise. We were not so happy with the oyster sandwich ($6.95), a travesty of four small oysters on a hamburger bun, and the "shrimpy caesar salad" ($7), a timid affair that lived up to its name in terms of size. Perhaps things get better at night, when there aren't apt to be so many tour groups around. Flounder and crab are featured in various guises, along with ribs, chicken and ribeye steak ($12 to $16). A widely advertised crab feast on Tuesdays and Thursdays was $14.99 for all you could eat, subject to a two-hour time limit.

Open daily, 11 to 9 or 10:30.

The Feast of Reason, 203 High St., Chestertown. (410) 778-3828.

This is a simple little place across the street from the Imperial Hotel with eight round tables, bentwood chairs and a few posters on the wall. Geoffrey Riefe and his wife Kathleen, who were innkeepers at the Williamsville Inn in the Berkshires for two years, are in charge, he doing the cooking and she the baking.

To eat in or take out, they offer things like buttermilk-oatmeal muffins, spinach and corn quiche ($4.75), flatbread pizza with shrimp or spinach and shrimp salad on a croissant, both $4.25. At our visit the soups were squash-honey and potato-scallion, and apple scrunch and butterscotch brownies were desserts of the day. We made a good picnic lunch of a roast beef sandwich with tomato-horseradish mayonnaise ($4) and a smoked salmon sandwich with dill and onion on pumpernickel ($4.75). Dinner entrées to go ($7 to $8) included chicken breast with pesto sauce and flounder with tomato-shrimp sauce. Beer and wine are available.

Open Monday-Friday 10 to 6; Saturday, 10 to 4.

Old Wharf Inn, Foot of Cannon St., Chestertown. (410) 778-3566.

A riverfront location commends this large, touristy restaurant of the old school. We wish we could commend the food and the service, both of which were lacking on the Monday night we ate here when it was about the only restaurant open in town. The light over our window table was much too bright; in retrospect, since it was too dark to see anything on the river anyway, we should have moved to a candlelit table in a corner.

From a long menu ($12.95 to $15.95), we chose crab imperial, which was so small we thought they'd served the petite portion that's available with many items, and seafood norfolk in a wine butter sauce. These came with frozen peas and french fries or rice, plus access to the salad bar and a $9 bottle of nondescript chardonnay from a pathetic wine list. Strawberry frozen yogurt from a dessert selection that included bread pudding and chocolate nut sundae managed to save the day.

Back by popular demand at our latest visit was the Friday night prime rib and seafood buffet, "featuring many new items" for $16.95.

Lunch, Monday-Saturday 11 to 4; dinner nightly, 4 to 9 or 10; Sunday, brunch 10 to 3, dinner 3 to 9.

Andy's, 337½ High St., Chestertown. (410) 778-6779.

Fr a change of pace, come here for a drink and a snack at the extra-long stand-up bar with high stools opposite or, better yet, in the rear "living room" with a fireplace, piano and numerous conversation corners with easy chairs, sofas and coffee tables.

Guest entertainers perform here on weekends and on some Thursday nights. The varied menu offers such things as a tomato-basil tart, ham and provolone sandwich, stuffed potatoes, burgers, quiche and gourmet pizzas in the $5 to $6 range.

Light fare, Monday-Saturday 4 to 11, to midnight on weekends.

Diversions

Historic Chestertown. The orderly grid of streets leading from the riverfront is a living museum of homes that stood in Colonial times. The sights along Water, Queen, High and Cross streets are best appreciated on foot, guided by annotations on a walk-

Maria Sommer and Carla Massoni show works of top artists at Massoni-Sommer Gallery.

ing tour brochure published by the Kent County Chamber of Commerce. More details are available in a booklet, "Chestertown: An Architectural Guide." A Kent County map outlines a 110-mile driving tour of this picturesque county, which includes the old-line waterman's community of Rock Hall and the beach at Betterton, considered the best swimming beach on the Chesapeake. Maps for nine bicycle tours are included in a Kent County Bicycle Tour brochure.

Waterman's Museum, 20880 Rock Hall Ave., Rock Hall, 778-6697. This little museum, nicely renovated from an abandoned house, was opened in 1993 by the owner of Haven Harbor Marina to preserve the history and lore of the watermen of Rock Hall. Three display rooms show exhibits on oystering and crabbing, plus fishing gear, local photographs, carvings and boats. "If it's been used on the water, we've probably got it," advises head curator Richard Burton, former marina manager who came out of retirement to oversee the well financed local venture. One of the more interesting exhibits involves a replica of a waterman's ark, a one-room shanty of a house on the scow of a boat. A pier was in the works to accommodate several workboats, including a skipjack, for visitors to board. Open daily, 10 to 5. Free.

St. Paul's Episcopal Church, Ricauds Branch-Langford Road, Chestertown. Actress Tallulah Bankhead, whose family lives nearby, is among the notables buried in the cemetery outside this historic church, built in 1713 and the oldest in Maryland. Giant oak trees, some more than 300 years old, rise among the boxwoods in the church yard. The interior is notable for embroidered kneelers and a beautiful stained-glass side window. A poster at our first visit piqued interest with word of an oyster roast celebrating the parish's 300th year.

Shopping. The shopping opportunities are wonderful in Chestertown. Start at the dramatic **Massoni-Sommer Gallery**, a two-story showplace at 210 High St. next to the Imperial Hotel. Here, former hotelier Carla Massoni teams with Maria Sommer, the artisan who's responsible for the fabulous vintage beads and glass earrings among the one-of-a-kind, classic contemporary crafts shown on the main floor. The deep blue pottery by a local teacher intrigued us and now a lovely shallow bowl sits on our coffee table. Sensational stoles woven by the wife of the college president, hand-blown glass, bonsai, jewelry made of Japanese rice paper, unique cards, colorful tiles and much more catch the eye, and the partners were expanding to offer more art clothing. Upstairs is a dramatic space displaying the works of nationally known artists as well as the finest regional artists.

Rhodes at 241 High St. is a mecca of the impeccable taste of Holly and Frank Rhodes, he a cabinet maker who will custom-make any furniture, for instance an exquisite Queen Anne lowboy for $4,800. Wonderful china, linens, fire screens, decoys, oriental rugs and estate jewelry are some of the other traditional wares. **Dockside Emporium** has everything nautical, from cookbooks for the boat to sweaters with crabs thereon, and has expanded its clothing line. We admired an oyster plate in the window of **Bittersweet,** an antiques store specializing in American country antique furniture. **Pride and Joy** has adorable clothing for children. Teddybears abound at **Singletree,** which also has a good selection of cards, toys and games. Casual and active wear for both men and women is featured at **Moon Bay Outfitters. The Finishing Touch,** which specializes in framing, offers nice prints. On Cross Street, we meandered into **Creative Cookery** to look at the gadgets and found cappuccino going for $1.50 at the coffee bar ($1 from 3 to 5 during "peppy hour." **The Butterfly Bush** has sophisticated and unique women's clothing and you'll find great sweaters at **Chester River Sweaters.** The works of more than 100 artists are on consignment at the interesting **Gallery 5.** Everything from gifts to cards to linens to books is available at **Twigs and Teacups.** We loved the birdhouses and things for the garden among the gifts and antiques at **The Village House.**

In the heart of Rock Hall, you can visit a restored corner drugstore, 1930s style, at **Durding's Store;** ice-cream sodas made with real vanilla beans are served at the original marble soda fountain amidst a selection of cards, gifts and sundries. Fine furnishings for the home and yacht are carried at **The Cat's Paw,** a gift shop at The Sailing Emporium.

Dixon's Auction Barn, Routes 544 and 290 off 30l, Crumpton, 928-3006. Every Wednesday is auction day at Dixon's, when you might find seven or eight pianos in a field, a tractor-trailer full of plants, a small Amish farm market and a warehouse stuffed with concession stands, furniture and antiques. Buyers and sellers of used and antique furniture come from across the country to deal here in something of a circus atmosphere. Auctioneer Norman Dixon takes no more than fifteen seconds to sell any item on his lot; if it's not sold, he gives it to anyone willing to take it. Table after table full of bric-a-brac leave some cold, and if you spot something you want, you have to wait until the auctioneer reaches that table and bid fast. When he and the crowd move in, things happen so fast the unwary bidder scarcely has time to think. As the typewritten handout says, "the auctioneer does not miss you, you miss him. So if you want something, holler out before he sells it, not afterwards." Open Wednesdays from 7 a.m.

Extra-Special

Remington Farms, Route 20, Chestertown. (410) 778-1565.

A driving tour leads through the 3,000-acre wildlife management demonstration area operated by the du Pont company in conjunction with Remington, the arms manufacturer. An informative brochure points out wildlife management practices being applied here. The self-guided tour takes one past ponds, swamps, woods and fields and involves fifteen marked – and some unmarked – stops for wildlife and plants. The leisurely drive is the closest thing we've found so far north to the famed J.N. "Ding" Darling National Wildlife Preserve on Florida's Sanibel Island, although the finds are neither so prolific nor so exotic. The quantity and variety of waterfowl you'll see depends on the season and the time of day. The habitat tour can take an hour or more, depending on stops. It's open free daily from February to Oct. 10, when it's closed to the public for hunting season.

Wide Lewes-Rehoboth Canal is on view from downtown Lewes.

Lewes, Del.
The First Town in the First State

Whoever thought up the "first town" slogan for Lewes was on the mark. The reference, of course, was to Lewes's founding by Dutch explorers in 1631, long before Delaware was to become the first state in the union. But age alone does not account for the popularity of this riverfront town that's pronounced "loo-iss" and takes its name from a town in Sussex County, England. As far as many are concerned, Lewes is first in charm and first in all-around appeal. For visitors, it's Delaware's most "visitable" – as opposed to its most visited – town.

Off the beaten path, Lewes is located on the lee side of Cape Henlopen, the strategic point where the Delaware Bay meets the Atlantic Ocean. It's long been home to skilled riverboat pilots who shepherd hundreds of cargo ships up the Delaware Bay to Wilmington and Philadelphia.

"This is a town with a beach – not a beach town," stresses JoAnne LaMere, executive director of the Lewes Chamber of Commerce. The distinction sets Lewes apart from its better-known neighbor to the south, Rehoboth Beach, and its glitzy sprawl of boardwalks and ballyhoo. This is a genuine town with a small but devoted year-round population (2,300), a working seaport town as opposed to a sailing or beachy town, a town that most folks (including us) would bypass on their way to or from the Cape May-Lewes Ferry.

No more. Now, restaurant waiters in Rehoboth are apt to steer their lunch patrons to Lewes for a rainy afternoon and innkeepers from across the bay in Cape May, N.J., come here for restorative day trips and overnights. In the last five years or so, Lewes has attracted fine inns and B&Bs, good restaurants and an uncommon array of small, sophisticated shops situated along Second Street beneath a canopy of unusual Bradford pear trees. It's now the side-by-side home of riverboat pilots, Delaware's first winery, the nation's first public park, an herb farm, some of Delaware's oldest homes, an inn

219

offering lodging on a houseboat, World War II bunkers, "walking" sand dunes, a working blacksmith shop and a fascinating new residential development in which every structure is at least a hundred years old.

All are true, small-scale, understated places, as the town fathers have strived to control development to avoid the all-too-evident fate of encroaching Rehoboth.

Once people discover the charms of Lewes, it seems, they become regular visitors or even residents. They like what one new innkeeper calls "a town of busy days and quiet nights."

Inn Spots

Blue Water House, 407 East Market St., Lewes 19958. (302) 645-7832.

There are times when we veteran inn-goers don't even want to look at another Victorian sofa or chair, much less sit on one. That's why we heaved sighs of relief when we checked into our room at the comfortably but minimally furnished Blue Water House. The bed didn't have a headboard, much less a canopy (sacrilege!). The seats were deck chairs, the lamps weren't tasseled, the carpet was a dark industrial gray and the only amenity was a TV set. How refreshing! The air-conditioned room was large, the art was fascinating, the bathroom modern, and the french doors opened onto a wraparound deck from which we watched an incredible sunset.

The shingled inn was built from scratch in 1993 by Chuck and Karen Ulrich and their children, Charlie and Kayla. Chuck, an architect, designed it and it is wonderfully whimsical, with little touches of the tropics all around – it reminded us of places we've seen in South Miami Beach. The ground floor, nicely landscaped, is open because the inn sits on wetlands. It includes a patio, picnic table, grill, hammock, bicycles and refrigerator for guests, and we enjoyed taking out dinner from a local restaurant and enjoying it by candlelight here. The first floor is for check-in and the family. Guests congregate here around the long dining room table for a hefty continental breakfast complete with cereals, sticky buns and homemade breads. The table is covered with a wild floral cloth and the seats are folding bridge chairs. This is a children-friendly inn and the Ulrichs even provide fruit loops for breakfast, to say nothing of all kinds of recreational equipment and the resident companions to go with.

Six ample bedrooms with private baths, four on the corners and all open to the wraparound porch, ring the third floor and are spaced for maximum privacy. Chuck has fashioned ingenious touches: the railing of the porch is a white picket fence. The decorative theme is bright colors and fish, which turn up on the juice pitchers, the shower curtains and the covers of the room diaries. Some bedrooms can be combined to make family suites. On the fourth floor is a large quasi-widow's walk with views of Lewes and the bay – its big TV set and wicker furniture make this a gathering spot.

Chuck, who practiced in the Baltimore area, and Karen fell in love with Lewes when

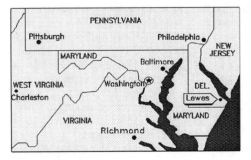

they visited and decided it would be a great place to raise the kids and to get out on the water. She works as a building inspector in Rehoboth, but is on hand nights and weekends. He runs the inn the rest of the week and, having become a licensed Coast Guard captain, leads charter fishing and bird-watching trips on the Lewes-Rehoboth Canal and Broadkill River. In fact, if you catch

Makeshift sign and carved fish on mailbox greet guests at Blue Water House.

some fish and want to eat them, the Ulrichs will provide a salad and a marinade for basting on the grill.

"It helped not going to B&B school," said Chuck, whose intuition makes him a good innkeeper. "We just opened our doors and did this by the seat of our pants." Again sacrilege, but it works. Staying here is "like joining old high school classmates and becoming part of the family," one guest wrote. Who knows? You could be treated to one of his great margaritas.

And if you miss your kitty, you might be comforted to find Spencer, the inn's orange cat, purring on your bed. He spent most of the night with us. The Ulrichs say he is an outside cat, but Spencer knows better.

Doubles, $90.

The Inn at Canal Square, 122 Market St., Lewes 19958. (302) 645-8499 or (800) 222-7902.

A coincidence led to the 1988 opening of the first and best-known new inn in Lewes. Bill Lucks, owner of a commercial real-estate firm, represented a client who was buying some rundown waterfront buildings. When the deal collapsed, the sellers suggested that he buy the property. The result: ex-banker Bill and his wife Amanda, a shopkeeper extraordinaire, decided to open an upscale inn with rooms facing the wide Lewes-Rehoboth Canal.

The brown-shingled facade of the main, four-story complex looks like a contemporary Cape Cod condominium. Hidden from street view are nineteen guest rooms on the three upper floors, most with large balconies facing the water (though some are screened by the adjacent lighthouse-turned-conference center). Rooms ascend in price and size by the floor. Ours on the top floor was quiet and comfortable and unusually spacious with 18th-century reproduction furniture including a kingsize bed, a sitting area with a loveseat and side chair, a dining table with two chairs and a TV hidden in

The Inn at Canal Square complex overlooks Lewes-Rehoboth Canal.

the highboy. The two-part bathroom came with a separate vanity area and all kinds of toiletries. The balcony yielded a fine view over the lighthouse onto the busy canal.

The next morning, we were impressed with the continental breakfast spread set out in the ground-floor library/lobby. Four kinds of juices, three sliced fruits (kiwi, watermelon and pineapple), yogurt and a choice of a dozen assorted breakfast pastries put us in good shape for the ferry crossing to New Jersey.

Three guest rooms in the adjacent Courtyard Suites building where the owners live compensate for their lack of balconies with more imaginative furnishings than rooms in the main inn. One draped romantically in mosquito netting has a brass bed; another has an antique sleigh bed, while a new room offers a Caribbean motif. The most prized quarters are on the two-story houseboat moored on a barge alongside the dock. Here, guests find a full kitchen, a contemporary living and dining area with fireplace and floor-to-ceiling windows, two bedrooms with full baths on the second floor and a rooftop sundeck, reached by a ladder through a narrow hatch in the ceiling.

Doubles, $115 to $150; houseboat, $225.

The New Devon Inn, 142 Second St., Box 516, Lewes 19958. (302) 645-6466 or (800) 824-8754.

Built in 1926, the former Valley of the Swans Hotel had deteriorated into a seedy boarding house. The "Ugly Swan" is how one newspaper described it. And when Rehoboth Beach realtor Dale Jenkins showed it to her investor-partner, Washington attorney Bernard Nash, they were met at the front door by a boarder emerging on a motorcycle.

Dale envisioned the possibilities, however. Acting as her own contractor and decorator, she gutted the building except for the main staircase, the pine floors in the bedrooms and a rickety elevator, barely big enough for two people with any luggage. She removed the kitchenettes and added baths for each of 24 bedrooms and two suites. Part of the lobby became a fashionable sitting area, with plush sofas and a couple of elephant chairs carved from solid teakwood in Thailand. A grand piano, a glass chandelier and a ficus tree lit by tiny white lights add elegance. The pool hall in the basement was converted into a breakfast area and a TV room.

The result is a small downtown hotel of considerable sophistication, one that wears its National Historic Register listing with pride. The rooms, though small, are squeaky clean and modern but for their original floors and antique beds. Ours, the largest of the standard rooms, looked from its fourth-floor corner roost onto the cemetery beside St. Peter's Episcopal Church. The bed was small enough that one's extremities continually had to be draped over the edges. But there were thoughtful touches: in-room telephones, floral sheets, good prints on the walls, nightly turndown with a couple of small cordials, crystal glasses on a silver tray and windows that open. All the beds are doubles, except for two with twins and two suites with queensize beds and sitting rooms.

The TV in the basement is serviceable, so long as everyone wants to watch the same program. Coffee and orange juice are put out on the breakfast bar here in the morning. Those with heartier appetites can order a full breakfast in The Buttery, the swish new restaurant that opened on the hotel's main floor in 1994 (see Dining Spots). Also available on the main floor and basement are a number of shops stocking everything from crafts to collectibles.

Doubles, $110 to $120; suites, $155.

Wild Swan Inn, 525 Kings Highway, Lewes 19958. (302) 645-8550.

Pink with white gingerbread trim, this Queen Anne Victorian is long on personality and turn-of-the-century charm. Owners Mike and Hope Tyler moved here from suburban Wilmington to open a B&B with two bedrooms and private baths.

The breezy wraparound porch is notable for a corner gazebo, as well as a small refrigerator for guests' use hidden away at the far side. Also hidden from the street is a nice swimming pool flanked by a patio and another gazebo. Inside, a small front parlor opens into a larger dining room, where one of the inn's many antique brass chandeliers presides over the dining table and a number of the couple's collections, from a glass cabinet bearing old miniature liqueur bottles to a 1940 Zenith radio.

The stairway to the second floor is lined with colorful door stops, all fruits and flowers except for swans, exceptions that are repeated throughout. Hope named the front bedroom Nan's Room because it holds her grandmother's furniture. A double bed is angled toward the center of the room from the far corner; its headboard matches the

Corner gazebo on porch at Wild Swan Inn.

bureau. The bathroom is decked out in lace. The side Rose Room takes its name from the wallpaper. A plate of cookies is put out at night on the outstretched hands of the wooden butler beside the double bed.

The dining room is the setting for some fairly fancy breakfasts cooked up by Mike. Besides a fruit dish like poached pears and fresh breads and muffins, expect such main courses as pumpkin waffles, asparagus pie or breakfast burritos, served with salsa made with ingredients from the Tylers' garden.

Doubles, $105. No smoking.

The Manor at Cool Spring, County Road 290, Route 2, Box 238, Milton 19968. (302) 684-8325.

Named for a hamlet about four miles west of Lewes, this farmhouse was converted into a four-bedroom B&B in 1994 by new owners Joe and Pauline Palenik. "We wanted to run a B&B and this house was a perfect fit," Joe explained.

The heart of the house is a sunken sun porch at the side. It holds a large jacuzzi tub, a wood stove and a glass table flanked by rattan chairs, where breakfast may be served. Also available to guests are a formal dining room, a living room containing a lineup of Pauline's Toby jugs from England as well as a display cabinet showcasing her collections of owls and glassware, and a big, turreted corner library with a fireplace, gaming table and chess board ready for action.

Upstairs are three guest rooms with private baths. They're furnished with what Joe calls 1920s and 1930s vintage furniture, enhanced by floral curtains that match the covers and pillows on the queensize beds. A fourth bedroom with bath was being readied for opening in 1995 in the attached garage.

Pauline's bountiful breakfasts reflect her British background and her cooking studies at the Sorbonne. A typical meal includes fruit, eggs any style, and sausage and Canadian bacon. Special treats could be fruit crêpes or eggs benedict. Among the ingredients are herbs, vegetables and shiitake mushrooms the Paleniks grow on their rural four-acre property. Their five cats also roam around the house and grounds.

Doubles, $80 to $100.

Dining Spots

Kupchick's Restaurant, 3 East Bay Ave., Lewes. (302) 645-0420.

Some of the area's finest and fanciest food is served in this unlikely looking building alongside the Delaware Bay beach. You'd expect burgers and frozen custard, perhaps. What you get is sophisticated continental and American fare, including some of the best crab dishes we've ever had.

Behind its undistinguished facade lie two dark, romantic dining rooms and a lively bar and grill. Traditionalists are partial to the formal restaurant, sedate with banquettes and windsor chairs at white-linened tables. Pink lalique-style shades over the candles and wall sconces and a few paintings provide accents of color.

The fare produced by chef-owner David Krasnoff is worthy of the setting. David is the grandson of Romanian immigrants who operated Kupchick's Restaurants in Toronto and Montreal in the first half of this century. His fairly lengthy menu is priced from $13.95 for grilled lemon chicken served sliced over linguini to $22.95 for grilled New York sirloin with maître d'hôtel butter. Other main courses include breaded flounder served on a bed of creamed spinach, sea scallops with prosciutto and parmesan cheese, jumbo pork chop stuffed with sage sausage, loin lamb chops, prime rib and steak au poivre. Blackened tuna, seared duck breast with port wine glaze and steak diane could be the night's specials.

Among starters are the family's special mushroom and barley soup, chiffonade salad, carpaccio, smoked bluefish and baked brie. Desserts could be Irish cheesecake, key lime cheesecake, strawberry shortcake, chocolate-walnut pie and crème caramel.

Banquettes and windsor chairs face white-linened tables in dining room at Kupchick's.

An extensive grill menu featuring pastas and light entrées is offered in the bar, which was obviously popular the weeknight we were there. The staff could barely keep up with the demand, although the food proved to be well worth the wait. One of us enjoyed pastry chef Daria Horn's favorite salad with assorted lettuces, bacon, egg, onion and mushrooms and the crab platter ($8.25), a succulent crab cake served with roasted potatoes. The other liked the zesty caesar salad and the lump crab linguini ($10.95), tossed with sherry and mushrooms and simply sensational. The heavy, coarse bread was served with real butter (as opposed to the ubiquitous foil-wrapped slices) and a $14 bottle of Chilean sauvignon blanc accompanied.

Dinner, nightly from 4:30; lunch, Monday-Friday 11:30 to 2, October to April. Closed Jan. 1 to Valentine's Day.

The Buttery Restaurant, 142 Second St., Lewes. (302) 645-7755.
New in 1994, this chic yet casual bistro leased space at the side of The New Devon Inn and opened to a receptive clientele. The high-ceilinged space holds a small bar, a display case containing charcuterie meats and salads, and close-together tables for 36. Bearing a coffee shop aspect at breakfast and lunch, the Buttery gets dressed for dinner. White tablecloths and candles lend a look of class, although we could have done without the rather raucous music in the background the night we dined.

Service was solicitous and highly professional as we enjoyed zesty house salads sprinkled with gouda cheese and dressed with fresh garlic and a basket full of sliced French sourdough bread, very crusty and more than we could eat. Main courses were priced from $14 for grilled chicken with spiced peach salsa to $19.50 for filet mignon béarnaise. We settled for the Maryland crab cakes (very tasty with a rémoulade sauce), red bliss potatoes and an interesting dish of sautéed kale, and a rather strange bouillabaisse with a thick tomato sauce that masked the advertised "fennel-flavored tomato-saffron broth" and gave priority to the mundane fish fillet rather than the expected shellfish. Perhaps the grilled Norwegian salmon with cilantro salsa or the broiled seafood platter would have been better choices.

The short list of appetizers (mussels marinara, cold poached salmon with sauce verde, hot and spicy Louisiana shrimp, clams in herb and garlic butter) struck us as a bit strange. So did the dessert choice, which was limited to three pies. Perhaps that was because chef Gary Papp and his wife Lorraine, the pastry chef, had the day off. For the young couple, recruited by the Buttery's Philadelphia owners from the Wycombe Inn in Bucks County, come with good credentials.

Breakfast daily, 8 to 10; lunch, 11 to 2; dinner, 5 to 9; Sunday brunch, 11 to 2:30.

Gilligan's Bar & Grille, Canal Square, Lewes. (302) 645-7866.

The kitchen is in a dry-docked boat, and the tropical bar, the side patio and the rooftop deck offer the best waterfront views of any local restaurant. New owner Patrick Sheehan planned to upgrade the decor, carpeting the interior and adding blue tablecloths with a colorful fish pattern to the dining room.

Chef Tim Euler, a Culinary Institute of America graduate, stayed on board to continue serving highly acclaimed cuisine that was considered locally to be on the pricey side. He's particularly known for his crab cakes, available broiled or blackened, and his pasta dishes, some of which change daily.

The short dinner menu starts at $18 for chicken breast stuffed with goat cheese, sundried tomatoes and kiwi, poached and served with a light lobster sauce, or grilled Norwegian salmon encrusted with red onions, pinenuts, herbs and a touch of honey. Prices top off at $21.75 for a sauté of veal and jumbo sea scallops with a sherry-mushroom demi-glace. Pasta dishes range from chicken mandarin over angel hair to seafood ravioli with a lobster cream sauce. Each item on the menu is paired with a recommended wine selection. Shrimp scampi over linguini was to be a special the night we booked there, but a tropical storm cut the power and the restaurant closed unexpectedly for the evening. Good starters are a sauté of mussels or clams, chicken satay or baked brie. Kentucky derby and caramel apple pies are among desserts.

Tarry with an after-dinner drink in the outdoor bar, with your back to a mural of a tropical island. Facing the boats passing by on the Lewes-Rehoboth Canal, you might think you were along the Intra-Coastal Waterway. Actually, you are.

Lunch daily, 11 to 3:30; dinner, 5 to midnight. Closed in winter, and Tuesday and Wednesday in off-season.

La Rosa Negra, 128 Second St., Lewes. (302) 645-1980.

This long and narrow Italian storefront restaurant is much loved by the locals, who rate the pastas the best around. The decor, a mix of black and white with red accents, is made gala by tiny white lights at night. The food arrives on black octagonal plates.

Good starters are seafood focaccia, steamed mussels and shrimp gnocchi. Pasta dishes ($7 to $10.75) are fairly standard, from spaghetti with meatballs marinara to fettuccine alfredo or puttanesca. More interesting was a special of the day, sautéed scallops with artichokes, prosciutto, parmesan and white wine over linguini. We also liked the chicken florentine gorgonzola, topped with sweet and sour bacon sauce and served with linguini. Other main courses are priced from $9.75 for chicken cacciatore to $16.75 for filet mignon or veal and shrimp marsala.

One couple we met, who were visiting Lewes for a week and had tried all the restaurants, liked this best and dined here twice.

Lunch, Monday-Saturday 11:30 to 2:30; dinner nightly, 5 to 9:30.

Jerry's American Cafe, 115 Second St., Lewes. (302) 645-9733.

Stylish decor and creative cuisine are the hallmarks of this narrow storefront restaurant, established in 1986 and expanded in 1991 with a pleasant rear bar called Chester's Alley. Chester, you quickly learn, is owner Jerry Scott's cat, who adopted the restaurant during a blizzard the year it opened. Recalled Jerry: "I said if he was still here the next day, I'd take him home with me. He was and I did."

226

The Buttery Restaurant is chic but casual bistro in New Devon Inn.

Cats turn up in the decorative scheme, from little ceramic felines on a stand near the entrance to a full-blown mural beside the bar, featuring seven "cool cats" being judged in a feline beauty contest. The yellow walls are lined on one side with good art – framed posters of the London subway at our visit – and assorted mirrors on the opposite side. Floral runners top the white tablecloths and votive candles flicker, making for a colorful, casual scene.

We found it fine for a breakfast of eggs benedict and a bagel heaped with smoked salmon and cream cheese (both $5.95). We also liked the looks of the lunchtime salads, which showed imagination and flair. Dinner treads a line between traditional and continental American, with a few nods to new American. Entrées are priced from $8.95 to $16.95. You'll find things like chicken pot pie, Yankee pot roast and leg of lamb with mint sauce side by side with chicken stir-fry, pan-fried catfish topped with tomato salsa, prime rib and veal oscar. Crab and artichoke are paired in one of the pasta dishes. The day's cakes are displayed in the pastry case at the entrance.

Breakfast, Monday-Friday 7 to 10, Saturday 8 to 10:30; lunch, Monday-Saturday 11 to 4:30; dinner nightly, 4:30 to 9 or 10; Sunday, brunch 9 to 1:30, dinner 5 to 8.

Rose & Crown, 108 Second St., Lewes. (302) 645-2373.

This restaurant and pub appears to be mostly bar, given the latter's position front and center and wrapping around the side. But appearances can deceive. Beyond the bar, way out back, the place opens up into a two-story dining room with skylights in the ceiling, flags hanging from the brick walls and a mix of tablecloth-covered booths and tables.

The night's seafood specials enticed for dinner, things like grilled salmon with tomato basil and grilled tuna with oriental sesame sauce going for a bargain $8.95. The rest of the dinner fare is rather British with a local accent. Expect main courses ($10.95 to $17.95) like fish and chips, diced chicken and mushrooms in puff pastry, stuffed flounder, pork tenderloin and crab imperial, the specialty. There's no roast beef on the menu, as in most British pubs, but there are pasta dishes and New York strip steak.

Two dinner items turn up on the lengthy lunch menu. We tried both the English cottage pie ($6.95 at lunch, $10.95 at dinner), a piping-hot dish of ground beef, peas and tomatoes, layered with mashed potatoes and melted cheese, and a ploughman's delight ($5.95 all day). The latter was mostly vegetables and wimpy cheese and came with the wrong kind of bread, but did have some Branston pickle. The taco salad at the next table looked to be a better bet.

We were mighty impressed with the lineup of international beers. And a pint of Watney's (one of several on tap) went down just fine.

Lunch, Monday-Saturday 11 to 5; dinner, Monday-Saturday 5 to 9 or 10.

Lighthouse Restaurant at Lewes, Anglers Road, Lewes. (302) 645-6271.

This sprawling establishment with a bakery and gift shop in front, waterside decks all around and a nautical inner dining room tries to be all things to all people – and succeeds, to the tune of feeding 1,500 guests a day in season. It opens at 5 a.m. for breakfast, serves lunches by the busload and caters wedding parties in a fairly dressy Upper Deck, where tablecloths are the rule for Saturday dinners.

The setting along the Lewes-Rehoboth Canal is the most nautical in town. The lengthy menu embraces everything from chicken and shrimp florentine to shrimp and scallops scampi. Main dishes are priced from $11.95 for grilled chicken to $26.95 for filet mignon and lobster tail. Crab imperial, grilled or blackened fish steaks, fried or broiled seafood sampler and grilled ribeye steak are other possibilities. Owner Paul Buchness is particularly proud of the "from scratch" breads baked for breakfast by his staff of four bakers, the fresh shrimp salad served for lunch, the individual dinner rolls, and the award-winning cappuccino brownie made by the head baker.

Breakfast daily, 5 to 11:30, weekends to 1; lunch daily, 11 to 4; dinner, 4 to 9 or 10.

Diversions

The sense of history and the quiet waterside attractions are what lure most visitors to Lewes.

History. The historic section of Delaware's oldest town – usually missed by motorists rushing to or from the Cape May-Lewes Ferry – is compact and eminently walkable. Most of the historic sites are spread out along Front, Second and Third streets in a quarter-mile stretch between Savannah Road and Shipcarpenter Street. The Lewes walking tour brochure points out 40 sites of special interest in the area that was discovered by Henry Hudson and settled by the Dutch in 1631. They range from the 1730 **Fisher-Martin House**, a gambrel-roofed structure moved from nearby Coolspring in 1980 to become the information center for the Lewes Chamber of Commerce and Visitors Bureau, to the 1850's Greek Revival **Doctor's Office,** a medical and dental museum, one of six buildings in the Lewes Historical Society complex. Other attractions include the 1797 **Cannonball House,** the last remaining Lewes house bearing a cannonball scar from the War of 1812 and now occasionally open as a marine museum, and **St. Peter's Episcopal Church Cemetery,** an unusual sight so close to downtown. You'll enjoy chancing upon the 1790 **Rodney House,** home of one of Lewes's first families and now the site of the Surf and Sands Florist sandwiched between stores on Second Street. It looks much older than the better-known 1665 **Ryves Holt House** at Second and Mulberry streets, believed to be the oldest house still standing in Delaware. Two little finds are at the far end of West Third Street: one of the few remaining Dutch-style homes from the 18th century at 320, its fence aglow in summer with morning glories, and across the street at 321, an 18th-century Sussex County saltbox restored in 1981 as a private home. Buildings in the **Lewes Historical Society**

Complex at Shipcarpenter and Third streets, next to Shipcarpenter Square, range from a 17th-century plank house, a log cabin that's one of the oldest extant buildings in the area, to the **Thompson Country Store,** where you obtain tickets for a $6 guided tour of the complex. Open June-August, Tuesday-Friday 10 to 3, Saturday 10 to 12:30. Admission, $5.

Zwaanendael Museum, Savannah Road and Kings Highway, 645-9418. Built in

Zwaanendael Museum is Lewes landmark.

1931 for the town's Tricentennial, this exotic Dutch Renaissance building could be straight out of Holland. It is an adaptation of the town hall at Hoorn. Now a state museum, it devotes its main floor to the story of the H.M.S. DeBraak, a British warship with a Dutch name that sank in a storm off Cape Henlopen in 1798 after it had stopped in Lewes for supplies. Supposedly laden with gold, it had defied treasure-seekers for nearly 200 years until 1986. It was found beneath 30 feet of sand in water 80 feet deep. More than 25,000 objects – but no gold bounty – were recovered from the shipwreck. A few hundred are shown in a dozen vignettes, of which many find the one reflecting the life of a seaman aboard the ship most interesting. Artifacts from religious medallions to clay pipes to galley pots and plates are on display. Some credit the widely publicized recovery of the DeBraak with having first put on the tourists' map this quiet town steeped in maritime history and riverboat pilot lore. The museum's second floor contains changing local history exhibits (at our visit, one on African-American education in Sussex County, including an intricate little dollhouse-like, one-room school). Open Tuesday-Saturday 10 to 4:30, Sunday 1:30 to 4:30. Free.

Shipcarpenter Square. The developer of this novel residential complex eschewed the new construction prevalent elsewhere and moved 35 rundown or abandoned structures to the western edge of the Lewes historic district. Built between 1720 and 1880, they came from around the Delmarva Peninsula. Now these ramshackle buildings that most people wouldn't have paid a cent for are restored as private homes, upgraded with modern kitchens and bathrooms and surrounded by railed patios, fancy gardens and homey outbuildings. Some liken it to Colonial Williamsburg, but this close-to-gether, close-in compound beats Williamsburg for livability, as attested by all the Mercedeses and Corvettes parked in the driveways. Particularly appealing are the looks of the 1795 timbered log house from Maryland and the dark red 19th-century school house from Milton, both now charming homes. You can walk or drive around the both the perimeter and the interior of the horseshoe-shaped community to see the unusual "telescope" house from Accomac, Va., or the colorful Victorian house from Wilmington College.

Cape Henlopen State Park, Lewes, 645-6852. A mile east of Lewes, just past the Cape May-Lewes Ferry Terminal, lies this 4,103-acre park at the mouth of the Delaware Bay. It offers four miles of beach on ocean and bay, as well as nature trails, a bird sanctuary, the famed "walking dunes" shifting across the pine forest, and the Great Dune, at 80 feet the highest between Cape Hatteras and Cape Cod. The **Seaside Nature Center** has aquariums, a touch tank containing two horseshoe crabs and other exhibits of particular interest to youngsters. The bathhouse is large and modern, and the ocean beaches relatively uncrowded. When the surf's up here, families tend to prefer the town beaches along the calmer bay. Worth the effort is the climb up a 115-step spiral staircase to the top of the restored observation tower, one of several relics from the abandoned Ford Miles military installation. Here, where patrollers watched for German submarines as arms were stashed in bunkers and gun emplacements below during World War II, you can scan the sea and landscape from the high-rises of Rehoboth Beach across the bay to New Jersey's Cape May. The views of the sunsets here are spectacular. Park open 8 a.m. to sunset, year-round. Cars, $5 in summer.

Cape May-Lewes Ferry, (800) 717-7246. Seldom are ferries tourist attractions, but this one is. The Delaware River and Bay Authority is giving its five ferries $5 million worth of renovations each, and the first three refurbished passenger-auto carriers came out feeling like cruise liners on the inside. Each is outfitted with televisions, a children's play area, cushioned high-back seats, pastel-colored dining areas, a deli and bar area, and even a canopied upper deck with tables for four. The ferry's 30th anniversary master plan also envisioned terminal improvements, new restaurants, lavish landscaping, recreational piers for fishing, and a maritime museum on the Lewes side. The seventeen-mile ferry ride takes about 70 minutes and runs roughly every hour or two in season. Vehicles, $18; adult passengers, $4.50.

Nassau Valley Vineyards, 33 Nassau Commons, 645-9463. The story of this fledgling winery, Delaware's first, is really that of 26-year-old Peggy Raley. A drama graduate of American University, the breathless and blithe blonde spent a couple of years "globetrotting" for Friends of Wine magazine before coming home to her father Bob's burgeoning office and retail complex in the Nassau section of Lewes. He launched her with 5 percent seed money. She borrowed the rest to open the winery after writing and personally shepherding the enabling legislation through the state legislature. Until the local harvest is big enough, supplemental grapes and production facilities have been offered by friends at Chaddsford, Ingleside Plantation and Meredyth wineries. Jill-of-all-trades Peggy, who's partial to red wines, touts her 1992 cabernet sauvignon ($12.50) and a limited edition 1991 cabernet, graced by an Old Testament painting by local artist Tom Wilson, first of an artist series ($20). Her early wines also include a sold-out chardonnay ($9) and a semi-sweet Meadow's Edge white ($6.95), with a rosé about to be bottled at our visit. Peggy pours samples in the tasting room after visitors take a self-guided tour alongside the production facility, an unusually showy and informative visual display that's almost like a museum on the history of winemaking. With 3,000 cases produced in 1994, her first full year, Peggy was talking of big things to exemplify the name of her winery, which she said is a play on the Napa Valley. Fifteen buildings that her father moved to the site "as a little restored Williamsburg" are to become retail shops. Open Tuesday-Saturday 11 to 6, Sunday noon to 6.

Shopping. For a small town, Lewes is blessed with unusually sophisticated shops and unusually friendly shopkeepers. Most are located along tree-shaded Second Street and a few along Front Street. Amanda Lucks, co-owner of the Inn on Canal Square, started with a small gourmet and coffee shop, hence the name **Sugar & Spice.** It has grown like Topsy and now stretches back through a warren of rooms displaying local artworks, handpainted birdhouses and weathervanes into a huge Christmas shop. Some of the most interesting wares are stocked by Gavin and Lou Braithwaite, who own **Puzzles** (all kinds of puzzles), **The Stepping Stone,** where we coveted everything from carved egrets to great windsocks, and the adjacent **Union Jack** (all things British). We liked the umbrellas bearing cats and dogs, respectively, at **Nature's Touch of Lewes,** a boutique full of nice gifts and clothing with an animal accent. A tall blue heron in the window lured us into **Thistles,** a wonderful trove of stained-glass lamps, hand-painted oyster Santas for Christmas tree decorations, silverware, children's clothing and a few items of women's apparel. Behind it is **Greenhorn,** featuring Southwestern jewelry, blankets and cookbooks along with enough vests, hats and mountain items to give it a distinctly Western flair. Underneath is **Auntie M's Emporium,** which the owners (one an antiquer and the other a writer) likened to "browsing in someone's basement." We were taken by all the old books and wrought-iron garden items here; the owners also have another store in the old firehouse and jail at 116 West Third.

Art, pottery and gifts with a statuary theme are featured at **The Saxon Swan**, where we were intrigued by a neat statue bearing bird feed in its outstretched hands. **The Gift Network** stocks handcrafts, quilts, wood crafts, dolls and miniatures, and the **Carolina Moon** unusual antiques and collectibles (check out the dollhouse furniture and the hand-dyed felt balls for kitties). The **Dockside Gift Shop,** here since 1977 ("long before Lewes was discovered," says owner Mary Perez), looks like your standard nautical gift shop but has unique touches, from shirts and bags silk-screened by a local artist to lighthouse replicas, birds and scrimshaw. Women's apparel is featured at **The Jetty, Figure Head** and **Twila Farrell.**

Antiques are everywhere, but nowhere in such quantity as with assorted dealers at the **Lewes Mercantile Antique Mall.** The owner of **Riverview** displays Haitian art at his somewhat avant-garde gallery, while across the street his **For the Child in All of Us** is chock-full of miniature everythings. The best view in town is of the canal from the side pergola and rear windows of **Simpler Days,** purveyor of fine antiques.

Health foods are featured at **Gertie's Greengrocer,** along with herb products from the new **Stillwater Herb Farm** out Route 9 toward Cool Spring. The farm is worth a visit to see 45 squares of display gardens and a shop full of herb and unusual local products, including honey candy, blended teas and handpainted herbal gourds. Farm manager and herbalist Linda La Plante Beatty writes a chatty newsletter and cracks lots of jokes during her guided tours of the gardens.

Take a break from your shopping rounds with ice cream from **King's Homemade Ice Cream Shop,** a Delaware institution to which many folks repair after dinner as well as all day long. Or stop at the **Lewes Bakery and Roasterie** for a cinnamon roll to accompany your morning espresso.

Extra-Special

Punkin' Chunkin'. The world-championship (not to mention only) event of its kind lures television crews and upwards of 10,000 people – Lewes's largest crowd of the year – to a cornfield north of town the Saturday after Halloween. They turn out to see which team can hurl pumpkins the greatest distance. Over the years, contestants have employed homemade slings, crossbow catapults and centrifugal devices with names like The Mean Green Pumpkin Machine to chunk their left-over pumpkins weighing eight to ten pounds. Three teams participated in the first event in 1986, and the winning pumpkin soared 50 feet. The main event in the 1994 competition attracted twelve teams and the world-record throw was 2,508 feet. The defending champion team was led by John Ellsworth, who happened to be chairman and founder of the event. It seems folks were sitting around his local blacksmith shop – the Preservation Forge, a real, live, working blacksmith shop at 114 West Third St. and a special place in itself – and started talking about anvil throwing. One thing led to another and Punkin' Chunkin' was born. Chunk on!

Court House that served as first state capitol is centerpiece of historic New Castle.

New Castle, Del.
The Smallest of Wonders

In the state that proclaims itself "Small Wonder," surely New Castle is the smallest wonder of all. And perhaps its most choice wonder.

This is the town where Peter Stuyvesant laid out the green in 1651, the town where William Penn set foot in the New World in 1682, the town that became the first state's first capital. But its early importance was eventually overshadowed by Wilmington and Dover. A plan to restore the old town into a second Colonial Williamsburg was aborted in the late 1940s. And so New Castle remains – the living example of a rare Dutch-English-American river town from the Colonial era. The population of this historic district roughly three blocks wide and five blocks deep numbers 1,500, about the same as in its heyday.

The old town is often bypassed, hidden just off Interstate 95 south of the towering Delaware Memorial Bridge. The past is everywhere apparent along the cobblestoned, tree-lined streets cozying up to the Delaware River. Like the better-known historic district of Charleston, New Castle has a Battery park, but it also has The Strand and The Green. There's a wonderful sense of access to a waterfront sheltered from the industrial disarray on all sides. Here you walk around the waterfront park, down Packet Alley, up the pedestrian path past the Presbyterian Church to the green and the gravestones beside Immanuel Episcopal Church and peer into the handful of stores along Delaware Street.

Two centuries of architectural styles are displayed in more than 50 landmark structures. Five are open to the public as museums showing the Dutch and English Colonial periods. Others, where life continues today amid a patina of yesteryear, are revealed to the several thousand visitors who come here the third Saturday of every May for A Day in Old New Castle, a local tradition since 1924.

Still, only about 30,000 tourists visit New Castle annually, many of them on bus tours. There is no information center for orientation purposes or brochures, and the fledgling New Castle Visitors Bureau operates through a post office box number. Until the mid-1980s, there was only one guest house. Now there are five, but the lack of accommodations means that many visitors must head for motels along the Route 13 strip, the other New Castle better known to transients.

For New Castle really has two identities. One is the modern-day sprawl away from the river, not really New Castle but bearing its address since the New Castle post office serves a wider area, a situation that "gets everybody confused," according to one local historian. The other is the easily defined old town, separate and apart – a small National Landmark Historic Area of Colonial and Federal vintage, likened to that of Charleston and the French Quarter but considered unique in the country.

The old section of New Castle is one of those rare places where the hackneyed phrase "step back in time" truly means something.

Inn Spots

Fox Lodge, 112 West 6th St., New Castle 19720. (302) 328-0768.

The Gothic Revival mansion known locally as "The Castle" was on its way in 1995 to becoming a European-style country B&B with a hunt theme. Elaine and William Class moved from Southern California for a change in occupation and lifestyle. Elaine, an interior decorator, was undaunted by the challenge of restoring a 33-room mansion that had seen better days. "I'm taking it one room at a time," she said, hoping to have the first bedrooms ready in mid-1995. Eventually, she planned to have nine bedrooms, all with private baths, on the second and third floors.

Built by a physician, the main floor with its thirteen-foot-high ceilings retains vestiges of its use as a doctor's office. Elaine pointed out the small waiting room, which was being converted by the Classes into their private family room, and the examining room, with its fireplace and pressed-tin walls. The physician obviously put more emphasis on his family living quarters than on his office. The original, eight-foot-high cast-bronze chandelier is the focal point of the manorial drawing room. All but one of the nine fireplace mantels are made of marble, the exception being the one of carved walnut and Mercer tiles in the dining room. The wood shutters on the windows of the library are "so beautiful that we're not going to cover them up with velvet swags," Elaine said. In fact, this won't be what people expect of a Victorian B&B. She was planning to enhance the Gothic colors and features with contemporary accents and California furnishings. "I'm not a slave to Bradbury and lace everywhere. The architecture here is so strong and masculine that I don't want the decor to detract."

Check out the trompe-l'oeil railing painted in the 1920s along the wall of the hand-carved, dark oak staircase. It's so real that many a guest undoubtedly will reach out to hold on. On the second floor are four bedrooms with twelve-foot-high ceilings, ranging from small with twin beds to considerably more sizable with queensize beds. Five

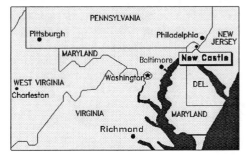

dormered rooms will be fashioned from servants' quarters on the third floor.

A lodge-style, hunt breakfast will adhere to the masculine theme of Gothic times, Elaine said. Juice and cereal will precede such possibilities as fresh oatmeal soup (inspired by Jacques Pepin), kippers, cold sliced ham, a cottage cheese sundae and grilled mushrooms and tomatoes. In the afternoon, guests will be invited into the former basement kitchen, now called Piglets Tavern, for beer, wine, herbal teas and snacks. Some of the foods and herbal products will incorporate the fruits of the restored Victorian and medieval gardens outside. Poetry readings, singing, music, seances and Gothic romance movies were in the works. You knew the Classes' plans would be realized: theirs was the first B&B we've encountered to have produced a full-fledged brochure more than a year prior to opening.

Doubles, $105 to $115. No smoking.

The Terry House, 130 Delaware St., New Castle 19720. (302) 322-2505.

This Federal brick townhouse, built in the early 1860s by a banker for his family, harbors some of New Castle's most comfortable lodgings. It also offers two rear verandas with views across the Battery to the water.

Brenda Rogers, a graduate in hotel management from Virginia Tech, and her father Don, who'd had his eye on the house for eight years, bought it in 1991. They inherited some furnishings from the previous owners and acquired others at auctions; Wilmington's Hotel du Pont turned out to be a bonanza when it sold its contents after closing its bedrooms in 1991 for two years of major refurbishing. Brenda, who's in residence, offers five spacious guest rooms, all with queensize canopy or poster beds, private baths, cable TV and air-conditioning. Those in front look onto Market Square and the Old Court House; two in the rear yield views of the park and river. Fresh flowers, dried-flower wreaths, bedside chocolates, scatter rugs on bare redwood floors and period antiques are the norm. Decorative touches include a shelf displaying a collection of cups and saucers in one room.

Guests enjoy a handsome parlor, quite elegant with ornate carved friezes, swagged draperies and a brass chandelier. A continental breakfast is served in the formal dining room, full of mahogany pieces in the Queen Anne and Federal styles. The fare includes fresh fruit, cereal and muffins baked by Brenda's mother, Peggy. Her father plans to open an antiques business in the rear of the house when he retires from du Pont.

Doubles, $80. No smoking.

The David Finney Inn, 216 Delaware St., New Castle 19720. (302) 322-6367 or (800) 334-6640.

The David Finney Inn is generally credited with putting New Castle on the tourist map. In 1985, Tom Hagy acquired a key corner property dating to the 1650s and converted what had been an antiques shop and tavern into a twenty-room inn and restaurant. The inn obviously filled a vacuum and was swamped until it was closed by a disastrous fire in May 1994.

Now retired in Florida, Tom Hagy rejected higher offers by apartment developers and sold to a local investment group that started rebuilding efforts in November 1994. William Condouris, on-site manager and principal for the New Castle Development Co., hoped the inn would reopen with thirteen rooms with private baths by early summer 1995. Enhancements include a new elevator and balconies offering river views from four suites, each with queensize sofabed in the living room, a bedroom with queen, kingsize or twin beds, and amenities including crackers and a complimentary split of wine. Otherwise, the inn was expected to retain its former style (more than 80 percent of the furnishings were spared from the fire). Most rooms had been done in beige with wedgwood blue trim. All were outfitted rather sparely, like the period, with antiques or reproductions from the 1700s.

The front reception parlor serves as the common room for overnight guests as well

Fox Lodge is evolving from Gothic Revial mansion known as "The Castle."

as for patrons arriving for meals in the dining room, the bar and the rear courtyard. The new owners expected the food and the rates to be comparable to what they had been before the fire.

Doubles, $60 to $90; suites, $120.

William Penn Guest House, 286 Delaware St., New Castle 19720. (302) 328-7736.

The restored 1682 house in which William Penn slept was the first of New Castle's modern-day lodgings. Irma and Dick Burwell bought the residence in 1956. "When I asked what I should do with it," Irma recalls, "someone suggested a B&B. I said I could do the bed, but not the breakfast." That's because she already was involved in the Coffee House, a restaurant next door.

Now retired, the Burwells do serve breakfast – continental style, with fresh fruit and homemade muffins or croissants – to overnight guests who stay in four air-conditioned bedrooms. It's taken amidst fancy lace and sterling in the dining room behind a pleasant parlor in this townhouse that's one room wide, a couple of rooms deep and three stories high. William Penn slept in one room, second floor rear, now outfitted with quilt-covered twin beds, an oriental rug and a little TV. It shares a clawfoot-tub bathroom with a front double-bedded room, also with TV. Two more bedrooms on the third floor share a tiled bath.

Doubles, $45. No credit cards.

Jefferson House B&B, 5 The Strand, New Castle 19720. (302) 322-8944.

Once the Jefferson Hotel, this 200-year-old hotel-residence occupies the prime historic location at Delaware Street and The Strand. It's a quite Southern and imposing-looking structure, flanked by screened porches and with park-like views to the water on two sides.

Mel Rosenthal, local chiropractor, and his wife offer this as a B&B with a difference: short- and long-term rentals, efficiency apartments and holistic health retreat.

The Jefferson includes seven apartments rented annually and four B&B facilities. The latter are the Hearth, a main-floor efficiency overlooking The Strand and containing a working fireplace; the basement Speakeasy, a budget efficiency that sleeps four; the Porch, a main-floor bedroom with porch that's the only room always available day-to-day, and another efficiency apartment above the chiropractic office at 208 Delaware St. All are air-conditioned, have private entrances and are furnished with a mix of antiques by Mel, who doubles as a collector and decorator.

Guests may use the outdoor whirlpool spa. A basic, pre-packaged continental breakfast is delivered to guests' rooms.

Doubles, $54 to $85.

Rodeway Inn, 111 South du Pont Hwy., New Castle 19720. (302) 328-6246 or (800) 321-6246.

Too bad this little local prize long known as the Dutch Village Motor Inn had to take on national airs with a Rodeway affiliation shortly before the first edition of this book went to press. But still special is this configuration of little duplexes that look not unlike haciendas, strung along a winding driveway back from the highway and amazingly quiet (testimony in part to the building techniques of the early post-war era). Lawn chairs are scattered about the grounds.

Two rooms go off an enclosed foyer in each duplex. The larger rooms in which we've stayed contain two double beds, large wraparound cantilevered windows that open and large closets with coat hangers and luggage racks. There's room to spare in each for a remote-control TV on a dresser, a table and two cushioned chairs.

The Rodeway connection coincided with the arrival of new owners Pierre and Peggy Olivero, who formerly owned the Terry House B&B. They said that, despite high AAA and Mobil ratings and a toll-free number, a local motel with a local name was no longer viable. This remains a good spot to know about – when the old town's accommodations are fully booked or you simply want motel conveniences at a reasonable price.

Doubles, $44 to $54.

Dining Spots

The David Finney Inn, 216 Delaware St., New Castle. (302) 322-6367.

The scene of some of New Castle's best dining, the restaurant in this historic building was closed by fire in 1994. New owners were rebuilding and promised to retain the tradition.

When reopened, take your choice of venues: a stenciled and beamed formal dining room in cream and rust colors with red accents and pewter service plates; a darker and more intimate Packet Tavern with ship's models, seascapes by local artists, oil lamps and a brick bar, and an outdoor courtyard with umbrella-covered tables, where the view across the Battery park to the river is quite idyllic on a summer's day.

Tin wall sconces were aglow and oil lamps flickered in the main dining room the busy Saturday night we first ate here. The inordinately slow service could be attributed to the fact that we and everyone else had ordered the caesar salad, a house specialty ($8.95 for two), prepared tableside and worthy of the wait. Among main courses ($15.95 to $22.95), we also liked the medallions of duck with peach glaze and the rack of lamb. These were accompanied by asparagus, rice or baked potato and a $17 bottle of Rodney Strong cabernet from a wine list heavy on Californias. Passion-fruit mousse and banana cheesecake were refreshing endings.

The courtyard and the tavern are appealing settings for lunch. The fare included an

Rear courtyard is popular attraction for diners and guests at The David Finney Inn.

interesting chicken salad with fried oysters, sandwiches, quiche or crêpe of the day and a dish called chicken George Bush (he visited here during the presidential campaign of 1988), stuffed with broccoli and cheese and topped with mushrooms.

Lunch, Monday-Saturday 11:30 to 2; dinner, 5:30 to 9 or 10; Sunday, brunch 11 to 2, dinner 4:30 to 8:30. No smoking.

The Arsenal on the Green, Market Street, New Castle. (302) 328-1798.

Built by the federal government as an arsenal in anticipation of the War of 1812, this handsome, cupola-topped building facing the green has served a variety of purposes, among them a school. In 1980 it was restored by Philadelphia caterer Claudia Brock into a restaurant called the New Castle Inn, nicely authentic and catering to bus tours and private parties.

Mrs. Brock closed the restaurant in 1994 shortly after the David Phinney Inn fire, leaving old New Castle without its two key dining spots, and put it up for sale. Along came local caterer Mimi Pawlowicz, who was born and raised in New Castle and took her culinary studies at Johnson & Wales University. She reopened the restaurant in January 1995 and revived its original name, saying the inn name was misleading.

Mimi inherited an elegant building with two large, high-ceilinged dining rooms on either side of the entry hall and more rooms for private parties upstairs. She converted the former rose dining room into a casual tavern for lunch and dinner and added seating for dining in the bar. The more formal dining room in blue and white was reserved for elegant dining at night. Traditional American fare was featured. Her chef's initial dinner menu listed seafood, steaks and chops in the $10 to $27 range, the highest prices being for lobster and filet mignon. Lighter, less expensive items ($2 to $12) were offered all day in the tavern.

Open Monday-Saturday 11 to 9; Sunday brunch, 11 to 3.

Lynnhaven Inn, 154 North du Pont Hwy. (Route 13), New Castle. (302) 328-2041.

Built years ago as a country inn/restaurant when this still was out in the country, the

Lynnhaven remains a beacon of good food and serenity in the midst of the frantic commercial strip that developing New Castle has spawned. The colors of the handsome facade – beige with burgundy trim – are repeated inside the two main dining rooms, which contain well-spaced tables and booths for two and an early American decor. Horsey paintings grace the walls and plates, trays and decoys line shelves here and there. The pleasant brick and beamed lounge with its curving bar displays ship models and nautical antiques.

More decoys and wood-carved fish are shown in lighted display cases in the foyer. They're the work of Andrew Asimos, brother of owner-manager George Asimos, whose family has run the restaurant for 37 years.

A team of four chefs, each with impressive credentials, prepares an extensive menu of basically American fare with an emphasis on local seafood. Dinner entrées run from $12.95 for fried oysters and broiled flounder to $26.95 for surf and turf. Shrimp aegean, Maryland crab cakes, seafood stir-fry over saffron rice, blackened chicken and shrimp, veal parmigiana, prime rib and steak diane are among the possibilities. House salads come with both the main courses and six pasta dishes. Start with escargots en croûte, clams casino or stuffed jalapeño peppers, or a cup of authentic snapper turtle soup. Finish with chocolate mousse, cheese cake or a changing selection of cakes and pies.

Some of the dinner dishes as well as selections listed under light fare turn up on the menu for lunch, which is popular with the business crowd.

Lunch, Monday-Friday 11:30 to 3:30; dinner, 3:30 to 10, Saturday 4 to 10, Sunday 1 to 9.

Air Transport Command, 143 North du Pont Hwy. (Route 13), New Castle. (302) 328-3527.

Near the airport is this Disneyland of a theme-park restaurant, an incredible mélange that's most un-New Castle-like but immensely popular for the novelty of it all. Only someone who has been to any of this growing restaurant chain's other extravaganzas with military air motifs from Florida to Illinois knows what to expect.

Here a sign at the parking-lot entrance warns of bridge bomb damage. Tanks and military craft are scattered about the outside of a building that's a cross between a castle and a military camp. Wend your way across a bridge and through a maze to the dining room – make that three, seating 200 in a collection of World War II memorabilia. This is candlelit, white-tablecloth dining at tiered tables with views of the airport runways. Get yourselves ensconced in one of the intimate side-by-side booths for two

Entrance to Air Transport Command.

and you can't get out – until the staff slides away the heavy table, which rolls on wheels.

The menu, all things considered, was relatively short and serious (although subsequently we were informed the entire chain's menus were about to be drastically revised). At our visit, the "specialties maison" were as diverse as calves liver, chicken moutarde, shrimp stir-fry and lemon veal, but most people seemed to go for the seven kinds of steaks and prime rib, $15.95 to $19.95. We went with the flow, choosing a large-cut prime rib and a petite filet mignon. Neither proved as memorable as the surroundings.

Blue and white dining room is dressed for dinner at The Arsenal on the Green.

When we returned for a second gawk, we surmised the reason why. At one end of the sprawl was the largest lounge we've seen, comfy as could be with sofas and chairs and quite a crowd for 4 o'clock on a weekday afternoon. No mere restaurant this. It's an all-hours watering hole.

Lunch, Monday-Saturday 11 to 3; dinner, 3 to 10 or 11; Sunday, brunch 10 to 3, dinner 3 to 10.

Wok's Chinese Restaurant, Airport Plaza, Route 13, New Castle. (302) 328-6833.

The first dim sum menu in Delaware is offered by Michael Fan at the branch of a Newark restaurant he opened here in a shopping center across from the New Castle County Airport. The dim sum is a separate menu, written in Chinese with English translations and slipped under the glass tabletops. It offers some 40 "salt" and six "sweet" items at $2 or $2.50 per serving of a few bites each; the small packages of interesting flavors come in soft or crisp wrappers. For an exotic tasting smorgasbord, pick and choose to sample a little of everything.

For the less adventurous, there's a full Chinese menu of the usual suspects, unusually highly rated. Prices range from $7.25 to $11.95. The room is a mix of high-back chairs at well spaced tables with a few booths separated by arched dividers. Ceramic camels and horses, hanging lanterns and a vivid frieze of dragons and chevrons provide plenty of color around the mirrored room. Chinese newspapers are available along with menus on a table in the entry.

Lunch and dinner daily, 11 to 10 or 11.

Cellar Gourmet, 208 Delaware St., New Castle. (302) 323-0999.

When chiropractor Mel Rosenthal purchased the 1802 Janvier House in the early 1980s, he was determined to turn the basement into a badly needed healthful and informal family restaurant. With a dirt floor and low ceiling, the project was quite a challenge and the front wall fell in. Now shored up with a new wall, the interesting room has local scenes etched into tables and benches built into the rocks.

We looked around and then settled down for breakfast at the counter between one of the old guard, who filled us in on the background of old New Castle, and a gadabout who kept interrupting to talk about places down the bay. One of us naturally had to try the "famous original tastiest-healthiest waffle in the world," billed as "the most delicious you've ever tasted" ($3.95, or $4.50 with strawberries and whipped cream). It turned out to be overrated – a hazard of superlatives. Also merely adequate was the sunshine cereal ($2.50), a hearty combination of oatmeal, almonds, sesame seeds and much more, served with whole milk rather than skim, for shame.

The lunch menu offers salads, sandwiches, melts, light bites and vegetarian items in the $2.75 to $5.75 range. Desserts range from a variety of ice creams to warm caramel-apple pie, and at one visit included a sticky bun à la mode. The ownership of the restaurant changed in 1994, but the menu and style remained.

Open daily, 8 to 4, to 8 p.m. in summer and on weekends in spring and fall.

The Green Frog, 114 Delaware St., New Castle. (302) 322-8898.

Eat, Drink, Be Merry," says the frog on the little green menu of this tavern in a 1724 house in the heart of old New Castle. The place takes its name from the early cast-iron frog doorstops used in the 18th century, some of which are on display behind the bar.

This is like an English pub, the bartender advised – a dark, long and narrow paneled room with green accents and leaded Tiffany lights. The drinks are priced out of the past and beers are available on draft and by the pitcher. A dozen sandwiches are priced from $3.25 for a BLT to $4.50 for crab cake. Under new ownership, the place added dinner service in 1994, filling a gap temporarily left by the closing of the David Finney and New Castle inns. The short menu was nicely priced from $6.50 for classic liver and onions to $9.25 for crabmeat simmered in garlic and white wine and served with roasted peppers over linguini. Chicken fajitas, mussels marinière and roasted turkey over homemade cornbread with a side of hobo potatoes and creamy gravy were other choices. Biloxi flounder and steamed shrimp were blackboard specials at our visit.

Lunch daily except Sunday, 11 to 3; dinner, Wednesday-Saturday 5 to 9.

Diversions

Not a reconstruction of replicas, New Castle is a living museum of superb restorations virtually unchanged since the mid-1800s. "The spirit of the town is not that of an antiquarian society at all," says the definitive book *New Castle on the Delaware,* a federal WPA writers' project compiled in the 1930s and revised in the 1970s. "The dwellers are as preoccupied with their own affairs as are Americans elsewhere. They take the town as a matter of course, a part of the background of their business, and like it as it is....The distinction of New Castle today is due to the busy daily life that has gone on in it without break through the centuries, achieving a fairly congenial blending of old and new in activity and interests. This is something rather rare in our country, rarer than in parts of Europe where a town normally has not only length, breadth and height, but also an imposing time dimension accepted as one of the realities of the place."

New Castle Heritage Trail. Most of the structures in the long two square blocks in the center of old New Castle are detailed in a brochure published by the town and the Trustees of New Castle Common. Walking is the best way to see the sites. Join New Castilians as they walk or jog around **The Battery** park beside the Delaware. Poke along the undulating brick sidewalks of **The Strand,** pausing to look at the vestiges of the old store with an early Ivory Soap billboard painted three stories high on the side of a brick dwelling along **Packet Alley.** Cut through a walkway beside the **Presbyterian Church** to the shady Green. Prominent Delawareans are buried in the graveyard at

Old railroad ticket office is part of New Castle's expansive waterfront park, The Battery.

Immanuel Episcopal Church, which since 1924 has sponsored the famed A Day in Old New Castle the third Saturday in May on the Green. Other sights worth noting are the **Old Town Hall** with an unusual open archway connecting Delaware Street and the Market Place, the 1789 **Academy,** the 1809 **U.S. Arsenal,** the original **ticket office** for the old New Castle-Frenchtown Railroad, and the **Town Wharf,** where little remains to validate the claim that New Castle was once an important shipping and transportation center.

New Castle Court House, Delaware Street, 323-4453. The largest structure in downtown New Castle, this is the oldest surviving courthouse in Delaware (1732) and also served as Delaware's first state capitol. The capital was moved to Dover and the county seat to Wilmington, and the scene of so much early history is now virtually still except for public tours offered by the Delaware State Museums. "We are interpreters, not docents," said the site supervisor. "We try to bring the building and the situations that occurred in it alive." The restored courtroom contains a judge's bench, witness stand and prisoner's dock. Open Tuesday-Saturday 10 to 3:30, Sunday 1:30 to 4:30. Free.

The Dutch House, 32 East Third St., 322-2794. This improbably low-slung house with a door, two windows and overhang roof is New Castle's only complete surviving house built prior to 1700. It's also believed to be the oldest brick house in Delaware. Typical of Dutch Colonial architecture, it is furnished with early Dutch furniture and artifacts, including a Dutch Bible and a courting bench. Open March-December, Tuesday-Saturday 11 to 4, Sunday 1 to 4; weekends in January and February. Adults, $2.

Amstel House, Fourth and Delaware Streets, 322-2794. George Washington was a wedding guest in 1784 in this imposing Georgian house built a half century earlier. Later the home of Gov. Nicholas Van Dyke, it has been maintained as a house museum since 1934 by the New Castle Historical Society. Antique furnishings and a complete Colonial kitchen are on view. Same hours as Dutch House. Adults, $2; combination ticket with Dutch House, $3.50.

Old Library Museum, 40 East Third St., 322-2794. Its fanciful hexagonal structure and three-level skylight make this an unusual site for a library. Philadelphia architect Frank Furness designed it in 1892 for the New Castle Library Company's collection of classics and law books. Today it is owned by the Trustees of the New Castle Common, which preserves 700 acres of early lands around the town in something of a

George Read II House is one of the more outstanding Georgian house museums anywhere.

civic coup for old New Castle. It's leased to the New Castle Historical Society for exhibits and a slide presentation on the town. Open Saturday 11 to 4, Sunday 1 to 4; also some Thursdays and Fridays 11 to 4. Free.

Shopping. Although this has always been a working town, most of the commerce has moved with suburbia up to Route 13. The Visitors Bureau's guide to old New Castle cites sixteen places of interest, four lodgings and ten places to shop, one of them a realty office. Biggest of the stores is O'Donald's **Variety Store,** one of the old school. Antiques and collectibles are featured at **Matilda's Treasures,** a shop run by old New Castilian Bill Challenger and his wife Jackie, who used to take in B&B guests at the River House on The Strand. Next door, **Bittersweet** carries more antiques and primitives. Lots of small gifts and accessories are displayed at **Etc. Shoppe, Ltd.** A dozen dealers show their wares in the **Antique Co-op of Historic New Castle.**

Extra-Special

George Read II House and Garden, 42 The Strand. (302) 322-8411. Considered one of the outstanding Georgian house museums anywhere, this was completed in 1804 by the prosperous lawyer-son of a signer of the Declaration of Independence. He imported both materials and craftsmen in an effort to build the grandest residence in Delaware. It's a huge house with an unimpeded view of the river, towering above its neighbors along The Strand. Now owned by the Historical Society of Delaware, it is a living museum of the decorative crafts from the Federal period. An iron balcony and palladian window surmount the handsome doorway, itself topped by a fanlight. Inside are incised marble window sills and lintels, a stunning Greek key trompe-l'oeil cornice decoration in the entry hall, and elaborately carved detailing in the woodwork, masonry and plastering. The house and its attached servants' wing are surrounded by formal gardens designed in the style of Andrew Jackson Downing, foremost landscape architect of the mid-19th century. The Colonial Revival taste of later owners is preserved in three rooms that contrast with the restored Read interiors. There is a small museum shop in the basement entry. Open March-December, Tuesday-Saturday 10 to 4, Sunday noon to 4; weekend hours in January and February. Adults, $4.

Chadds Ford, Pa.
Wyeth and du Pont Country

Although the Battle of the Brandywine stamped Chadds Ford's place in history, the Wyeth family has given it cachet.

This two-bit hamlet along the Brandywine is named for the farmer and tavern-keeper who ferried travelers across the river at "John Chad's fording place." Here is where George Washington made his stand in 1777 against British troops on the march from nearby Kennett Square to the new nation's capital at Philadelphia. Some of the British crossed here as expected; others outwitted Washington by outflanking him to the north. The biggest battle of the Revolution went to the Crown.

The bucolic landscape later inspired many an artist, among them Howard Pyle, father of modern American illustration. Most famous of his students in classes at Chadds Ford was N.C. Wyeth, who settled his family along the Brandywine early in the 20th century and launched three generations of artistic talent here. Andrew Wyeth was born in Chadds Ford and still is said to go out on foot daily to seek inspiration for his work. The works of America's foremost family of artists are the cornerstone of the famed Brandywine River Museum.

The Brandywine winds past forests, meadows and hillsides in a rural, almost Vermont-like strip through encroaching exurbia. Side by side with pastoral landscapes that are the backdrops of Wyeth paintings lie the du Pont estates, substantial tract houses, shopping areas and office parks of the Philadelphia-Wilmington corridor. Busy U.S. Route 1 traverses the area's midsection and crosses the Brandywine, as did the British, at Chadds Ford.

The hamlet's appeal derives partly from its scenic landscape, its trademark houses and barns of gray fieldstone and its abiding ruralness, utterly unexpected in the midst of so much development. Its winding, back roads are made for getting lost.

The appeal of the broader Brandywine Valley, which fans out on all sides from Chadds Ford, comes mainly from its uncommon concentration of sophisticated museums. Most owe their existence to one branch or another of the du Pont family, a name as strongly identified with the area as that of the Wyeths.

Together they lend sophistication to one of America's most celebrated landscapes.

Old wagon is on view outside stone barn housing Chadds Ford Historical Society museum.

243

Inn Spots

Accommodations range from country hotels and chain motels to small inns and home-stay B&Bs. We concentrate here on a variety situated near Chadds Ford or reflective of its particular ambiance. The geography involves a narrow section along the Route 1 corridor from Glen Mills to Kennett Square and along the north-south Route 52-100 corridor from Lenape to Fairville and across the state line into Delaware.

Fairville Inn, Route 52 (Kennett Pike), Box 219, Mendenhall 19357. (610) 388-5900.

Fifteen of the Chadds Ford area's most comfortable and attractive rooms are located in this welcoming, personal complex of a country house, a carriage house and a converted barn at the edge of Fairville, the heart of Château Country. The welcome and the personality come from Ole and Patti Retlev, he a fun-loving Swede and she a native Delawarean who moved here in the 1980s after selling their Deerhill Inn in West Dover, Vt.

The Retlevs moved for the climate, the quality of life and a less-seasonal business. Success was assured by the combination of luxurious accommodations and the year-round demand for them by museum visitors and business travelers.

The inn in the main 1820s house, the rear carriage house and a small barn was designed by Patti's uncle, architect Rodney Williams, owner of Vermont's famed Inn at Sawmill Farm, who also had a hand in the Deerhill. Patti, who did the decorating, seems to have inherited her aunt Ione Williams's design flair.

The original 1826 house has a spacious living room with a stunning copper table bearing some of the magazines that are displayed throughout the inn, a tea and breakfast room dressed in pink and white with copper utensils hanging about and five upstairs guest rooms.

Most choice rooms are the ten out back in the carriage house, built by an Amish family, and in the nearby barn. Accented with barnwood, beams and occasional cathedral ceilings, seven rooms have fireplaces, and some boast decks looking across three acres of fields toward a pond. All have spacious private baths (our suite had two vanities and a separate dressing area; the towels were thick and matched the decor), oversize closets, unobtrusive TVs, telephones, elegant country furnishings, crisp and colorful chintzes, and fresh flowers. Aforementioned suite had a balcony with wrought-iron furniture, a sitting room with a loveseat, and a bedroom with a kingsize bed and two wing chairs by the fire. Its pale yellow and moss green decor was altogether cheerful, enhanced by pink tulips in a green vase.

The Retlevs are forever embellishing their rooms, adding kingsize canopy beds, doing stenciling here and replacing fabrics there. They even repainted a room in the

barn in one day for arriving guest Barbra Streisand. Newly hung in guest and public rooms are magnificent paintings copied from old masters by a New Jersey artist.

The Retlevs and staff serve a continental-plus breakfast on fine linens and china in the main house. As classical music played, we enjoyed a generous cup of kiwi, melon, grapes and strawberries, as well as Patti's delicious homemade tomato juice,

Innkeepers Patti and Ole Retlev welcome guests to Fairville Inn.

cinnamon-raisin buns, sticky buns and Swedish coffee bread. Not to be missed is afternoon tea, accompanied by at least ten kinds of yummy homemade Swedish butter cookies.

Doubles, $125 to $170; two suites, $180. No smoking.

Hamanassett, 725 Darlington Road, Box 129, Lima 19037. (610) 459-3000.

What a manse is this! What gardens and grounds! What a nice place to stay, thanks to the heritage of an uncommon manor house and the straightforward, no-nonsense charm of its owner, a retired school teacher who has lived here since her marriage in 1949.

The mistress of the manor is Evelene Dohan – "every other letter is an E – when I was born, my mother must have screeched, 'eeee,'" quips this eminently quotable woman who must have been a memorable teacher. Here, single-handedly except for a commercial cleaning and grounds service, she offers six comfortable guest rooms and a suite, all with private baths and television sets and most with oversize beds. Her literature conveys the grace of an heiress as well as the strictures of a school marm.

"I want people to feel at home when they're not at home," says Evelene. We'd gladly stay in any of the guest rooms on the second and third floors of this manor house in which she raised five children. All are quite spacious, nicely furnished in traditional, unshowy decor and outfitted with "an abundance of antiquities, many of which have been in the family for centuries." Rooms have sitting areas, full baths, big windows, well-worn oriental rugs and an air of lived-in comfort. Some rooms contain small refrigerators stocked with wine, beer and snacks. A two-bedroom suite comes with a formal living room. A two-room affair with two double beds and a living room would be a suite anywhere else, but because the rooms are "connected through an open archway, it is not a suite," the lodging literature insists. It's quite a pad, nevertheless, for $95.

Guests spread out around the large Federal-era fireplace in the main living room/

library, its shelves stocked with more than 2,000 volumes; in a cozier Green Room parlor with another fireplace outlined in Delft tiles (except for three substitutes made by her late father-in-law, and she defies you to determine which); in a huge, brick-floored and plant-filled solarium to end all solariums, and on the majestic front loggia overlooking the gardens. Guests enjoy strolling through the formal English boxwood gardens with statues of Psyche and Aphrodite and inspecting the colorful flower gardens everywhere. "This is no Longwood," the owner apologized, but the plants are so prolific they keep the weeds at bay from July on.

Breakfast is taken at individual lace-covered tables in a chandeliered dining room open to the solarium. Evelene "studied at the Cordon Bleu, so cooking doesn't bother me." She prepares an extravagant buffet spread: juices, stewed fruit and melon, cereals, a couple of hot dishes such as tomato-mushroom omelets and pancakes with raspberries from the garden, Virginia ham, turkey sausage, Philadelphia scrapple, creamed mushrooms with basil sauce and assorted pastries from croissants to sticky buns.

You leave Hamanassett's 48 hilltop acres well-fed and restored, returning down the winding driveway past forests and gardens to Route 1, a half mile and a world away.

Doubles, $90 to $100; suite, $120 to $170. Two-night minimum May and June and October-Dec. 15. Smoking restricted. No credit cards.

The Inn at Montchanin Village, Route 100 at Kirk Road, Box 134, Montchanin, Del. 19710. (302) 888-2133.

A deluxe inn and restaurant were scheduled to open in the summer of 1995 on the site of a charming 19th-century workers' village. Local preservationists Missy and Daniel Lickle planned 26 bedrooms and suites plus a 55-seat restaurant in eleven buildings on twenty acres. The buildings were formerly occupied by mill laborers who worked at the nearby du Pont powder mills and factories along the Brandywine River.

Guest rooms were emerging in a row of turn-of-the-century duplexes facing Rockland Road and the railroad station that helped make this a thriving workers' village in the midst of du Pont country. One house has four bedrooms, a living room and a dining room and will operate as a true B&B, said Missy, with guests taking breakfast there. Most other units in various duplexes and dependencies are one- or two-bedroom suites with sitting areas. These have kitchenettes with microwaves and refrigerators; guests are served a continental breakfast at the restaurant. Missy planned to furnish the rooms in formal Victorian style, each with private bath and fancy toiletries, TV/VCR, handpainted wardrobes, Frette bed linens from Italy, terrycloth robes and the like. Guests will register in an 1890 stone schoolhouse, home of a resident innkeeper.

Dining for inn guests – and the public on a space-available basis – is offered in **Crazy Cat's Cafe.** It occupies an old blacksmith shop and is named for an old maid who once lived there "and was crazy as a cat," as Missy's grandmother described her. Serving dinner nightly, the restaurant offers regional American fare in the $13.95 to $24.95 range. It is more formal than her other restaurant, The Back Burner, part of her huge gourmet emporium known as Everything But the Kitchen Sink in nearby Hockessin.

The inn site, a rural area sloping toward the Brandywine, is architecturally notable for 19th-century stone, frame and stucco construction and paths, gardens, carriage ways and such. It represents the core of the old village named in honor of Ann Alexandrine de Montchanin, mother of Pierre Samuel du Pont de Nemours.

Almost next door are Winterthur and the Hagley Museum, and not far away are the Brandywine River Museum and Longwood Gardens. "We're surrounded by treasures and have everything right here," says Dan Lickle. "How could we miss?"

Dinner nightly, 5:30 to 9:30. Doubles, $100 to $250.

Potted flowers on front loggia welcome guests to Hamanassett manor house.

Sweetwater Farm, 50 Sweetwater Road, Box 86, Glen Mills 19342. (610) 459-4711.

Part of a William Penn land grant to the Hemphill family, this inviting 1734 Georgian fieldstone mansion has been around since before the nation. The 50 acres of meadows and woodlands on the surrounding working farm impart a rural feeling. Add elegance and comfort to the guest quarters with an outdoor swimming pool, working fireplaces, a sweeping center-hall staircase, a formal parlor and a pleasant library with stereo.

The six guest rooms in the main house vary considerably in size and decor. Three have private baths and four have fireplaces. All are handsomely furnished in styles from Williamsburg to Laura Ashley and accented with period antiques, hand stenciling, Wyeth prints, dried or fresh flowers, quilts and eyelet-ruffled pillows. Lafayette's portrait is over the fireplace in the room in which he once stayed. The master bedroom with a queensize canopy bed and fireplace has three windows onto the sunrise. Wicker headboards and Laura Ashley coverlets enhance the two double beds in the third-floor loft room. We liked the fan-window suite, private and peaceful, where you can watch the sun set and the queensize bed feels as if it's in the treetops.

Off to the side of the house are five cottages fashioned from farm buildings and farmhand quarters. The Hideaway has a living room with a corner fireplace, a kitchen, and an upstairs bedroom with a canopied four-poster. Like most of the cottage rooms, it has a telephone and TV.

Fancy breakfasts are served family style by resident manager Lee Hunt in the dining room. She might offer shirred eggs, cheese soufflé, gougère with scrambled eggs or sweet potato pancakes to accompany fresh fruit and homemade muffins.

Some guests have found the atmosphere less convivial than it had been under the previous ownership. But the house and the grounds are as attractive as ever.

Doubles, $145 to $165; cottages, $150 to $225.

Scarlett House Bed & Breakfast, 503 West State St., Kennett Square 19348. (610) 444-9592.

Victoriana reigns in this stone house with rust-colored shutters astride a hill at the edge of Kennett Square. Susan Lalli Ascoci left a career in marketing at the University of Pennsylvania Hospital to open a B&B in 1990 with her husband, an engineer who describes himself as Susan's supervisor of maintenance. They and their young son are only the second family to occupy the house purchased from the Scarlett family, to which the lady of the house came as a bride in 1923.

Guests enter a wide foyer notable for chestnut woodwork, doors and stairs. Each of two window nooks on either side of the door contains facing benches that are replicas of originals in the old Quaker Meeting House in Kennett Square. Off the foyer are two fireplaced parlors. One is Susan's "fantasy room," an explosion of red, from the floral maxi-print wallpaper to the velvet chairs and sofas. The other is less Victorian with a country feeling, comfortable seating and a TV/VCR.

Upstairs is another sitting area, this one beside sunny windows full of plants on the landing, plus three guest rooms (two with shared bath) and a suite. A dish of candies, a basket of fruit, a guest diary and Gilbert & Soames toiletries are in each room, and a fresh flower is put on the pillow at turndown. The suite offers a queensize bed with the head of Shakespeare carved in the top of its solid walnut headboard and a sofa in the rear sitting area. "We have a penchant for fancy furniture," Susan says by way of explanation for the elaborate headboards in the various rooms, which remain uncluttered, despite their propensity for Victoriana. Miniatures collected on their travels are displayed in a cabinet in the hallway.

Susan serves a deluxe continental breakfast by candlelight in the dining room or on the wraparound front porch in summer. She uses low-fat recipes for all the fare, even the chocolate-chip scones and the chocolate-amaretto bread puddings that are among the breakfast pastries. The interesting coffee turns out to be a special blend with vanilla, walnut and Irish cream. "I did it once by accident and everybody liked it," says its originator. She serves tea and cookies in the afternoon.

Doubles, $65 to $95; suite, $105. No smoking.

Lenape Springs Farm Bed & Breakfast, West Creek Road, Box 176, Pocopson 19366. (610) 793-2266 or (800) 793-2234.

Get explicit directions before trying to reach this restored, three-story 1850 stone farmhouse on 32 acres above the Brandywine Creek. It's barely three miles north of Chadds Ford, but one wrong turn and three false stops took us an extra half hour. Our jaunt was worth it to find a large and livable B&B and an expansive property on which Sharon and Bob Currie raised three sons, cattle and horses.

The sons now gone, the Curries offer three spacious bedrooms and two suites, all with private baths. The Dutch suite on the second floor of the main Quaker house has a queensize bed, shag carpeting, Dutch prints of the town in Holland where the Curries once lived and a new sitting room with TV. A two-bedroom suite on the third

Lenape Springs Farm dates to 1850.

248

Stone structure is now the Scarlett House Bed & Breakfast.

floor pairs a queensize bed and two twins with a private bath across the hall. Also with a bath across the hall on the third floor is the new Cozy Corner with a queen bed. The attached carriage house at the other end of the house has two large rooms with kingsize beds above a huge game room. One decorated with bottles found around the farm is named for the bow window looking onto the barn and the old spring house over the Lenape Spring that runs down the property. The Doll Room contains quite a collection of miniature dolls from all over, some given to Sharon as presents while she was growing up.

The dolls are a feminine counterpoint to the sunken game room with a billiards table a floor below, a casual place where men and youngsters are particularly entertained and where breakfast may be served in a sunny corner. Breakfast also may be taken in the dining room and on a spacious back deck complete with outdoor jacuzzi. The meal is a hearty country-farm affair, involving fresh fruit, homemade muffins and Bob's buttermilk waffles on weekends. At other times you might get Sharon's scrambled eggs, french toast or sliced mushrooms in dijon sauce over poached eggs and English muffins.

Guests also enjoy use of the farmhouse living room, where a brass rubbing from Holland is displayed over the fireplace. Or they can join Bob, a retired engineer, as he does his farm chores.

Doubles, $70 to $85. No smoking.

Meadow Spring Farm, 201 East Street Road (Route 926), Kennett Square 19348. (610) 444-3903.

Santas and dolls dressed in their Christmas best made this farmhouse-turned-B&B a highlight of the annual Candlelight Christmas tour in Chadds Ford. It's kind of a Christmas fantasyland all year long. Innkeeper-collector Anne Hicks has turned her home into a gallery of whimsical animals in all guises, dolls and country antiques, from

249

Meadow Spring Farm is a B&B plus a 200-acre working farm.

Noah's ark on the fireplace mantel to surplus dolls stored in the attic. We were charmed by the hundreds of cows of all varieties, many sent by guests.

The Hicks family has lived in the 1836 farmhouse for 50 years; daughter Sissy Hicks, chef and co-owner of the Dorset Inn in Vermont, grew up here. With her daughter Debbie and occasional help from one of eight grandchildren, Anne opens the farmhouse to guests in six air-conditioned rooms, each with TV and four with private baths. One queensize room has a fireplace and a sleigh bed and another, the Chippendale, has a crocheted canopy bed and a huge bathroom that was converted from a bedroom. Both beds are covered with Amish-made quilts. Antique wedding gowns hang on the wall in a twin bedroom featuring Laura Ashley linens and quilts. Two rooms over the garage are newer and furnished in more contemporary country style.

Guests enjoy the living room full of inanimate animals, a dining room with the long table centered by a carved cow and her calf, a lovely porch with garden furniture looking onto gardens and a swimming pool, and another enclosed porch with a hot tub. Fruit pancakes and mushroom omelets with scrapple or sausage are specialties at breakfast. It's served in the dining room or on the screened porch, where Anne offers tea or wine in the afternoons. She also puts up 200 jars of jam made with local fruit each year.

Guests are welcome to fish in the farm pond or play ping-pong or pool in the downstairs game room. Families particularly like the feel of a 200-acre working farm, although the rooster crowing at dawn jars some.

Doubles, $65 to $75.

Brandywine River Hotel, Route 1 at Route 100, Box 1058, Chadds Ford 19317. (610) 388-1200.

Claiming to be "the focal point of historic Chadds Ford village," this brick and shingle hostelry is set back on a hill away from busy Route 1. Opened in 1987, it's shielded from highway view by a cluster of rustic buildings called the Chadds Ford Barn Shops and the historic Chadds Ford Inn.

250

Among its 40 deluxe guest rooms are ten suites with fireplaces and jacuzzi baths. Room appointments were designed to resemble a traditional Colonial home: Queen Anne reproduction furnishings in cherry and classic English chintz, wing chairs, oriental rugs, brass sconces and paintings in the Brandywine tradition. Telephones, bathrooms and remote-control TVs hidden in armoires are thoroughly up to date.

A complimentary buffet continental breakfast of cereals, bagels, croissants and English muffins is served in the fireplaced hospitality room, decorated in the style of a Colonial meeting hall. It also is used for functions. Afternoon tea (iced tea on a warm day) and homemade cookies are set out by the fireplace in the inviting lobby.

Doubles, $109; suites, $140.

Hedgerow, 268 Kennett Pike (Route 52), Chadds Ford 19317. (610) 388-6080.

Massed plantings of impatiens brighten the facade of the handsome Victorian home that had been in owner John Haedrich's family since the 1950s, and lately has been showy enough that passersby along Kennett Pike paused for a closer look. When John and his wife Barbara moved in 1988, friends asked why they didn't open it as a B&B. With a "house full of kids," John said, it was more practical to use their rear garage/carriage house instead.

The Haedrichs started by offering two guest rooms in the air-conditioned carriage house, set well back from the road beyond a spreading sycamore that shades much of the back yard. The bedrooms, perfect for joining as a suite, share a bathroom, living room, kitchen, dining room and porch. All are pleasantly furnished in country style. One bedroom holds a step-up queen pineapple poster bed; the second contains two twin beds. The living room is equipped with telephone and TV. The Haedrichs provide a continental breakfast in the dining room: fresh fruit, cereals, fresh baked goods and beverages.

As their family moves on, the Haedrichs anticipate converting the main house into a four-bedroom B&B. They also plan to add rooms to the carriage house.

Doubles, $85; suite, $140. No smoking.

Pace One, Thornton and Glen Mill Roads, Thornton 19373. (610) 459-3702.

Since 1985, Ted Pace has offered B&B lodging in the restored upper levels of a 250-year-old fieldstone barn in which he started a restaurant in 1978.

The six guest rooms and a suite, all with private baths, are distinguished for the Lancaster oak queensize beds made by the carpenter who built the inn, the original watercolors of Brandywine Valley scenes by a local artist and the variety of striking wreaths fashioned by the decorator. Though different in each room, all the sheets, pillowcases, comforters and shower curtains match. All rooms have handsome tables and chairs, and the carpentry is beautiful throughout.

A continental breakfast of fresh fruit, juice, and breakfast cake is set out in an upstairs sitting room for guests.

Doubles, $65 to $85.

Dining Spots

Chadds Ford Inn, Routes 1 and 100, Chadds Ford. (610) 388-7361.

The house built by Francis Chadsey, the English Quaker who purchased 500 choice acres here from William Penn's commissioner of land grants in 1703, is now the Chadds Ford Inn. His eldest son, who lived nearby, ran the ferry that crossed the Brandywine. In 1736, John Chad turned the house into a tavern, a role it has upheld virtually ever since.

The place where Colonial officers were entertained during the Revolution now provides sustenance to Andrew and Betsy Wyeth, who live up the road, and to countless travelers who eat better here than they might expect.

The low beamed ceilings and wainscoting enhance the works of three generations of Wyeths hung on the walls of the restaurant. It has two main dining rooms on either side of the center entry hall downstairs and three more upstairs, plus a tavern in back. Tables, each bearing a slender rose, are attractively set in beige and brown. Candles are lit at lunchtime, even though sunlight streams through the windows recessed in the thick stone walls.

It was here we first learned that the area's ubiquitous snapper soup is made not with red snapper but with snapper turtle. It tastes like the turtle soup we've had in New Orleans and is thick and spicy. We also had chicken crêpes garnished with carrots, cole slaw, a piece of melon and rippled potato chips. Roasted turkey salad served with marinated artichoke hearts and roasted sesame seed dressing was another good choice from a menu that ranges widely from a grilled chicken and jack cheese sandwich to boboli with montrachet and crab cakes with lobster-chive sauce ($5.75 to $10.95).

The dessert tray held old favorites like pecan and pumpkin pies, chocolate éclairs, sour-cream peach pie, chocolate mousse cake and a strawberry-kiwi tart

The enormous wine list offers a Chaddsford chardonnay as well as a number of Californias at fair prices. The bill comes on a doily, with a dollop of M&Ms.

At night, the historic atmosphere is grand, the presentation stylish and the service leisurely, at least the autumn midweek evening we dined. Everything on the contemporary dinner menu ($14.95 to $23.95) appealed, from baked salmon served over basil and spinach to grilled free-range chicken with sweet corn puree. We were especially smitten by the mustard-sauced Australian loin of lamb and the tender grilled venison steak topped with port wine and plum sauce. These were accompanied by broccoli and roasted potatoes. A hot popover came first; a key lime puff finished.

Lunch, Monday-Saturday 11:30 to 2; dinner, 5:30 to 10 or 10:30; Sunday, brunch 11 to 2, dinner 4 to 8.

Dilworthtown Inn, Old Wilmington Pike at Brinton Bridge Road, Dilworthtown. (610) 399-1390.

For historic atmosphere and fine food, locals head to the quaint hamlet of Dilworthtown and this rambling old wood, stone and brick structure dating to 1758. The French fare is classic and the wine list the area's best, as evidenced by the Wine Spectator award of excellence.

The original inn and its late 18th-century wing were restored in 1972 into a mélange of fifteen dining rooms, bar and lobby, complete with plate-glass windows and plantings in a mini-atrium. Eleven fireplaces, stenciling, oriental rugs, antique furnishings and candlelight combine for a romantic atmosphere, and the restaurant shows no effects from a kitchen fire that required its closing for most of 1993.

The leather-like, eight-page dinner menu starts with fourteen appetizers ($5.50 for the house pâté of duck liver, port wine and truffles to $8.25 for shrimp cocktail or hickory-smoked salmon).

Among entrées ($14.25 to $22.25) are three steaks, South African lobster tail, Maryland crab casserole, and specialties like lobster thermidor, Long Island duck with apricot nectar sauce, rack of lamb and medallions of veal with local mushrooms. The chef shines with the nightly specials: perhaps salmon poached with ginger, quail sautéed with fresh pears and venison sauced with green peppercorns. Desserts include chocolate mousse, crème caramel and homemade sorbets and gelatos of exotic flavors.

Dinner nightly, 5:30 to 10:30, Sunday 3 to 9.

Works of three generations of Wyeths hang on walls of Chadds Ford Inn.

Chadds Ford Cafe, Route 1 at Heyburn Road, Chadds Ford, Pa. (610) 558-3960.

Two sisters and their husbands opened this sprightly deli with a counter in 1991 and quickly expanded to a full-fledged dining room. "We're family-owned and geared for family dining," said Joan Winchester, who's proud of her bright and cheery addition enhanced by Amish-made table tops and a bench and a corner cupboard made by Amish farmers.

The "family" description and the simple, somewhat plain-Jane surroundings mask a rather ambitious menu offering three meals a day. Some of the area's most sophisticated fare emanates from the kitchen of chef Frank Perko, who came on board as a partner in 1994. His dinner menu starts with such appetizers as duck and potato napoleon, wild mushroom polenta, almond-coated fried brie with raspberry coulis and goat-cheese strudel. Treats like lobster ravioli, sea scallops barcelona and shrimp shanghai (with bok choy and oriental garlic-ginger sauce) tempt the pasta-lovers. Up to fifteen entrées are priced from $13.95 for citron chicken or chicken wellington to $18.95 for veal scampi or grilled filet of beef with roasted garlic demi-glace and wild mushroom potato hash. Caesar salad and roasted head of garlic come with all pastas and main dishes. One reviewer wrote that the food looked almost too good to eat, but practicality prevailed, as well it should.

Good salads and sandwiches in the $4.95 to $6.95 range are featured at lunch. Breakfasts run from the basic to the creative. Consider the tour de cafe, a sautéed veal medallion topped with fresh tomato confit, poached eggs and green onion hollandaise sauce ($8.95).

Open Monday, 8 to 2:30; Tuesday-Saturday 8 to 9 or 10 p.m., Sunday 8 to 8. BYOB.

Buckley's Tavern, 5812 Kennett Pike (Route 52), Centreville, Del. (302) 656-9776.

Built in the late 1700s, this consists of an intimate, noisy tavern in front, a pretty, white-linened interior dining room and an airy garden room at the back. There's also an open-air bar on two upper levels outside. Votive candles flicker on bare, rich wood tables flanked by comfortable, cushioned chairs in the garden room, our choice for dining on two occasions.

The former tavern and dinner menus have been combined into one short, interesting menu appealing to a variety of tastes and pocketbooks. That no doubt accounts for the fanciful juxtaposition of an expensive foreign car parked next to a pickup truck in the delightful drawing of the tavern exterior on the menu cover, as well as for the actual mix of singles, on-the-town foursomes, du Pont executives, foreign businessmen and couples that seem to pack the place every time we're there.

Burgers or hummus, barbecued pork sandwich or goat cheese bruschetta, chicken chili with black beans or Thai beef and noodle salad, spinach fettuccine with smoked salmon or roasted Long Island duckling – here's the ultimate grazing menu at prices from $4.95 to $16.95.

At one visit, we liked the crab cakes with a fresh coriander tartar sauce and the linguini with smoked chicken and red peppers. At another, the shrimp ravioli with tomatoes and rosemary and the shrimp and scallops with green peppercorns in puff pastry were winners.

The wine store located in the front of the building keeps the tavern's wine selection interesting and reasonably priced.

The special cappuccino-pecan-praline ice cream was a hit among desserts ($3 to $5), as was a fuzzy navel peach pie with a peach brandy custard sauce, which looked and tasted like a creamsicle.

Lunch, Monday-Saturday 11:30 to 2:30; dinner nightly, 5:30 to 9; Sunday brunch.

The Farm House Restaurant, McCue Road, Avondale. (610) 268-2235.

The restaurant in the clubhouse at Loch Nairn Golf Course is getting increasingly high marks locally, thanks to a former chef from Wilmington's Hotel du Pont. Particularly appealing is the canopied outdoor patio, glamorously set for dinner with white linens on large, well-spaced tables flanked by solid wooden chairs.

The blackboard menu might list dinner entrées from $15 for roast pheasant to $22 for surf and turf. Shrimp provençal, salmon florentine, veal madeira, venison with lingonberry sauce and steak au poivre are other possibilities. Appetizers could be assorted smoked seafood, clams casino and breaded portobello mushrooms.

Homemade desserts include chocolate-pecan tart, poppyseed butter-lemon cream cake and strawberries romanoff with slivered almonds.

The lunch menu is fairly standard, except perhaps for sautéed Norwegian salmon on a kaiser roll. But you can't beat the outdoor patio for location.

Lunch daily, 11 to 3; dinner, Thursday-Monday 5 to 9.

Lenape Inn, Routes 52 and 100, Lenape. (610) 793-2005.

For dining with a view of the Brandywine, head for this 1852 landmark refurbished into one of the area's larger and fancier restaurants and banquet facilities.

The view is consistent, even if the food is not. Baby ducklings parade in spring by the expansive windows of the main dining room, which is on two levels to take advantage of the view. Christmas lights illuminate a large tree much of the year, and the river is spotlit at night. A single rose graces each table; crisp white linens, stenciled chairs and huge chandeliers add elegance.

The continental-American menu prices dinner entrées from $15.95 for breast of capon with madeira sauce to $29.95 for lobster tails and filet mignon. Crab imperial, dover sole with lump crabmeat, poached salmon, veal oscar, rack of lamb dijon, wiener schnitzel and steak au poivre are among the choices.

Buckley's Tavern, dating to the late 1700s, is one of the area's most popular eateries.

Salads, sandwiches and a number of entrées from the dinner menu are available at lunch, $6.75 to $10.75.

Lunch, Tuesday-Saturday 11:30 to 3; dinner, Tuesday-Saturday 4:30 to 10:30, Sunday noon to 9.

Mendenhall Inn, Route 52, Mendenhall. (610) 388-1181.

Named for the Mendenhall family that built barns throughout the Brandywine Valley, the restaurant that began this expanding hotel/conference center complex occupies a large, century-old barn. The comfortable fireplaced lobby with wing chairs, barnwood walls, and farm implements sets the stage for entry into the Blue Room, Garden Room, Tavern or the upstairs Mill Room and a ballroom – 350 people can be served at once.

The lower floor of the mill is now the main dining room, where the old beams are still intact. It combines rustic charm with contemporary appointments, upholstered chairs, linened tables, fresh flowers and candlelight.

The conservative, continental dinner menu seldom changes. You might start with Chincoteague oysters on the half shell, Kennett Square mushrooms stuffed with crabmeat, jumbo Panamanian shrimp cocktail or North American whitefish caviar ($8.50 for two). The two dozen entrées, served with ample tossed salads, are priced from $16.95 for broiled flounder to $32.95 for South African lobster tail stuffed with crabmeat. Most of the other seafood dishes also are paired with crabmeat. Meat dishes range from calves liver sauté and prime rib to rack of lamb for two. Fresh strawberries are a featured dessert, teamed with ice cream and grand marnier, or served in champagne or red wine. Cherries jubilee and bananas foster are other possibilities.

Lunch, Monday-Saturday 11:30 to 2:30; dinner, 5 to 9 or 11, Sunday 1 to 9.

Pace One, Thornton and Glen Mill Roads, Thornton. (610) 459-3702.

Ted Pace, who hails from a Pittsburgh restaurant family, is the guiding light behind this restaurant in a 250-year-old fieldstone barn. Located off the beaten path and only

Chef Ted Pace dishes out one of his soups for lunch patrons at Pace One.

lately granted a liquor license, which accounts for the new entrance and bar, the place is known for creativity and consistency.

Diners sit in a dimly lit interior room with stucco walls, bare pine floors and low ceilings or in a bright outer room enclosed like a porch. Inside, good artworks and vases of fresh flowers provide color.

Our lunch began with a cup of snapper soup served with a small pitcher of sherry and a terrific vegetable pâté that looked like a colorful mosaic. The generous seafood salad niçoise ($7.95) and the puff pastry filled with crabmeat, spinach and sweet red peppers ($9.50) were excellent. We also remember fondly a Sunday brunch that included a lobster, crab and shrimp casserole. The pumpkin-brandy cheesecake was as delicious as the menu said it was.

Dinner entrées run from $16.50 for baked flounder with a saffron cream sauce and beluga caviar to $26.95 for rack of lamb with a mushroom demi-glace. Other choices might be veal tenderloin stuffed with crabmeat, roast duckling with a sweet and sour sauce, cornish game hen stuffed with vegetables, and a mixed grill of lamb, venison sausage and quail, served with apple-pepper chutney. A soup cart offers all you care to eat of, perhaps, squash-apple bisque, shrimp and corn chowder, and clear mushroom soup. Among desserts are hazelnut cheesecake, pecan pie, warm New England pudding and key lime pie.

Lunch, Monday-Friday 11:30 to 2; dinner, Monday-Saturday 5:30 to 10; Sunday, brunch 10:30 to 2:30, dinner 5 to 9.

Pizza by Elizabeths, 4019A Kennett Pike, Greenville, Del. (302) 654-4478.
Two Elizabeths – Greenville residents Betsy Stoltz and Betty Snyder – run this high-style, gourmet pizza parlor in the heart of du Pont country. No ordinary pizza parlor, this. The place is a beauty in beige and green, with a Mediterranean terra-cotta tile floor, oversize dried-flower wreaths on the walls and half a dozen booths and tables. The pizza toppings are displayed in containers at the pizza bar. The crisp, chewy crusts are baked in a wood-fired oven. And the beverage list includes not only Evian and cappuccino but Samuel Adams beer and a connoisseur's selection of wines, priced up to $39.

256

You can try some of the owners' favorite pizza creations named after famous Elizabeths, from $7.50 for the Barrett Browning to $11 for the Taylor (with goat cheese, onions sautéed with rosemary, sundried tomatoes and black olives). Or you can create your own pizza from a selection of three sauces and about three dozen toppings. Breadstick appetizers, green salads and cookies make up the rest of the menu.

Open Monday-Saturday, 11 to 8:30 or 9. No smoking.

Diversions

Museums are chief among the Chadds Ford area's myriad attractions. The big three:

Brandywine River Museum, Route 1, Chadds Ford, (610) 388-2700. The Civil War-era grist mill converted into a modern museum is known for its incomparable collection of art by the Wyeth family as well as fine collections of American illustration, still life and landscape painting associated with the Brandywine heritage. Spectacular glass additions overlook the river as well as the adjoining wildflower gardens and nature trail developed by the Brandywine Conservancy, which marked its 25th anniversary in 1992 and preceded the museum by a few years. Andrew Wyeth's work, reflecting the valley and its people as well as the Maine coast, is shown in the special Andrew Wyeth Gallery, which constantly changes with additions loaned by the family. Open daily, 9:30 to 4:30. Adults, $5.

Longwood Gardens, Route 1, Kennett Square, (610) 388-6741. One of the world's great horticultural displays is showy year-round, thanks to the gardens and conservatories that once were the 350-acre private preserve of Pierre S. du Pont. Spring begins in January and the spectacle changes monthly through Christmas in the twenty Crystal Palace-type conservatories, which we find even more colorful and exotic than the outdoor gardens. Illuminated fountain displays are choreographed to music on summer evenings. Open daily, 9 to 6 or later. Adults, $10.

Winterthur Museum and Gardens, Route 52, Winterthur, Del. (302) 888-4600. The world's premier collection of American decorative arts and antiques, assembled by Henry Francis du Pont, is displayed in 175 period room settings in the main house and in a new building with three exhibition galleries. Only some are on view at any one time, such is the scope of the collection and the size of the nine-story mansion. The interior can be seen on an assortment of guided tours, sometimes fully booked well ahead. The layman may be well enough served by Winterthur's new building dedicated to the art of looking at (and learning from) things. The Galleries at Winterthur shows 1,000 of the museum's pieces arranged in galleries on two floors. The self-guided tour is immensely enlightening. Trams take visitors on tours of the lavish gardens developed by "head gardener" du Pont on his 980-acre estate. Open Monday-Saturday 9 to 5, Sunday noon to 5. Adults, $8; tours from $13.

Brandywine Battlefield, Route 1, Chadds Ford, (610) 459-3342. In the biggest battle of the Revolution, 18,000 British and 11,000 Americans met at Chadds Ford. This one went to the Brits. They outflanked George Washington, who was defending Chadds Ford, and encircled his troops from the north. Now a 50-acre state park, it has a visitor center that shows a thirteen-minute slide show on the battle. Washington's headquarters in the Benjamin Ring House and Lafayette's quarters in the Gideon Gilpin House are open periodically for tours for a fee. The actual battlefield is on unmarked lands, "two miles north as the crow flies and five roundabout miles by car," according to a park guide. Open Tuesday-Saturday 9 to 5, Sunday noon to 5. Free.

The **Chadds Ford Historical Society** has a new museum and visitor center in a barn across from its **John Chads House,** Route 100, a quarter mile north of Route 1. The 1725 house is furnished as it was when the ferryman and farmer for whom the village was named lived here – that is to say, sparely. The society also operates the **Barns-Brinton House,** a restored 18th-century tavern nearby. Houses open May-October, weekends 11 to 6, rest of year by appointment. Adults, \$1.

Chaddsford Winery, Route 1, Chadds Ford, (610) 388-6221. This boutique-style winery with lots going on has been producing good wines since 1981. Operating from a converted barn, it imports grapes from around the area to make "new American classics from the Brandywine Valley." These include the Proprietors Reserve White (rated a model for regional whites), classic European varietals and a first-class chardonnay. Proprietor Eric Miller comes from a winemaking family (his father owns Benmarl Vineyards and Winery in New York's Hudson Valley); wife Lee has authored a book about wine. Open Tuesday-Saturday 10 to 5:30, Sunday noon to 5.

Shopping. A very special country gift shop is to be found at **Pratt & Company,** a good-looking emporium run by Margaret DeMarco and Joy Juliano beside the train station in Glen Mills. Their collectibles, gifts and period reproduction furniture are displayed in several rooms. Dried flower arrangements, pretty linens, chandeliers and, at one of our visits, gorgeous Christmas things, especially the stockings, abound. More country wares are to be found in Dilworthtown, where the **Dilworthtown Country Store** is chock full of sophisticated American country crafts and folk art. The largest selection of Wyeth reproductions anywhere is featured at **Chadds Ford Gallery,** in a brick house in front of the **Chadds Ford Village and Barn Shops.**

The area's most sophisticated shopping extends along Kennett Pike (Route 52) from Fairville, site of a cluster of antiques shops, through Centreville to Greenville, Del. We're particularly partial to Centreville, where old buildings along the wide street have been converted to house such favorites as **Troll of Scandinavia** (for interesting takeout food), the **Jolly Needlewoman** and **Wild Thyme,** all neatly detailed in a new brochure touting it as "still the perfect rest stop, from 1750 until today." We're drawn to **Communiques,** a great new paper, book, card and gift shop, where coffee's always on tap and poetry readings are among the special events. **The Horse is** an exceptional gift shop run by one of the du Ponts and frequented by many of the others.

Extra-Special ⎯⎯⎯⎯⎯⎯⎯⎯⎯⎯⎯⎯⎯⎯⎯

Hagley Museum, Route 141, Wilmington, Del. (302) 658-2400.

The original du Pont mills and powder works, estate and gardens offer 230 acres of Brandywine history. More than the other museums, this lives up to its slogan, "something for everyone." A shuttle bus takes visitors around the tranquil grounds along the Brandywine. The Henry Clay Mill exhibits trace America's industrial expansion. Water flowing through the mill races power the massive stone mills in the powder yard. Pause for lunch in the simple Belin House Coffee Shop atop Blacksmith Hill and visit the workers' housing area. Then see how the boss lived in Eleutherian Mills, the first du Pont family home built by E.I. du Pont in 1803. The Georgian-style residence is furnished to reflect the tastes of five generations of du Ponts who lived there. Espaliered fruit trees set off the beautiful yet functional French garden outside. The Hagley, we contend, is most evocative of the Brandywine heritage. Open daily 9:30 to 4:30; weekends only, January to mid-March. Adults, \$9.75.

Monuments and cannons are everywhere at Gettysburg National Military Park.

Gettysburg, Pa.
Trappings and Treasures

There are two aspects to Gettysburg, the small town that embraces the decisive battlefield of the Civil War. One side is the tourist trappings that draw 2.5 million visitors annually and threaten to out-Niagara the Niagara Falls scene in the annals of tourism. The other is the rural tranquility and sense of history that prompted Dwight and Mamie Eisenhower to make a Gettysburg farm their first and only permanent home. The two aspects manage to co-exist quite nicely, thanks in part to a semi-rural location and to the tenure of the National Park Service.

Sure, there are incursions that should not demean such hallowed ground: the domineering National Tower, the Civil War Wax Museum, the countless ancillary attractions ranging from war stores to a family fun center to a General Lee's Family Restaurant. Even the commercialism of the National Park Service's electric map and cyclorama programs is jarring. Not a particularly distinguished-looking town, Gettysburg gets downright tacky in places.

Yet there also are the treasures: the 1,432 monuments and markers that dot the rolling hills of the vast battlefield and cause Civil War buffs to choke up, the site of Lincoln's Gettysburg Address, the picturesque Eisenhower Farm full of poignant memories, the stately brick Gettysburg College campus, the rural byways that lead to all kinds of pleasures and discoveries.

259

The composite makes Gettysburg a classic middle American tourist destination, just as the Eisenhowers were the classic middle American couple of the post-World War II era.

The epic 1994 movie and mini-series on "Gettysburg," adapted from the Michael Shaara novel *Killer Angels* and shown on Ted Turner's TV network, cast the town in the national spotlight and gave it a banner year for tourism.

Despite all its history, the inns and B&Bs of the modern idiom came late to a Gettysburg where high-rise motels were the rule. The first B&B emerged only in 1984. Many have followed, in town and in the surrounding countryside, especially to the south and east – the part of the area that we feature here. They make a choice base for experiencing the best that Gettysburg has to offer.

Inn Spots

Antrim 1844, 30 Trevanion Road, Taneytown, Md. 21787. (301) 756-6812 or (800) 858-1844.

The most upscale inn in the area – indeed, one of the more upscale anywhere – is this paragon of elegance twelve miles southeast of Gettysburg in the Maryland border town of Taneytown (pronounced Tawneytown).

The Antrim dates to 1844, when a Pennsylvania farmer began building the seventeen-room manor house and outbuildings for a working plantation. During the Civil War, Union Gen. George Meade made this his headquarters and watched Confederate troops move toward Gettysburg from its widow's walk. The house had been boarded up for 60 years when Dorothy and Richard Mollett, Baltimore restorationists, acquired it in 1988 to fulfill their dream of running an inn. They started in 1989 with four rooms and now have fourteen, plus a restaurant of distinction (see Dining Spots), a black-bottom marbleite swimming pool that looks like a reflecting pond, a gazebo, an Omni tournament tennis court, a croquet course and a putting green, all for people with means and leisure time.

Guests arrive to find their names calligraphed on cards with their room assignments at the entry. Fourteen-foot-high ceilings dignify the spacious common rooms on the main floor and four original bedrooms on the second. No expense has been spared to make everything perfect. Each guest room has a different personality but the same amenities – private marble baths, step-up canopy feather beds, oriental rugs, swagged valances. Crisp and pristine, they are cloaked in luxury. Men tend to favor the vast George Washington Clabaugh Room with a 19th-century half-tester bed from New Orleans. Women are partial to the Lamberton Room, pretty in white and floral prints. The footed, free-standing shower in the Meade Room is like nothing we've seen. The posts on the 1820 Honduras mahogany canopy bed weigh 150 pounds each. We liked the Boucher Room, with a canopied kingsize feather bed, well-worn oriental rugs, a front morning porch and an evening garden porch from which we watched the sun set over the Catoctin Mountains.

What Dorothy calls four funkier rooms with canopies hanging from sloping ceilings and bathrooms with two-person jacuzzis now grace the third floor. Most prized are fireplaced rooms and suites with jacuzzis or two-person steambath showers in four plantation outbuildings. The private decks beside the stream that come with the deluxe Sleigh and Carriage rooms in the small yellow barn are perfectly idyllic. So is the Ice House Suite with queensize four-poster bed and chintz loveseat. Half-doors open onto the garden on one side and the pool on the other, and clouds are painted on the ceiling to complete the indoor-outdoor transition.

The main house is an architectural and decorative masterpiece. All shows to great

Canopied rear porch dressed in wicker overlooks plantation outbuildings at Antrim 1844.

advantage in the dining room with cobalt-blue lacquered walls and a crystal chandelier above a table for fourteen and in the two formal rear drawing rooms opening one onto the other, brimming with fine antiques, marble fireplace mantels and a profusion of fresh flowers. A corner of the library harbors a nifty English mahogany telephone booth that Richard found on an antiquing expedition and was just the ticket for sophisticated privacy. The library is "where everyone hangs out," in Dorothy's words, on facing plush leather sofas. That is, when they're not enjoying the formal gardens or the views of the Catoctin Mountains from the large back veranda dressed in wicker.

The Molletts pamper guests with a complimentary bar containing wine and champagne, turndown service with chocolates, port and a rose, and a wakeup tray placed on a butler stand outside the door of each room an hour before breakfast. Don't overindulge on its muffins and fruit, however. Ahead lies a leisurely feast of belgian waffles, scrapple, ham and hash browns, or perhaps eggs benedict, beautifully served amidst fresh flowers, gold-edged china, silver and crystal goblets. Dorothy decorates the plates with all kinds of garnishes, just one more example of an innkeeper who cares.

Doubles, $175; suites, $250 to $300.

The Old Appleford Inn, 218 Carlisle St., Gettysburg 17325. (717) 337-1711.
The town's oldest and largest B&B, this 1867 Italianate Victorian mansion is close to the Gettysburg College campus and next door to a fraternity house. Frank and Maribeth Skradski of Chicago bought it in 1988 and furnished it with family heirlooms, remarkable collections and TLC.

Consider their library-reception room. You register at a desk facing shelves full of antique Kodak cameras dating from 1900 to 1910, hundreds of Chinese ceremonial teapots, music boxes and a Dickens village. There's a lineup of cannons on the fireplace mantel. Tea, coffee and cookies await on a table near a chest covered with Civil War books. Beyond is the stenciled dining room, where a long oak table is set for twelve at breakfast and early china and wavy glass are on display in corner cabinets. Adjourn to the high-ceilinged living room, a spacious affair furnished with Victorian antiques, a baby grand piano, a tray with a decanter of sherry and bowls of munchies and a stash of local apples from Pennsylvania's largest apple-producing county. Or relax upstairs in the wicker-filled plant room, which has a stunning garden mural on one wall and harbors books to exchange and a refrigerator for guests' use. A tiny back porch for two lies beyond.

Classical music plays throughout the common rooms. A jar of candy and a decanter of sherry are in each of the twelve guest rooms, all with private baths. Antique collectibles, fringed lamps, Victorian flowers, dainty pillows, dried flower arrangements, sinks in oak cabinets and Lord & Mayfair toiletries are the norm. Maribeth's last childhood doll is in the corner of the General Lee Room, once a children's playroom and now a showplace for a wedding dress, hatboxes and shoes. The country decor of the General Custer Room with its maple bed and a quilt wall hanging offers a break from the prevailing Victorian theme. Particularly prized are two rooms with queen canopy beds, one with a fireplace. We liked the lavender clawfoot tub in front of the stained-glass window in the third-floor General Burnside Room. The rear carriage house contains a two-room suite as well as the innkeepers' quarters.

Given the inn's name, it comes as no surprise that apples are featured in the fare: Appleford french toast, apple sausage ring, apple muffins, apple juice – "not all at once," says Maribeth, "or you'd get apple'd out." A more typical breakfast might include a citrus sparkler, fresh melons or strawberries with amaretto cream, apple-pumpkin spice bread and blueberry pancakes with sausage.

Doubles, $103 to $113. No smoking.

The Brafferton Inn, 44 York St., Gettysburg 17325. (717) 337-3423.

"Experience Gettysburg in the home where its history began," proclaims the advertising for this interesting inn. And history it has in spades. Built in 1786, the original fieldstone house was the first in Gettysburg's historic district. A ricocheting bullet fired during the Civil War battle left its mark on an upstairs fireplace mantel. Troops flanked the stairway as Catholics worshipped in a bedroom while their church became a hospital for the wounded. The dining room is encircled by a fascinating mural of eighteen local structures, painted by artist Virginia Jacobs McLaughlin, who lately was involved in the restoration of Mount Vernon.

New innkeepers Sam and Jane Bock, former education administrators in Connecticut, have made some of this history more comfortable. All ten rooms now have private baths and two are suites, their sitting areas equipped with pullout sofas and TVs. The sitting room of one suite on the main floor occupies what had been a small shop. The new family suite on the third floor is a great space with beamed cathedral ceiling and a wall of stone and brick.

Six of the guest rooms are in a brick and clapboard house connected to the main structure by a glass-covered brick courtyard that the Bocks call an atrium. It opens onto the rear patio and a small garden, a pleasant refuge given that this is the heart of downtown Gettysburg. Some rooms in this house lack windows and are lit by skylights; they're small and somewhat stark in the Colonial style, with room for only one chair (for more comfortable seats, head to the atrium or the long front parlor that the Bocks have decorated in elegant early 19th-century style). The bedrooms have whitewashed walls with woodwork in Williamsburg colors, quilts, samplers and coverlets that match the remarkable stenciling. Benches and rockers, braided rugs, Civil War books, hats on racks and masks on the beds carry out the theme. A local potter made the salad bowls that form some of the sinks. We're partial to the quiet garden room in back with a carved four-poster queen bed. Upstairs in the main fieldstone house are the other four guest quarters with 200-year-old floors and walls. One of the three larger bedrooms here holds a queensize bed, as does the third-floor suite.

Mural of local structures encircles dining room at The Brafferton Inn.

Tables in the appealing dining room are set with white ironstone plates and assorted bowls. The Bocks serve a breakfast of juice, fresh fruit and a main course like strawberry or apple pancakes or peaches and cream french toast with bacon.

Doubles, $75 to $95; suites, $110 to $125. No smoking.

Gaslight Inn, 33 East Middle St., Gettysburg 17325. (717) 337-9100.

The newest and most upscale inn in Gettysburg emerged Cinderella-like in 1994 from a ramshackle downtown apartment house. Dennis and Roberta Sullivan were putting the finishing touches on what they envisioned as "a deluxe in-town oasis" with eight custom-decorated guest rooms, all with private baths, five with gas fireplaces and four with two-seat steam showers.

As workmen rushed it to completion, the Sullivans led a tour of their facility, waxing enthusiastic over its accoutrements. They showed the see-through gas fireplace in the Lily Room, open to both the jacuzzi tub in the bathroom and the queensize bed in the room, where the walls were ragrolled in shades of taupe, shrimp and blue. A Louis XV bedstead with French Provincial end tables and bureau were set for the Daisy, a handicapped-accessible room on the main floor. An antique Persian carpet was ready for use as a bed cover in the rear Sweet William Room, rich in burgundy and cream. It shares the third-floor balcony with the Aster Room, dressed in beige and blue and bearing a loveseat and a chaise lounge.

The rear of the second floor holds a TV room with video library and a balcony for guests' use. Other common areas include a formal parlor decked out in oriental draperies puddled on the floor, a dining room with a large cherry table and a gateleg cherry table for overflow, a side porch and a gaslit brick patio beside gardens and a tiny pond.

"Food is very much a feature here," according to Roberta, formerly a caterer in

Monuments frame The Doubleday Inn, only B&B located on the Gettysburg Battlefield.

Montgomery County, Md. Breakfast can be a healthful, light continental affair or a full meal, always with an egg dish and perhaps crêpes with strawberries and champagne sauce. Coffee or cold beverages are served with a variety of baked goods in the afternoon.

Prix-fixe dinners are available to guests and the public on Saturday evenings. The $35 tab includes hors d'oeuvre in the parlor, soup, salad, homemade breads and a main course like bouillabaisse, stuffed roast pork or rack of lamb. There's a choice of two desserts ("one decadent and one healthful," says Roberta), plus complimentary wine. Simpler bistro dinners are offered to house guests on Fridays and Sundays. Roberta was planning to conduct cooking classes in her professional kitchen as well.

Doubles, $85 to $120. No smoking.

The Doubleday Inn, 104 Doubleday Ave., Gettysburg 17325. (717) 334-9119.

The only B&B on the Gettysburg Battlefield, the Doubleday occupies a splendid location in a residential section atop Oak Ridge. On view are monuments and battle markers in front, the college campus and the town in back, and busloads of tourists going between.

In 1994, Charles Wilcox, a Chicago area banker, and his wife Ruth Ann purchased the white clapboard house built in 1929 and started redoing one room at a time. They offer nine guest rooms, five with private baths and two sharing at either end of the house. The Civil War is the theme and rooms are named after people involved, says Ruth Ann. "This was the site of the first day's battle and a lot of soldiers died on our grounds."

Rooms are rather small (one large enough only for a bed and a luggage rack) but sprightly, as the Wilcoxes have decorated for an English country look. Murals of two seasons are painted on the walls of the Loft Room, everybody's favorite, with a double and twin bed up a staircase from the bathroom. The two largest are on the main floor, the dainty Bell Jefferson Room in pink and green and the more masculine Marse Robert, with a paneled library air and an open bathroom screened by a lace partition.

The Doubleday makes up for any shortcomings in lodging space with marvelous public areas. Besides an elegant parlor and dining room, there are a rear patio, a side porch with a hanging swing and another patio, and a second-floor balcony. Civil War memorabilia is displayed throughout. Gary Gross, a licensed battlefield guide, holds forth in the parlor Wednesday and Saturday evenings with an entertaining two-hour dialogue on the war.

A country breakfast is served by candlelight on fine linens and china or, in summer, on the side porch. The meal includes juice, fresh fruit and a main dish like egg and cheese strata, rum-apple french toast or blueberry pancakes.

Doubles, $79 to $100. No smoking.

Baladerry Inn, 40 Hospital Road, Gettysburg 17325. (717) 337-1342.

Once a field hospital for the adjacent battlefield, this restored 1810 farmhouse is nicely located out in the countryside and outfitted with the creature comforts that are important to the ratings guidebooks and their inspectors. Ex-New Yorkers Tom and Caryl O'Gara try to provide the kind of accommodations they seek on their travels. They offer four bedrooms with private baths in the original main house and its addition, and four larger rooms (two with corner fireplaces) in a recently converted carriage house in back. All but one have queensize beds and come with tiled baths, light painted walls, plush carpeting and Pennsylvania House reproduction furniture. They're crisp and serviceable, but somewhat lacking in charm.

The latter commodity is more evident in the main inn's two-story, beamed great room, a manorial expanse with individual breakfast tables, sitting areas, wood stove and a decorative loft backed by a remarkable stained-glass window that is illuminated at night. Soft drinks are available in a help-yourself wet bar. Off the great room is a large, trellised brick patio, a good spot for taking in the tranquil woodland scene. A common room and wicker-furnished sun porch in the new carriage house doubles as a conference center. The spacious grounds include gardens and a tennis court.

Breakfast in the great room or on the dining terrace consists of juice, a fruit plate, cereal and a main course such as french toast or bacon and eggs.

Doubles, $78 to $89.

The Old Barn, One Main Trail, Carroll Valley 17320. (717) 642-5711.

John and Janet Lee Malpeli came well prepared for their new venture in an old barn. He was a landscaping contractor and she an interior designer in the Valley Forge area, so redoing the 1853 barn as a B&B and country inn in 1994 "seemed a logical thing," in John's words. Refurbishing the vast structure room by room, they have created quite an assortment of eleven sprightly, lodge-style bedrooms, nine with private baths. Some are standard doubles; others have kitchenettes and some adjoin to become three-bedroom suites. One bedroom in the loft is light and airy with wicker furniture, floral bed covers and a green picket fence serving as a headboard. A downstairs suite offers a full kitchen, fireplace, a kingsize brass bed and a huge sitting area with sofabed and TV. The windows here are recessed into the original stone walls that are two feet thick.

The main-floor common rooms are uncommonly large: a formal sitting room with country and primitive furnishings and a large living room with fireplace and TV/VCR (in addition, an attic space is equipped with a billiards table and games). A meandering mural of area scenes by local artist Virginia McLaughlin graces a wall in the dining room, where three lace-covered tables are set for breakfast. The meal is billed as continental-plus but is really more, with quiche or omelets offered on weekdays. Sunday brings a gourmet feast – "always something exotic that nobody has ever had before," says John. "My wife likes to experiment. I'm just the waiter and I can't remember the names." Janet Lee also will prepare dinner by reservation for eight or more.

The four rural acres include a spacious rear deck and a 20-by-50-foot swimming pool. Youngsters like to explore the covered bridge nearby.

"The Old Barn may have been a barn formerly, but it is now a lovely country inn," said the blurb for the 1994 Pippinfest house tour, of which this was a part.

Doubles, $75 to $80; suite, $100.

Beechmont, 315 Broadway, Hanover 17331. (717) 623-3013 or (800) 553-7009.

Fancy leaded windows surround the entry to this red brick Federal townhouse at the edge of downtown Hanover, an out-of-the-way town that seems much bigger than its population of 15,000 suggests. Susan and William Day run it as a B&B with four bedrooms and three suites.

The main floor harbors a glamorous living room done in soft greens with oriental rugs on the polished floor, a library with a games table and a rear dining room with a lace-covered table and dried flowers arranged in a swan. Beyond are an inviting back porch, a courtyard area beneath a trellis and a deep lawn.

The other side of the house contains two side-by-side suites. One with a fireplace sports a bronze cat at ease on the fishnet canopy bed and a whirlpool tub in the bathroom. The other has a separate sitting room, gas fireplace and a private entrance.

Upstairs is another suite plus four bedrooms with private baths, some of them in the hall. One room is big enough for two queensize beds. The smallest has its bathroom in the closet and an antique rope bed, the only one in the house that isn't queensize. The Hampton Suite has a TV, and television sets are available for other rooms.

Susan prepares a full breakfast and also offers a tray for breakfast in bed. The fare includes fresh fruit, homemade granola, breakfast breads and a main dish like apricot puff pancakes, florentine cheese tart or country eggs. Afternoon refreshments might be tea and brownies or lemon cookies.

Between meals, Susan steers guests to her favorite antiques shops or to the nearby Hanover Shoe Farms, the largest standardbred horse breeders in the world.

Doubles, $80 to $90; suites, $115 to $135.

The Herr Tavern & Publick House, 900 Chambersburg Road, Gettysburg 17325. (717) 334-4332 or (800) 362-9849.

Five B&B guest rooms in the Colonial style were added above a restaurant rebuilt after its west wall blew out during a windstorm in 1987. Lately upgraded to appeal to what a fellow innkeeper calls "the new money crowd," all have been given private baths, fireplaces and television, and some have jacuzzi tubs.

Two large rooms facing the busy highway retain their Colonial feeling with creaky floors and period furnishings, stenciling and dried flowers. Three formerly small rooms that shared a bath have been converted into two rooms with private baths. One is small with a double bed; the other is big enough for a kingsize canopy poster bed, VCR, a mirrored double jacuzzi with shower and twin vanities. The crowning touch is a new attic suite. Any semblance of Colonial style has been taken over by an oversize round bed, wicker furniture, gray carpeting, a mini-refrigerator, microwave and private deck, plus a day mattress covered with pillows on the floor beside the wood stove.

Guests have use of an upstairs sun porch with reading materials and card games. The downstairs sun room is where innkeeper-owner Steve Wolf serves breakfast, perhaps eggs or crêpes, fruit and danish pastries.

Doubles, $90 to $170.

Tartan plaids and Civil War paintings dignify dining room at Antrim 1844.

The Historic Farnsworth House Inn, 401 Baltimore St., Gettysburg 17325. (717) 334-8838.

Three Confederate sharpshooters fired on Union troops from the garret window above the bedrooms in this 1810 house, and more than 100 bullet holes remain in the south wall. Ghosts have been known to stalk its corridors, and a psychic had confirmed their presence shortly before our visit. There's a lot going on in the Farnsworth House complex, which includes a restaurant and lounge, a dining garden, a book store, a Civil War art gallery, house tours, Saturday night ghost stories in the cellar and a garret museum.

In 1990, a quirky B&B was added to the array. Although not a typical inn, it offers four guest rooms with private baths and clawfoot tubs, some with patterns painted on the outsides. Each is decorated in high Victoriana, with vivid Bradbury wallpapers, ornate lamps and accents that reflect, as the brochure states, "the Victorians' flair for the extreme in color and design." An old victrola and a sewing machine decorate one room. Fishnets provide both the canopy and the spread for the queensize bed in the front Gideon room, whose bathroom is commodious enough to contain a wicker seat and dressing table. Guests keep journals in the rooms, some telling of hearing footsteps in the hallway or doors opening and closing unexpectedly.

There's a small upstairs common room with a TV. A full breakfast is served in the dining room or the garden by one or the other of the Loring H. Shultz family, owners of the complex.

Doubles, $75 to $85.

Dining Spots

Antrim 1844, 30 Trevanion Road, Taneytown, Md. (301) 756-6812.

Knowing diners are being drawn from far and wide to this wonderfully restored plantation complex a dozen miles southeast of Gettysburg. Innkeepers Richard and Dorothy Mollett have fashioned three elegant dining rooms seating 65 in their old smoke house, summer kitchen and slave's kitchen – each a dramatic setting in brick, tartan plaid and hunter green – as well as on their canopied rear veranda, which needs little to compete with the rural, mountain vistas. To complement the setting and ensure flawless service they hired as maître d' and general manager Stewart Dearie from the famed Conservatory restaurant at Baltimore's Peabody Court Hotel.

We enjoyed a fabulous, well paced dinner here prior to the arrival of talented young chef Sharon Ashburn, who's taken the restaurant to even greater heights. The experience begins at 6:30 with cocktails and complimentary hors d'oeuvre in the bar, where two loveseats face each other beside the huge brick hearth. At 7:30, diners adjourn to the restaurant wing, where oil portraits of major Civil War generals watch over the proceedings and a pianist plays on weekends. Dinner is served in four or more courses, prix-fixe for $50. One December meal started with an antelope picadillo burrito with papaya salsa and a green salad dressed with toasted nuts and fruited vinaigrette. Sorbet cleared the palate for the main course, a choice of wild rockfish baked with fennel and saffron, barbecued quail with hot German potatoes and braised cabbage, filet of angus beef tenderloin with wild mushroom-bourbon sauce and garlic mashed potatoes, and roasted rack of lamb with spaghetti squash and Smithfield ham.

Crème brûlée flavored with pumpkin and an apple strudel with crème fraîche completed what a Baltimore magazine reviewer called "a near-perfect dinner." The latest entry in the guest book at our visit touted "the best meal we've had west of Europe."

Lunch, Wednesday-Friday 11 to 1:30; dinner nightly by reservation, 7:30.

Dobbin House Restaurant and Tavern, 89 Steinwehr Ave., Gettysburg. (717) 334-2100.

Almost everybody's favorite restaurant locally is the 1776 Dobbin House, upstairs on two floors of Colonial dining rooms or in the basement in the stone-walled Springhouse Tavern that is most people's vision of what eating out in Gettysburg should be about.

The tavern is illuminated by candles even at noon. It was so dark we could barely read the menu, a lengthy affair with an historic theme. When finally we could see – and decide – one of us settled for an excellent baked French onion soup and a so-so spinach salad ($5.25), accompanied by a glass of sparkling cider. The other was tempted by the tavern's special mile-high sandwich ($5.95), "meats and such piled almost as high as the stone walls of the Dobbin House but much straighter!" But with a choice of only two meats it seemed no bigger a deal than the No. 33 club sandwich, roast beef and swiss cheese, which also added bacon, for $5.25. There was no denying the atmosphere, although service was slow as molasses. And the roll that one of us requested to go with the salad turned out to be cold and stale and cost an extra 50 cents.

Afterward, we adjourned upstairs for a look at the main floor, a ramble of small rooms with bare tables and high-back or windsor chairs. Proceed to the second floor where you'll find more dining rooms, some with tables covered by glass. The largest called the Bedroom contains the startling sight of three tables for six under bed canopies, "wherein one can actually dine in bed," according to promotion materials. For some, the gas-fired fireplaces diminish the otherwise authentic Colonial atmosphere. But most praise the food listed on a lengthy menu that rarely changes. Entrées ($14.95 to $21.95) run the gamut from "drunken scallops drowned in chablis" and crab cakes to veal madeira and prime rib. A Colonial meal of the day is offered for $15.25.

Desserts run to cheesecake, pecan pie, black forest cake and warm gingerbread. The bound wine list contains affordable varieties, except for the special Chaddsford Gettysburg chardonnay at $42.

Lunch and dinner in tavern, daily 11:30 to 11; dinner in Dobbin House, 5 to 9.

268

Upstairs dining room at Dobbin House.   Pedestal chairs in Herr Tavern dining room.

Blue Parrot Bistro, 35 Chambersburg St., Gettysburg. (717) 337-3739.

The chef trained at the Culinary Institute of America and gives cooking lessons, so you expect the food to be a cut above. The menu is not particularly innovative, however. And the surroundings are downright funky: a bar in front with three booths and some parrot paraphernalia to live up to the name (from a previous incarnation), a rear dining room with another bar and a pool table, and at the end of it all the kitchen, quite a hike from the front. Tables are covered with paper mats over striped cloths over white linens, a case of decorative overkill. Assorted lamps or candles and dried flowers in marmalade pottery jars complete the picture.

From a large lunch menu we sampled a hot chicken salad ($5.50), a grilled brochette on a bed of tossed greens that left one of us still hungry. The other was more than satisfied with a delicious, hearty corn chowder and a vegetarian pita pizza ($3.75), whose leftovers helped fill up the salad-eater. Each meal was served on a different platter, and ice water came in oversize glasses. Oyster crackers for munching at the bar were an added touch.

The nightly specials are supposed to be the best part of the dinner menu, upon which eggs benedict, of all things, once headed the list of entrées. More recent possibilities ($8.50 to $14) range from fried brown rice with beans and veggies or fettuccine tossed with pesto and vegetables to pan-fried catfish with bistro slaw, breaded chicken on creamed white beans with tomato and sweet pepper salsa, and two versions of steak. Desserts could be crème caramel, mocha swirl cheesecake and fruit with zabaglione.

Open Tuesday-Saturday, 11:30 to 8:30 or 9:30.

The Herr Tavern Publick House, 900 Chambersburg Road, Gettysburg. (717) 334-4332.

Rebuilt in 1987, this restaurant founded in 1828 is out in the country, atop Herr's Ridge where it saw action in the Civil War. The new establishment is squeaky clean, in contrast with the creaky old of its compatriots, the Dobbin House and the Farnsworth House. The biggest room is the contemporary-style tavern, light and airy with big windows and a long faux-marble bar.

The original tavern is known for a "salty past," according to old newspaper accounts. It's now the main dining room, pretty with green fanned napkins on white-over-salmon tablecloths, stenciled walls and a working fireplace. Most striking are the unusual wood and leather chairs on pedestals, which the hostess likened to those in church choir lofts. Altogether, 180 diners can be seated on the main floor, the stone basement rooms or the rear Livery Barn and Grill.

The extensive menu covers all the bases. Dinner appetizers range from potato skins to escargots with prosciutto. Entrées are priced from $13 for pork dijon to $18 for filet mignon béarnaise. Other possibilities are broiled ham steak, veal parmesan, chicken kiev, trout imperial, seafood creole and blackened prime rib. Four pastas also are offered. Complimentary cheese and crackers precede the meal. The changing dessert tray might yield fuzzy navel peach pie, french silk pie and "berry sinful" pie.

Sandwiches and a few light entrées like scampi sauté and nutty chicken in a pineapple comprise the lunchtime fare, served in the tavern. There's a pleasant outdoor patio for drinks.

Lunch, Monday-Friday 11 to 4, Saturday 11:30 to 2; dinner nightly, 5 to 9.

Historic Cashtown Inn, 1325 Old Route 30, Cashtown. (717) 334-9722.

Built in 1797 as the first stagecoach station west of Gettysburg, this gained prominence as a location for the filming of the 1994 movie and the mini-series "Gettysburg." Innkeeper Charles Buckley is proud of his "rogue's gallery" of film stars pictured on the lobby wall.

He's also proud of his wife Carolyn's cooking. In 1987, they took over what had been "a redneck saloon" and turned it into a fine restaurant serving dinner three nights a week year-round. A mural of the inn graces one wall of the large rear dining room, an open space done up in blue and gray with white-clothed tables set amid ficus trees.

Carolyn's menu is short and rarely changes, such is the popularity of such specialties as slow-roasted prime rib and baked individual chicken pie. Other main dishes are priced from $11.95 for country ham steak to $16.96 for crab imperial, stuffed shrimp or filet mignon. Honey-glazed sausage rounds, baked french onion soup and stuffed mushroom caps are among starters. The homemade cheesecake and peanut-butter ice cream pie are favorite desserts.

The inn's second and third floors house four guest rooms and a suite, available for $80 to $135.

Dinner by reservation, Thursday-Saturday from 5.

The Historic Farnsworth House Inn, 401 Baltimore St., Gettysburg. (717) 334-8838.

This nice-looking theme restaurant, part of a complex of Shultz family enterprises, is devoted to the Civil War period. Oil paintings of opposing generals Meade and Lee hang over the fireplaces and the walls bear Civil War photos, letters and even a carpetbag in a frame. Pewter tankards and plates top the bare wood tables, dimly lit by lalique-style oil lamps. Taped Civil War music plays in the background, and sometimes it can be a bit much.

Chef Steve Shultz adapts the menu to the period as well. Goober peanut soup, game pie, "real Virginia ham – salty and dry," Yankee pot roast, pumpkin fritters and sweet potato pudding are specialties. Baked flounder and prime rib are available for the less adventurous. The fare, priced from $12.95 to $17.95, includes a relish tray, homemade spoon and Jennie Wade breads with local apple butter and choice of vegetables. Among homemade desserts are rum cream pie, black walnut ice cream and walnut-apple cake.

Dinner nightly, 5 to 9 or 9:30.

The Altland House, Route 30, Abbottstown. (717) 259-9535.

Contemporary dining in an historic atmosphere is offered by the Haugh family in this landmark facing Abbottstown's Center Square. In 1986, Michael Haugh refurbished the restaurant started by his parents in 1954. The main dining room is a serene and stunningly sleek, hotel-style space with a few booths, round tables set with white linens, upholstered chairs and pinpoint overhead lighting rather too bright for our tastes.

The food and atmosphere are highly rated, drawing many from Gettysburg fifteen or so miles to the west. Dinners including a choice of salad run from $11.95 for chicken Hawaiian or chicken and biscuits to $18.95 for veal oscar and filet mignon béarnaise. Oyster pie, stuffed flounder imperial, scampi and veal marsala are other possibilities A favorite starter is York County turtle soup served with sherry, and we liked the sound of the avocado egg rolls.

Downstairs is the **Underside Restaurant and Bar,** popular for sandwiches, burgers, light entrées and dinners in the $8.95 to $16.95 price range. Two can order a sirloin steak dinner with salad bar for $24.75.

Upstairs are seven guest rooms with kingsize beds, TVs and telephones. Two new rooms have fireplaces and jacuzzis. They rent for $74 to $89 a night.

Lunch, Tuesday-Sunday 11 to 5; dinner, 5 to 10, Underside to 11. Closed Monday.

Diversions

Gettysburg National Military Park. Gettysburg is virtually surrounded by 25 square miles of battlefield, where the Civil War's bloodiest battles were fought on the first three days of July 1863. President Lincoln delivered his Gettysburg Address later that year when he dedicated the Gettysburg National Cemetery. More than 1,400 monuments and markers, countless cannons and stone walls, three observation towers and 31 miles of marked avenues comprise the park. Start at the park visitor center to avoid being overwhelmed by it all. The best way to experience the site is to hire one of 90 licensed guides at the visitor center for a two-hour tour ($20) in your own car. Most retired history teachers and Civil War buffs, they are passionate about their subject as they point out the obvious and not so obvious. You also can tour the battlefield on a double-decker bus ($10.95), one with a guide and the other with earphones for listening to a taped narration, or you can rent tour tapes for $12. A map points out highlights along a 23-mile self-guided tour that takes two to three hours, varying with stops and traffic. Bicycling may well be the most rewarding way to go. The Eternal Light Peace Memorial, the North Carolina and Pennsylvania memorials, Little Round Top and the optional Culp's Hill side tour are personal favorites. The visitor center contains a theater with an electric map program that shows with colored lights various troop movements during the battle (the 30-minute show costs $2). Nearby is the Cyclorama Center, where an 1884 painting of Pickett's Charge is displayed with a sound and light program inside a circular, 26-foot-high auditorium (adults, $2). Park open daily, 6 a.m. to 10 p.m. Free.

Scenic Drives. The Gettysburg Travel Council details a **Scenic Valley Tour** covering 36 miles through the rolling orchard country of the west and north sides of Adams County. It also details an **Historic Conewago Tour** of 40 miles to the east and northeast of Gettysburg. Make your own tour to the southeast to include Taneytown, Littlestown, the horses at Hanover Shoe Farms, the lakes of Codorus State Park and the Stone Mill shop at Brodbecks.

Antiquing in New Oxford. East of Gettysburg is New Oxford, a Victorian town with a beautiful circle in the heart of downtown. It's a mecca for antiquers; 28 dealers within a few blocks of the circle are designated in a brochure.

Shopping. Gettysburg is full of stores specializing in Civil War memorabilia (the best is **Fields of Glory**) and tacky souvenirs. Some of the town's better shops are gathered under the **Old Gettysburg Village** umbrella at Baltimore Pike and Steinwehr Avenue. A downtown favorite is **Arrow Horse International Market,** purveying all sorts of unusual treats from Guatemalan baby overalls to piano rolls, samosas to toblerone chocolate. **Codori's Bavarian Gift Shop** is worth a look, as are **Fremantle** for dried flowers and pottery, and three establishments linked in a country craft shop tour south of town, **The Quilt Patch, Koony's Barn** and **Smokehouse Crafts.**

Our favorite shopping is a half-hour's drive away at **Stone Mill Clay and Woodworks** in Brodbecks, four levels with room after room of tasteful things. It's the gallery and shop of Inez and Jerry Fenster, she a potter and he a woodworker, who live upstairs in the old paper mill dating from the 1700s and whose studios and output flow through a most intriguing building. Her hand-thrown pottery and his inlaid tile tables and cupboards are showcased with the works of other artisans. Wooden spoons, Amish paintings, floral arrangements, quilts, linens, specialty foods, painted birdhouses, folk art, jewelry, decorative accessories – you name it, they've got it. The year's highlight is Stone Mill's annual Christmas show, when the shop is open Tuesday-Sunday. Otherwise, it's open Wednesday-Sunday, but closed in January.

Extra Special

Eisenhower National Historic Site, Gettysburg. (717) 334-1124.

There's something altogether endearing about this monument to the 1950s, the only home President Dwight D. Eisenhower and his wife Mamie ever owned. Fifty Norway spruce trees, birthday presents from each of the state Republican chairmen in 1955, line the long driveway into the 231-acre farm, which is reached by a five-minute ride on a shuttle bus leaving every fifteen minutes from the National Park Visitor Center. The rural site is very different from the Gettysburg that many tourists see; the bus driver pointed out two separate herds of deer as we arrived. The Eisenhowers bought a seven-room brick farmhouse in 1950 and added wings on either side for entertaining. The self-guided tour starts in the living room, where a guide notes that "the house was furnished in gifts" from friends and dignitaries. You learn that Ike considered this "the stuffiest room in the house," far preferring the long rear sun porch where the couple ate breakfast while watching the farm scene and had dinner in front of the TV. An easel bears a copy of the painting Ike was working on at his death. Among Mamie's collections are two gold plates from Tiffany & Co., juxtaposed with a plate she bought at Stuckey's and figurines of presidents and first ladies from cereal boxes. Ike's library contains favorite books plus U.S. Army Registers and volumes of Order of Battle Maps from operations in Italy. A glass door allows a peek into the linen closet, where most of the towels are pink, Mamie's favorite color, and monogrammed "MED" and "IKE." Past a funny little 1950s kitchen is Ike's paneled den, a favorite haunt. The self-guided tour ends outdoors with a look at Ike's brick barbecue, his putting green and a garage containing a Crosley runabout with a fringe on top, its front fender emblazoned with "Ike and Mamie" in stenciled script. Ike used the last to show guests like Winston Churchill and Charles DeGaulle around his farm. Visitors get to share part of the 1950s and the great middle American experience. Unfortunately, all the shades inside the house are drawn so you can't see the views the Eisenhowers could. Hour-long tours, daily 8:30 to 4:15; closed Monday and Tuesday, November-April. Adults, $3.60.

Curving driveway leads to The Cameron Estate Inn, one of county's finer properties.

Western Lancaster County, Pa.
Beyond the Tourists

Much of the Lancaster County of Pennsylvania Dutch fame is a land of strange names and quaint places – a sea of smorgasbords, outlets, motels and commercial enterprises taking advantage of the Amish-Mennonite connection and, alas, undercutting the very notion of "The Plain People."

That applies to eastern Lancaster County, where tourists arrive by the busload, three million a year strong. Western Lancaster County is, for the most part, a place apart.

Here, the picturesque rolling farmlands of the east flatten as they approach the broad Susquehanna River. The Amish and Mennonites are far less conspicuous. So are the trappings of tourism. The western section wears an equally historic face, but one unfettered by the commercialism of its eastern counterpart.

Mount Joy, Marietta and Columbia. These are the sleepy rural villages and river towns that dwell in the western county, surrounded by the ubiquitous farmlands that manage to survive in the face of creeping Lancaster suburbia.

Mount Joy, the biggest town, marks something of a dividing line between the frenzied quaintness of Pennsylvania Dutch country and the serenity beyond. Marietta is a long and narrow strip of a river town, as authentic as they come; nearly half the town is on the National Register. Columbia was a gateway to the west when it was Wright's Ferry, crossing point to the Susquehanna frontier. It was an important enough river site in the 1790s that it was one of the potential locations for the new nation's capital.

Congress ultimately chose a capital along the Potomac River, not the Susquehanna. The development of the area, which blossomed during the heady river and railroad days of the 19th century, was stunted in the 20th. Buildings now considered historic were bypassed by the building boom. They stand as mute testimony to an earlier era.

Betty Groff, the guru of Pennsylvania Dutch cookery, and her Groff's Farm restaurant put Mount Joy on the national culinary map. The sophisticates who came to this

273

Overseeing broad lawn is Mount Gretna Inn, the biggest house in town.

side of the county were charmed by its lack of clutter and tourism. The Groffs opened a country inn nearby, more inns and B&Bs followed and lately, western Lancaster County is becoming a destination in search of an identity.

No one – not tourism directors, innkeepers nor restaurateurs – has come up with a name for the area other than western Lancaster County. But they all see it as different from the rest of Lancaster County, a place apart.

Inn Spots

The Cameron Estate Inn, 1895 Donegal Springs Road, Mount Joy 17552. (717) 653-1773.

Betty Groff, a tenth-generation Mennonite (an Herr of Herr's Potato Chip fame), started visitors beating a path to her farmhouse door for weekend dinners more than 30 years ago. Such was the success of Groff's Farm Restaurant – still going strong (see Dining Spots) and now adding a golf course – that in 1981 she and husband Abe bought the Cameron estate to open as an inn in the grand manner.

A grand manor it is, indeed. Out in the country on fifteen acres beside historic Donegal Church is a majestic 1805 Federal mansion built by the great-grandfather of President McKinley and owned in the 1870s by Simon Cameron, Abraham Lincoln's first Secretary of War. Converting it into an eighteen-room country inn and restaurant was Abe's task. Now, although he is on the premises regularly, he has turned day-to-day duties over to a trio of innkeepers.

The inn is grandiose, from the sweeping entry foyer and central staircase to the third floor where an enormous skylight is filled with hanging plants. Rooms range from spacious baronial chambers on the first and second floors to third-floor hideaways tucked beneath dormers that the Groffs describe as intimately cozy and some call cramped. All but two have private baths, most have king or queensize beds and seven have working fireplaces. Creature comforts there are, but most rooms are decorated in staid brown colors and retain some of the starkness of earlier times.

Folks gather in the library-sitting room beneath the watchful eyes of Washington and Lincoln portraits. Although the Groffs' hectic schedules too frequently prevent them from being visible at the inn, they try to compensate with a "Dear Guests" letter in each room. It spells out services, including tennis at Groff's Farm and swimming at their home pool, and concludes "please don't hesitate to ask."

A continental breakfast of juices and sweet rolls is served in the sun porch section of the restaurant (see Dining Spots). The grounds are a rural paradise of lawns, woods and artesian wells, one of them flowing into a century-old pool edged in limestone blocks. A trout stream meanders beneath an arched stone bridge. At the front of the property is Donegal Presbyterian Church, founded in 1721 and famous for its Witness Tree, a 350-year-old oak beside which the congregation gathered in 1777 to pledge support for the new nation. The setting leads some to call this the perfect weekend retreat.

Doubles, $65 to $115.

Mount Gretna Inn, 16 West Kaufman Ave., Mount Gretna 17064. (717) 964-3234 or (800) 277-6602.

Opened in 1988, this is the only B&B in the Cinderella town of Mount Gretna, a hilltop aerie of pine groves, religious campgrounds, arts and music, and Lake Conewago. And it's some B&B.

It was built in 1921 in the American Arts and Crafts style by local entrepreneur Abraham Lincoln Kaufmann, who developed the 50-acre subdivision known as The Heights. His was (and remains) the biggest house in Mount Gretna. Bill Cook, a former Hershey Foods executive who had a year-round home nearby in Pennsylvania's Chautauqua, turned it into an elegant yet convivial B&B that belies its 1960s tenure as a dormitory for 90 girls from a summer camp.

The inn was purchased in December 1994 by Robin and Keith Volker from nearby Elizabethtown, who inherited a turnkey operation and planned to "maintain all the traditions Bill started." They had spent many a summer vacation in Mount Gretna, Keith said, and "for fifteen years my wife had been trying to talk me into becoming an innkeeper, when this perfect place became available." Keith was continuing work as a field engineer for a computer company while Robin became fulltime innkeeper.

The main floor is dramatic in lodge style with a fireplaced living room big enough for the occasional concert on the grand piano, two dining rooms set with china and crystal, and a great wide, deep front porch overlooking a manicured lawn. Upstairs on the second and third floors are eight bedrooms of varying size. All have new private baths and queensize beds. Stickley Arts and Crafts furniture and original paintings by local artists are featured. Most in demand is the huge Louisiana Room with a Victorian bed from the Louisiana plantation owned by the former owner's family and a serene

wicker sitting area amid oriental rugs, side table, dresser and armoire. Also popular are the Veranda Room with burl maple furniture and private porch and the rear Bay Window Room with antique poster bed made of a solid piece of black walnut and a plush chaise with matching ottoman.

Candlelight breakfasts are gala here. The day of our visit had begun with cantaloupe and blueberries, a choice of orange juice or mimosas, a mini-quiche with turkey link sausage, and crois-sants with black raspberry jam. Cheese danish was offered to finish. Other main dishes could be sausage casserole, Scottish griddle scones and stuffed french toast. After-noon tea is served with crudités or snacks on the porch; wine is substituted on week-ends.

Although the inn had changed hands, Bill left most of the furnishings and assured that the festive atmosphere would remain. "We don't plan to miss a beat," Keith agreed.

Doubles, $95 to $125.

Maison Rouge, 2236 Marietta Ave., Box 6243, Lancaster 17607. (717) 399-3033 or (800) 309-3033.

Little wonder that the imposing – some say formidable – Second Empire Victorian structure near the main intersection in the hamlet of Rohrerstown has always been called the Red House. It's painted a shiny, wine red color with white trim and almost gleams in the sunlight. Rodney Petrocci and William Stomski chucked their budding careers and a Victorian townhouse in Philadelphia for a different lifestyle in 1993. They bought the residence long occupied by a physician from an interior design firm that had used it as a showroom. They added their furnishings and antiques to rooms that had been papered by Eisenhart as a backdrop for an advertising brochure. The decorative masterpiece is now a showplace B&B.

The foyer opens into a small but lavish parlor in which a crystal chandelier reflects in a gilded mirror above the fireplace. On the other side are a study fashioned from the former doctor's office and a cozy TV room, once the doctor's waiting room. Beyond is a formal dining room, where breakfast is served on antique china, silver and crystal beneath another glistening crystal chandelier. At our visit, the repast included fresh peaches and blueberries, banana muffins, and french toast stuffed with cream cheese and black walnuts and topped with orange sauce. Other main dishes include quiches, oatmeal pancakes with sausage and apples, and ricotta cheese wrapped in phyllo and baked with ham.

Upstairs are four spacious bedrooms, two with private baths and all with queensize beds. The master bedroom is dark and masculine in Ralph Lauren wallpaper and fab-rics, all deep navy, hunter green and burgundy. It comes with a cannonball four-poster bed, two wing chairs in the bay window and an oriental carpet. It shares a bath with the lady's bedroom, light and feminine in off-white tones and possessor of a remarkable bed canopy "headboard" formed by the wallpaper pattern. Here a display case shows Rod's collections of antique perfume bottles and wedding miniatures. Ralph Lauren floral chintz covers the bed and windows in the Garden Room, which is outfitted with a white wicker loveseat and rocker. Our favorite is the Empire Room in back, its choco-late brown walls contrasting with the cool blue sofa and comforter on the Chippendale canopy bed. The prized fine antiques everywhere reflect Rod's passion for acquiring and living with fine pieces. Comments in the room diaries indicate that guests enjoy sharing them, too.

Doubles, $80 to $120. No smoking.

The Columbian, 360 Chestnut St., Columbia 17512. (717) 684-5869 or (800) 422-5869.

A magnificent tiered staircase passes ornate stained-glass windows at the entry to this turn-of-the-century brick mansion with beige trim and a wraparound veranda. An outstanding example of Colonial Revival architecture, it was painstakingly restored in 1988 and converted into a fine B&B.

New owners Chris and Becky Wills offer five air-conditioned bedrooms, each with

Imposing Second Empire Victorian structure lives up to its name, Maison Rouge.

private bath, and a two-room suite with its own balcony. All have queensize beds with extra-firm mattresses, comfortable sitting areas, TVs, and fresh flowers and fruit. They are decorated in Victorian or country style, accented by paintings, crafts, needlework and quilts. Our room, though smaller than some of the others, came with a dainty window seat outfitted with lots of pillows. A rear suite offers a painted brass bed and sofa, plus an adjoining sitting room with a twin bed.

Centerpiece of the foyer is an antique victrola. At our visit, Chris "couldn't wait" for Christmas when it was to get quite a workout from his collection of old records. Principal listener other than guests was infant daughter Katy, whom her parents describe as "our entertainment committee."

Becky serves a hearty country breakfast. A typical repast could start with half a grapefruit, banana-nut or applesauce-raisin bread and a hot fruit dish, perhaps blueberry kuchen, for which Becky has printed copies of the recipe. The main dish could be baked egg casserole, strata, waffles or french toast. We were offered a choice of peach pancakes with peach sauce or a dish of hard-boiled eggs chopped in a cheese sauce on an English muffin with ham. Both were excellent.

Doubles, $55 to $70. No smoking.

Cedar Hill Farm B&B, 305 Longenecker Road, Mount Joy 17552. (717) 653-4655.

Stay in this handsome 1817 fieldstone-stucco farmhouse and you're really on a working farm, blessedly out in the country on a wooded hillside beside Little Chiques Creek. Gladys and Russel Swarr (he was born here and his family has owned the property since the 1870s) raise 56,000 chickens as well as corn and soybeans on 51 acres.

The five air-conditioned bedrooms with private baths are more elegant than city-slickers might expect at a farm. Each is nicely decorated with family heirlooms. One with a queensize, carved-oak bed (the bedroom suite was made by Russel's grandfather) overlooks the creek. Access to the front balcony belongs to the queensize honeymoon room, country pretty with a wicker sitting area. Its large bathroom contains a sit-down shower. A third room with a double bed is small and furnished in Victorian style. The largest room at the rear has two double beds, a full bath with a separate vanity under a skylight and a desk chair from the school Russel attended. The newest room has two brass twin beds that can be joined as a kingsize. A whirlpool tub was in the planning stage here.

Common facilities include a double parlor, a TV room with VCR and stereo, and a front porch furnished in wicker. Gladys serves breakfast in the original kitchen in front of a walk-in fireplace that's atmospheric as can be. She calls it continental-plus "because I don't serve eggs" – everything but, perhaps a fresh fruit and cheese platter, fruit cobbler, cereals, muffins and coffee cake.

Doubles, $65 to $75.

The River Inn, 258 West Front St., Marietta 17547. (717) 426-2290.

They don't get much more historic than this 200-year-old house, lovingly tended by Joyce and Bob Heiserman and once featured in a Colonial Homes magazine cover story on Marietta.

The Heisermans live in half of the fourteen-room duplex house and turn over to guests the other half, including a parlor-library, tavern room and dining room. The entryway features magnificent crown molding and a painted checkered floor. All three guest rooms have queensize beds and private baths. They are decorated simply to the Colonial and Federal periods with oriental rugs, plaster walls and painted woodwork. The nicest, across the back of the house, has a fireplace, a canopy bed and a sofa. The largest is in front, facing the railroad track and the Susquehanna River. It contains both a queen and a twin bed. At our visit, the Heisermans were thinking of adding two more bedrooms.

Guests spread out in the cozy fireplaced parlor-library, well stocked with books and a TV set, and a tavern room with a reproduction bar modeled after one in Williamsburg. Here they can store food in the refrigerator, mix drinks and imagine themselves back in the 18th century. The adjacent Colonial dining room is notable for a large pierced-tin chandelier, handmade wall sconces, braided rugs and a fireplace. Here or on the long rear screened porch outfitted in wicker, the Heisermans serve a full breakfast, perhaps herbed omelets, pancakes or french toast with bacon or sausage. The couple also have bicycles for guests to use, and Bob will take people fishing in his boat with advance notice.

The porch is a grand spot for taking in the 200-foot-deep back yard with its formal holly garden, Colonial herbs and flowers that turn up in colorful arrangements throughout the house.

Doubles, $60 to $70.

Country Gardens Farm Bed & Breakfast, 686 Rock Point Road, Mount Joy 17552. (717) 426-3316.

The name here says it well, but let us embellish. The gardens are prolific, their bounty used to decorate the house and play a big role at breakfast. The 170-acre farm, primarily cattle and crops, includes a pen with four sheep, a goat and chickens. The bedrooms are homey and comfortable, and the breakfasts are something else.

Andrew and Dotty Hess, who have spent most of their lives working on the farm, raised seven youngsters in their house before turning it into a B&B in 1992. "We'd been doing B&B for 38 years," quips Dotty, "and figured it was time we were paid." They offer four bedrooms, two with private baths – one of them attached to the cov-

Original kitchen at Cedar Hll Farm B&B includes a walk-in fireplace.

eted Balcony Room, which comes with a queensize bed and an outside balcony for viewing the surrounding farmlands.

Quilted wall hangings are draped over the chairs and sofas in the extra-large living room. Made by an Amish woman, they're for sale, as are Dotty's floral wreaths and dried flower arrangements. The living room also holds quite a conversation piece – a photograph of the Hess family reunion, showing three generations and 213 people (of a possible 239) descended from Andrew's parents (he was one of nine children, each of whom had up to nine children, who in turn have had up to seven children). Most live in Lancaster County, and it turns out that Dotty is a cousin of noted restaurateur Betty Groff (see Dining Spots); both grew up close to each other in eastern Lancaster County, were married about the same time and "moved up here about the same distance apart as before."

Most guests seem to congregate in the family room off the dining area and country kitchen at the side of the house. Here is where the Hesses serve a bountiful country breakfast. The meal includes bowls of fresh fruit from the garden, baked oatmeal and a succession of main dishes served family style: perhaps scrambled eggs with cheese or cheese strata and ricotta cheese pancakes or french toast, accompanied by vegetables of the season, from asparagus and snap peas to corn and tomatoes. "Some folks go out of here thinking they've just had dinner," Dotty concedes. After breakfast, the Hesses take any children to the pen out back to gather eggs and feed the sheep.

Doubles, $55 to $70. No smoking.

Morning Meadows Farm, 103 Fuhrman Road, Marietta 17547. (717) 436-1425.

The driveway winds through cornfields as high as an elephant's eye. From the main road, owner Barbara Frey says, "you go three-quarters of a mile before you see a house." And it's quite a house, this stately brick edifice, with four soaring pillars and two stories worth of verandas.

Cornfields and barns surround stately brick house at Morning Meadows farm.

Barbara and husband Harold (he works this 240-acre farm of mostly cornfields along with nearly 1,000 acres nearby) opened their home to help put their children through college. They offer four air-conditioned bedrooms with private baths, each with queensize bed, color TV, wing chairs and working fireplaces, and some with extra beds for families. The entire house is stylish in French country decor, except for the dining room, which is Victorian, and the country kitchen, where a collection of antique Santas adorns the fireplace. Barbara does all the "decorations," from a massive cornucopia of plants and vegetables on the kitchen table to the Raggedy Ann theme executed with abandon in Room 2.

The accommodations are more luxurious than most farm B&Bs, so it comes as a surprise to learn that families with children comprise the bulk of the clientele in summer (couples predominate the rest of the year). Youngsters gather eggs, feed the lambs, chickens and ducks, and enjoy the petting barnyard, playhouse and sandbox. The dining room table off the formal living room was set for thirteen people at our visit – "we can get quite a crowd in here," Barbara acknowledges. Breakfast that day was fresh blueberries, granola and yogurt, bacon and french toast with blueberry sauce.

Doubles, $55 to $65.

West Ridge Guest House, 1285 West Ridge Road, Elizabethtown 17022. (717) 367-7783.

Her children having left the nest, Alice Heisey decided to share the family home in an outlying residential section of West Donegal with overnight guests. That proved successful, so in 1990 she and husband David turned the onetime chicken barn that had been headquarters for his contracting business into a guest house with five spacious bedrooms, a large living room with dining area and a carpeted room with a jacuzzi and exercise equipment.

This is not your typical B&B, even though it does everything a B&B should and more. The Heiseys cater more than others to corporate business and have outfitted their rooms accordingly. Each contains a modern bath, air-conditioning, TV and telephone. Some have private decks overlooking sections of the 23-acre farm, broad lawns, a gazebo, two fish ponds and a swimming pool.

The modern rooms in the guest house are individually decorated in different styles. The Williamsburg Suite is the biggest, possessing a four-poster bed, cherry furniture, a blue and red color scheme, a sitting area with two stuffed chairs and a sofabed, and a new whirlpool tub. The Wicker Room is in pale pinks, greens and whites – even the bed is wicker. Country curtains and spreads identify the Country Room, which has two double beds. Ornately carved chairs, fringed lamps and a crocheted bed cover mark the Victorian Room, a fantasy in teal and red. We liked our quarters in the Anniversary Suite, where the whitest, laciest kingsize bed imaginable is reflected in the mirrored headboard. Black floral wallpaper strips break up the white of the walls, mauve wing chairs and carpeting provide color, and a fireplace adds romance. Candles in many guises are the theme here.

Four more rooms are available upstairs in the Heisey home next door. They range from a small room with an oval bed built into the wall to a two-bedroom suite with a whirlpool tub in one bedroom. The main floor of the Loft Suite is all bath with forest green tiles, mirrors, whirlpool tub and separate shower. The upstairs loft is a knockout in mauves and greens with a large sitting area and sofabed and a queensize bed on the other side of the room.

Bowls of assorted candies are placed in the rooms, which have such unexpected flouncy touches as little wool puffs on the coat hangers and fake flowers around the candle bases. A refrigerator in the hallway is stocked with sodas and snacks for sale. Alice serves a full breakfast in the dining alcove off the large living room. Guests write their choices on a checklist the night before. Eggs any style, french toast and cereal were the offerings at our visit.

Doubles, $60 to $70; suites, $80 to $90.

The Olde Square Inn, 127 East Main St., Mount Joy 17552. (717) 653-4525 or (800) 742-3533.

From the front porch, guests enter directly into the living room of this neoclassic residence built in 1917 by a local builder who apparently did not want a foyer. Later a boarding house, it was opened in 1991 as a B&B by Fran and David Hand, York

Main house and converted chicken barn face swimming pool at West Ridge Guest House.

County residents who drove by, saw the house for sale and knew it was for them. After two years of work, they were ready with four guest rooms, all with private baths, TVs and VCRs.

The largest is the Royal Room, which "we bill as fit for a king and his queen," says Fran, and is decorated with castles and such. The deep red wallpaper bears large blue flowers, and the twin beds can be joined as a king. The Charleston Room, which Fran named for her favorite city, holds a queen bed and its bathroom has a double shower with two seats. The Ivy Canopy Room comes with ivy and roses on the wallpaper and handpainted on the bed, the armoire and chest of drawers. The Garden Room has a double bed and a wing chair.

On the main floor are two living rooms, one with a fireplace. Beyond is a dining room elegant in beige and teal. Fran, who has run a food stand in the historic Columbia Market, serves guests a full breakfast of fresh fruit, juice, homemade muffins and breads, and a main dish like baked sausage casserole, pancakes and sausage, or a baked egg casserole.

Doubles, $65 to $85.

The Country Stay, 2285 Bull Moose Road, Route 1, Box 312, Mount Joy 17552. (717) 367-5167.

Candles glow year-round in the windows of this beautiful 1880 brick Victorian farmhouse, and you may hear church bells chiming in the distance upon arrival. You also will no doubt be greeted by one of the barnyard cats, fifteen at last count, and perhaps by a pervasive odor of manure–a seasonal accompaniment in much of Lancaster County farm country.

Owners Darlene and Lester Landis, who have three children, raise beef and grain on their 98-acre farm. A Victorian suite in a separate section of the house has a private bath, while two other bedrooms here share a bath. A hat is perched on one post of a carved Victorian headboard on the old rope bed in a room with thick brown carpeting, a bay window with frilly curtains and a window seat. Another bedroom contains braided rugs and a queen canopy bed covered with an Amish quilt. Homey touches and country crafts abound in the bedrooms and in the small guest parlor adjacent to the breakfast room. "We try to make this feel like home for guests," says Darlene.

In the morning, she dons a period costume to serve a continental-plus breakfast of fresh fruit and homemade pastries, perhaps rhubarb bread, shoofly cake, blueberry buckle and coffee cake. She makes the crafts she sells in her Country Craft Cupboard on the premises.

Doubles, $55. Closed December-March. No smoking.

Railroad House, West Front and South Perry Streets, Marietta 17547. (717) 426-4141.

A four-story Federal structure with a double-decker front veranda, this was built in the 1820s to serve river and canal traffic and was in its heyday when the trains stopped next door. It fell on hard times a century later and was derelict when Donna and Richard Chambers acquired it in 1989. They have restored it into a bustling restaurant and tavern (see Dining Spots) and also fixed up the bedrooms.

They offer twelve rooms, eight with private baths. Original wood floors, twig rockers, ornate bedsteads, antiques and Victoriana are the norm. Two rooms on the second-floor front share a small sitting room and one has access to the balcony. The Wicker Room is a favorite. So is the Old Proprietor's Room, which has a side porch; a patchwork quilt tops the brass bed, the bathroom is in a closet and the shower is in the room. Most prized is the Summer Kitchen Room off the patio, which has a queensize bed

White candles stand tall on tables in dining room of Accomac Inn.

angled in the corner, a sitting area with two rockers, Caswell-Massey toiletries in the bathroom, a kitchenette and, up a spiral staircase, a loft with twin beds.

There's no common room as such, though the courtyard might serve the purpose in season. Rick Chambers prepares a full country breakfast, served in one of the dining rooms or outside in the courtyard. He also owns the railroad station across the street, which he hopes to make into a transportation museum and banquet hall.

Doubles, $59 to $79; Summer Kitchen, $89.

Dining Spots

Accomac Inn, South River Drive, Wrightsville. (717) 252-1521.

Dating to 1775, this fieldstone inn overlooking the Susquehanna across from Marietta at what used to be the landing for Anderson's Ferry is known far beyond the region for fine dining. For more than twenty years, owner H. Douglas Campbell Jr. and a staff of pros have maintained both quality and service.

The historic dining room could not be more elegant. It's all white with dark brown trim and a white fireplace at one end. White tapered candles stand tall on each well-spaced table, set with fanned napkins, pewter service plates and fresh flowers in pewter vases. Fine paintings adorn the walls, and window tables catch a glimpse of the river across a screened porch (everyone gets a water view when the porch is put into service in summer).

It's an altogether lovely, authentic 18th-century setting for executive chef Kevin Anderson's classic French fare at prices considered high for the area. One of us started with an excellent warm salmon and shrimp terrine with a pernod-spinach-cream sauce. The other chose a salad of belgian endive, toasted pinenuts, grapefruit sections and watercress with a raspberry dressing. A small loaf of French bread, surrounded by an army of sweet-butter curls, accompanied.

Entrées are priced from $17.50 for tuna steak with tomato coulis to $28.95 for rack of New Zealand lamb. Good choices were grilled duck au poivre, served with wild rice and julienned peppers, carrots and leeks, and an outstanding dish of sautéed venison with duck liver mousse in a port cream sauce. Portions were small but exquisite. Bananas foster made a worthy ending.

Prices on the extensive wine list were staggering, starting in the high teens and rising rapidly. The teak wood bar in the small side lounge is the place for an after-dinner drink. We might have tarried had we not faced the roundabout way back to the highway – small signs mark the way in, but you're on your own going home.

The Sunday champagne brunch includes fresh baked goods, soup, fruit salad and sorbet, a choice of twelve entrées and dessert for a prix-fixe $17.95.

Lunch, Monday-Saturday 11:30 to 2:30; dinner nightly, 5:30 to 9:30; Sunday, brunch 11 to 2:30, dinner 4 to 8:30.

Groff's Farm Restaurant, 650 Pinkerton Road, Mount Joy. (717) 653-2048.

Betty Groff started serving weekend dinners in her home as a hobby more than 30 years ago for visitors who wanted to meet a farm family and taste the local cuisine. Betty, who grew up as a tenth-generation Mennonite on the other side of Lancaster County, had married Abe Groff and felt isolated without family and friends in Mount Joy, so this was her way of keeping in touch with people.

The rest, as they say, is history. They turned a 1756 fieldstone farmhouse into a thriving restaurant. They opened the high-style Cameron Estate Inn in 1981. A few years ago, they expanded their original restaurant with a glamorous sun porch and acquired a liquor license. Lately, they were converting their farmland into a golf course. Betty, the author of four cookbooks, is nationally known as the guru of Pennsylvania Dutch cookery.

Although housed on a farm, Groff's no longer is really a farm restaurant. Rather it is a fashionable, social place where the patrons ask after Betty and trade gossip with the waitresses. The food has taken on a sophisticated air, thanks to the lighter touch that Betty has given to the hearty dishes associated with the area as well as her son Charlie's additions of seafood and an à la carte menu to the traditional family-style menu. Charlie, a Culinary Institute of America grad, is the executive chef and manages the restaurant with his wife Cindy.

Certain things never change, says Betty. All the coffee cups are turned up at each place setting, and the waitress asked "would you like coffee now?" as we were seated for lunch in the sun porch, pretty in peach and white. A platter of four relishes – corn, cole slaw, pickled celery and chow-chow – and apple butter for the bread arrived soon after. One of us had to try the house specialty, chicken stoltzfus ($6.50), a luscious and filling dish of tender chicken smothered in cream sauce and served over flaky diamonds of buttered pastry – perfect for lunch. This came with thick stewed tomatoes and Southern-style green beans cooked in ham broth, served family style. Our other choice was a chicken and Canadian bacon melt ($4.50), garnished with chips and pickles. For dessert, we shared an excellent Amish vanilla pie embellished with butterscotch ice cream ($2). The $13 tab wasn't bad for lunch in a country-club setting.

The menu is considerably expanded at night. Most first-timers order off the family-style menu; each person gets to choose an appetizer and dessert, but the whole table shares the main course – served family style, all you can eat. Main courses are chicken stolzfus, hickory-smoked ham, prime rib and seafood, available singly or in various combinations. Prices for each person range from $15 for the chicken to $24.50 for all four choices and include everything from soup to dessert. You may not want the latter, especially if you have sampled the moist chocolate cake and Betty's cracker pudding served as you are seated – "so you can enjoy these treats while you still have room for them," the menu advises.

Diners in new sun room overlook golf course outside Groff's Farm Restaurant.

If the entire table so decides, diners can order à la carte – much the same fare, plus New York strip steak, baked stuffed flounder and broiled lobster tail, $13.75 to $16.25.

After lunch, we perused copies of Betty's best-selling cookbooks, which are displayed in stacks here and there, and acquired some Groff's Farm relishes to take home.

Lunch, Tuesday-Saturday 11:30 to 1:30; dinner by reservation, Tuesday-Saturday 5 to 7:30, Saturday 5 to 8.

Alois's, 102 North Market St., Mount Joy. (717) 653-2057.

The creative menu for six-course meals changes weekly in the old Central Hotel portion of Bube's Brewery. This is the nation's only microbrewery surviving intact from the 1800s and is now home to three separate restaurants under the ownership of young entrepreneur Sam Allen.

Named for Alois Bube, a German immigrant who built the brewery during Lancaster's heyday as the Munich of the New World, this section was the brewmaster's house. You think the hotel's brick exterior with its aqua and purple wood trim and shutters is colorful? Check out the flamboyant interior, four intimate dining rooms themed to their names (Canopy, Peacock, Dragonfly and Trophy), an upstairs banquet room with incredible handpainted walls and a Victorian bar to end all bars. Furnished like a Victorian parlor, it has an old gaming table with shelves underneath for drinks in one corner and, over the massive bar, a revolving silver ball like those we remember from '40s and '50s dance floors, casting beams of light around the room.

Chef Ophelia Horn mixes cuisines and styles – Sam calls it all "interpretive international" for the leisurely dining experience that begins in the bar. Oil lamps flickered and new age music played here as we had drinks and the hors d'oeuvre course, a small portion of roast beef pâté with onion pastries. We asked not to be seated in the Trophy Room, where patrons dine beneath the mounted heads of animals. Instead we were assigned to the Canopy Room, named for the ceiling shaped like a canopy. As in all the others, its walls were lavishly decorated with a mix of intricate handpainted and handstenciled art.

Our white-clothed table bore a candle, napkins and nothing else. Utensils came with each course, and salt only upon request. The glass of ice water contained a slice of lime.

The only choices involved soups, entrées and dessert, the price of the full meal being determined by the entrée (from $19.95 for chicken franconian to $26.95 for steak diane). Service was inordinately slow for a quiet night and a meal that was supposed to be paced. Gradually we got our soup course (one was cock-a-leekie and the other white gazpacho), a garden salad with creamy pepper dressing and strawberry sorbet. Our main courses arrived on salad-size plates, the veal medallions with port and ginger accompanied by potatoes and the filet mignon by rice, carrots and zucchini. The blueberry cassis pie was chilled, intense and refreshing. Also good was the praline-pumpkin-rum pie. Chocolate twigs came with the bill.

Although the meal is competently prepared and represents exceptional value, be forewarned: the bar bill for a couple of house drinks and a bottle of wine likely will approach the tab for the food.

Also look forward to the opening of a six-room B&B on the third floor in a few years. Sam had no particular target date, saying "I won't open until the rooms are as nice as the rest of the place."

Dinner by reservation, Tuesday-Sunday 5:30 to 9 or 10.

The Catacombs, 102 North Market St., Mount Joy. (717) 653-2056.

If Alois's is the height of Victoriana, the Catacombs is positively medieval. A serf in medieval garb greets diners and leads them on a tour of the brewery as they descend 43 feet into the stone-lined vaults that were the aging cellars of Bube's Brewery. Here are round-ceilinged rooms totally lit by candles; in fact, the stone wall at the end of one room is covered with candle drippings, the better to hold steady more candles. Owner Sam Allen and his father made the heavy pine tables, dressed in white linens and set with pewter tankards and plates. This is the setting for medieval feasts staged most Sundays at 5 year-round. The $30 tab includes wine and ale, live music and entertainment, tax and tip; everyone gasps as burly chefs carry in a whole roasted pig.

On other nights, a fairly versatile menu is offered. Entrées, most of which are available in full or light portions, are priced from $15.95 for flounder stuffed with crabmeat to $21.95 for tournedos of beef with cracked peppercorns. Seafood mornay in a pastry shell, shrimp sautéed with garlic and pinenuts, roast duckling and veal dijon are other choices. Chicken satay, stuffed mushrooms and sausage en croûte are among the appetizers. Dessert could be chocolate-chip cheesecake or kahlua pie.

Upstairs in the brewery's original bottling plant is **The Bottling Works,** an atmospheric restaurant and tavern serving lunch and light fare. Interesting salads and sandwiches, gourmet burgers and bargain-priced entrées are featured. An adjacent outdoor **Biergarten** adds 80 seats to the 300 inside the brewery's three restaurants.

Dinner nightly, 5:30 to 9 or 10. Lunch in Bottling Works, Monday-Friday 11 to 2, dinner nightly from 5:30.

The Country Chef, 1444 Cloverleaf Road, Mount Joy. (717) 653-2783.

Ex-veterinarian Ed Hitz says he gave up his practice and became a country chef for a simple reason: "I like to eat." So do the cognoscenti who come to his converted barn for a six-course, no-choice dinner–planned according to his whims, not those of guests. He started serving dinners at his home as a hobby, which got out of hand. So he moved to larger quarters in the two-story barn in which he formerly treated steers and sheep. Up to 60 people can be served nightly at a single seating.

The event begins at 7 with complimentary wine, aperitifs and hors d'oeuvre in a

Beamed lounge is setting for pre-dinner aperitifs at The Country Chef.

huge, stone-walled basement with many sofas, sectionals and seating areas around a central fireplace. At 8, guests move upstairs for the main event in a barn of a room in which each table is screened off from the others for privacy. Couples who do not want an intimate tête-à-tête would be advised to form a group.

Over the next two and one-half hours, customers are served in dinner-party style. Ed, who does the cooking, uses local produce, dairy products and meats almost exclusively for his always-changing French fare. The meal the night we were there started with vegetable-beef soup and baked zucchini stuffed with ground veal and topped with cheese. A salad of fresh greens was tossed with a sweet and sour tomato dressing – the recipe for which is his most requested. The main course was swordfish provençal, served with broccoli and homemade French bread. Dessert was an almond meringue shell filled with homemade peach sorbet, black raspberry sauce and liqueur-flavored whipped cream. Partager wine was poured during the meal. Everyone adjourned for coffee downstairs after dinner.

The event costs $35. Guests are urged to inquire as to the menu when they reserve (the main course is set several months ahead), and reservations are to be made at least 24 hours in advance. Occasionally the entire restaurant is booked for a private party.

Dinner by reservation, Tuesday-Saturday at 8.

The Cameron Estate Inn & Restaurant, Donegal Springs Road, Mount Joy. (717) 653-1773.

The estate-like dining room here is attractive, its widely spaced tables covered with blue-over-white linens, candles in hurricane chimneys, bud vases with fresh flowers and pewter service plates. The adjacent sun porch is more intimate and less formal in peach and white.

The fare is American-continental, far removed from its Plain People heritage but well regarded under chef Dave Ritchey, a Culinary Institute of America grad and protégé of Betty Groff. Betty describes it "classic American country cuisine," using the same ingredients found in Pennsylvania Dutch cooking, but combined in a more sophisticated way. Simon Cameron, who owned the place in the 1870s, was "a world traveler who had caviar and champagne for breakfast," says Betty. "This was his summer house and the food served here, like rainbow trout Simon Cameron and chicken and shrimp Versailles, is based on his lifestyle."

Eight entrées are priced from $12.95 for lemon-pepper chicken to $21.95 for broiled veal chop with a shiitake and portobello mushroom sauce or filet mignon stuffed with smoked oysters and topped with hollandaise sauce. (Dave has borrowed a page from the butchers in Betty's family background, and smokes all his own meats and seafood on the premises.) Crab-stuffed mushrooms, smoked salmon crêpes with asiago cheese and sea scallops au gratin are among the appetizers. The selection of homemade cakes, pies and ice creams changes frequently.

The Sunday champagne brunch is priced from yesteryear, with all but two main dishes in the $5.25 to $6.95 range.

Dinner, Monday-Thursday 6 to 8:30, Friday and Saturday 5:30 to 9:30; Sunday brunch, 10:30 to 1:45.

Railroad House, West Front and South Perry Streets, Marietta. (717) 426-4141.

Dining is in several venues at this architecturally significant old hotel, lately rejuvenated by Donna and Rick Chambers. One is the Music Room, where handsome yellow and green swag curtains match the walls, oriental rugs cover the dark wood floors and a sheet of "America" is on the music stand next to a victrola. Another is the large Blue Room, stenciled and wainscoted. Beyond is the Country Room, where a collection of clocks is backlit on the mantel of the huge open fireplace that served the original kitchen. Light fare is available weekends in the downstairs **Arrivals Tavern,** where posters of the Orient Express and railroad memorabilia complement the beamed ceiling and the 30-foot-long copper bar. You also may dine on an outdoor courtyard with black wrought-iron furniture overlooking flower and herb gardens. There are whimsical touches: a Victorian shoe on the wall here, two stuffed rabbits in an Adirondack twig loveseat there.

The same care extends to the kitchen, where Rick's brother-in-law, Brian Mills, oversees an ambitious menu featuring beef and seafood in the $13.95 to $19.95 range. A pasta dish called straw and hay – lobster, scallops and shrimp over spinach and egg fettuccine – is a favorite with customers. Rick also touts the veal normandy, chicken champagne and steak diane. Stuffed mushrooms, clams casino and caesar salad are among the starters. Desserts could be any number of flavored cheesecakes (oreo, mocha, amaretto and pumpkin-pecan), cappuccino torte and peanut-butter pie. Strolling minstrels play on Saturday nights.

Soups, salads, sandwiches and a few entrées are offered for lunch and on the light-fare menu.

Lunch and dinner daily, 11 to 9 or 10; Sunday brunch, 10 to 2.

The Country Table Restaurant, 740 East Main St., Mount Joy. (717) 653-4745.

A Mennonite family runs this large, family-style restaurant known for good homemade food and reasonable (make that bargain) prices. Despite its size, patrons expect an hour's wait for a table on Saturday night. Floral wallpaper, candle sconces and a solarium along one side lend a touch of class to the vast dining room.

The extensive menu is served family style on platters, each including rolls and a choice of two vegetables. The prices are from a couple of decades ago, running from $5.75 for fried chicken or oven-baked ham loaf with gravy to $9.95 for the broiled seafood combination incorporating haddock, shrimp, scallops, salmon cake and crab cake. Imagine, breaded veal cutlet topped with stewed tomatoes for $5.80 or T-bone steak for $9.25. Hamburgers and most sandwiches are in the $2 to $4 range.

On your way out, stop at the full-service bakery between the restaurant and banquet hall to take home some luscious pastries.

Open Monday-Thursday 6 a.m. to 8 p.m., Friday and Saturday to 9 p.m. Saturday breakfast buffet, 7:30 to 10. No liquor. No credit cards.

Bully's On Union, 647 Union St., Columbia. (717) 684-0811.

This Victorian eatery featuring "food and spirits" in a three-story brick building in the old Union Hotel could be anywhere, but it fills a niche in up-and-coming Columbia. Brick walls and a pressed-tin ceiling enclose three dining areas, barely partitioned from a long oak bar.

The extensive menu is priced right, from $8.95 for grilled chicken to $19.95 for the combo filet mignon and crab imperial with béarnaise sauce and Swiss cheese. We found dining in the small no-smoking room a convivial if noisy affair. The rolls were hot but lacked butter and the salad consisted of iceberg lettuce. The oriental flank steak with broccoli was fine, although the yellow squash never arrived. The steak slices in onions, mushrooms and provolone cheese were okay, although not the advertised tenderloin. The curly fries were excellent.

Open daily, 11 to 11, weekends to midnight; Sunday brunch, 11 to 3.

The Meyer Family, 869 Sunhill Road, Manheim. (717) 392-8678.

A neighboring B&B innkeeper once asked Dee Dee Meyer to cook for his guests. She demurred, saying she wanted to stay home with her six children, but suggested that visitors could come to her house for dinner. They did and still do. Up to two dozen guests join the Meyer family for home-cooked, family-style dinners in a phenomenon that has garnered international publicity and become so successful that reservations now are taken 30 days ahead and booked by credit card – "no exchanges or refunds."

Guests arrive at the appointed hour at the rural house the Meyers built themselves and are greeted by Jack Meyer in the sitting room, large enough to accommodate the River Brethren congregation that holds services here. They sit with the Meyer family at a long, fourteen-leaf table and enjoy a communal meal. Food is passed around the table, the conversation gets interesting after the man of the house overcomes early stiffness on the part of guests, and the hosts sing Brethren hymns at meal's end. People who come here want more than a good dinner, says Jack. "They are looking for solutions – how to live a simpler life." So as guests enjoy relishes, green and gelatin salads, pot roast and chicken, mashed potatoes, breads, strawberry pie, cherry delight and such, Jack leans back from the table and expounds on life as lived by the Brethren.

The entire happening lasts about two hours and costs $18.95. One food writer said that better Pennsylvania Dutch food cannot be found anywhere, and the Amish Country News reports that the Meyers are "the only Old Order church family that will sit down and actually eat with the guests." By day, Jack runs a horse and buggy tour business in eastern Lancaster County, while Dee Dee prepares the evening's dinner.

Dinner by reservation, seatings nightly except Wednesday and Sunday, 4:30 and 7.

Diversions

All the attractions of Pennsylvania Dutch Country are at hand from a base in western Lancaster County. The tour buses head to Bird-in-Hand, Paradise, Intercourse and such; we prefer the more staid, picturesque towns of Ephrata and Lititz. Innkeepers in this section say it makes a central base for touring not only its own attractions and those of eastern Lancaster County but also nearby Hershey and Gettysburg.

The Watch and Clock Museum, 514 Poplar St., Columbia, 684-8261. Tick-tocking away the seconds in unison, the country's largest collection of precision watches and clocks draws visitors from across the country. Since opening in 1977, the museum has grown to more than 8,000 timepieces divided chronologically into galleries, from early pocket sundials to moonphase wristwatches. A turtle floating in oil in a silver bowl tells the time by swimming to the numbers on the side of the bowl of the tortoise clock; a mouse climbs along the numbers to show the time on the hickory dickory dock wall clock. A statue of a woman stands atop a pedestal and dangles the pendulum that drives a French clock. The masterpiece is the Engle Monument Clock, whose creator called it the eighth wonder of the world, fourteen feet high with 48 moving figures illustrating Greek mythology and the twelve apostles. Open Tuesday-Saturday, 9 to 4; Sunday (May-September), noon to 4. Adults, $3.

Wright's Ferry Mansion, 38 South Second St., Columbia, 684-4325. This stone house was built in 1738 for a remarkable English Quaker, Susanna Wright, whose pursuits spanned a spectrum from writing to the raising of silkworms. It contains an outstanding collection of Pennsylvania furniture and accessories in the William and Mary and Queen Anne styles from the early 1700s. Textiles, English ceramics and glass also are displayed to good advantage. Open May-October, Thursday-Saturday 10 to 3; hours and days may vary. Adults, $5.

Veterans Memorial Bridge, Columbia. The multi-arched, reinforced concrete bridge stretches 6,657 feet across the broad, shallow Susquehanna to Wrightsville. When built about 1930, it was the longest of its type in the world. Ironically, the walls totally obscure any view of the river as you drive across. The bridge is closed one Saturday in October for the annual Bridge Bust. A double-decker bus shuttles back and forth the 20,000 area residents who turn out to enjoy arts and crafts, food and entertainment.

Chickies Rock County Park, Route 441, Chickies. Good hiking trails lead to the edge of the cliffs and what one enthusiast advises is one of the best overlooks in the East, high above the Susquehanna. Named for a native tribe that once lived here, the park won the award for "best view" in a Lancaster County magazine poll.

Walking Tour of Marietta. Two and a half miles long and three blocks wide, this town of 2,700 grew up along the Susquehanna River. Basically unchanged from the 18th century, its eight-block center representing nearly half the town was placed on the National Register of Historic Places as a well-preserved example of a 19th-century industrial town. A map with a detailed guide to 90 historic places is published by the Marietta Restoration Associates, which sponsors a popular candlelight house tour the first Sunday in December. There's also a walking path along the river.

Nissley Vineyards, 140 Vintage Drive, Bainbridge, 426-3514. Thirty-five acres of rolling farmlands have been converted to vineyards, their French-hybrid or American grapes used to produce the Nissley family's varietal and proprietary wines. A booklet outlines a self-guided tour of the large stone-arch winery. The property includes an 18th-century stone mill with an adjacent arch bridge, a rushing brook and pleasant areas for picnicking. The site is perfect for the highly rated Music in the Vineyards series, open-air lawn concerts scheduled Saturday evenings from July through Labor Day. Open Monday-Saturday 10 to 5, Sunday 1 to 4.

Shopping. For real Pennsylvania Dutch flavor, you need head no farther than **The Country Store,** 906 Mount Joy-Manheim Road, Mount Joy. The Mennonites run – and also patronize – this place, where you'll find all kinds of bulk foods, cheeses, luncheon meats, pretzels, apple butter and Martin's handcooked potato chips, which we hear are the very best. Oh yes, you'll also find baseball cards and inspirational music tapes. Otherwise, western Lancaster County is not prime shopping territory, the eastern part of the county having cornered the market.

We liked all the handmade dolls and wreaths among the gifts and collectibles offered by Althea Johnson at her large **Country Haus Gift Shop,** located in her home at 558 East High St., Elizabethtown. In Columbia, **Hinkle's** combines a pharmacy, restaurant and gift shop of the old school. **C.A. Herr Family Hardware** is a three-story jumble where the basic hardware has been supplemented by household goods, work clothes and even a toy train display. It's been augmented by the **C.A. Herr Annex,** a co-op space that spreads antiques and collectibles through three buildings. The **Susquehanna Glass** outlet store also has a clearance center for extra savings; local innkeepers have had their B&B glasses engraved with their logo here. Across the Susquehanna River in Wrightsville is the **John Wright Warehouse,** host to changing enterprises, among them the large **Country Store** and the **Riverside Foundry** restaurant, a casual place for breakfast or lunch on a canopied terrace beside the river.

Farmers' Markets. Shopping for local foods and crafts is usually at its best at farmers' markets, and Lancaster area markets are some of the best. Locals tout the **Columbia Market House** at Third and Locust Streets, built in 1869 and operated continuously since. Visitors can tour the dungeon underneath, originally storage space for farmers and the borough's lockup for drunks and felons during the Gay 90s. Also worth a look is the old opera house next door, newly restored as a municipal building. The market here operates Fridays from 7 to 4 and Saturdays from 7 to noon. Columbia's market was surprisingly empty the Friday morning we were there, and seemed to stress crafts over food. For the real thing, we headed for the **Central Market** on downtown Lancaster's Penn Square. The nation's oldest publicly owned, continuously operating farmers market is a wonderful sight to behold, smell and taste. The Amish and Mennonites are much in evidence. So are such other local luminaries as a bake shop owned by Lancaster's fancy Windows on Steinman Park restaurant. We picked up salads, breads and cheeses for a ready-made picnic from Plum Street Gourmet, the Baker's Corner and Marion Cheese. Open Tuesday and Friday 6 to 4:30, Saturday 6 to 2.

Extra-Special

Le Petit Museum of Musical Boxes, 255 West Market St., Marietta. (717) 426-1154.

After David Thompson and George Haddad sold their gift shop and old country store in northern New Jersey and retired to Marietta, they found they missed their customers. Their trim green brick Federal townhouse also was overflowing with antique treasures they wanted to share. So in 1994 they opened a museum in their home. The name is a bit of a misnomer. The museum is not particularly petite and the 76 music boxes represent only the tip of the iceberg. Visitors will find such remarkable collections of New England art glass, clocks, Bennington pottery, baskets, toys, china and more tastefully displayed throughout the main floor that a special exhibit is mounted for each collection once a month. "Visitors are stunned – they're not ready for so much," says David. In the library he points out a rare American horse trough basket and a painting of Westminster Abbey that chimes. The largest Swiss 1896 disc musical box resides in the living room next to the museum's smallest music box, hidden in an album on a table. Lift the bread basket on the dining room table and it plays; ditto for the seat on a child's chair and the statue of an inebriated man leaning against a lamp post, whistling "Show me the way to go home." There's so much in this fascinating house museum that David guides up to eight people through on hourly tours. Open March-December, Saturday and Monday 10 to 4, Sunday noon to 4. Adults, $3.

Canadensis, Pa.
Heart of the Poconos

For all its glitz and glitter, its honeymooners and heart-shaped tubs and honky-tonk, the Pocono Mountain area suffers a bum rap. There's a section of the Poconos where the glitz image does not apply – a quieter, more old-fashioned and more rural refuge, less sullied by all that mars much of the region.

That refuge is the area around Canadensis, a dot on the map and a traffic light at a crossroads. Add its neighbors in the tight little stretch from Cresco and Mountainhome to Skytop and South Sterling. Country inns, restaurants, antiques stores, hiking trails, mountains and waterfalls are mixed in just the right blend for "unhurried leisure," as one innkeeper bills it.

Elsewhere in the four-season vacationland known as the Poconos, tourism has taken on immense proportions. Resorts, whirlpool tubs, golf courses, ski areas, souvenir shops, outlet stores, theme parks – you name it, they've got it, almost too much. Studies show that by the end of the century, the four-county region will host eighteen million visitors a year.

People come here from the cities for the outdoors – "the near country," the Pocono Mountains Vacation Bureau hypes it. But the onslaught threatens to blight the natural assets that are sought. Some of the Poconos are becoming rather like what visitors are escaping from.

The happy exception is the section around Canadensis, a place not that many outsiders have heard of. Its name is taken from the botanical name for the hemlock tree that furnished the bark for the leather tanning industry, which was the lifeblood of this region before tourism took hold. This area has managed to retain the natural attractions that originally beckoned Pocono-goers. It's a mountainous, forested retreat surrounded by three state parks, the home of the venerable Pocono Playhouse and the focus for a cluster of old country inns and new B&Bs.

Here, away from the fray, is the heart of the Poconos, the way they used to be.

Inn Spots

The French Manor, Huckleberry Road, Box 39, South Sterling 18460. (717) 676-3244 or (800) 523-8200.

The crème de la crème of lodging spots in the Poconos is the fieldstone château built in 1932 atop Huckleberry Mountain for Joseph Hirschorn, the mining tycoon whose art collection is now housed in the Smithsonian. He modeled this house after his manor

in the south of France. Later sold to Samuel Kress of department store fame, it was transformed in 1986 into a small country inn of distinction and was acquired a few years later by Ron and Mary Kay Logan, who had taken over the nearby Sterling Inn in 1982.

Despite (or perhaps because of) its attributes, this is a low-profile establishment that's little known in the area and relatively unknown outside. Beneath its imported Spanish slate

Fieldstone château built in 1932 for Joseph Hirschorn is now The French Manor.

roof and beyond the Romanesque arched entry are a manorial restaurant (see Dining Spots) and six guest rooms and suites, each with private bath, plus a downstairs lounge that looks like what it was: a huge, dark-paneled basement recreation room with a TV set in the corner.

Often kept open (perhaps to entice curious diners into a future stay?) is the Monte Carlo Room near the entry foyer. It is on the majestic side, its walls and ceiling paneled in cedar. A fancy headboard dresses the kingsize bed, two bright blue armchairs await nearby and there's a full bathroom. Go upstairs to the Florence Room with its canopied four-poster, massive dresser and elaborate bath-shower curtain and on to the spacious Venice Room. Here you'll find another ornate headboard and two armchairs, one on either side of the room.

The pièce de résistance is the Turret Suite, whose living room has a TV in the armoire and windows on three sides to take in the mountaintop view. Even that pales beside its bedroom, one floor above and again with windows on three sides. A colorful Southwest-looking quilt tops the kingsize bed, and baskets in recessed shelves provide decorative accents.

The woods throughout the house are cedar and pecky cypress. Leaded glass doors and windows, stone fireplaces, paintings, sculptures and antiques attest to the care lavished by Hirschorn and the 165 craftsmen and artisans he imported from Europe to build and furnish the structure, a task that took five years.

There's more. The main floor of the Carriage House is home to the lavish new Genevieve Suite, with a canopied kingsize mahogany bed facing a gas fireplace and a sitting area with loveseat and TV. A corner of the room holds a double whirlpool tub on a platform and the bathroom contains a shower. Upstairs, the Brigitte Suite offers two more bedrooms and a living room.

The grounds contain trails for hiking and cross-country skiing. Guests also may use the recreational facilities of the Sterling Inn less than two miles away. A full breakfast is included in the rates.

Doubles, $120 to $180; suites, $160 to $225.

Brookview Manor occupies hilltop property facing Broadhead Creek.

Brookview Manor, Route 447, RR 1, Box 365, Canadensis 18325. (717) 595-2451.

Built in 1911 as a summer vacation home for a prominent Scranton family on four hilly acres across from Brodhead Creek, this was renovated into a B&B in the mid-1980s and has had three owners since. As current owner Lee Cabana tells it, "the first ones brought it back from the brink and did what no one sees. The second owners did the cosmetic things that everybody sees. And now we get to show it off."

There's a lot for Lee, who left a career with the Red Cross in Erie, his wife Nancie and their seven-year-old daughter to show off. The entire first floor is given over to guests: a living room, a music corner with a grand piano, flute and guitar next to three bowed windows with remarkable curved glass and window sills, a den and TV room, a game room with the Cabanas' collection of Monopoly games from across the world, a wraparound porch containing rockers and what could be the biggest swing in the county, and a lineup of three adjoining rooms in which breakfast is served – a fireplace room, a sun porch and a picture-window room with striking stained glass.

That breakfast offers a choice of five juices, granola, fresh fruit, homemade muffins and perhaps an omelet, pancakes or french toast. Afternoon refreshments are served on the porch or in front of one of four fireplaces.

Upstairs in the main house are two bedrooms and two suites, all with private baths and outfitted with country furnishings and antiques. The Rose Room has two armchairs by a corner fireplace and an antique double bed, while the other front room has a kingsize bed and country calico decor. The Gold Suite has a queensize bed, corner reading room and a private rear porch. The innkeepers' favorite is the Sun Porch Suite, with rattan queensize bed and two rattan rockers, a sun porch outfitted in wicker, a third room with a day bed and a huge bath with decorative tiles and stained glass.

A fifth room with private bath is available in the rear carriage house, where part of the main floor is given over to a ping-pong and pool room. Upstairs is what Lee calls "our inn within an inn." It's a three-bedroom suite, two with double beds and one with twins, sharing a large living room and a bath.

The main house, attractive in yellow with dark red and green shutters, is shaded by giant hemlocks. Behind the Brookview property are an additional hundred acres that guests can explore. Almost everyone takes the 30-minute hike to a hidden waterfall.

Doubles, $85 to $135; carriage-house suite, $145 to $185. No smoking.

Farmhouse Bed & Breakfast, Grange Road, HCR 1, Box 6B, Mount Pocono 18344. (717) 839-0796.

An antiques collector and professional chef runs this restored 1850 homestead that's not like any farmhouse we've seen. Jack and Donna Asure turned the home of his parents, who formerly owned Memory Land across the street, into a B&B of character and comfort. Part of a complex of family residences on six treed, landscaped acres, this has five suites, all with private baths, remote-control television, telephones, small refrigerators and air-conditioning.

The enormous, wood-paneled living room-dining area is a showcase for the Asures' antiques and collections. "We collect everything," says Jack. That ranges from an authentic cigar-shop Indian in the entry to Stangl pottery to depression ware to shot glasses. A large TV is ensconced in the old bake oven. Guests take breakfast at a long table in a sunny corner of this wondrous room. "Donna bakes," perhaps carrot and pineapple muffins or blueberry croissants, says Jack. "I'm just the cook and bottle washer". He offers a choice of eggs, from benedict to broccoli and cheese omelet, or rum-raisin french toast, potato pancakes and belgian waffles.

The other side of the main floor contains the wood-paneled Parlour Suite with a queensize bedroom, a pretty quilt in peach and green, and a library-like living room with a stone fireplace. Upstairs is the Master Suite with a free-standing cast-iron fireplace in the living room and a queen bedroom. Outside, the farm's original ice house is now a cottage. You enter into a cozy living room, where a fireplace has been built into the now-whitewashed stone walls. Stairs lead to a balcony and a bedroom.

In 1994, the Asures divided a ranch house on the property into two suites. The Sundown offers a large living room with fireplace, a bedroom with queensize four-poster and a bath with a sunken garden tub. The Sunup lacks a fireplace but adds a full kitchen, a queensize bedroom and a combination tub-shower.

Doubles, $85 to $105. No smoking.

The Sterling Inn, Route 191, South Sterling 18460. (717) 676-3311 or (800) 523-8200.

This is the most with-it of the area's old country inns, and the recreational facilities on the 103-acre property give it a bit of a resort flavor. The place is as old as some of the buildings dating to the mid-19th century on its park-like campus and as new as the indoor pool and spa added in 1989.

Big draws are cross-country skiing, tobogganing, ice-skating and horse-drawn sleigh rides in winter and a small private lake for swimming and boating, the Wallenpaupack Creek, tennis, a nine-hole putting course and a 90-minute, self-guided nature trail at other seasons. Perhaps folks who hike the nature trails make use of all the walking sticks stowed in a milk pail beside the inn's front door.

Nearly half the 56 lodging units are in the sprawling main inn, where a large living room separates the reception area and restaurant (see Dining Spots) from the new indoor pool and bar area. Most rooms here are rather small and pleasantly old-fashioned, some with twin beds and two armchairs, others with king or queensize beds and perhaps a daybed.

Definitely worth the extra tab are the inn's four deluxe suites and the eight new Victorian fireplace suites in converted buildings out back by the creek. Our corner suite on the inn's second floor was a nice surprise with two large rooms, two closets, television and lots of space to spread out. A mix of fancy French provincial off-white furniture blended with modern tweedy sofa and chairs, and two more chairs were available in a reading area with windows on three sides beside the kingsize bed in the bedroom.

The road noise that was the only disturbance here is not a problem in the eight fireplace suites in the Nearbrook and Wayside buildings out back. You'd never guess these deluxe, carpeted rooms with potbelly stoves, queensize four-posters and decks or balconies onto the babbling brook started as garages. The rest of the accommodations include standard rooms in an old lodge and guest house and four cottages of one or two bedrooms.

Three meals a day are served in the dining room. The day's breakfast choices are recited by the waitress and yield such dishes as eggs any style with local ham or sausage, pancakes and corned-beef hash.

Doubles, $130 to $160, MAP; suites and cottages, $170 to $220, MAP.

Veranda across front of The Sterling Inn.

The Pine Knob, Route 447, Canadensis 18325. (717) 595-2532 or (800) 426-1460.

After a few years of "retirement," Dick and Charlotte Dornich are back where they belong – at the helm of this 1847 inn that occasionally shows its age. They took it back in 1992 and promptly hired a chef for the dining operation, the nemesis that had burned them out a few years previously.

The L-shaped common room in this homey inn is a real common room. It's full of Victorian and traditional sitting areas, with a Christmas village of ceramic houses on the fireplace mantel lighted year-round.

"People asked us not to take them down," said Dick, so the holiday decorations remained up – slightly camouflaged by flowers interspersed in summer. Walls here and in other common areas are hung with artworks painted by participants in the annual art workshops the inn sponsors.

There are seventeen guest rooms (nine in the main inn and eight in the North and South guest houses out back), plus a two-room cottage for two. All have private baths, and most have brass, cherry high back or oak beds covered with cheery quilts. Most beds are twins or doubles, but the twins in two rooms can be joined as kings. Carpeting covers the floors, and rooms have accents of little wreaths, a stenciled stool here and poof curtains there. Furnishings include collectibles and pieces from the owners' antique glass collection. Bathroom amenities amount to clean towels and a little bar of Ivory soap, plus the occasional quilted shower curtain. The clientele approves. "At least once a week people say they feel like they're in Grandma's house, meaning it's comfortable," reports Dick.

White Adirondack chairs are scattered about the lawn. The property includes a tennis court, volleyball court, a 60-by-40-foot swimming pool and a pagoda between the pool and Brodhead Creek, a mecca for fly-fishermen.

Doubles, $95 to $110, B&B; $148 to $156, MAP. Cottage, $166 MAP. Two-night minimum on weekends.

Fresh snow provides mantel of white around main house at The Pine Knob.

The Overlook Inn, Dutch Hill Road, Canadensis 18325. (717) 595-7519.

Quiet and out in the country atop a Pocono ridge, this unusual-looking structure with a pillared portico used to yield a view of the lights of Stroudsburg at night (hence the Overlook name). Trees have long since obscured the view, but guests get a feeling of being away from – if not above – it all at this old-fashioned place that's been an inn or a boarding house for 120 years and does show its age.

The portico collapsed in the rough winter of 1994 about the same time the inn collapsed into bankruptcy. The portico was quickly rebuilt and the inn was on the rebound as well under new management. Innkeeper Peter Wawra, who was watching television as we arrived, provided few specifics beyond stressing that "nothing has changed." We saw no signs of the lavish afternoon tea that had been a traditional drawing card here. The tea was taken in three homey parlor rooms that run one into the other across the front of the inn, with a little barroom at one end.

On our previous visit we were advised "there are no saunas or heart-shaped beds, but we have plenty of crooked walls." Some of those walls bear interesting framed advertisements from days gone by, we discovered on a tour of the facility. Twelve guest rooms with private baths are on the inn's second and third floors. They are country quaint with such homey touches as white frilly curtains, crocheted afghans and the like. But they are not exactly color-coordinated (one room had two faded armchairs on an orange shag carpet and another, two brown chairs on a new pinkish carpet). A bit more up-to-date with queens or two double beds, TVs and telephones are six guest rooms in the Lodge conference center and two more in the Guest House.

Guests may watch TV in the library, and join the public for dinner in the 84-seat restaurant across the rear of the building (see Dining Spots). A full breakfast is served here or on the porch, from which you might see a wild turkey, deer or a black bear. The fifteen-acre property includes shuffleboard, bocce, badminton and a swimming pool.

Doubles, $150 to $170, MAP; suites, $190 MAP.

Pump House Inn, Skytop Road, Canadensis 18325. (717) 595-7501.

This 1842 inn north of town is best known for its elegant restaurant, a Poconos institution since the 1960s (see Dining Spots). But owner John Keeney also offers three guest rooms above the restaurant, as well as four more in a rear carriage house.

Those upstairs are fairly simple, small and basic with twin beds, Bates spreads, a dresser, bathroom and little else. There's also a suite with a double bed and a sitting room with a sofabed and a couple of deck chairs.

More modern, brighter and welcoming are carpeted rooms and suites in the Carriage House with queen beds, modern baths and reproduction furniture. A guest cottage with living room, sun porch and terrace serves two to four people.

Continental breakfast is included in the rates.

Doubles, $65 to $85.

Skytop Lodge, Route 390, Skytop 18357. (717) 595-7401 or (800) 345-7759.

Off by itself just north of Canadensis is this grand mountaintop resort built in 1928, commanding 5,500 acres of private woodlands, lakes and hills and a devoted repeat clientele. It's a favorite for conferences (one of us attended a newspaper seminar here a decade ago and found it perfect for the purpose, but not the kind of place to which we'd return for a tête-à-tête).

Skytop has all the sports facilities you could want, from a golf course by the lake to its own ski slope, a toboggan run, indoor and outdoor pools and a fitness center. Three meals a day, served in formal dining rooms, are included in the rates.

The tiered, angled fieldstone hotel contains 130 rooms and mini-suites. There also are 36 guest bedrooms in nine cottages – four bedrooms each with porches, refrigerators and laundry facilities. Half the cottage rooms have queen beds and the rest are twins. Sixty-five of the hotel rooms contain twin beds; 29 rooms have queen beds and five, kingsize. Seven mini-suites have queensize beds and sitting areas, while two VIP suites come with a separate bedroom and parlor. Skytop so far has eschewed the oversize canopy beds and jacuzzis of similar resorts of its standing, and has suffered in guidebook ratings as a consequence.

Doubles, $246 to $266, AP; cottages, $289, AP; suites, $321 to $388, AP.

Dining Spots

Homestead Inn, Sandspring Drive, Cresco. (717) 595-3171.

Consistently good food in pleasant surroundings is the hallmark of the Homestead, established in 1980 and, at our visit, about to gain a view of a new manmade lake in back. Philadelphia caterers Drew and Susan Price converted a large barn-like skeleton into an attractive restaurant that's country casual. Three dining rooms in prevailing brown and white seat a total of 95 amid barnwood or redwood walls, an occasional aquarium, starched green floral linens, votive candles and Wyeth prints on the walls.

The Homestead gained a measure of fame in 1990 when TV producer Woody Fraser, a Poconos vacationer and fan of the Homestead, featured the owners on ABC's Home show.

Susan oversees the kitchen, from which come such entrées ($14.25 to $22.95) as crabmeat-stuffed brook trout en croûte, broiled crab cakes with basil-mustard sauce, broiled Norwegian salmon with peppercorn-parmesan-hollandaise sauce, sautéed chicken wrapped with prosciutto, roasted pork tenderloin with peach sauce, filet mignon au poivre and rack of lamb bordelaise. Hot biscuits and breads, tossed salad and fresh vegetables accompany.

Among starters are snapper soup, escargots in puff pastry and smoked mozzarella with tomatoes and basil. Raspberry cheesecake, apple crisp, rum cake and chocolate mousse are favorite desserts. The well-chosen wine list is priced from the teens to the

Artworks and hanging plants adorn rear dining room at Homestead Inn.

$40s. It includes the Homestead's private reserve seyval blanc from New Hope's Bucks Country Vineyard.

Dinner, Monday-Saturday 5 to 9, Sunday 4 to 9.

Pump House Inn, Sky Top Road, Canadensis. (717) 595-7501.

The red pump in the original well outside the entrance provides the name for this elegant bastion of special-occasion dining. The imposing foyer inside is like a library, where proprietor John Keeney takes telephone reservations at an old desk and greets patrons upon arrival. He leads them to the Pub Bar, dark and intimate and atmospheric as can be, or to a couple of small, dark dining rooms brightened with pink linens, the front porch whose four tables are highly prized or the far grotto room with its waterfall wall and all kinds of nooks and alcoves. Trenton oyster crackers, flickering oil lamps and place settings of three forks and three spoons each are on the tables.

It's a sumptuous backdrop for French-American fare that has been pleasing a well-heeled clientele since the early 1960s. Chef Paul Guthy's short menu is supplemented by daily blackboard specials. For starters ($4.95 to $6.95), you might try the sensational baked pecan brie over warm spinach, beer-batter shrimp with pungent fruit sauce or poached shrimp and scallops on a bed of grilled eggplant and tomatoes with a ginger-lime sauce.

Main courses run from $13.95 for chicken breast topped with grilled tomatoes, smoked mozzarella and tomato-basil sauce to $24.95 for rack of lamb. The poached salmon could be stuffed with grilled scallops and crabmeat, the basil shrimp served with garlic on a bed of pasta and the veal sautéed with grilled shrimp and a mustard-marsala sauce. There's no wine list; instead the wines are displayed on racks between dining rooms. Patrons view the array, affordably priced from the mid-teens and up, and pick their choice.

To finish with a flourish, how about chocolate mousse, raspberry crème brûlée or white chocolate cheesecake?

Dinner nightly 5 to 9, Sunday 2:30 to 8:30. Closed Monday-Wednesday, December-April.

The French Manor, Huckleberry Road, South Sterling. (717) 676-3244.

The dining room in what was the great room in Joseph Hirschorn's manor home has 40-foot-high peaked and beamed ceilings and massive fireplaces at either end, each with a gigantic grape wreath above. The setting reminded us of a certain lovely pousada at which we once dined in Portugal.

A plush beige carpet with borders of burgundy and green covers the floor, the linens are pink and green, and a bouquet of carnations and baby's breath was on each table at our visit. From picture windows on one side of the room, you can see the slate terrace and mountains beyond. Oriental screens and lamps and a mix of chairs from ladderback to French provincial complete a look that's rather sophisticated for the area. Classical music adds to the splendid setting in which to try some of the splendid fare of chef George Filak.

But it's not cheap, especially at lunch when "les sandwiches" are $8.95 to $9.95 and "les salades" go up to $12.95 for one of "blended seafood." The onion soup sells for $5.25. We liked the poached chicken, broccoli and pasta topped with fresh tomato

Majestic dining room at French Manor.

concasse and the vegetables with melted cheese and artichoke mayonnaise. The latter was listed under hot platters but came as an open-face sandwich on whole-grain toast.

A pianist plays at night, when appetizers are priced from $5.25 for melon with prosciutto to $11.95 for poached prawns and crab claws on watercress with a spiced cocktail sauce. A green salad with balsamic vinaigrette and a sorbet intermezzo are included in the price of the entrées. They run from $19.50 for sautéed chicken on an eggplant crouton to $30 for rack of lamb with choice mustards. Salmon nantua, grilled pheasant, roast duckling in cointreau, medallions of veal with wild mushrooms and tournedos hongroise are other choices on the French menu, whose execution seems to live up to the pretensions of its prose. Desserts could be raspberry linzer torte, chocolate mousse, apple custard torte and cannoli. The wine list is short and expensive.

Lunch daily, noon to 2, May-October; dinner nightly, 6 to 9; weekends only, November-April. Jackets required. No smoking.

The Sterling Inn, Route 191, South Sterling. (717) 676-3311.

A stone fireplace helps divide into two intimate sections the long dining room at this inn hidden behind towering rhododendron bushes. It's pretty in pink and white, but rather too brightly lit for intimate dining and with tables rather too close for comfort on busy nights.

The changing menu is printed daily. Among appetizers, we tried the chicken liver pâté with crackers and mussels on the half shell with tarragon and tomatoes; unfortunately, the mussels were not as fresh as they should have been. The tossed salad was mostly iceberg lettuce, but this lapse was redeemed by the savoyard potatoes and the excellent mix of sautéed snow peas and yellow squash that accompanied our prime rib with dijon cream sauce and broiled loin lamb chops with a homemade tomato chutney.

A $19 Mirassou cabernet was one of the cheaper selections from the short wine list. Other entrée choices ($13.95 to $17.25) might include blackened red snapper, baked sea scallops provençal and veal marsala. A perfect key lime pie was an excellent choice from desserts that ranged from tapioca pudding and rainbow sherbet to walnut pie and honey cheesecake with raspberry topping.

Although there's quite a range in prices on the menu given the public, all items on the same but unpriced menu are available to house guests on the MAP plan without surcharges – a rare policy that we find refreshing. Innkeepers Ron and Mary Kay Logan know how to keep their guests happy.

Lunch daily, noon to 1:30; dinner, 6 to 8:30. No smoking.

The Overlook Inn, Dutch Hill Road, Canadensis. (717) 595-7519.

Two large dining rooms are pleasantly old-fashioned with beamed ceilings, captain's chairs and tables bearing ivory-over-beige cloths, blue fanned napkins, oil lamps and two big wine glasses at each setting. Chef Sharon Rose presents an ambitious menu that attracts the public as well as inn guests.

Entrées run from $9.50 for grilled chicken to $21.75 for rack of lamb and $44 for châteaubriand bouquetiere for two. Among the favorites are local rainbow trout, shrimp champagne, veal with prosciutto and melted provolone, stuffed quail, grilled rabbit and roast duckling with an apple-walnut-citrus sauce,.

You can also get a sample of that duckling as an appetizer, along with smoked salmon, shrimp cocktail and oysters rockefeller. Among desserts are white chocolate cheesecake, chocolate mousse and homemade banana or cappuccino ice cream.

Dinner nightly except Tuesday, 6 to 9; Sunday, 5:30 to 8; fewer days in off-season.

The Pine Knob, Route 447, Canadensis. (717) 595-2532.

The menu arrives in an old book in this inn's 65-seat dining room, sprightly in pink with white floral overcloths, rose napkins and lalique-style candle-holders. It makes for interesting reading to embellish the menu proper, which is short and to the point.

Among entrées ($13.95 to $22.50), expect standards like stuffed flounder, shrimp scampi, grilled salmon, chicken cutlets sautéed with Italian sausage, roast Long Island duckling with orange sauce and filet mignon. Appetizers include herring in sour cream, smoked trout and eggplant rollatine. Seasonal pies are featured desserts.

Dinner nightly, 6 to 9; fewer days in off-season, Friday-Sunday in winter.

Crescent Lodge, Routes 940 and 191, Cresco. (717) 595-7486.

This refurbished, contemporary lodge in the Paradise Valley section offers a glamorous setting for dining in two large rooms with heavy leather and wood armchairs at well-spaced tables and artworks hung in gilt frames.

Chef Wayne Dunlop, representing the third generation of Dunlops at the family-owned lodge, oversees an ambitious menu with continental flair. Seven veal specialties join two dozen other entrées and specials in the $14.50 to $24.95 range. Here you'll find almost anything from coq au vin and broiled brook trout to Long Island duckling with orange sauce, beef wellington and broiled African lobster tail.

A complimentary bowl of marinated vegetables starts the meal. Appetizers include such standards as fruit cocktail and marinated herring as well as beer-batter shrimp and scallops nantua. Ditto for desserts: parfaits, strawberry ice cream pie, coupe romanoff and peach melba. The wine list is slightly better than the area's norm and is value-priced. A pianist plays on Friday and Saturday nights.

Dinner nightly, 5:30 to 9 or 10, Sunday 3 to 8; closed Monday and Tuesday in off-season.

The Forks at Buck Hill, Route 390, Mountainhome. (717) 595-7335.

French doors open onto the enclosed side porch from the main contemporary-style dining room in cranberry and green, with mini-print wallpaper, pine tables and windsor chairs, and a few country accessories here and there. It's a simple but stylish setting for a something-for-everyone menu, and so well received that a second dining room has been added.

Dining room at The Forks at Buck Hill.

The chef also has expanded the menu, adding continental offerings to the traditional roster of steaks, seafood, veal and chicken dishes. Thus chicken piccata, veal marsala, shrimps provençal and pork chops pizzaiola co-exist with baked stuffed flounder, lemon sole, grilled swordfish, pan-fried brook trout, chicken stir-fry and steak au poivre in the $10.95 to $18.95 range. There are six pasta entrées as well.

An autumn lunch on the pleasant side porch brought a chef's salad with home-made blue cheese dressing, pea soup and a hefty hamburger on a kaiser roll. The large bar is a favorite haunt of locals and the Pocono Playhouse crew.

Lunch daily, noon to 3; dinner nightly, 5 to 10.

Jaegermeister, Route 390, Mountainhome. (717) 595-9978.

The best German food this side of Germany is how one local innkeeper refers to it. The owner cooked in Germany and transplanted part of his homeland to this inauspicious looking roadhouse, transformed inside into a German gasthaus. The name translates to game warden in German, and boar heads are mounted on the walls.

The short menu features veal and wursts, but you also can get the best cheeseburger in Pennsylvania, according to our innkeeper informant. Expect such main courses ($6.95 to $12.95) as bratwurst, knockwurst, kassler rippchen and jaeger schnitzel. Order pierogies, German potato salad, sauerkraut or spaetzle on the side.

Lunch and dinner daily, noon to 8, weekends to 10.

Hazzard's Rainetree Restaurant, Route 191, South Sterling. (717) 676-5090.

You want "gourmet American food at reasonable prices," as chef-owner David Hazzard describes it? In a summery, country setting with a view of a fountain in a duck pond surrounded by willow trees?

That's the attraction of this twenty-year-old restaurant, taken over in 1991 by Laurie and David Hazzard. David made a name for himself in Bucks County where he was a wholesale caterer and executive chef at Conti Cross Keys Inn in Doylestown. The beamed bar with dining room beyond is much bigger than its 65 seats would indicate, the space filled with changing collections like antique cycles loaned by a collector-friend.

The menu is geared to the family trade, but with sophisticated touches. Prices generally are in the $10.95 to $15.95 range, except for a rather astonishing $38.95 for surf and turf (seven-ounce filet and fourteen-ounce lobster tail). You also can order a 64-ounce filet for a cool $72.50. Advises the menu: "eat all four pounds in an hour and it's yours free, but no help!" You also could order grilled halibut with garlic butter over linguini, grilled salmon with montpelier butter, brook trout sautéed in sesame seeds and honey-mustard sauce, bouillabaisse, maple and raspberry glazed ham steak, and chicken stuffed with shrimp, crab and scallops and topped with three sauces. Appetizers are equally varied, from grilled vegetable terrine to pickled herring to marinated mussels. Among desserts are crème caramel, fresh fruit turnovers and what David calls the best bread pudding this side of the Mississippi.

The homemade bread and raspberry-mustard salad dressing are sold for takeout.

Lunch, noon to 3; dinner, 5 to 10; Sunday buffet brunch, 11 to 2. Closed Monday and Tuesday.

White Cloud Inn, Route 447, Newfoundland. (717) 676-3162.

This rural, old-fashioned inn founded as a retreat for members of Self-Realization Fellowship includes a small, laid-back restaurant known for vegetarian dishes and natural foods. Well-balanced, meatless meals are served with produce grown from the organic garden of owners George and Judy WIlkinson.

Two women oversee the cooking chores. Lunch offerings include cashew nut soup, salads, sandwiches like tahini, nutloaf with cheese and tofu with tomato and sprouts or a hot pizza muffin, plus blender drinks and carrot cake or peanut pudding.

The dinner menu is more ambitious. Entrée prices ($9.50 to $14.75) include soup, whole-grain bread, salad, vegetable and hot beverage. Among the possibilities are sautéed vegetables with cheese, cheese nut balls in Mexican sauce, tofu parmesan and baked nut loaf with mushroom sauce.

Founded by George Wilkinson in 1970, the Self-Realization Fellowship retreat opened to the public as a means of support. It operates the restaurant and inn "as our contribution toward making the world a better place in which to live."

Meal schedules vary, and Judy Wilkinson strongly advises calling for reservations. Summer hours, generally: breakfast, 8 to 10; luncheon, noon to 2 on weekends; dinner nightly, 6 to 8.

Diversions

From golf courses to ski areas, fishing lakes to mountain trails, the Poconos are a four-season recreation destination. The specifics are outlined in countless brochures and periodicals, including "This Week in the Poconos" and "News of the Poconos."

Promised Land State Park, ten miles north of Canadensis, is the most popular of three state parks in the vicinity. The area along Route 390 into Promised Land is as notable for the profusion of rhododendron and mountain laurel, a majestic sight in the late spring, as it is for the funny little cabins that line the highway year-round. The 3,000-acre state park at an elevation of 1,700 feet is surrounded by 8,000 forested acres. Good fishing and swimming are available in a tranquil setting – power craft are banned from the lake, though you can rent rowboats, sailboats, pedal boats and canoes. For more exciting boating, head a few miles north to **Lake Wallenpaupack,** Pennsylvania's largest. **Gouldsboro** and **Tobyhanna** state parks also offer good swimming, boating and picnicking.

Waterfalls. Bushkill Falls is billed as the Niagara of Pennsylvania and is quite commercial. **Buck Hill Falls** is reached by a well groomed trail from a parking lot near the old Buck Hill Falls resort. The falls tumble 200 feet in three major drops along a mile of picturesque glen. It's not as spectacular as Bushkill, but most people like it better. Innkeepers at area lodging establishments can steer visitors to their own favorites.

Pocono Playhouse, Mountainhome, 595-7456. One of the nation's longest-running summer playhouses has brought Broadway to the Poconos for 48 years. The 1994 season opened in June with Neil Simon's "The Goodbye Girl" and closed in mid-October with "La Cage aux Folles." "Oklahoma" and "Phantom of the Opera" were two of the hits in between. Shows are staged Wednesday-Sunday nights, plus three matinees. Tickets, $17 to $20.

Shopping. Antiquing and the new Tannersville outlet stores have their devotees, but the main intersection of Canadensis tells something of its priorities. It has a Gulf station, an Indian Trading Post, the Sunrise Foodmart, the Calico Kitchen, a Methodist church and that's about all. The better shopping is along Route 390 in Mountainhome and Cresco.

Holley Ross Pottery at La Anna is widely advertised for "distinguished china and threefold entertainment" – demonstrations, woodland park and large factory show-room. Bus tours descend here, and you might find a nice bean pot, a mixing bowl or a coffee mug at a good price. As for the rest of it, take it, puh-leeze. Much more tasteful are the clothing, home accessories and artificial floral arrangements and outdoor furniture at **Viva** in Mountainhome. **Welcome Home** in Mountainhome bills itself as a unique country store, but stocks sophisticated cards, crafts, soaps, coffees and specialty foods among its wares. Also in Mountainhome, **Christmas Memories** claims to display the Poconos' largest line of collectibles. More collectibles, dolls, teddybears and gifts are on display at **Wonderful Things.** The relocated and expanded **Cooks Tour,** in something of a hardware store setting in Mountainhome, is a kitchen shop without peer, especially in terms of cookware, gadgets and utensils you can't find elsewhere.

Theo. B. Price Inc. at Cresco must be seen to be believed. It's part lumber company and part country store, with a mysterious jumble of things from oyster crackers to light bulbs, dried flower arrangements to carved decoys and Santas, all mixed in together. The **Ella C. Ehrhardt General Store** in Newfoundland is like a time capsule, purveying some of the same kinds of items it did when it opened in 1860. Also near Newfoundland is **Reece Pottery,** where Thomas Reece crafts interesting functional and sculptural stoneware.

Extra-Special

Callie's Candy Kitchen and Pretzel Factory, Route 390, Mountainhome and Cresco. (717) 595-2280 and 595-3257.

We never thought we'd see so much candy until we – and a few tour buses – met up with Callie's Candy Kitchen, founded in 1952 in Mountainhome and now a three-generation family enterprise that opened a pretzel factory in Cresco in 1985. The family patriarch still gives occasional candy-making demonstrations, which attract young and old, and there are plenty of free samples. We defy anyone to get through the huge store showroom without succumbing to one of the tempting fudge flavors from macadamia nut to piña colada. Or the new chocolate-covered potato chips with the texture of chips and the taste of chocolate. Or the Pocono Mountain Crunch, a mix of butterscotch, crispied rice and ground cashews that is the best-seller. What next? Pretzels, that's what – plain or chocolate-covered, filled with peanut butter, available in bite-size chunks, sticks and rings, plus pretzel dogs and pretzel pizzas. The pretzel factory just down the road in Cresco also makes gourmet popcorn in 60 flavors, from hot jalapeño to apple pie. The pretzel factory is all glassed-in so viewers can watch the goings-on. Both the candy kitchen and pretzel factory are open daily from 10; pretzel factory, open weekends only in winter.

Delaware River is viewed from second-floor balcony at Bridgeton House.

Bucks County, Pa.
Romance Along River Road

What could be more special than the River Road section of Bucks County, sixteen miles of pristine paradise along the Delaware River? William Penn called it "the most beautiful of landscapes," even more beautiful than England's Buckingham, the shire in which he was born and after which this was named. We call it romantic, even magical, any time of year.

River Road, the winding state Route 32, hugs the river and its adjacent canal as it wends north from New Hope to Upper Black Eddy, linking hamlets that have changed little since the Revolution. The river remains largely untouched by development; its flow varies from rushing to gentle, depending on location and season. Beside it is the Delaware Canal, which flourished for a century as mules plied the towpath, drawing barges behind. The canal's quaint wooden bridges, moss-covered locks and stone aqueducts attest to times past.

There are treasures: Phillips Mill, the cradle of the Bucks County Art Colony; Centre Bridge, an area of substantial edifices in keeping with its English name; Lumberville, a string of houses, stores and inns up against the river; Point Pleasant, the area's population center, if a few hundred souls can be called that, and Erwinna, where large historic landmarks are spread across a river plain.

Hillsides awash with mountain laurel and rhododendron tumble down to the flatland strip along the river. Sturdy stone houses punctuate the countryside, looking for all the world like those of Britain's Cotswolds. Authentic country inns provide lodging and sustenance for travelers, as in the past.

This is Bucks County at its best, away from the hustle and bustle of touristy New

The Inn at Phillips Mill, as depicted by artist Raymond E. Halacy.

Hope and the encroaching suburbia from Philadelphia and Doylestown. It's a place tailor-made for a rural retreat, for canoeing, walking the towpath, browsing the few shops, eating well and rejuvenating one's spirits at a country inn or B&B. Ramble along the river and succumb to its romance.

Inn Spots

The inns here, as well as the restaurants that follow, are covered in geographical order from south to north.

The Inn at Phillips Mill, North River Road, New Hope 18938. (215) 862-2984.

Hanging pots overflowing with fuchsias, wooden casks filled with all colors of mums, wreaths of Christmas greenery or a profusion of spring bulbs – depending on the season, these mark the entrance to this small and adorable yet sophisticated inn. When you see its facade of local gray stone, smack up against an S-turn bend in the River Road, with its copper pig hanging over the entrance, you would almost swear you were in Great Britain.

That impression is heightened as you register at the reception desk and observe the low-ceilinged dining rooms (see Dining Spots). Upstairs are four charming guest rooms

and a suite, cheerily decorated by innkeeper Joyce Kaufman, whose architect husband Brooks did the restoration of the 1750 barn. One has its own sitting room. Honeymooners request the third-floor hideaway suite, where fabric covers the ceiling. Most beds are four-posters or brass and iron and are topped with quilts. Antiques, handpainted trays, dried-flower arrangements and embroidered cloths on the nightstands abound. They don't advertise it, but sometimes the Kaufmans rent a cottage in back of the inn. A small swimming pool also may be used by guests.

A continental breakfast (juice, flaky croissants and coffee) is delivered to your room, wrapped in a blue and white checked tablecloth in a basket.

Doubles, $75; suite, $85; cottage, $125. No credit cards.

Centre Bridge Inn, 2998 North River Road, New Hope, Pa. 18938. (215) 862-2048.

This striking white structure with red shutters built in Colonial Williamsburg style has a large restaurant-tavern (see Dining Spots), nine guest rooms and an advantageous location beside the Delaware River across the bridge from Stockton, N.J. Fires destroyed inns that had occupied the site since 1705, so this reconstruction is of early 1960s vintage.

Overnight guests enter an enormous formal vestibule, with a fireplaced parlor on the river side. Ahead are a pair of two-room suites, one with a foyer leading into the main room with queensize canopy bed, two plush blue chairs on thick carpeting, TV set, cedar-lined bath and private river-view deck – "our nicest room," according to our guide. The other suite in front has a queen brass bed and sitting room with sofa, loveseat and TV. Upstairs are seven more rooms, many with canopy beds and four with TV. All are air-conditioned, have private baths and are notable for antiques and colorful Schumacher wall coverings, though some appear a bit tired lately.

A continental breakfast is served in the suites, the parlor or outside on a deck off the main floor, which has one of the nicest views of the river anywhere.

Doubles, $80 to $135. Two-night minimum on weekends.

1740 House, River Road, Lumberville 18933. (215) 297-5661.

For serenity, motel-style privacy and a quiet location in a quaint hamlet beside the Delaware, this appeals to repeat visitors who book the same rooms year after year. The 1740 House was opened in 1967 by well-traveled New Yorker Harry Nessler and his wife. They built it to look old, each room in two wings opening from a front corridor and extending to patios or balconies perched out back at canal's edge.

Individually decorated, the 24 spacious rooms on two floors have king or twin beds, large bathrooms (a few with showers only), comfortable chairs with reading lights, nightly turndown service, detachable wooden coat hangers, and pleasant outdoor seating areas overlooking the river. There are no televisions or phones to intrude.

Instead, enjoy the peace and quiet of the river from your balcony or porch, catch some sun around the small pool, read in a couple of small parlors, and meander up River Road to the center of Lumberville to walk the canal towpath or cross the foot-bridge to an island park in New Jersey.

A buffet-style breakfast is served in the cheery garden dining room, where you're

1740 House at Lumberville.

likely to end up sitting family-style with other guests. Help yourself to juice, cereal, croissants and a hot dish like scrambled eggs or creamed chipped beef, and toast your own homemade bread or English muffins.

Since the death of Harry Nessler in 1994 (the 92-year-old manned the front desk at the inn until the end), the 1740 House has been run by his grandson, Robert John Vris, who lives with his wife and young children in nearby Ottsville. Robert planned no major changes, but he did stop serving dinners for house guests, which he said really had been a service used more by his grandfather. Mr. Nessler's living quarters on the second floor were being converted into a deluxe two-room suite in 1995.

Doubles, $84 to $122. Two-night minimum on weekends. No credit cards.

Tattersall Inn, Cafferty and River Road, Box 569, Point Pleasant 18950. (215) 297-8233.

This manor home of pale aubergine plastered fieldstone with wood trim of cream and dark green is set amid holly trees and rhododendrons. It was once the home of Ralph Stover, the best known member of the ubiquitous Bucks County clan of mill owners. The B&B originally was opened in 1983 by the owners of the Inn at Phillips Mill to accommodate their overflow. Herb and Gerry Moss have been running it for the past few years with aplomb, plus some fun music from Herb's assortment of ancient phonographs (he worked for RCA, which explains his interest).

They offer six bedrooms, all with private baths and queensize beds. The Highland Room is done in Black Watch tartan. The Royal Lavender Room has lavender moiré covering the walls and a lace canopy over the bed, and the Wintergreen Suite adds a sitting room. Gerry crocheted the canopy for the bed in the main-floor Squires Room, which also has a sofabed.

Cider and cheese are served in the afternoon in the beamed rear tavern room, now a common room with a wonderful big fireplace, old wood floors, hunting prints and comfy rust-colored velvet sofas.

Breakfast is taken amid Herb Moss's collection of early victrolas and talking machines. His 1903 Edison cylinder talking machine is the oldest, and the 1915 Edison retains its original diamond needle. Juice, croissants, homemade breads and muffins accompany the jollity in the dining room. Or you can have breakfast in your room, on the veranda or on the back porch.

Doubles, $85 to $109. Two-night minimum on weekends.

Centennial Barn, 26 Cafferty Road, Box 139, Point Pleasant 18950. (215) 297-5615.

Sequestered in greenery, the large brick veranda with oversize twig furniture awash in pillows sets a stage for the dramatic. You get it here in two comfortable apartment-suites that are just the ticket for the celebrities who come here to escape.

Quite unprepossessing is the exterior of this stone and clapboard barn, built for the Barns Across America exhibit at the 1876 World Fair in Philadelphia. So the interior of what once was the ground-floor stables comes as a surprise.

Enter the kitchen of one suite, a homey country-style affair with windows onto the courtyard, flagstone counters, an adobe fireplace and planters abrim with hibiscus. Beyond is an enormous bedroom-living room with beamed ceiling, plaster walls, oriental carpets and a poster bed, and a bathroom with a bidet and a floor of Portuguese tiles. The other suite has a large living room with free-standing adobe fireplace, separate bedroom and a kitchen and bathroom with Italian tile floors.

The decor defies categorization, but has a Southwest motif and Italian and American antiques. "It's my style – eclectic," says owner Linda Ward, a designer, a writer,

Set back from the river on broad lawns is Evermay-on-the-Delaware.

an art and antiques dealer and, well, sort of bohemian. She designs and her son, a builder, executes. She and her husband Palmer, a composer, live upstairs on three floors of the restored barn, a central portion of which has been turned over to an art gallery.

Linda, trying to embellish a romantic escape for guests, puts out wine and a tray of fruit and cheese in each suite in the afternoon. She stocks the kitchens with yogurt, cereal, fruits, breads and croissants for guests to help themselves to in the morning.

Catering to long-term stays as well as to transients, she does not advertise – "we're sort of exclusive," says she. Nor is there a sign to identify the place, which is just behind the Tattersall Inn.

Suites, $225; two nights or more, $175.

Golden Pheasant Inn, River Road, Erwinna 18920. (610) 294-9595.
In the fashion of the French countryside, well-known local chef Michel Faure and his wife Barbara live upstairs over their acclaimed restaurant (see Dining Spots). Since taking over the 1857 fieldstone inn, they have renovated six guest rooms to offer "a taste of France on the banks of the Delaware," according to Barbara.

The number of guest rooms seems to vary with the number of Faure offspring in residence. All have private baths and queensize four-poster beds, one so high that you need a stool to climb up. The rooms we saw were decorated with country touches, antiques and interesting window treatments. We particularly liked the main-floor suite with its private entrance and deck, a stereo set and handsome furnishings.

A continental breakfast of juice, coffee and croissants is served in the morning. Overnight guests also enjoy a rear patio beside the canal.

Doubles, $110 to $135.

Evermay-on-the-Delaware, River Road, Erwinna 18920. (610) 294-9100.
Dating to the 1700s and enlarged in 1871, this three-story gold and tan Victorian mansion has the patina required for a listing on the National Register of Historic Places. It's set back from the road on a broad lawn facing the river, the perfect setting for the

air of calm and quiet that the innkeepers try to project – though we were a bit startled to find chickens pecking away on the side lawn at one of our visits.

Evermay is the bed-and-breakfast and gourmet-dinner venture of Ron Strouse and Fred Cresson, who were known for their cuisine at the Sign of the Sorrel Horse in Quakertown and who have enhanced their reputation with weekend meals here (see Dining Spots). Their sixteen guest rooms, all with private baths and telephones, are furnished with fine collectibles and antiques from the Victorian era. We found ours in the Carriage House a bit austere, despite the presence of fresh flowers and a large bowl of fresh fruit. Some inn rooms retain the original fireplaces. Walnut beds, oriental rugs, marble-topped dressers, fancy quilts and lacy pillows are among the furnishings.

A fire often burns in the fireplace and decanters of sherry are at the ready downstairs in the double front parlor, where afternoon tea with cucumber or watercress sandwiches and cookies is served at 4. At bedtime in your room you may find fruit and candy and a liqueur in a little glass with a doily on top.

Although continental, breakfast in the rear conservatory room is quite special, with orange juice, incredibly flaky croissants and pastries, one with cream cheese in the center, and the pièce de résistance at our visit: a compote of fresh strawberries, red seedless grapes, bananas and honeydew melon, garnished with a sprig of mint and dusted with confectioners' sugar – colorful and pretty.

Doubles, $85 to $170; two-bedroom suite, $200. Two-night minimum on weekends.

Bridgeton House, River Road, Box 167, Upper Black Eddy 18972. (610) 982-5856.

With sweat and TLC, restorationists Charles and Bea Briggs have transformed this onetime wreck of an apartment house built in 1836 into a comfortable B&B with a great location beside the river. Although smack up against the road, the inn has been opened to the rear for a water orientation.

A rear parlor and upstairs balconies look onto a landscaped courtyard beside the canal. Lovely stenciling, fresh or dried flowers, a decanter of sherry and bowls of potpourri grace the dining room, where breakfast is served. Following a fruit course (perhaps baked pears in cream or a fresh fruit plate) comes a main dish: waffles with strawberry butter, eggs Roxanne, or mushroom and cheese omelets. Fresh lemon breads, muffins, and apple cake likely accompany.

Most of the ten guest rooms overlook the water. Each was exceptionally fashioned by Charles, a master carpenter and renovator, and interestingly decorated by Bea. Some contain four-posters and chaise lounges; all have private baths, country antiques, colorful sheets, fresh flowers and intriguing touches. Our main-floor room came with lovely stenciling and a private porch.

Bea calls the dramatic penthouse suite Bucks County's ultimate. It has a twelve-foot cathedral ceiling, a kingsize bed, black and white marble fireplace, marble bathtub, backgammon table, black leather chairs, a stereo-TV center and a full-length deck onto the river.

An eleventh river-view room with a kingsize bed and a more elaborate bathroom than most was being readied in 1995 in space vacated by a staff member.

Doubles, $79 to $149; suites, $149 and $199. No smoking.

Dining Spots

Hotel du Village, River Road at Phillips Mill Road, New Hope. (215) 862-9911.
The food is country French, but the chef-owner is Algerian and his hostelry is Tudor

English in an early boarding-school setting. The main dining room in the former Lower Campus building of Solebury School looks like one in an English manor house, with a glowing fire at each end, a beamed ceiling, small-paned windows and a fine Persian carpet on the floor.

Chef Omar Arbani arrived in Bucks County from Algeria by way of culinary endeavors in France, Denmark, London and Washington, D.C. His aim is "the kind of home-style country cuisine you'd find in the restaurants of Bordeaux or Burgundy on a Sunday afternoon," according to his wife Barbara, a former New Jersey teacher who manages the dining room and inn.

Appetizers, including clams casino, escargots and shrimp sautéed in garlic butter, are $5.50 to $5.95, except $6.50 for lamb sausage, one of the few additions to the menu since we first dined here ten years ago. The crusty, piping-hot French bread was excellent, particularly when spread with the house pâté ($5.50 for a small crock as an appetizer).

Entrées run from $13.95 for chicken tarragon to $18.95 for tournedos or steak au poivre. Our tournedos with artichoke heart and béarnaise sauce were heavenly. So were the sweetbreads with green olives, mushrooms and madeira sauce. Potatoes sautéed with lots of rosemary, crisp beans and grilled tomato with a crumb topping accompanied. Moist black forest cake, crammed with cherries, and cafe royale were sweet endings to a rich, romantic meal.

Dining here takes precedence over the accommodations. Twenty rather spare rooms, all with private baths and air-conditioning, are in a converted stable in the rear and reflect their boarding-school heritage. Continental breakfast and access to a pool and two tennis courts on the ten-acre estate are included in the rates (doubles, $85 to $100).

Dinner, Wednesday-Saturday 5:30 to 9 or 10:30, Sunday 3 to 9. Closed mid-January to mid-February.

The Inn at Phillips Mill, 2998 North River Road, New Hope. (215) 862-9919.

Looking as if it had been transported from the British Cotswolds, the quaint gray stone building right at the S-turn bend in the River Road has a copper pig above the entrance – a symbol of the stone barn's origin as a gristmill that stood next to the village piggery. Architect Brooks Kaufman and his innkeeper wife Joyce transformed it into a country French restaurant.

The dining setting is romantic as can be. Candles augment light from the fireplace in low-ceilinged rooms with dark beams and pewter service plates and water goblets. Arrangements of flowers are all around.

The menu, written in French with English translations, is executed by three chefs whose names are listed at the bottom. The terrine of veal, pork and foie gras and the escargots with garlic-walnut demi-glace are favored appetizers. We enjoyed a springtime special, Maryland crabmeat in half an avocado, which was really special. Entrées are priced from $14.50 for chicken with herbs and wild mushrooms to $23 for rack of lamb with garlic, lemon and lavender. We've never tasted such a tender filet mignon with such a delectable béarnaise sauce nor such perfect sweetbreads in a light brown sauce as on our first visit. We liked the sautéed calves liver in a cider vinegar and the veal medallions with roasted shallots in cognac sauce on another occasion.

Hearty eaters may find the portions small, but they can fill up on the crusty French bread that comes with.

Desserts are triumphs, among them a lemon ice-cream meringue pie, about six inches high and wonderfully refreshing, and a vanilla mousse with big chips of chocolate and chocolate fudge sauce.

Dinner nightly, 5:30 to 9:30 or 10. BYOB. No credit cards.

Centre Bridge Inn, River Road, New Hope. (215) 862-2048.

The downstairs tavern-dining room with beamed ceilings, stucco walls and huge open fireplaces could not be more attractive, nor the glass-enclosed porch overlooking the river more inviting. Outside by the river is a brick patio with white wrought-iron furniture and a circle of granite tables around a fountain.

The food has been upgraded with the arrival of a new chef in 1994. The presentation is good, the product more consistent and the fare more innovative, according to staff members who felt the kitchen had tired under the same hands for thirteen years. The short continental menu is supplemented by nightly specials. Appetizers (each $8.50) include country-style pâté with champagne sauerkraut and whole-grain mustard, wild mushroom strudel, lobster and shrimp lasagna, and smoked goose breast sliced thin over a red currant and port wine mayonnaise, served with toasted sourdough bread. Main courses start at $18.95 for roasted half duckling stuffed with cornbread and black peppercorns and rise rapidly to $28.95 for pan-seared loin of lamb topped with a red wine-mint sauce. Sautéed salmon over a sweet potato-rum sauce, hickory-smoked pork loin with black bean sauce and julienned jicama, baked venison steak en croûte and veal scaloppine with fresh figs, pistachios and an applejack cider sauce are tempting possibilities. A house salad comes with. Cappuccino and international coffees are available, and we recall a happy evening sipping after-dinner drinks at the bar as a pianist entertained.

Dinner, Monday-Saturday 5:30 to 9:30 or 10, Sunday 3 to 9.

Cuttalossa Inn, River Road, Lumberville. (215) 297-5082.

Although the food here may not live up to the surroundings, it's not for lack of trying. Owner Marilyn MacMaster, something of a showperson, travels the world to find new recipes.

The place is big and the setting is great: an 1833 stone landmark, with three history-filled dining rooms inside and a series of outdoor terraces beside a millstream and waterfall, where we'd gladly have an al fresco lunch anytime.

The dinner menu is rather extensive in an effort to appeal to the diverse tastes and ages of the clientele. The menu mixes continental and American ($18.95 to $28) and some unusual presentations. Broiled red snapper comes with a white peach-almond-praline glaze, braised sea scallops with a honey-curry coating, baked salmon with a crunchy cucumber sauce, baked St. Peter's fish with Spanish olive salsa and grilled pork filet with cranberry chutney, and the breast of chicken is topped with camembert and strawberry glaze. More traditional tastes are served by items like prime rib, veal oscar and filet mignon. Even skeptics say good things about the crab imperial, whose recipe has been printed by national magazines. Start with smoked oysters with raspberry vinaigrette or sliced smoked duck breast with raspberry coulis. Finish with homemade strawberry cheesecake.

If you can't dine, stop for a drink in the outdoor bar, illuminated at night by twinkling white lights. With the woods and the stone walls and the roar of the falls in the background, it's the epitome of the River Road experience – romantic and magical.

Lunch, Monday-Saturday 11 to 2; dinner, Monday-Saturday from 5:30.

Black Bass Hotel, Route 32, Lumberville. (215) 297-5770.

For rustic charm, you can't beat this 1740 establishment straight out of England and so loyal to the Crown that, when George Washington crossed the Delaware just below here, the hotel supposedly wouldn't let him in. Wander around the dark, beamed dining rooms and look at all the British memorabilia collected by veteran innkeeper Herbert Ward, as well as the pewter bar that came from Maxim's in Paris.

312

Fountain is centerpiece of courtyard beside canal and river at Centre Bridge Inn.

Though we recall a memorable dinner from some years ago, we like the Black Bass best for lunch, when you can feast on the riverside scenery outside the long rear dining porch. Many favor the Charleston Meeting Street crab, a fixture on the short menu for $12.95. We enjoyed the New Orleans onion soup, thick with onions and cheese, which came in a proper crock. The crisp greens in the house salad were laden with homemade croutons and a nifty dressing of homemade mayonnaise, horseradish, dijon mustard and spices. Hungry after a lengthy hike along the towpath, one of us devoured seven of the nut and date mini-muffins that came in a basket. You also can order a poached seafood and grapefruit salad with poppyseed dressing, old-fashioned chicken and dumplings or grilled salmon with potato-horseradish galette, priced from $6.95 to $12.95.

The short dinner menu ranges from $18.95 for grilled pork chop with ginger-sweet potato custard and cider glaze to $24.95 for aforementioned crab. Poppy-crusted tuna with red onion confit and fennel, seared salmon with leek compote and savoy cabbage, and roast duck with oyster stuffing are other possibilities. Desserts here are exceptional: perhaps walnut cheesecake with sour cherry sauce and crème fraîche, chocolate turtle pie with macadamia caramel, or fresh fruit cobbler with wild turkey whiskey sauce. Happily, there's also a selection of homemade ice creams and sorbets.

Upstairs are seven bedrooms sharing two baths ($80) and two suites ($150 and $175).

Lunch, Monday-Saturday noon to 3, dinner, 5:30 to 9; Sunday, brunch 11 to 2:30, dinner 4:30 to 8:30.

Golden Pheasant Inn, River Road, Erwinna. (610) 294-9595.

The glamorous plant-filled solarium here was the setting for one of our more memorable meals, so we're glad that the rest of the place has been fixed up as well.

French chef-owner Michel Faure, who was well regarded at the nearby Carversville Inn and Philadelphia's Le Bec Fin, and his wife Barbara, who oversees the front of the house, have restored the two dark inner Victorian dining rooms to an elegant country

French look of the 1850s. They have been brightened with accents of copper pots, oriental rugs and the Faures' extensive Quimper collection from Brittany. The bar is in the front of the wallpapered main dining room, which has a working fireplace. The inner Blaise Room has hardwood floors, a beamed ceiling and exposed stone walls.

We'd still choose the solarium, where you can see the canal and the trees illuminated at night, to enjoy some of Michel's dinner creations. Start perhaps with his renowned lobster bisque, pheasant pâté, homemade gravlax with mustard-dill sauce or escargots in a hazelnut garlic butter. Continue with such entrées ($21.95 to $26.95) as bouillabaisse, poached Atlantic salmon with a champagne and lobster sauce, roast boneless duck, filet mignon bordelaise or rack of lamb with a rosemary, mint and garlic sauce. Worthy endings include cappuccino cheesecake, pecan pie, crème caramel, homemade sorbets and Belgian white chocolate mousse with a raspberry coulis.

Dinner, Tuesday-Sunday 5:30 to 9 or 10; Sunday brunch, 11 to 3.

Evermay on the Delaware, River Road, Erwinna. (610) 294-9100.

The weekend gourmet dinners offered by innkeepers Ron Strouse and Fred Cresson are acclaimed, drawing not only house guests but the loyal following they gained while running the Sign of the Sorrel Horse in nearby Quakertown. The six-course meal costs $48, with little choice except between two entrées and two desserts. It's served at a single 7:30 seating, usually booked far in advance.

The meal is taken in a main dining room where the draperies match the upholstered chairs, in a rear garden room or at tables for two in an intimate porch-conservatory pretty in white and light brown, with windows onto the back lawn. Our meal here was one of the best we've had, nicely presented and paced. Hors d'oeuvre of smoked trout salad, sundried tomato crostini and country pâté with green peppercorns were served first. Next, in order, came a suave chicken and leek soup, sautéed chanterelles on a saffron crouton, and a salad of boston and mache lettuces, garnished with violets and toasted walnuts and dressed with a fine balsamic vinaigrette.

These were mere preliminaries to the entrées: Norwegian salmon poached in white wine, served with hollandaise sauce and garnished with shrimp, and tender lamb noisettes wrapped in bacon and topped with a green peppercorn butter. These came with thin, crisp asparagus from Chile, rice pilaf and a sprig of watercress.

A cheese course of perhaps St. André, montrachet and gorgonzola precedes dessert. Ours was a perfect poached pear, set atop vanilla ice cream, butterscotch sauce, golden raisins and pecans. Nowadays a choice is offered, perhaps chocolate cones filled with white chocolate mousse and raspberries or coffee-kahlua-honey-almond ice cream. Ron handles the chef's duties. Fred does the baking, makes the sorbets and ice creams, and is responsible for the knockout flower arrangements all around.

Dinner by reservation, Friday-Sunday at 7:30; jackets requested.

Bucks Bounty, 20 River Road, Erwinna. (610) 294-8106.

The Adirondacks meet the Southwest in this expanding restaurant and pub put together by a Dutch chef. The result is a spectacular setting, one worthy of the photo layout in Restaurant/Hotel Design International magazine shortly after it opened. It has also proven quite popular for good country fare at pleasant prices.

Johan Van der Linden, who used to be at the old Wilson Inn in Lambertville, N.J., opened his own restaurant here in 1991. It's notable for the unique vaulted ceiling, extravagantly colorful in yellow, red, turquoise and black – the design taken from an Alaskan Indian blanket. Long, narrow mirrors atop the wood wainscoting that doubles as the back for banquettes are bordered by Adirondack scenes. Sturdy Adirondack chairs are at green-clothed tables covered, alas, by glass tops.

Adirondack motif prevails at Bucks Bounty.

It's a trendy, unexpected setting for food that Johan calls American-continental with German influences and Italian specialties. He's at his best at dinner, when the menu is nicely priced from $9.95 for a couple of pastas to $15.95 for grilled New York strip steak with herbed butter. Crispy roasted Long Island duck with his own Chinese barbecue sauce and chicken dijonnaise are signature dishes. A pub menu, an abbreviated version of the dinner menu, is served on weekdays. In either case, you might start with sautéed brie, onion soup au gratin or wilted red leaf salad with feta cheese and sesame seeds. Favorite endings are peach cobbler, crème brûlée and shoofly pie.

The new weekend brunch menu is more enticing than was the fare offered at lunch the weekday we ate here. One of us had a good tuna salad sandwich ($3.50), while the other got the soup and half-sandwich special ($3.50). The caramelized onion soup was tasty and the half liverwurst sandwich with a big slice of raw onion more than substantial. But we would have preferred some of the interesting luncheon salads (like oyster caesar or smoked turkey and ham) that had been added at our latest visit.

Ever-improving, Johan has converted the old section with a take-out window into a cozy little pub. The former bar at the other side of the restaurant was to become a combination coffee, wine and juice bar.

Lunch, Tuesday-Friday 11:30 to 4; dinner, Tuesday-Sunday 5:30 to 10 (pub menu only, Tuesday-Thursday); weekend brunch, 8:30 to 3.

Diversions

The Delaware River and the adjacent Delaware Canal provide diversion enough for most. For action, New Hope and its galleries, shops and nightlife are just down River Road – but all that is a different world.

Walk the Towpath. The best way to experience both river and canal and their surroundings is to walk the towpath, which also is used by joggers and the occasional bicyclist. Start in Lumberville at the footbridge to Bull's Island, a New Jersey state park. The gardens, back yards and architecture of English-type manor houses edify and intrigue. A footbridge leads to the Cuttalossa Inn, where the outdoor terrace begs one to pause for lunch or a drink. For the makings of a picnic, cross the highway bridge at Centre Bridge to Stockton, N.J., to pick up food to go at Errico's Market and a bottle of wine at the well-stocked Phillips wine store. Not far downriver is Phillips Mill, an ever-so-British looking cluster of stone houses hugging the River Road. The old miller's house and surroundings were taken over by artists around 1900, thus launching New Hope's reputation as an art colony. The 1756 grist mill has been preserved by the Phillips Mill Community Association as a landmark, cultural center and site for its highly regarded annual fall art exhibition. Not far beyond is Lenteboden, the business and residence of Charles Mueller, the bulb specialist whose gardens – lavish with daffodils, tulips and hyacinths – herald the arrival of spring. Like almost everything else along the towpath, they're free and open for the exploring.

River Pursuits. Canoeing, rafting and tubing are so popular here that the Point Pleasant Canoe and Tube enterprise has become the East's largest water recreation facility. Tubing is its biggest operation, with up to 3,500 people a day renting inner tubes for floats of three to six miles. Canoeists are transported up to Tinicum, Upper Black Eddy or Riegelsville for trips downriver of six to twelve miles. The New Hope Mule Barge Co. hauls tourists on mule-drawn barges along the old Delaware Canal past Colonial homes, artists' workshops, gardens and countryside from downtown New Hope north to the Route 202 bridge and back.

Parks. The entire River Road area is so utterly unspoiled that it seems like one big park. And so some of it is. The aforementioned towpath is part of the **Delaware Canal State Park,** a 60-mile strip following the canal along Bucks County's riverfront. **Tinicum Park** offers picnicking, boating, hiking and more on its 126 acres beside the river in Tinicum, just north of Erwinna; here also is the historic **Erwin-Stover House,** which is open to visitors on weekends. **Ralph Stover State Park,** just north of Point Pleasant, has 45 hilly acres for fishing, hiking and swimming along Tohickon Creek. It adjoins **Tohickon Valley County Park,** one of the largest of Bucks County's parks.

Shopping. A complex of buildings centered by a picturesque red wood and field-stone barn built in 1749 is part of **River Road Farms** in Erwinna. The barn houses **Chachka,** one of our favorite stores anywhere. An interesting gift shop, it has been accenting more unusual food items (many Thai and Indonesian) lately. "People say they have to go to many different stores in New York to find what we have here," says proprietor Dick deGroot, who makes the wild and wonderful Gentleman Farmer preserves and relishes at his home next door. Chachka also hosts outdoor festivals with seasonal food and entertainment on certain weekends. The **Lumberville Store** is an institution in Lumberville, a country store with a post office, book section, sundries, antiques and a deli (great sandwiches). Small antiques shops are scattered here and there along the River Road. If you want still more shopping, just cross the river to the New Jersey side (Milford, Frenchtown and Stockton) or head down river to New Hope.

Sand Castle Winery, 755 River Road, Erwinna, (800) 722-9463. Two brothers from Czechoslovakia moved to a 72-acre estate above the Golden Pheasant Inn to grow vinifera grapes – the "noble vines of Europe," they call them – in the old-world tradition. Paul and Joe Maxian offer wine tastings beneath a tent canopy and in a reception trailer on a hilltop overlooking the countryside. They lead tours through their underground wine cellar and show pictures of their planned winery building patterned after a 10th-century Czech castle. The winery started production of riesling and chardonnay before adding expensive barrel-aged cabernet sauvignon and pinot noir, priced at $18 and $19 respectively.

Extra-Special _____

Bucks County Covered Bridges.
Nostalgia and romance are triggered by covered bridges that preserve a vanishing piece of Americana. Bucks County still has eleven of its original 36 covered bridges, all excellent examples of the lattice-truss construction patented in 1820 by Ithiel Town, a Connecticut architect. The oldest bridge was built in 1832. Five of the bridges are in the River Road area between Point Pleasant and Frenchtown. One at Uhlerstown spans the Delaware Canal; the shortest, at Erwinna, crosses Lodi Creek. Another was relocated for preservation purposes but burned in 1991. A Bucks County Tourist Commission brochure touts the virtues of covered bridges and provides a detailed map for a day's tour. Make a wish as you enter a wishing bridge or steal a kiss on one of the kissing bridges.

Sign tells story of the swallows of Lambertville at Delaware River entrance to town.

Lambertville, N.J.
On the Verge of Chic

Some time ago, the New York Times referred to a village of our acquaintance as "on the verge of chic." The same could be said today for Lambertville.

This sleepy New Jersey river town, a product of the Industrial Revolution and the 19th century, languished until lately. It was at the edge of chic, overshadowed by New Hope, Pa., its better-known neighbor across the Delaware River. History, artists and an enduring quaintness gave New Hope the best of everything. But Lambertville? This was the town through which New Yorkers had to pass to get to New Hope. Even that need was obviated after the new Route 202 toll bridge bypassed Lambertville.

Time was on Lambertville's side, however. The three A's – arts, authors and antiques – strained New Hope's limits and spilled into Lambertville. They found a receptive host, one untouched by the 20th-century building boom and urban redevelopment.

The first restaurant of note opened in 1980; the first B&B in 1983. Next a group of investors turned the old train station into a restaurant and built an adjacent luxury inn-hotel. Suddenly, Lambertville was "in." Now its main streets are chock-a-block antiques stores and art galleries. It has a wider variety of quality restaurants than does New Hope. Visitors are discovering the advantages of staying in Lambertville – close to New Hope, but without the crowds, the expense, the hassle.

Lambertville has its own identity, that of an emerging town of 3,900 on the way to becoming the little city it calls itself. In 1994 for the first time, its Chamber of Commerce even produced a helpful brochure to guide tourists. Just up river is Stockton, itself a class act, centered by the old inn with the wishing well immortalized in the song, "There's a Small Hotel." Beyond is Rosemont, a crossroads hamlet where an old chicken farm has been turned into a complex of business enterprises, one of them advertising the largest selection of handcrafted furniture in the country. Most of the area's riverfront with its parallel Delaware & Raritan Canal has been turned into the longest and narrowest strip of state parkland in the nation.

Although Lambertville is on the verge of chic, its surroundings are about as rural as they get in the nation's most densely populated state.

Inn Spots

The Inn at Lambertville Station, 11 Bridge St., Lambertville, N.J. 08530. (609) 397-4400 or (800) 524-1091.

A group of investors spent more than $3 million to build this architecturally impressive, luxury hotel-inn on abandoned land that had been an eyesore along the Delaware River.

Check-in is at a counter resembling the ticket office of an old train station, but you'll probably be awed more by the soaring, three-story lobby, which is higher than it is wide. Prized antiques are in the 45 guest rooms and suites, each named for a major city and decorated accordingly by an antiques dealer who spared no expense.

Ours was the corner New York Suite, high in the trees above a rushing waterfall that lulled us to sleep. There were chocolates at bedside, the bathroom had a whirlpool tub and a basket of good toiletries, and around the L-shaped room were heavy mahogany furniture, leather chairs facing the fireplace and TV, handsome draperies, ornate mirrors and fine art. Afternoon tea or drinks from an honor bar are available in the lobby or on the adjacent creekside deck, a shady refuge in the trees. A small continental breakfast with carrot-nut muffins arrived at our door with the New York Times the next morning.

The large Riverside Room, facing the river with windows on three sides, is used for Sunday brunch ($18.95 for quite a spread).

Doubles, $90 to $110; suites with fireplaces and whirlpool baths, $150.

Chimney Hill Farm, 207 Goat Hill Road, Lambertville 08530. (609) 397-1516.

Three deer were grazing in the back yard the day we revisited this rural retreat. "There are lots more," said Terry Ann Anderson, new owner and innkeeper with her husband Rich. "They ate every chrysanthemum and daisy off our porch this fall. We also have a brood of wild turkeys, rabbits and big fat groundhogs."

The animals are appropriate at this opulent manor house, sequestered atop a wooded hill beyond a high-rent residential area on the southeast edge of Lambertville. It was once a working farm, and the restored gardens put in by former owner Edgar W. Hunt, an internationally known attorney, are quite spectacular in season.

The inside of the house borders on the spectacular as well. Vacant when it was acquired by two aspiring innkeepers in 1988, they first put it on display as a designer

show house to benefit the Delaware River Mill Society. The designers took everything with them but the living room wallpaper, however.

The former owners used their own restoration and design instincts to good advantage to create a B&B with great potential. They lost interest and ultimately the house to bankruptcy. It was left to the Andersons, who moved here in July 1994 from northern New Jersey to put the B&B back

Manor house of Chimney Hill Farm is part of what once was a working farm.

on track. All it took was live-in owners who decided this was to be their home, an infusion of money, a woman's touch and plenty of TLC.

The Andersons inherited most of the furnishings for the eight guest rooms, all but one with king or queensize beds and private baths and two in the north wing with fireplaces. Each is awash in splashy fabrics, all Schumacher or Colfax & Fowler, we were told. The smallest room has space enough only for a double bed and one chair. The rear Terrace Room is bigger with tapestry fabrics, kingsize bed, a large bath with clawfoot tub and its own balcony. We liked the looks of the Hunt Room master suite, where the covers and canopy on the step-up queen bed match the gently swagged curtains, and the sofa and the oriental carpet pick up the theme. As we peeked into the Library Room at the end of the North Wing, a large space with a queensize canopy bed, fireplace and two armchairs, a departing honeymooner returned to snap a photo. "We want to take every inch of this house with us," he said.

We also liked the looks of the sunken main-floor sun porch, with windows on three sides and floors, fireplace and walls of fieldstone. Warmth and color come from ficus trees and the chintz that covers four wicker loveseats angled around a huge glass cocktail table. The splashy sun porch makes the attractive living room pale in comparison.

Breakfast is served by candlelight at six tables for two in the 1820 dining room that was the original room in the house (the wings were added by attorney Hunt in 1927). Terry offers fresh fruit, cereals and plenty of homemade pastries, from muffins with farm-made raspberry jam to croissants filled with fruit or cream cheese. Baked french toast is one of the additional treats on Sunday mornings. In the afternoon, port and cream sherry await in the butler's pantry, where tea, cider and snacks also are available. The Andersons have added bathroom toiletries, and guests find in each room a "gift snack pack" with candy, goldfish and peanuts.

The new owners had their eyes on the rear carriage house, which they planned to renovate in 1995 to provide four more guest rooms. They hoped to convert the barn into a conference and entertainment center, and to add a tropical hot tub in the rear greenhouse.

Doubles, $110 to $145.

The Stockton Inn, 1 Main St., Stockton 08559. (609) 397-1250 or (800) 545-3804.

You want a sense of history plus contemporary comforts? At many inns, the two are mutually exclusive. The Stockton Inn offers both.

History it has in spades, this stone edifice with the pillared veranda dating to 1710. Remember the Rodgers and Hart Broadway show song, "There's a Small Hotel?" This is that small hotel, the lyrics were written here and guests still make wishes at *the* wishing well.

Band leader Paul Whiteman used to sign off his national radio shows from Trenton with the announcement that he was going to the Stockton Inn for dinner (one of the fascinating murals in the dining room pictures Whiteman fallen from his horse on his way home to nearby Rosemont after imbibing too much). In 1935, the inn gained national fame as the press headquarters during the Lindbergh kidnapping trial.

Besides making history, the inn preserves it in its overnight accommodations. The three rooms and eight suites all have private baths, lavish period furnishings and color TV, and most have queensize canopy beds and fireplaces. We were comfortably ensconced in the upstairs suite in the Federal House, one of three outbuildings holding the bulk of the accommodations. It was handsomely appointed in deep greens, with the fabric on the canopy and bedspread matching the curtains and the loveseat. A fireplace, a selection of timely magazines, a mini-refrigerator and a basket with packets of instant coffee, teabags and broth were among the amenities. More extras were found in the bathroom, where another basket offered everything from the usual shampoos and lotions to mouth wash, a mending kit and a toothbrush.

"New Yorkers love the creaky floors," innkeeper Andy McDermott said when the floor underneath the thick carpeting squeaked with every footstep as we toured the Colligan Suite, upstairs in the inn. It and the adjacent Stockton Suite share access to the front balcony, from which guests get a straight shot down Bridge Street to the Delaware River and can see most of the goings-on in town.

The popular Loft Suite in the rear of the stone 1832 Wagon House is large and airy, thanks to high windows and a vaulted ceiling from which hangs a brass chandelier with a dimmer switch. Rich Williamsburg colors, striking trim (blue here, black in the Carriage House), good art works and mahogany furniture are the rule. The range of accommodations includes a basement kitchenette suite running the length of the Federal House, entered through a rear garden.

Next on innkeeper McDermott's agenda was conversion of the Victorian gingerbread house beside the inn into four more luxurious suites in 1995.

A continental breakfast buffet is put out in the inn's dining room. We enjoyed quite a spread of fresh fruit (kiwi, strawberries, pineapple and cantaloupe), carafes of juices and an array of pastries from croissants to muffins to nut bread.

Doubles, $85 to $125; suites, $150 to $165.

The Woolverton Inn, 6 Woolverton Road, Stockton 08559. (609) 397-0802.

Built in 1792 as a manor house by pioneer industrialist John Prall Jr., whose mill is nearby, this is a B&B on six bucolic acres – where curious black-faced sheep and goats may mosey up to your car from a field next to the parking area. Its location on a country road, atop a hill away from the river, guarantees a noiseless night.

Elizabeth and Michael Palmer, new owners in 1994, have been reconfiguring and upgrading eight bedrooms in the main house, all now with private baths – the lack thereof had been a major shortcoming since we stayed here a decade ago. The Palmers redecorated all the rooms, adding mostly king and queensize beds. Each room has been furnished to reflect the personality and era of its namesake, a past owner or local figure. Thick soft towels, monogrammed terrycloth robes and extra pillows are pluses.

Ornate railings mark facade of The Woolverton Inn.

The Michener Suite is particularly handsome with a kingsize four-poster canopied in a striking fabric, a few wood side chairs, a fireplace and a large bathroom with dressing area. The new Pearl S. Buck Suite has incorporated what had been the inn's smallest bedroom and now claims a jacuzzi tub, a king bed and fireplace. A third bedroom on the second floor opens onto the front balcony. Five more rooms occupy the third floor. Guests seeking seclusion might opt for the George Washington Suite or the small Martha Washington Room in the former barn that also contains the innkeepers' quarters.

Guests have the run of the grounds, plus an elegant large living room with a portrait of Michael's mother over the fireplace. Family heirlooms have been interspersed among the sofas, wing chairs and oriental rugs that testify to the Federal period and the traditional style of what Michael calls "a classic country home." The dining room is big enough for the banquets and wedding parties to which the inn caters. Elizabeth and her husband, who works in Princeton, offer a full breakfast daily rather than just on weekends as in the past. Fresh orange juice, baked apple and a vegetable frittata with fried potatoes and bacon were served the day of our visit. Pocket french toast, stuffed with cream cheese and walnuts and sautéed on the grill, was on the next day's docket. In the afternoon, tea and cocoa or lemonade are served with homemade cookies.

Doubles, $95 to $160.

Coryell Bed & Breakfast, 44 Coryell St., Lambertville 08530. (609) 397-8292.
Gingerbread trim and a small front porch holding an Adirondack twig couch grace this 1870 brick Victorian house, spiffed up by new owners Denise Kortunik and Garry Duda. The interior is eclectic and quite unusual, much of it with an arty, oriental theme. The decor is the work of live-wire innkeeper Denise, a counselor by trade and an interior designer by heart. "Our guests get some of both," she advises.

The partners offer three "suites" with queensize beds and private baths. One bedroom on the first floor front comes with poster bed, armoire, chaise lounge and a long, narrow bathroom running along the side of the house. Overhead on the second floor is another bedroom notable for bright colors, floral prints and oriental rugs. A genuine suite has a small sitting room with a wicker loveseat and chair and a bedroom beyond, with an English pine bed, another wicker chair and a green Korean kimono displayed on the wall. A fourth bedroom with private bath on the third floor was in the works for late 1995.

Interesting art prevails throughout the house. A door between living room and dining room is painted as a trompe-l'oeil bookcase, realistic as all get-out down to the copy of the New York Times on the bottom shelf.

Breakfast here is different from those B&Bs where guests eat what the innkeeper chooses, Denise says. "We tell people what we can serve and then they make a choice." Fresh fruit, blended juices, blended Italian-American-African coffee, cereals and breakfast meats accompany such main dishes as blueberry pancakes and eggs benedict – "basically whatever anyone wants." Denise adds that Garry, who's involved in building construction by day, is a good cook who's known for "outrageous omelets."

Doubles, $120; suite, $130.

York Street House, 42 York St., Lambertville 08530. (609) 397-3007.

This large Georgian brick home was opened as Lambertville's first B&B in 1983 after it had been glamorized as a designers' show house. It wasn't the first time it had received wide publicity – the Massey Mansion was featured in 1911 in House and Garden magazine shortly after a local coal merchant had built it as a 25th wedding anniversary gift for his wife.

Today's visitors are greeted by an imposing brick mansion set back from the street with pillared verandas on the front and side. Mercer tiles compliment the working fireplaces in the main-floor common rooms and an original Waterford chandelier glitters over chintz sofas and chairs in the elegant living room. Besides the living room, big enough for a couple of separate sitting areas, guests can spread out in front of the book shelves or TV set in a cherry-paneled library evocative of a London club.

Crystal knobs open the walnut doors to the six large guest rooms. Three on the second floor have private baths and three on the third floor share two baths. One favorite has a lace canopy queen bed, two high wing chairs in the corner, an extra sink in another corner and – a startling sight in the bathroom – a free-standing toilet in the front bay window of what once was a dressing room.

A full breakfast is served at white-clothed tables in the formal dining room. The fare could be bacon and scrambled eggs with English muffins, french toast or pancakes.

The welcome here is more personal than in the past, thanks to resident innkeepers Jeff and Claire Shoemaker. They became partners with his uncle, James Bulger, the inn's founder and also owner of the Swan Hotel. Jeff is a local house painter and Claire is a nurse who commutes to Philadelphia, but they're in residence here and one or the other is generally on hand.

Doubles, $80 to $100.

The Bridgestreet House, 75 Bridge St., Lambertville 08530. (609) 397-2503.

A pair of pre-Victorian structures started in the 1980s as a restaurant with a B&B adjunct. The restaurant failed in 1991, and the establishment was taken over by couple who moved their retail Heritage Lighting operation into the old restaurant and ran the B&B for a period. Now it has a new owner, Sharon Lykins from northern New Jersey, who offers seven cozy guest rooms on three floors of the B&B house.

Four bedrooms have private baths and three share. Each is air-conditioned and has thick carpeting and remote-control TV. Sharon and her husband Randy have redone one bedroom with a queensize bed; the rest have doubles. Victorian antiques embellish

Chef-owner Bobby Trigg takes break on Delaware River near The Ferry House.

the rooms. A couple have beamed ceilings, and floral comforters and draperies brighten one room. The rear Garden Room has a private bath and a private entrance off a small stone courtyard. Elaborate stenciling decorates the doorways off the narrow corridors

Chocolate mints and a decanter of brandy await guests in each room. In the morning, Sharon sets out a continental breakfast buffet in the small parlor. It consists of juice, seasonal fruit and homemade muffins.

Doubles, $75 to $95. No smoking.

Dining Spots

The Ferry House, 21 Ferry St., Lambertville. (609) 397-9222.

The restored 18th-century edifice at the site where the original Coryell ferry crossed the Delaware River to New Hope houses the newest culinary gem in Lambertville. The interior is sleekly contemporary in black and white, as evidenced by the table for two on full display in the window of what used to be the front entry.

We were lucky enough to have lunch here (since discontinued, but enough to testify to chef-owner Bobby Trigg's culinary prowess). One of us enjoyed a roasted red pepper, prosciutto, marinated goat cheese and arugula sandwich on toasted focaccia. The other was amazed by a salmon BLT with ginger and cilantro, an explosion of tastes lurking between slices of a man-size English muffin. Each was artistically presented on parsley-flecked plates with crispy sweet potato fries and garnishes of fresh strawberries and raspberries. Both were representative of what you might expect at Sunday brunch, a cornucopia of exotic dishes priced from $7.50 for grand marnier french toast to $16.50 for grilled baby lamb chops with watercress and feta cheese salad.

The exotica reaches its zenith at dinner. You could start with smoked salmon, asparagus and bay scallops wrapped in puff pastry, resting on a cilantro and corn coulis, or duck confit wrapped in a green onion crêpe with an avocado and lime vinaigrette. Expect main courses ($16 to $23) like pan-seared rare tuna on a fried artichoke and cherry tomato compote with a curry-basil butter sauce or grilled pork loin marinated in

Samuel Adams ale, set on a poached pear and kale sauté with a caramelized fennel coulis.

The dessert tray includes an acclaimed crème brûlée, lemon mousse cake, mocha swirl cheesecake, caramel nut torte and a signature miniature bittersweet chocolate canoe (patterned after the restaurant's logo) filled with small scoops of chocolate ice cream and laden with strawberries and raspberries.

At our latest visit, the energetic young owner had just received the zoning approvals necessary to open an upstairs bistro serving a lighter menu. He also stages frequent special events, ranging from a chile pepper fiesta (the dessert was soft banana taco with papaya and strawberry salsa and black pepper ice cream) to a shellfish and truffles dinner.

Dinner, Wednesday-Saturday 5:30 to 9:30 or 10; Sunday, brunch noon to 3, dinner 4:30 to 8:30. BYOB. No smoking.

Anton's at the Swan, 43 South Main St., Lambertville. (609) 397-1960.

Shortly after it opened in 1990 in the Swan Hotel, this was picked by the New York Times as one of the year's ten best restaurants in New Jersey. It's still going strong, thanks to the inspiration of talented chef Anton Dodel, who leases the space from Swan owner James Bulger.

Anton is, in his words, spontaneous and eclectic. He's also versatile; at our latest visit, he was sprawled on the floor preparing to rehang curtains an hour before a special wine-tasting dinner. His short menu changes monthly. We'd gladly have tried any of his seven November entrées ($19 to $27), but particularly the roast cod on ginger-pumpkin sauce, the sautéed duck with juniper, the grilled venison loin with cranberries, and the grilled rack of lamb with goat cheese flan. Starters ($7.50 to $12) included salad of wild turkey and avocado, mussels with saffron and brandy, and sautéed foie gras with persimmon.

Desserts ($6) always include something chocolate and always a flan, but you might find a poached pear in caramel sauce or a cornbread pudding.

The backdrop for these culinary triumphs is a subdued room with paneled wainscoting, a wall of mirrors, step-down windsor chairs and white-linened tables topped with candles in hurricane chimneys. Anton rebuilt the hotel's kitchen in order to produce a sophisticated menu and style, "one like a well-established restaurant in France." He cooks more casual fare for the hotel's bar, where you might enjoy penne with parmesan cheese, swiss chard and cream or grilled sweet sausage on a black bean and red pepper salad ($6.50 to $13).

Dinner, Wednesday-Saturday 6 to 10, Sunday 4:30 to 8. Bar, Tuesday-Sunday 5 to 11.

Hamilton's Grill Room, 8 Coryell St., Lambertville. (609) 397-4343.

Former Broadway set designer Jim Hamilton and his daughter Melissa opened this little gem that used to be Gerard's, hidden at the end of an alley in the Porkyard complex beside the canal and towpath. Jim, an architect who designs restaurants, installed an open grill beside the entrance and built the wood-fired adobe pizza oven himself. Melissa moved on in 1994, turning over the Mediterranean grill concept to executive chef Marc BrownGold, who moved here from New York's Tavern on the Green.

Marc created the option of grazing portions to let weekday diners try "a little of everything." Most items are available in standard and smaller portions (at about half the price). You might start with Tuscan roasted garlic soup or a salad of belgian endive, radicchio, gorgonzola and pears. Then it's on to an adobe oven pizza ($6.25), or perhaps penne with spinach, anchovies, mussels and saffron. Or graze with half por-

Wall of mirrors and paneling are backdrop for dining at Anton's at the Swan.

tions of entrées ($13.25 to $19.25) like grilled fillet of salmon with roasted green tomatoes and ginger or grilled ribeye steak with crisped leeks and onion rings.

The menu is similar but pricier ($15.50 to $28) on weekends, when the open grill yields things like rack of lamb with roasted garlic and mixed grill of quail, duck breast and rabbit sausage with macerated figs and apples in red wine.

Our convivial meal began with grilled shrimp with anchovy butter and a crab cake on wilted greens and sweet red pepper sauce, chosen among appetizers priced from $5.75 to $8.25. Main courses were an exceptional grilled duck on bitter greens with pancetta and honey glaze and sautéed calves liver with pancetta, scallions and wine. The oversize plates were filled with fanned razor-thin sliced potatoes and grilled zucchini and green and red peppers. The signature grappa torta and the grand marnier cheesecake were good desserts, and two biscotti came with the bill.

Patrons dine at tables rather close together in the grill room, the Bishop's Room beneath angels and clouds surrounding a huge gilt mirror on the ceiling, beside a sensuous mural of a nude in the dining gallery and, in season, outdoors around the fountain on the courtyard.

Hamilton's is BYOB with a twist. It serves its regular menu weekends at the **Wine Bar** annex, a small house across the courtyard for folks who want full liquor service from the adjacent Boat House wine bar. In the main grill, the white wine we toted was stashed in a pail full of ice, and red wines and even water are poured in large handblown globes made locally.

Dinner nightly, 6 to 10 or 11, Sunday 5 to 10. BYOB.

Manon, 19 North Union St., Lambertville. (609) 397-2596.

An air of whimsy reigns here, from the colorful exterior of orange and blue-green with gingerbread trim to the pictures drawn by customers and posted on the front of the pastry case. Patrons doodle with an assortment of crayons at each table as they await the fine south-of-France fare furnished by young chef-owner Jean-Michel Dumas, who grew up in Provençe. He and his American wife Susan gave a French name to the 32-seat charmer they opened in 1990 in the tiny space vacated by The Cafe, which moved to Rosemont, near Stockton.

The downtown storefront has tables rather close together, outfitted with white butcher paper over white cloths. Besides a basket of crayons, each has a plant that changes with the seasons and a candle in a tall hurricane chimney. But there's room left for the gutsy food that is served in robust portions.

Jean-Michel, who previously was a chef at the Inn at Phillips Mill in New Hope, relies on fresh ingredients cooked simply. The dinner menu usually starts with his trademark anchovy relish and an assortment of raw vegetables ($6), the house pâté, or one of the three salads (goat cheese, duck with cider vinegar, or watercress with pear, endive, walnuts and roquefort). Soup of the day could be garlicky mussel or pistou ($4).

Among the eight entrées ($16.50 to $22) are white bouillabaisse, grilled salmon with sorrel cream sauce, breast of chicken with garlic sauce, calves liver with a shallot-wine sauce, sautéed lamb chops with garlic confit and tournedos with a mustard sauce. Desserts include the classic crème caramel, tarte tatin, chocolate mousse, marjolaine and nougat ice cream with raspberry sauce.

Similar fare is offered in three courses at a prix-fixe Sunday brunch ($15.50).

Dinner, Wednesday-Sunday 5:30 to 9 or 10; Sunday brunch, 11 to 2:30. No credit cards. BYOB.

The Stockton Inn, 1 Main St., Stockton. (609) 397-1250.

The food at this venerable inn has improved markedly since innkeeper Andy McDermott, a former New York restaurant manager and a food and wine connoisseur, took over in 1989. He and chef Stuart Pellegrino present a contemporary American menu that mixes the traditional with the trendy – prime rib and Maine lobsters from the inn's own tank along with grilled salmon with a shallot-zinfandel butter on braised vegetables and roasted rack of lamb with minted apricot chutney. National recognition came in 1994 when they were invited to prepare a special dinner at the James Beard House Foundation in New York.

Dinner appetizers ($6.75 to $9.95) include wild mushroom strudel, smoked brook trout and crab cakes with two sauces. We found the trio of salmon (vodka-cured gravlax, hot smoked salmon from the inn's smoker and salmon rillettes) a sensational presentation, thanks to an assortment of sauces, capers, red onions and delicious baguette toasts. We also liked the special salad, an arrangement of arugula, goat cheese, roasted red peppers and sundried tomatoes with a complex, smoky taste.

Among entrées ($16.75 to $26.75), the boned and rolled chicken stuffed with mushroom duxelles and flanked by an array of green beans, carrots, braised red cabbage and layered potatoes was excellent. So was the veal sauté with sundried tomatoes and roasted garlic. Rain forest crunch ice cream with fresh raspberries was a refreshing ending.

The setting is comfortable and romantic in six historic dining rooms seating a total of 175. We particularly enjoy the intimate front rooms with fireplaces, crisp white tablecloths and candles, and subtly illuminated local murals on every wall. Painted by artists during the Depression in exchange for room and board, they are quite remarkable. In season, there's dining on five outside terraces amidst two waterfalls and a pond stocked with golden trout, near the wishing well made famous by the Rodgers and Hart song. The Old World Garden Bar on the upper terrace has a dance floor. The main inn has a glamorous bar and a cozy pub in front.

Murals enhance Stockton Inn dining room.

Fireside dining at Stockton Inn.

Lunch, Monday-Saturday 11:30 to 3:30; dinner, Monday-Thursday 4:30 to 9:30, weekends 5 to 10; Sunday, brunch 11 to 2:30, dinner 3:30 to 9.

Rick's, 19 South Main St., Lambertville. (609) 397-0051.

The decor of this new storefront restaurant is negligible (pine paneling, a linoleum floor and tables topped by red and white checked oilcloths). And there's no menu – the night's fare is scrawled on a couple of blackboards. But the place is packed with people who appreciate good, true food at fair prices.

A couple of the town's best chefs tipped us off to what was going on at Rick Buscavage's new place. He'd tired of his role as a partner in a large Japanese restaurant on Philadelphia's waterfront. He bought this hole-in-the-wall restaurant of 35 years, moved with his wife Kathy into space upstairs, and started serving up his favorite Italian "comfort" foods.

The blackboard descriptions are deceptively straightforward, but the delivery is worthy of many a highfalutin' northern Italian trattoria charging twice the price. A dish of chopped tomatoes with arugula and herbed olive oil arrived with Italian peasant bread as our bottle of wine was uncorked and we studied our options. There were a ravioli sampler, an arugula salad with aged provolone, caesar salad; pastas like tortellini alfredo, penne arrabbiata, potato gnocchis with gorgonzola sauce, and spaghetti with mushrooms and leeks, and heavier dishes like veal parmesan on pasta or chicken bolognese on spinach fettuccine, priced up to $15.95. "I add a lot of seafood, especially shellfish, on the weekends," Rick said later.

This was early in the week, so we sampled Kathy's antipasti ($7), an array of Italian meats and cheeses, most of which we took to our cooler to make excellent sandwiches the next day, followed by a salad of baby field greens tossed with goat cheese, hazelnuts and roasted red pepper dressing ($5.50). Then we shared pencil points (penne) with prosciutto, roasted garlic, asparagus and mushrooms, a heaping portion for $10.95. The dinner bill for two totaled $25, not counting the sensational tirami su that Rick had just made and insisted we try, over our faint protests.

Lambertville Station restaurant is illuminated at night.

Rick's is that kind of place, totally unpretentious but with class. The crowd is young and convivial, the owner tablehops between or after cooking stints and everyone seems to know each other, or does by the end of the evening. Remarkably, Rick does almost everything (except service) himself. Kathy works a fulltime job but comes in to prepare her antipasti and give him a hand in the restaurant. And a waitress writes the menu on the blackboard.

Dinner, Wednesday-Sunday 5:30 to 9. BYOB. No credit cards.

De Anna's, 18 South Main St., Lambertville. (609) 397-8957.

Here's another small, convivial place in which De Anna Menzel continues the culinary magic launched by her predecessor, Paul Blasenheim. She took over the former Chef Paul's in 1990 upon his retirement. The only physical change involved partitioning off the open kitchen from which Paul liked to converse with customers. De Anna confesses to being too shy to be part of the dining scene; her statement is her food, which is robust Italian.

The menu lists a dozen homemade pasta entrées, from $8.75 for pasta with marinara sauce to $15.25 for pasta with calamari fra diavolo. We were smitten by two flavorful pastas, one with prosciutto and peas and the other with sundried tomato and pinenut cream sauce, and also a couple of gutsy breads. The portions were ample and the leftovers made a great lunch the next day.

Desserts, for those who leave room to indulge, include blackberry jam tart, mocha fudge cake, ricotta cheesecake and Italian ice.

The place couldn't be smaller – six tables seating twenty. Illumination is entirely by candles that flicker in hurricane lamps, reflecting on the glass tabletops. Big pillows and cushions rest on the long wall benches.

Dinner, Wednesday-Saturday 5:30 to 9:30 or 10, Sunday 5 to 9. BYOB. No credit cards. No smoking. .

Siam, 61 North Main St., Lambertville. (609) 397-8128.

Musical instruments from the hill tribes in northern Thailand and swaths of Thai fabrics on the high walls comprise the decor of this small Thai storefront eatery. It is owned by an American and her Thai husband, who cooks with his two brothers and a sister-in-law.

The food is true Thai, much loved by local foodies but vastly underrated, in the estimation of one of the area's top chefs. Much of it is flavored with garlic, onion, lime juice, lemon grass, ginger and hot pepper, and garnished with peanut and cucumber sauces. A special of fillet of red snapper with three-flavor sauce (sweet, sour and hot) with hot and sweet peppers was offered at one of our visits. Appetizers are in the $3.75 to $5.25 range; entrées, $8.50 to $13. The stir-fried pork with spicy peanut sauce on a bed of watercress sounds especially appealing. We also like the sound of crispy fish with ground pork, shiitake mushrooms and a ginger-scallion sauce. Sticky rice, kiwi and mango are among desserts.

The American serving staff helps decipher the ins and outs of the extensive menu embellished with the Thai script.

Lunch, Wednesday-Sunday 11 to 2; dinner, Tuesday-Saturday 6 to 9 or 10, Sunday 4 to 9. BYOB.

Lambertville Station, 11 Bridge St., Lambertville. (609) 397-8300.

Once abandoned, Lambertville's 2 1/2-story train station has taken on new life as a stylish Victorian restaurant and lounge. Diners on several levels of the glass-enclosed Platform Room can watch geese glide by and lights reflect off the waters of the Delaware & Raritan Canal. And the food is so good and fairly priced that we've returned more than once – an unusual occurrence given our normal wanderlust.

The first time, our party of four sampled the unusual appetizer of alligator strips ($7.95), which we dipped into a mustard and green peppercorn sauce – novel, and so popular that it's now a menu fixture. The rattlesnake Arizona that replaced it for awhile has been superseded by carpaccio of buffalo, also very good.

Among entrées ($11.25 to $19.95), the jambalaya was spicy, the boneless roast duck was properly crispy and came with a raspberry sauce and polenta, the medallions of buffalo sautéed with mushrooms and brandy cream sauce were more than ample and the veal medallions with jumbo shrimp in garlic butter were excellent. The honey-mustard dressing on the house spinach salad was super. Lime-almond cheesecake and key lime mousse pie were good desserts.

At our latest visit, a new chef had added a few innovations to the menu, among them grilled albacore tuna steak served over wilted spinach, potato pancakes served with grilled vegetables and tomato jam, and a main dish called lobster sweetbread salad — chilled lobster and sweetbreads with mushrooms and onions in a curry dressing, served over fresh spinach. Yum.

The Sunset on the Delaware special, served weekdays from 4 to 6:30, draws crowds for one of the best bargains around: soup or salad, entrée and dessert for $9.95. A Victorian lounge is on the mezzanine, and a dance club is on the lower level.

Lunch, Monday-Saturday 11:30 to 3; dinner, Monday-Thursday and Sunday 4 to 10, Friday and Saturday 5 to 11; Sunday brunch, 11 to 3.

Meil's Restaurant, Bridge and Main Streets, Stockton. (609) 397-8033.

Fresh American fare with an old-fashioned slant is the theme on the extensive menu at this cramped little bakery and restaurant, which moved from Lambertville to an old gasoline station here in 1990. On a warm winter's day, we eyed the picnic tables on the blacktop parking lot in front before deciding to sit inside. The decor is simple but jaunty: colorful balloon curtains over the windows, quilts on the walls (one wall has a montage of black muffin pans) and tables covered with mint-colored oilcloths.

We sampled a classic salad niçoise ($9.75) and a not-so-classic huevos rancheros ($9.95), with an unexpected and unwanted ton of chili between the eggs and the tortilla, and the accompanying salsa lacking fresh coriander. All kinds of interesting salads, sandwiches and egg dishes are featured at lunch, when something called "Day after Thanksgiving" – who doesn't know what that means? – may top off the menu at $9.95. Night brings some of the daytime fare as well as hefty pastas and main courses from $12.95 for meatloaf and mashed potatoes to $19.95 for shrimp in creamy peanut sauce with cucumber relish or grilled filet mignon with roasted garlic sauce. The fisherman's spaghetti is $17.95. If you don't feel like paying so much to eat in an old gas station, be advised that there are plenty of "supper" items, from chili with cornbread to country ham with baked beans, for under $10.

The place packs in the hungry. You also can get almost anything from buttermilk biscuits and blueberry muffins to beef stew and chicken pot pie to go. Exotic omelets are available at breakfast, served with seasoned red-skin potatoes and French bread.

Breakfast daily, 9 to 3; lunch, 11 to 3; dinner, 4:30 to 9. No credit cards.

The Cafe, Route 510 at 604, Rosemont. (609) 397-4097.

Lola Tindell and Peg Peterson moved their little cafe from Lambertville to Rosemont. In the 1885 old general store, they have a lot more room to offer "fresh food at its simple best," as their business card attests.

It's a casual, drop-in kind of place with bare floors, wooden tables and a mix of chair styles. Shelves are filled with the cookbooks they use, plus things for sale like gourmet foods, Botanicus soaps and striking ceramics, some done by one of the waitresses. A case along one side displays cheeses, desserts and baked goods. At night things get more formal with candles, cloth napkins and Lola's 1940s tablecloths on the tables.

Stop in for a breakfast burrito or the Adirondack breakfast, muesli and a bran muffin, which "gives you the strength to climb mountains," says the menu. Omelets include Russian peasant and rhubarb-ginger chutney with cream cheese. Potatoes from heaven are grilled with olive oil, rosemary, garlic, onion and cayenne. At lunch, we enjoyed an excellent turkey quesadilla ($6) and a hefty turkey sandwich on whole wheat ($4.75). The menu also offered vegetarian black bean chili, eggplant and mozzarella boboli, pasta with wild mushroom sauce and red pepper ravioli with garlic and olive oil, most in the $6 to $7 range.

At dinnertime, when entrées are priced from $13 to $16.50, you can still find sandwiches and omelets for much less. Try broiled flounder with herbs, chicken brazilia or pasta Wilhemina (named for the resident ghost) with chicken, broccoli, mushrooms and garlic. There's a large selection of natural soft drinks, mineral waters, teas, coffees and juices, and you may BYOB. Mocha pot du crème is a popular dessert, and Peg's cheesecakes (maybe rum raisin, apple cinnamon or lemon) are also in demand. An ethnic menu is offered on Wednesday nights.

Open weekdays at 8, weekends from 9, dinners Wednesday-Sunday to 9. Closed Monday. BYOB.

Victorian Gardens, 19 North Franklin St., Lambertville. (609) 397-0881.

The daintiest of tea rooms and bake shops, Victorian Gardens has seven tables topped with lace and teacups. Dried flowers abound, and the prevailing color is pink.

Margaret Powers and Sally Richardson offer continental breakfast (maybe English muffin, lemon curd, juice and coffee, $4.50), lunch like a ploughman's ($8.50) or a bacon, leek and apple pie and salad ($5) and, of course, a proper English afternoon tea. A $7.50 tab brings finger sandwiches (perhaps watercress, egg salad, cream cheese and walnut), scones, tea cakes and pastries, and a selection of teas served in china pots.

High tea (thank goodness they know the difference, because hardly anyone we have met does) is served on Fridays and Saturdays from 5 to 7:30 and, in the English style, includes such savories as Cornish pasties and Scotch eggs. There are a couple of soups for lunch every day, and lots of yummy baked goods like English toffee cookies, apricot-poppyseed scones and cranberry-raspberry coffee cake, and desserts like bread pudding and chocolate-banana cream cake.

Teas and tea cozies and pillows are for sale, and the partners do a lot of catering – how about a pre-wedding breakfast or a rehearsal high tea? Take out a Chelsea bun or a Bakewell tart to enjoy with a pot of tea at home.

Breakfast, Wednesday-Sunday, 7:30 to 11:30; lunch, 11:30 to 2:30; afternoon tea, 2:30 to 5; high tea, Friday and Saturday, 5 to 7:30. Closed Monday and Tuesday.

Diversions

A Lambertville phenomenon that's rather diverting is that of wine bars and pubs. Local entrepreneur James Bulger is the inspiration behind two, The Boat House and The Swan Hotel. **The Boat House** at 8 Coryell St. in the Porkyard is an elegant bar, where wines are featured by the glass and where the walls are paneled with old twelve-foot-high doors. Hamilton's Grill and the Boat House team up to provide food and drinks at the adjacent **Wine Bar.** Another good place for a drink and maybe a snack is **The Swan Hotel,** where the public rooms are filled with art and antiques. The main bar has comfortable leather chairs to sink into and a greenhouse wall looking out onto a small garden with a fountain, which is spotlit at night. A pianist plays show tunes on weekends. **The Inn of the Hawke,** 74 South Union St., is a neighborhood pub with a long horseshoe-shaped bar in the center room and a dining room looking onto a pleasant outdoor courtyard. Two young sisters have upgraded both the dining operation and the seven upstairs guest rooms, but this remains essentially a drinking establishment.

Walking Tour. The Lambertville Area Chamber of Commerce has published a walking tour for historic buildings and points of interest. The self-guided tour takes about 45 minutes. The map details 22 buildings, the oldest being the landmark Lambertville House, built in 1812 and for years abandoned and derelict but always rumored to be in line for renovations. Other buildings on the tour date to the late 19th century, and one (the Massey Mansion, now the York Street House B&B) is as recent as 1909. For more ancient history, visitors have only to walk across the bridge to New Hope, where 18th-century structures are much in evidence.

Delaware & Raritan Canal State Park. For nearly a century, the old D&R Canal was one of America's busiest. A 22-mile-long navigable feeder canal stretching from above Stockton at Raven Rock south through Lambertville to Trenton brought water from the Delaware River to the main canal, which ran from Bordentown to New Brunswick. The canal and its adjacent towpath by the Delaware River are now part of New Jersey's longest park. The towpath is a favorite of joggers and hikers.

The Prallsville Mills, Route 29, Stockton. Once a thriving little commercial center, the 18th-century mills were abandoned until 1973, when they were included on the National Register of Historic Places and became part of the D&R Canal State Park. Local citizens formed the Delaware River Mill Society to restore and interpret the mill site, which includes a four-story grist mill now used for periodic arts and crafts exhibits, lectures and concerts. Original mill machinery is on display.

Shopping. The old **Acme Market** and the **Ben Franklin Store** are two landmarks at either end of downtown Lambertville; they also happen to be the only chain stores here. Antiques stores and art galleries are proliferating lately along Bridge and North Union streets, where the shopping seems to get better every year. One of the nicest and newest is the avant-garde **A Mano Gallery** of contemporary crafts, an offshoot of one across the river in New Hope. **Something Different** bills itself as a year-round craft show with booths by more than 100 craftspeople; we admired some cute handpainted stools for children, the pillows emblazoned with cows or strawberries, and a bench with a Noah's ark design on the seat. Lots of flowery and garden-y things are featured at **Joanna Hearts,** whose stock runs from cards and teacups to fabrics and aromatic home accessories. Not to be missed is the **Porkyard,** a former sausage factory complex now given over to a restaurant, wine bar, **Porkyard Antiques** and **Coryell Gallery.** A rear terrace overlooks the Delaware River behind **Rivergate Books;** pick up a good book and start it outside. We like the cappuccino bar at **Lambertville Trading Co.** on Bridge Street, where Dean Stephens offers single or double espresso, cappuccino or mochaccino and the aromas are luscious. Pumpkin truffles, Bavarian espresso cake, black currant scones, oils and vinegars, cheeses and many varieties of coffee beans are available. Also on Bridge Street, **Pinch Penny & Dress Well** has some interesting casual clothes for men and women, including sportswear from Jackeroos. **Sojourner** is a treasure trove of gift items from around the world; a huge selection of dangling and colorful fish earrings was $10 a pair. **The 5 & Dime** on North Union Street specializes in toys, comic watches, plastic, paper, advertising and the like from 1900 to the '70s.

South of town is the **Laceworks,** a mill complex with a changing array of outlet stores, among them **The Gipsy Horse** for clothing and **The Gipsy Pony** for children's apparel, **Descamps** for French linens, towels and bathroom accessories, **Bucks Country Dry Goods** ("honest clothing" for men and women) and the **Cross-Country Ski Outfitter. Riverrun Gallery** here features contemporary art and was having a show of original artworks and crafts, all priced for under $300. **Prestige Antiques** operates out of a warehouse of a place. Antiquers in the know head for the **Lambertville Antique Market,** a mile and a half south of town along Route 29 and rated by the New York Times as one of the nation's ten best. This is where many local shopkeepers and innkeepers find their prizes, and dealers come from across the country to buy and sell authentic pieces. The market and its companion **Golden Nugget Antique Flea Market** operate weekends year-round.

Extra-Special _____

Cane Farm, Route 519, Rosemont. (609) 397-0606.

Three generations of Canes have transformed a 94-acre farm once home to half a million chickens into a furniture-making center and a complex of crafts workshops and retail showrooms in old chicken coops. The idea was that of Charles Cane, who gave up one of New Jersey's largest poultry operations for more versatile pursuits upon his retirement in 1965. The implementation was left to son Phil Cane, a woodworker at heart. Lately joined by his two sons, Phil and staff make much of the handcrafted furniture on display in a 580-foot-long showroom called **Cane Farm Furniture.** You'd never know these were once chicken houses and hatcheries, so complete is the transformation with windows along one side, carpeted or brick floors, and classical music playing. One old coop after another stretches nearly the length of two football fields, showing what Phil calls the largest collection of country furniture in America. The stock ranges from reproductions of antique tables, Shaker cupboards and windsor chairs to decoys, pewter, brass light fixtures, hunting prints and, lately, aviation art. Talented Phil, who restores old cars and builds racing boats, says he's also "a collector and an accumulator." He needs little persuasion to show his antique guns, Indian relics, historic documents, old postmarks and what-not in an area marked "Ephemeral and Miscellaneous." Showrooms open daily 10 to 5, Sunday 1 to 5.

Victoriana and verandas reign in typical Cape May scene along Jackson Street.

Cape May, N.J.
Grande Dame of Victoriana

Bed and breakfast as an American phenomenon got its start in Cape May. It also has been elevated here to its highest form.

Tom and Sue Carroll are credited with launching the phenomenon in the early 1970s when they turned the Windward House on Jackson Street into a Victorian B&B in this most Victorian of towns. Within two decades, the registered National Historic Landmark city spawned about 100 more B&Bs. And entrepreneurs in what they call the B&B capital of the United States were hosting seminars for prospective innkeepers from across the country. The phenomenon locally was raised to high art through formal teas, exotic breakfasts and even B&B house tours. Lately the inns' brochures have become state-of-the-art and as showy as the rest of the B&B experience here.

In the 19th century, America's first seaside resort was the playground for no fewer than five presidents, and Benjamin Harrison made Cape May his summer White House. Less than a century later, it was down at the heels when citizens banded together to save the landmark Emlen Physick House from demolition. Thus was born the Mid-Atlantic Center for the Arts (MAC), a community dynamo that not only promotes the arts but restores structures (the latest is the Cape May Point Lighthouse), stages tours and sponsors events. Thanks to MAC, Cape May seems to be a series of festivals all year long, from Crafts in the Winter to a Christmas Candlelight House Tour. Cape May's celebrated Victorian Week is now a ten-day extravaganza in mid-October.

The year-round population of 4,800 swells many-fold in the summer in this town at the southern end of a peninsula, a point actually below the Mason-Dixon Line, where the Atlantic Ocean meets the Delaware Bay. Visitors come to ogle the largest collection of authentic Victorian structures in the country, to relax on the beaches and enjoy the wildlife, including some of the East's best bird-watching. At the heart of it all are the inns and B&Bs, an integral part of the Cape May experience.

Inn Spots

Almost every house in Cape May's historic district seems to be turning into a B&B. In a whimsical turn, a sign in front of the 1882 Christopher Gallagher House notes its distinction from all its Jackson Street neighbors: "a private residence." Many B&Bs here require minimum stays of two to four nights, do not allow smoking inside, and access is only via push-button combination locks installed in the doors. Breakfasts tend to be lighter in summer, more formal and filling the rest of the year. The Cape May custom is for the innkeepers to serve – and often sit with – guests at breakfast, and later to help with dinner plans as they review the menus during afternoon tea or beverages.

The Mainstay Inn, 635 Columbia Ave., Cape May 08204. (609) 884-8690.

Preservationists Tom and Sue Carroll launched the B&B movement in Cape May at the Windward House, now under different ownership, and purchased the Mainstay in 1975. The 1872 Italianate villa was built by two gamblers as a gaming and entertainment club for gentlemen. It is one of the town's few Victorian structures that has gone through more than a century with no transitions. The fourteen-foot-high public rooms are lavishly furnished in Victoriana, right down to the sheet music on the piano. Especially notable is the ceiling of the entrance hall, where a stunning combination of seventeen wallpapers makes a beautiful pattern.

The twelve rooms with private baths in the inn and in the pleasant 1870 Cottage next door are named for famous visitors to Cape May. Lace curtains, stenciling, brass and iron bedsteads, armoires and rockers comprise the museum-quality decor. The Henry Ford room has its own small porch and the Bret Harte room (with many of his books in a case) opens onto the entire second-floor veranda. Climb a steep ladder with a wavering rope for a railing to the tower on the third floor, where, with cushions on two sides and windows on all four, you get a good view of the town. The inn and the cottage, both with wide verandas and green rocking chairs, are separated by a brick walk and a handsome trickling fountain. The front gardens are brilliant with flowers.

Four modern, two-bedroom suites with queensize beds are located in the Mainstay's new annex, the Officers' Quarters, a restored naval officers' building across the street. It's an appropriate addition, since Tom is a Naval Reserve officer. Each suite contains a spacious living room with a dining area, a loveseat facing the gas fireplace and the TV in a corner cupboard, a kitchenette with a mini-refrigerator, and a marble bathroom with whirlpool tub and shower. They are decorated in country style, giving "a totally different experience than at the main inn –contemporary elegance rather than Victorian splendor," says Sue. She mixed in a few modern furnishings like loveseats, but many items are antiques. The stairway railing came from the old Lafayette Hotel here,

thanks to a former mayor who had saved it in storage. The Mainstay's trademark green wooden chairs also appear on the front porches of each suite. Guests who stay here have tea at the main inn; continental breakfast is delivered to their quarters.

Sue's recipes for her breakfast and tea goodies are so sought after that she has published six editions of a small cookbook called "Breakfast at Nine, Tea at Four." In summer,

The Mainstay Inn is headquartered in landmark 1872 Italianate villa.

breakfast at the main inn is continental-plus, served buffet-style on the veranda; other seasons it is formal and sit-down at two seatings at 8:30 and 9:30 at a table for twelve in the dining room. Chicken-pecan quiche, ham and apple pie, hash browns quiche, western oven omelet, California egg puff, cheese strata and stuffed french toast with strawberry sauce are among the specialties.

Tours of the Mainstay's ground floor ($7.50) are given Saturday, Sunday, Tuesday and Thursday at 4. Participants are invited to join inn guests afterward for a formal tea, the tea served from a copper container and accompanied by cucumber sandwiches, cheese straw daisies, chocolate streusel bars, spiced shortbread and the like.

"Young children generally find us tiresome," the inn's brochure advises sensibly. Except for the spiffy Officers' Quarters, the Mainstay is, as Tom Carroll says, "a total Victorian experience."

Doubles, $130 to $190; suites, $190; three-night minimum in season and most weekends. Open mid-March through December; Officers' Quarters open year-round. No smoking.

The Queen Victoria, 102 Ocean St., Cape May 08204. (609) 884-8702.

Toned-down Victoriana and creature comforts are offered by Dane and Joan Wells in Cape May's largest B&B operation, the only one open every day of the year. The Wellses, who along with Tom and Sue Carroll are considered icons by their fellow innkeepers, started with twelve rooms and eight private baths in their original 1881 corner property. In 1989, they turned the Victorian house and carriage house next door into eleven luxury suites. Here they offer the niceties that many of today's travelers want: queensize brass or iron canopy beds, bedside clocks and reading lights, sitting areas or rooms, mini-refrigerators, whirlpool baths, television, fireplaces and air-conditioning.

In 1994, they took over the former Heirloom 1876 House across the street, closed it for major renovations, and reopened it in 1995 as **The Queen's Hotel,** a small European country hotel. It was to have beds without breakfast: ten smaller rooms and a suite with private baths, TVs, affordable prices and more privacy. "Twenty percent of our guests have been looking for this kind of thing," said Dane, which he likened to a hotel's concierge floor. "It's for the person who wants historic surroundings without all the B&B trappings."

Back in the main facility, furnishings in both guest and public rooms are not so high Victorian as in other inns here. They are authentic in the post-Victorian Arts and Crafts style. Each house has a parlor, one in the original building with a piano and a fireplace and the newer one with TV, games and jigsaw puzzles. Pantry areas are stocked with the makings for popcorn, tea, sherry and such. The library in the original inn contains volumes on architecture, art and history collected by Joan when she was executive director of the Victorian Society in America.

Breakfast at our latest visit included choice of juice, homemade granola, blueberry-cinnamon muffins and three kinds of homemade breads, a main course of hash-brown potato bake with ham slices, plus a basket of toasting breads. Baked eggs, cheese strata, spinach or corn casserole and stuffed baked french toast with warm strawberry sauce are other possibilities. The meal is served at a long table beneath a portrait of Queen Victoria in the dining room of the main house and in a dining room outfitted similarly in the addition. Joan presides at one breakfast table and Dane at the other.

Inn: doubles, $155 to $200; suites, $210 to $240. Hotel: doubles $130 to $150; suite, $200. No smoking.

The Abbey, Columbia Avenue and Gurney Street, Cape May 08204. (609) 884-4506.

If all is prim and proper and rather like a museum at the Mainstay, its across-the-street neighbor, The Abbey is intimate, theatrical and laid-back. Jay and Marianne Schatz, corporate and academic dropouts, purchased the showy 1869 Gothic villa with its 60-foot tower and incredible gingerbread trim in 1979. It's their fourth restoration, and they've done a splendid job.

The parlor, library and dining room on the main floor have ornate twelve-foot ceilings and eleven-foot windows (decorated with lace curtains and striking lambrequins, designed by Marianne). Among their priceless possessions is the largest freestanding bookcase (which comes apart in 27 pieces) we've ever seen.

Fourteen people can sit around the banquet table in the dining room with its Teutonic sideboard. "We have the noisiest breakfasts in town," says Marianne. That's partly because Jay keeps guests regaled both with his stories and his selection of hats from a closet that holds a choice of more than 250 – perhaps an Australian bush hat or a "Hagar the Horrible" beauty. His act and Marianne's repartee nearly upstage their breakfasts, which are continental-plus in summer and more elaborate at other times. You might have pink grapefruit juice, a dish of peaches and whipped cream, an egg and ham casserole with garlic grits on the side, and buttered English muffins. Marianne's cream cheese strata with strawberry sauce and bacon or sausage also is popular.

Seven bedrooms on the second and third floors, all with private baths and interesting period light fixtures, are named for cities. We stayed in the Savannah, a sweet room with white enamel bedstead, oriental carpets, a white wicker sofa with purple

Owner-manager Curtis Bashaw oversees deluxe Virginia Hotel.

cushions and a small refrigerator in the bathroom. The Schatzes also restored the Second Empire-style summer cottage next door as a bright and airy adjunct, offering seven less formal guest rooms, all with private baths, and a couple of parlors and verandas.

Jay gives public tours of the first floor of the main house ($5) on Monday, Wednesday and Friday at 4, followed by tea and tidbits at 4:30. He and Marianne, who works during the day in real estate, join guests at 6 over beer, wine and popcorn on the porch or in the parlor, steering their dinner choices and the next day's itinerary.

Doubles, $90 to $200; two- to four-night minimum stay on weekends. Open April to mid-December. No smoking.

The Virginia Hotel, 25 Jackson St., Cape May 08204. (609) 884-5700 or (800) 732-4236.

Built in 1879 as Cape May's first hotel, the Virginia has been grandly restored as what general manager Curtis Bashaw, co-owner with his father, calls a deluxe "boutique" hotel. Tiny white lights frame the exterior year-round, newspapers hang from a rack outside the dining room and appear at your door in the morning, and a pianist plays in the pleasant lounge during the dinner hour.

On your way upstairs check the stained-glass window in the landing; a local craftsman spent a year looking for old glass with which to restore it. The second and third floors contain 24 modern, comfortable guest rooms that vary widely in size and shape. Like the public rooms, they are furnished in a simple yet sophisticated manner. Bedrooms are equipped with private baths with new fixtures, telephones and remote-control TVs and VCRs hidden in built-in cabinets. Room service is available, terrycloth robes are provided and the hotel's guest services packet is one of the more informative we've seen.

The decor is mostly soft peaches and grays, for a restful look. There are eleven standard-size rooms, eleven premium and two extra-premium at the front of the second floor with private balconies. Five have a sofa and two upholstered chairs each, though we were surprised that one premium room with a kingsize bed had room enough for only one chair. The wraparound balcony on the second floor gave our already expansive room extra space and was particularly pleasant the next morning for a continental breakfast, delivered to the room at the time specified, of fresh orange juice, fruit, danish pastries and croissants.

At age 34, co-owner Curt is the oldest person on his talented staff, except for his chef for the acclaimed Ebbitt Room (see Dining Spots). He sees this as the prototype for other small luxury hotels that he and his father want to develop along the East Coast. A fine prototype it is.

Doubles, $190 to $260.

The Manor House, 612 Hughes St., Cape May 08204. (609) 884-4710.

Amid Cape May's haute Victoriana and large inns with owners usually around only at breakfast or teatime, the Manor House is a refreshing change. The impressive, gambrel-roofed house with warm oak and chestnut foyer and striking furnishings seems almost contemporary in contrast. "We're not trying to be high Victorian," explains Mary Snyder, innkeeper with her husband Tom, both of whom are very much in evidence here. "This is more homey and we want people to feel comfortable."

Guests spread out for punch or tea in a living room with a striking stained-glass-front player piano or a library with two plush loveseats in front of a fireplace. Upstairs are ten rooms, eight with private bath and nine with queen or kingsize beds. They are nicely furnished with antiques, brass and wood beds, handmade quilts and light Victorian print wallpapers. The newest is a third-floor suite that stretches across the front of the house with a kingsize bed, a sitting area and a whirlpool tub by the window in the bathroom.

The Snyders offer a choice of two main dishes (from a repertoire of more than 100) for one of the town's more elaborate breakfasts. A french toast sandwich stuffed with cream cheese, "asparaeggs" (poached eggs and asparagus on homemade English muffins with mornay sauce), frittatas, corn quiche and breakfast pizza are favorites. They're accompanied by Mary's signature sticky buns and non-stop monologue by Tom, who rivals the Abbey's Jay Schatz as a standup comic and has been known to lead walking tours of town when he isn't singing with his barbershop quartet. The Snyders also teamed up to produce their own cookbook with a twist, called "Mary's Buns and Tom's Puns."

Doubles, $98 to $146; suite, $160. No smoking.

The Inn on Ocean, 25 Ocean St., Cape May 08204. (609) 884-7070 or (800) 304-4477.

A billiards table greets guests as they enter this new B&B, which is furnished in light-hearted Victorian style. It's part of a billiards room just off the front entry, where owner Jack Davis's model Pontiac racing cars line the fireplace mantel and two of his seven sets of golf clubs are stashed in the corner. The room has a distinctly masculine air, an aspect that sets it apart from most B&B rooms in Cape May. Also unusual is this inn's theme of accommodations: five suites with private baths, oversize beds, TVs, wet bars, microwave ovens and thick carpeting.

Jack, who retired from General Motors, and his wife Katha opened their B&B in 1993 after a total overhaul of a three-story apartment house that was "barely fit for human habitation," in Katha's words. The walls are colorfully painted in sage green, pale yellow or pink, with coordinated fabrics and comforters. The bath in the Veranda Room was designed around an elaborate pedestal sink. A working clawfoot tub occupies a rear corner of the Promenade Room, while the shower is located in the bathroom. Besides sitting areas and the aforementioned amenities, Katha's lilting decor includes straw hats and accents like a pin cushion here and an old shaving brush and bowl there. A third-floor suite with two bedrooms and a sitting room sleeps four.

Wide front porch at The Inn on Ocean.

Guests enjoy a wicker-filled front porch, an open porch on the second floor with a good view of the ocean at the end of the street, a parlor with a fireplace and a pleasant pink dining room, where the table can extend to seat twenty. This is the setting at 9 o'clock for some memorable breakfasts, employing different table settings every day. An apple baked in chardonnay, an omelet supreme with salsa and cornbread, and cinnamon coffee cake were the treats at our visit. French toast with fruit was the main event the next day. The professional nurse in her spurs Katha to "try to mitigate our sins with a lot of fresh fruit." She also offers heart-healthy breakfasts. Afternoon tea time brings sherry in front of the fireplace, lemonade and brownies on the front porch, and tea or wine and cheese.

Jack, who says his innkeeping wife is the toughest boss he ever had, gets in his licks as a golf instructor and as a basketball coach for local youth leagues. He also may tempt you into a game of billiards.

Doubles, $135 to $145; two-bedroom suite, $165 for two, $265 for four.

Inn at 22 Jackson, 22 Jackson St., Cape May 08204. (609) 884-2226 or (800) 452-8177.

Presiding over the front parlor at this new B&B is Minerva, a lady (?) ensconced at the edge of the sofa with her shoulders wrapped in mink, a wine bottle in the pocket of her apron and a wine glass in hand. "Minerva was our resident housekeeper," says co-innkeeper Barbara Carmichael. "But guests kept sending her expensive gifts and she's too prissy now to clean house. So she minds Eliza, my mother's doll."

The presence of Minerva sets a whimsical tone for this B&B that was opened in 1992 by Barbara, an interior designer from Gettysburg, Pa., and her partner, contractor Chip Masemore. They won a 1992 county beautification award for their restoration of this former apartment house, whose facade is strikingly vivid in navy blue and bright purple with white trim. Five suites come with oversize beds, TVs, wet bars, microwave ovens and such. "We wanted to serve a different niche in Cape May," Barbara explained. "We tried to determine what Chip didn't like about B&Bs. He missed having TV, a gin and tonic at 5 o'clock and not being able to reheat his doggy bag from dinner for lunch the next day. So we offer modern conveniences, yet retain the charm of Victoriana."

Victoriana there is aplenty, from the unusual curved armoire in the Holly Suite to the clawfoot tub in the bathroom of the Windward Suite. And there are collections everywhere: Barbara's are dolls and majolica; Chip's are toys, games and depictions of bawdy women from days of yore – "the higher up in the house you go," says Barbara, "the bawdier they get." A mounted boar's head and a life-size cardboard cutout labeled Betty Boop oversee the sitting room of the Jackson Suite, whose porch faces

Jackson Street. The two-bedroom Turret Suite on the third floor comes with a deck and a bathroom yielding an ocean view and a secret balcony for two overlooking Jackson Street. In back of the house is a two-story apartment annex that the innkeepers advertise as a cottage. It has a living room and kitchen on the main floor and two bedrooms with bath on the second floor, where a balcony affords an ocean view.

A full breakfast is served in the stunning dining room with bleached solid oak furniture, deep red painted walls and a ceiling trimmed with several showy Victorian wallpapers. The fare could be blueberry buckle and baked omelet with Canadian bacon, or baked apples with raisin-bread french toast and sausage. If you're so inclined, there's "fresh cereal right off the truck," a reference to the cereal boxes stashed in a truck on a shelf displaying toy vehicles and dolls. Afternoon tea also follows the alternating sweet and savory themes: chocolate-chip cake one day, baked crab spread the next.

Doubles, $165; two-bedroom suites, $220 for two, $280 for four.

Leith Hall, 22 Ocean St., Cape May 08204. (609) 884-1934.

In their colorful Victorian B&B (moss green with accents of deep peach and mustard), preservationists Elan and Susan Zingman-Leith are working miracles with wallpaper and paint. "We're trying to create an 'aesthetic movement' house," says Susan. Since Japanese things were the rage at that time, the parlor, with its Bradbury & Bradbury wallpaper dotted with swallows, plum blossoms and the rising sun, has an anglo-Japanese look.

Seven guest rooms – one a suite and all with private baths – reflect the fun the couple has had with the painting techniques popular at the time. The Iris Room off the parlor has rag-rolled walls and a dragonfly and butterfly pattern on the ceiling. The floors are stenciled with lily pads. Bedrooms on the second and third floors have views of the ocean (especially good on the third floor) and beds have been positioned so you can lie in bed and see the water. There are exotic touches, such as the white net draped from a ring over the bed in the checkerboard-stenciled Empire Room and silver and gold stars painted all over the ceiling in the Turkish Suite. The latter has an Arabian Nights feel (and the only queensize bed). Bathrooms sport nifty reproductions of ads from magazines of the era.

Breakfast is served in the small parlor (and the even smaller library off it) at two seatings, 8:30 and 9:30. Elan, the cook, loves to serve big breakfasts of perhaps scrambled eggs with cream cheese and dill, mixed berry pancakes or apple and cheese crêpes. There are always granola and fresh fruit as well. At teatime you might find scones and crumpets, brownies or even chocolate mousse cake. In summer it's served outside on the big wraparound porch.

Let us not overlook the sub-theme of Scotland. There are engravings of the town of Leith, the Highland Room on the second floor has wonderful murals from the highlands and stenciled thistles, and in December Susan wraps balls for the Christmas tree in tartan. After only a few years of decorating, she says, "already my tastes are getting more complicated." We can't wait to see what she and Elan come up with next.

Meanwhile, they've co-authored a beautiful, insightful coffee-table photographic book called *The Secret Life of Victorian Houses*. Their own house shares many of the secrets.

Doubles, $95 to $180.

The Humphrey Hughes House, 29 Ocean St., Cape May 08204. (609) 884-4428 or (800) 582-3634.

"For ladies and gentlemen on seaside holiday," defines the sign marking this imposing shingled Colonial Revival house erected in 1903 and belonging to the Hughes family until 1980. Lorraine and Terry Schmidt now run it as a B&B, which their brochure calls "perhaps the most spacious and gracious of them all."

Spacious it certainly is, from the large wraparound veranda to the downstairs common rooms. You enter directly into the living room, which opens into a big parlor, complete with an Italian game table and an 1870 square grand piano. The parlor flows into a large fireplaced dining room, graced by silver pieces left by the Hughes family. There's also a side wicker sun porch, given over to smokers. The original chestnut and oak trim throughout has never been painted. Also notable are the leaded transom windows in the living room and beside the door.

Victorian antiques and a few reproductions decorate the ten air-conditioned guest rooms, all with private baths and three with sitting rooms and television. Half the beds are queen or kingsize.

Lorraine cooks a full breakfast, served at 9 at a large table in the dining room and at an oak table in the living room. Omelets, french toast, pancakes and welsh rarebit are part of her repertoire. Afternoon tea with cookies and cakes is best taken on the veranda, full of rocking chairs and gliders. It's offered to the public for $5.

Doubles, $80 to $150; suites, $175 to $205. Minimum three-night stay in season.

The John F. Craig House, 609 Columbia Ave., Cape May 08204. (609) 884-0100.

Some of the best breakfasts in town are served in this attractive carpenter gothic summer cottage dating to 1866. New owners Frank Felicetti, formerly a lawyer in Wilmington, Del., and his wife Connie live in the house, so are more involved than was former owner David Clemans, who sold to open the Cucina Rosa restaurant here. The B&B came with most of its furnishings, so about the only changes for longtime guests are hands-on innkeeping and evening turndown service, accompanied by homemade fudge or cookies – "whatever we've baked that day," say the enthusiastic cooks.

The house, which comes in two sections, contains nine air-conditioned guest rooms (seven with private bath), including a suite. They are done in typical Cape May style, with lots of wicker and oriental rugs, lace curtains and elaborate period wallpapers. Eastlake and Renaissance Revival antiques and original gasoliers prevail. Guests have use of the parlor and the requisite Cape May porches.

Blended coffees and teas are put out for early-risers at 7. Breakfast is served at 8:30 and 9:45 seatings in the pretty dining room with its lace tablecloth and scallop-shell wallpaper. There are always seasonal fruits on the table as well as homemade muffins and buttermilk coffee cake. The entrée, which comes out on a piping-hot plate garnished with fruit, could be anything from lemon french toast spiked with rum to a bacon and gruyère cheese casserole to eggs with cream cheese and scallions in a ramekin, accompanied by rosemary-flavored new potatoes. Blueberry-cornbread pancakes with grand marnier sauce are a house favorite. Herbed popovers, homemade sourdough or dark molasses breads, biscuits and coffee cake might accompany.

Frank does the cooking, while Connie serves. She also bakes the pastries and the goodies that accompany afternoon tea, put out on the sideboard in the dining room. Ginger cake, lemon-poppyseed bread, French pineapple upside-down cake, mushroom pâté with swiss cheese, hot artichoke dip and guacamole are among her specialties.

In lieu of tea, the Felicettis serve picnic suppers on the major summer holidays – perhaps roast chicken, potato or tomato-orange salad and cornbread. "It was the holiday thing we did at home," Connie explained, "and so we continue it here." They also serve Thanksgiving dinner and Easter brunch for guests.

Doubles, $105 to $165. Closed January and first two weeks of February.

341

Rhythm of the Sea, 1123 Beach Ave., Cape May 08204. (609) 884-7788 or (800) 498-6888.

The name of this new B&B derives, of course, from the ocean surf across the street. It also reflects the spring and fall concert series presented by visiting musicians in its huge living room centered by a concert grand piano. Innkeepers Carol and Richard Macaluso aren't musicians themselves –"somebody has to listen," says Carol – but they import professionals who stay at the B&B and entertain inn guests and invited friends at afternoon tea.

Besides music, the Macalusos have set themselves apart from other B&Bs here by furnishing the 1915 summer house simply in the Arts and Crafts style with Stickley furniture and Mission-style lanterns, wooden blinds and table linens. Almost everything is handmade in the Craftsman style. "Many of our guests say they're tired of Victoriana," says Carol. "They find this to be more open and spacious." The six large bedrooms come with queensize beds and private baths, and the painted walls are done in the rose, pumpkin and olive palettes of the period. The look is spare and pure, except for the linoleum-covered floors in the bedrooms.

Carol, who studied at the Cordon Bleu, offers a full breakfast at three tables in the huge dining room. French toast with orange marmalade is one of her specialties; Richard is known for his potato pancakes. Fruits and pastries accompany, among them a banana split with fresh fruit and cream and unusual crab muffins. Russian tea biscuits, scones and sandwiches turn up at afternoon tea.

Doubles, $150 to $210.

The George Allen Estate, 720 Washington St., Cape May 08204. (609) 898-9694.

All Cape May was agog in 1994 over the goings-on at the historic George Allen House, also known as the Crilly Estate, a 14,000-square foot mansion that occupies a full square block near the heart of town. It was acquired by a pair of 28-year-olds, Barbara Bray and Rick Wilde, who set about converting it into an elegant boutique hotel, which she said would be "the biggest and best in town."

The daughter of a Philadelphia Main Line physician who helped finance the project, Barbara said they would start with fifteen "humungous," twenty-by-twenty-foot guest rooms with private baths, fireplaces and fifteen-foot-high ceilings with crown moldings. The mansion, designed by well-known 19th-century architect Samuel Sloan as an Italianate American bracketed villa, is topped with a huge cupola containing four-seater benches.

The building was said to be structurally perfect and came "lock, stock and barrel with fabulous furnishings and antiques." Barbara and Rick said they only had to make cosmetic changes. Emerging from the foundations at our visit – "we're basement moles now," Barbara apologized – they said they were doing the grunt labor under the guidance of a good architect and contractor.

They hoped to open in June 1995, at which time they would get married here in a "humungous wedding" to launch the new venture. They said that breakfast and dinner would be available for house guests – they were interviewing chefs the last we knew – and that gardens and lawns would be restored. They envisioned nine more guest rooms opening in late 1995.

Doubles, $200 to $350, EP.

Dining Spots

The Ebbitt Room, The Virginia Hotel, 25 Jackson St., Cape May. (609) 884-5700. Named for the original owners of Cape May's first hotel, the small, candlelit dining

Elegant Ebbitt Room provides fine dining at Virginia Hotel.

room in the restored Virginia Hotel is an exceptionally pleasant setting for some of the best food in Cape May. In a town where restaurants get noisy and hectic, this remains an oasis of calm and professionalism, one worthy of owner Curtis Bashaw's aspirations for a small boutique hotel. Elegant in peach and gray, the high-ceilinged room has swagged draperies, crisply linened tables, delicate wine glasses, art deco wall sconces and birds of paradise standing tall in vases on dividers.

Chef Christopher Hubert, whose progressive American cuisine is exciting and innovative, changes his menu seasonally and adds nightly specials. Main dishes ($18.50 to $24) range from grilled swordfish with caramelized lobster, shallots and arugula, served with a pomegranate vinaigrette to sautéed venison with spaetzle and caramelized pearl onions.

At one visit, excellent hot rolls with a crisp crust preceded our appetizers, one an eggplant and gorgonzola crostini served with red onion pesto and the other a very zesty caesar salad, served on black octagonal plates. The roast cornish game hen was heavily herbed and rested on a bed of caramelized vegetables on a parsley-flecked plate, and the filet mignon came with a grilled three-onion salad and roasted potatoes. On another occasion we liked the shrimp margarita, flamed in tequila and served with avocado cream sauce and roasted tomato salsa, and the pan-roasted quail with grapes and green peppercorns. These came with a medley of zucchini and carrots, and potatoes shaped like mushrooms.

For dessert, we enjoyed an upside-down fig cake and pecan-praline cheesecake. The good wine list tends to the expensive side, but we've found a Danfield Creek chardonnay for $17 and a Rutherford Hill merlot for $22. Service by young waitresses is graceful and competent. And the live piano music emanating from the lobby lends a glamorous air to this addition to the Cape May dining scene.

Dinner nightly, 5:30 to 9:30 or 10; Sunday brunch, 9 to 2.

Restaurant Maureen, 429 Beach Drive, Cape May. (609) 884-3774.
Consistently good food and flawless service distinguish this sophisticated place run by Maureen and Stephen Horn on the second floor of what once was a bath house and

saloon. Particularly inviting is the enclosed porch, all pristinely white with pink napkins and affording a great view of the ocean. Inside is a long chandeliered dining room, where an unobtrusive, waist-high divider nicely separates parallel lineups of tables for two, providing privacy in a configuration that we ordinarily find too close.

A zesty sauce of ginger, garlic, soy and scallions accompanied an appetizer of shrimp oriental. One might also start with lobster ravioli or Steve's crab cake with a puree of red pepper. Chef Horn showed his deft hand with seafood and sauces in crab Abigail, fresh jumbo lump crab seasoned with a sauce of cream, mustard and shellfish stock and baked in a casserole, and the house specialty, poisson jardinière – at our visit, a succulent salmon baked in parchment with an array of tomatoes, leeks, carrots, basil, olives and lemons. Crisp asparagus and red potatoes sautéed with onions accompanied. Other entrées ranged in price from $18.50 for crab fritter or duck stuffed with pecans to $26 for lobster caribe served on a puree of mangos and chardonnay. Beef and shrimp gorgonzola, salmon natsuky, bouillabaisse, grilled venison with polenta and sliced lamb sautéed with a sauce of scotch, mint and mustard hint of the chef's range. When we were there, the pastry-laden dessert cart held a good strawberry tart.

As we lingered over coffee and cordials, it was obvious to us why the Horns have attracted such a following after seven years in Philadelphia and thirteen in Cape May.

Dinner nightly in summer, 5 to 10; fewer days in off-season. Open mid-April through October.

Water's Edge, Beach Drive and Pittsburgh Avenue, Cape May. (609) 884-1717.

Chef-owner Neil Elsohn and his wife Karen, who is hostess, offer some of the best and most inspired food in town in this sleek, hotel-style dining room in front of La Mer Motor Inn. The well-tailored expanse of banquettes and booths is dressed in white cloths topped with rose-colored runners and flickering votive candles.

On one occasion, we enjoyed an appetizer of strudel with escargots, pinenuts and an ethereal garlic cream sauce before digging into poached fillet of Norwegian salmon with lime and salmon caviar, and sautéed sea scallops with tomatillos, cilantro and grilled jicama. On our second visit, we grazed happily through appetizers and salads. These included scallop chowder, spicy pork and scallion empanadas with pineapple-ginger chutney, fusilli with grilled tuna, oriental vegetables and Szechuan vinaigrette, and grilled chicken salad with toasted pecans, grilled red onions, mixed greens and citrus vinaigrette.

Main courses ($18 to $21) include such standouts as veal sausage with cappellini, plum tomatoes, basil and roasted garlic; veal scaloppine with three varieties of mushrooms, served with squares of parmesan-tossed polenta, and grilled tenderloin of pork with spicy black bean sauce and crispy sweet plantains. Desserts could be fruit shortcakes, banana-bread pudding with hot chocolate sauce and bittersweet chocolate-walnut pâté with espresso and vanilla sauces.

In summer, a lounge menu is served in the spacious bar. Salads and appetizers are available there anytime. The brunch menu contains some exotic items; the meal is quite salubrious when taken on the outdoor deck with ocean beyond.

Lunch in summer, 11:30 to 3; dinner nightly, 5 to 9:30 or 10; Sunday brunch, 11 to 2:30. Dinner only, Thursday-Monday, mid-October to May.

410 Bank Street, 410 Bank St., Cape May. (609) 884-2127.

This restaurant's outdoor courtyard, covered by a big green and white awning and surrounded by plants, tiny white lights and Victorian lamps, is a lovely setting for dinner. Owners Steve and Janet Miller, who also run Frescos next door, are theater set designers and their background shows.

One of few ocean views for dining in Cape May is offered by Restaurant Maureen.

Chinese chef Sing Cheng offers a gumbo of New Orleans, French and Caribbean dishes, many grilled over mesquite wood and most with cajun-creole overtones. We loved the special seviche and butterflied quail on warmed greens for appetizers, which also included Bahamian yellowfin tuna beignets and fresh Jersey asparagus amandine in a puff-pastry cornet. Among entrées ($19.95 to $24.95) are shellfish filé gumbo, sautéed soft-shell crabs grenobloise and coconut-battered catfish fillet with bananas, tomatoes and lime-jalapeño sauce. Our choices of blackened red snapper with pecan sauce and yellowfin tuna in Barbadian black bean sauce, served with crisp vegetables and rice pilaf, were too much to finish. After all, we had to save room for the highly rated key lime pie, which was the real thing. So is everything else, from crawfish bisque to possibly the best bread pudding with hot bourbon sauce you'll ever taste. There's even a French-style roast, a special meat, fowl or game dish offered nightly.

If you can't eat on the courtyard, settle for one of the screened porches or the small, intimate dining rooms adorned with New Orleans posters inside the restored 1840 house. Lately, we've heard reports that even those with reservations may face a lengthy wait for their table.

Dinner nightly, 5:30 to 10. Closed November-April. BYOB.

Frescos, 420 Bank St., Cape May. (609) 884-0366.

Some patrons like this northern Italian bistro even better than its parent next door. The main dining area is intimate, with faux marble columns and unusual three-dimensional fish artworks around tables that are rather close together. The narrow wraparound porch has tables for two far enough apart for privacy.

The pasta dishes ($12.95 to $21.95) are Cape May's most extensive, ranging from fettuccine alfredo with home-smoked salmon to pappardelle with shrimp and scallops in champagne-lobster cream sauce. Other entrée choices ($17.95 to $21.95) include pan-grilled swordfish in a crabmeat and mushroom cream sauce, shrimp scampi over a bed of spinach, chicken with polenta and gorgonzola, veal saltimbocca, osso buco and veal chop sautéed with roasted garlic and smoked red pepper aioli. Among delectable

345

desserts are a key lime cream-filled cannoli and a rum-soaked sponge cake with mascarpone cream and grated chocolate.

Dinner nightly, 5 to 10:30; Thursday-Sunday, Oct. 15 to New Year's. Closed January-April. BYOB.

The Washington Inn, 801 Washington St., Cape May. (609) 884-5697.

Surrounded by shade trees and colorful banks of impatiens, this historic white building run by brothers David and Michael Craig is considered far and away the best of the larger restaurants in town. Originally a plantation house built in 1840, it contains four elegant dining rooms, including a Victorian garden room and a pretty wicker-filled front veranda done up in pink.

The fairly extensive menu starts with scallops and shrimp on horseback, sautéed filet mignon strips with tamari-ginger sauce, provençal tart and crab cakes with a roasted red pepper sauce. Entrées ($15.95 to $24.95) include flounder stuffed with crabmeat and monterey jack cheese and laced with brandy, grilled salmon with a six-onion compote, bouillabaisse, chicken baked in puff pastry, grilled veal chop with a tomato-basil sauce and grilled strip steak with beet-horseradish butter. Desserts could be frozen key lime pie, pumpkin-pecan cheesecake and fresh strawberry napoleons.

The basement wine cellar won the Wine Spectator Grand Award. The wine list is reasonably priced, and diners like to finish with international coffees.

The Craig brothers have opened a less formal, family restaurant they call their country cousin. **The Old Grange Restaurant** at 735 Seashore Road in nearby Cold Spring is open for lunch and dinner and is considered good value.

Dinner nightly, 5 to 10; fewer nights in off-season. Closed in January.

Peaches at Sunset, 1 Sunset Blvd., West Cape May. (609) 898-0100.

Arguably Cape May's prettiest restaurant is this establishment with an offbeat name, derived from chef-owner George Pechin's nickname and its location at the head of Sunset Boulevard. A decade ago, "Peach" Pechin and partner Craig Needles opened a small sidewalk cafe in downtown Cape May. Their debut as a gourmet-to-go cafe quickly evolved into a serious small restaurant, one that finally gained the space it deserved with the new location in 1992. Peaches Cafe remained behind in the old quarters for a while, before giving way in 1994 to a Japanese restaurant, Kuishimbo.

A nicely restored Victorian house, vivid in peach with aqua trim, holds Peaches at Sunset. Two small dining rooms are divided by a walnut-trimmed aquarium full of tropical fish beneath a stained-glass panel and a wild tropical design on the ceiling. Peach-colored napkins stand tall in wine glasses at each candlelit table. Dining is al fresco on a raised rear deck leading to a gazebo with a few pint-size tables.

The contemporary dinner menu offers eight entrées ($16.95 to $24.95), among them Thai-style sweet and sour whole fish of the day, baked halibut with caramelized vidalia onions, shrimp and scallops in Thai-spiced carrot juice, medallions of veal with lobster and béarnaise, and Santa Fe filet mignon served over polenta with smoked ancho chile sauce. Start with the creamy clam chowder that we once savored during lunch at Peaches Cafe, an endive salad with herbed goat cheese and asparagus or roasted garlic served with mascarpone cheese and grilled sourdough bread. Finish with bourbon-pecan pie or crème caramel.

Dinner nightly except Tuesday, from 5. BYOB. Closed January and February.

Cucina Rosa, 301 Washington St. Mall, Cape May. 898-9800.

David Clemans, who has a reputation as one of the best cooks in town, opened this authentic and popular Italian restaurant in 1993 after selling the John F. Craig House,

Colorful tropical design enlivens ceiling at Peaches at Sunset.

his B&B of many years. "We take relatively standard southern Italian dishes and make them very carefully," says David. Everything is done from scratch, from the marinara and meat sauces to semolina bread.

His stepson, Guy Portewig, is the chef. Appetizers run from $3.95 for eggplant parmesan to $5.95 for clams oreganata, a house favorite. Main dishes are priced from $6.95 for basic pastas to $19.95. Widely acclaimed is the chicken portofino, stuffed with mozzarella cheese and Italian sausage specially made for the restaurant, rolled and baked with tomato sauce and served with pasta ($14.95). Other treats include grilled swordfish and lamb chops, each marinated in olive oil and Italian spices and served with fried potatoes sautéed with peppers and onions or pasta with a choice of sauce.

Desserts are David's forte. He makes fruit pies that change daily, lemon cheesecake and a rich chocolate cake. He also offers ice creams and sherbets.

The 64-seat restaurant is at a corner location along the mall, with sixteen tables on a sidewalk patio in season. The interior decor is soft and romantic in rose and green tones, with candles flickering on white-clothed tables amid brass railings and plants.

Dinner nightly, 5 to 10, Sunday from 4:30 to 9:30. Closed January to mid-February. BYOB. No smoking.

The Rose Garden Restaurant, Perry Street and Congress Place, Cape May. (609) 884-8336.

There's a new rose garden outside this gem of a restaurant ensconced at the side of Congress Hall. Culinary Institute-trained chef Chris Holl and partner Jerry Emery have softened the soaring space with an abundance of hanging plants and potted greenery and – a striking touch – swags of roses and ivy hand-painted on the pink walls. The pair added latticework to the front veranda to give al-fresco diners more privacy.

The seasonal menu offers a dozen entrées, priced from $17 for grilled vegetable lasagna or chicken alsace surrounded by spinach spaetzle to $24 for bouillabaisse. Other choices are grilled Norwegian salmon garnished with scallops, spicy grilled shrimp pesto served atop grilled eggplant slices and pasta, rack of lamb stuffed with feta cheese and served over tomatoes flavored with pernod, and veal and shrimp fricassee laced with cassis and armagnac.

Starters at our visit included carpaccio, seafood mousse tagliatelle, grilled herbed shrimp served in an artichoke cup, and escargots and wild mushrooms in puff pastry. Among the acclaimed desserts are sixteen-layer chocolate cake over champagne sabayon, mascarpone-chocolate mousse with passion fruit and raspberry sauce and, in summer, fresh fruit ices and sorbets.

Dinner from 5:30, nightly in summer, Thursday-Monday rest of year. BYOB.

The Peter Shields Inn Restaurant, 1301 Beach Drive, Cape May. (609) 884-6491.

Local innkeepers recommend this new restaurant, owned by Culinary Institute-trained chef Ron Panczner, who opened his own place after fifteen years of training in some of Cape May's best restaurants. The setting is the main floor of the oceanfront Peter Shields Inn.

Ninety diners can be seated in two elegant, high-ceilinged dining rooms, graced with crystal chandeliers and Victorian wallpapers. "This is the only restaurant in town where you can sit in front of a fireplace and see the ocean," Ron noted. Popular in summer is the wraparound porch, which seats another 70 outside.

A choice of caesar or garden salad is included in the price of all dinner entrées ($19.95 to $24.95). The menu changes every three weeks, but among the possibilities are grilled tuna étouffée, grouper baked in parchment paper with julienned vegetables, grilled Norwegian salmon served with tomato salsa on a bed of chilled cucumber noodles, steak au poivre and pan-fried veal topped with spinach, mushrooms, Jersey tomatoes and cheeses.

Good starters are Prussian pearls (chilled Long Island blue point oysters topped with Russian vodka, sour cream and caviar), a medley of seven smoked seafoods, and brie and crabmeat in puff pastry with raspberry coulis. Desserts are done with flourishes: bananas foster, strawberries flambé, chocolate-chip cheesecake and tirami su.

Dinner nightly, from 5; Sunday brunch, 10 to 2. Closed in January.

Louisa's, 104 Jackson St., Cape May. (609) 884-5882.

A tiny storefront with colorful flowers banked around its window, Louisa's serves some of the most innovative and affordable meals in town at a handful of close-together tables surrounded by molded plastic chairs in wild colors.

The changing seasonal menu might offer hot and spicy ginger sesame noodles, roasted eggplant salad, garlic tomato soup or fresh salmon salad as starters ($3.75 to $4.50). For main courses ($10.50 to $14.50), how about grilled polenta with savory greens, grilled red drum fish with Thai spices or crab and carolina shrimp gumbo? Among desserts for $2.75 are ginger-butternut squash pie, sweet potato pudding and kahlua mousse pie.

It's no wonder the place is usually jammed and there may be quite a wait for a table. Louisa's is not the place to go to if you feel like having a private conversation.

Dinner, Tuesday-Saturday 5 to 9. Open March-October. No smoking. No credit cards. BYOB.

Kuishimbo, 322 Carpenter's Lane, Cape May. (609) 884-0712.

The name is a Japanese term describing "one who loves to eat, a good eater," according to owner Daniel Takayama. Billed as a Japanese charcoal and sushi restaurant, it occupies the diminutive quarters vacated in 1993 by Peaches Cafe, now consolidated at Peaches at Sunset. Daniel, who previously owned and operated several restaurants in Los Angeles, raised the ceiling and brightened the interior of the intimate downtown spot, where black chopsticks accent the white tablecloths.

The place still seats only twenty inside and sixteen outside on the sidewalk patio. Those lucky enough to get a table enjoy such main-course treats ($13.95 to $17.95) as broiled salmon with tangy green scallion sauce, tuna tataki, shrimp tempura and charbroiled beef marinated in sesame ginger sauce.

Starters include miso soup, shrimp gyoza and squid with shiitake mushrooms. A section of the menu is devoted to nigiri and maki sushi in the $3.95 to $5.25 range. A deluxe sashimi plate goes for $19.95.

Dinner, Thursday-Monday from 5. BYOB. No checks or credit cards.

McGlade's On the Pier, 722 Beach Drive, Cape May. (609) 884-2614.

One of the best-kept dining secrets in Cape May, this is treasured for its ocean view and creative food. We've had breakfast here several times and thoroughly relished a shrimp and garlic omelet ($7.95), the bacon, egg and cheese on a croissant ($4.75) and Uncle Tuse's bacon, tomato and cheese omelet ($7.25), which was more than enough for two to share. Everything on chef-owner Mickey McGlade's large menu has zip. The omelets are accompanied by fresh fruit garnishes and great hash-browns with lots of onions. A surprise treat at one visit was the school of dolphins that passed just off shore on their way to breakfast.

At lunch, the crab cake platter is superb, and the salads are as enticing as the breakfast fare. We know folks who come here for a casual dinner by the water to feast on shrimp butter rosa (with mushrooms and garlic over linguini), grilled swordfish or the triple-threat salad of crab, shrimp and lobster (entrées, $9 to $18). Although the high-end prices have escalated lately, the interesting food and that glorious view compensate.

Open daily in summer, 7 a.m. to 9 p.m.; otherwise, breakfast and lunch, 9 to 3. Open May-September. BYOB.

Diversions

Victorian Cape May. The nation's largest concentration of Victorian gingerbread structures – some 670, ranging from tiny cottages to sprawling hotels – is on display in the historic district. The best way to see them is on foot or bicycle or, better, through a variety of tours offered by the Mid-Atlantic Center for the Arts. MAC offers two distinct **guided trolley tours:** the East End (the best if you only have time for one) and the West End. Each takes about half an hour and costs $4.50. MAC guides also lead several **walking tours,** each 90 minutes and $5. MAC sponsors boat cruises, moonlight trolley rides, kitchen tours, an Inns and Outs of Cape May tour and Cape May INNteriors Tours and Teas. Individual inns are opened for tours under their own auspices as well as through Mansions by Gaslight, Victorian Sampler and Christmas Inns tours.

Emlen Physick House and Estate, 1048 Washington St., 884-5404. The eighteen-room house designed by Victorian architect Frank Furness was the first to be saved by MAC and the property serves as its headquarters. Many of the original furnishings have been returned to the house for display purposes. Tour highlights include an upstairs library with Japanese wallpaper, even on the ceiling, the owner's bachelor bedroom and the fan collection in his mother's bedroom. Hour-long tours cost $5.

Cape May Point Lighthouse, Cape May Point State Park. MAC continues to restore this 1859 landmark, reopened for tours in 1988. The hardy climb the 199 tower stairs to the Watch Room Gallery just below the lantern for a panoramic view (adults, $3.50). A visitor center in the newly restored Oil House on the lighthouse grounds contains a photo mural showing the lighthouse view, a twelve-minute video detailing the structure and a museum shop.

Performing Arts. MAC sponsors a spring series of chamber music concerts known as the **Cape May Music Festival.** The East Lynne Company, an equity group in residence here in summer, presents a **Victorian Theater Festival** July through September. **Cape May Stage** mounts a number of summer shows at the Welcome Center, while the Chalfonte Cabaret is staged weekends at the Chalfonte Hotel. MAC also sponsors a summer **Vintage Film Festival** at the Chalfonte.

Birding and Wildlife. Cape May lies on the heavily populated Atlantic Flyway and more than 400 species of birds head north and south through Cape May Point. Good areas for nature-watching are South Cape May Meadow, Cape May Point State Park, Higbee's Beach Wildlife Management Area and the Cape May Bird Observatory.

Swimming is fine along Cape May's beach (the required beach passes may be purchased, and often are complimentary to inn guests), and at Higbee's and Sunset beaches and Cape May Point State Park.

Shopping. Despite its Victorian charm and influx of tourists, Cape May's forte is not shopping, although the situation has improved lately. The Washington Street Mall is where most of the action is. Our favorite here is **The Whale's Tale,** a ramble of rooms containing everything from shell magnets to an extraordinary collection of cards. Other good gift shops are **McDowell's Gallery of Gifts** and **The Victorian Pink House Gift Shop,** the latter with an incredible array of Victoriana. **For the Birds** carries excellent things for nature lovers and **Swede Things in America** speaks for itself. Check out the wallpaper borders and elegant fixtures at **Fralinger's** original saltwater taffy emporium, even if you're not into taffy. The **Cape May Linen Outlet** offers good bargains, especially in placemats. The Virginia Hotel's Curt Bashaw oversees the tenant mix in the new Shops Amidst the Columns at Congress Hall. We were impressed with the stock at **Environs** (artful living inspired by nature), **Colleen and Quinn** cards and gifts, **The Best Vest Co., Emmie Galleries** and especially **Love the Cook,** a gourmet kitchen shop par excellence, run by Rhona Craig of the Washington Inn.

Extra-Special

Cape May Diamonds, Cape May Point.

A lot of fuss is made over the quartz pebbles found only locally and known as Cape May Diamonds. The semi-precious stones of diverse colors vary from the size of little peas to marbles and walnuts. They're bright and clear when found in the wet sand, but, alas, they become dull as they dry. When cut and polished, they can be set in gold or silver to make attractive jewelry such as rings, bracelets and necklaces. One of the best places to find Cape May diamonds is at Sunset Beach in Cape May Point, where you'll also see the shell of the USS Atlantis, a World War I concrete ship that ran aground in a storm and has been trapped here ever since. We burrowed into the sand here looking for "diamonds" and finally latched onto someone who seemed to know what he was doing. He demonstrated how to separate the good stones from the bad, or we'd never have known.

Landmark St. Catharine's Church faces parkland across Spring Lake.

Spring Lake, N.J.
Jewel of the Jersey Shore

Among the seaside towns strung out along the Jersey shore is one that stands apart. No boardwalk bric-a-brac. No honky-tonk. No video arcades. No hangouts for young singles.

Spring Lake planned it that way. A century of tight zoning regulation and community resolve has produced a genteel enclave of substantial homes, manicured lawns, a tree-lined shopping district, a pristine boardwalk and not one but three lakes a stone's throw from the sea. All this within a long hour's drive of New York City or Philadelphia.

Enterprising developers launched Spring Lake in the late 19th century. They planned four neighboring towns, each having its own railroad station and a lavish hotel catering to a wealthy clientele from Philadelphia, northern New Jersey and New York. Additional hotels, large guest houses and elegant estates followed. The four communities united to become Spring Lake, which celebrated its centennial in 1992.

The town retains the elegance of its past. The Warren Hotel clings to its summer social season and Green Gables, an oceanfront residence that occupies an entire block, has two regulation-size croquet courts still used by croquet clubs. The stately Spring Lake Community House accommodates a library and theater groups in manorial surroundings. The recreation commission sponsors summer concerts at the park gazebo and model-boat regattas on Spring Lake.

This is an eminently livable community for those who can afford houses starting at $200,000 and oceanfront properties of $1 million or more. The two-mile shoreline is pristine, its boardwalk uncluttered by anything more than two pavilions containing swimming pools at either end. Weeping willows frame and wooden footbridges cross

351

Spring Lake, the meandering, natural spring lake in the center of town. It and two other lakes at either end of town yield a landscape rare for a seaside community.

No chain motels are among the 26 lodging establishments, ranging from old hotels to B&Bs, and no more can be licensed. The population of 5,000 year-round increases only to 7,000 in summer. "The town consciously chose to stay a community rather than become a resort," says Michael Robertson, executive director of the Chamber of Commerce. "For a quiet, romantic getaway, this is the place – only an hour away from everything, but an island of tranquility."

Inn Spots

Hollycroft, 506 North Blvd., Box 448, Spring Lake 07762. (908) 681-2254.

Hidden behind a curtain of holly in a wooded residential area, this 1908 mountain-style hunting lodge is unique in the area. You'd expect to find it in the Adirondacks, perhaps, but not at the Jersey Shore. When you're sitting in the living room, you can look out across Lake Como and see the Atlantic beyond. In summer it's like being in the country with an ocean view; in the winter, when the towering ironstone fireplace is ablaze, it's like a ski lodge with an ocean view. That's the way the original owners planned it – one partner wanted a shore house and the other a mountain house, so this oversize log cabin in the Arts and Crafts style was their compromise.

"We bought it in 1985 as a private home, tore it apart and have been putting it back together ever since," said Mark Fessler, an architect and innkeeper with his wife Linda. Their handiwork has produced one of the more inviting and charming B&Bs we've seen. The public areas on the sprawling first floor include a large and welcoming living room paneled in knotty pine, a log-beamed dining room and a brick-floored sun porch beside the flagstone terrace, all taking advantage of the lake/ocean view. Stylishly and with great taste, the house displays portions of Linda's multitude of collectibles, from miniature English cottages to a Sicilian donkey cart chair.

The Fesslers have decorated in eclectic country style seven comfortable guest rooms with private baths. All but two have king or queen beds and three have fireplaces. Each room comes with bottles of Perrier and the Hollycroft's own soaps. Unusual touches abound: a custom-made iron bed with a twig bird cage atop the canopy and lace curtains around the headboard in the Grassmere room, a twig accessory hanging from the rafters and on the wall behind the queen bed in the Somerset. The Ambleside has an English scrub pine canopy bed shipped back from one of the couple's many trips to England, a clawfoot tub and a private porch with a hanging swing seat. A favorite room is the spacious Cotswold Cottage at the far end of the main floor. It has a king bed, ivy painted on one wall, a wicker sofa, a window seat, Cotswold cottages pictured on the wallpaper border and in prints on the walls, and floral fabrics on the bedspread, curtains and table skirts.

Another favorite was emerging in 1995 above the dining room: a cathedral-ceilinged suite with stone fireplace, sitting room and french doors onto a private balcony.

Talented Linda decorates lavishly for the seasons and makes all the handicrafts, which are for sale in her little Hollycroft Country Store off the entry.

The Fesslers put out a substantial

Formal dining room is set for breakfast at Sea Crest by the Sea.

buffet breakfast on a sideboard and table in the dining room. It's likely to include juices, fresh fruit, black-raspberry crumbles, Irish soda bread, raspberry-chocolate chip muffins and creamy scrambled eggs or ham and cheese egg strata. In the afternoon, sherry awaits in a crystal decanter atop a silver tray in the living room in the afternoons.

Doubles, $95 to $135. Smoking restricted. Two-night minimum weekends in summer.

Sea Crest by the Sea, 19 Tuttle Ave., Spring Lake 07762. (908) 449-9031 or (800) 803-9031.

Energetic owners John and Carol Kirby from Short Hills have infused this oldtimer on a residential street half a block from the ocean with a sprightly new lease on life. In a town where Victoriana reigns only slightly less preciously than in Cape May, their twelve-bedroom inn finds its own niche. "We're more eclectic," says John. "We're reliving memories from our past lives and catering to adult fantasy and romance."

That translates to flamingos galore in the Flamingo Grove Room, a Christmas wonderland in the Sleigh Ride Room, the Velveteen Rabbit Room reflecting Carol's favorite childhood tale, a stars and stripes ribbon around the portrait in the G. Washington Room, and a beaded curtain through which you enter the Casablanca Room. A favorite is the third-floor Yankee Clipper, where windows yield a view of the ocean both to the east and south. The bureau contains John's original sextant and old sailing logs from his service in the Merchant Marine, and a Kings Point Academy pin and pennant rest on the bed. A card lists the furniture in each room and guest diaries reveal the thoughts of previous occupants.

All rooms possess queensize beds and private baths with Caswell-Massey toiletries, and the Teddy Roosevelt Suite comes with a TV – "good for the news," John explains – and a luxurious soaking tub for two. Seven rooms have fireplaces and several have feather beds. All beds are dressed in linens of Egyptian cotton, French damask and Belgian lace and have six pillows on top. Equally fetching are the common areas, from a graceful living room and wicker-filled library, both with fireplaces, to a wraparound veranda and a dining room with a majestic French oak table and sideboard.

The Kirbys serve a bountiful gourmet breakfast starting, as their brochure puts it, at the civilized hour of 9 o'clock. Fresh fruit, homemade granola, John's breads and muffins and Carol's scones are accompanied by a Scandinavian blend of coffee reduced in caffeine. The main event could be frittata, featherbed eggs or french toast. Afternoon tea is served beside the player piano.

Doubles, $139 to $159; suite, $239. Two-night minimum in summer (three nights on weekends); two-night minimum weekends rest of year. No smoking.

Normandy Inn, 21 Tuttle Ave., Spring Lake 07762. (908) 449-7172.

Haute Victoriana reigns inside this five-tone olive green and gold Italianate villa with Queen Anne accents. That's the work of innkeepers Michael and Susan Ingino, who note that only two pieces of furniture remain from the inn they purchased in 1982. They have renovated and replaced with prized antiques and authenticity.

The mood is set in two fancy pink and red common rooms containing a rococo damask parlor set, an antique English tall case clock and marble sculptures. A Chickering grand piano occupies center stage in the huge, pillared dining room, where an extensive breakfast menu as well as daily specials are served to house guests. Complimentary wine is available all day on the side sun porch, where there's a television set, baskets hang from the ceiling and wicker furniture makes a comfy retreat.

Upstairs on the second and third floors are fifteen air-conditioned guest rooms and a suite, all with private baths. The two large second-floor front corner rooms are most prized. One has a tester bed whose posts stretch at least ten feet high, two upholstered chairs beside a table and a private porch. The other has a queen bed with a nine-foot burled wood headboard. Among the treasures are an 1860 signed Herter bed, a woven Brussels carpet and a reproduction of the bedroom wallpaper from the home of Robert Todd Lincoln. Victorian lamps, old portraits and antique furnishings dignify the rooms. Some on the third floor are rather small, although two at the rear have been turned into a suite with TV in the sitting area, a gas-fired fireplace, a kingsize bedroom and a soaking tub. Out back, two rooms upstairs in the carriage house have been converted into a deluxe suite with a more contemporary feeling: a queen-bedded room, a small kitchen, a marble bath with a family-size jacuzzi, a big cathedral-ceilinged sitting room with corner fireplace, a sofabed and loveseat, and two TVs with VCR and stereo. Telephones lately have been incorporated into all bedrooms, and the inn's Victorian Times newsletter polled guests as to whether they want in-room TVs. The verdict: half do and half don't, so the Inginos make them available for those who wish.

Doubles, $108 to $161; suites, $240 and $252. Two-night minimum weekends except in winter.

Hamilton House Inn, 15 Mercer Ave., Spring Lake 07762. (908) 449-8282.

Every room has a swan somewhere in this deluxe new B&B fashioned by Anne Benz, who was born and bred in Spring Lake, which is known for its swans, and her husband Bud, who grew up in neighboring South Bellmar. The two longtime AT&T employees raised four sons and cooked many a meal for their sons' friends and later their wives before deciding to move across town to open a B&B. "Now we have paying guests and only have to cook breakfast," said Anne. "We're having the best time ever."

Theirs is Spring Lake's only B&B with a swimming pool, and it's also one of the closest to the ocean. The facade of the 1877 Victorian is rather plain, but the inside is a beauty. You'd never guess that eighteen months before the Benzes opened in 1994 it

Guests are accommodated in high style in Normandy Inn and its rear carriage house.

was a wreck. Eighteen months of renovations created inviting public rooms and eight comfortable bedrooms, all with private baths.

Cross the threshold from a small porch and enter a huge, square living room, 27 feet by 27 feet, lovely with salmon-colored walls and groupings of traditional-style sofas and chairs. An enclosed sun porch harbors a TV and a decanter of sherry waiting to be poured. The chandeliered dining room is papered in a floral pattern that matches the Villeroy & Boch china put out each day for the candlelight breakfast. That breakfast is quite a spread. Ours began with orange juice and honeydew melon, plus honey french bread and apple strudel muffins. The main dish was belgian waffles with crisp bacon. The kitchen remained so tidy we marveled that any cooking actually was done there.

Upstairs are five fresh and pretty bedrooms on the second floor and three on the third. Each is decorated according to its name. A wallpaper border of swans along the ceiling graces the Spring Lake Serenity suite with kingsize bed and sitting room at the front of the house. A border of seashells and castles coordinates with the bedspread in the summery Seashells and Castles room, which includes a private porch from which to view the sun rising over the ocean. We liked the extra-large Victorian Splendor with kingsize brass bed, elegant loveseat, and oversize bathtub and marble shower. The lack of Victorian clutter was manifest even in a room named for its splendor. The swan theme here was an intricate twig swan resting on the bureau. Seawatch on the third floor harbors an old desk, a ship's model in a bottle and a ship's lantern. Poet's Retreat comes with a wallpaper border of Shakespeare books and a wall of Bucks County photos by Bud, a talented photographer. Each room has a sitting area, and fireplaces were being added to four in 1995.

Doubles, $125 to $165; suite, $195. No smoking. Two-night minimum weekends in season.

Ashling Cottage, 106 Sussex Ave., Spring Lake 07762. (908) 449-3553 or (800) 237-1877.

Every morning at breakfast in the gazebo-shaped solarium at the front of this engaging Victorian cottage, innkeeper Jack Stewart runs a contest. He asks folks to guess in 30 seconds how many window panes there are in the solarium. "No one ever comes within a hundred," says Jack. "They're always too low." We won't spill the beans, but the answer lies well into the hundreds.

Those windows, containing the original glass dating to 1877, yield views onto Spring Lake across the street and a glimpse of the ocean beyond. "You couldn't face a better way to start the day," says Jack, and few would disagree. Against that watery backdrop, he and wife Goodi serve a sumptuous breakfast, buffet style. The fare includes a fresh fruit compote, cereal, bread and muffins and perhaps a special egg dish like California cheese puffs with hot peppers or a corn quiche.

The Stewarts are apt to pour wine for afternoon get-togethers in their living room, handsome with red ribbon walls, dark green velvet swagged draperies and a sectional in front of the TV/VCR.

Despite period touches, there's no fussy Victoriana here. All ten guest rooms hold queensize beds and eight have private baths; two on the third floor with in-room wash basins share. The front Peach Room, the largest, offers a lovely lake view as well as an armoire, dresser and headboard in old oak. Jack's favorite is No. 4 on the third floor, up in the treetops surrounded by century-old sentinel sycamores. Most in demand in summer is a rear first-floor room with a private porch.

Doubles, $85 to $150. Smoking discouraged.

La Maison, 404 Jersey Ave., Spring Lake 07762. (908) 449-0969.

"I wanted this to be everyone's house," says former IBM sales executive-turned-innkeeper Barbara Furdyna. And as a college French major and a francophile who studied for a summer at the Sorbonne, she wanted hers to be a house with a French accent.

She started in 1982 with four rooms and a cottage in what had been Spring Lake's oldest guest facility. Within ten years, she had left IBM and renovated the entire house for upwards of $300,000 to produce a spiffy, French-style B&B. She now offers four rooms and two suites, all with private baths, TVs, telephones, queensize French-style sleigh beds, country French reproduction furniture, all-white duvets and down comforters, balloon curtains on the windows, Monet prints or original artworks on the walls and cozy sitting areas. The honeymoon room on the third floor, enhanced by beautiful French wallpaper, is the only one with a tub. Two pairs of rooms are rented as suites, each with a queen bed and a single bed.

The French theme continues during the champagne breakfast each morning. Mimosas and creative fruit dishes, perhaps poached pears in an orange-raspberry sauce, precede a main dish of belgian waffles, quiche lorraine or french toast. Tartes tatin, baguettes, breakfast pastries, granola and cappuccino or espresso accompany. The meal is taken in a chandeliered dining room, where a fanciful bird cage is situated in the corner, or on the wraparound front porch. In the afternoon, there's an open bar for happy hour, as Barbara hosts guests as she would for a private party.

Besides exuberant hospitality, La Maison is known for fine art. The walls of its entry and living room are hung with paintings, some of them by watercolor artist Paula Jordan, who lives across the street and is the assistant innkeeper here. Another staff member's watercolors as well as paintings gathered on one of Barbara's frequent trips to France are also for sale. "We've sold 30 paintings in the year we've had our gallery," she said at our visit.

Doubles, $120 to $165; efficiency cottage, $190. No smoking.

Victoria House, 214 Monmouth Ave., Spring Lake 07762. (908) 974-1882.

Masses of impatiens and a giant hydrangea bush brighten the exterior of this gray-green, Eastlake-style residence with white gingerbread trim and an extra-large wrap-

Gazebo-shaped solarium at Ashling Cottage contains hundreds of window panes.

around porch. Built in 1882 and a guest house for some years, it was revived in 1993 by new owners Robert and Louise Goodall. "We've hung 150 rolls of wallpaper and refinished all the floors," said Louise, who was busy performing both functions at our midweek visit to get the house ready for Spring Lake's Christmas tour in 1994 .

What do-it-yourself elbow grease, modest carpentry talents and an eye for design can do is manifest throughout the Goodalls' house, but most particularly in their ten guest rooms, six with private baths and four of them new. Two of the most popular rooms make the most of their corner turrets. "There seems to be something about being in a turret that guests like," Louise surmises. Both turret rooms hold kingsize beds. One has a handpainted bench and the other is smart in Laura Ashley fabrics. An armoire made from a gun cabinet enhances the Garden Bouquet Room, while a colorful quilt tops the kingsize bed in Cottage. The Delft and Wicker Room lives up to its name with a blue and white decorative scheme and lots of wicker. Two rooms at the rear of both the second and third floors share a bath each.

The common areas are equally appealing. There's a TV in the turreted parlor, and four original stained-glass windows brighten the stairway landing. Hand-carved Italian walnut chairs are at individual lace-covered tables in the dining room. A full breakfast is served here or on the side porch. Typical fare involves juice, fruit, granola and a main dish, perhaps cheese strata, quiche, waffles or french toast. One guest wrote in the hall diary that the waffles with peach sauce were out of this world.

Louise, who did the decorating, is a fulltime mother as well as a hands-on innkeeper. Her husband works at AT&T but is on hand nights and weekends.

Doubles, $80 to $125. No smoking.

The Chateau, Fifth and Warren Avenues, Spring Lake 07762. (908) 974-2000.

Billing itself as the Tiffany of Spring Lake's small hotels, this is gradually becoming less hotel-like and more like a large B&B. The evolution involves a conscious decision of young owner Scott Smith to offer elegant accommodations, personal service and, given the size of rooms and their amenities, good value for Spring Lake. The main lobby has been expanded to include a showy breakfast area, full of chintz floral armchairs at pink-linened tables. Continental breakfast is offered here – free midweek in the winter and $4.75 the rest of the time.

The hotel, dating to 1888 and in Scott's family for 46 years, is located at the end of Spring Lake and overlooks two parks and the town gazebo. Thirty-nine guest rooms and suites are in three buildings characterized by lots of public spaces, from decks to porches to a second-floor gazebo. Wicker furniture and Waverly fabrics are the common denominator in each room. All also have TV/VCRs, refrigerators and phones. The ultimate are luxury suites with wood-burning fireplaces, marble bathrooms and soaking tubs for two. We were happy to be ensconced in a large "classic parlor" with a sitting area, wet bar and two double beds in the Villa. A former residence facing the town gazebo, it contains six rooms that had been the Chateau's best until they were surpassed by the addition built in 1989 to house luxury suites.

Doubles, $95 to $170; suites, $160 to $195; three-night minimum weekends in summer, two nights in spring and fall.

The Hewitt-Wellington, 200 Monmouth Ave., Spring Lake 07762. (908) 974-1212.

This turn-of-the-century lakefront condominium hotel was totally renovated in 1988 into the most inviting of Spring Lake's other small hotels. Twelve bedrooms and seventeen suites are offered in two three-story wings connected by a breezeway beside a small heated pool. Suites consist of a bedroom and a living room with a queensize sofa bed and can accommodate four persons.

Most of those in the east wing face a park and afford views of the lake and the ocean. Two in the front corner tucked into the turret are particularly intriguing. Rooms are light and airy, outfitted with Drexel-Heritage furniture and thick carpeting. Queensize beds, TVs, mini-refrigerators, telephones and marble baths with brass fixtures are the rule. All rooms are decorated in similar style. Rates vary with location and view.

A complimentary continental breakfast is served in season. Dinner is available in the hotel's leased restaurant, Whispers (see Dining Spots).

Doubles, $140 to $200; suites, $200 to $220. Closed January-March and weekdays in November and December.

Villa Park, 417 Ocean Road, Spring Lake 07762. (908) 449-3642 or 974-8672.

This interesting looking, three-story square house with wraparound porch a few blocks from the ocean is colorful in beige with lavender trim and a lavender and green door. The quirkiness continues inside where Alice and David Bramhall share their home with guests in eight homey bedrooms decorated in country style, four with private baths.

David, a retired policeman, is a master mechanic and handyman, whose efforts show throughout the house. Ask to see the enormous kitchen he remodeled in tiger oak and stained glass with all kinds of sliding shelves and useful space fashioned from nooks and crannies – a homemaker's dream. From it Alice serves guests a full breakfast of fresh fruit, cereal, biscuits and perhaps french toast, apple-nut pancakes or eggs any style. It's taken in a pink, oak-filled dining room opening off a cozy fireplaced parlor.

Upstairs, Alice's collection of dolls takes up most of the second-floor landing and hall. A favorite room at the rear of the third floor has a queensize bed, a wing chair, small TV set, stenciling and private bath. Another favorite is on the main floor front, with ornate molding, two rocking chairs, a TV and a handmade quilt. Another beautiful quilt covers a wall in the upstairs hallway. Alice swapped it a few years ago for lodging for a craftswoman from Ohio.

Doubles, $60 to $100. Two-night minimum in summer. No credit cards.

Window tables in Green Room overlook pond outside Old Mill Inn.

Dining Spots

Spring Lake's restaurant choices are limited by zoning regulations and a lack of liquor licenses. But there are plenty of options nearby. The Normandy Inn offers guests a file of menus from 70 recommended restaurants, only five of them in Spring Lake proper.

Old Mill Inn, Old Mill Road, Spring Lake Heights. (908) 449-1800.

Overlooking a tranquil mill pond with an eight-foot water wheel just west of town is this impressive establishment that's almost everybody's favorite for fine food and surroundings. If it no longer looks much like the grist mill it once was, that's because the restaurant established here in 1938 has burned five times, the latest in 1985. From the ashes emerged a behemoth with two main-floor dining rooms seating a total of 240, a lobby bigger than most restaurants and an upstairs function room that caters 100-plus weddings a year.

A remarkable stained-glass rendering of the New York skyline takes up most of one wall in Joe's New York Cafe, dark and plush in rich wood and hunter green. Most diners choose the larger main Green Room, which is frilly and feminine and obviously popular for a Saturday lunch outing. Best of all at midday is a window table in the bar, away from the hubbub and seemingly perched over the water beside a flotilla of ducks. The taped piano music was so pure we thought it was live. We enjoyed a spicy Manhattan clam chowder, an abundant spinach and avocado salad, and two crab cakes on a pool of herbed cream sauce, nicely presented with a side of yellow and green squash, cauliflower and green peppers. A bread basket with good, crusty rolls and a blueberry and a bran muffin came with. The french fries were made by hand with the skins left on, and the excellent salad accompanying the crab cake was tossed with a zesty raspberry vinaigrette. It was obvious that the kitchen cares and maintains interest and quality along with quantity.

For dinner, owner Joe Amiel recommends any of the seafood dishes ("we have wonderful lobster, crab and fresh fish"), the extra-crispy roast duck with raspberry-port wine sauce and the prime rib with horseradish sauce. Prices start at $17.95 for chicken and artichokes or pasta of the day and go to $29 for T-bone steak. Start with

359

lobster bisque, carpaccio or oysters rockefeller. Finish with cheesecake, Swiss chocolate pie or ice cream. The wine list offers a good mix between high end and low end, with lots in between.

Lunch, daily 11:30 to 3 (closed Monday in winter); dinner nightly, 3 to 10 or 11; Sunday, brunch 11 to 3, dinner noon to 10.

Robinson's, 415 Highway 71, Spring Lake Heights. (908) 449-3223.

Charles and Dolores Robinson, whose Water's Edge restaurant in Bayville was ranked among New Jersey's best four years in a row by New Jersey Monthly magazine, moved to Spring Lake in 1994 in an effort to transplant their success. They took over the old P.J. Ruggle's restaurant, redecorated elegantly, brought in a pair of chefs from New York and Palm Beach, and catered to haute tastes and adventuresome palates.

Although the Ruggle's heritage was proving to be something of an albatross, the Robinsons were elevating local dining with a short continental menu supplemented by creative nightly specials. Dinner entrées are priced from $15.95 for pork chops stuffed with smoked mozzarella, sage and a green garlic sauce to $20.95 for garlic-crusted rack of lamb with a coarse mustard demi-glaze. Salmon au poivre with toasted shallot spinach, grilled swordfish medallions with a sherry and caper sauce, veal française, New York strip steak, filet mignon and seven pasta dishes are other possibilities, although we understand the night's specials offer more adventure. Good appetizers are cornmeal-crusted calamari with a basil vinaigrette and balsamic-glazed chicken livers with potato pancakes and vidalia onions. Dinner ends with a flourish, perhaps bananas foster, strawberries romanoff or a highly touted sabayon.

Dining is formal in several Victorian rooms decked out in splashy black and burgundy wallpapers, white-linened tables, leather chairs, black shaded oil lamps and colorful Parisian china. Eleven kinds of house-made salad oils – from citrus-thyme-basil to jalapeño-red pepper – are showcased in a mirrored niche at the rear of the main dining area.

Dinner nightly, 4 to 10; Sunday brunch, 11 to 3.

Whispers, 200 Monmouth Ave., Spring Lake. (908) 449-3330.

The owner of The Sandpiper restaurant has taken over the elegant dining room in the Hewitt-Wellington Hotel, which had been leased to Anne's of Spring Lake for a couple of years, and returned it to its maiden name. Brian Flynn retained the elegant decor: a beige and pink room with a marble floor, upholstered chairs, and four crystal chandeliers that coordinate with the long-stemmed crystal vases and wine glasses on the tables.

Young chef Dan Hurley is known for adding creative touches to classic dishes. Main courses ($17.96 to $21.95) could be grilled salmon with a cilantro-pesto sauce, pan-fried brook trout with shrimp and red seedless grapes, linguini with shrimp and arugula in a tomato cream sauce, veal and shrimp sautéed in white wine and steak au poivre. Starters include baked mushroom caps stuffed with crabmeat and cheese, spicy steamed clams with julienned red peppers and garlic, and roasted eggplant soup served with croutons and melted mozzarella.

Dinner, Wednesday-Sunday 5 to 9. Closed January and February. BYOB.

The Sandpiper, 7 Atlantic Ave., Spring Lake. (908) 449-4700.

Hidden in the walkout basement of a century-old hotel of the same name is this little gem, purchased in 1991 by John Nagle and Brian Flynn. They and 25-year-old chef Greg Weightman have made quite a culinary mark for themselves in a U-shaped room that's mostly windows, pretty in pink with ruffled curtains, Villeroy & Boch china,

Country-pretty look prevails in the Sandpiper dining room.

pink-stemmed glassware and good art for sale on the interior walls. With candles flickering and a pianist playing, it's all quite romantic.

Vodka rigatoni ($13.95), garnished with peas and prosciutto, is the chef's pasta specialty. Among other main dishes ($16.95 to $21.95), chicken and veal each take top billing in three presentations. Grilled salmon topped with wildberry schnapps and basil cream, sesame-seared tuna and shrimp in a light teriyaki sauce, stuffed filet mignon and steak diane round out the menu. Sandpiper garlic bread – fresh semolina bread topped with garlic butter, basil, sundried tomatoes and mozzarella – is a favorite appetizer.

The hotel, which offers fifteen guest rooms on three upper floors under separate management, boasts Spring Lake's only indoor pool.

Lunch daily, 11:30 to 3; dinner nightly, 5:30 to 9:30 or 10; Sunday brunch, 11:30 to 2:30. Closed Monday and Tuesday in off-season and January to mid-February. BYOB.

Armadillo Crossing, 16th and Main Streets, South Belmar. (908) 280-1880.

The ice water comes with lemon wedges in mason jars, a muddy cowboy boot rests on a shelf and a stuffed beaver stands near the restrooms in this interesting little Southwest haunt just north of Spring Lake in South Belmar. The blackboard menu reads like Tex-Mex with a cajun accent, although young chef-owner Brian Mahoney demurs. "Up-and-coming Southwest food," the Spring Lake native calls it. "No tacos or burritos or anything like that."

The complimentary plate of white bean dip with tortilla chips, cucumber and zucchini slices and black olives nearly made redundant our dinner appetizers of roasted garlic with feta cheese and red peppers (sensational) and a salad of exotic mushrooms on assorted baby lettuces (sublime). The waitress who explained the ins and outs of the menu employed a lot of "very hot" adjectives, which turned out to be particularly true in the grilled jerked chicken with kiwi salsa, accompanied by interesting sweet potato fries and a zesty corn salad. Slightly milder, as it was supposed to be, was the Arizona chicken with avocado and kiwi sauce and Mexican rice. Both main dishes

361

were excellent and arrived in such abundance that part left in doggy bags for lunch the next day. Desserts included an acclaimed key lime pie, strawberry-amaretto cake and cappuccino-hazelnut cake, but alas no icy refreshments to cool such assertive fare. The peppermint candies that came with the bill had to suffice.

We'd gladly return to try some of Brian's other main courses ($12.95 to $16.95), perhaps blackened tuna with pineapple salsa, a sixteen-ounce Texas steak with red chile onion rings, or tequila-lime chicken with roasted red pepper sauce. Steamed spiced shrimp and 'gator à la bayou are possible starters.

The place is tiny, the music soft and the barn-red walls glow at night when the lights are dimmed and the oil candles lit. You don't even notice that the tablecloths are mismatched and that the decor is of the tag-sale variety.

Dinner, Monday-Saturday 5 to 10. BYOB.

Ragin' Cajun, 1110C Main St., Belmar. (908) 280-8689.

Self-taught chef Tracey Orsi had never even been to Louisiana when she and her boyfriend, Brian Mahoney, opened this 40-seat wisp of a restaurant in 1993. Brian moved down the street to open Armadillo Crossing in 1994, but still marvels at Tracey's skills. "It's a real show to watch her cook," he said. "I designed the restaurant for her to be on stage."

From her open kitchen at the rear come complimentary roasted garlic appetizers and such true-blue cajun offerings as conch fritters, crawfish étouffée and shrimp vermilion ($8.95 to $16.95), the variations spelled out nightly on a blackboard menu. Desserts could be lemon mousse cake and mocha-amaretto torte.

The setting is simple: floral print tablecloths and coral-colored pressed-tin walls. There's little to detract from the show in the kitchen.

Dinner, Monday-Saturday 4 to 10. BYOB.

The Avon Pavilion, Ocean Avenue, Avon. (908) 775-1043.

They dole out hot dogs and hamburgers by day at this snow-white pavilion right over the beach. Come evening, they dress up the place with tablecloths and candlelight and offer a menu featuring gourmet, low-sodium and low-fat entrée specials denoted by heart symbols.

The lapping waves are the backdrop for interesting pastas and main dishes ($12.95 to $16.95) like grilled chicken forestière, broiled salmon with a lemon-lime sauce verte, grilled yellowfin tuna with spicy creole sauce, stir-fried shrimp and vegetables on steamed rice and grilled strip steak smothered with mushrooms, sweet vidalia onions and garlic.

The "New Joisey" clam chowder with a Jersey Shore zip is a favorite starter. Otherwise, begin with bay and booze shrimp (steamed in beer and Old Bay spice) or caesar salad with a unique chardonnay caesar dressing.

Dinner nightly from 6, summer only. BYOB.

Chrisandra's, 900 Ocean Ave., Bradley Beach. (908) 774-7000.

"Dynamite food," our knowledgeable Spring Lake informant advised of this newcomer ensconced in the wraparound porch and two small dining areas on the main floor of the Bradley Inn. Owners Lori and Gerard Morano oversee a colorful dining operation amid lavender painted walls and bright floral tablecloths.

The food is colorful as well. Dinner dishes are priced from $10.95 for sundried tomato fettuccine tossed with grilled vegetables and garlic to $16.95 for filet mignon in a pinot noir demi-glace. Choices include lobster pasta in a spinach-ricotta cream sauce over black linguini, pan-seared sea scallops finished with a Thai chile butter and grilled chicken with a black bean salsa.

Dessert could be a bittersweet chocolate pâté with grand marnier, bread pudding with caramel sauce or banana crème brûlée.

Lunch daily, noon to 3; dinner, 5 to 10. BYOB. No smoking.

Scarborough Fair, 1414 Meeting House Road, Sea Girt. (908) 223-6658.

The name of this atmospheric spot reflects its former incarnation as a farmhouse-turned-mini-mall full of gift and craft boutiques. The marketplace failed and so did a health-food eatery that followed. William Suckow turned it into a "gourmet" restaurant in 1986 and, judging by the wait we had after arriving for an 8 o'clock reservation one autumn Friday night, success was achieved.

Continental is a more apt description than gourmet for such standards ($15.95 to $22.95) as chicken marsala, veal française and steak au poivre. The chef adds an international flair with things like spanakopita, quesadilla, chicken jambalaya, cajun shrimp, amaretto sole and beef with broccoli stir-fry. We were tempted by a special of prime rib with cognac sauce, but they'd run out. We settled for appetizers of baked escargots topped with brie and a lovely pernod-garlic sauce and a not-so-special pasta with shrimp in a tomato cream sauce (which turned out to be a small bowl of fettuccine with pink sauce) and entrées of veal saltimbocca and tournedos dijonnaise. Rice, red-skin potatoes and an assortment of vegetables were served family style. Salads were nicely dressed with honey-mustard or the house herb vinaigrette. The bread basket consisted mainly of cellophane-wrapped crackers.

Stick to the tried and true and you'll likely do all right. Maybe you'll luck into a round booth for four up the staircase in the tiered front atrium, overlooking all the action below. We found it more private than the crowded upstairs dining room or the rear carousel room, where at Christmas carousel horses are hung from the ceiling.

Lunch, Monday-Friday 11:30 to 3:30; dinner nightly, 5 to 8:30, weekends to 10, Sunday 3 to 8:30. BYOB.

Rod's Old Irish Tavern, 507 Washington Blvd., Sea Girt. (908) 449-2020.

Favorite among a number of Irish pubs in an area only lately shedding its moniker as the Irish Riviera is this large green house with white trim and a canopied entrance at the edge of downtown Sea Girt, an attractive residential town on Spring Lake's southern border. Green and white is the color scheme inside as well, from the checkered tablecloths in the enormous pub to the curtains separating leather booths and tables in the dining room. There's a garden cafe beyond.

The same menu is served throughout the establishment. This means you can enjoy grilled swordfish or sirloin steak while watching one of the dozen or so big-screen TVs around the central bar, or a burger or barbecued ribs in the dining room, and vice-versa. Mix and match chicken pot pie, shrimp scampi, fettuccine primavera, a nacho platter, chef's salad, oysters on the half shell and such. The extensive menu runs from $3.50 for a jumbo hot dog to $17.95 for blackened sirloin steak.

Lunch daily, 11:30 to 2:30; dinner, 5 to 11.

Jon Anthony's, 713 Riverview Drive, Brielle. (908) 223-0769.

This new Italian bread and specialty store isn't a restaurant per se, but it might as well be for all the folks stopping by after work to pick up dinners to go. People from up and down the shore come here for party fare as well as sumptuous picnics and at-home meals. Some of Spring Lake's best dinner parties are catered by Jon Anthony's.

The display cases are chock full of Italian meats, cheeses and prepared foods at reasonable prices. Among the fabulous array of 40 salads was a seafood salad made with those ghastly sealegs (at least they were honest). The chicken scampi looked wonderful, as did the veal marsala and the roast loin of pork. Desserts, frozen foods, baked goods – they have it all.

Open daily from 8 to 7, Sunday 8 to 4.

Who's on Third, 1300 Third Ave., Spring Lake. (908) 449-4233.

This deli and grill with the neat name and a bit of a baseball theme occupies a prime corner location in Spring Lake's shopping area. There are a few tables on a covered porch beside the sidewalk, a revolving cake display inside the entry, a counter and a family-style dining room.

It's a real deli and grill (as in grilled cheese), and is especially popular for breakfast. We were impressed with one of the breakfast specials, the one with three scrambled eggs, toast, home fries, juice and coffee for a cool $2.75. Other tempters were the breakfast sandwiches (one a pork roll with egg), the kitchen sink omelet ("this has it all") and the pizza omelet.

For lunch, order subs, sandwiches and burgers by the numbers. An open roast beef or turkey sandwich with gravy goes for $6.25. Desserts are the likes of jello, chocolate pudding and homemade pies.

Open Monday-Saturday, 7 a.m. to 8 p.m., Sunday 7 to 5; shorter hours in off-season.

Diversions

A New York Times article claimed that "it's not so much what there is to do, it is what there is not to do that makes Spring Lake special." The prime attractions, of course, are the quiet boardwalk and pristine beach, plus the parklands surrounding the town's namesake lake. Within easy striking distance are Atlantic City, New York, Philadelphia, gambling, racing, arcades and what have you. From these you can return quickly to Spring Lake's refuge.

The Beach. A two-mile-long boardwalk separates the Atlantic Ocean beach from sand dunes and Ocean Avenue. Unlike neighboring Belmar where a McDonald's occupies the prime boardwalk location, Spring Lake's boardwalk contains only two buildings at either end: pavilions harboring saltwater pools, rest rooms and food stands. Beach passes are sold here.

Theater. The Spring Lake Theatre Company has expanded its repertoire and schedule to stage eight shows year-round in the Spring Lake Community House. The English Tudor building built in 1923 by a former mayor and state senator includes a library and a 360-seat theater. Tickets are in the $15 range and sell out early; they're available through the Chamber of Commerce, 449-0577, or direct, 449-4530.

Gazebo Concerts. The town recreation commission sponsors outdoor concerts in Potter Park on varying nights roughly every other week in summer. Jazz bands, the Atlantic Wind Ensemble, the Ocean Grove Band, the Happy Days String Band, a folksinger and an Irish balladeer were among recent performers. Townspeople and visitors bring chairs or blankets and pretty well fill the park.

St. Catharine's Church, Third and Essex Avenue. Built beside the lake between 1901 and 1907 by a wealthy resident as a memorial to his daughter, this striking edifice resembles the Romanesque St. Peter's Basilica in miniature and is well worth a visit. Two 800-year-old bronze standards from Rome line the entrance to the church. The high altar is made of the same Carrara marble used by Michelangelo and the stained-glass windows were made in Bavaria. A professor from Rome painted the interior frescos. The church is one of two in the same parish in Spring Lake, a heavily

Roman Catholic community once known as the Irish Riviera. The total enrollment of Spring Lake's single public elementary school is less than that of the parochial school.

Green Gables Croquet Club, Ocean Avenue between Washington and Madison streets. The first such croquet club on the East Coast hosts an invitational tournament that attracts about twenty teams and an enthusiastic gallery every summer. A substantial private home and two regulation-size courts are set on award-winning lawns that occupy an entire block facing the ocean. The owner turns over the lower part of her home for use as a clubhouse. The putting-green quality expanse is arguably the most impressive of many in Spring Lake, where commercial lawn services must rank as the town's single most prosperous business niche. Another manicured masterpiece surrounds the Coleman residence at 301 West Lake Drive. The whole lawn is clipped to one-fourth inch high and maintained daily like a putting green.

Vitale & Vitale, 315 Morris Ave., 449-3000. Housed in an impressive neoclassical white building that would be at home on Rodeo Drive in Beverly Hills is this clock shop and gallery/museum like no other. Calling themselves horologers and antiquarians, staffers claim the finest and most extensive selection of antique timepieces in the world. Prices start about $5,000 and rise to $500,000. We're told the owner runs it as a hobby. Open Thursday-Tuesday 10 to 5:30. Free.

Shopping. Four blocks of tree-lined Third Avenue are home to small stores and an unusually high number of real-estate offices. The only chain store is a branch of **Crabtree & Evelyn,** although the local **Karen's Boutique** has a branch at the Warren Hotel to display its women's wares. Perhaps the biggest drawing card is the **Irish Centre,** which features all kinds of Irish imports reflecting the resort's heritage. Another is the old-fashioned **Spring Lake Variety Store** filled to the brim with all kinds of things, including beach chairs hanging from the ceiling. Clothing and accessories are more sedate specialties of **The Camel's Eye, Village Tweeds** and **Courts & Greens,** whose names indicate their priorities, as does **Spring Lace,** full of lace and Victoriana. Adorable bears clad in little smock dresses are in the windows of **Teddy Bears by the Seashore,** a children's wear outlet. We admired the sweaters at **The Clover Leaf** and the cute clothes at **Samantha's.** Some of the most sophisticated cards, stationery, books and desk accessories we've seen anywhere are stocked at **Noteworthy By-the-Sea.**

Sweets lovers get their fill at the **Third Avenue Chocolate Shoppe** and **Jean-Louise Homemade Candy,** where the day's special at our visit was chocolate-covered grapes. Snacks are available to eat in or take out at **Freedman's Bakery** and **The Victorian Bean Cafe & Gifts,** where afternoon tea is offered daily in summer. Gourmet pizzas and sophisticated entrée specials are offered at the new **Spring Lake Pizzeria,** a sleek and squeaky clean place that lives up to its claim of being "not just another pizzeria." The **Spring Lake Bottle Shop** is the place to pick up a good bottle of wine for restaurants where you bring your own.

Extra-Special

Historic Allaire Village, Allaire State Park, off Route 524, Allaire, 938-2253. This outdoor living-history museum re-creates the days of New Jersey's early iron industry. Interpreters dressed in the work clothes of the 1830s portray the daily life and times of early iron workers and their families. They demonstrate early crafts and open-hearth cooking in several houses and buildings. Other buildings include a snack bar and a general store/museum shop. Listed on the National Register, this mini-Sturbridge is part of 3,000-acre Allaire State Park just west of Spring Lake. Village buildings open daily 10 to 5, May to Labor Day; Wednesday-Sunday in off-season. Closed in winter. Parking fee.

East Hampton, N.Y.
Village Beautiful

East Hampton, let it be said up front, is too-too. Too posh, too trendy, too social, too expensive, too precious, too much.

At the same time, let it be said that it is also beautiful. Classy. And, at other than peak visiting periods, rather serene. Almost perfect. Not too-too perfect.

For New Yorkers, there is no better-known summer place than the Hamptons, some

Old Hook Windmill frames Mill House Inn.

110 miles east on the South Fork near the tip of Long Island. The Hamptons collectively embrace, from west to east: Westhampton and Hampton Bays, which for most are quite skippable. Southampton, perhaps the best known of the Hamptons, the Palm Beach of the North. Bridgehampton, which is consciously understated. And East Hampton, more subdued than flashy Southampton.

It's not hard to understand why this was called "America's Most Beautiful Village" in the early 1960s by a national magazine. Town officials differ over whether it was the Saturday Evening Post or National Geographic; their indecision suggests that to East Hampton it doesn't matter.

The wide main street of the historic village passes a long green with a pond and a graveyard, a windmill, English-style edifices and substantial old homes before it reaches shady, suave downtown East Hampton. Take Ocean Avenue down to the

beach, arguably the nation's cleanest and one of its most beautiful. Meander along the side streets of the estate area, where thick privet hedges screen the manicured estates of the rich and famous. Some of the more illustrious – and less flamboyant – make up the Blue Book of the Hamptons, discreetly stacked for sale on the counter at the local bookstore. Pause for a look at Home Sweet Home, the Mulford House, Clinton Academy, Miss Amelia's Cottage, Guild Hall, the Tudoresque library and the Old Hook Mill, one among the nation's largest collections of windmills. This is the East Hampton that the transient visitor sees.

The East Hampton that the New Yorkers take over in the summer is the one where the scene is seeing and being seen: in restaurants charging Manhattan prices, at chi-chi inns demanding minimum stays of three to five nights, in boutiques catering to the celebrity and carriage trade, in the slick newspapers and maga-

Pine pencil-post bed is draped in lace in Blue Room at The Pink House.

zines touting the Hamptons' social scene, in all the fitness centers and beauty salons and cosmetic makeover clinics that show where priorities lie.

Some New Yorkers would give their bottom dollar for an invitation for a weekend or for a share in a house in the Hamptons each summer. Others would be advised to visit at off-peak times to enjoy East Hampton's many charms, without its hassles.

Inn Spots

Accommodations vary from old inns to small, home-stay B&Bs taking in guests on summer weekends. Weekends, when minimum stays of at least three nights are the rule, are booked far ahead. Many inns require four-night stays on holiday weekends and two-night stays on spring and fall weekends.

The Pink House, 26 James Lane, East Hampton 11937. (516) 324-3400.

Despite an abundance of established inns here, architect/builder Ron Steinhilber felt there was a market for an upscale B&B. "People will pay a little extra for something really luxurious, that goes the extra mile," he said. So he took over a National Register-listed house, built by a local whaling captain across from the village green and pond in the mid-1800s, and imbued it with taste and personality – except for the pale pink exterior, which he inherited and cannot be changed. The interior is not the locally prevailing Victorian look but country light.

Ron and a friend renovated the house themselves in 1990 and his architectural genius shows. So do his collections, from a platform light from Brooklyn's Myrtle Avenue subway line in a corner of the living room to his grandfather's watercolors and Salari bells from New Mexico. A row of lights illuminates the entry hall and focuses on collections in two shelves at the top of the stairs.

All five guest rooms come with private baths and telephones. The Blue Room has a cushioned window seat, queensize pine pencil-post bed, and a huge marble shower and sink bearing the inn's own toiletries. The Twin Room, where the beds with pretty pink and green sheets can be joined as a king, contains a wall of iron artifacts. The Green Room has an Adirondack chair and a wicker queensize bed. Already a favorite is the new Elk Room, with Southwest decor, a jacuzzi and TV. On the main floor is the Garden Room with a four-poster bed, a private entrance and its own flower-filled patio, where "guests feel like they're in a cottage at the Beverly Hills Hotel," says Ron. Calla lilies adorn the bathroom sink to carry out the garden feeling.

Recessed ceiling lights spotlight selected art in the living room with two facing loveseats and in the dining room, both of which have fireplaces. Iced tea and nibbles are served on the wicker-filled front porch. Guests may help themselves to soft drinks and ice from a refrigerator, and chocolates are on the beds at night.

Breakfast in the dining room or on the screened rear porch includes fresh fruit and juices, delectable muffins (strawberry, banana and blueberry muffins came in red, white and blue for the Fourth of July), homemade granola and European roast coffee. The crowning glory might be banana-walnut pancakes, sourdough french toast with sautéed pears, heart-shaped waffles topped with raspberries or a cream cheese and chive omelet.

Outside is a lovely back yard, where guests enjoy a hedge-screened swimming pool. "Although our aim is to be elegant and deluxe," says he, "we're also rustic and homey. People feel at home here."

Doubles, $245 to $285.

Bluff Cottage, 266 Bluff Road, Box 428, Amagansett 11930. (516) 267-6172.

"We felt this was a house to share," say owners Clement Thompson and John Pakulek. They'd bought the oceanfront place as a summer home in 1971 and had proceeded to rent it out from Memorial Day to Labor Day, so rarely got to use it. When they decided enough was enough and moved in, they converted the 100-year-old summer cottage into a year-round house. "For years people had wanted to see it," Clem says. "Our friends were after us to do a B&B, so we did."

And a very inviting one it is. The only thing cottagey about the place is its name. It's situated amidst a stretch of substantial residences cosseted behind privet hedges with the open Atlantic across the street. The air-conditioned house, full of fine antiques, has four guest rooms with queensize beds and private baths, elegant common rooms and porches on two levels overlooking the ocean. A refined, house-party atmosphere derives from affable hosts, relaxed company and a posh setting beside the beach. "This was our retirement project," says John. "And we've never worked so hard."

Every guest gets a tour of the main floor. See the focal point of the den: the huge English partner's desk with intricate carvings all the way around (and a little sign warning not to use the desk for writing). Admire the 18th-century confessional in the corner and an old French dome chair beside the fireplace in the living room. Note the parquet-inlaid refectory table and one of the last surviving French tapestry screens in front of the fireplace in the dining room. In the country kitchen are shelf after shelf of antique English ironstone dinnerware. "You can see we're partial to French provincial and English country," says Clem.

Upstairs, the bedrooms are color-coordinated around a specific color, some more coordinated than others. The rear Peach Room is peach from its carpet to its walls to its hand-ironed sheets, interrupted only by the antique English mahogany poster bed and the curved English armoire. The front Green Room is a Ralph Lauren hunt scene lookalike in burgundy and dark green, although this was done like the rest of the house with fabrics from Calico Corners. The front Blue Room takes its name from just one of the colors in the draperies and isn't particularly blue, "so we *could* call it the Cameo Room," advises Clem. The Beige Room is, well, mostly beige. Each four-poster bed is

Wicker-furnished front porch at Bluff Cottage faces lawns and ocean.

draped in down comforters and duvets. Sturdy antique furniture abounds, but the look is uncluttered.

You'll be well fed in the morning after John picks up the makings for continental breakfast from the nearby Amagansett Farmers Market: luscious croissants, blueberry or bran muffins, English scones, fresh grapefruit and juices. They're served buffet-style in the dining room, and often taken on trays to the front porch.

The special charm of Bluff Cottage is enhanced by the wide front porch awash in wicker and a smaller upstairs balcony big enough for four. Both are good for ocean-watching and soaking up the salubrious seaside air.

Doubles, $180 to $210. No smoking. Closed October-April.

Centennial House, 13 Woods Lane, East Hampton 11937. (516) 324-9414.

This shingled Victorian hugging the main road at the edge of the estate district was built in 1876, the date having been inscribed in plaster in the Bay bedroom by one of the village's celebrated builders. It was owned by only two families before it was acquired in 1987 by David Oxford, a lawyer who had his office in the rear barn until he retired, and Harry Chauncey, a television executive in New York. In the midst of restoration, they turned their home into a B&B when the Perles of the 1770 House inn followed up a casual suggestion by calling one night with a problem, the need for overnight lodging for a desperate couple. Their friends obliged, and one thing led to another.

Now the partners offer five bedrooms with private baths and a three-bedroom cottage. Each is decorated to the Victorian hilt with antiques garnered mainly from estate and yard sales. Sherry and port, chocolate truffles and turkish robes are in each room, and a small refrigerator at the top of the stairs is stocked with drinks and snacks.

The Bay Room with the builder's initials inscribed in the wall beside the bookcase is most in demand. Its queensize four-poster is topped by a comforter, a mohair afghan and chintz floral pillows that match the balloon curtains in the bay window. The bathroom has a clawfoot tub and a sink ensconced in a 19th-century pulpit. The Lincoln Room is so named for its Lincoln bed, designed the year he became president. The clawfoot tub that goes with the canopy four-poster in the Rose Room is draped with heavy fabric. The third floor holds a loft bedroom, its ceiling sloping down to a kingsize bed. There's a TV with a chair beside. This is not for tall people, who have to bend over in the shower and are apt to hit their heads on the ceiling as they go down the steep, curving staircase. The Sleigh Room off the parlor contains a double sleigh bed and an armoire. In some respects the most comfortable lodging is in the rear cottage, fully winterized and boasting a full kitchen, breakfast area, living room with a TV and stereo, gas fireplace, two baths and a front porch. It has a small twin bedroom and a queen bedroom downstairs, and a room upstairs with a king bed, bare floor, TV and one antique rocker.

The interior of the main house is dark and done in the high Victorian style. Twin crystal chandeliers illuminate the double parlor, where prized doggies Earl and Edwinna are apt to preside in front of the Italian marble fireplace. Outfitted in Williamsburg fabrics (the chair seats are coordinated with the wallpaper), the formal Georgian dining room is set as if for dinner with cut-linen napkins and Rosenthal china. Breakfast is served here at a lace-covered table for eight and a smaller round table in a corner beside the bookshelves. Guests rave about the buttermilk pancakes, french toast or omelets prepared by Harry, David or the house manager. Fruits, muffins and breakfast meats accompany.

Out back is a secluded pool behind Harry's rose and herb gardens, where you're feel as if you're a guest at someone's summer home. Entry to the house is "by appointment only." A Cape May-style combination lock discourages transients, since Harry is at work and David is out and about during the day and they don't want their guests' tranquillity marred in the evening.

Doubles, $175 to $325; cottage, $475 (breakfast not included). No smoking.

The Maidstone Arms, 207 Main St., East Hampton 11937. (516) 324-5006.

Nicely located across from the town pond and the gravestone-lined village green, this white clapboard structure looks the way a summery country hotel should look. It was converted from a private home in the 1870s, and upgraded from a seasonal inn into a year-round hotel in 1992. A porch with white rockers faces the tranquil green. Inside two three-story buildings connected by a sun porch is a ramble of rooms, from restaurant and dining porches to sixteen bedrooms with private baths, TVs, phones and air-conditioning. Out back are three garden cottages that represent the crème de la crème.

New owner Coke Anne Saunders, a New York architect whose late father was Texan Clint Murchison, poured big bucks into a cosmetic renovation and refurbishing of the old inn. A major rehab was precluded by zoning restrictions, but visitors today find modernized bathrooms, new furniture and beds, new wallpapers and draperies, and what general manager Christophe Bergen calls "a brighter, more cheery feeling." Accommodations vary in decor and size. Two small rooms we saw in the main inn – one with a double bed and another with twins – retain a snug, understated look even with the upgrades. More impressive are the garden cottages, each large and airy. We liked the one with vaulted ceiling, queensize poster bed, angled fireplace, sitting area with sofabed and armchair, and Waverly wallpaper and fabrics. Another cheerful bedroom, its wallpaper patterned with seashells and paired with tartan lampshades, won an honorable mention in Waverly's 1994 Country Inn Room of the Year contest. Besides the usual toiletries, a little sampler bag of local fragrances from Antonia's Flowers is in each room.

Waverly wallpaper and fabrics enhance cottage at The Maidstone Arms.

Guests share the wicker-filled front sun porch that doubles as a sitting room and breakfast room. It opens into a plant-filled room leading to gardens out back. A continental breakfast of scones, English muffins and such comes with the room. Breakfast also may be ordered à la carte.

The new owner has renovated the kitchen to enhance the restaurant operation (see Dining Spots), which the Maidstone Arms is running itself rather than leasing it out as in the past. It's seeking to become known as *the* local hotel, serving three meals a day year-round.

Doubles, $165 to $235; suite, $275; cottages, from $295.

Mill House Inn, 33 North Main St., East Hampton 11937. (516) 324-9766.

Facing the parkland and gravestones surrounding the Old Hook Windmill, this is a country charmer of a B&B with eight guest rooms, all with private baths. The original 1790 colonial saltbox was turned into a Dutch Colonial during expansion a century later. Katherine and Dan Hartnett, former northern New Jersey social workers and parents of two toddlers, bought the place in 1994 and undertook a major renovation the following winter.

The beamed living room and dining room are properly historic and nicely decorated. When we stayed there, the guest rooms on three floors could best be described as homey. Our second-floor room had pretty floral stenciling in peach and green, a comfy lace canopy bed, three chairs, a skirted table and green and white awning-like curtains. At our latest visit, Katherine had begun buying antiques, armoires, oriental screens and paintings to upgrade and redecorate all the guest rooms in a Colonial style. She planned to stress the history and character of the area with an equestrian theme in the Hampton Classic Room, a floral theme in the Hampton Gardens Room, and mill memorabilia in the Mill Room. Several rooms were to gain fireplaces in an effort to boost winter business. Two large third-floor rooms now have private baths.

There's room to spread out on a long enclosed front porch, which the Hartnetts opened up with french doors, and in a spacious back yard. They also added french doors in the dining room, which opens onto a rear patio. Afternoon tea is served by the living-room fireplace in the off-season.

The Hartnetts installed a commercial kitchen so they could augment their continental-plus breakfast with hot entrées. Expect fresh fruit, fresh juice, granola and a variety of fresh pastries, from cornmeal blueberry muffins to Irish soda bread. In winter they add things like stuffed french toast with apple preserves, cornmeal waffles with sausages, and scrambled eggs with smoked salmon and croissants. Breakfast is taken on colorful Mikasa china with a peach pattern in the dining room, or on trays delivered to the bedrooms.

Doubles, $160 to $195.

1770 House, 143 Main St., East Hampton 11937. (516) 324-1770.

Seven guest rooms with private baths and a dining room of note (see Dining Spots) are offered by Miriam Perle and her offspring in this white clapboard house beside the old Clinton Academy, New York State's first accredited high school.

Mim Perle, a cooking instructor and caterer, and her late husband Sid, a clothier, bought the structure, which had seen many lives, in 1977. Planning this as a semi-retirement project, the Perles found it quickly became a hands-on, family operation. They eventually moved into the Philip Taylor House nearby, leaving the 1770 House in the capable hands of daughter Wendy Van Deusen, who shares cooking duties with Mim, and son Adam, who presides over the Colonial taproom with its old hickory beams and open dutch hearth. Guests gather here or in a paneled library with fireplace.

Mim Perle's decorating touch is evident in the guest rooms. We liked Room 10, a junior suite that has a queen bed in a recessed alcove, a floral print on the walls and some of the period clocks and antique furnishings that abound throughout. It comes with a little sitting room with a desk and one of the inn's two working fireplaces, as well as a small dressing room and a private entrance. A suite in the carriage house with a queen canopy bed, a loft with twin beds, a cathedral-ceilinged living room and a 2,000-volume library is the only place in town, we heard, where Yoko Ono will stay.

After Sid Perle's untimely death in 1993, Mim put up for sale their Elizabethan manor house, **The Philip Taylor House,** at 181 Main St. Until its sale, she continued to offer three regal bedrooms to B&B guests, who walk to the 1770 House for breakfast. That's the specialty of Mim, who ran a cooking school in Great Neck after studying at the Cordon Bleu. She offers fresh juice or fruit, cereal and perhaps french toast made out of challah bread, belgian waffles or fresh herb omelets with scones.

Doubles, $105 to $185; carriage house and Philip Taylor House rooms, $225.

The Huntting Inn, 94 Main St., East Hampton 11937. (516) 324-0410.

The closest inn to the center of town, this is within walking distance of stores and yet back from the street beside a shady English country garden, of which innkeeper Linda Calder is rightly proud. The only problem is that inn guests have to walk outside and halfway around the building to get to the garden retreat. The owners hope eventually to put in french doors allowing access from the sun porch to the garden, but in strictly regulated East Hampton such things take time.

Resembling a New England country inn, this white clapboard structure with green shutters is really ancient and protected (some would say prevented) from changes that would bring it into the 20th, let alone 21st, century. It was built as a home in 1699 by the Church of England for the Rev. Nathaniel Huntting; his widow turned it into a public house in 1751, a status it has maintained since. The front porch and main floor are given over to The Palm (see Dining Spots), one of two New Yorkish restaurant operations run here by co-owners Wally Ganzi and Bruce Bozzi. The other is at the associated Hedges Inn.

Upstairs, a narrow maze of corridors leads to eighteen air-conditioned guest rooms on two floors. Rooms vary widely in size and style. One of the largest harbors a beamed ceiling, kingsize four-poster bed and a velvet sofa. The bathroom has pine wainscoting stained to look like oak and a double jacuzzi and separate shower. Another is small with an old-fashioned tub. Most rooms are decorated with vivid floral prints and dark carpeting. One charming room, sprightly with yellow paint and yellow floral duvet that matches the draperies, was awarded an honorable mention in Waverly's 1994 Country Inn Room of the Year contest. Our room was part of a two-room suite with a small bath in the middle. It had the floral wallpaper typical of the inn, tied-back lace curtains, a kingsize bed, a TV hidden in a corner armoire, new carpeting and a dark sitting room in which only one of the three lights worked. Ice was delivered with a complimentary bottle of S. Pellegrino water and one of the bureaus displayed a basket of toiletries, a little bag of local Antonia's Flowers fragrances and lotions, and two Lindor truffles.

A good continental breakfast buffet is spread out atop the Palm bar or, at peak periods, in the restaurant. Those who get there first may eat on the front sun porch so coveted by diners at night.

Doubles, $145 to $195; suite, $250.

The Hedges' Inn, 74 James Lane, East Hampton 11937. (516) 324-7100.

Beautiful flowers line both sides of the brick walk leading to this yellow clapboard inn dating to 1774. It stands at the entry to the village at the west end of the town pond – where the road makes a turn from the city to country life, according to one writeup. The secluded setting is residential, although much of the main floor gets busy at night as the James Lane Cafe, formerly the Palm Restaurant. Like the Huntting Inn, it's owned by Wally Ganzi and Bruce Bozzi of the Palm restaurants.

Some of the eleven guest rooms on the second and third floors here seem brighter and more up to date than those at the Huntting. Room 1, for instance, is light and airy with a queensize bed, a small fireplace, a dark red velvet loveseat, baskets of fruit and flowers, and a modern bathroom with a double black marble vanity. Room 6 offers a king bed against sky-blue wallpaper. A small upstairs corner room has a double bed with a wicker headboard, but has no chairs. Each room has a private bath.

Fruit, cereal, bagels, muffins and croissants are put out in a cheery breakfast room. Wicker furniture on the front porch faces the pond.

Doubles, $145 to $195.

The House on Newtown, 172 Newtown Lane, East Hampton 11937. (516) 324-1858 or 329-0672.

This modest 1912 house built by a sea captain doesn't look like much, at least by East Hampton standards. Owners Mike and Marianne Kaufman ran it as a low-key B&B for eight years, filling by word of mouth and then branching out to lease four other houses they own around town to summer renters. Their house-rental service, the first in town, made a difference.

In August 1994, they received "a modicum of fame," as Mike tells it. First, the White House travel office called for accommodations for "some very important people" in connection with a fund-raising visit by Vice President Al Gore. Although their houses were already booked, the calls continued daily for possible cancellations. In the midst of all this, upon the recommendation of the Maidstone Arms, ABC News asked if it could use the Kaufmans' Victorian living room as a backdrop for an interview with White House counsel Lloyd Cutler on "This Week with David Brinkley." The next morning the TV crews arrived, as did Cutler from his nearby home on Georgica Pond. All the goings-on at The House on Newtown made the front page of The East Hampton Star in a story headlined simply "Certainly Never in Kansas" – a reference to Mike's quote that if they had a B&B in Kansas, they wouldn't have the same stories to tell. "East Hampton is so exciting. We're at the epicenter of everything here."

The Kaufmans are fonts of lore regarding the epicenter, Mike having been a seventh-grade teacher here for twenty years. Like its owners, the B&B is welcoming and down-to-earth. Two of the four bedrooms have private baths, and plans were to add a fourth bath so all would be private. Except for one room with twins, all have double beds ("we couldn't get queen beds up the stairway," Mike advised). They're full of sturdy oak furnishings and a lived-in look. Over the bed in one is a nifty painting of sandpipers by an artist who had once lived in the house. In the hallway a display case overflows with son Eric's wrestling trophies, and these are only the tip of the iceberg.

A continental breakfast buffet of bagels, croissants, muffins, cereals, yogurt and fresh fruit is taken at little round tables for two on the front sun porch. Guests also enjoy a small sitting room outfitted in wicker and the larger Victorian living room. The latter has a shelf lined with tea kettles, Victorian side tables, three sofas and one chair, now to be forever known as the Lloyd Cutler chair.

Doubles, $140 to $180.

McErlean House, 152 Montauk Hwy., East Hampton 11937. (516) 329-2212.

Breakfast is a big deal at this newish five-room B&B, owned by Lee and Artie McGurk, former restaurateurs from Mineola, who lately have been moonlighting on weeknights at Michael's at Maidstone Park. Served in the dining room or on the brick patio overlooking a big back lawn, it starts with a mix of cranberry-raspberry and orange juice, bowls of fresh fruit, yogurt and granola, and a variety of muffins, from multi-grain to pear-orange. Try to save room for the main course, perhaps a crabmeat, mozzarella and basil omelet, grand marnier french toast garnished with peaches, sourdough pancakes or crab cakes on toasted English muffins with salsa.

The place is named after Artie's mother. Most of the main floor is devoted to a kitchen (from which Lee does catering), a dining room and an airy great room with a fireplace and a piano, where hors d'oeuvre are offered in the afternoon.

Upstairs are five guest rooms, three with private baths and all with ceiling fans. Lee puts little vases of fresh flowers on each bed to welcome guests, and each room has a teddy bear, a swan, a duck, a mouse or a little bird attached to the curtain. She named one front corner room Moonlight Sonata, "because it's kind of gentle when the moon comes up." It has lace curtains and a queen bed. The Symphony Suite is the master bedroom, decorated by Lee's mother "as she'd like to have it." The curtains match the spread, the sheets and the material draped behind the bed.

Doubles, $95 to $140. No smoking.

The Bassett House, 128 Montauk Hwy., East Hampton 11937. (516) 324-6127.

A homey, masculine air pervades this 1830 house run since 1977 as a country B&B just west of town. That's because owner Michael Bassett does almost everything himself and it's a big house to keep up.

Guests enter through a small sitting room that flows into a spacious living room. A barber chair occupies a corner of the former, while the latter contains a TV, piano and fireplace. Beyond is a dining room with an extra-long table. The veranda is a mix of twig and wrought-iron furniture and wooden rockers.

Of the twelve guest rooms, eight have private baths. They range from singles with

Sleek, summery look prevails in rear dining room at Nick and Toni's.

in-room sinks to suites. The decor is eclectic, "blending comfortable furniture of varied vintages in a setting which is purposely informal and relaxing," according to the inn's chatty brochure written by Michael to "Dear Friend." One downstairs bedroom has dark wood walls, a sofa in front of a fireplace and a queen bed topped by a comforter. One upstairs contains a queen bed, old-fashioned wallpaper and dried flowers in an old wash pitcher. Room 5 has a Laura Ashley comforter on the bed, a fireplace and two upholstered chairs. The most coveted is Room 1, the old master bedroom facing west; it's large, has two wicker loveseats, a hooked rug depicting many birds, and a huge bathroom with a double jacuzzi and a corner shower. Michael has been known to rent his own room at busy times. That's not all. "One night I was about to sleep in a tent out back," he recalls. "People said they'd take it and I slept on the lawn."

Michael, a bachelor who's known locally for his outspokenness, offers a full breakfast of the guest's choice. "Anything you want I can cook to order," he says. "I can make you a nice omelet in a couple of minutes with herbs from my garden. Or perhaps you'd like pancakes or waffles." Juices, grapefruit and bananas accompany. Breakfast is taken in the dining room or on the interesting grounds, full of gardens and statues.

Doubles, $115 to $225.

Dining Spots

East Hampton is a place for eating and eating well, often at prices approaching those in Manhattan. Many restaurants require gratuities in cash rather than on credit cards, and reservations often are hard to come by.

Nick and Toni's, 136 North Main St., East Hampton. (516) 324-3550.

New and tony, this is one of East Hampton's "in" places, and not simply because of its wood-burning oven. We could tell the moment we arrived and were led through the entire place to a rear table, which was fine with us. We became aware of the Hampton

375

glance – all eyes on new arrivals to see who they are and with whom. Even the deuces are angled with backs to the wall so each person can watch the passing parade. And why not, when the restaurant's backer was Steve Ross, the late Time-Warner mogul who had a home in East Hampton, the place is run by his daughter and son-in-law, Toni Ross and Jeff Salaway, and chef Gail Arnold is an inspired cook with a devoted following?

There's a variety of summery rooms with big windows and no curtains. Seating is on sleek, cushioned European contemporary chairs at tables set with crisp white cloths. The look is unadulterated: no candles, no flowers and fairly bright overhead lighting.

Dinner begins with dense Tuscan bread served with olive oil for dipping. For starters, we tried the night's soup, grilled tomato with a very smoky flavor ($6) and a sensational wilted dandelion salad with a bacon and mustard vinaigrette ($7). Among main courses, we fell for the loin of pork with nectarines and swiss chard and the fettuccine with rabbit, lemon and rosemary (both $17). The house wine we had with appetizers was poured from an Italian pitcher, and meals came on various pottery serving pieces. With our meal we chose an $18 sauvignon blanc from the nearby Hargrave winery among a number of good, affordable choices. Dessert ($6) was the day's special blueberry-peach buckle from a selection that included tirami su, "serious" chocolate cake and homemade ice cream.

The changing menu involves about seven appetizers, four pastas and six main courses, priced up to $22 for black angus ribeye steak with onion and vegetable fritters. Roasted squid stuffed with sea scallops and basil, blackfish with roasted peppers and zucchini and grilled tuna niçoise were other choices the night we were there.

Although the clientele is haute, this fortunately is not a haughty place, as many in the area are. Its culinary magic, prices and lack of pretension are refreshing.

Dinner nightly, 6 to 10 or 11; Sunday, brunch 11:30 to 2:30, dinner, 5 to 10. Closed Tuesday and Wednesday, September-May.

Della Femina, 99 North Main St., East Hampton. (516) 329-6666.

In East Hampton, don't be surprised by the improbable. Here in 1992 was Jerry Della Femina, arguably the world's most famous ad man and full of Brooklyn bravado, opening a restaurant – named after himself – across the street from Nick & Toni's. Nine months later, he took over another restaurant on the waterfront, East Hampton Point. Soon followed an Italian food market and deli to go, also bearing his name. And in 1994 he acquired a propitiously located lumber yard for, at the time, who-knew-what-purpose (not, wife-TV newscaster Judy Licht hoped, another restaurant). As New York magazine put it in an article headlined "The Adman Who Ate East Hampton," Jerry Della Femina has a way of making his presence known.

His first restaurant is understated, except perhaps for the prices and the flurry of reservations that are taken ten days ahead and sell out in a few hours at peak periods (there's a "power list" for VIPs). The 80-seat dining room is stark white except for beige cane chairs at well-spaced tables, a wood-paneled ceiling, tall straw wall sconces that look like sheaves of wheat and, near the far corner, a decorative fireplace with colorful jugs on the mantel. Boxes of fruits and vegetables add color in an opening between the dining room and the skylit bar, its walls plastered ever-so-suavely with framed caricatures of restaurant patrons. Trying to make that wall quickly became part of the restaurant's cachet.

Drew Nieporent, the Manhattan restaurant superstar (Montrachet and TriBecCa Grill), was one of Jerry's partners here before departing in 1994. He had a hand in the food presentation and occasionally filled the role of maître-d' at East Hampton Point.

The menu changes monthly. Look for starters ($7 to $11) like green gazpacho, grilled local oyster mushrooms with prosciutto, house cedar-smoked salmon with frisée and tapenade dressing and a terrine of shiitake mushrooms and goat cheese with leeks and sesame oil. Fettuccine with lobster, asparagus and sundried tomatoes is one of the stellar pastas. The eight main courses ($21 to $28) could be crispy soft-shell crabs with couscous, grilled salmon with fava beans, seared grouper with horseradish whipped potatoes, magret duck breast with creamy balsamic polenta and roasted veal chop with wild mushrooms, marsala and fried leeks.

Except for crème brûlée, summer desserts ($6 to $8) are refreshingly cooling, among them Italian plum and blackberry cobbler with blueberry ice cream, banana tarte tatin with gianduia ice cream, root beer float with chocolate ice cream and something called a fudge brownie and malted milkball ice cream sandwich.

Dinner nightly, 6 to 10:30, fewer nights in off-season.

Dining room at Della Femina.

The Maidstone Arms, 207 Main St., East Hampton. (516) 324-5006.

New ownership has enhanced the grande dame of East Hampton restaurants. A spectacular floral arrangement in the entry hall is the only showy accoutrement in the low-key refurbishment. The front dining room with corner service bar is traditional and masculine with dark wood floors, a fireplace and ship's models and seascapes on the walls. The larger rear dining room is carpeted, light and airy. It's notable for Clarence House wallpaper imprinted with trompe-l'oeil shelves and panels of plates that match the real china displayed along the front wall.

Such is the setting for meals that measure up to the expectations of resident East Hamptonites, young and old, celebrating special occasions. Chef William Valentine returned to his native Long Island and the Maidstone Arms after a stint in Los Angeles. California and Pacific Rim influences show up in his masterful roast lacquered duck, everybody's favorite hereabouts. Flavored with five spices, its crisp mahogany skin and tender meat are perched atop soba noodles tossed with julienned vegetables and crowned with crunchy white rice noodles. The lacquered duck also turns up in an appetizer of Vietnamese summer roll on arugula dressed with soy-scallion vinaigrette. Other starters run from $6.50 for chilled smoked salmon and cucumber soup to $13.50 for seared New York State foie gras on a crisp potato cake with a summer truffle sauce.

Main courses ($16.50 to $29.50) vary from a vegetarian dish (cauliflower and potato korma with stir-fried local okra) and fusilli with lobster, summer vegetables and swiss chard to soy-grilled tuna with tropical fruit salsa and tequila-grilled pineapple, grilled filet mignon with herbed goat cheese and smoked wild mushroom sauce, and rack of Colorado lamb with a puree of chickpeas and roasted garlic. Desserts could be blueberry cobbler, crème brûlée and a trio of homemade ice creams and sorbets.

The restaurant takes pride in being open for lunch and dinner daily year-round. Lunch is $12.50 prix-fixe for soup or appetizer and entrée, or may be ordered à la carte from an appealing menu offering pasta and salad-y items like seared salmon with mesclun and fried leeks or sliced grilled sirloin with greens and french fries, $8.50 to $15.50. Similar fare is available for the weekend brunch, along with eggs benedict, omelets and the like.

The wine cellar is one of the Hamptons' best. In the summer of 1994, the restaurant attracted a number of visiting chefs for its Sunday evening series of Star Chef dinners.

Lunch, Monday-Friday noon to 2:30; Saturday and Sunday brunch, noon to 3; dinner nightly, 6 to 9:30, to 11 on weekends.

East Hampton Point, 295 Three Mile Harbor Road, East Hampton. (516) 329-2800.

Formerly Wings Point, this used to be the place that everyone locally recommended for cocktails on an outdoor terrace beside the water. They didn't seem to eat here, which is why we were able to get an 8 o'clock reservation for a window table on a weekday evening when other restaurants were full. We like to eat as well as drink beside the water, and this is one of the lamentably few waterfront places in which to do so in East Hampton.

Enter adman Jerry Della Femina and Manhattan restaurateur Drew Nieporent (now departed), who took over Wings Point in 1993 and renamed it East Hampton Point. They whitewashed the dining room and removed walls so that every seat on two levels looks onto boats bobbing to and fro in the marina and the sunset across Three Mile Harbor – or into mirrors reflecting same. Now its tables are coveted as much for dining as for the view. The place looked appealing for a summer lunch, except that we (and other latecomers) were thoroughly ignored, we felt underdressed amid all the fashion and media peacocks, and we didn't care to spend $11 for a chicken BLT sandwich or a tuna niçoise salad. View carries only so far.

For dinner, the young staff delivers such standouts ($20 to $29) as steamed halibut over savoy cabbage with bliss potatoes and tomato marmalade, grilled Moroccan swordfish on a lentil cake with haricots verts, shelled lobster drizzled with orzo and a perennial favorite, barbecued braised lamb shank over red onion and corn risotto. Start with chilled tomato and avocado soup, seared yellowfin tuna tart, a swiss chard and wild mushroom risotto with white truffle oil and parmigiano-reggiano or the king salmon and crab cakes with celery root slaw and avocado tartar sauce, priced from $7 to $12. The pastry chef makes a mean glazed berry tart with linzer crust and mint syrup, and some of the kicky desserts here bring back childhood memories: root beer float with chocolate-chip cookies and toasted marshmallow and chocolate s'mores with tahitian vanilla bean ice cream, at un-childhood prices in the $7 range.

And wouldn't you know? At our visit, chef Gerard Hayden was about to appear on NBC's Today show. His theme: how to prepare and grill burgers, including grilled ahi tuna burger with Asian spices, a jalapeño and cumin cheeseburger, and a grilled turkey burger with marinated eggplant and sundried tomatoes.

Lunch daily in season, noon to 3; dinner nightly, 5:30 to 11; Sunday brunch, noon to 3.

Bostwick's Seafood Grill, 313 Three Mile Harbor Road, East Hampton. (516) 324-1111.

This spacious new seafood grill commands the same water view as its higher-profile neighbor, East Hampton Point, but without the prices and pretensions. It's named for young chef-partner Chris Eggert's favorite fishing area in Gardiner's Bay, which shows where his priorities lie.

The seasonal place seats 140, most on a covered outdoor deck that can be enclosed in plastic and heated for use on chilly evenings. This is obviously the dining venue of choice, both for the setting and for the fact that its well-spaced tables are covered with white butcher paper over linens rather than the hard-edged glass topping the linened tables inside.

Tiny white ribbed lights on the canopy barely gave off enough light to read the menu as we staved off hunger with a basket of lavasch and hot rolls served, for shame, with foil-wrapped butter. The lobster ravioli was the meal's highlight, a superior appetizer with a divine basil and garlic cream sauce. The caesar salad also was good, and we liked the looks of the thin-crust, brick-oven pizza topped with spinach, bacon, garlic, tomato and more delivered to the next table. Main courses are priced from $13.95 for pan-seared chicken tossed with bowtie pasta, smoked wild mushrooms and sundried tomato pesto to $17.50 for Maryland crab cakes or swordfish steak, pan-blackened or grilled over mesquite. One of us settled on a special of grilled yellowfin tuna, nicely charred and served on an oversize white plate bearing three swirls of mashed potatoes and a bed of sliced carrots and haricots verts. The other sampled the stuffed yellowtail flounder, a less successful dish with more of the same accompaniments. A $16 Buena Vista sauvignon blanc was a satisfying choice from the affordable wine list. Desserts included Mississippi mud pie, chocolate mousse cake, key lime pie and raspberry sorbet.

In the fall of 1994, the chef and his partner, Kevin Boles, who handles the front of the house, opened Santa Fe Junction, a year-round Southwestern restaurant, in town.

Lunch, Saturday and Sunday noon to 3 in summer; dinner nightly, 5:30 to 10 or 11, Thursday-Sunday in off-season. Closed late September to May.

Santa Fe Junction, 8 Fresno Place, East Hampton. (516) 324-8700.
Tucked away on a back street (and rather hard to find) is this trendy year-round venture, opened in late 1994 by Chris Eggert and Kevin Boles, who earned their spurs at Bostwick's. It was formerly the site of the late, great Fresno, which closed inexplicably earlier in the year. The new owners undertook a substantial renovation, adding brick and rough-hewn cedar and french doors in place of windows.

The menu features Southwest fare – "not Tex-Mex," chef Chris pointed out. Dinner entrées range from $11.95 to $17.95 for the likes of assorted fajitas, smoked ribs, crab cakes, local seafood, steaks and chops, Start with quesadillas, tamales, clams or oysters. Finish with sopaipillas, flan, chocolate-pecan pie or pumpkin cheesecake.

Although Chris oversees the food in both restaurants, his summer priority remains Bostwick's, because he's a water person at heart.

Dinner nightly, from 5:30; closed Wednesday in winter.

The Laundry, 31 Race Lane, East Hampton. (516) 324-3199.
Only in place like the self-assured Hamptons could a restaurant converted from a commercial laundry call itself that. This really was a laundry, and you still can see the big extractor outside. Inside all is dark and glamorous, with seating on two levels, a long bar against the outside wall, and seating in green booths or on red chairs and banquettes. A spectacular flower arrangement at the entrance is a trademark.

Chefs come and go here and the prices are considered high locally, perhaps because the Laundry hamburger with fries costs a cool $12.50, salads and vegetables cost extra, and there's a $14.50 dinner minimum. The menu changes daily and is very with-it. You might start with carpaccio of local tuna with mustard sauce or a basket of sweet potato skins with yogurt, honey and mint or a choice of two tapas for $10.50. The soup could be Tuscan tomato or chilled cantaloupe and the salad local bibb lettuce with lump crabmeat, pink grapefruit and red onions.

Other than the hamburger, entrées are priced from $18 for pan-roasted chicken with rosemary and garlic to $24 for grilled New York sirloin strip steak "dry aged 14 days." Roasted salmon on a bed of creamed corn with roasted cipollini onions and grilled swordfish with sundried tomato puree are other possibilities.

Desserts run to strawberry sour cream brûlée, vol-au-vent of lemon curd with raspberry coulis, fresh fruit crisp and banana bread with chocolate crème anglaise and pistachio ice cream.

Locals consider this a good late-hour dining spot. It's also popular with singles.

Dinner nightly, 5:30 to 11 or midnight.

Palm Restaurant, 94 Main St., East Hampton. (516) 324-0411.

Everybody raves about the Palm Restaurant at the Huntting Inn, one of a chain extending from Manhattan to ritzy points south and west. They love the huge steaks and chops and lobsters. They warn about being talked into ordering more potatoes and vegetables than you need (the menu says they're served family style for two or more but they can feed an entire family). And they love the scene, dark and clubby and masculine, with lots of booths and caricatures framed on the walls. And, of course, they love it for the celebrities. "Billy Joel would go there, not here," we were advised by an insider at the Hedges' Inn, whose former Palm Restaurant recently was converted into the James Lane Cafe.

This is a typical Manhattan steakhouse, transported to the summery Hamptons by the Huntting owner, whose grandfather was the founder of the Palm. We can't imagine why people would come out here to pay $26 to $29 for a steak or prime ribs ($56 for a 36-ounce New York strip for two), add $6 for hash browns or fried onions or string beans ($7 for creamed spinach that we hear is great), and $30 or more for a cabernet sauvignon. But thousands do, even lobster-lovers who always come at least once a summer to order lobsters weighing four or more pounds. Who's to question why?

Dinner nightly, 5 to 11; closed Monday and Tuesday in off-season.

The 1770 House, 143 Main St., East Hampton. (516) 324-1770.

The owners' master clock collection is the backdrop for dinner in this dark and cozy beamed dining room with accents of stained glass. The bare oak tables are set with rose medallion china, and the setting is like that of an old New England country inn. Which may be why the New York Times cited it as the most beautiful restaurant on Long Island.

Miriam Perle, who studied at the Cordon Bleu and ran a cooking school for thirteen years in Great Neck, shares cooking duties with her daughter, Wendy Van Deusen. They recently changed the traditional prix-fixe menu to à la carte but retained their Mediterranean-inspired fare.

Typical entrées ($19.50 to $24) are lobster and chicken paella, grilled swordfish salsa verde with orange-mango relish, roast duck with lingonberry sauce, rack of lamb with garlic mashed potatoes and filet mignon marchande de vin with potato pancake. Among starters ($7.50 to $9) are Mediterranean antipasto, grilled tuna au poivre and sundried tomato ravioli with wild mushroom sauce. Desserts include the specialty chocolate cake, profiteroles with three sauces, key lime meringue pie or old-fashioned fruit syllabub.

Dinner, Thursday-Sunday, seatings at 7 and 9:15; weekends only in off-season.

Sapore di Mare, Montauk Highway, Wainscott. (516) 537-2764.

The Hamptons have perhaps no more glamorous restaurant than this, with dining on several levels inside and on a porch backing up to Georgica Pond. Up to 160 diners

Porch next to Georgica Pond is choice dining spot at Sapore di Mare.

can be accommodated at well-spaced tables topped by white linens, mod dispensers of extra-virgin olive oil and balsamic vinegars, and sleek glass oil lamps in various styles.

This is one beautiful restaurant and the beautiful people usually keep it packed, though not quite the way they did before the arrival of that adman-turned-restaurateur, Jerry Della Femina. Sapore countered with its own advertising: "It takes more than an Italian- or French-sounding last name to offer a real Italian dining experience....Beware of imitations."

The contemporary Italian menu changes seasonally. Antipasti range from $9.50 for a selection from the display table to $12.50 for carpaccio of tuna or filet mignon. Six pastas run from $17.50 to $19. Salads are $7.50 for seasonal greens to $9.50 for baby artichokes with sliced parmigiano cheese. The ten entrées range from $24 for grilled chicken paillard or roasted cornish hen to $32 for grilled ribeye steak with french fries. Others include grilled swordfish, spicy seafood stew and osso buco. Wines start in the twenties and rise rapidly, though some are available at $6 to $11 a glass.

Among desserts ($7) are tirami su, chocolate mousse, country-style apple tart, soft polenta cream with strawberry sauce and espresso granita with whipped cream.

Owner Pino Luongo also owns Le Madri and Coco Pazzo in New York, Piccola Cucina in Dallas and a second Sapore de Mare in St. Barts. He has published a cook-book, *A Tuscan in the Kitchen.* He also has run a summer cooking school here, as well as the Sapore di Mare Piccola Cucina store and takeout service in Bridgehampton.

Lunch, Saturday and Sunday noon to 3; dinner nightly, 6 to 10:30 or midnight; closed Tuesday and Wednesday in off-season.

James Lane Cafe, 74 James Lane, East Hampton. (516) 324-7100.

The old Palm Restaurant at the Hedges' Inn has been renamed the James Lane Cafe. The owners are the same and the menu still offers the pricey sides of potatoes and vegetables served family style, though updated to include mashed sweet potatoes and grilled seasonal vegetables. But gone are the weighty steaks and lobsters; in their place are pastas and seafood with an Italian accent. The main dining room has been lightened up as well in shades of pale yellow and white. The tented flagstone patio remains inviting as ever with rattan chairs, votive candles and fresh flowers on white-clothed tables, twinkling white lights and geraniums here and there.

The menu is priced from $16 for chicken dijon to $28 for New York strip steak, a holdover from Palm days. Other main dishes include champagne salmon, peppered swordfish, lobster and shrimp shepherds pie, broiled crab cakes, two presentations of veal and five pastas, from fettuccine with tequila shrimp to linguini with clam sauce. Among starters are fried calamari, lobster corn cakes and baked clams oreganata. Dessert favorites are chocolate ganache cake, key lime pie, tirami su and pineapple or melon sorbet, each served on a slice of the corresponding fruit.

Dinner nightly from 5, May-October.

Cafe Max, 85 Montauk Hwy., East Hampton. (516) 324-2004.

The former chef at the Maidstone Arms has moved his operation a mile west and found his niche in this cozy roadside cafe. It's nicely rustic in a Hamptons kind of way with rough-hewn wood paneling and barn rafters under the pitched ceiling. Tiny lamps with fancy fabric shades light the crisp, white-clothed tables.

Owner Morris (Max) Weintraub has kept some of his clientele from the Maidstone Arms (and earlier, the Maidstone Club) with main dishes ($16 to $20) like lobster linguini, cioppino, blackened cajun bass, grilled shrimp in a light ginger and scallion sauce and veal topped with shrimp. He offers honey-roasted salmon fillet on a bed of spinach, mushrooms and tomatoes, and teams cold poached salmon with marinated lentils and cucumber salad. Rosemary herbed chicken, veal topped with shrimp, grilled delmonico steak and three pasta dishes are the only non-seafood items.

Expect such starters as bruschetta, scotch smoked salmon, crab cake and fried calamari. Desserts could be chocolate mousse cake, lime pie and homemade raspberry or mango sorbets. Nearly half the wines are priced at $21 or under.

Dinner nightly except Tuesday, 6 to 11. No smoking.

Estia, 177 Main St., Amagansett. (516) 267-6320.

This started as a luncheonette, became known for extravagant breakfasts and now specializes in pastas at night. It was named by the former Greek owner for the Greek word for hospitality, and young chef-owner Colin Ambrose liked the name and its comfortable feeling.

Come here for breakfast and a wide selection of omelets, pancakes, french toast and Mexican dishes like ranch eggs, breakfast burrito and veggie white quesadilla, nicely priced from $3.25 to $6.75. The extensive lunch menu yields sandwiches, eight kinds of burgers, four club sandwiches and nine salads. Colin, who takes over the kitchen at night, makes his own pastas and prepares sauces to order, and again the selection is enormous. Try Mediterranean tomato, olive and feta; shrimp primavera; basil pesto or arabiata ($9 to $14.50). Add a salad plate or starters like smoked trout over a corn pancake, sesame shrimp on a bed of napa cabbage or grilled goat cheese with field greens. Eat at the counter or at one of the lipstick-red vinyl booths. Estia has a beer and wine license.

Breakfast and lunch daily, 7 to 2; dinner nightly from 5:30 in summer, weekends rest of year.

The Honest Diner, Route 27, Amagansett. (516) 267-3535.

Leave it to the folks from Nick & Tony's. Rather than branch out with a glamorous waterfront restaurant or an upscale market, they opened a diner – a trendy but true one, at that. Here, in a silver and blue wraparound replica with the requisite counter and great big booths, folks like to feast on southern fried chicken with biscuits, mashed potatoes and gravy ($10.95) or Grandma Rose's brisket of beef (the most expensive posted dinner item at $13.95).

Yes, they also offer such contemporary fare as pan-roasted salmon cakes with sautéed spinach and crispy leeks. This is the Hamptons, after all, and customers are as likely to want huevos rancheros or a bagel with salmon and cream cheese for breakfast as they are the basic corned-beef hash with eggs and toast ($7.95). At lunchtime, look for some of the dinner specials along with sandwiches, from tuna melt to a soft-shell crab club. Desserts are baked at the diner's retail facility next door.

Long Island wine choices are printed on a card at each table. There also is a good selection of local beers.

Breakfast, 8 to 11:30; lunch, 11:30 to 3; dinner, 5 to 10 or 11.

Diversions

Many people come to "America's most beautiful village" for the beaches, which have been ranked among the nation's cleanest. But there is much more to see and do.

Beaches. Parking at any village or town beach along Long Island's south shore is limited to fifteen minutes or requires a parking sticker indicating residency. All parking is banned from 10 a.m. to 4 p.m. on the residential streets lined with great estates near the beaches. For those without stickers, parking is available at Main Beach and Atlantic Avenue Beach for $10 daily. Many inns have beach passes for guests.

Walking Tour. Walk Main Street in the heart of East Hampton's historic district from Montauk Highway to Newtown Lane. The **Town Pond** is a tranquil spot at the end of the village green, between Main Street and James Lane. Tombstones date back to the 17th century in the adjacent **South End Cemetery,** where many gravestones are so worn they are no longer legible. **Home Sweet Home,** the 1680 saltbox that was the boyhood home of poet John Howard Payne, who wrote the song of the same name, is open for guided tours and features fine furniture collected over three centuries. Nearby is an early windmill. The **Mulford Farmstead,** long the center of a working farm, also is open for tours in summer. **Guild Hall,** given to the town in 1931, is an art museum with three galleries and the John Drew Theater, the oldest playhouse on Long Island, the site for plays, musicals and concerts. Across the street is the charming brick and stucco, English-looking **East Hampton Library.** There's not a computer terminal in sight, but stacks of newspapers and two old typewriters can be seen through the front office windows of the **East Hampton Star,** the thick and newsy local weekly. Beside it is **the Wild Flower Garden of Long Island,** a shady oasis of native plants, the gift of the Garden Club of East Hampton. **Clinton Academy,** built in 1784, is marked as the oldest "academical" institution in New York State. It's used for Historical Society exhibits of period furniture, artifacts, decoys and dolls. School desks, handwriting lessons and quill pens are on view next door in the shingled **Town House,** a former school and town hall built in 1731. The 1735 **Osborne-Jackson House** is the headquarters of the East Hampton Historical Society. In the triangle between North Main and Pantigo Lane is the **Hook Mill,** a still-operable windmill open to the public for tours in summer.

Driving Tours. Residential streets in the estate area between Main Beach and Georgica Pond are worth a look-see. Tall trees, privet hedges and deep lawns screen some estates from view, but others are visible from the road and most show signs of big money and good taste. Another pleasant drive is along the dunes on Further Lane to Bluff Road in Amagansett.

Shopping. East Hampton's tree-shaded shopping district along Main Street and

Newtown Lane is quite villagey and low-key, as opposed, say, to Southampton. Two stores that everybody seems to like are the ultra decorated **Polo Country Store,** the second of summer resident Ralph Lauren's country stores, and the **Coach Factory Store,** occupying a former bank where the handsome and expensive bags are sold at a slight discount (we got a discontinued model for half price, however). At one visit, the rear vault was the setting for an exhibit of East Hampton resident Sinai Waxman's abstract paintings of local scenes in the $4,000 range; the next time it displayed a Japanese artist's collection of "small prints," all $250. There are so many designer clothing shops that you wonder if visiting New Yorkers are simply too busy to shop in Manhattan; ditto for antiques and interiors stores. More to our taste and price range were the handful of upscale outlet stores, spread out around sculptures and benches flanking the large lawn at **Amagansett Square.** The trendoids pick up their gourmet foods at **Jerry and David's Red Horse Market,** owned by Jerry Della Femina and a partner from Dean & DeLuca, at 74 Montauk Hwy. One of the more exotic salad bars is located across the plaza at Red Horse to Go. Other good lunchy spots with salads, focaccia sandwiches, gourmet foods and such are **JL Bean** and **Barefoot Contessa,** both along Newtown Lane.

Farm Stands. Long known for potatoes and ducks, eastern Long Island has become a center for fresh produce. **Round Swamp Farm** at 184 Three Mile Harbor Road was featured in the New York Times as one of summer resident Craig Claiborne's favorite markets. It sells everything from fruits and vegetables to preserves, fish, cheese, baked goods and more, and we picked up a couple of jars of their good salsas. We thought Round Swamp couldn't be topped, but it was – at least in terms of size and crowds – by the **Amagansett Farmers Market** on the Montauk Highway in Amagansett, a privately owned "stand" bigger than any we've seen. Here, at what is obviously a local gathering spot, everyone was buying cut flowers for the weekend, picking up oyster mushrooms and baby pattypan squash, and sifting through every salsa, mustard, oil and vinegar ever made. An incredible bakery produces the best sticky buns, and folks sit out front with croissants and cappuccino from the espresso bar. There also are a section of prepared foods and a great meat market.

Extra-Special

The Bridgehampton Winery, Sag Harbor Turnpike, Bridgehampton. (516) 537-3155.

Long Island has become known for fine wines, since the Hargrave Vineyard pioneered on the North Fork in the 1970s. This, the first winery to be established in the Hamptons in 1982, is causing North Fork vintners to take notice. In 1984, the federal government awarded "appellation" status to the Hamptons, the first such designation of a Long Island winemaking region. Bridgehampton is known for its premium viniferas, which show "French elegance rather than California brawn," in one writer's words. It won a bronze medal with its first vintage of chardonnay and has scores of awards since for chardonnays (sold at the winery for $10.99 to $14.99), cabernets and merlots. The winery's striking labels were selected for the permanent collection of New York's Metropolitan Museum of Art. The dramatic contemporary showroom has windows onto a deck with chairs overlooking the vineyard. After tasting the chardonnays, the tour guide led our group downstairs to the cellar – "how romantic," one visitor said – for a tasting of red wines. This is for serious connoisseurs; only a few hundred show up on the busiest weekends. After a year's hiatus, Bridgehampton was on the move again after it was purchased in 1994 by the owner of the larger Lenz Winery on the North Fork. Tours and tastings, daily 11 to 6.

Cold Spring faces Hudson River and Storm King Mountain, as viewed from 3 Rock B&B.

Cold Spring/Garrison, N.Y.
From Highlands to River

"G.W. Drank Here '79," claims the mural along a brick wall in the center of Cold Spring. No, George Washington didn't sleep here, but during a trip up the Hudson River he did eat in Garrison and drank from a spring that gave Cold Spring its name.

Cold Spring, population 2,000 and as unspoiled as they come, and its even smaller neighbor to the south, Garrison, hug the Hudson in the area where it is at its narrowest and deepest. Surrounding mountains created a fjord-like gorge of military significance and unsurpassed beauty. On a curve in the river just across from Cold Spring and Garrison lies West Point, home of the U.S. Military Academy. It's as commanding a presence in its own way as such grand natural assets as Storm King, Breakneck and Bear mountains are in theirs.

During the Revolution, great iron chains were laid across the Hudson from West Point to Constitution Island to prevent British warships from sailing up the river. In the 19th century, Cold Spring became an early company town as immigrants arrived to work in the West Point Foundry and iron mine. Twentieth-century development and urban renewal passed these towns by, leaving two of the last river towns with their waterfronts intact. The train station beside the river at Garrison's Landing was a backdrop for the filming of "Hello, Dolly."

"Cold Spring looks in many ways like it did a hundred years ago," says Carolyn Krebs, owner of a bookshop in the old Salamagundi Works. "It's been taken care of and not chi-chied up." Most of the center of town is on the National Register. Main Street descends from the highlands down to the river, with Victorian houses, antiques shops and restaurants along the way. When it confronts the Metro North line, it stops,

385

detours around, goes up and over, and comes back opposite – this is one of the few main streets blocked by a train track in the country. Main Street then continues a bit farther to a town bandstand, a waterfront park and a river dock undergoing restoration.

There's a bit of a California air – as in Sausalito or Carmel – to this riverside region tumbling down the highlands 50 miles north of New York City. Life is laid-back, entrepreneurial and preservationist (no malls, no chain stores, and no waterfront honky-tonk). This is an area where palatial estates co-exist with forgotten hamlets, where tranquility triumphs over suburban sprawl. The Appalachian Trail here has as many takers as Boscobel, the great house museum.

The Hudson Highlands are as delightful a slice of scenery as you'll find.

Inn Spots

Pig Hill Inn, 73 Main St., Cold Spring 10516. (914) 265-9247.

Commuting weekends from New York, Wendy and Dan O'Brien found themselves frequently entertaining guests at the family farm near Cold Spring. "I just loved cooking and entertaining," Wendy recalls. "One day my sister said I'd been doing this for years and it's about time I got paid for it."

So in 1987 the O'Briens bought a 150-year-old brick building in downtown Cold Spring, converting it into an antiques shop and an eight-room B&B with great panache. Here you'll find brass pigs, hand-carved wooden pigs, pig quilts, pig chopping blocks and pictures of pigs – all for sale, as are the antiques and furnishings in the rooms. Wendy raises pet pigs along with cattle and lambs at her Glenwood Farm, which contributes many of the ingredients for Pig Hill's gourmet breakfasts.

Trailing ivy is painted on the stairways and halls leading to guest rooms, four each on the second and third floors. Each is furnished in a different style, from Adirondack to English country to Southwest to French. Four rooms have private baths and four share. All but one has a wood-burning stove or fireplace. They are decorated to the hilt with whimsy and flair, down to the patterned porcelain door knobs. Wendy says the rooms are even nicer than those in her farmhouse, which has been pictured in House Beautiful. The room to which we were assigned on the rear of the second floor was lovely in deep green. A discreet sign indicated that the iron brass bed was available for $1,025 and the armoire for $550. Two sachets were interspersed amidst all the pillows atop the bed, and the bathroom was outfitted with pig-shaped soap, colorful towels and bubble bath. Tea was available upon arrival, and a tray with mints and a miniature of brandy was distributed in the evening.

Although Wendy used to cook all the breakfasts and be more involved, lately she has turned over innkeeping duties to a young staff. We were mighty impressed with

our breakfast, a leisurely feast of fresh orange juice poured in an oversize wine glass, half a grapefruit, pumpkin muffins and a piping-hot baked omelet with sausage and stewed tomatoes in a pastry crust. Shirred eggs, egg potato pie, eggs benedict over asparagus tips and soufflé roll (which Wendy describes as basically a jelly roll of eggs, cream cheese and mushrooms) are other favorites.

We were not impressed with paying $150 for a room and finding that a family with two small children (one of whom

Adirondack theme prevails in one guest room at Pig Hill Inn.

cried most of the night) had just arrived and decided to settle into the room next door. Fortunately, the table for six that we noticed set for breakfast as we left for dinner had been separated upon our return. We ended up breakfasting with the New York Times in a small rear space that doubles as a sitting room and wondering why anyone would want to bring toddlers to a fancy B&B and why it would accept them.

Out back is a tranquil sitting area on several landscaped levels, where you'd hardly know you were in the heart of Cold Spring.

Doubles, $100 to $150.

3 Rock Bed and Breakfast, 3 Rock St., Cold Spring 10516. (914) 265-2330.

The area's best view, bar none, is offered from this curving, contemporary showplace. That it's so unexpected as you approach, a block off Main Street, makes it the more awesome. Up a winding driveway atop a bluff in the center of Cold Spring, the spacious house of one's dreams looks over the rooftops of the lower town to the Hudson and the mountains beyond.

Peter Hold, who designs and builds houses on St. John's in the Virgin Islands, built this in 1989 as his Cold Spring residence. He offers three suites with queensize beds, whirlpool baths and separate two-person showers. The only drawback is that the place is often booked for weddings and private parties on weekends, so the transient guest may get lost in the shuffle.

Part of the spacious foyer opens onto a sunken, two-story breakfast room full of windows facing West Point, across and down the river. To the right is a modern living room where floral-covered sofas are grouped in front of a huge fireplace and a grand piano occupies a windowed alcove. Farther to the right is a suite in which the jacuzzi looks out onto Storm King mountain. To the left is a kitchen where a resident innkeeper prepares a continental breakfast of fruit, breads and cheese, and private quarters where Peter planned to add a fourth suite with fireplace and jacuzzi.

Upstairs are two more suites. The larger one, done in shades of blue, has an outdoor balcony and a jacuzzi overlooking West Point. The smaller one is done in chintz; its bathroom is as large as a bedroom (which it used to be). An office is on a balcony over the open breakfast room. Above that on the third floor is a reading room with a 180-degree view and a telescope at the ready.

Outside is a wraparound veranda, looking across a landscaped lawn toward the river below. It's a majestic site for the social functions to which 3 Rock caters.

Doubles, $140. No smoking.

The Bird & Bottle Inn, Nelson Corners, Route 9, Garrison 10524. (914) 424-3000.

This pretty little yellow inn with white columns supporting a two-story veranda dates to 1761, when it opened as a way station for travelers between New York and Albany. Were it not for the fact that it served as a private home for nearly half its years, it might be the oldest inn in the country – a distinction accorded to the Beekman Arms in nearby Rhinebeck, operating continuously since 1766.

The grounds were aglow with azaleas and dogwoods for our first visit to the Bird and Bottle, tucked away on eight acres off a dirt road beside rippling Indian Brook. Charm and quaintness it has in spades, as well as surprising comfort, given the building's age.

The main floor is devoted to an acclaimed restaurant (see Dining Spots), as well as a neat little tavern called the Drinking Room.

Upstairs are two air-conditioned rooms and a suite, all with private baths and working fireplaces. The last make this a particularly appealing place to stay in the fall and winter. Cuddle up in wing chairs in front of the fire in the sitting room of the Robinson Suite and imagine life more than two centuries ago, before retiring to a queensize canopied bed. The fireplace is at the foot of the double four-poster bed in the John Warren Room, the smallest room with a single armchair. Also available are the Emily Warren Room with a queensize canopy bed and, outside, a recently redecorated barnwood cottage that shelters a large bedroom with a queensize poster bed, a loveseat and a fireplace. Lord & Mayfair toiletries, hair dryers and baskets of fresh fruit are amenities in each room. Decor is generally dark and historic, the draped canopied fabrics matching the curtains and braided rugs scattered across the wide-board floors. Some might miss having a common room or TV, but this is a place for escape.

A full English breakfast is served in the morning. Guests receive a menu to check off their choices when they finish dinner the night before.

Doubles, $210 and $220 MAP; suite and cottage, $240 MAP. Two-night minimum on weekends.

Netherby, Avery Road off Route 9D, Garrison 10524. (914) 424-3807.

The name, taken from a Scottish poem "The Highlands," means away from things. And this somewhat contemporary private residence, out in the country where Avery Road becomes a dirt road, certainly is away from things. Innkeeper Wynn Mackey converted the main floor into a B&B when he and a partner bought the house in 1991.

The setting is dramatic, on a hillside beside a farm pond used for swimming, with three acres of forests and exotic gardens, a greenhouse in which Wynn starts his plants, chickens and roosters wandering about, and a huge deck from which to take it all in. The inside is also dramatic, from the sunken dining room with large windows onto the gardens to the lodge-style living room with high ceiling, leather sofa and chairs, and a collection of pewter plates and mugs lining the fireplace mantel. Three small guest bedrooms are situated at the far end of the main floor. The nicest has a queensize bed and a little balcony over the garden, but its only other amenities are a single club chair,

Historic accommodations and fine dining are offered at The Bird & Bottle Inn.

the carpeting and the bed quilt. It shares a full bathroom with two other bedrooms on the other side of the hall. A second corner room, with another queen bed and a single chair, has the advantage of its own attached half-bath. The adjacent room, which was functioning as an office at our visit, can be pressed into service.

Continental breakfast is prepared by Wynn, who also works four days a week as a manager and all-around Man Friday at the Hudson House in Cold Spring. The day's offering might be a dish of cantaloupe and raspberries or a baked apple with raisins and walnuts, followed by blueberry muffins.

Doubles, $90.

Plumbush, Route 9D, Cold Spring 10516. (914) 265-3904.

Renowned for their dining rooms, Swiss-born restaurateurs Gieri Albin and Ans Benderer opened their upstairs to overnight guests in 1986. Although the B&B tends to play second fiddle, its two bedrooms and a suite have private baths and convey a feeling of being away from the action.

Ornately furnished in the Victorian style, the Washington Irving room and the Marquesa suite go off a wicker-filled sitting room outfitted with a TV. The Hendrik Hudson room is set apart and looks more comfortable. The sofa and chairs in the suite are upholstered in pink to complement the colors of the oriental carpet and the floral pattern on the slanted walls.

A continental breakfast with homemade croissants is served to guests in their rooms. Doubles, $95; suite $125.

Hudson House, 2 Main St., Cold Spring 10516. (914) 265-9355.

Its riverfront location across from the town bandstand and its air of history dating to 1832 keep this hotel filled on weekends. It has had its ups and downs since its restoration in 1981, closing in 1989 but reopening a year later under new owner Gary Pease.

Fifteen rooms on the second and third floors have private baths, but remain hotel rooms of the old school – clean but sterile. Floral wallpaper matches the dust ruffles on the beds and tin cake molds adorn the walls, but that's about it for decor. Most rooms

389

have twin beds (the rest are doubles), there are few chairs and these are rooms for sleeping, not lingering, despite the Reader's Digest Condensed Books placed on the bureaus. Soap and Kleenex are the bathroom amenities. Some rooms on the second floor have balconies from which to enjoy the river view. Overnight guests partake of a complimentary continental breakfast.

The main floor contains a restaurant (see Dining Spots) and the **Half Moon Bar,** a large lounge. At one end opposite the bar, two sofas face each other across a hooked rug in a sitting area with a TV. Tables for breakfast take up the rest of the space. The weekday continental breakfast includes fruit plate, muffins, bagels and cream cheese. A hot breakfast buffet is offered on weekends.

Doubles, $125 to $135; suites, $175.

Village Victorian Guest House, 7 Morris Ave. (Route 9D), Cold Spring 10516. (914) 265-9159.

A pretty white brick house near the main intersection in upper Cold Spring, this was opened in 1991. Jim and Mary Ann Zatlukal offer four upstairs guest rooms that share two side-by-side baths.

Black floral curtains and wallpapered wainscoting dress up the Gold Room, which has a double four-poster bed. A pretty floral comforter atop a king bed matches the pillows and curtains in the Blue Room. The other two rooms have queen and twin beds, respectively. Bottles of Great Bear mineral water are set out in each room, and baskets of toiletries are in the bathrooms. Juice, muffins and coffee are served in the morning on a table in the second-floor hallway.

Doubles, $85.

The Front Parlour, 11 Main St., Cold Spring 10516. (914) 265-3607.

Full of fine furnishings and antiques, the Victorian parlor here used to serve as an antiques shop of the same name. Susan Crofoot, a widow, occupied the rest of the brick townhouse down by the river at the foot of Main Street and took in guests on her many-windowed third floor. Now retired, she still opens her home to B&B guests on occasion, primarily to family groups or at peak periods when the town is otherwise full and other innkeepers send her their overflow.

She offers three air-conditioned bedrooms, all with ceiling fans. Two on the second floor share a hall bath. One has a double bed, a settee and Victorian chair, while the rear room contains a twin day bed, a trundle bed and two chairs. The prize accommodations are on the third floor, where a long window seat against the west window commands a great view of the Hudson. A floral comforter covers two brass beds joined as a kingsize. A dressing room contains the bathtub, while a separate water closet encloses the toilet and vanity. Guests stow their clothing in a cedar-lined closet.

The owner serves a continental breakfast in her formal, antiques-filled dining room. Juice and fruit (perhaps fresh berries or spiced applesauce) precede two kinds of pastries, ranging from muffins or zucchini bread to croissants or hot sticky buns.

Doubles, $65 to $75.

Dining Spots

Xaviar's, Route 9D, Garrison. (914) 424-4228.

In a place like this, "you couldn't do anything else but grand dining." So says talented young chef-owner Peter X. (for Xavier) Kelly of his highly acclaimed restaurant at the Highlands Country Club.

And grand it is, from the arched windows overlooking the golf course to the massed

Chef-owner Peter Kelly is the guiding force behind Xaviar's.

floral displays to the Sunday champagne brunches that are booked weeks in advance. Except for the wedgwood blue walls with white trim, the long, high room is a sea of white, its well-spaced tables decked out in white china and linens, fanned napkins, gleaming wine glasses, crystal candle-holders and white candles, with a Baccarat dolphin here and a silver pheasant there. The only touches of bright color come from the artworks by noted Rockland County artist Charles Yiser and all the arrangements of exotic flowers (roses at our winter visit) in crystal vases on each table, on the fireplace mantels, on sideboards and even in the rest rooms. Light is provided by candles everywhere and blazing fireplaces at each end. The canopied terrace has its own magic for outdoor dining in season.

To make the most of such glamorous settings, Peter has canceled weeknight dinners to concentrate on special-occasion dining on weekends. He also opened **Xaviar's at Piermont,** across the Hudson, where he serves lunch and dinner daily as well as a bistro menu in the adjacent **Freelance Cafe and Wine Bar.** Both Xaviar's earned the first near-perfect 29 ratings ever accorded in the Zagat Restaurant Survey. Peter has chefs at both restaurants, but is usually here on weekends.

Dinner here is prix-fixe, $68 for six courses and a pairing of six wines, with a choice between two menus that change every five weeks. The $28 champagne brunch represents unusual value.

We have sampled a number of Peter's dishes, each a triumph of taste, texture and presentation. Consider his lobster ravioli in saffron sauce, garnished with the ends of lobster tails (they look like butterflies so that's what Peter calls them) and bearing a mound of caviar in the middle and two long chives on top. Or the seared sea scallops, served with potato pancakes and raspberry vinaigrette with a few fresh raspberries for good measure. Or the New York foie gras, surrounded by sliced kiwi, strawberries and sliced pears and served with a glass of sauternes. Best of all is the seared Pacific tuna tartare with wasabi and soy sauce, resting on an oversize plate, the rim garnished all the way around with dollops of red, gold and black caviar.

Finger bowls were presented before the main courses: mignon of venison with grand

391

veneur sauce and the best spaetzle we've tasted, and saddle of veal with wild mushrooms and pommes parisienne, garnished with a tomato carved to look like a rose. Both came with tiny, barely cooked haricots verts.

Desserts here are hardly after-thoughts. One of us had an ethereal hot raspberry soufflé, light as air. The other tried the grand assortment, nine little samples including hazelnut dacquoise, chocolate chestnut terrine, frozen caramel mousse, raspberry sorbet and praline ice cream. A plate of petits fours, chocolate strawberries and chocolate truffles finished a meal to remember.

The silverware that came and left with each course was as noticeable as all the extra touches that went into food and presentation. "We try to give people a little more than anyone else does," explains Peter. That extends to the Sunday brunch, an unbelievable buffet spread supplemented by numerous extras – from wild mushroom raviolis to grilled quail to rack of lamb – passed from table to table by the staff.

Dinner, Friday and Saturday 5 to 9:30; Sunday brunch, noon to 3.

Riverview, 45 Fair St., Cold Spring. (914) 265-4778.

A wood-burning oven at one end of the dining room and a convivial bar beside enliven this intimate establishment that's sleek in gray, black and white. White paper tops gray cloths at tables rather close together, except for the deuces along the side windows where you can get a look at the Hudson River and Storm King Mountain. Fresh flowers and cactus plants provide color.

The food here sets the standard for consistently good dining in Cold Spring, according to the local consensus. In fact, owners Jim and Lori Ely have made the Riverview such a success that they branched out in 1993, taking over a much larger restaurant and rechristening it NorthGate at Dockside Harbor

What some locals call California-style pizzas are featured, though Jim Ely considers them more "old world, Italian-style." Whatever, you'll find six to eight pizzas, some named for regions of Italy, in the $5.75 to $6.75 range at lunch, $6.95 to $8.95 at dinner. Try the torino (marinated artichoke hearts, roasted garlic, red onions, fontina and parmesan) or the diablo (spicy Italian sausage, bell peppers and mozzarella).

A number of interesting pastas and entrées ($13.75 to $17.50) are added at night. They might be fettuccine with smoked ham, peas and gorgonzola cream; duck confit with arugula salad and shoestring fries; braised lamb shank with white bean ragout, or grilled shell steak with red wine and shallots. Starters include a signature cold antipasto plate, grilled and roasted garlic polenta with roasted bell pepper puree, smoked duck breast with cranberry-orange relish and carpaccio served with grilled onions, herbed olives and shaved parmigiano-reggiano. The changing dessert selection might include tirami su and crème brûlée.

Penne pasta with chicken, garlic and mushrooms ($6.75) is a lunchtime hit.

Lunch daily, noon to 3; dinner, 5:30 to 10; Sunday brunch, noon to 3.

NorthGate at Dockside Harbor, 2 North St., Cold Spring. (914) 265-5555.

Colorful wooden fish dress the tables and the walls at this new establishment housed in the former Dockside Harbor restaurant. But there's little else to upstage the view of the Hudson River from wraparound windows on three sides or from outdoor tables beneath a large canopy.

Fortunately, the food offered by Cold Spring restaurateur Jim Ely is up to the smashing waterfront setting. Many of the luncheon dishes show up on the dinner menu and vice-versa, which may make dinner a better value for those who don't like to make their midday meal the main event of the day. Grazing is encouraged, however, and for a weekday lunch, we were quite impressed with a large cobb salad ($7.75) and a thick

Dining room at Riverview is sleek in gray, black and white.

garlic and potato soup ($3.75). The latter was teamed with a hearty appetizer of Caribbean conch fritters with coconut-curry sauce ($6.75). All three items also are available on the dinner menu.

Nighttime prices start at $9.75 for aforementioned cobb salad, and pastas are priced in the low teens. Main courses run from $13.75 for thyme-roasted chicken with garlic mashed potatoes to $16.50 for seafood stew. Creative culinary touches turn up in such dishes as baked Boston cod with soy and ginger sauce and Asian charred duck with a scallion pancake. Among starters are fresh oysters with ginger and scallions, fried calamari with black bean aioli, a leek and chèvre tart and a salad of farfalle, wild mushrooms, garlic and asparagus.

Seasonal desserts include pumpkin crème brûlée, apple cobbler and cheesecake with cranberries.

Lunch, Monday-Saturday noon to 3; dinner nightly, 5:30 to 10:30; Sunday brunch.

Plumbush, Route 9D, Cold Spring. (914) 265-3904.

On a hill above the Hudson close to the Boscobel restoration is this purple Victorian house trimmed in yellow, known for fancy dining. The house was built in the early 19th century for the Marquise Agnes Rizzo dei Ritii and the Victorian frills were added later in the century.

Inside are several handsome dining rooms with rich oak-paneled walls or flowered wallpaper, spotlit oil paintings, oriental rugs, fireplaces and a general air of luxury. In summer, these is also dining on the wraparound porch. Part of the porch lately has been enclosed into a greenhouse room, all quite glamorous, with seven well-spaced tables at windows onto the park-like surroundings.

The house has an intimacy that masks the fact it can accommodate 250 to 275 diners at once on busy days.

Its Swiss owners, chef Ans Benderer and host Gieri Albin, formerly were at Stonehenge in Connecticut, and that restaurant's influence shows on their continental menu. An extensive choice of appetizers and entrées is offered at lunch and dinner. You can order à la carte (dinner entrées are $23.50 to $25) or have the prix-fixe dinner, three courses and salad for $34.

Specialties are trout au bleu with a mousseline sauce, crispy tarragon roast squab and medallions of veal with smoked mozzarella. Other dinner entrées include sautéed breast of chicken with apples and calvados, Long Island duckling glazed with brandied plums, and tournedos of beef with wild mushrooms and gorgonzola. Four or more people can order a whole roasted suckling pig with three days' notice.

Those partial to the shrimp in beer batter and pungent fruit sauce made famous at Stonehenge can get it here, $7.50 for a dinner appetizer or $9.95 for lunch. Typical lunch entrées ($8.50 to $14) are vol-au-vent of shrimp and scallops, baked trout or broiled fillet of sole in beer batter, sautéed calves liver and broiled baby lamb chops with mint jelly.

The chef recommends the Swiss apple fritters for dessert ($5), but chocolate praline mousse and frozen orange soufflé grand marnier are hard to resist.

Lunch, Wednesday-Friday noon to 2; dinner, Wednesday-Saturday 5:30 to 9:30; Sunday, brunch noon to 2:30, dinner 2:30 to 8.

The Bird and Bottle Inn, Nelson Corners, Route 9, Garrison. (914) 424-3000.

Another "oldie but goodie" is this pretty yellow inn with white columns, built as a tavern in 1761. Classical music plays in the background in the dark and cozy dining room. White linens, gleaming silver, wall sconces, wide-board floors, windsor chairs and wood wainscoting create a lovely setting. The focal point is a stuffed pheasant with a bottle of wine – hence the inn's name. A cheery tap room and a smaller dining room are on the other side of the main entrance hall.

Under the aegis of ex-hotel and restaurant consultant Ira Boyar, innkeeper here since 1982, the dining room has gained a reputation far beyond the area. Co-chefs Loren Centrello and Robert Carpino have been here for the duration, so it's hard to fathom the occasional complaints we hear of inconsistency in the kitchen.

Five-course dinners are served for a fixed price, the charge depending on choice of entrée (from $33.95 for fettuccine with sautéed shrimp, tomatoes and arugula to $48.95 for roasted New Zealand rack of lamb with mustard-herb glaze and garlic sauce). You might start with smoked salmon mousse layered with puff pastry, curried oysters with cucumber sauce, herbed goat cheese baked in puff pastry with pear sauce or grilled garlic shrimp with roasted red and yellow pepper vinaigrette. A salad of five greens follows. For the main course, how about poached Norwegian salmon with lemon vinaigrette or grilled swordfish with onions, balsamic vinegar and sweet bell pepper compote? Or roast pheasant with pâté and truffle sauce for two? Still hungry? Homemade pumpkin bread is available for a surcharge of $2.50 a loaf.

Desserts are to groan over: pecan sponge cake with whipped cream and caramel sauce, a trio of baked mousses with raspberry and chocolate sauce, three-layered chocolate pâté with pistachio cream and a "celebration cake" of hazelnut meringue layered with vanilla, chocolate and praline butter cream. After all the food before, we'd settle for one of the great homemade ice creams, perhaps praline with prickly pear sauce, a trio of sorbets with Scottish shortbread, or a refreshing frozen raspberry soufflé.

The Bird and Bottle puts on quite a Sunday brunch that's also good value, the fixed price varying from $16.95 to $19.95 depending on choice of entrée. Start with crab cakes or smoked salmon mille-feuille before moving on to salad, muffins and rolls. Enjoy eggs benedict, belgian waffles, chicken divan or sirloin steak and finish with one of those great desserts. Gourmet feasts, six courses of food and wine for about $85 each, are scheduled several times a year, and lately the Bird & Bottle has started serving lunch three days a week.

Lunch, Thursday-Saturday noon to 2; dinner, Wednesday-Saturday 6 to 9; Sunday, brunch noon to 2, dinner 4:30 to 7.

Vintage Restaurant & Bar, 91 Main St., Cold Spring. (914) 265-4726.

The shelves along the walls here hint at the name. They're laden with glasses, pictures, artifacts, an old cash register. A skylight is the centerpiece of the small, L-shaped dining room flanked by banquettes with a black and floral tapestry pattern. Cooking pans and utensils hang from the ceiling. The remarkable tables were handpainted by a friend of the former owner and left bare to show the parcheesi, chess or checker game boards, for example.

Kevin Lee, who operated a couple of restaurants in his native England, brought in a chef from New York's Upper West Side upon acquiring the restaurant in 1994. They had quite a reputation to live up to and, after a shaky start, were on their way to succeeding. Veal, lamb and steak specials supplement the short dinner menu priced from $14.75 to $22. Expect main dishes like homemade seafood ravioli, grilled tuna with a white bean puree and roasted red peppers, baked walnut-crusted salmon with a three-citrus beurre blanc, pork tenderloin in a port wine sauce, and roast duck with a star anise sauce and a vegetable pancake. Most of the appetizers are salads: perhaps warm goat cheese with mesclun greens and balsamic vinaigrette or arugula and radicchio with shaved parmesan. Desserts could be fresh fruit with grand marnier zabaglione, fruit tortes and chocolate bags filled with fresh fruits and liqueurs.

After dinner, adjourn to the bar to play one of the twenty or so board games. Or linger with a brandy at one of the handful of umbrellaed tables on the new garden courtyard in the rear.

Lunch daily, 11:30 to 2:30; dinner, 6 to 9:30 or 10.

Breakneck Lodge, Route 9D, Cold Spring. (914) 265-9669.

At the foot of breakneck Mountain, which rises 1,400 precipitous feet above the Hudson across from Storm King Mountain, perches this German restaurant with an old-school menu and updated surroundings. Lately, the main dining room of the vast establishment dating to 1935 has been gussied up with pink linens, stemware, swagged curtains, track lights and a fireplaced alcove that give it a more formal, contemporary look. The high-ceilinged bar with artifacts on the walls and a stunning stained-glass piece remains true to its origins.

German Owner Ludwig Link's wife does most of the baking, and two German chefs turn out old-world fare for a rather considerable operation. Large windows framed the Hudson as we lunched on some of the Bavarian specialties. Prices are not cheap (after all, you do have that million-dollar river view), but we felt we received good value. A choice of soup (a good lentil), salad or juice was included with our entrées of grilled knockwurst with sauerkraut and whipped potatoes and a special of venison ragout with burgundy and onions, served with delicious homemade spaetzle and red cabbage.

At night, duckling Bavarian style, beef à la Deutsch, wiener schnitzel, sauerbraten and smoked pork loin are featured on a large menu that also lists jumbo scampi, broiled or fried sole, chicken française and minute steak, $13.50 to $18. Linzer torte, warm bread pudding, apple strudel and lemon cheesecake are favorite desserts.

Lunch daily, noon to 2:30; dinner, 5 to 9 or 10, Sunday noon to 8.

Henry's on the Hudson, 184 Main St., Cold Spring. (914) 265-3000.

Down-home American food, with an emphasis on seafood, steaks and burgers, is offered here by Wendy and Dan O'Brien, owners of the Pig Hill B&B. The casual uptown American bistro is decked out in green checked cloths, green walls hung with framed posters and a tin ceiling, with a long bar along the side wall. A heated, wrap-around sidewalk cafe can be used year-round.

The extensive menu features sandwiches, salads, platters, raw-bar items and "snackitizers" for both lunch and dinner. A number of entrées ($12.50 to $19.95) are added at night. They range from grilled chicken and barbecued baby back ribs to Maryland crab cakes and grilled filet mignon with béarnaise sauce. Expect desserts like chocolate mousse cake, tirami su and pumpkin cheesecake.

Open daily, noon to 11.

Hudson House, 2 Main St., Cold Spring 10516. (914) 265-9355.

The food is said to have improved lately at this restored hotel, which is held in higher esteem by tourists drawn to its riverside location than by locals. Three little dining rooms with chintz tablecloths catch a glimpse of the river outside. A porch is used in summer.

The short dinner menu is priced from $16 for Yankee pot roast with whipped sweet potatoes and steamed vegetables to $18.50 for grilled New York sirloin with woodland mushroom sauce. Also offered are charred yellowfin tuna with a warm bean and cilantro salad, honey-glazed salmon baked on a cedar plank and served with a garden slaw, and crispy Long Island duckling with seasonal fruit sauce.

Appetizers ($4.25 to $7.25) include mushrooms sauté on a cornmeal and scallion waffle, lobster and lump crab cakes with citrus mayonnaise, and grilled shrimp over a lemon cole slaw. Among desserts are lemon mousse, cherry cobbler and fruit tarts.

Lunch, Monday-Saturday 11:30 to 3; dinner, 5:30 to 9 or 10; Sunday, brunch 11:30 to 2:30, dinner, 4:30 to 9.

Jasmine's Courtyard, 76 Main St., Cold Spring. (914) 265-5520.

This new offshoot of a casual gourmet eatery in Peekskill takes its name from the large, canopied rear courtyard outfitted with white wrought-iron furniture. It's a great spot for outdoor dining in season. A small inside dining room is rather formal, with swagged curtains and tables draped in butcher paper over layers of white and salmon cloths.

This appears to be a good place for lunch, with creative salads and sandwiches in the $6 to $7 range. It was closed tight the day we stopped by, however, so we could only look longingly at the menu and vow to return.

The with-it dinner menu also appealed. Main courses ($12.95 to $15.95) included grilled salmon in apple cider sauce, grilled swordfish in a tequila-lime marinade, shrimp and scallops sautéed over fettuccine with a vodka cream sauce and loin lamb chops crusted with rosemary mustard and served with minted hollandaise. There's a vegetarian accent in such items as baked eggplant cakes filled with three cheeses, polenta, plum tomato sauce and fresh basil, and a creative hand at work in such light fare as a chèvre and grilled shrimp salad with avocado.

Among starters were baked brie with pinenuts and raisins, vegetable tempura with ginger plum sauce and herbed flatbread with grilled mushrooms, onions, wilted spinach and sour cream.

Open, Thursday-Sunday, noon to 10; closed in winter.

Karen's Kitchen, 55 Main St., Cold Spring. (914) 265-1083.

When Karen Ferencz opened a gourmet and natural-foods deli and store in 1990, it was planned as a takeout establishment. But so many vegetarians and new-agers sat around and talked over herbal tea and bean sprouts, that she added a full lunch menu and started serving breakfast as well.

On bentwood chairs at small round tables, you may lunch on such things as wild rice and lentil cakes, a Zen (tofu) burger, smoked chipotle chili or a middle eastern plate ($4.95 to $6.95). There are also several sandwiches in the $5 to $7 range, with extras like sundried tomatoes or pesto costing 75 cents. Smoked salmon with sesame mayonnaise, spinach and scallions on pumpernickel is $7.25. Brunch (waffles, pancakes, huevos rancheros) is served on weekends, and bagels, bialys, oatmeal crunch and muesli during the week. You also might find a brie, herb and tomato omelet, and just-squeezed carrot-apple juice. Desserts look yummy (everything except the sandwich bread is made in house) and there's a wine and beer license.

Open Monday to Wednesday, 6:30 a.m. to 5 p.m., Thursday and Friday to 8, Saturday, 7 to 8, Sunday, 7 to 6.

Marika's, 137 Main St., Cold Spring. (914) 265-4375.

Caterer Marika Vittori opened this gourmet takeout shop with three tables and lately has expanded into the back garden with seating for about twenty under a huge maple tree. She has all kinds of goodies with which to put together a fancy picnic or to sup at home. Specializing in French fare, she offers duck sausage confit, caponata with crackers, a tortilla casserole, smoked duck with french lentils, and a green bean salad with walnuts and feta cheese from a display case that looked so enticing we could have eaten everything in it. Prices are in the $4.50 to $9.95 range. We thought the day's specials of grilled vegetable sandwich with pesto mayonnaise and bread pudding with bourbon sauce would make a great lunch.

Marika sells a few food items like herbes de Province and some funny little potholders crocheted by her aunt in Germany.

Open Wednesday-Friday noon to 7, Saturday and Sunday 11:30 to 6. Marika's sign says "Monday and Tuesday, diet."

Diversions

Boscobel Restoration, Route 9D, Garrison-on-Hudson, 265-3638. Twice saved from demolition and finally sold for $35 to a wrecker, the house that Gov. Nelson A. Rockefeller called "one of the most beautiful homes ever built in America" was moved from Montrose in Westchester County and rebuilt piece by piece beside the river in Garrison. Lila Acheson Wallace, co-founder with her husband of the Reader's Digest, was the fairy godmother who funded much of the project. Originally saved because of its architecture, Boscobel now is a major house museum displaying furniture and decorative arts of the Federal period. Ironically, in 1975, fourteen years after it had been rebuilt on the site, researchers determined that the European interiors were inaccurate. Mrs. Wallace was advised of the cost of completely refurnishing with authentic New York Federal pieces and said, "Do what you have to do." Graceful wooden swags on the facade of the house are repeated inside on chair backs, a looking glass and a wardrobe. Swags of laurel are incorporated in the designs of china and the base of a candlestick. Rooms contain Duncan Phyfe furniture, fine paintings and unusual lighting fixtures. The collection is full of rarities, among them a winged secretary-bookcase bearing what's believed to be the first coat of arms incorporated into a piece of American furniture. The riverside property includes beautiful gardens and vistas of the Hudson. Open daily except Tuesday, 9:30 to 4 or 5; closed January and February. Adults, $6.

Nature Sanctuaries. Reached from Route 9D via Indian Brook Road in Garrison, **Constitution Marsh** is a public wildlife sanctuary with a self-guided nature trail and boardwalk near the river. Owned by the Taconic State Park Commission, it is managed by the National Audubon Society and is open daily, 10 to 6. Canoes may be rented here. To the south is **Manitoga,** Route 9D, Garrison, a woodland preserve created by famed industrial designer Russel Wright on his estate overlooking a 19th-century quarry. Among the trails is an access route to the **Appalachian Trail,** which crosses the Hudson at Bear Mountain Bridge and cuts through the property. Manitoga is open Wednesday-Friday 10 to 4, weekends to 6; adults, $2.

State Parks. Hiking trails through the Hudson Highlands yield spectacular views, some of the best from Breakneck Mountain and the undeveloped **Hudson Highlands State Park,** a wilderness with trailheads off Route 9D just north of Cold Spring (see below). More pastoral surroundings for hiking, picnicking and swimming are offered in **Fahnestock State Park,** an unexpectedly large complex along Route 301 near the Taconic Parkway.

In **Cold Spring,** walking tours are led by Donald McDonald, a public-spirited soul, Sundays at 2 from mid-May to mid-November. The Putnam County Historical Society's **Foundry School Museum** is an austere little place dedicated to memorabilia from the West Point Foundry. It also shows paintings and a school room with a dunce stool and a schoolmaster's desk from the first private school in Cold Spring. Open for weddings and special services is the **Chapel of Our Lady,** a restored Greek Revival Chapel built on a riverside bluff in 1834 to serve Catholic workers at the foundry. Speaking of churches, two of New York State's most beautiful of the Episcopal persuasion are located along Route 9D, **St. Mary's Church in the Highlands** in Cold Spring and **St. Phillip's Church in the Highlands** in Garrison. **Graymoor,** a Franciscan monastery above Route 9 in Garrison, welcomes visitors for picnicking, retreats and more.

Shopping. Antiquing is big business in Cold Spring, where some two dozen shops occupy storefronts along Main Street. Everything from European antiques to 1930s collectibles can be found here. **Taca-Tiques** specializes in silver and the **Brass Pear** is all brass. **Other's Oldies** is one of the more reliable. **Cold Spring Trading Co.** is a little mall with three antiques stores. **Cat's Cradle** purveys country crafts and gifts, including great dolls. Cards and gifts are the specialty at **Sarsaparilla,** where we especially liked the froggy things. China, mugs, potpourris, kitchen gadgets and lots of specialty foods are featured at **Country Goose.** Known for its services is **Salamagundi Books,** which always offered better local information than the now-defunct visitor center next door at the **Hudson Valley Gift Gallery**. One-of-a-kind clothing, accessories and collectibles are displayed at **Staley Gretzinger.** Marguerite Diblasi and her pudgy dog Broadway preside at **Cold Spring Express,** where you can find silk shirts and crinkle skirts for $15 each, and Indian pendants for $6. Somewhat more expensive are silk velvets, and tuxedo suits for $400. At **Irish Imports** you'll find Celtic jewelry, tweed hats, Irish teas and oatmeal, crystal and china.

Extra-Special ⸻

Hiking. Where else can you arrive by commuter train at the edge of downtown, have everything you need close at hand, and even be able to hike in the nearby mountains? That's what makes Cold Spring so special, especially for city-dwelling New Yorkers a short train ride away, according to local partisans. Disembark at the Cold Spring train station and walk down Fair Street about three quarters of a mile to the trailhead for Mount Taurus (Bull Hill), one of three offshoots of the Appalachian Trail in the eastern Hudson Highlands. You can hike up Bull Hill to the top of Breakneck Mountain, a precipitous 1,400-foot drop to the Hudson opposite Storm King Mountain. The trip takes a few hours, or you can continue on from Breakneck to Beacon for an all-day hike – it's as easy or as arduous as you want. If you don't want to walk to start your hike, you can ask the conductor to have the train stop at the foot of Breakneck. The only problem is, there's no way to get the southbound train to stop at Breakneck for the return home.

Georgian Revival brick buildings present attractive vista in Saratoga Spa State Park.

Saratoga Springs, N.Y.
The City in the Country

Ever since George Washington came here following the decisive battle of the Revolutionary War nearby and tried – unsuccessfully – to buy one of the Saratoga springs, the high and the mighty have been drawn to Saratoga.

They come for the restorative powers of its mineral-water springs, the only carbonated waters east of the Rockies. They come to watch the horses at America's oldest and most scenic thoroughbred race track. They come for the amenities of the meticulous Saratoga Spa State Park, a complex of columned brick Greek Revival buildings and archways harboring a resort hotel, a theater, swimming-pool pavilions and baths, all set among lawns and towering pines sheltering a golf course, a skating pond and more. They come for the concerts at the Saratoga Performing Arts Center, summer home of the New York City Ballet, the Philadelphia Orchestra and many a visiting pop-rock performer. They come to eat and drink, to bet and be merry, to see and be seen.

Saratoga, recently promoted as "the city in the country," is many things to many people. It's too many to be totally encompassed unless you come – as the Vanderbilts and Whitneys, the Paynes and the Phippses do – for the season. The season here is August, the traditional thoroughbred racing period (lately extended to five weeks and five days and opening in late July). With Saratoga's increasing emphasis on the arts, however, a secondary season is all summer long.

Many a superlative applies to Saratoga. A Fortune magazine cover article in 1935 said the convergence of society and big money in Saratoga each August creates "America's dizziest season in America's daftest town." From the Gay Nineties on, more than 20,000 visitors could be housed in one of the world's great concentrations of grand hotels (all but two long since torn down). The rich and famous built "cottages" of 30 to 40 rooms along North Broadway and Union Avenue.

Some of those Victorian mansions are still occupied by the moneyed regulars who come each summer. Others are rented out by Saratogans who flee the August frenzy. Still others have been turned into lodging establishments.

Lately, Saratoga "has become a haven for B&Bs," according to Kate Benton, a native who returned with her husband to open her own. Indeed, B&Bs are opening "faster than we can keep track of them," adds Linda Toohey, executive vice president of the Saratoga County Chamber of Commerce. The Chamber has adopted guidelines that new B&Bs must have innkeepers living on the premises, must serve breakfast and must operate at least six months a year.

Saratoga bills itself as "the August place to be." But that's Saratoga at its most frenetic and most expensive. Go to Saratoga in August if you're into the racing scene. If not, go at less crowded, less pricey times to better savor the splendors of this urbane small city in the country.

Inn Spots

Accommodations are at a premium during the racing season, now the last week of July and all of August, and for major Skidmore College weekends. Reservations should be made far in advance for those dates, and prices usually double or triple. Almost as quickly as the crowds descend, however, they leave. Accommodations tend to go begging from after foliage season until the next June.

The Mansion, Route 29, Box 77, Rock City Falls 12863. (518) 885-1607.

When Gary Collins televised ABC's Home show live from The Mansion a few years back, innkeepers Tom Clark and Alan Churchill put on an outdoor buffet breakfast for the TV entourage of 40 under the lights at 4 o'clock in the morning. "We had a full house, too," Alan said. The overnight guests got the usual breakfast spread a little later that day, after the excitement was over.

The incident tells two things about this remarkable establishment seven miles west of town. One is that of all the possible Saratoga settings, this was the one chosen for a national telecast from Saratoga. The other is that breakfast here is quite an event, TV crews or not.

The setting is the 23-room Venetian villa built in 1866 as a summer home by self-made industrialist George West, known as "The Paper Bag King" for his invention of the folded paper bag. It was acquired in 1986 by Tom, then president of Rockland Community College, who had restored four other houses in Saratoga. He and Alan converted it into a fine Victorian B&B with four guest rooms and a suite, all with private baths.

The mansion is full of striking details, like the six marble fireplaces with massive

carved mantelpieces soaring to the fourteen-foot-high ceilings, brass and copper chandeliers with etched Waterford globes, etched-glass doors, parquet floors of three woods, and Currier and Ives prints. The monogram of George West is inscribed near the top of the front parlor's fireplace mantel, a hefty combination of black marble, walnut, ebony, rosewood and beech, all inlaid with gold. Two matching etched-glass doors stand side by side at the end of the entry foyer. Covered with dirt and grime in the base-

Double parlor at The Mansion.

Statue of St. Francis in Mansion library.

ment, "they were one of those magical finds you come across when you're doing restoration," Tom says. Another was the array of original chestnut shutters stashed in the attic. Now in place inside all windows, they obviate the need for draperies, keep interior temperatures stable and keep out unwanted early morning light.

A double parlor goes off a central hall striking for an unsigned Tiffany chandelier. One parlor is furnished in Empire furniture and the other in Eastlake. Tom built the handsome new floor-to-ceiling shelves in the front parlor and in the suite to hide utility pipes. Three chairs in the front parlor came from Saratoga's old Grand Union Hotel and have been refurbished with the original tapestry fabrics. Ditto for the hotel's couch. It's now ensconced in the sitting room of the main-floor suite, which has parquet floors, marble fireplaces and a pink marble sink in the full bath. The bed here is a double four-poster; the partners deemed a queensize bed too overwhelming for a room we thought large enough for a kingsize.

Queensize beds are attributes of the four upstairs guest rooms, where small private bathrooms (showers only) were fashioned from dressing areas. Mahogany four-poster beds, mirrored armoires, wing chairs and puffy comforters are among the furnishings. Each room contains a dish of hard candies plus fresh flowers and plants that attest both to Alan's green thumb and his knack for arranging the results in his collection of 200 vases. The second floor also harbors a small, plant-filled area, where guests may sit on bentwood rockers and admire the river across the road.

Classical music from Alan's extensive collection of tapes plays in the front library, a fascinating room with a beautiful life-size carved wood statue of St. Francis in a window area and so full of coffee-table books and magazines that one of us could hardly be pried away for breakfast.

A bowl of exotic fruits centered by an alstroemeria blossom was followed by fresh orange or grapefruit juice. Next came a platter of half a dozen breads – lemon, zucchini, banana-bran, applesauce, pumpkin and six-grain toast. Cooked to order was an entrée of the guest's choice. We enjoyed a masterful eggs benedict and a vegetable omelet with a slice of ham. Chocolate-almond coffee was poured throughout at five rose-linened tables graced with fresh roses and tulips (this in January). A flame flickered from an Aladdin's lamp in front of the mirror on the fireplace mantel.

All is not inside. The cupola is open for a rooftop drink, if you'd like. There's a restored side porch, and the four acres of landscaped grounds include a swimming pool. The roaring waterfall that gives Rock City Falls its name is across the street.

Doubles, $95, $165 in August; suite, $110 and $180.

The Batcheller Mansion Inn, 20 Circular St., Saratoga Springs 12866. (518) 584-7012 or (800) 616-7012.

The outside of this new, drop-dead B&B is a sight to behold, as befits what historians variously call Saratoga's most spectacular, conspicuous and architecturally fanciful residential landmark. Park on the side lawn where your special grass-covered parking space is posted with a sign bearing your name. Open the arched mahogany doors and prepare to be overwhelmed. The living room with its gilt-edged mirrors and enormous crystal chandelier is extravagant. The mahogany-paneled library with its plump red velvet sofas beside the fireplace and towering ficus trees by the tall windows in the bay is dramatic. The impressive dining room holds a long table set for twelve and four side tables for two. Just when you think you've seen everything, you enter a kitchen to end all kitchens. It's a breathtaking space, long and narrow and 26 feet high – contemporary and stark white except for three soaring, twenty-foot-tall arched windows that bring the outside in. Oh to have a kitchen like that, except surely the cook must feel on stage as passersby along Whitney Place stop to gawk. After all this, the nine guest bedrooms may be a bit of a letdown, even though they are decorated to the utmost and one is so large it holds a billiards table in the middle.

The house was built in 1873 in what has variously been called flamboyant French Renaissance and High Victorian Gothic styles with Moorish minarets and turrets. Original owner George S. Batcheller was a lawyer, judge and ambassador, who eventually spent most of his life abroad but retained the 28-room castle as his pied-à-terre. It had been condemned and abandoned as a rooming house when a bachelor attorney bought it for $25,000 in 1972. He started a restoration that culminated in 1994 in two whirlwind months of conversion from a residence into one of the grandest B&Bs of all.

The current owner, local developer Bruce J. Levinsky, had failed in efforts to sell the mansion as a residence and ultimately decided a B&B would be more feasible. He wooed a friend, retired adman Stuart Williams, to move with his partner, Lorena Lund, from Georgia in 1994 to get the B&B up and running. "I did this more or less as a lark, to get it going and hopefully in the black," said Stuart, one of whose fortes is marketing. After all the renovations and redecorating, he's still intrigued with the house "because every day I see something new."

There is, indeed, a lot to look at. Purists praise the structural restoration while scoffing at the modern kitchen and some of the decor. The interior was put together by a local decorator who executed the wants of the owner and his two innkeepers, all "very pestering individuals with strong tastes and no background," admitted Stuart.

The nine bedrooms on the second and third floors come with private baths, queen or kingsize beds, fancy wallpapers and coordinated fabrics, oriental rugs atop thick carpeting, writing desks, television sets, telephones, mini-refrigerators, monogrammed bathrobes, thick towels and Haversham & Holt toiletries. They vary widely in size from two small front rooms with hall baths to the third-floor Diamond Jim Brady Room, outfitted with a billiards table, kingsize iron canopy bed, a sitting area and a huge bathroom with an oversize jacuzzi, large stall shower and mirrored wall (two other rooms have smaller jacuzzis). Some rooms, with their TV sets and phones prominent atop their large working desks, would be at home in a business hotel. The Lillian

Saratoga's most conspicuous residential landmark is now The Batcheller Mansion Inn.

Russell Room has two queensize beds and only a single settee for seating, while the Katrina Trask Room comes with a circular porch – reached by ducking through a window. The Rip Van Dam Room with its horsey theme and maple furniture is the only non-Victorian room. "We're not purists," Stuart concedes. "More than half the furnishings were already here."

An elaborate continental breakfast is prepared by Lorena, whose background was in the food and beverage trade. Set out buffet style on the kitchen counters, it includes fresh fruit (perhaps melon wrapped in prosciutto), cold cuts and cheeses as well as homemade muffins and breads from local bakeries.

So extravagant in scope and size is the mansion that it remains a work in progress. No more guest rooms are planned, but seven fireplaces were to be converted to working gas installations. Stuart planned to hang more than 100 artworks, "which will be absorbed in no time." Already accenting living room, kitchen and back porch are some of his amazing replicated paintings – copies of Van Gogh, Picasso, Degas and others, and so true to the originals that even the trained eye cannot tell the difference except for the "SW" initials signed in the corner. Stuart's paintings make for quite a story, and are just another ingredient elevating this inn into a one-of-a-kind place. Though among Saratoga's priciest, the rooms represent unusual value for the high-end vacationers and businessmen for whom they are intended.

Doubles, $110 to $220; racing, $190 to $340.

The Westchester House, 102 Lincoln Ave., Box 944, Saratoga Springs 12866. (518) 587-7613.

One of Saratoga's oldest guest houses, this Queen Anne Victorian structure has been accommodating guests for more than 100 years. But it has been greatly enhanced since its 1987 purchase by Bob and Stephanie Melvin of Washington, D.C. They had traveled extensively and stayed at B&Bs before they opened their own, and Stephanie said they approached the endeavor differently than others in town. "Comfort was paramount to us," she advised. "So while we have fine things, we encourage people to feel at home. We want the rooms to be restful and our guests to feel special." The hallmarks here are hospitality and attention to detail, amidst a residential garden setting.

Hospitality comes easily to Stephanie, an opera singer who performs occasionally in Saratoga. She has arranged antiques, "old" art and contemporary artworks to co-exist in a welcoming environment. Brass and copper chandeliers, oriental paper-cuttings on the walls, high ceilings and gleaming wood floors topped with oriental rugs dignify the common rooms. Rich woodwork, oak newel posts on the staircase banister, blue tiles, two elaborate fireplaces and distinctive wainscoting are all original. "We just had to clean up the house and update the systems," says Bob. He makes the stained glass and both collect antiques and art.

All seven upstairs guest rooms have handsome private tiled baths and all but one have king or queensize beds. We were comfortable in the Jefferson Room, where the new kingsize iron bed is dressed in fine linens. Air-conditioning, ceiling fans, fresh flowers and chocolates with the raised Westchester House logo are among amenities in all the rooms.

Guests relax amid terraces and Victorian gardens on the extra-large side lawn bordered by a thick hedge of spirea – a real in-town oasis in summer. Or they gather on the wraparound porch overlooking the Melvins' colorful, old-fashioned perennial borders for tea and cookies or wine and cheese. They relax at other times in either of the two main-floor parlors, where decanters of sherry are at the ready.

A continental breakfast is served stylishly and with lively conversation amid pink linens, china, crystal mugs and stemmed glasses in the dining room or on the porch. Juice, fresh fruits, fresh breads and muffins and sometimes cheese are the fare. After breakfast, Bob snaps photos of guests, which he and Stephanie forward with a thank-you note to remind them of their stay. Happy customers, they know, are repeat customers.

Doubles, $75 to $125; racing, $180 to $225. Closed in January.

Adelphi Hotel, 365 Broadway, Saratoga Springs 12866. (518) 587-4688.

One of only two of the great old Saratoga hotels still standing, this is the place to stay if you want to relive Saratoga's glory days. The four-story beauty with the columned veranda in the heart of downtown was built in 1877. The Adelphi had been closed for four years when Gregg Siefker and Sheila Parkert of Nebraska bought it in 1978 and started its ongoing restoration restoration into a fantasy of Victoriana.

"It was a complete wreck, but we were lucky because it was never modernized," said Sheila, who made the curtains, sought out the antiques and now arranges the spectacular towering floral arrangements that grace the lobby.

We've seldom seen so much lace or so many crazy quilts in the 34 air-conditioned guest rooms, each with private bath, telephone and television. All are spacious and feature lofty ceilings, ornate woodwork, antiques and lavish doses of Victoriana. For a change of pace, check out Gregg's favorite Adirondack Mission Room with its twig furniture, a sitting room in Stickley Arts and Crafts style, and a bathroom paneled in dark wood slats. Across the hall is a suite furnished in French country style.

A complimentary continental breakfast of fresh fruit and coffee cake is served in bed, on the second floor in the High Victorian Parlor or outside on the Grand Piazza, the geranium-bedecked porch overlooking Broadway.

Flanked by pergola and flagstone terrace, Adelphi Hotel's pool is sylvan oasis.

In 1994, the owners completed a total overhaul of the elaborate Victorian lobby, bar and upstairs parlor. The sight-to-behold lobby is an extravaganza of palms, chandeliers, crystal chandeliers and plush sofas and chairs. The walls and ceiling have been newly hand-stenciled in an exotic, over-the-top Neoclassic style by a stencil master from California.

Cocktails, tea, supper, dessert and coffee are served daily in summer in the **Cafe Adelphi,** a Victorian bar incorporated into the rear of the lobby and extending beyond to a back porch and a charming courtyard garden. The latest addition here is a swimming pool surrounded by an elaborate pergola and flagstone terrace, a sylvan oasis in the heart of Saratoga.

Doubles, $105 to $125; racing, $180 to $220. Suites, $140 to $170; racing, $255 to $295; three-night minimum on meet weekends. Closed November-April.

The Wayside Inn, 104 Wilton Road, Greenfield 12833. (518) 893-7249.

Built as a stagecoach inn and farm in 1789, this B&B reflects the much-traveled background and enthusiasm of owners Karen and Dale Shook. In the main house, they offer four bedrooms and a two-bedroom suite, all with private baths and furnished with exotica. Their big blue barn (the largest in Saratoga County) was home to assorted sheep, goats, chickens, cats, dogs and an evolving "arts in the country" center until it was destroyed by fire in December 1994. A community barn-raising was in the works to help the Shooks rebuild.

Both house and barn have great appeal. The Shooks lived in many parts of the world while he taught on military bases before he came here in 1987 as a professor of international business at Saratoga's Skidmore College. The oriental screen and a shelf display of collections in the large fireplaced living room hint at things to come.

Upstairs, puppets are pinned to the curtains in the Toy Room. Canadiana prevails in the Captain St. John Room. Furniture from China and Korea marks the Madame Butterfly Room, which has an incredible screen framing an equally incredible chair in the corner, a queensize brass bed, TV set, oriental throw rugs atop the carpeting and an enormous bathroom-dressing area with double vanity, shower and small jacuzzi. The third-floor Scheherazade Suite, a son's former hideaway, was transformed by furnishings from the couple's years in Saudi Arabia. There's a kingsize bed with a rocker sitting area; a connecting room has a daybed and a double bed draped in blue mesh netting.

On the main floor in what had been the summer kitchen is the Maria Theresa Room, with a queen brass bed, private entrance and windows on three sides. It provides reminders of the Shooks' days in Holland, Belgium, Germany and Italy. All rooms share a vivid decor of quilts, curtains, pillows and such in lush deep colors, many reds and greens. Each contains a mini-refrigerator, which you could easily miss because there's so much to look at.

Karen has compiled a good little cookbook of her breakfast menus and recipes. A typical day's fare could be layered granola and strawberries, Mexican eggs, potatoes with onions and cheese and pineapple upside-down cake, along with juices (guava and passion fruit), yogurt, cereal, fruit, bagels and pastries. Sunday might bring fig-peach tarts, bacon popovers, and layered mushrooms and eggs. The feast is taken at a table in the formal dining room, at rattan tables on a sun porch or at a couple more tables in the entryway off the kitchen, which used to be a woodshed.

Until the fire, the artists' cooperative in a restored gallery in the front of the former dairy barn was home to a award-winning potter John Visser as well as a resident weaver, a painter and a candlemaker. Another section of the barn was the summer home of the Victor Herbert Festival and of Merlin the Magician's lunch and dinner theater. With both those enterprises booked for 1995 and a groundswell of support from the community, Karen hoped to rebuild quickly. "I have a million plans and projects to make this a destination point for visitors," she said. She had already planted an herb garden and a wildflower layout with paths and benches beside a creek and added a fountain and gazebo beside the pond on the ten-acre property since our previous visit. So you knew her arts center would be, from the ashes, quickly reborn.

Doubles, $100 to $135.

The Eddy House, Nelson and Crescent Avenues, Saratoga Springs 12866. (518) 587-2340.

"Welcome home...to your private Saratoga estate," begins the brochure for Saratoga's first B&B, a winner of a place operated by Barbara and Tom Bertino. "Staying home should be this good!" it concludes.

We agree, but don't let their "home away from home" theme mislead. This is a sophisticated house where a continuing house-party atmosphere draws a sophisticated repeat clientele partial to horses and the nearby tracks. The only drawback is a lack of private baths, the five guest rooms sharing two in a rather home-like situation.

The Bertinos – he a retired athletic director and she a former interior designer on Long Island – used to summer in Saratoga so their children could be exposed to the ballet, arts and horses. When the children left the nest, Barbara recalls, they urged their parents to move to Saratoga "and do what you like best – to cook and entertain." That was in 1984, and they've been cooking and entertaining since in a house and property that are suited to the role.

Guests may use every downstairs room in the 1847 Federal house. They include a summery parlor, pretty in pale yellow and blue with a collection of rare flow blue china on the wall, another living room in pink and teal, a cozy wormwood-paneled library with TV and a winterized rear porch. The formal dining room is a sight to behold, what with a large oak parquet table, the original white brick fireplace, an unused corner staircase upon which figurines and pictures are displayed and a table with

Two acres of farmland surround The Eddy House and barn.

every imaginable cordial to which guests may help themselves. Between the pre-dinner setups and vegetable dips and the after-dinner nightcaps, the house-party atmosphere is understandable.

Upstairs in the rear are three rooms sharing a bath. They're named Lavender, Yellow and Teddybear for their decor. The Lavender is particularly striking for its floral-print wallpaper on walls and ceilings, nicely color-coordinated with a rainbow of towels. In the front of the house sharing a bath are two larger corner bedrooms. One has a queensize bed and an antique fainting couch that opens to a double bed; it's a fantasy in black and burgundy against pink walls. The other is in navy and white with a kingsize bed and white wicker.

Barbara's buffet breakfasts are such a hit that friends of guests often show up for the meal. Fresh berries and fruits from the Bertinos' organic gardens in back get things off to a good start and turn up in her homemade preserves that get lathered on the bran muffins and breads. The main course might be Swedish pancakes with lingonberry sauce, frittatas, oat waffles or orange french toast. Smoked pork chops or ham steaks cooked on the outdoor grill might accompany.

The party continues outside with volleyball, badminton, bocce and even a golf ball net, plus a game room in the garage. A twelve-foot-high hedge surrounds the nicely landscaped, two-acre property.

Doubles, $90 to $100; racing, $140 to $160. Smoking restricted.

Saratoga Bed and Breakfast, 434 Church St., Saratoga Springs 12866. (518) 584-0920.

When Noel and Kathleen Smith and their three daughters started one of the area's first B&Bs in their 1860 farmhouse, four of their five rooms shared baths. "That's no good any more," conceded Noel, who said they managed to survive for six years but realized they were losing business.

In 1991, the Smiths attacked the problem with a vengeance. They added two bathrooms over an entryway, eliminated one bedroom and ended up with four bedrooms, each with private bath. What's more, they bought a brick house across the street and restored it into four sumptuous suites, each with modern bath, fireplace and TV. Add their small motel next door and, as Noel proudly describes it, "we've now got all the bases covered."

The four lodgings in the original farmhouse vary from a couple of small rooms with double beds and maple and oak furniture to two larger rooms with fireplaces, wicker furniture and queensize beds topped by colorful quilts made by a local church guild. All have private baths.

Kathleen would prefer to dwell on – and in – the new 1850 House with its four suites, three with kingsize beds. All have splashy coordinated fabrics, antique walnut and mahogany furniture, glistening hardwood floors, TVs, telephones and bottles of Saratoga water. The most lavish is the rear Irish Cottage Suite, quiet and private with two queensize beds and two curved loveseats facing the TV and fireplace. The Waverly violet fabrics match the curtains and wallpaper; even the clawfoot tub is painted violet. One man who stayed here claimed it was like "waking up in a Bonwit Teller shopping bag," Kathleen reports.

The sun porch here is the summertime setting for a full breakfast. Noel might prepare french toast with sausage one day and cream-cheese omelet with bacon the next. Juice, fresh fruit and corn muffins or toast round out the fare.

Doubles, $65 to $95; racing, $95 to $135. Suites, $100 to $185; racing, $150 to $210.

The Lombardi Farm, 34 Locust Grove Road, Saratoga Springs 12866. (518) 587-2074.

A solarium with a hot tub/jacuzzi, gourmet breakfasts and Nubian and French Alpine goats in the barn are diverse attractions at the B&B that Kathleen and Vincent Lombardi run on the outskirts of town. The focal point is the large solarium that joins two houses, one old and one new. Here is where Kathleen serves leisurely breakfasts at four lace-covered tables overlooking a jungle of plants and a jacuzzi.

Off one side of the solarium, in the new house to the rear, is a guest living room with a TV and a piano. Off another side, again in the new wing, is a large main-floor bedroom with a canopy queensize bed, a wicker sitting area and a private bath outfitted with all kinds of lotions and colognes. This room has doors to an outside deck "so private that guests can sit out in their pajamas and enjoy their first cup of coffee," says Kathleen. Upstairs in the rear wing are two guest rooms with private baths. One decorated in a native American motif has a carved walnut bed with a headboard reaching the ceiling. The other has a double and a twin bed with hand-carved headboards..

Off the front of the solarium is the new country kitchen, the heart of the old house (circa 1840). Guests gather here around the wood-burning stove for hot mulled cider and home-baked goodies.

Upstairs is a master bedroom with kingsize canopy bed and private bath. Vince built an ingenious partial canopy decorated with silk roses above a queen bed tucked between the chimney and an outside wall in another bedroom. The bed in a nearby room has a lace canopy hand-crocheted by Kathleen's great-grandmother. An attic suite comes with a kingsize bed, a sitting room and a Niagara massage chair.

Kathleen's breakfasts start with an individual fruit platter, presented like a picture. Then might come coeur à la crème featuring the goat cheese made on the farm or toffee toast that is like candied bread – made with thick slices of french bread dipped in an egg batter and baked with a toffee syrup. Corned-beef hash with poached eggs, chocolate crêpes, ham soufflé with raspberry meringues and peach strudel, crème caramel

The Six Sisters Bed & Breakfast, as viewed from house across Union Avenue.

and orange-oat waffles are among her imaginative dishes. There are always four or five courses.

Doubles, $100; racing, $115.

The Six Sisters Bed & Breakfast, 149 Union Ave., Saratoga Springs 12866. (518) 583-1173.

Saratoga native Kate Benton, daughter of a former mayor, didn't want to leave Saratoga during the August racing season, as so many locals do. Upon returning to her hometown after fourteen years in Hawaii, she and her husband, Steve Ramirez, sought to be where the action is. So they opened a B&B in an 1890 Victorian facing Union Avenue, the main route to the racetrack. Verandas on the first and second floor give front-row seats onto all the comings and goings.

They named the architecturally unique building with a scalloped-edge roof for Kate's sisters; "my six brothers are still waiting," she quips. The four air-conditioned guest rooms, all with private baths, are quite large (two have kingsize beds, one a queen and one two doubles) and are furnished in different styles. The master bedroom suite comes with a small sun room with etched-glass windows and a private front balcony. Wicker and floral prints mark a room furnished in the style the couple enjoyed when they met in Hawaii. The Elizabeth Marie room has a tropical look with wicker chairs and pictures of flowers. The rear Parlor Suite offers a living room with TV, a wet bar and a huge back porch.

Steve, an accomplished cook, prepares a family-style breakfast in the large dining room. Fresh fruit and baked apples might be followed by vegetable quiche or frittata, a side plate of bacon or sausage, and zucchini or nut breads. Kona macadamia nut coffee accompanies.

The pleasant front parlor with new flooring, oriental carpets and Italian marble around the fireplace harbors considerable local information, plus Steve's chatty little offbeat guide to Saratoga dining. At our visit, he had just been elected president of the New York State Bed & Breakfast Association and was the proud father of the couple's first-born.

Doubles, $60 to $105; racing, $200 to $225. No smoking.

Union Gables, 55 Union Ave., Saratoga Springs 12866. (518) 587-7122 or (800) 398-1558.

Locally known as the Furness House, this three-story mansion with a corner turret was converted in 1992 into a ten-room B&B, Saratoga's largest and one of its more laid-back and comfortable. Local realtor Tom Roohan, whose office is across the street, his wife Jody and four children make the restored house their home.

The Roohans offer ten bedrooms with private baths in the circa 1901 Queen Anne Victorian with a corner turret and wraparound veranda, and out back in a renovated carriage house. The rooms – spacious, airy and uncluttered – have been professionally decorated with partial-canopy beds and colorful fabrics. Each is named for one of the couple's brothers or sisters. Annie, a front-corner turret room, has a painted sideboard, interesting periwinkle glaze painted walls and a white floor painted with ribbons, a kingsize bed and a single wicker chair. Edward also has a king canopy bed, two armchairs and a bay window awash in pillows. Kate's room is dark and horsy; a horse's collar is wrapped around the mirror in the bath, and a great wreath hangs above the kingsize bed. All rooms come with king or queen beds, TV and telephones, airconditioning and a Victorian country – as opposed to haute – decor. "We want to provide the best of both worlds," Tom said, referring to the contemporary amenities in a Victorian masterpiece.

Rich paneling abounds throughout the house, especially in the large foyer and the huge living room/dining area, where you may be left to rattle around on your own. The Roohans put out a continental breakfast of fresh fruits, yogurt, cereals and pastries from the Bread Basket in the morning. It can be taken at a table for eight or outside on the great veranda with 80 feet of frontage on storied Union Avenue.

The house, designed by noted Saratoga architect R. Newton Brezee for a local manufacturer, blends Richardson and shingle styles. The variety of exterior surfaces (limestone, sandstone, pressed brick, wood shingles and slate) and their diverse planes produce an ever-changing play of lighting effects enhanced by the deep red, beige and dark green color scheme.

Doubles, $90; August, $200.

Gideon Putnam Hotel and Conference Center, Saratoga Springs 12866. (518) 584-3000 or (800) 732-1560.

Head deep into Saratoga Spa State Park past verdant golf-course fairways barely visible through the trees along the glorious Avenue of the Pines. Around the corner is this impressive, five-story Georgian brick structure that looks as if it's been there forever. A long green awning extends out from the entry between Corinthian columns to a circular drive upon which carriages and limousines once arrived. The latter still do, of course. The marbled, chandeliered lobby contains lighted cabinets displaying porcelain and china collections. Beyond are five dining rooms and countless lounges.

This is a state-owned resort of the old school, built as part of Franklin Roosevelt's WPA project in the 1930s and named for the man who sensed the springs' potential and opened Saratoga's first guest house. Lately, the resort has been upgraded and turned into a year-round facility by a concessionaire that also runs the national park lodges at Yellowstone, Bryce and Zion. The $5 million investment includes new and renovated bathrooms, better air-conditioning and heating, and new carpeting and lighting. The concessionaire also renovated and manages the nearby Roosevelt Baths.

Each of the 132 guest rooms has at least a glimpse of the park. Rooms are furnished in Colonial reproductions and wicker in rose or blue color schemes. Because two double beds didn't fit well, most rooms combine a queensize and an extra-long twin bed. All have enormous closets, television sets and telephones. Guests who spend the season

Local art enhances decor of Eartha's Grill & WIne Bar.

usually snap up the eighteen parlor and porch suites. The latter have large screened porches furnished in bamboo overlooking a forest. No longer do guests in August have to eat every meal here; the hotel now offers a no-meals (EP) plan.

Doubles, $135, EP; suites, $160 to $175. August, doubles, $270; suites $420 to $455.

Dining Spots

Saratoga offers more restaurants per capita than any town in upstate New York. We offer here a selection of our favorites. Serving days and meal hours vary widely, especially off-season. To avoid disappointment, check ahead.

Eartha's Grill & Wine Bar, 60 Court St., Saratoga Springs. (518) 583-0602.

Some of Saratoga's most interesting and assertive fare is served at this intimate grill and wine bar, formerly known as Eartha's Kitchen and lately run by Kevin and Juliet Morrill. He's the young chef who worked for the restaurant's founder and she's the hostess out front. The surroundings are stylish and congenial, and the background jazz and classical music is played at just the right volume.

The name derives from the six-foot wood stove that the founder called Eartha. From it come eight or nine entrées, mostly grilled but with an occasional sautéed dish, as in shrimp and scallops with artichokes and capers or veal scaloppine with sundried tomato and oregano sauce. The menu changes frequently.

When we were there, the huge wood stove was ready for mesquite, charcoal and applewood. It produced a super grilled mahi-mahi with avocado mousseline and a remarkable grilled catfish with pickled ginger and a mango glaze, among entrées from $14 to $20. They were accompanied by good rice and the best zucchini we've tasted in a long time.

Another visit yielded grilled breast of chicken with melted brie and apple-cranberry chutney and roasted rack of lamb with a hunter sauce, accompanied by a julienne of squash, carrots and snow peas and scalloped potatoes baked with herbs.

The only problem was that our appetizers were so filling we barely had room for the main courses (either would have been enough to share). The seafood sampler was a platter full of gravlax, smoked trout, smoked tuna and shrimp mousseline. The unusual grilled country game pâté was a man-size slab surrounded by garnishes, chutneys and toast rounds. A $16 bottle of Rosemount Estate shiraz accompanied from a choice but expensive wine list that's considered the best in the city.

Desserts are to sigh over: chocolate grand marnier torte, Italian rum cake, plumapricot kuchen, cinnamon bread pudding with sabayon and warm tollhouse pie. We enjoyed a creamy cheesecake with strawberry puree on top.

The decor is upscale bistro – white tablecloths and china, fresh flowers in carafes, bentwood chairs, wood wainscoting and local art on the cream-colored walls.

Dinner nightly in summer, 6 to 9 or 10; closed Monday rest of year.

43 Phila Bistro, 43 Phila St., Saratoga Springs. (518) 584-2720.

Culinary excitement also issues from this suave American cafe-bistro opened in 1993 by Michael Lenza, an ex-South Jersey chef who cooked locally at Sperry's before launching his own venture. He and chef John Winnek earned rave reviews for their contemporary fare served with finesse. They're also on the cutting edge: How else to explain the monthly Cigar Nights, when a $5 cover charge produces free cigars to savor with the finest in vintage ports, beers, wines or single-malt scotches? These proved so successful that they were about to stage a holiday cigar dinner in December 1994.

Thank you, no. We were quite happy with our November dinner that opened with a dish of assorted spicy olives marinated in olive oil, the oil useful for soaking the accompanying homemade bread. Among starters ($5 to $9.50) were a smooth chicken-liver pâté served with crostini and cornichons, a terrific trio of smoked seafood (with capers in a little carrot floret and roasted red-pepper crème fraîche) and an enormous pizzetta, a meal in itself.

Had we eaten more than a sliver of the pizzetta we never would have made it through the main courses, a choice of three pastas ($16 to $18.50) and eight entrées ($15.50 to $22). The Tuscan chicken pasta with roasted peppers, olives and white beans was a lusty autumn dish; the fillet of sole in parchment on a bed of julienned vegetables and rice, a signature item, turned out a bit bland. Other possibilities included cedar-planked broiled salmon with braised belgian endive and pears, grilled Idaho brook trout stuffed with prosciutto and served with gorgonzola, and pan-roasted lamb chops with a sweet onion custard, wilted swiss chard and a cider shallot compote. A $15 bottle of our favorite Hogue Cellars fumé blanc accompanied from a varied, well-chosen list that earned the Wine Spectator award.

The pastry chef is known for distinctive desserts, including a white chocolate raspberry tart, bananas foster and a peanut butter mousse in a chocolate ganache shell with mocha crème anglaise. We settled for a dish of plum-port sorbet, a refreshing ending to an uncommonly good meal.

Caricatures of local businessmen brighten one wall of the 50-seat dining room, which is lovely in peach and terra cotta. The bar and banquettes are custom-made of bird's-eye and tiger's-eye maple. Tables, some rather close together, are covered with white linens topped with paper mats bearing the 43 Phila logo (a curious but attractive touch that we far prefer to glass). Atop each are fresh flowers, a lucite pepper grinder and a bottle of red wine – a different label at each table.

In season, chef Winnek offers some mighty good crab dishes, from soft-shell crabs with Thai curry sauce to Maryland crab cakes with rémoulade, corn piccalilli and hush puppies. He also bottles for sale the 43 ketchup that accompanies his black angus steaks.

Breakfast daily in summer, 7 to noon, Wednesday-Sunday 8 to noon in off-season; dinner nightly from 5; Sunday brunch, 11 to 3.

The Wheat Fields, 440 Broadway, Saratoga Springs. (518) 587-0534.

A pasta machine in the front window attracts passersby to one of Saratoga's newer restaurants, which features what it calls "unique pasta dining."

Pretty wallpaper accented with baskets of wheat dresses the two long and narrow

storefront dining rooms. Modern blonde tweedy chairs, glass-topped tables and Saratoga mineral water bottles filled with dried pasta topped with dried flowers complete the decor.

Every dish contains pasta and all the pasta is made by the owner, former New York advertising exec Joseph Loiacono, according to his advertising – allowing for some license that goes with the trade. Each time we've been there a young man or woman was working at the pasta machine and Joseph was nowhere to be found.

The 30 pasta dishes are priced at night from $9.95 for ravioli formaggio to $16.95 for sliced Tuscan flank steak on a bed of spinach and egg fettuccine with tomato-mushroom sauce. The chicken breast stuffed with asparagus mousse is served over fettuccine, while the shrimp and mushrooms with fresh snow peas comes on a bed of linguini. Starters include a hearty

Table for four at The Wheat Fields.

soup of pasta and beans, stuffed pasta and fried pasta sticks with salsa or a dipping sauce. Even the day's quiche has an angel-hair pasta crust, topped with imported cheeses.

Five sandwiches are served with soup or salad for $5.75 to $6.75 at lunchtime. Two of the more interesting are chicken with walnuts and Sicilian eggplant with red clam sauce and melted cheese. One of us tried the cream of artichoke soup (delicious) and the fiesta Italiano – chilled pasta salad, garnished with edible nasturtiums. The other chose the pasta sampler ($7.25), an uninteresting cavatelli with house sauce, a better spinach fettuccine with herb butter, and a tasty tomato-basil rotelle with sweet basil cream. Good, chewy bread with a sesame seed crust and a generous glass of the house chardonnay accompanied. The sugar that came with coffee was flavored with anise.

Favorite desserts are pumpkin-pecan cheesecake, cappuccino pie and a "killer" chocolate cake described as like fudge.

Lunch, Monday-Saturday 11:30 to 3; dinner, Monday-Saturday 5 to 9, 10 or 11, Sunday 4:30 to 9.

Sperry's, 30 1/2 Caroline St., Saratoga Springs. (518) 584-9618.

Once owned by Charles "Chubby" Sperry, a thoroughbred owner and trainer, this unlikely-looking establishment attracts a racetrack crowd in summer and locals the rest of the year. It looks like a gin mill, and only those in the know would venture inside. The decor is quite forgettable: a long bar, a black and white tile floor and, at either end of the room, dark old booths and tables covered with blue and white checked cloths. Beyond is a large covered patio for additional seating in season.

Chef-owner Ridge Qua is known for consistently good food at reasonable prices. The menu rarely changes, but some of the preparations do, and there are always several specials.

For lunch, one of us enjoyed a great grilled duck breast salad with citrus vinaigrette ($7) and the other a cup of potato-leek soup with a huge open-face dill-havarti-tomato sandwich ($5.25), served with a salad. Unfortunately, service was so laid-back as to be slow and disinterested. We had to go to the bar to ask for – and then pay – the bill.

The dinner menu runs from $10.95 for jambalaya to $17.95 for steak au poivre, veal with a demi-glaze of port wine and wild mushrooms and some of the night's specials. Grilled Atlantic salmon with cucumber-dill crème fraîche, cajun-spiced catfish with southwestern salsa and guacamole, rock shrimp with apples and walnuts in a sage cream sauce over whole wheat linguini and grilled chicken with roasted peppers, ham and aged provolone were specials at our latest visit. Desserts include seasonal fruit tarts, cheesecakes, crème caramel and chocolate-cointreau mousse.

Lunch, Tuesday-Saturday 11:30 to 3:30; dinner nightly, 5 to 10 or 11.

Caunterbury Restaurant, 500 Union Ave., Saratoga Springs. (518) 587-9653.

The interior of these huge horse and dairy barns borders on Disneyland, but the food is consistently good and locally popular. Stage-set scenes and rooms on several levels surround what once was a lagoon in the middle – the lagoon was covered after a customer fell in. The Waterfall Room comes with a wooden footbridge across a pond full of goldfish; there's a wicker table for two near a waterfall, and it's all very tropical. Other rooms in five "village houses" are smaller and more standard. The posh, two-story lounge with lofts is favored in winter. Here, lights twinkling on trees and vines are reflected in the mirrors on the angled roof, a fire blazes in the walk-in-size hearth, and all is cozy and romantic.

The food, once secondary to the atmosphere, is now considered its equal. A new hickory wood grill produces such treats as red snapper with changing sauces, pork tenderloin with grilled mushrooms and cider-rosemary sauce, New York strip steak with roasted garlic and peppercorn butter, and a mixed grill of beef tenderloin, chicken and shrimp. Other entrées ($10.95 to $18.95) include three interesting pasta dishes, shrimp in puff pastry, seafood crêpes, beef wellington and steak diane.

The traditional appetizers have been enlivened with the addition of things like bruschetta and carpaccio served on crostini. The dinner menu also adds a few salads, sandwiches and pasta dishes for lighter fare. Desserts include tollhouse pie, English toffee cheesecake, trifle and mud pie.

Dinner nightly except Wednesday, 5:30 to 10, Sunday from 4:30.

The Olde Bryan Inn, 123 Maple Ave., Saratoga Springs. (518) 587-2990.

All gray stone and flanked by tubs full of geraniums and white petunias, this is the oldest building in Saratoga, a tavern and inn dating to 1773 and located near the High Rock Spring that George Washington tried unsuccessfully to buy. The place is jammed day and night, no doubt because of its moderate prices (the same menu is served all day) and a pleasant atmosphere of brick, brass and booths. There's also a covered outdoor terrace that we found torridly uncomfortable on a sunny day. It was being replaced by a large addition for dining overflow and functions at our 1994 visit.

For lunch, try a grilled chicken BLT, a cajun burger ($4.50), a french dip sandwich or one of six salads ($5.95 to $6.95) served with homemade nut muffins or garlic bread. Light entrées go from $3.75 for chili to $8.95 for stir-fried chicken maui or petite sirloin with homefries. Dinner entrées range from an old-fashioned turkey dinner for $10.95 to blackened steak or New York sirloin for $16.95, with plenty of options in between. The signature dessert is chocolate oblivion, a dense, fudge-like creation topped with whipped cream and resting on a pool of raspberry sauce.

The atmosphere is as casual as the menu, but locals consider the food outstanding.

Two-story lounge with lofts is a favorite place for dining at Caunterbury Restaurant.

The owners have opened another restaurant with the same format and menu, the Old Homestead, in nearby Burnt Hills.

Open daily, 11:30 to 11 or midnight.

The Inn at Saratoga, 231 Broadway, Saratoga Springs 12866. (518) 583-1890.

Back in the kitchen at this Clarion Inn is chef Frank D'Aluisio, who was nicknamed François by the French chef he worked for here six years earlier. His food is highly rated and more approachable than that of his immediate predecessor who had taken it to the cutting edge.

These days, expect dinner entrées priced from $13.95 for chicken cacciatore to $18.95 for the chef's specialty, steak au poivre laced with courvoisier. On the fall menu you might find broiled salmon with lemon-caper hollandaise, grilled duck breast with sweet plum glaze, grilled pork chops with dried cranberry gravy and potato pancakes, and a hearty venison pot pie. Lobster bisque is the house favorite, although the four-onion soup with parmesan crouton is no slouch. Or start with grilled shrimp quesadilla with spinach, chèvre and warm sundried tomato salsa, a superior appetizer for $7.95.

Also held in high regard here is the Sunday brunch buffet ($14.95) featuring live jazz groups. Among the buffet "stations" is one for smoked salmon, served with a variety of bagels, cream cheeses and condiments.

The main dining room is formal Victorian in pink and black. Drinks are offered at bamboo club chairs or at the marble bar in the adjacent Ascot Lounge with walls of glass. A small garden courtyard is also available for dining.

The refurbished inn is something of a misnomer, for this is really a blend of hotel and motel with an English theme. Redone from top to bottom, the 38 former motel rooms go off a wide hall in back. They are comfortably outfitted with traditional reproduction furniture, heavy draperies and comforters. There's no common room as such, and the public spaces are rather impersonal. Doubles are priced from $105 to $125.

Dinner nightly, 5 to 9 or 10; Sunday brunch, 10 to 2.

Hattie's, 45 Phila St., Saratoga Springs. (518) 584-4790.

After 55 years as Hattie's Chicken Shack, this well-known institution changed hands and shortened its name in 1993. Hattie Austin, still doing the baking here at age 93, sold to Christel Baker, then a 33-year-old Wall Street investment banker. "We're old friends," explained Christel. "Our families go way back."

Christel, who was making apple butter in the kitchen at our first visit, retained Hattie's chef and staff. She broadened the emphasis from soul food to Southern home cooking, but kept the homey, cozy red-and-white-checked-tablecloth decor. She also expanded the hours and obtained a liquor license to feature Southern drinks like mint juleps and planter's punch.

The food, according to local consensus, is better than ever. Such traditional favorites as dirty rice and turkey and rice soup have yielded to things like creole jambalaya and broiled lamb chops, although regulars still go for the crispy southern fried chicken and barbecued spare ribs ($11.25 to $13.50). Dinners are served with hot biscuits, soup, green salad and choice of two Southern accompaniments, among them mashed potatoes and collard greens. Starters and light fare include cornbread, catfish fingers with Mississippi salsa, sautéed chicken livers on toast and a vegetarian sampler. These along with sandwiches and a fried chicken plate are available for lunch ($3.75 to $5.75).

Among desserts are peach cobbler, berry pies, puddings and cakes.

Regulars and visitors alike swear by Hattie's Southern farm breakfast. For $6.50 you get eggs, grits, homefries, ham, bacon, sausage and biscuits.

Open daily in summer, 7 a.m. to 10 p.m.; rest of year, lunch daily 11:30 to 5, dinner 5 to 9 or 10.

Villa Luisa, 780 Saratoga Road (Route 9), Wilton. (518) 581-0234.

Great food at reasonable prices is the hallmark of this relatively new restaurant run by the Cirelli family. Owner Luisa Cirelli is an Italian who sang in opera choruses in Italy until her marriage to a surgeon. Here she plays the personable hostess who goes from table to table to ensure that her guests are being well fed.

Her sons, Michael and Rick, are the chefs. The food is northern Italian and the menu wide-reaching. Tagliatelle with vegetables, chicken parmigiana, calamari and mussels marinara, and veal marsala are the house specialties ($8.95 to $12.95). We've heard raves about the chicken Luisa (sautéed in a light vodka cream sauce) and the julienned vegetables baked in parchment paper. Dinner prices are mainly in the low teens, and the most expensive item is the mixed shellfish served over linguini ($16.95). The food is of such quality and value that area food connoisseurs forgive the roadhouse decor.

Lunch, Monday-Friday 11:30 to 2:30; dinner nightly, 4:30 to 9 or 10.

Little India, 423 Broadway, Saratoga Springs. (518) 583-4151.

Another well received newcomer is this authentic Indian restaurant in a downtown storefront. Tables are dressed in white and blue beneath a pressed-tin ceiling.

The usual appetizers and breads are priced nicely from $1.50 for chapati to $5.95 for a platter of chicken tikka, seikh (beef) kabob, fish pakora, samosa and papadum. Vegetarians have a good choice of entrées, from baigan bahajia (roasted eggplant cooked with onions, tomatoes and green peas) to malai kofte (balls of minced vegetables simmered with cardamom, saffron, garlic, cashews and cream). Lamb, chicken, beef, seafood and biryani (rice) dinners are $8.75 to $11.95 (for three shrimp dishes). We like the sound of lamb shami korma, with cashews, almonds and cream.

You may have your food spiced as hot as you like. Cool it down with raita, and end with punjabi style pistachio and cashew ice cream.

Lunch daily, 11 to 3; dinner, 3 to 10 or 11.

Diversions

There are so many things to do and see here that we cannot possibly do them all justice. And any visitors who tried to do them all in one trip would wear themselves out. Here is a brief selection:

The Horses. Drive around the east and south sides of Saratoga and you'll be amazed at the number of stables, racetracks, horses, horse people and hangers-on, especially in August. Louisville has its Kentucky Derby and Baltimore the Preakness, but the real high-rollers come to Saratoga for five-plus weeks of racing and allied activities. Socialite Marylou Whitney's annual gala at the Canfield Casino to benefit the National Museum of Dance launches a whirlwind of balls and fund-raisers all through August. The **Saratoga Race Course** off Union Avenue, oldest thoroughbred flat track in the country (1863), attracts the highest average daily attendance of any track (about 28,000) for its recently extended season from late July through August. As many as 50,000 show up for its major Travers Stakes race. Because so many winners of Triple Crown events have lost at Saratoga, the track has become known as "the graveyard of favorites." The place is massive: 17,000 seats, hundreds of stables, five restaurants and an infield with a pond upon which floats an Indian canoe, painted the colors of the owner of the last Travers winner. Breakfast at the track – watching the morning workouts and mixing with the trainers – is a tradition. Folks eventually move into the sprawling grandstand, rife with red and white striped awnings, gilded cupolas and thousands of geraniums and petunias, to bet an average of $3.5 million a day. Races, daily except Tuesday at 1. Admission, $2 to grandstand, $5 to clubhouse.

Open from February-November is the **Saratoga Raceway,** near Crescent and Nelson avenues, the standardbred harness track that opened in 1940. Races are staged Tuesday-Sunday in July and August. Revived in 1978 after a 40-year lapse, the **Saratoga Polo Association** at the Whitney Polo Field, Bloomfield and Denton roads, schedules games in August every Tuesday, Friday and Sunday at 6.

National Museum of Racing and Hall of Fame, Union Avenue and Ludlow Street, 584-0400. Enter not through a turnstile but a set of starting gates next to a life-size fiberglass horse and jockey frozen at the moment of a race's start. The sounds of horses loading, jockeys yelling and stalls flying open propel you into an arena that does for horse racing what Cooperstown's Hall of Fame does for baseball. This museum, founded in 1955, was renovated in 1988 to the tune of $6 million. It relates the past, present and future of thoroughbred racing through the latest in you-are-there museum gadgetry. An impressive, fifteen-minute film called "Race America," a montage of racing from coast to coast, is shown in the Hall of Fame auditorium. Famous jockeys and trainers explain their techniques through videos in a simulated racetrack area. Open daily in August, 9 to 5; rest of year, 10 to 4:30. Adults, $3.

The Canfield Casino, Congress Park, 584-6920. John Morrissey, the U.S. Congressman who was principal sponsor of the thoroughbred racetrack, opened the gambling casino in 1870 in what is now a downtown park separating Broadway from Union Avenue, the main corridor to the racetrack. In the casino-turned-Canfield Museum, the Historical Society of Saratoga Springs traces the town's growth from a frontier village into a flamboyant international resort in two museums and an art gallery on the upper floors. Open May-September, Monday-Saturday 10 to 6 and Sunday 1 to 4; daily to 4, October to late December. Adults, $2.

Saratoga Performing Arts Center, Saratoga Spa State Park, 587-3330. An amphitheater at the edge of the state park has seats for 5,100, and up to 25,000 more crowd the lawns for performances here. The New York City Opera is in residence in June, July brings the New York City Ballet and August the Philadelphia Orchestra. The

Newport Jazz Festival-Saratoga and the Saratoga Chamber Music Festival also take place here. Special-event superstars range from Bonnie Raitt to James Taylor, Linda Ronstadt to Steve Winwood. Prices vary, generally from $6 to $13 on the lawn and $20 to $40 for reserved seats.

National Museum of Dance, 99 South Broadway, 584-2225. The nation's only museum devoted exclusively to professional dance occupies the former Washington Baths, now beautifully restored through the beneficence of the Cornelius Vanderbilt Whitneys. Since its opening in 1986, three exhibitions relating to the history of dance have been mounted each year. The focal point is the Mr. and Mrs. C.V. Whitney Hall of Fame, honoring the principals of American dance. Open May 29 to Labor Day, Tuesday-Sunday 10 to 5. Adults, $3.

Saratoga Spa State Park, off Route 9 South, 584-2535. Perhaps the grandest park of its kind, this is a 2,000-acre island of serenity at the edge of the Saratoga hubbub. Enter through the soaring Avenue of the Pines past one of two golf courses. All the Georgian Revival brick pavilions, arched promenades, domed ceilings and marble arcades are flanked by pools, fountains and deep, pine-shaded lawns. Of special interest are the Hall of Springs, the Spa Little Theater, the classical Victoria Pool and the larger, Olympic-size Peerless Pool. Besides swimming, there are places for walking, running, cross-country skiing and ice-skating. The park was created to protect the springs, which at the turn of the century were in danger of being commercialized into oblivion. Most of the construction took place in the mid-1930s as a WPA project. "The park is unique in the state and maybe the world," said the assistant manager. "You couldn't build this today." Open daily, 8 a.m. to dusk. Parking $3, Memorial Day to Labor Day.

The Springs. Long before racing took hold here, Saratoga was renowned for its carbonated mineral springs. What made Saratoga different from other watering spas, however, was the racing and the high-rollers it attracted. The fizzy waters, often smelling like eggs gone bad, can be sampled at more than 50 springs around town. A pavilion recently was built around the original Congress Spring in Congress Park, the downtown layout designed by Frederick Law Olmsted. Nearby are the domed Columbian Spring pavilion and the Hathorn Spring on Spring Street. North of downtown near Excelsior and High Rock avenues are the High Rock Spring and Red Spring, named for the color of its water. The heaviest concentration is in Saratoga Spa State Park. You can drink the waters, if you like, or soak in them (see below).

Mineral Baths. Opened in 1935, the **Roosevelt Baths** in Saratoga Spa State Park offer mineral water baths and massages year-round. (They are being renovated and upgraded by the concessionaire that runs the Gideon Putnam Hotel, but the baths and the facility still looked fairly primitive – the purists say authentic – at our visit.) You pay $14 for a mineral bath, taken in small private rooms in the men's or women's wings. Each is equipped with a tall bathtub and a cot with a sheet on top. Bubbly, brown water from the springs is heated and pumped into the tubs; you soak for twenty minutes, then wrap yourself in the sheet on the bed and nap for half an hour. For $26 more, you can add a 45-minute massage by appointment (584-2011). Open in July and August are the **Lincoln Baths,** recently redone by the state and offering semi-private baths. For more upscale surroundings (Italian marble and crystal chandeliers), head for the privately owned **Crystal Spa** at 92 South Broadway, fed by the Rosemary Spring outside the Grand Union Motel. Opened in 1988, this modern facility offers fifteen private rooms in separate men's and women's sections for mineral baths, massages by appointment, saunas, manicures, facials and such.

Saratoga Springs Urban Cultural Park, 297 Broadway, 587-3241. The visitor center in the Beaux Arts-style Drink Hall provides information and displays on the city and its six National Register historic districts. There are self-guided walking tours. Guided walking tours are offered daily in summer.

Yaddo, Union Avenue, 584-0746. A private estate turned into a working arts community, the 55-room mansion just east of the flat track has played host since 1926 to 200 artists, writers and composers each year in an environment free of distractions. Some get their inspiration from the atmospheric rose and sculpture gardens, which are open to the public and well worth seeing. Modeled after formal turn-of-the-century Italian gardens, they have a colonnaded, rose-covered pergola as the dominant feature. On the terrace below are four oblong beds of red and white roses joined by a central Florentine fountain. Tucked among pine trees above the pergola is a rock garden of Japanese design. Grounds open daily, 8 a.m. to dusk. Free.

There's more, folks. Outside town is the **Saratoga National Historical Park,** site of the Battle of Saratoga, a turning point in the American Revolution. But that's another day's outing.

Shopping. Most of the good stores in this real, working downtown are stretched along wide, tree-lined Broadway and side streets, Phila and Caroline. The top floor of the City Hall has been converted into a music hall for downtown concerts and the Saratoga Film Festival. In 1994, a series of community forums shaped a vision for downtown Saratoga and things will start happening soon, several merchants advised.

You won't find one of the ubiquitous Benetton or Gap stores here; about the only "chain" store is a branch of the **House of Walsh,** the classic clothing store based in Williamstown, Mass. Nearby on lower Broadway is **Symmetry,** where we ogled some of the most beautiful works in glass we have seen. It's really more like a glass art gallery. The **Santa Fe Trading Post** is chock full of Southwestern goodies, such as jewelry and luminous pottery. We liked the white coffee mug with the red chile pepper for a handle. **Nostalgia** is a good place to pick up a gift, perhaps a scented candle, a wreath, a picture frame or a mohair throw. **Designers Studio** shows fine contemporary American crafts. At **Brushstrokes,** artist Barbara Bishop has handpainted her colorful designs on everything from sweatshirts to lamp shades to umbrellas. The best hats for the track, many made on premises, are available amidst the "vintage ladies' finery" **at Saratoga Trunk.** Gifts for the horse lover are featured at **Impressions;** many convey an animal or a Saratoga theme. **Antiques 400** is considered one of the better antiques and Victorian accessories stores. **Bookworks** ranks among our favorite independent bookstores, and the **Lyrical Ballad Bookstore** qualifies as one of the better antiquarian booksellers. Stop for a coffee, latte or pastry at **Madelines Espresso Bar** or **Uncommon Grounds,** both classics of their genre.

Extra Special

Caffé Lena, 47 Phila St., Saratoga Springs. (518) 583-0022. The oldest continuously operated coffeehouse in the country, this was run from 1960 until her death in 1989 by Lena Spencer, called "the Mother Teresa of folk music." Her friends and patrons have banded together to continue the tradition since. "It's been a struggle, but we've endured," said one of the promoters for the 35th anniversary year. "It's time to celebrate – 30 years under the loving hand of Lena Spencer and four years on our new feet." Her legacy remains in the small upstairs room full of atmosphere as patrons enjoy the music along with good coffees, teas and homemade pastries (no smoking and no alcohol). Many is the name folksinger and cabaret singer who has entertained at Lena's. Bob Dylan and Don McLean first found an audience here; Arlo Guthrie sang here long before the rest of the world heard his music. The tradition, as they say, continues. Open Thursday-Sunday from 6 or 7.

Westport/Essex, N.Y.

Where the Adirondacks Meet Lake Champlain

Is there a less likely place than a corner of the nation's second most populous state to find quaint 19th-century villages relatively unscathed by time? This is the region where the Lake Georges, the Lake Placids and the Old Forges have been sullied by wanton commercialism on the edges of the East's largest forever-wild area. So it is an agreeable surprise to leave the Adirondack Northway and head east through unspoiled countryside to the area where the Adirondack Mountains meet Lake Champlain.

Here is Westport, a hillside village where a library, rather than a town hall or a church, dominates the village center and the green is called the Library Lawn. A tradition of local beneficence began with the gift of both library and lawn in the early 1800s. It continued in 1991, when the land across the street was given for a village park leading down to the Northwest Bay of Lake Champlain and a sandy swimming beach open to one and all.

Here is Essex, an old-fashioned place containing one of the most intact ensembles of pre-Civil War village architecture in America. The entire village is on the National Register of Historic Places and persists as a living history museum. One cannot help but be impressed by the beauty of its lakeside setting as well as by its architecture.

Something of a B&B and retailing boom is under way in the mid-1990s, especially in Essex. "Several of us decided independently that Essex needed a good B&B," said new innkeeper Susan Callahan. "We started a B&B association and now there are nine of us." The night's vacancies are posted on a blackboard in front of the reopened Essex General Store with the notation, "Thank you for staying with us."

Both Westport and Essex occupy particularly scenic sites beside Lake Champlain. Looming behind are the Adirondack High Peaks. Across the lake are the Green Mountains of Vermont.

History gave this section of Lake Champlain pivotal roles in the American Revolution and the War of 1812. The lake became the primary route for travel and commerce between Canada and the growing American republic. By 1850, Westport and Essex were among the largest and busiest communities on the lake, each with populations of 2,300. The coming of the railroad brought summer visitors, who filled the area's hotels and inns to overflowing. "Social Notes from The Westport Inn" was a feature in the New York Times and the Boston newspapers. Prestigious Camp Dudley prospered here as America's oldest summer camp for boys.

The reduction of train service and the rise of the interstate highways freeze-dried the

area's development in the 1950s. One finds here not mere vestiges but rather the essence of the look and the lifestyle of half a century or a century ago.

Contrary to trends elsewhere, most of Westport's old inns have been converted into private residences of distinction. The railroad depot is now an equity summer theater. The yacht club is a public restaurant. The country club is open to the public. Boats are launched from public launching sites and busy marinas. The Lake Champlain ferry arrives in Essex

Greek Revival facade masks contemporary interior of Blockhouse Farm Bed & Breakfast.

every half hour in summer from Charlotte, Vt. Tourists find excellent brochures for walking tours of Westport and Essex and their historic sites.

What these villages don't have is traffic lights, chain stores or fast-food outlets. Such things weren't needed in days of yore, nor are they needed here today. Westport and Essex offer other virtues. They are two of the more appealing lakefront towns we know of, far from the hordes yet with touches of sophistication interspersed amid the charms of yesteryear.

Inn Spots

Blockhouse Farm Bed & Breakfast, Route 22, Box 353, Essex 12936. (518) 963-8648.

Little wonder that this new B&B was the subject of a photo case study in a 1991 edition of Remodeling magazine. Susan Callahan acquired the 1836 house at auction and did a total rehab. Named for a blockhouse near the property, it retains its stunning 1836 Greek Revival facade, a beauty in yellow with green and white trim and four white columns in front.

Inside all is strikingly contemporary. There's an open living room/dining room/kitchen that Susan calls her Great Room. Tall rear windows frame beautiful lake and mountain views beneath the arched ceiling. The room opens onto a great rear deck looking across the gardens and down the hillside to Lake Champlain. Here is where guests enjoy wine and cheese in the afternoons.

A collection of decoys lines the staircase to the second floor. Jugs of Poland Spring water await guests in the bedrooms. The spacious Lake Room holds a queensize bed, a loveseat and a full bath. The two-level Princess Room in front offers a queensize bed and a bathroom with shower. A third guest bedroom will open when Susan and her husband, Ron Allbee, convert space in an adjacent barn into their quarters.

Susan, who used to own our favorite Cheese Outlet in Burlington, Vt., serves a continental breakfast during the week and a full breakfast on weekends. She features all natural foods and fresh fruit from the gardens. A choice of eggs, waffles or pancakes is offered.

421

The lakefront property includes heirloom vegetable and flower gardens reflecting its status as a commercial flower farm.

Doubles, $95.

Champlain Vistas, 183 Lake Shore Road (Route 22), Willsboro 12996. (518) 963-8029.

You want vistas? From this new hilltop B&B two miles north of Essex, Lake Champlain and Vermont's Green Mountains are the front yard, so to speak, and the High Peaks of the Adirondacks are the back yard. The views were what prompted Barbara Moses to move here upon her retirement as business manager of the computer center at Rensselaer Polytechnic Institute in Troy.

She had sailed on Lake Champlain for years, so was quite keen to buy part of the historic Owens Farm on the western shore, renovate its mid-18th-century farmhouse (listed on the National Register of Historic Places) and make it her year-round home and B&B. She offers four guest rooms, two with private baths and the others sharing. The rooms are named for their views. The main-floor Champlain room has a queen bed and a private bath, as does the Green Mountain Room with its original wallpaper of yellow jonquils on the second floor. Closets hold bathrobes for the occupants of the Mount Mansfield and Adirondack rooms.

A striking mahogany table made by Barbara's father-in-law graces the formal dining room. A delightful sun porch adjoins. Guests also enjoy the square, beamed living room that is both stylish and homey. Quite spacious, it has a spinning wheel in one corner and a fireplace made from fieldstones gathered on the 300-acre property.

Barbara serves a full country breakfast of fruit, juice, cereals, homemade muffins and a main course of perhaps bacon and eggs, french toast or waffles. In the evening, guests sit on the side lawn and watch the moon shimmering across the waters of Lake Champlain.

Doubles, $60 to $80. No smoking. No credit cards.

The Stonehouse, Church and Elm Streets, Essex 12936. (518) 963-7713.

This restored 1926 Georgian stone house looks as if it's been transplanted from the British countryside. Which is why it attracted Sylvia Hobbs, who lives in England and spends the summer and holidays here.

She shares her gracious home full of antique furnishings with overnight guests in four bedrooms, all with queensize beds and two with private baths. We liked the looks of the master bedroom with its coffered ceiling. Others prefer to escape to the attic hideaway with a queen and an extra single bed and a bath with clawfoot tub.

On the main floor are a large and elegant living room, a formal dining room and a small room for TV, "which we don't encourage," advises Sylvia. Wine is offered at the end of the day on the candlelit porch, and sherry is poured on chilly evenings in front of the fireplace.

Breakfast is a treat at individual tables on the sunny garden terrace. Sylvia calls it "superior continental," which translates to a fresh fruit platter, juices, cereals, homemade breads and muffins, and bagels obtained from a specialty shop in Montreal.

Doubles, $65 to $95. Open May-October and some holidays. No credit cards.

All Tucked Inn, 53 South Main St., Box 324, Westport 12993. (518) 962-4400.

The new name was "the first thing that dawned on me," Tom Haley said of his 1993 purchase of the former Gables adjunct to the nearby Inn on the Library Lawn. He entered it in a national contest and, lo and behold, the name won fourth place.

The cutesy name perhaps does not do justice to this rather stylish, full-service inn

Side lawn is the place for relaxing and taking in views at Champlain Vistas.

with a guest dining room and nine bedrooms, all with private baths. Or perhaps it does. Energetic Tom, a former lobbyist for the state Civil Service Employees Association in Albany, shelters guests in rooms with sitting areas and coordinated sheets and bed covers and plies them with caloric afternoon refreshments, home-cooked dinners and ample breakfasts. "Dining here is not a low-cholesterol event," he says.

He'll prepare anything from a chicken and ribs back-yard cookout ($8) to a candle-light dinner with soup, salad and steak or chicken piccata ($15). He might make peasant soup (sausage with white beans and leftover veggies) or clam chowder ("which people tell me is the best they've ever had"). Dessert is likely to be an ice-cream sundae. "Sweets are my weakness," he explains, "and I make what I like." Dinner is optional and BYOB, served by reservation around 7.

Breakfast is not optional. Tom prepares fruit, homemade raspberry or apple muffins, sausage and bacon, and offers a choice of three main courses: eggs, pancakes or french toast.

Bedrooms are scattered about the summery, country-style house and reached by different stairways. Most have queen or king beds and sitting areas with wing chairs, and three have fireplaces. A main-floor suite comes with a private porch. They're cheerfully decorated down to their coordinated sheets and quilts. Horse prints and memorabilia reflect the owners' love for the Saratoga racing season.

Tom runs the inn on weekdays while his wife, Claudia Ryan, a lawyer, is in Albany. Claudia sheds her lawyer's mantle on weekends and becomes a waitress, serving Tom's meals to receptive guests.

Doubles, $65 to $95.

The Inn on the Library Lawn, 1 Washington St., Westport 12993. (518) 962-8666.

This is the largest inn in a village that once had many, including the storied Westport

Three architectural styles are combined in The Victorian Lady.

Inn across the street. The Westport was torn down in 1966, and its abandoned site was given to the village in 1991 as a public park with a new swimming beach beside the lake. The site of the old inn's foundation has been a public ice-skating rink for years.

Actually, this inn occupies what used to be annexes of the Westport Inn. The inn, whose entry is on the side across from the Library Lawn, wears its age well. New owners Ron and Liz Van Nostrand from northern Maine took over in 1994 and keep the place impeccably. All ten air-conditioned rooms have private baths and seven have television. Decor is simple but fresh. Rooms have high ceilings, European wallpapers, traditional furnishings and braided rugs, and five yield views of the lake. Some rooms have TV sets. Rates vary according to size, type of bed (twins, double and queen) and view.

Guests share an old-fashioned common sitting area full of books and magazines in the upstairs hall. The ground floor contains a fireplaced lounge area where complimentary beverages are served. This opens into an antiques shop and a gallery of local artists in space formerly occupied by the inn's restaurant.

It also serves as the setting for some mighty interesting breakfast fare, served with blended premium coffee that the owners advertise as "among the finest in the world." Expect fresh orange juice, a fruit cup, and a choice of a no-cholesterol eggs soufflé, french toast or pancakes. Liz is known for her exotic baked goods, among them Norwegian kringles, rugalach, croissants, sticky buns and cinnamon rolls. The Van Nostrands were also considering options for the restaurant, which had been a local institution. At our visit, Liz was talking of opening a pancake house because her pancakes are so popular.

Doubles, $69 to $95. Closed November-April.

The Victorian Lady, 57 South Main St., Box 88, Westport 12993. (518) 962-2345. Colorful in shades of pale yellow with light blue and brick red trim, this charmer dating to 1856 combines three architectural styles. The original 1856 home is Greek Revival, the front facade with mansard roof and three-story tower is Second Empire, and the full veranda added in the 1880s is of the Eastlake style. Wayne and Doris Deswert, who winter in Florida, took over the former Doll House B&B and spent a year refurbishing before reopening in 1994.

The main floor contains a high Victorian parlor furnished with antiques, plus an informal living room with TV and modern wicker. The parlor is notable for its English embossed wall coverings. Rich paneling and woodwork are evident throughout.

Upstairs are three bedrooms with private baths, plus a bunk room good for children. A front room offers a queensize brass bed and a day bed, while a second room opens onto a wicker-furnished porch. Grammy's Room in the back comes with a canopied double bed, a few dolls and stuffed animals. It has an old dresser converted into a lavatory sink and a long closet for a bathroom, which may be shared with occupants of the bunk beds in the adjacent Garden Room.

Continental breakfast is served upon request in an upstairs sitting room. Most guests wait for the four-course breakfast served by candlelight in the formal dining room, however. Fresh fruit, orange juice and homemade muffins precede the main event, perhaps quiche or blueberry waffles.

Tea is served in the afternoon. It's often taken on the 1,200-square-foot front veranda that catches a glimpse through the trees of Lake Champlain. The veranda contains a swing and a hammock, just like at Grandma's house – to which many guests liken The Victorian Lady.

Doubles, $75 to $85. Closed mid-October to Memorial Day. No credit cards. No smoking.

The Gray Goose, 42 North Main St., Box N, Westport 12993. (518) 962-4562.

Shades of gray and geese are the decorative themes for this little Victorian B&B and gift shop lovingly run by Elizabeth Kroeplin, a New Jersey transplant who had spent summers here. She offers three guest rooms with private baths, one with a double bed and the others with twins. Two on the first floor on either side of the shop open onto a front porch, with a view of Lake Champlain beyond buildings across the road. Each has its own private entrance and is decorated with period furniture, white frilly curtains and gray, geese-covered bedspreads that match the shower curtains. A third bedroom on the second floor has antique maple beds, a wicker loveseat and a clothing hook in the form of a wooden goose. The atmosphere is simple and homey.

Guests may use Elizabeth's skylit sun room, cozy with a wood-burning stove, as well as the front porch. She offers an optional continental breakfast for $3, including juice and homemade muffins, served at a table set with cloth placemats in her shop or on the front porch.

The shop is a family affair. She and her sister and an aunt make most of the handicrafts for sale. Grapevine wreaths are Elizabeth's specialty.

Doubles, $62 to $68. Closed mid-November to mid-May.

The Westport Hotel, Pleasant Street (Route 9N), Westport 12993. (518) 962-4501.

This dates to 1876 when the railroad opened a new era for Westport and the hotel was built across the tracks from the new depot. It has operated under eight names since and is well known as a restaurant (see Dining Spots).

The last part of its billing as "a small, friendly, family-operated country inn" is a bit misleading. For it is squashed in a commercial area between the railroad tracks and the Ideal Garage, across from the Essex County Fairgrounds. Evergreen trees all around screen the outside distractions and give a semblance of privacy.

Upstairs off a long central corridor are ten guest rooms, clean but spartan. Six have private baths. Two are tiny singles with hallway baths. A couple have twin or queen beds. One, suitable for four, contains a double bed and bunk beds. Rita Warren, inn-keeper with her chef-husband Ralph, has prettied up the rooms with colorful stencil-ing, botanical prints, thick pastel towels and touches like dried-flower wreaths and a crib full of dolls.

A full breakfast is complimentary for guests in the winter. Rates in summer do not include breakfast, which is available in the restaurant. Although there are no common parlors, there are places to sit in the lounge, on the front terrace or in the side yard.

Doubles, $45 to $70.

The Essex Inn, Main Street, Box 324, Essex 12936. (518) 963-8821.

Its pillars and verandas on the first and second floors running the length of the house, this 1810 Federal structure with a Greek Revival colonnade lends quite a pres-ence to Essex's little main street.

The inside is a presence as well. All is arty and ever-so-eclectic, courtesy of owner David Millstone, who purchased the inn in 1989 after a short-lived fling with his Mill-stone Gallery and Restaurant in downtown Burlington. David is an artist of merit and some of his works hang in the downstairs restaurant and cocktail lounge (see Dining Spots) as well as in the three guest rooms and four suites. We found it all quite deco, although we stand corrected by David, who said there was nothing deco about it. "We have antiques and modern art," he stressed.

They appeal to a certain element, one that would not be surprised to find a huge stuffed alligator on a built-in bed or large carved wood figures by the back stairs. Huge paintings are everywhere in the Kerouac Suite, which has a clawfoot tub. The Ben-jamin Franklin Room contains a kingsize bed atop a platform with built-in drawers and a single bed, while a chaise lounge graces the Fitzgerald Room. David's Suite, also known as the e.e. cummings, has beds for six and a kitchenette, harkening back to the days when this was an apartment building.

Breakfast on the veranda is complimentary for overnight guests. Although some find it pricey, "I serve a helluva breakfast for $7.95," David insists. He likens it to brunch, and offers it seven days a week.

In winter, this versatile innkeeper operates a shop called Pizazz, featuring fine art, wines and fashions, in North Palm Beach, Fla.

Doubles, $79 to $89; suites, $89 to $149.

Canopied deck of Westport Yacht Club appeals for dining beside Lake Champlain.

Baskets shading lamps hang from ceiling of porch at Westport Hotel.

Dining Spots

Westport Yacht Club, Old Arsenal Road, Westport. (518) 962-8777.

Long a focus of Westport social life with its dances and regattas, the old yacht club was sold in the 1940s as Westport experienced a decline in tourism, and was converted into a private home. After a fire in 1982, the place was rebuilt as a public restaurant.

We know of no better lakefront location for a restaurant than this, perched like a yacht club along the shores of Northwest Bay, with a panoramic water view up and down the lake. A front cocktail platform, a side deck, a lovely canopied porch and a serene inner dining room take full advantage.

That the decor is so sophisticated and the food so inventive is a bonus. The airy interior is full of curvy lines resembling waves. Blonde windsor arm chairs are at white-linened tables, and striking watercolors are on the walls.

The canopied outdoor porch is perfect for a leisurely summer lunch beside the lake. The pâté, fruit and cheese platter ($7.95) was pretty as a picture, with garnishes ranging from radicchio to fresh dill. A big basket of French bread accompanied. We also liked the salade niçoise ($5.95), the albacore tuna set off with sliced red potatoes and green beans. Grilled chicken salad with walnuts and apples, shrimp louis, spinach ravioli, broiled salmon and burgers were other choices, priced from $5.95 to $9.95.

The kitchen also shows its stuff at dinner, when prices range from $9.95 for char-broiled chicken breast to $19.95 for steak au poivre or seafood fettuccine. Chicken oscar, salmon béarnaise, grilled swordfish with raspberry salsa, veal scaloppine with grand marnier and wild mushroom sauce, and noisettes of lamb roasted in a dijon mustard and herb crust are possibilities. You might start with gazpacho, escargots bourguignonne or smoked trout with raspberry-horseradish mousseline. Finish with desserts like banana-chocolate chip cake, raspberry pie and hazelnut torte.

The wine list is sophisticated. Used bottles hold candles for patio dining at night.

Lunch daily in summer, 11:30 to 2:30; dinner, 5 to 9:30 or 10; closed Sunday and Monday in June and September. Closed October to May.

The Westport Hotel, Pleasant Street, Westport. (518) 962-4501.

If its unprepossessing exterior in a commercial area prompts you to pass on, don't. Hidden behind the evergreens is an elongated restaurant of great appeal, particularly the rear porch screened by trellises and evergreens and looking like something you might find in California – or in an old Adirondack lodge. Hanging bushel baskets contain the lamps. Brightly painted wooden tulips are on the tables and shelves, and there's quite an assortment of mismatched chairs. All the wooden posts and beams and greenery provide lots of atmosphere. There's additional outdoor dining on the front and side porches. The interior dining rooms are more traditional, with white-clothed tables, beamed ceilings and walls enhanced with paintings by local artists. A pot of impatiens decorates each table, inside and out. A huge picture of a dog team and sled dominates the bar.

Chef-owner Ralph Warren used to own the College Inn Restaurant and Lounge in South Hadley, Mass. Here he's gone more upscale with a fairly extensive, changing dinner menu. Entrees run from the $10.50 range for peanut-ginger chicken and vegetarian dishes to $16.25 for oven-roasted New Zealand rack of lamb with honey, garlic and thyme. Choices include Jamaican shrimp spiked with Myers's rum, baked halibut with lemon-dill butter, bouillabaisse, seafood au gratin, veal sautéed with applejack brandy and Montreal peppered sirloin steak. Bacon-wrapped scallops and baked blue cheese mushrooms are among the appetizers. The house wines are some of our favorites from Corbett Canyon.

The lunch menu is considerably shorter. Five sandwiches on toast or pita bread, including seafood salad, are $3.25. Luncheon plates include turkey club and open sirloin ($4.75 to $5.50). There are pizzas and salads for those who prefer.

Breakfast daily, 8 to 2; lunch, 11:30 to 2; dinner, 5 to 9.

The Galley, Westport Marina, Foot of Washington Street, Westport. (518) 962-4899.

What owners Dee and Bob Carroll call Lake Champlain's most active marina includes a busy restaurant operation in the old sea plane hangar, whose arched roof gives it something of a boathouse feeling. It's a cavernous place, made more cozy with such personal touches as a gallery of Westport waterfront scenes along one wall, newspapers and games in the restored desk from the old freight office on the dock, and a free paperback book exchange in the pigeon-hole pass-throughs once used for selling tickets to steamboat passengers.

The Carrolls preserved as much as they could when they converted the old hangar into a restaurant in 1988. They keep the place jumping with activities like weekly lakeside barbecues with visiting entertainers on summer Saturday nights. A choice of london broil or cold poached salmon, shell pasta with mushrooms and sour cream, caesar salad and key lime pie were on the docket with guitarist Joan Crane at our visit; the price, a bargain $14.90 for adults and $9.50 for children.

The all-day menu also is affordably priced. Specialties include tortilla salad ($4.25), charbroiled steak sandwich on a sesame-seed roll ($5.50) and teriyaki sirloin sticks from an old family recipe ($5.50). Among dinner platters are poached salmon, a kabob of grilled scallops and chicken marinated in pineapple and ginger, $9.35 to $12.95.

All this is taken on redwood picnic tables inside or outside under umbrellas beside the boats.

Part of the marina includes the excellent **Ship's Store,** where you'll find everything for boats and cottages and those who reside in them.

Breakfast daily, 8 to 11, Sunday to noon; lunch and dinner, 11 to 8 or 9. Open mid-June through Labor Day.

Diners enjoy lunch on canopied deck beside water at Le Bistro du Lac.

Westport Country Club, Liberty Street, Westport. (518) 962-4470.

The clubhouse here is open daily to the public as a restaurant, and the food is said to vary yearly, according to the chef at the time. In 1994, we were advised, a new manager and chef had upgraded the dining operation, which was well received locally.

The lunchtime fare sticks to basic burgers and sandwiches in the $5 to $6 range. For dinner ($9.95 to $13.95), the chef shows his stuff with things like shrimp and crab alfredo, linguini pescatore, scampi, New York strip steak and steak au poivre. Starters could be stuffed jalapeño peppers, potato skins and nachos. Desserts might be chocolate nemesis cake and snickers pie.

Open daily in season, 8 a.m. to 11 p.m.

Le Bistro du Lac, Essex Shipyard, Essex. (518) 963-8111.

American, French and Canadian flags fly over the entrance to this jaunty bistro with tables inside and out at the Essex Shipyard. It's run by Bernard Perillat, co-owner of the popular Chez Henri at Sugarbush in Warren, Vt., who was wooed across the lake by the shipyard owner who has a ski house in Warren.

The bistro theme is carried out in a couple of dining rooms with tables covered with blue floral oilcloths and big brass oil lanterns, in a pine-paneled lounge with captain's chairs at tables and bar, and on a couple of levels of canopied outside decks with white molded tables and chairs overlooking the lake.

It continues on the bistro-ish menu, which is quite like the Sugarbush model and changes monthly. Dinner entrées run from $12.75 for changing preparations of chicken to $21.50 for rack of lamb with rosemary herb sauce. Duck with fruit or pepper sauce, salmon with beurre blanc and filet of beef au poivre are standards. They're supplemented by such nightly specials as blackened tuna with mustard sauce, grilled mahi-mahi with salsa, pork tenderloin charcuterie and ragout of sweetbreads and shiitake mushrooms. The classic onion soup gratinée, country pâté, escargots in puff pastry and endive salad are popular starters. Desserts run to mousses, ice cream and sorbet.

Parisian music was playing and the geraniums and begonias were in full bloom in window boxes around the deck as we lunched on the house pâté with a side salad ($4.75) and salade niçoise ($7.50), tasty but different with cauliflower substituting for the usual potatoes and bits of bacon, anchovy and warm tuna. A signature dessert – frozen sorbet cake ($5), layers of passion fruit, raspberry and black currant topped with kiwi and served on a raspberry coulis with lady fingers – was a fabulous ending.

Open daily from noon, dinner from 5:30. Closed mid-October to end of May.

Millstone's Gallery Restaurant at the Essex Inn, Main Street, Essex. (518) 963-8821.

The restaurant taking up the front veranda, a rear patio and several main-floor rooms is as funky as the rest of this establishment. It defies description; suffice to say that it's deco – and decorated – to the max.

The menu also defies description, partly because there is no menu as such and the servers are expected to recite from memory. As best we could determine, dinners are $18 prix-fixe for three courses (salad, sorbet and entrée) and $29 prix-fixe for five courses.

A typical menu, if there is such a thing here, might start with a choice of scallops with peach brandy sauce, fettuccine alfredo or shrimp dijon. Salad and sorbet clear the palate for the main course, perhaps fillet of bluefish in puff pastry, fillet of salmon, lobster crêpes, shrimp dijon, pork tenderloin or tournedos au poivre. Dessert could be fresh blueberries with cream, chocolate strawberries, or lemon bundt cake with peach brandy.

Pillars identify facade of The Essex Inn.

The menu changes nightly. Owner-innkeeper David Millstone, who ran a restaurant and gallery in downtown Burlington, claims an award as one of the top 100 restaurants in the world. He's the chef, cooking three meals daily whenever there are takers.

Brunch/lunch daily to 2:30; dinner nightly by reservation, 6 to 9:30. Shorter hours in off-season.

The Old Dockhouse, off Main Street, Essex. (518) 963-4232.

Ensconced beside the ferry terminal where passengers and cars debark from Charlotte, Vt., this is the last surviving dockhouse on Lake Champlain. It was built in 1815 as a warehouse for the sloop trade before the coming of canal boats.

The interior is a mélange of bare wood and oilcloth-covered tables in a room with fishing, hunting and nautical artifacts on the walls and sliding screen doors opening to the outside. On either side are two outdoor terraces, one with round tables and molded chairs beneath a canopy and the other with tiny tables under and beyond a gazebo.

The new owners present a light American/international menu that gives little hint of their other restaurant across the lake in Burlington, Coyotes Tex-Mex Cafe. Here they offer dinner entrées like shrimp genovese, shellfish alfredo, English fish and chips, New England lobster and shellfish pie, chicken oriental, cider-smoked duck breast and prime rib in the $8.95 to $16.95 range. Crab cakes, quiche and shellfish crêpes supplement the lunchtime fare of burgers, sandwiches and salads ($4.95 to $7.95).

Open daily, 11:30 to 10. Closed November to mid-May.

Diversions

Westport's prime location on one of Lake Champlain's largest bays has always offered a protected port for boats of all kinds. The old steamboat Ticonderoga – now on display across the lake at the Shelburne Museum – berthed here nightly early in the century. Visitors today have considerable access to the lake from the new Ballard Park, the public boat-launching site, the Westport Marina and the Westport Yacht Club.

Westport Walking Tour. An exceptional guide to the town was prepared in 1989 by the Westport Historical Society and the Westport Chamber of Commerce. A 36-page booklet with photos, descriptions and maps outlines the tour, which totals five miles and can be covered in two to three hours. The starting point is the landmark **Westport Library,** a restored beauty whose all-wood interior with cathedral ceiling resembles an Adirondack lodge. The library is as much the dominant force as it is the dominant structure in town. The Library Lawn is the setting for concerts each summer. You'll likely be struck by the number of buildings that at one time served as inns.

The Depot Theatre, Pleasant Street, Westport, 962-4449. Westport's newly refurbished Delaware & Hudson railroad station now serves as a town museum and as the summer home of the professional Depot Theatre (the Amtrak train also stops here daily in each direction on its run between New York and Montreal). Founded in 1979, the equity theater presents four shows a season, one of them sometimes a new American musical, in the old freight room. The summer of 1994 saw "Sleuth," "Tell Me on a Sunday," "Someone Who'll Watch over Me" and "Oklahoma!" There are also special mid-week shows and art shows in the depot. Shows generally run for two weeks over long weekends. Adults, $15.

Meadowmount School of Music, Lewis-Wadhams Road, Westport, 873-2063. Students ranging in age from 8 to 30 converge each summer on this summer school for accomplished young violinists, violists and cellists training for professional careers. You might hear a budding Itzhak Perlman or Yo-Yo Ma, both alumni, at free concerts given in the Memorial Concert Hall Wednesday and Sunday evenings at 7:30.

Essex Tour. This is one interesting village, from the sunburst of mustard and maroon splashed across the facade of the 1800 firehouse greeting visitors at the main intersection in town to the 1790 Wright's Inn now serving as a town office across the street. Twenty-eight village landmarks are detailed in "Essex: An Architectural Guide;" 24 more also are shown in the outlying town. The descriptions plus the accompanying maps make your travels more informed. The entire village is on the National Register and contains one of the more prized collections of Federal, Georgian Revival and Greek Revival architecture in the country.

Sunburst Tea Garden, South Main Street, Essex, 963-7482. The Sorley family serve English cream teas at tables beside a garden with a fountain on their back lawn overlooking the lake in summer, Wednesday-Sunday 2 to 5, weather permitting. Homemade scones with jam and fresh whipped cream, cakes and a variety of teas are featured. They also offer a modest room for overnight guests in their 1813 house.

Shopping. There's not a lot, but the situation is rapidly improving – particularly in Essex – and you will find a number of places in which to spend your shekels. In Westport, we liked **The Westport Trading Co.** at 2 Pleasant St., where Kip Trienens makes gorgeous stained-glass hangings and lamps. Pottery, baskets, twig furniture, windchimes and birdhouses abound here. **The Bessboro Shop** at 26 Main is a small department store with classic clothing and gifts. Paintings and crafts by local artists, collectibles and antiques dating to the early 17th century are shown **at Elizabeth V's Antique Shop & Gallery,** occupying part of the former restaurant space at the Inn on the Library Lawn. The **Ship's Store** at the Westport Marina is fun to wander through; from things for the cocktail hour to novelty hats to inflatable boats, there's a lot to look at. If you need a pick-me-up after shopping or walking tours, stop at **McQueen's Food & Fountain** in Westport, a restaurant and ice-cream parlor from yesteryear.

Essex, which had only a couple of stores of note as recently as 1992, now is experiencing a mini-burst in retailing. **The Store** on Main Street has changed from an old-fashioned emporium into an upscale center of eclectic folk art, featuring works of New York and Vermont artisans. Beside it is **Adirondack Spirit,** offering sophisticated country woodsy merchandise. Ed and Martha Hourihan reopened the **Essex General Store Co.** and stock food, gifts, crafts, Adirondack furniture, books and souvenirs. Potter Judy Koenig claims her **Sugar Hill Pottery** is the oldest business in town; we particularly liked her teapot with iris, garlic bakers and bowls, all hand-thrown and appealing in earth colors. Furniture, clocks, linens, china and collectibles are among the offerings at **Margaret Sayward Antiques & Untiques.** A gift shop was in the works for the **Cupola House.** The little wood cats with the sign "Better to feed one cat than many mice" intrigued at **Wade's Woods and Crafts.** Jim and Mary Wade also design wooden replicas of Essex's Main Street. The new **Bread & Butter Bakery** offers a view of the lake from the dining area as you partake of breads, muffins, sandwiches and salads. Beside the lake is **Polly's Garden & Gift Shop,** a special place where Polly McKenna and her teenagers display her handmade wreaths and dried-flower arrangements along with glycerine soaps, flavored Italian olive oils, Tuscan seasonings, clay pots and more. "I've been a frustrated decorator for years," she explains. Polly and husband Stephen also offer their version of bed and breakfast, **Cabins by the Lake,** 953-7374. Four small renovated 1930s-style cabins sleep two to four (rates $59 to $79), and morning coffee and muffins are served on the porch of the shop.

Extra-Special

Camp Dudley, Camp Dudley Road, Westport. (518) 962-4720.

The historic marker near the entrance designates this as the oldest boys' camp in continuous service in the United States (1885). It's extra-special to one of us, who was a happy camper here back in the late 1940s when half the fun was getting there on the

special Camp Dudley train from Albany, New York, Syracuse and points beyond. Today's campers fly in from Sri Lanka and St. Louis or drive in with their parents, who boost occupancy rates at local inns and B&Bs. To a venerable alum, the sprawling camp complex looks the same except for a new-fangled curving slide at Swim Point and an indoor gymnasium with two basketball courts and, sign of the times, a weight-lifting room. Still the same are all the eight-bunk fireplaced cabins spread along the lakeshore and the perimeter of the 250-acre campus, the cavernous Dining Hall, the nightly shows at Witherbee Hall, the activity at Avery Boathouse and enough sports facilities to handle a small army of 480 campers whose parents spend a small fortune for the month or two-month stay. Casual visitors may introduce themselves at the main office and ask for a look around.

Lakeside scene at Camp Dudley.

Cooperstown shows its patriotism and serenity in Lakefront Park.

Cooperstown, N.Y.
The All-American Village

Few places its size (population, 2,200) are so embedded in the American consciousness as the upstate New York village of Cooperstown.

Native son novelist James Fenimore Cooper gave it and Otsego Lake, his "Glimmerglass," a romantic place in the history of literature through his *Leatherstocking Tales*. Abner Doubleday supposedly invented the game of baseball here, and the Baseball Hall of Fame stands as the shrine to America's national pastime. The Farmers' Museum captures the spirit of New York State's rural life of the 19th century.

Although Cooper and Doubleday get most of the credit, the impetus for the Cooperstown we know today stemmed from latter-day native sons, the Clark family of Singer sewing machine fame. The house that Edward S. Clark built in 1932 on the Cooper property beside Otsego Lake is now the Fenimore House Museum, a showcase for the New York State Historical Association's masterful collections of folk and decorative art. Stephen C. Clark Sr. paid $5 for an early baseball that led to the formation in 1939 of the National Baseball Hall of Fame. He founded the Farmers' Museum in 1943, the third prong in his visionary effort to develop for Cooperstown a clean industry, tourism. Another prong has emerged with the evolution of the Glimmerglass Opera, thanks to more local benefactors, the Busches of beer fame. A fifth prong arrived in 1993 with the opening of the Corvette Americana Hall of Fame, one newcomer's astonishing tribute to cars and pop culture.

The four museums – celebrating baseball, art, rural life and pop Americana – reflect the essence of small-town America and inspire for Cooperstown the logical moniker, "The Village of Museums." But Cooperstown is no mere display-case relic. It's the living Norman Rockwell town where flower baskets hang from the downtown lamp posts, flags fly in front of homes large and small along its tree-shaded streets, there's only one traffic light and no outside chain store or motel has been allowed to sully its all-American purity.

"Time has stood still here and people fight tooth and nail to keep it that way," says Laura Zucotti, the ex-New York restaurateur who now operates the J.P. Sill House here as a B&B. And well they should. No tourist town with the credentials of Cooperstown remains so unspoiled by the trappings of tourism. It's a neat and tidy-looking community with an air of obvious prosperity. The Bassett Hospital, affiliated with Columbia University, is the village's biggest employer and a training site for doctors. The impressive new Alfred Corning Clark Gymnasium is a multi-purpose counterpoint to baseball's historic Doubleday Field. Main Street is dominated by the institutional presence of the Hall of Fame and the lakeshore by the stately Otesaga Hotel resort.

The Otesaga, a few old inns and small up-the-lake motels monopolized visitor accommodations until 1984, when the first B&Bs emerged. That year, four pages in the 36-page Cooperstown Area Guide were devoted to accommodations; a decade later, the guide had swelled to 72 pages, 27 of them for lodgings. Many of them were opened by metropolitan New Yorkers who found nirvana here away from the mainstream.

Cooperstown, enveloped in hills, is not really on the way to anywhere else and therefore access is difficult. That helps explain its singularity, but scarcely prepares unsuspecting visitors for what they find – a picturesque, tranquil lakeside village that's far more than a baseball shrine. Here is a Brigadoon dreamland suspended in time from a century ago.

With its physical beauty and ties to what is most honored in our history, Cooperstown is as close as you may get to the nearly perfect all-American place.

Inn Spots

Thistlebrook, County Road 28, RD1, Box 26, Cooperstown 13326. (607) 547-6093.

Except for a few Gothic-patterned windows, nothing about the facade of this big red barn prepares one for the treasures found inside. Paula and Jim Bugonian, corporate types from the Kingston area, crossed the mountains to visit her parents in Cooperstown, found the 1866 barn, bought it the same day and started creating one of the more dramatic, stylish and all-around comfortable B&Bs anywhere.

"We don't have children," says Paula, "so everything we've done – all the gifts we've given – have been for our home. And we love to share it."

The shared home is also a work in progress. The Bugonians opened with two guest

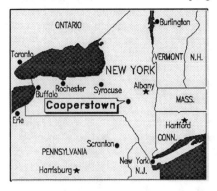

rooms, had four at our visit, and were about to embark on two more in the rear of the barn. In the process, they've thought about, and provided, just about everything a guest could want.

The interior spaces, formerly occupied by working artists who used them as galleries, soar to ceilings sixteen feet high in the living room. French doors and tall windows open onto an expansive new deck, overlooking a meadow, stream and hillside alluring to deer, ducks and red-winged blackbirds.

434

Potted plants surround pool in sunken sun room at Thistlebrook.

The living room, elegantly outfitted like the rest of the place in a mix of European and American furnishings and antiques, is big enough for a dining table at one end. But that's just for show, and the occasional card game. The main dining room holds an antique table big enough to seat twenty, an intricate Queen Anne bar cabinet from which port is dispensed in the evening, and a 200-year-old Chinese china cabinet that is Paula's pride and joy. The stairway landing harbors an array of books and upscale magazines to occupy guests "since we don't have TV," Paula notes. Take a batch to your room, the common areas or the sunken sun room with a small swimming pool – you'll find the perfect nook or cranny since, as the hostess says, "I love little groupings of seats where people can sit and read or chat."

Such groupings are evident in the spacious guest rooms, the first four of which all are sited on different levels for utmost privacy. Two in the rear are light and airy, with windows onto the meadow, white walls and floral prints. The least expensive is Paula's favorite. It comes with a double bed (the others are queen or king) set between French kidney-shaped night tables, a comfy chaise and wing chair, a little French armoire and a unique writing desk hidden inside a chest of drawers. Upstairs in the darker front of the house is the master suite, where a kingsize bed resides on a raised platform beneath a nicely angled, vaulted ceiling. It's flanked by plush chairs and faces a wall of books and a sitting area with sofa and an overstuffed chair and ottoman big enough for two. Gothic-style doors lead into a sight-to-behold bathroom with tub, separate shower, bidet and a long double vanity in front of mirrors implanted in a Gothic window frame. Downstairs in front is another bedroom with four-poster twin beds and a high-riser daybed. Two new bedrooms, again with private baths, another large common room and a new screened deck were in the works in 1995.

The Bugonians' brand of hospitality matches their luxurious accommodations. They put out coffee and fruit at 7:30 in the morning, prior to serving a full breakfast with fresh fruit cup, banana or corn bread and a main dish like french toast with ham and browned cinnamon apples, blueberry-orange pancakes with ham or lemon-dill

Opera performers Gwen and Fred Ermlich entertain at Creeekside Bed & Breakfast.

scrambled eggs with mini bagels or croissants. On Saturday evenings by reservation, they offer festive, prix-fixe dinners for $25 to $35, BYOB. Paula changes her menu and hours seasonally, but expect such treats as shrimp and dill canapés or antipasto baguettes, oriental cucumber or pasta salad, swordfish kabobs with grilled portobello mushrooms and wild rice, and a zesty orange-berry shortcake. Afternoon libations are offered on the decks or around the small pool in the sun room full of plants and wicker.

Doubles, $95 to $125. Closed November-April. No smoking.

Creekside Bed & Breakfast, Fork Shop Road, RD 1, Box 206, Cooperstown 13326. (607) 547-8203.

The hosts at this elegant B&B on the delightfully named Fork Shop Road beside the delightfully named Fly Creek are among the most interesting people around. Fred and Gwen Ermlich – he a former priest and she a onetime Playboy centerfold – helped found and still perform with Glimmerglass Opera. And their B&B digs are a bit theatrical in three rooms, two suites and a cottage, all with private baths, queen or kingsize beds and TV/HBO.

"This is my Saints and Sinners gallery," Gwen said as she led us up the stairs lined with photos from her shows and modeling career, including one as a centerfold (clothed) in the Japanese edition of Playboy magazine in 1970. We were to be ensconced in the Penthouse Suite, an open, third-floor hideaway complete with sitting room and dining area. That was more spacious for a rainy evening than the one we'd booked, the Bridal Chamber, a mostly white cocoon of lace and frills, plus a canopied queen brass bed, a skylight and a beautiful curved armoire. This room has since been enlarged into a suite with an 18-by-22-foot living room harboring a year-round Christmas bridal tree decorated in wedding memorabilia, a parquet floor, tapestries, bisque lamps and a grouping of leather chairs and sofa beneath a crystal chandelier – not to mention a Romeo and Juliet balcony or a Rapunzel tower with circular staircase. Less extravagant but functional is the three-room cottage out back, where there's lots of room to spread out on peach-colored sofas in the living room with wet bar beneath a dramatic twenty-arm brass chandelier. The bedroom has a canopied bed, and a spacious side deck overlooks lawn and creek. The new Garden Room comes with an antique kingsize bed and a fifteen-foot expanse of picture windows overlooking the garden.

The Ermlichs and their teen-aged sons share with guests the rest of their home, including an atrium entry and a wraparound deck off the beamed and paneled rear family room – an expansive space that's perfect for the opera parties the Ermlichs frequently host. "This house is so happy when it's filled with people," Gwen says.

The actress in her demands that she serve her husband's lavish breakfast on a dining-room table set with lace cloth, dainty china, elaborate silver, lit tapers in the candelabra and a showy centerpiece of dried flowers. Tiny white lights twinkle here and there to add to the charm, and she changes the place settings daily so that "the meal becomes as dramatic as an opera." At our visit, orange juice, fresh fruit cocktail and coffee cake preceded Fred's dilled scrambled eggs, bacon, baked apple slices and English muffins, on which we tried Gwen's three sensational liqueur-flavored butters (peach, raspberry and strawberry).

The energetic Ermlichs founded Glimmerglass Opera in 1975 with a director-friend as an outlet for local musical talents (not to mention Gwen's old La Boheme costumes). Fred is "the last singing treasurer" in operadom, and also is dean of the School of Continuing Education at the State University of New York in Oneonta. He served as first president of the Bed & Breakfast Association of New York State.

Doubles, $70 to $85; suites, $85 and $125; cottage, $99.

The Bassett House Inn, 32 Fair St., Cooperstown 13326. (607) 547-7001.

Built in 1816 as an inn, this was long occupied by the Bassett family for whom the local hospital is named and is directly across the street from the Hall of Fame. "With a history and location like this," says former Wall Street lawyer Steve Collins, "we couldn't miss." He and wife Peggy were living in Greenwich, Conn., when he decided to quit his job. "We could have just moved to our lake house and died," quipped

Large side lawn goes off flagstone terrace and brick piazza outside The Bassett House Inn.

Peggy. "But my parents and grandparents still go to the Otesaga and I had been coming here since I was a kid, so I said, why not go up to Cooperstown and buy one of those big beauties for a B&B? This was waiting for us and it was a perfect fit."

The Collinses fitted out the handsome Federal-brick house with their Greenwich houseful of antique furnishings, collections (from American clocks and game tables to miniature cannons and guns) and a dash of ingenuity. Everyone seems to want canopy beds, Peggy learned, so she found some netting in the Spiegel catalog and fashioned fancy mesh canopies for beds that lacked them. The second floor has five spacious bedrooms with private baths, all but one with queensize beds (it has two twins joined as a king). All have sitting areas, TVs and antiques, and a couple are appointed in high Victorian style. We think the nicest is the rear room with windows on three sides, light and airy in white, where versatile Peggy has painted trees on the walls and draped ivy over the lace curtains.

Continental breakfast is served stylishly in the Victorian dining room. Cut-up fruit comes in a crystal punch bowl and coffee and tea in silver pots. Cereals, danish pastries and donuts complete the repast, which may be taken on trays to the large dining table or out to the side brick piazza and flagstone terrace, facing a hedge-rimmed lawn, geraniums, a fountain and sturdy cedar lawn chairs that Peggy picked out from a Plow and Hearth catalog. Board games and a pool table occupy prominent positions in the living room.

The Collinses live on the third floor and do all the work themselves, from house cleaning to yard maintenance. They deliberately categorize themselves as an inn so as not to mislead about their breakfast.

Doubles, $109 to $125. No smoking.

The J.P. Sill House, 63 Chestnut St., Cooperstown 13326. (607) 547-2633.

The architectural magnificence of this yellow brick Italianate Victorian built in 1864 by Cooperstown bank president Jedediah P. Sill has landed it on both the state and national historic registers. Add its remarkably lavish handprinted Victorian wallcoverings, prized antiques and an aura of status cultivated by the innkeepers, former owners of New York's famed El Morocco restaurant. The accommodations are fit for royalty, though it's hard to imagine royalty sharing bathrooms, as do people in the four guest rooms here.

Angelo and Laura Zucotti literally stumbled upon Cooperstown shortly after they closed El Morocco in 1988 because of a decline in their carriage trade. "I'd always wanted a B&B," she said. "We found this house and thought, wouldn't it be nice to fix it up?" The sale was closed in three weeks and they started restorations designed to make the carriage trade take note.

The most striking aspects of the decor are the reproductions of Victorian wallpaper designs created by William Morris and others. The front parlor sports seven different papers on the walls and even the ceiling; the dining room has eight. The parlor is awash in oriental rugs, Victorian furnishings, bookcases reproduced by a preservationist and a replica of the house holding a TV inside. Decanters of port and cream sherry await guests in the parlor, and the Zucottis offer complimentary drinks from a full bar.

Japanese-Italianate paper adorns the dining room, where El Morocco's first menu from 56 years ago hangs framed near the kitchen door. Here is served a bountiful breakfast: perhaps strawberries and cream, fresh juice, homemade granola, orange-buttermilk pancakes and little homebaked danish pastries and cinnamon rolls. Laura, who studied at the Cordon Bleu, is known for her lemon and coconut breads. On Sundays she likes to serve a smoked salmon platter and cream cheese along with the

Ex-banker's Italianate Victorian home has been transformed into The J.P. Sill House.

New York Times. The repast is taken around the formal table, set with tapestry mats atop a lace cloth, or on the wicker-filled side porch off the dining room.

A front corner of the main floor is given over to a suite that's arguably the most extravagant in town. It's the only guest accommodation with a private bath. And what a bathroom – a huge space with a whirlpool tub and a vibrator for one's back, a wicker rocker and chair, floral wallpaper and windows onto the side lawn. The suite, decorated by Laura Ashley's son, is papered with eight different patterns to represent the Iris and the Dragonfly. A Laura Ashley duvet covers the ornate queensize brass bed angled in a corner and an armoire hides the TV-VCR and stereo system facing an armchair and two wicker chairs.

Upstairs are four more guest rooms, all with queensize beds and more showy wallpapers. One has a wicker sitting area. Another has a fireplace, a signed Eastlake armoire and a new powder room with Laura Ashley appointments. Otherwise the four rooms share two bathrooms, one containing the original pewter tub and a new shower and the other with shower only.

Constantly upgrading, Laura has acquired Frette bedspreads from Italy for summer, to stand in for the Laura Ashley quilts and comforters she favors in winter. She also furnishes new linen bathrobes for summer, Ashley robes for winter. All bathrooms are outfitted with hair dryers, shaving mirrors and a complete line of Perlière toiletries.

The Zucottis aren't through yet, however. On the third floor are three servant's rooms that they hope to convert into one long gaming room with a billiards table. At the side of the house is a carriage house with two apartments that they plan eventually to convert into deluxe suites.

Doubles, $100; suite, $150. No smoking.

Angelholm, 14 Elm St., Box 705, Cooperstown 13326. (607) 547-2483.
Painted mint green with dark green trim, this 1805 house on a residential street backs up to Doubleday Field, and guests can frequently hear – if not see – baseball games being played. Fred and Jan Reynolds retired here from Ridgefield, Conn., in 1992 after having stayed frequently with the original owners over five years. "This

was almost like moving into our own house," says Jan. They changed the decor from Victorian to Federal, built a small addition to expand the rear side veranda and two rear bedrooms, and added two private baths.

They now offer five bedrooms with private baths, good swivel reading lights over the beds, countless oriental rugs and runners, and collections of dolls here and there. Most in demand are three large corner rooms, two with queensize beds and one with antique twins. Two smaller center bedrooms have their own baths across the hall. The rear Doubleday Room with antique iron bed and a day bed comes with plush carpeting made out of recycled pop bottles. "We use only recycled stuff in this house," Jan points out.

The hosts share the main floor with guests. The fireplaced living room with fine oriental rugs opens into a snug little library with TV and another fireplace. The library opens onto the rear side veranda, where formal tea or iced tea and lemonade are served in the afternoons and the guests help themselves to Jan's "never-empty cookie jar."

Breakfasts are an occasion. A former caterer who knows and loves good food, Jan offers assorted juices, a fruit course like blueberries with lemon-yogurt sauce or peaches with honey-cinnamon glaze, braided coffee bread with pecans and cinnamon or fresh croissants, sausage or bacon and a main dish like blintzes filled with sour cream and topped with toasted coconut or country egg scramble incorporating red potatoes, leeks, and red and green peppers. Fred, the raconteur, holds forth in the dining room.

Doubles, $85 to $95. No smoking.

Strawberry Hill Farm, Greenough Road, RD3, Box 245, Cooperstown 13326. (607) 547-8619.

"Peace and quiet" are what Jocelyn Rauscher and her husband Andrew, a physician at Bassett Hospital, like most about their 120-acre farm. They offer two grand rooms with private baths and television, as well as abundant common space and gardens. With their children off to college, the Rauschers have plenty more room options, although Jocelyn says she quite likes her sitting room and her husband likes his, so further guest rooms in the rambling three-story Federal farmhouse with seven working fireplaces are in limbo.

Meantime, guests enjoy their own handsome rear living room with fireplace and a formal dining room and frequently spill into the enormous country kitchen, which

Surrounding countryside is on view from large side deck at Wild Turkey Farm.

Strawberry Hill Farm faces field of wildflowers and backs up to English gardens.

opens onto the hosts' family room. A front main-floor bedroom has a lace canopy queensize bed and a small bathroom with a European sink handpainted with flowers. Upstairs is a secluded bedroom with queen wicker bed, ivy stenciling and dark green carpeting, and Gilbert & Soames toiletries in the full bath. A connecting bedroom with twin beds is available for families.

The British-born Rauschers' floral interests are manifest in the delightful English gardens they have created in back. Water trickles in fountains, morning glories climb a trellis and a rope hammock beckons. If you don't become immobilized here, you can amble along the walking path they have blazed through the eight-acre field of wild-flowers across the road.

Jocelyn prepares a full breakfast with fresh fruit salad, cereal, a main dish like eggs benedict or blueberry pancakes with bacon or sausage, and homemade zucchini bread or muffins.

Doubles, $70 to $85. No smoking.

Wild Turkey Farm, West Hill Road, RD 1, Box 121B, Worcester 12197. (607) 397-1805.

Commanding its own hilltop with a panoramic view a dozen or so roundabout miles east of Cooperstown is this special, two-bedroom B&B. It's named for the rafter of wild turkeys that Rod and Beatrice Bird first encountered upon arriving in 1993 from Bergen County, N.J., at what was to become their retirement home. Make no mistake. Even with a small barn, this is not your traditional farm. It's a remote and posh hilltop aerie of sixteen acres with a modern, four-year-old house embracing all the creature comforts, a front veranda and a side deck that won't quit, and endless vistas of valleys and hills that "we from New Jersey call mountains," Rod says.

As one arrives at a clearing after negotiating a winding wooded driveway that you wouldn't want to tackle in winter, the view lengthwise through the front veranda al-most takes one's breath away. That's mere prelude to the side deck beyond, a 40-by-20-foot patch of paradise that the Birds added for their daughter's wedding reception and now lures guests back early from their day's rounds in Cooperstown. Wicker furniture and umbrellaed tables are perfect for relaxing and enjoying the vibrant perennial gardens and rose arbor in the foreground and verdant valley views beyond. The panoramic landscape is so undeveloped that you can distinguish only three farms.

Inside the house are a living room, a country kitchen open to a dining area that enjoys the fabulous view and a cozy rear sitting room with plump chairs. The view from this side of the house is such that the formal dining room in the rear had been used only once – for Thanksgiving dinner. Upstairs are two large, light and airy guest rooms with kingsize beds, each with private bath and an eclectic country look. Each room opens onto a small adjunct with extra beds that appeal to families. The Birds also have been known to relinquish their kingsize bedroom on the main floor for overflow.

Breakfast on the deck or adjacent dining area is apt to be scrambled eggs with chives and cream cheese, blueberry pancakes with a streusel-like topping or "hoppel poppel", described as a Virginia egg dish with vegetables. Guests may use the outdoor grill to barbecue their own dinner on the deck, a welcome consideration given the distance to the nearest restaurant.

Doubles, $75. No smoking.

Evergreen Bed & Breakfast, Route 33, RD 2, Box 74, Cooperstown 13326. (607) 547-2251.

Their five offspring having left the nest, Long Island transplants Emily and David Morris open to overnight guests the stately red brick Victorian house astride a hill just outside town. The four elegant but homey quarters range from a single to a two-bedroom suite. The rooms are seldom rented all at once to avoid shared-bath situations.

A Mother Goose doll and her offspring rest on the nifty window seat of a twin-bedded front corner room, lovely in lavender and rosy brick colored wallpaper (designed to coordinate with the remarkable exterior brickwork and repeat the theme inside). Beyond is a queen-bed room with a large bath that may be shared with the twin room. Another rear bedroom has pretty floral paper, a modern, with-it decor and a bed with beautiful monogrammed sheets.

Guests enjoy a delightful little front porch in which the moss-colored lattice vinyl chairs exactly match the Lynchburg green trim of the house. Inside is a comfy common room in green and purple, where a huge TV is ensconced in a hand-carved cabinet. French doors from a more formal fireplaced parlor lead onto a porch used on sunny mornings, outfitted in beige wicker with mauve accents. A backgammon table occupies a prime spot at the entrance "and my husband will challenge anybody who walks in the front door," says Emily.

The formal rear dining room from which deer can be seen is set with linens, goblets and silver for breakfast. Emily serves juice, fresh fruit with various sauces (one version is pears, bananas and cantaloupe topped with celery-seed dressing), cereals and homemade pastries, perhaps cinnamon twists, blueberry-ricotta coffee cake or crescent rolls stuffed with cream cheese – anything but the muffins endemic to B&Bs. A favorite is her variation on English trifle: warm custard with blueberries, peaches and yogurt, sprinkled with granola.

Doubles, $50 to $80; two-bedroom suite, $120 to $140.

Overlook Bed & Breakfast, 8 Pine Blvd., Cooperstown 13326. (607) 547-5178.

Another family home, this one along a stately boulevard near the heart of town, the Overlook has been taking guests since 1989 when six of Jack and Gayle Smith's seven children had left the nest. The main section of a manse that required five servants in its heyday dates to 1888.

A harmonium in the foyer and an extensive collection of music boxes hints at this

Murals adorn Toad Hall living room walls. **Toad Hall library is full of exotica.**

family's musical interests. A spacious, fireplaced living room has lots of seating and oriental rugs. A corner TV room contains a leather sofa and a wall of family pictures. Guests help themselves to an extended continental breakfast on the sideboard in the fireplaced dining room; they can eat there at a table for six or head outside to one of the commodious porches.

Upstairs are three light and spacious guest rooms and a suite, created when the Smiths vacated the master suite and "moved up to the servants' quarters – which was quite fitting," Gayle quips. That opened up a huge room with queensize poster bed, a sitting area with a beige leather sofa that converts to a bed in front of a console TV, a large bath and walk-in closet. A room in the front corner has a double four-poster bed; it shares a hall bath with a larger turret room, pretty in blue and pink with twin poster beds, a floral sofa and a wall of decorative plates from the musical "Annie." A rear room with a double poster bed enjoys a private bath and small sitting area.

Doubles, $65 to $75; suite $95.

Toad Hall, Route 28, RD 1, Box 120, Fly Creek 13337. (607) 547-5774 or 547-2144.

A dead tree carved into a totem pole with all kinds of critters marks the entrance to one of the more unusual B&Bs we've encountered. The tree was planted around 1820, when the house was built near the hamlet of Oaksville. Allen Ransome and Randy VanSyoc, owners of the fabulous Toad Hall store in Cooperstown, bought the house in 1988 and have turned it into a mini-folk-art museum that was the subject of a photo spread in Country Living magazine.

The living room walls are covered with murals in the style of Rufus Porter. In the book and art-filled library is a Thai temple guardian. A collection of Pennsylvania redware decorates the dining room, and even the kitchen is filled with folk art. On the 80 acres of property are walking trails and a trout pond; the men raise and show Newfoundland dogs.

Staying in one of the four upstairs guest rooms would be like staying in a museum, a rather eclectic one. Paintings from Allen's travels in India adorn the India Room, outfitted with a tiger maple queensize bed, a chaise lounge and a TV. Its hall bath is shared by a small single room. The walls and floors of the other two baths, both private, are made of slate. The Bovine Room with another queen bed has, you guessed it, cows painted on the dresser and on a twig chair, plus a collection of frogs. The Trinidad Room is named for a friend, Trinidad Gilmore, who painted its incredible wall mural of animals toting furniture to Toad Hall. The room has a queen poster bed, a French Victorian loveseat and an armchair.

At breakfast, taken on the long wooden table in the fireplaced dining room, a big espresso machine provides frothy cappuccino or caffe latte. Seasonal fresh fruit, juices, waffles, pancakes, french toast with homemade bread and New York maple syrup make up the fare. The hosts like to use local eggs, butter, milk, cheddar, ham and sausage.

On the pillared veranda out front, even the Adirondack chairs are the background for some wonderful art.

Doubles, $85. No smoking.

Cooper Inn, Main and Chestnut Streets, Box 311, Cooperstown 13326. (607) 547-2567.

On broad lawns in the center of town, this distinguished brick mansion dating to 1812 is owned by the famed Otesaga Hotel. It's quite inn-like, with a graceful double parlor and TV/game room off the entry foyer, and a cozy breakfast room in which donuts and danish are served at five tables in the morning.

The facility's ten rooms and five suites are all quite different, furnished in period hotel style with double or twin beds, desks, TV sets, telephones, walk-in closets and non-working fireplaces. The wing hidden behind dense trees contains five two-bedroom suites. Guests here have access to all the facilities of the Otesaga Hotel.

Doubles, $130; two-bedroom suites, $160 to $190.

The Inn at Cooperstown, 16 Chestnut St., Cooperstown 13326. (607) 547-5756.

Built in 1874 in Second Empire French style as the annex to the old Fenimore Hotel across the street, this is the baby of Michael Jerome, a Cornell Hotel School grad and thirtysomething preservationist from Elmira, who occupies an apartment on the property. He acquired the hotel in 1985 and quickly received a state historical preservation award for a restoration that is ongoing.

The seventeen rooms with private baths on two floors vary widely. One rear room with a queensize bed was barely big enough for a chair and a dresser. A front corner room with a kingsize bed and two armchair-rockers was a surprise, because all the rooms are billed as having twins or queensize beds. Frilly sheer curtains, plain decor and a minimum of furniture are the rule, although Michael points out that he is continually adding furnishings and most rooms now have a table and a couple of chairs.

The main floor offers two pleasant sitting rooms in a double parlor, where a television set and telephone are available. Complimentary coffee, juice and hot muffins are served in a couple of small breakfast rooms. Rocking chairs on the wide front veranda offer relaxation and a view of the passing scene.

Doubles, $85 to $95.

The Otesaga Hotel, 60 Lake St., Box 311, Cooperstown 13326. (607) 547-9931 or (800) 348-6222.

No mention of Cooperstown lodging facilities would be complete without a reference to one of New York's grand resort hotels, opened in 1909 and still owned by the

Canopied outdoor garden terrace is popular summer dining spot at Terrace Cafe.

Clark family. A doorman beneath a columned portico and a palatial lobby in green and red chintz greet arriving visitors; a pianist plays in the lobby during afternoon tea. A sweeping rear veranda looks across the swimming pool, a luncheon terrace and the broad lawns to Otsego Lake, with an eighteen-hole golf course beside.

The four-story brick hotel offers 124 rooms, six parlor suites and eight two-bedroom suites. The standard rooms are nicer than we had been led to expect, fresh in pale blue with twin beds, two armchairs, yellow floral spreads and curtains, lamp stands painted with flowers, television sets and large, modern baths. The six deluxe parlor rooms are quite spiffy in wicker with matching fabrics.

A sumptuous breakfast buffet and prix-fixe dinners are served in two beautiful, connecting dining rooms (see Dining Spots), while a lunch buffet is available on the Lakeside Patio. Lunch and dinner also are served in the new Hawkeye Bar & Grill, a favorite of locals. There's live musical entertainment nightly in the Templeton Lounge. Jackets are required for the evening meal in the dining room and are strongly recommended after 6 p.m. in all public rooms except the Hawkeye Bar & Grill.

Doubles, $240 to $260, MAP; deluxe and suites, $300 to $335. Open late April through October.

Dining Spots

Terrace Cafe, 10 Hoffman Lane, Cooperstown. (607) 547-8938.

Local consensus anoints this establishment the area's best for fine dining. Under owner Robert Paul, the two-story contemporary restaurant named for its attractive garden terrace has gained a reputation for consistency. And Baltimore-trained chef Lynn Hathaway has been given free rein with the menu.

"We try to do things nobody else around here does," says Lynn, citing particularly his seafood and veal dishes. If not exactly cutting-edge, Manhattan style, the fare has its moments, as in the tangy goat-cheese lasagna, layered with prosciutto and marinara sauce, a dish we found surprisingly refined, and the veal scaloppine sautéed with zucchini, tomatoes and pernod. Zero in on nightly specials like these to give the chef a chance to shine. Otherwise the entrées are fairly standard, priced from $11.95 for grilled pork chops with applesauce to $17.95 for mixed grill of filet mignon, spiced shrimp and lemon-pepper chicken breast. There's nothing standard about the specialty dessert, bread pudding with a delicious whiskey sauce, so rich that a little goes a long way. A velvety Beaulieu pinot noir for $14 was a good choice from a short wine list.

Dining is on three levels: the main-floor bar, a mezzanine landing with stained-glass pieces in the big windows and an airy second floor with green-inlay butcherblock tables and track lighting focusing on paintings by local artists. In summer, the trellised and canopied terrace with its expanse of white tables is positively idyllic.

Lunch, Monday-Saturday 11:30 to 2:30; dinner, Monday-Saturday 5 to 9 or 10. Closed Sunday, also Monday and Tuesday in off-season.

The Dining Room, 171 Main St., Cooperstown. (607) 547-2211.

This is quite sleek in black and white with black cane chairs and votive candles shining on the twelve glass-topped tables. It's small and intimate and not at all what you'd expect from the name or the "approved by AAA" designation.

Chef-owner Larry DeCarr offers a reasonably priced menu ($11.95 to $15.95) for the likes of panéed chicken alfredo, grilled albacore tuna steak with a peppercorn sauce, shrimp dijon, sweet and sour seafood stir-fry, deviled crab cakes topped with garlic-hollandaise sauce, veal with artichokes and scallops in a dill cream sauce, teriyaki London broil and broiled or blackened New York strip steak. Pasta el greco (linguini tossed with shrimp, crabmeat and clams with olive oil, oregano, garlic and romano) and other pasta dishes ($8.95 to $10.95) come with salad and vegetable of the day.

Deli sandwiches, quiche, pizza for one on a boboli cheese crust and good salads (caesar or spinach and orange) are lunchtime favorites. For dessert, how about chocolate mousse torte or lemon meringue pie? The short wine list is as undistinguished as the Inglenook house wine.

Lunch, Monday-Saturday 11:30 to 2; dinner, 5 to 8:30. Closed Sunday.

Otesaga Hotel, Lake Street, Cooperstown. (607) 547-9931.

Nobody in town goes here – it's too stodgy, the locals say repeatedly. Then you find that, like most resorts of its ilk, it's a local favorite for a summer lunch or Sunday brunch on the outdoor terrace or in the beautiful, chandeliered dining room. We were headed here for lunch, until we found they weren't serving outside on a mild September day and the lunch buffet in the dining room cost $12.50 for an array that looked like a glorified salad bar with seafood newburg, rice and green beans at the end.

The fancy setting lends itself less to a quick weekday lunch than to a leisurely Sunday brunch. The extra tab for brunch ($15) yields scrambled eggs, roast turkey and steamship round as well as the salad-y fare and the venue is usually on the outside terrace overlooking the lake.

A new general manager has upgraded much of the food operation lately. The printed dinner menu (prix-fixe, $27.50) changes daily. Au courant choices are mixed in with traditional fare, offering a range from fresh fruit cup with sherbet to belgian endive with ham mousse, chicken broth with rice to chilled strawberry soup, prime rib with yorkshire pudding to broiled lamb chops with baked tomato and mint jelly, bread pudding with English sauce to chocolate ice cream pie with marshmallow topping.

And local people certainly do favor the new downstairs **Hawkeye Bar & Grill,** where the fare is more contemporary and the decor casual in pink and dark green with white exposed pipes overhead. The grill has become immensely popular with people

Crisp black and white decor prevails in The Dining Room.

who like the Otesaga cachet, the lakeside setting and the reasonable prices. They speak highly of such dinner entrées as Eastern salmon steak with red onion and juniper marmalade, thick lamb chops with mint chutney and pork tenderloin with a champagne and cider cream sauce, priced from $11.50 to $15.75. You can settle for a burger or a couple of hearty sandwiches, or graze on appetizers like baked brie, deep-fried potato skins with herb dip and caesar salad with grilled chicken. Sandwiches, salads and pizzas are available for lunch here in the $3.75 to $6.75 range.

Dining Room, lunch or brunch on Lakeside Patio, depending on weather, noon to 2; dinner nightly, 6 to 8:30; jackets required at night. Hawkeye Bar & Grill, lunch daily, 11:30 to 3; dinner nightly, 6 to 9:30. Open late April through October.

Black Bart's B-B-Q, 64 Main St., Cooperstown. (607) 547-5656.

"It ain't for sissies," says the trademark for this long, narrow downtown storefront that opened in 1994 and serves specialties of the South and Southwest. Local foodies gave it the highest marks for solicitous service and quality fare.

Pass the open kitchen and settle at one of the booths and tables in the back, where colorful papier-mâché Mexican figures soar overhead. Owner Judith Cooper and her chef do a lot of Texas and Louisiana specials, from jambalaya to baby back ribs, smoked in their own smoker. Everything is made from scratch except for the potato chips, the manager advised. Highly rated are the barbecued beef and pork and the smoked beef, pork and turkey, served on fresh French bread, with a choice of baked beans, potato salad, cole slaw or papafritas. Expect to find also the usual Tex-Mex items, as well as salads and sandwiches. Prices are in the $3 to $5 range, except for dinner samplers and platters from $8.95 to $11.95. There's a beer and wine license.

For a different breakfast, how about huevos rancheros, biscuits with country gravy or a breakfast burrito?

Open Monday-Thursday 7 a.m. to 10 p.m., Friday and Saturday, 7 to midnight.

The Rose & Kettle, 4 Lancaster St., Cherry Valley. (607) 264-3078.

For fine dining in a charming setting, local people highly recommend this "quaint and adorable" restaurant well north of town in an 1810 house in Cherry Valley. The setting is cozy but elegant, and the 35 seats are much in demand. Everything from soup to bread to dessert is prepared on premises in the chef-owned restaurant.

The eclectic menu is ambitious for the area. Consider such entrées ($11.50 to $16.95) as grilled swordfish Jamaican jerk style, chicken Louisiana sauté, hot and spicy chicken with Chinese chile and black bean sauce, pork schnitzel, pork tenderloin marsala, veal piccata, lamb on a skewer or filet mignon au poivre. Among appetizers are escargots, scallops seviche and chicken yakatori with a tamari dipping sauce.

Dinner, Monday-Saturday 5 to 9:30. Closed November-April.

The Red Sleigh Restaurant, Lake Road (Route 80), Cooperstown (607) 547-5581.

Popular with opera-goers because of its location 200 yards from Glimmerglass, this old-timer has improved lately in its food delivery.

The young chef-owner oversees a prodigious output, with no fewer than 60 items on the six-page menu, priced from $11.95 to $19.95. Seven veal dishes range from wiener schnitzel to cordon bleu and the nine beef dishes from steak diane or au poivre to Italian stuffed tenderloin. Among ten seafood dishes, how about scallops flamingo, cajun shrimp or dill seafood flambé over fettuccine? Can't decide? Try one of the seven combination dishes (steak and fried clams, steak and chicken mornay) or one of the dozen selections labeled "Little Italy." Vegetarian and low-cal items are listed under heart-healthy entrées. Chicken sautéed with herbs, mushrooms, scallions and finished with a layer of melted cheese is billed as the house specialty. Starters run the gamut from potato skins and nachos to shrimp cocktail and escargots bourguignonne.

The setting for all this is a low-slung house that reminds some of an old Catskills country summer home. A photograph in the lobby showing snow above the Red Sleigh's roof line became quite a conversation piece following the record snowfall in 1994.

Breakfast in summer, 7:30 to 11; dinner nightly, 4:30 to 9:30. Closed mid-November to April.

Hickory Grove Inn, Route 80, Cooperstown. (607) 547-8100.

Antiques, beautiful wallpapers and a lakeview dining porch create a homey elegance that makes some summer folks want to dress for dinner at this former stagecoach stop, an inn since 1805 at Six Mile Point, six miles north of Cooperstown. The fare is continental, with a couple of menu sections featuring Italian specialties and "for your heart's delight."

Expect such main dishes ($9.95 to $15.95) as stuffed jumbo shrimp (stuffed with crabmeat and "flavored for the true garlic lover"), broiled trout, seafood fra diavolo, hunter chicken, veal parmesan or marsala, delmonico steak remo or broiled filet mignon topped with mushrooms. Prime rib is offered on weekends.

Appetizers here run to french onion soup, baked stuffed clams, mussels marinara, escargots or antipasto.

Dinner nightly, 5 to 9 or 10, Sunday 4 to 9. Closed Monday and Tuesday in off-season and mid-December to April.

Doubleday Cafe, 93 Main St., Cooperstown. (607) 547-5468.

Bottles of ketchup and mustard are on every table in this downtown cafe in the heart of baseball country. A big jukebox may be playing CDs and the TV is likely turned on atop the bar in the long, narrow, high-ceilinged room with brick walls and track lights spotlighting local art.

This is where we were advised to head for breakfast, and with good reason. An order of excellent eggs benedict was a mere $4.50 and garnished with enough bananas, watermelon and grapes to skip the fruit course. We also liked the huevos rancheros for $4.50. The lunch menu yields sandwiches in the $3 to $4 range, burgers, omelets and salads up to $6.95. Much the same fare is available at dinner, plus hearty appetizers and a few entrées.

Breakfast daily, 7 to 11; lunch, 11 to 4; dinner, 4 to 10 or 11.

Diversions

In baseball land, you'd expect to find a baseball theme, from the Short Stop restaurant and the Walker Gallery ("the fine art of baseball") to the Cooperstown Bat Co. and the Doubleday Batting Range. But there's much more to this appealing village, some of which we concentrate upon here.

National Baseball Hall of Fame and Museum, Main Street, Cooperstown, 547-9988. Enshrined here in 1939 on the apparently erroneous theory that Abner Doubleday invented the game in Cooperstown a century earlier, the four floors dedicated to America's national pastime are what draw most visitors to Cooperstown. This is the only museum we know of in which hordes of men and boys can stand mesmerized for hours – in front of an old uniform, a signed baseball, a recital of statistics. Since a major addition in 1979, it has been transformed from a primitive museum with table-top glass cases and encyclopedic sweep into a scattershot, state-of-the-art story of the game. The zoom-in, flashback approach is tailor-made for today's attention spans and the increasing enormity of the subject matter. Everyone has his favorites (ours include the section on baseball parks and the lifelike statues of Babe Ruth and Ted Williams carved from single pieces of laminated basswood); others prefer the awesome cathedral dedicated to the more than 200 Hall of Famers or the statistics spewed out by IBM computers. Who can fail to appreciate the magic of the animated, twelve-minute multimedia presentation in the Grandstand Theater? The audience sits in grandstand seats, shouts of "play ball" and "get your popcorn here" punctuate the ever-so-realistic crowd noise, the organ pumps up the fans and, well, it's just like being in the old ballpark. Little wonder that everyone joins in the rousing "Take Me Out to the Ballgame" finale. Visitors exit through the ultimate baseball gift shop. Open daily, May-October 9 to 9, rest of year 9 to 5. Adults, $8.

The Farmers' Museum, Lake Road, Cooperstown, 547-2533. This, not the Hall of Fame, was the primary destination for our seventh-grade class trip back in upstate New York in the late 1940s. Only five years old at the time, the museum was already famous among educators and made a worthwhile outing for a day's immersion in early New York State history. The main barn displays agricultural artifacts and early crafts. Nearby is the relocated resting spot of the memorable Cardiff Giant, originally foisted on an unsuspecting public as a petrified prehistoric man and looking mighty big to seventh-graders. Beyond is the Village Crossroads, a dozen historic buildings assembled from within 100 miles of Cooperstown, nestled against the hillside with cows grazing and chickens wandering about nearby. Buildings are furnished and staffed for the period. The Toddsville Store has a cast-iron stove, a printing office issues leaflets and the old Bump Tavern ought to dispense food and grog instead of relegating visitors to the mundane but very reasonably priced fare of the nearby snack bar. But on a gorgeous autumn day, strolling the grounds, admiring the old buildings and looking across the stone walls to the golf course, Otsego Lake and the flaming hillsides, we felt this was close to paradise. Open May-October, daily 9 to 6; April, November and December, Tuesday-Sunday 10 to 4. Adults $8.

Fenimore House, Lake Road, Cooperstown, 547-2533. Magnificent, yet somehow personal and homey, is the lakeside edifice built in 1932 on the site of novelist James Fenimore Cooper's farm. It's been the home of the New York State Historical Association since 1945. The stately portico leads to room after room of fine and decorative arts. A twelve-minute slide show provides a good orientation, and the descriptions throughout the galleries are unusually informative. The paintings in the ballroom include many from the Hudson River School. Thomas Cole's landscape scene from Cooper's *Last of the Mohicans* is especially appropriate in a gallery holding works associated with the novelist. At our visit, a major exhibition, "Worlds of Art: Worlds Apart," showcased the association's unsurpassed collection of folk art, only a small portion of which normally is displayed at any time. Upstairs, a fascinating, interactive exhibit exploring the impact of portraiture on everyday life was on display in seven galleries. A new wing was being readied for opening in 1995 to exhibit the acclaimed Eugene and Clare Thaw Collection of more than 500 works of American Indian art. Open daily, May-October 9 to 6; November and December, Tuesday-Sunday 10 to 4. Adults, $6.

Corvette Americana Hall of Fame, Route 28, Cooperstown. (607) 547-4135. What could be more related than "baseball, hot dogs, apple pie and Chevrolet," as the old ad campaign suggested? The first three were already associated with Cooperstown, so this was a logical site for Allen Schery's one-man tribute to Corvette and American pop culture. The son of a New York City fireman, the graying, pony-tailed Corvette collector, cultural anthropologist and former rock band manager spent more than $7 million to realize his life-long dream in a warehouse-style arena that's bigger than the Baseball Hall of Fame it emulates. He personally oversaw every detail, from photographing the mural backdrops on two whirlwind 1991 cross-country jaunts to editing the lively audio-visual presentations that accompany. His 35 heavy-hitter collector Corvettes are displayed each in their own color-coordinated Hollywood sets that Allen calls "time tunnels," complete with TV, movie, news and sports snippets and commercials from the year involved. The extravaganza starts with the first 1953 model (the year he was born). It shows Allen's first white convertible bearing a sticker price of $3,860 (it's now worth $125,000) and a life-size cutout of Marilyn Monroe, plus posters and artifacts of her films from that year. The museum integrates each Corvette into the cultural milieu from which it emerged. The backdrops (from Ebbets Field to the Golden Gate), the featured pop heroes (from James Dean to Madonna) and the memorabilia (from hula hoops to pet rocks) are the images and symbols of Americana as portrayed by Schery. His collections are awesome; the 1978 display of Chevrolet billboards touting the 25th anniversary of Corvette stresses that "these are the original billboards – they are not reproductions." The museum also contains an interior display room featuring every Corvette sales brochure, plastic model, magazine, wheel cover and owner's manual ever made. The whole astonishing affair is dedicated to Woody Guthrie of "This Land Is Your Land" fame: "What Woody did with a guitar and a song has been done here with a camera and a car." Baseball star Reggie Jackson was so impressed that he put his 1963 Corvette on indefinite loan here. Open daily, 10 to 8 in summer, to 6 in off-season and weekends in November and March-April. Adults, $8.75; children, $6.75.

Sightseeing. Catch the **Cooperstown Trolley** for a scenic ride between three free outlying parking lots and the village's major attractions. The trolley runs daily from 8:30 to 8 in summer and 8:30 to 6 on weekends in spring and fall. An all-day pass costs $1.50. This may be the best way to get around on busy days, when visitors outnumber the resident population. The Lake and Valley Garden Club publishes a brochure outlining a walking tour of 44 local sights. **Classic Boat Tours** offers daily hour-long excursions on Otsego Lake aboard two all-wooden boats that cruised the lake at the turn of the century for the Clark and Busch families; adults, $8.50. Swimming and picnicking are available at Glimmerglass, Fairy Spring and Three Mile Point parks.

Shopping. Baseball cards and paraphernalia are on sale everywhere, of course, from the **Home Plate** to **Mickey's Place** (for Mickey Mantle memorabilia) to **Cap City,** which sprung up to capitalize on the baseball cap craze. Even the venerable **Church & Scott Pharmacy** sells baseball bats. A long garden path leads to the hidden courtyard outside **Moon Dreams,** an inspirational music, book, crafts and jewelry store; it offers a pleasant tea room with lunch specials and pricey pastries. If coffee's your thing, head for **Stagecoach Coffee Roastery & Espresso Bar.** Some of the village's more interesting shops are clustered along Pioneer Street. They include **Tin Bin Alley** for gourmet jelly beans, among lots of other candy and gifts, **Lake Classic Designs** and **Toad Hall,** a showcase for the most incredible pottery, crafts, gourmet foods and more. Here are imports from across the world, as well as many items by local artists. We coveted a table with frogs for legs, not to mention a bed with bears at the head and foot. From fancy soaps to Hudson Bay blankets, everything here is fascinating and fits in with that certain look sought by owners Allen Ransome and Randy VanSyoc, who also operate the stylish Toad Hall B&B.

Just north of town in Fly Creek are two worthy side-by-side destinations. **Fly Creek Cider Mill** is a complex of weathered buildings dispensing a variety of ciders, plus apple bread, apple butter, apple pies, candied apples, specialty food items and much more. You can watch cider being made from a vantage point upstairs off the gift shop, where the owner sells pretty dried arrangements from flowers and weeds she collects and air dries. Exotic ducks frequent the pond out back. The nearby **Tins and Bins Country Store** has bins of candies (as it has at its Cooperstown store, Tin Bin Alley). But here you'll also find really special Christmas things. Dozens of trees, all with different themes, display hundreds of ornaments. Just about everything else for Christmas decorating is here as well. Tins and Bins is open from May to Dec. 24, and Fly Creek Cider Mill from mid-August through November.

Extra-Special

Glimmerglass Opera Festival, Route 80, (Box 191), Cooperstown. (607) 547-2255. The high retractable walls roll down as the lights dim in the 900-seat Alice Busch Opera Theater on Thomas Goodyear's former turkey farm above the lake James Fenimore Cooper called Glimmerglass. The sense of drama heightens as another performance by one of the nation's best regional companies begins. Founded in 1975, this has become a major attraction, drawing 27,000 enthusiasts to Cooperstown for its 20th anniversary season. The $5 million, semi-open-air theater funded in 1987 by the Busch family represents the first major opera house built from scratch in America in several decades. And a sophisticated place it is for so rural a setting. The gilded ceiling is staggered in a quilt pattern for acoustical purposes, lamps adorn the balconies and the European-opera-house look is elegant and intimate, remarkable for a building designed to resemble a hops barn. Concessions sell anything from turkey croissants and cornish game hens to champagne and desserts for picnics before the opera. These can be consumed beside a reflecting pond or on the hillside across the road, overlooking Otsego Lake. "Opera previews," free 35-minute talks, are scheduled one hour before performances. Thirty-three performances of four operas run in repertory from early July to late August, Sunday and Monday matinees at 2, Thursday-Saturday evenings at 8. Tickets, $15 to $55.

Cazenovia, N.Y.
Picture-Perfect Place

There's little commercial hoopla surrounding Cazenovia and its lake. No visitor information center (not even a tourist booth or a Chamber of Commerce office). No brochures touting its attractions. No marinas or amusement parks. No chain stores or fast-food restaurants, a solitary McDonalds at the far edge of town excepted. The weekly newspaper claims on its masthead to be Cazenovia's oldest industry.

And yet the knowledgeable traveler has likely heard of this picture-perfect village, most of it still stuck in the 19th century, at the end of Cazenovia Lake. It offers three full-service inns of considerable renown, and bed and breakfasts are popping up. It possesses enough historic structures to prompt the Cazenovia Preservation Foundation to produce a brochure outlining five walks in the village of Cazenovia and another detailing five drives in the surrounding township. It harbors a small college that adds activity to an already sophisticated community. It has a much-photographed main street whose storefronts are occupied by local entrepreneurs, most of them thriving. An outlying suburb of Syracuse but with an identity of its own, it exudes an unmistakable air of prosperity.

Despite its lakeside setting beside sylvan hills 1,250 feet above sea level, this is no summer resort. It did have something of that reputation in the late 1800s when lakeside farms gave way to estates with their summer "cottages" and some of the nation's first tennis courts and golf courses were laid out here. Today, summer greenery blocks water views for motorists who circle the four-mile-long Cazenovia Lake along East and West Lake Roads to look at the substantial year-round homes. Lake access is limited to town residents and their guests.

The opening of the New York State Thruway some twenty miles to the north in the 1950s stifled the development of Cazenovia and nearby towns along U.S. Route 20, the old Lincoln Highway that spanned the continent on the path the stagecoaches took.

This area turned its isolation to advantage, however. Cazenovia retained much of its early character, which had been inspired by young Dutch naval officer John Lincklaen. He established a Holland Land Company office beside the lake in 1793 and named his new community in honor of Theophilus de Cazenove, the Philadelphia-based banker for the Dutch investors. Most of the village is listed on the National Register of Historic Places.

To the east, sleepy Bouckville and Madison have become a mecca for antiquers, lining Route 20 with 39 antiques shops in the space of a few miles and staging the

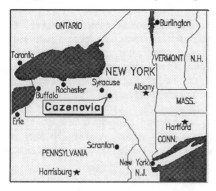

East's second largest outdoor antiques show every August.

Visitors are drawn by Cazenovia's character, its lakeside setting, its varied architecture and historic charm.

They sense what the Syracuse Standard was alluding to in a newspaper article a century ago: "Amid the vast aggregation of summer resorts, of spas, beaches, points and harbors, Cazenovia stands by itself...for certain distinguishing characteristics, for its individuality." It is, indeed, a special place.

Cazenovia Lake is on view from balcony outside Harden Room at Brewster Inn.

Inn Spots

The Brewster Inn, 6 Ledyard Ave. (Route 20), Box 507, Cazenovia 13035. (315) 655-9232.

Gloriously situated at the southern end of Cazenovia Lake, the old Lake Meadows inn and restaurant gave way to the Brewster in 1984. Syracusan Dick Hubbard, who had managed the Sherwood Inn in Skaneateles for five years, and his wife Cathy from Ohio have upgraded into a class act the 1887 summer home built by financier Benjamin Brewster, who with John D. Rockefeller established the Standard Oil Co.

Not that everything is perfect. The inside of the house is finished entirely in hardwood, and the lobby with its deep-coffered ceiling is particularly dark. Trooping up two long flights of stairs to our third-floor room was gloomy. And the room with two double beds and a tiny bathroom (shower only) – despite a lake view through a couple of tiny windows – turned out to be small and undistinguished. Fortunately, no one seemed to know or care about the third-floor common room to which our room was attached, so we took it over and quietly made it our suite.

A tour the next morning proved our room to be an aberration. For half again more money, we could have stayed in the Harden Room, newly fashioned from former servants' quarters. It has a crocheted canopy queensize four-poster bed, elegant Harden furniture set against cherry walls, a two-section bathroom with brass fixtures, two reclining armchairs in front of a huge TV set and a balcony overlooking the lake. Also on the second floor is a cheery room in mint green and pink with a kingsize brass bed and, the first thing you notice, a double jacuzzi beside the bay window. Dark and more formal with oriental rugs and an ornate carved wood double bed is another second-floor suite with a sun porch. The three-room Stickley suite on the third floor has a jacuzzi and a magnificent lake view. All nine inn guest rooms and suites contain private baths, TVs and phones, but vary markedly in size and spirit. Six offer lake views. Ours, in the mid-price range, actually was not the smallest.

Proprietors Jim and Grey Barr welcomes guests to The Brae Loch Inn.

New in 1993 were eight more air-conditioned rooms on two floors of the renovated Carriage House Annex at the side of the main inn. Here, all have queensize beds (except for one with two doubles) and full baths with tubs and showers. Two on the main floor boast jacuzzis; two on the second floor, cathedral ceilings.

Everyone gets to enjoy the lawn leading down to the lake where sailboats bob up and down, although it was taken over for a private party by a business group when we were there. A buffet spread of juice, cereal, mini-bagels (which you can toast in the toaster provided) and pastries is set out for continental breakfast in the lovely dining room (see Dining Spots). There's an appealing cocktail lounge, where we picked up after-dinner drinks to sip on the lawn, and a small gift shop.

Doubles, $70 to $140; suites, $130 to $195.

The Brae Loch Inn, 5 Albany St., Cazenovia 13035. (315) 655-3431 or (800) 722-0674.

"As close to a Scottish inn as it can be this far west of Edinburgh," says the brochure for this dark brown gabled landmark across from the park near the head of Cazenovia Lake. Occasionally attired in kilts, longtime innkeeper Grey Barr and his son Jim oversee a bustling establishment with a good downstairs restaurant and lounge (see Dining Spots), banquet facilities, a large Scottish gift shop and fifteen guest rooms.

Grapevine wreaths wrapped in tartan ribbons adorn the doors to the rooms, which vary from small (with two three-quarter beds) to deluxe with kingsize canopy beds. All but two have private baths and most have remote-control TVs. Nicest are the luxury rooms on the second floor in front and in a new section in back.

Grey Barr was ebullient as he pointed out special touches: Stickley furniture, prized antiques, in-room coffee-makers, reclining chairs, a mix of carpeting and oriental rugs, extra insulation and firm mattresses ("because I have a bad back and want the best beds one can get").

A continental breakfast is served buffet style in the entry lobby, much of it displayed in an antique serving cupboard Grey had just acquired after seeking one for years. Guests have swimming privileges at the town park across the street.

Recently, Grey added a selection of antiques to supplement the Scottish gift items in his "Wee Hoose" and renamed it the Wee Gift and Antique House.

Doubles, $75 to $125.

Lincklaen House, 79 Albany St., Cazenovia 13035. (315) 655-3461.

The handsome brick landmark that bears Cazenovia founder John Lincklaen's name was built in 1835 by a group of investors who felt the village needed an elegant hotel to care for its prominent visitors, who were to include Grover Cleveland and John D. Rockefeller. Dating to horse and buggy days, rooms vary from small, for those arriving by horse in back, to spacious, for those arriving by carriage in front. Some of the smallest rooms have been joined to make fewer but larger rooms.

Each of the eighteen air-conditioned rooms and three suites comes with private bath, phone and TV. Rooms are generally light and airy, with stenciled borders, floral curtains, antique highboys or armoires, and Lord & Mayfair toiletries. They look surprisingly comfortable, despite their age, although those in front suffer from street noise. One suite we saw had a queensize Hitchcock stenciled bed, an armoire with a TV, and a sitting room with a couch, an armchair and a table for three.

Afternoon tea and a continental breakfast, including cereals and pastries, are put out in the East Room off the main lobby. An aura of history and elegance pervades the entire main floor with its high ceilings, large fireplaces, classical carved moldings and chandeliers. Before or after dinner (see Dining Spots), some guests like to pause downstairs in the intimate, often smoke-filled little tavern, **Seven Stone Steps.**

Doubles, $70 to $99; suites, $120 to $140.

Willowbank, 21 Forman St., Cazenovia 13035. (315) 655-9868.

In their grand lakeside home of thirteen years, Bonnie and Roger Bradstreet were empty-nesters and had a decision to make. "Should we stay put with only two people or move on?" asked Bonnie. "I hoped to stay put." So the Bradstreets began taking in overnight guests, enjoyed the company, and in 1991 renovated the third floor to offer a total of eight guest rooms. Three on the second floor have private baths, while five on the third floor share two baths.

Located beside village park, Willowbank occupies property sloping to Cazenovia Lake.

Right beside the village park and with lawns sloping to the lake, this 1810 beauty was meant to be a B&B, according to neighbor Cathy Hubbard of the Brewster Inn, who saw it on a house tour and suggested that use to the Bradstreets. They offer a variety of lived-in rooms, one with a porch and a walk-out deck, another with twin four-poster beds and a ceiling fan. A high-ceilinged second-floor suite with a king bed and a sitting room was light and airy. The attic rooms have window seats in the dormer windows.

Guests have use of a pretty pale yellow front parlor with oriental rugs, a rear family room with a pool table and a wood stove, and a third-floor exercise room outfitted with all kinds of equipment. There's a pantry for kitchen privileges. The Bradstreets serve a hearty continental breakfast in a Federal-style rear dining room overlooking the lake.

The name comes from the willow trees outlining the park next door. The original house on the site – the first home of John Lincklaen, founder of Cazenovia – was destroyed by fire. This was rebuilt on its foundation in 1810.

Doubles, $65 to $85. No smoking.

Edgewater Hollow Bed & Breakfast, 4880 West Lake Road, Cazenovia 13035. (315) 655-8407.

A long driveway leads off West Lake Road to this handsome year-round home, centered on a grassy lawn sloping down to the lakeshore and a dock with a waiting canoe.

Eleanor Karl Rooney opens her home to guests in five bedrooms, one with private bath. The main feature is a two-story-high central living room with a huge, curving off-white sectional facing windows onto the lake. On one side of the living room are the kitchen and a rather medieval-looking dining room.

On the other side is a carpeted guest room with private bath, queensize bed, TV, a wicker settee and french doors onto the rear deck. It's summery in white and light pink. Upstairs off one side of the mezzanine are two bedrooms, one in front with twin beds and a striking African print, and one in the rear with a queensize bed. They share a full bath. On the other side of the mezzanine are two more bedrooms, one with a king bed and one with a queen. They also share a bath. All are furnished in simple, homey and uncluttered style.

Eleanor serves a continental breakfast of fresh fruit and baked goods ("whatever I feel like baking.") Fried dough dipped in cinnamon and sugar is a house favorite. She also serves afternoon refreshments on the back porch and terraces running the width of the house or, in cold weather, beside the fire in the living room.

Mrs. Rooney had the house up for sale at our visit in 1994. Had we had an extra half-million dollars, it might have been ours on the spot!

Doubles, $60 to $90.

Abigail's Straw Hat Bed & Breakfast, Route 20, Box 242, Madison 13402. (315) 893-7077.

Biggest and most serious of the home-stay B&Bs popping up around Cazenovia is this circa 1830 village home, acquired in 1993 by Gail and Don Hergert. They had run a B&B at their ten-acre Mutton Hill Farm outside Cazenovia since 1990 and wanted to be more in the thick of things.

Now located close to Route 20 in the heart of tiny Madison, the Hergerts have added three bathrooms and switched from a homey farm theme to country Victorian. A hat stand at the entry holds some of the little straw hats that Gail makes and places strategically in each bedroom and around the house.

Upstairs are four air-conditioned bedrooms with private baths. A favorite is Aunt

Curving polygonal building houses Ye Olde Landmark Tavern, an inn and restaurant.

Grace's, named for the aunt who crocheted the canopy and bedspread for the antique double bed; its couch opens into a twin bed. A third person also can be accommodated in Mary-Patricia's Room in back with twin brass beds and a sleeping nook containing a built-in child's bed. The double bed and windows are draped in white lace in Veronica's Room, while Eileen-Sarah's Room features an antique quarter-canopy oak bed and matching dresser.

The main floor holds a pleasant guest parlor with TV and piano, a side porch furnished in wicker, and a fireplaced dining room. In the morning, Gail puts out coffee before serving a full breakfast by candlelight with the family china and crystal. Crêpes stuffed with eggs, diced ham, peppers and tomato and topped with hollandaise sauce are her specialty these days. Eggs benedict, egg and bacon cheese pie. strata or french toast are other choices. "I ask the first guests what they want," says Gail. "The rest get told." Fresh fruit and biscuits accompany.

Doubles, $60.

Ye Olde Landmark Tavern, Route 20, Box 5, Bouckville 13310. (315) 893-1810.

At the antiquey end of Madison County near Colgate University is this landmark. It's an imposing, curving polygonal building with four cobblestoned facades and a peaked roof topped by a gingerbread-trimmed cupola with six sides. Legend has it that the builder's wife wanted an octagonal structure and only half of it would fit on the pie-shaped lot, so what she got was one-half an octagon.

Visitors today get a good restaurant (see Dining Spots) plus four new second-floor guest rooms, all with private baths. The rooms ooze history, but are thoroughly up-to-date with canopy four-poster beds, carpeting, cable TV and air-conditioning. Each is stenciled and furnished in antiques. A suite offers a canopied queen bed and a sitting room with blue accents and a writing desk.

Juice, fruit, yogurt, cereal and danish are put out amid the magazines in a small dining-common room in the morning.

Doubles, $73; suite, $83. Closed January and February.

The Horned Dorset Inn, Route 8, Leonardsville 13364. (315) 855-7898.

Next door and across a garden from their famous restaurant, the owners of the Horned

457

Dorset have restored a once-decrepit late 19th-century house into a handsome B&B. They offer two bedrooms, two suites and a distinct sense of isolation and privacy, although in summer guests may run into the elderly relative of one of the owners who maintains an apartment there. An off-site innkeeper comes in to serve a continental breakfast with linens, china and a silver coffee pot on a silver tray to the bedrooms in the morning. The fare includes juice, coffee and croissants with homemade preserves.

Otherwise, guests are on their own. There's a dark and elegant, richly paneled living room with a grand piano occupying a corner alcove and an abundance of antiques, as is the case throughout the house. The main floor also holds two main-floor bedrooms, one with a double four-poster bed and a full bath with a black tub and black sink, and the other with twin beds and a shower. Up a curving staircase are the suites, one over the living room with a table in the alcove, a kingsize bed and a pullout sofa. The other has twins joined as a king bed and a bathroom with a bidet and many amenities.

Two of the original partners left in 1988 for Puerto Rico to open the Horned Dorset Primavera, a secluded 24-room inn that has won rave reviews. The hearts of the two owners who stayed seem to be in their restaurant.

Doubles, $75; suites, $95.

Dining Spots

The Horned Dorset Inn, Route 8, Leonardsville. (315) 855-7898.

Wow! That's the first-timer's initial – and lasting – impression of this dramatic space carved out of a two-story commercial establishment that started as a 19th-century stagecoach stop and became a general store and an antiques store. It had been unoccupied for ten years and its roof was falling in when four partners acquired it and converted it into a restaurant in 1977.

Out in the middle of nowhere, this had to be good – and good it is, earning acclaim (and fame) far beyond the territory. It takes its name from the horned Dorset sheep that original partners Harold Davies and Kingsley Wratten raised here after they graduated from Colgate University in nearby Hamilton.

Replicas of horned Dorsets are scattered throughout the bigger-than-expected establishment (the only real ones are pictured in the men's room). The side dining room with three palladian windows is a stunner, its well-spaced, white-clothed tables flanked by windsor chairs and topped with fresh flowers, candles in hurricane lamps and gleaming crystal and sterling. Black walnut woodwork acquired from a house being torn down in Syracuse accents the soaring room that's otherwise all pristine white. Chef-owner Don Lentz calls the decor Victorian; we call it medieval or baroque, more at home in Europe than Leonardsville. Church-like elements are seen in the paneled banquet room and the main dining room on two levels, one beside a library of bookshelves. It's paneled, has stained glass and a great hanging tapestry. Upstairs is a cocktail lounge with more bookshelves and high-backed Victorian furniture.

Such is the spectacular backdrop for the food, which is classic, high-cholesterol French and has won even more accolades than has the architectural restoration. The changing menu is recited nightly and includes five or six appetizers and an equal number of entrées, priced from $19.95 to $27 (for veal oscar). One evening's dinner started with broiled scallops in a superb sauce and tossed salad with a dressing whose recipe the chef guards jealously. Main courses were sweetbreads and twin tournedos, extra-tender and served in ample portions. Chocolate bombe and a chocolate roll wrapped around chocolate mousse were desserts of choice. Neither the menu nor the prices were shown, and this is not the place to ask. The wine list was expensive and the service slow.

Room with a medieval look is setting for fine dining at The Horned Dorset Inn.

At our latest visit, Don was preparing appetizers like cold marinated mussels with lime vinaigrette, sautéed scallops and lobster in phyllo with green onion beurre blanc, duxelle lasagna with tarragon cream sauce and slices of smoked duck breast with apples, cabbage and peppers. Main courses that night were to be swordfish with basil beurre blanc; chicken with cream sauce and sundried tomatoes; filet of lamb with brown sauce, ginger and raisins; loin of veal stuffed with peppers, onions, prosciutto, brie and served with curried brown sauce, and tournedos with wild mushroom-peppercorn brown sauce. Raspberry mousse cake in genoise, frozen lemon soufflé, strawberry-blueberry tart, homemade apricot ice cream in a cookie cup and five sorbets were on tap for dessert.

Head chef Don and partner Bruce Wratten, who runs the front of the house, met at Ithaca College and have been here from the beginning. Bruce's brother Kingsley and Harold Davies have left to operate the Horned Dorset Primavera in Puerto Rico. But the original still draws a knowing clientele from Syracuse, Cazenovia, Cooperstown and beyond.

Dinner, Tuesday-Saturday 6 to 9; Sunday 3 to 8.

The Brewster Inn, 6 Ledyard Ave., Cazenovia. (315) 655-9232.
Sliding glass windows open onto the lake in the wraparound dining room elegant in white and mint green. Swagged curtains top the windows, candles flicker in oil lamps and our only quibbles are that the atmosphere is fairly close and track lights make the window tables overly bright. An interior dining room is serene in white and beige, with windsor chairs at well-spaced tables, and a fireplace.

Innkeeper Dick Hubbard, who has a restaurant background, acts as host and puts together the excellent, expensive wine list. A choice of good salads comes with the meal: in our case, romaine with mandarin oranges, almonds and a creamy dijon dressing and a classic caesar salad with homemade croutons. Entrées are priced from $14.25

for baked scrod or tomato-basil chicken to $18.25 for veal atlantis (sautéed veal cutlets with lobster and béarnaise sauce). We found the pork tenderloin au poivre a bit heavy handed, but liked the delicate poached salmon with dill sauce, rice and nicely julienned vegetables. Raspberry crème brûlée was the most interesting of many desserts.

Other possibilities on the changing menu could be country pâté, smoked duck breast, shrimp cocktail, clams casino and escargots for appetizers. Entrées could be blackened swordfish, shrimp provençal, roast duckling with bing cherry and cinnamon sauce, and tournedos of beef with artichoke hearts and mushrooms.

Dinner nightly, 5 to 9, Saturday 6 to 9; Sunday brunch, 11 to 2.

Brae Loch Inn, 5 Albany St., Cazenovia. (315) 655-3431.

Back in the days when we lived in the area, this was our place for special-occasion dining. A summer ritual was a trip to Cazenovia, roast-beef dinners in what we re-

member as the Wee Little Pub, and then nightcaps at the Seven Stone Steps across the way.

The Wee Little Pub has given way to a series of three dark, cozy dining rooms paneled in butternut or pine, the one in the middle called the Grill Room because of the open brick grill at the side. In front is a large Victorian cocktail lounge. The motif remains Scottish, from the tartan carpeting on the floors, the white tablecloths with red napkins and the pewter service plates to the staff wearing kilts and Glengarry hats.

Beef remains a fixture on the menu, as it has since the Barr family opened the restaurant in 1946. The prime rib ties with filet mignon as the priciest item on the menu ($17.95). Other choices from $12.95 include shrimp scampi, baked Boston scrod, open steak sandwich with onion rings and french fries, chicken stuffed with crabmeat en croûte, roast Long Island duckling and

Table for two at Brae Loch Inn.

veal piccata. Changing specials could be mustard-fried catfish with cajun mayonnaise, chicken Tuscany or tournedos of lamb in phyllo with spinach, garlic and feta cheese.

Start with coconut shrimp with drambuie marmalade, escargots en croûte, baked brie or, the first time we've seen this as an appetizer, lobster newburg ($7.25). Finish with a choice of sundaes and parfaits, cheesecake, pastries or ice cream pie.

The Friday night surf and turf buffet packs in the crowds. Roast leg of lamb is a standard at Sunday dinner.

Dinner nightly, 5 to 9:30 or 10:30; Sunday, brunch 11 to 2 (no brunch in summer), dinner 1 to 9.

Lincklaen House, 79 Albany St., Cazenovia. (315) 655-3461.

In our college days and for a while afterward, one of us considered the Lincklaen dining room a bit stuffy. But the **Seven Stone Steps** tavern in the basement was such a quiet, impressive place for a few drinks that we sometimes made a night out of it. Seven stone steps lead from the sidewalk to an intimate tavern with wood tables in which many a name has been inscribed.

Columns and fireplace mark formal dining room at Lincklaen House.

Nowadays the columned, high-ceilinged dining room seems quite romantic, dimly lit with an oriental screen gleaming in the fireplace at the far end and windsor chairs at nicely spaced tables set with white linens and floral china. The short dinner menu has risen to nouvelle heights. It's priced from $15.95 for pistachio-crusted chicken served with a citrus butter sauce or shrimp and mussels tossed with tomatoes, spinach, asiago and rigatoni to $17.95 for roasted veal chop on a sauce of cinnamon and port with crispy forest mushrooms and garlic whipped potatoes. Among the treats are grilled rare tuna served with a warm Asian pasta salad and ginger mustard and grilled Pennsylvania lamb with a hint of curry, raisin-almond sauce and peppermint tea rice.

Look forward to starters ($5.95 to $6.95) like pan-roasted sea scallops with fennel salsa, lime cream and crispy fried noodles or grilled plum tomatoes on chive risotto with black olive tapenade. The featured salad might be composed of asparagus, pearl onions and beets, drizzled with tarragon vinaigrette and topped with crisped parsnips. Hazelnut cappuccino torte and chocolate chambord cake are favorite desserts.

A screened, shaded outdoor courtyard is a pleasant setting for lunch in season.
Lunch daily, 11:30 to 2; dinner, 5:30 to 9; Sunday, 11 to 2 and 5 to 8.

Wheatberry, 63 Albany St., Cazenovia. (315) 655-2102.
One oldtimer calls Wheatberry "bohemian, serving things like quiche and salads." We and the standing-room-only crowd that jammed it one weekday lunchtime call it neat. The decor is something else, all right. Fake leopard skins frame the door and the pastry freezer and cover the chair seats and bar stools. The long, narrow room on several levels is dark in hunter green and brick, its high ceiling bearing gold designs. Lighting is from upside-down, parasol-like hanging glass lamps. There are assorted marble-top tables and banquettes in the rear.

It's a witty backdrop for a with-it international menu. At lunch, we enjoyed a combination salad platter (curried chicken, crunchy tuna and tabbouleh served on romaine,

$6.25) and the chilled gazpacho with a spinach, bacon and mushroom salad ($4.95). Everything was served in glass cups, bowls or plates. The spiced iced tea packed a punch. The day's Wheatberry News on each table offered quotable quotes, a secret-word contest and a handful of ads. In short, this is fun, noisy and convivial.

At night, you can still get sandwiches, salads, Greek pizza and quiches in the $4 to $6 range. You'll also find a dozen more substantial entrées, from $10.95 for spanakopita to $14.95 for shrimp à la griglia, sole with shrimp and mushrooms, veal champagne or strip steak stuffed with blue cheese and scallions. The homemade desserts are delectable, and a good little wine list is easy on the wallet. Beer and wine only.

Lunch, 11 to 3:30; dinner, 5 to 9 or 10; Sunday brunch, 11 to 3. Closed Monday, also Sunday January through April.

Stoker Homestead, 4955 Nelson Road, Cazenovia. (315) 655-9835.

This was a new one on us. "Country dining by reservation," said the ad, which piqued our interest. We stopped by, found a good-looking farmhouse a half-dozen miles out of town and chatted with the lady of the house, Nancy Stoker.

It turned out dinners were being served Saturdays only at communal tables for 30 people in two rooms. Served family style at one sitting, they start with a variety of salads from molded to cabbage to melon, and homemade rolls. Then come the hot dishes: roast beef, baked ham or stuffed chicken (or perhaps all of the above) with twice-baked potatoes, green bean casserole and scalloped onions. Cream puffs and chocolate mousse could be the desserts. The tab: $20 each, payable in advance. "Cancellations allowed only for impassable roads."

Mrs. Stoker, a widow who is helped in the kitchen by her eldest daughter Lou Ann, said she got the idea from farm dinners in nearby Brookfield and Turin. "I've been cooking all my life," says Nancy, "plus farming isn't a very prosperous business now. So I thought we'd branch out and keep the family homestead. We're doing basic, old-fashioned cooking – there's enough gourmet cooking out there."

No liquor is served, but guests may bring "a limited amount of wine" to accompany dinner. The Stokers serve groups and private parties by reservation on other nights, but have been doing the Saturday night dinners for the public quite successfully since 1991.

Dinner by reservation, Saturday at 7.

Ye Olde Landmark Tavern, Route 20, Bouckville. (315) 893-1810.

This odd-looking landmark (half an octagon, with four cobblestoned facades) has been a restaurant since 1970, when it was acquired by Andrew Hengst, head of the food service department at Colgate University, and his sons Jock and Steve.

Theirs is an attractive operation, seating 120 in four beamed and stenciled dining rooms, the wainscoting and trim in each painted a different color.

The menu is basic upstate New York traditional, running from $8.95 for baked stuffed chicken or broiled steer liver with a rasher of bacon to $15.95 for filet mignon or New York strip steak. In between are roast duckling à l'orange, chicken cordon bleu, broiled pork loin, broiled or deep-fried sea scallops, brook trout amandine and three versions of turf and surf. The day's special at our latest visit was veal marsala, $13.95.

Appetizers are tomato juice, soup, shrimp cocktail, french-fried onion rings, deep-fried mushrooms, deep-fried cauliflower and deep-fried clams. The short, rather appalling wine list is priced from $7.95 to $16.95. The house wines are $8.95 a liter.

The dessert list includes five kinds of parfait, cheesecake, apple crisp à la mode, pies and bread pudding with bourbon sauce.

Dinner nightly, 5 to 9 or 10, Sunday 1 to 8.

462

Diversions

Cazenovia and environs are a do-it-yourself kind of place. Guests at some inns have lake privileges; otherwise Cazenovia Lake is generally viewed from afar. Swimming in Lakeland Park is reserved for village residents.

Sightseeing. The 33-year-old Cazenovia Preservation Foundation, whose land-use guide is a model for groups across the country, publishes two self-guiding maps. One details five walks in a village known for its architecture. The planned community was laid out by Holland Land Company agent John Lincklaen, whose taste in building kept the Federal style in Cazenovia long after it was out of favor elsewhere. Although Greek Revival and Gothic styles also are prominent, the village reflects the gamut of 19th-century architectural styles. One tour takes in the out-of-the-way village green and the campus of Cazenovia College, a former seminary and junior college for women, now a co-ed four-year institution with 1,050 students. The other map outlines five driving tours, one around the lake and the others taking off in all four directions. Not to be missed is **Chittenango Falls,** where Chittenango Creek drops 136 feet.

Shopping. Seemingly every other store along tree-lined Albany Street has the name Cazenovia in it, from **Cazenovia Jewelry** to **Cazenovia Fabrics** to **Cazenovia Cookware.** One of our favorites, **Cazenovia Abroad,** displays European and Asian giftware, including a double-decker checker bus for kids, nutcrackers resembling Scotsmen and Mounties, stained-glass vases and paper weights, sterling silver tree ornaments and Cazenovia tote bags. The store opens into **P.E. Mulligan's,** an updated dry goods store with handknit sweaters and cute children's clothes. **Details,** an interior design studio, stocks the fabulous hand-painted china from MacKenzie-Childs in nearby Aurora; we coveted a small pitcher but balked at the price. The emphasis at **Serendipity Gifts & Crafts** seems to be on dried flower creations. The most versatile gift shop is **The Cheshire Cat,** with a mix of toiletries, kitchenware, cards, Cazenovia T-shirts, Lorenzo towels and a small Christmas shop.

Antiquing. The Cazenovia area has ten antiques shops, but the biggest concentration is along Route 20 to the east in Bouckville and Madison. A guide details 39, some harboring a number of dealers. More than 1,000 dealers attend the annual mid-August **Madison-Bouckville Antiques Show,** the biggest in New York State.

Extra-Special

Lorenzo State Historic Site, Route 13, Cazenovia. (315) 655-3200.

Every area should be so lucky as to have a treasure like this in its front yard. The showy brick mansion was built in 1807 by John Lincklaen, the Holland Land Company agent who founded Cazenovia. He is thought to have named it for Lorenzo di Medici, the Renaissance patron of Florence, whose work he admired. The visitor center in the restored carriage house is an excellent introduction to the man, the house and the times. Here you see a huge curtain quarter coach and other carriages and sleighs. Guided tours leave here every half hour for the mansion, which was occupied by Lincklaen descendants, including Ledyards, Fairchilds and Remingtons (of Remington Arms) until it was given to the state in 1968. The furnishings are original, reflecting the different periods and styles of the occupants over 160 years. Visitors can't help but be impressed by the majestic entry hall with its vivid pink patterned wallpaper, the Federal-style drawing room, the bedrooms and a library of 4,000 volumes. A brochure details a self-guided tour of the formal gardens and grounds, site for numerous community events. Open mid-May through October, Wednesday-Saturday 10 to 5, Sunday 1 to 5. Grounds open all year, dawn to dusk. Free.

Ithaca, N.Y.

The Little Apple

"Ithaca Is Gorges," say the ubiquitous bumper stickers hereabouts. The play on words is apt. Gorges slice through and around the biggest city in the Finger Lakes region, creating waterfalls that cascade almost into downtown. And the scenery is gorgeous, thanks to all the gorges, the surrounding hills and Cayuga Lake. The Cornell University campus, which straddles some of the most gorgeous of the gorges, is to our minds the most scenic in America.

Hills rise sharply all around this city cradled at the southern end of Cayuga Lake. Only the downtown and west side are flat. Everything else in Ithaca is on hillsides, some as steep as any in San Francisco. The views from parts of the Cornell campus and the posh Cayuga Heights residential section are as dramatic as those in Berkeley.

Cornell landmarks overlook Cayuga Lake.

Ithaca is also called "The Little Apple," a reference to its big-city status as a cultural and arts center. Ithaca is home to both Cornell University (an Ivy Leaguer with 12,500 undergrads and 5,600 graduate students) and Ithaca College (the largest private residential college in New York State with 6,400 students). The ivied Cornell and the modern Ithaca campuses sprawl across hilltops on opposite sides of town, though Cornell is much the larger presence. Together their student bodies nearly equal the year-round population of the city (29,500). The students and their faculties make for a lively academic and arts community.

Ithaca remains a small town at heart, however. One of our visits coincided with a flying trip by then Vice President Dan Quayle to visit his son at a summer soccer camp and to take in the panoramic view of Ithaca, as everyone does, from the fifth-floor gallery of the Herbert F. Johnson Museum of Art. The Ithaca Journal ho-hummed the story the next day under a one-column inside headline, "Quayle Drops In."

Where there is such scenery and sophistication, good restaurants, shops and inns are sure to follow. Ithaca harbors more than its share. One block of North Aurora Street in downtown has five restaurants in a row for starters. Downtown, with its main street turned into a pleasant pedestrian mall, bustles at all hours, thanks to good shops, galleries and eateries. The area has the only four-diamond, four-star country inn in New York State as well as more than 30 bed and breakfasts at last count. Ithaca has the largest farmers' market on the East Coast for a city its size. It also has a new winery

Sherry and Charles Rosemann have built Rose Inn into highly rated inn and restaurant.

inside the city limits, and is the starting point of the Cayuga Wine Trail. Three large state parks with waterfalls and gorges have Ithaca addresses, as do the spectacular Cornell Plantations gardens and the Sapsucker Woods wildlife sanctuary.

All these assets add up to a quality of life that ranked Ithaca first in the East in a book, "Rating Guide to Life in America's Small Cities." Little wonder that the Ithaca area is one of the fastest-growing in New York State.

Inn Spots

The Rose Inn, 813 Auburn Road (Route 34), Box 6576, Ithaca 14851. (607) 533-7905.

In less than a decade, the old "House with a Circular Staircase" has been transformed into New York State's first four-star, four-diamond country inn, as rated by Mobil and AAA. That comes as no surprise to those who know Charles Rosemann, who moved to Ithaca to manage the Cornell University hotel school's Statler Inn, and his dynamic wife Sherry. The large and classic Italianate mansion they bought in 1983 had such potential that Charles left his Statler job to devote full time to the inn that Sherry seemingly had started somewhat as a lark.

Located in the hilly countryside twelve miles north of Ithaca, this has become a destination for travelers. Starting with five guest rooms and mostly shared baths, the Rosemanns have worked constantly to improve the guest quarters. They now have ten rooms with private baths, plus five glamorous suites with fireplaces and jacuzzis for two. A parlor with a game table, a living room with Victorian furniture, TV, books and games, outdoor terraces and a rear rose garden are also available for guests' enjoyment.

The Rosemann's latest addition, planned for 1995, was to be a casual restaurant and lounge in their new conference center, discreetly located out of the way on the main floor of a carriage house at the side of the property. The conference center, which accommodates up to 44 people for meetings and meals amidst barnwood and oriental carpets, is used during the day. On weekend evenings, Sherry planned to transform it into **The Carriage House** to offer northern Italian cuisine, grilled seafood "and the best burgers in town." Live jazz in the non-smoking lounge was expected to draw the public as well as house guests.

Despite the growth, the man who answers the inn's phone and welcomes guests is apt to be Charles, a hands-on innkeeper if ever there was one, and Sherry still is involved in cooking first-rate dinners in the inn.

The inn's guest rooms are individually decorated by Sherry. Those in a newer two-story addition capture the classic flavor of the rest of the house. They are luxurious, from their lace curtains, ceiling fans and fresh flowers to their luggage racks, terry robes, Vitabath and other amenities. In two, the bathroom fixtures (including a stretch-out tub) are from the Eastman House in Rochester. Folk art and antiques abound. Our rear suite contained a sunken jacuzzi in a garden-like space filled with plants, a majestic kingsize bed and antique furnishings in the bedroom, a large closet and a modern bathroom. At nightly turndown, a candle is apt to be lit beside the bed, the towels replenished, your toiletries neatly lined up on the bath vanity and your clothing hung in the closet. A thank you note wishes "Sweet Dreams."

Breakfast is an event worthy of the rest of the Rose Inn experience. It's served in the parlor, the dining room or the foyer with its beautiful parquet floor. Rose mats are on the polished wood tables, as are white baskets full of seasonal flowers. The juice glasses sport the Rosemann crest. Because fifteen varieties of apples are picked from their orchard, homemade cider is often poured. Also on the table are Sherry's jams and preserves – maybe spiced blueberry or strawberry-rhubarb. Local fruit is served in summer (we loved the raspberries), often with the Rosemanns' own crème fraîche. The main dish could be an omelet with smoked salmon and croissants, or perhaps cream cheese, bagels and lox. Charles's specialty is his puffy Black Forest apple pancake with raspberry syrup, which we found absolutely yummy. The coffee is his own blend of beans, including Kona from Hawaii.

The Rosemanns set an elegant dinner table as well, with candles, flowers, sterling silver and sparkling wine glasses. The many-course dinner at $50 per person is optional for inn guests and must be booked in advance. A few non-guests may reserve if space is available.

Our dinner started with smoked oysters in a puff pastry and a hot artichoke strudel on a bed of pureed tomatoes. The colorful salad was a work of art: Boston lettuce with snow peas, radicchio, watercress and sprouts, dotted with red and yellow peppers and red and yellow tomatoes, and dressed with a raspberry-dijon vinaigrette. The rack of lamb (done by Charles on an outdoor grill, even in winter), served on a glaze of madeira with red currant jelly and cumin, and a veal chop with chanterelles were garnished with baby ears of corn. Scampi Mediterranean style is served on a bed of acini, the sauce including a touch of curry with pinenuts on top. Our favorite vegetable was the potato basket, which comes with every dinner. Individual grand marnier soufflés with chocolate or a foamy brandy sauce are a perfect end to the meal. The wine list is well chosen and affordably priced.

Whether it be for food or lodging, the Rose Inn is a class act.

Doubles, $110 to $160; suites, $185 to $250. Two-night minimum on weekends. Dinner by reservation, Tuesday-Saturday at 7. Carriage House, dinner and music, Thursday-Saturday 5:30 to 10:30; Sunday brunch, 11 to 2. No smoking.

Hanshaw House B&B occupies restored 1830 farmhouse with a second-story addition.

Hanshaw House B&B, 15 Sapsucker Woods Road, Ithaca 14850. (607) 257-1437 or (800) 257-1437.

She loves country inns, decorating and entertaining, so the wife of an Ithaca College dean put it all together in this sumptuous country B&B. Helen Scoones, who used to work for a decorator, did the decorating herself in this restored 1830 farmhouse with a second-story addition and a new rear wing for the couple's living quarters.

Hanshaw House has four air-conditioned guest rooms, all with private baths and two with sitting areas. Each is furnished with great panache and an eye to the comforts of home. We lucked into the second-floor suite, with a queensize feather bed, down comforter and pillows, English country antique furnishings, a modern bath and plenty of space to spread out. We didn't need so much space, for we had the run of the house – a stylish living room outfitted in chintz and wicker with dhurries all over, a side TV room, and Adirondack chairs in a pleasant yard backing up to a small pond and woods full of deer, woodchucks and other wildlife.

Helen greets guests with iced lemon tea or mulled cider and cookies in the living room. Always upgrading her rooms, at our latest visit she showed the newly tiled bathroom, the floral sheets and the new curtains in a main-floor bedroom that she decorated in "MacKenzie-esque style," a reference to the colorful pottery from the nearby MacKenzie-Childs studio.

Gardens are now on view on both sides from the refurbished television room. Beyond it in the new wing is "my pièce de résistance," a formal dining room with a crystal chandelier, oriental rugs on pegged floors and french doors opening onto the rear patio and gardens

Early-risers are pampered with a choice of exotic coffees, best taken at a table in the country kitchen as Helen prepares a gourmet breakfast. Ours included fresh orange juice, an orange-banana yogurt frappe and Swedish pancakes puffed in the oven with peaches and crème fraîche. Other main courses could be quiche, frittata with homemade popovers, baked french toast with caramel sauce, baked eggs and heart-shaped waffles.

Breakfast is served in the new dining room on blue and white china. The table is set with crocheted lace mats and field flowers in colorful MacKenzie-Childs pottery. The candles are dressed with MacKenzie-Childs lamp shades and the glasses are handpainted with rosebuds. They epitomize the interesting touches that abound at Hanshaw House.

Doubles, $72 to $98.

Buttermilk Falls B&B, 110 East Buttermilk Falls Road, Ithaca 14850. (607) 273-3947.

Guests leave this very personal B&B with full stomachs and hugs from innkeeper Margie Rumsey. You'd expect no less, for breakfast is quite a riot with guests in the dining room bartering and exchanging jams, seconds and whatnot with those on the porch, and Margie encouraging it all as she cooks up a storm on her new AGA cast-iron cooker in the kitchen in the midst of all the fun.

First you help yourself to juices, including local grape and apple cider. Then you build your own "cereal sundae" with a hot whole grain (rye, at our visit), several kinds of fruits, local honey, yogurt sauce and four kinds of milk from skim to heavy cream. A big loaf of French or Italian bread is placed on each table, where people break off chunks and lather it with butter and one of Margie's homemade jams, perhaps gooseberry or apricot with ginger (here starts the bartering). There follow sticky rolls (as if anyone needs them), bacon and scrambled eggs jazzed up with herbs Margie manages to pick from the garden between courses. All the while she keeps up a steady chatter with guests on all sides.

Such is the start of a typical day – if there's any such thing as typical here – at this attractive white brick 1825 house, the closest private building to the foot of Buttermilk Falls. Energetic Margie, a one-woman dynamo, came to the home of her late husband's grandfather as a bride in 1948. When her youngest son graduated from Cornell in 1983, she opened it as Ithaca's first B&B and has been improving it ever since.

Now all four guest rooms have private baths, and some retain a homey look (including built-in cupboards like one of us grew up with). Good art of Finger Lakes scenes, oriental rugs and early American antiques grace each room. We enjoyed the luxurious downstairs bedroom with a woodburning fireplace and a double jacuzzi surrounded by plants in the corner, from which Buttermilk Falls can be glimpsed through a hedge. Recently, Margie painted pink the mahogany walls of an upstairs room with a little kitchen and out came the fancy Rose Room. She also redid the living room in a Colonial English tavern look, with Queen Anne loveseats facing each other in front of the fireplace. A rear carriage house contains a two-room cottage good for families.

Classical music plays throughout the public rooms. They include the plant-filled dining room notable for a long cherry table flanked by twelve different styles of windsor chairs made by her son Ed, the aforementioned eat-in kitchen and an attractive screened porch where we had breakfast, facing a garden in one corner.

Doubles, $88 to $125; jacuzzi room, $195. Smoking restricted.

The Federal House, 175 Ludlowville Road, Lansing 14882. (607) 533-7362 or (800) 533-7362.

Antiques collector Diane Carroll closed her former Decker Pond Inn south of Ithaca and reopened north of town in the historic mill hamlet of Ludlowville. An antique carriage is a signature decorative item on the front yard, as it was at Decker Pond. Here, instead of a pond, Diane has Salmon Creek Falls within earshot, plus a park-like setting. She has fashioned a great side yard, complete with prolific flower gardens, a gazebo, a trellis and an old bench. There's an expansive wicker-filled side porch for taking it all in.

Diane stripped the interior of the gracious 1815 house to its original woodwork and floors before decorating it elegantly in the Federal style. The fireplace mantels are

Side porch at The Federal House overlooks park-like setting.

believed to have been hand-carved by Brigham Young, who worked as an apprentice carpenter in the area in the early 1800s. Candles flicker by day in the handsome living room and at breakfast in the formal dining room.

Any cook would covet Diane's enormous country kitchen that stretches across the back of the house and includes a center island and a dining area. Here she prepares lavish breakfasts for guests. One day it might involve fresh orange juice, an apple-banana crisp with sour cream sauce, banana bran muffins and orange french toast with cinnamon-peach sauce. Another day could bring cantaloupe with lime-yogurt sauce and fresh mint, a zucchini frittata, bacon and blueberry muffins. Individual vegetable soufflés are served with steamed asparagus and broiled tomatoes on the side.

Upstairs in the front of the house is the Seward Suite, named for William Seward of nearby Auburn, secretary of state under Abraham Lincoln. He courted his future wife in this, her uncle's summer house. The suite comes with a queensize canopy four-poster and a sitting area with a fireplace. Also with air-conditioning and private baths are two more bedrooms reached by a steep rear staircase. Each is decorated with flair and appointed with antiques. An adjacent sitting room with ivy painted on walls and ceiling is equipped with a TV and a refrigerator. It has day beds that may be pressed into service if the need arises.

A collector with great taste, Diane sells antiques and gifts in her little Blueberry Muffin Gift Corner at the side entrance.

Doubles, $100 to $115; suite, $120. No smoking.

The Hound & Hare, 1031 Hanshaw Road, Ithaca 14850. (607) 257-2821.
Lace, antiques and family heirlooms abound in this stately white brick house in a residential area, surrounded by tall trees and manicured lawns and gardens. Innkeeper Zetta Sprole's ancestors built the house in 1829 on property given them by George Washington for service in the Revolutionary War.

Guests settle into three upstairs bedrooms with private baths, two with queensize beds and each resplendent with eyelet trimmed sheets, down pillows and fluffy comforters. One bedroom adjoins a porch-like room with twin beds, so its occupants have a choice of sleeping accommodations.

Zetta bills as "a Victorian fantasy" her well-dressed living room and a cozy library with TV and stereo. She offers afternoon tea and crumpets, and directs guests out to the back yard to enjoy herb gardens, rose beds and a lily pond and fountain.

Morning brings a candlelight breakfast served with fine china, silver and crystal in the dining room or on the porch. Apple pancakes or quiche could be the main course, supplemented by turkey sausages and fruit compote.

Zetta also offers a two-bedroom country Victorian cottage named **The Cudde Duck** on Cayuga Lake, twelve miles north of Ithaca in Lake Ridge. The suite holds a queen bed, while a second bedroom contains four twins. The kitchen is stocked and breakfast is help-yourself, the hostess says, since "I can't be in two places at once." Cottage rates range from $125 to $150 a night.

Doubles, $65 to $95. No smoking.

Peregrine House, 140 College Ave., Ithaca 14850. (607) 272-0919.

This 1874 brick Victorian located three blocks from the Cornell campus has been a B&B since 1986. At our latest visit, the cozy parlor with its two wing chairs beside the fireplace was decorated with vases of black-eyed susans and Queen Anne's lace, and fresh fruit and candy were set around for guests.

Each of the eight bedrooms on the second and third floors (four with private baths, four with w.c. and sink and sharing showers) are different. Most have a fresh Laura Ashley look. All are air-conditioned, and all have TVs and clock radios. Pretty linens, thick towels, soaps and shampoos (and even Woolite) are nice touches. Room 203, the largest, has tulips on the comforter and cabbage roses on the shower curtain.

Innkeeper Nancy Falconer, who was a social worker for 25 years, serves a full breakfast of juices, plates of fresh fruit, and always a choice of two main courses; maybe french toast, blueberry pancakes, belgian waffles or a tomato, cheese and bacon omelet. Coffee beans from Gourmet Delight in the Triphammer Mall are delivered still warm from roasting. In the afternoon, tea or lemonade and gingersnaps are served on the front or side porches or in the parlor.

Doubles, $79 to $109.

La Tourelle, 1150 Danby Road (Route 96B), Ithaca 14850. (607) 273-2734 or (800) 765-1492.

A French-style country inn or a glorified motel? We've heard plenty of references to both, though this white stucco building trimmed with brown certainly looks more like the former than the latter. The points of interest on a walking map of the grounds given to guests are listed in French, and what could be more French country inn-like than that?

La Tourelle was built in 1986 by Walter Wiggins, a partner in the well-known L'Auberge du Cochon Rouge restaurant next door (which was damaged by fire in 1994 and reopened as the John Thomas Steakhouse). The building is set back from the road on a 75-acre property descending to Buttermilk Falls State Park.

The glamorous, plant-filled lobby is notable for colorful tiled floors. Three comfy sofas are in front of a stone fireplace, blazing in winter. Thirty-three spacious rooms and two executive suites, one with a fireplace, are handsomely appointed in elegant country French style. Each has king or queen beds, good art, color TVs, VCRs (movies are available at the front desk), and tiled and marble bathrooms. A decanter of Spanish sherry awaits in each room.

The most memorable are the two round "romantic tower suites," which must be seen to be believed. Each has a sunken circular waterbed, a double jacuzzi just behind it, a TV mounted over the door and a mirrored ceiling.

An optional continental breakfast will be delivered to the room for $5.95 per person. Meals from the restaurant are available through room service.

Doubles, $75 to $110; suites, $110 to $125.

Thomas Farm, 136 Thomas Road, Ithaca 14850. (607) 539-7477.

Electric candles glow in the windows year-round at this trim white farmhouse along a rural road southeast of Ithaca. Glenn Schneider and his wife Edie, whose family has owned the house since it was built about 1850, offer four bedrooms, two with private baths, and a coveted main-floor suite with a kitchenette and hand stenciling on the ceiling. All are handsomely appointed with antique wallpaper, quilts and brass beds, all but one of them queensize.

Edie Schneider greets guests with lemonade or tea and cookies on the side porch or on a patio on the other side of the house. In the morning, she prepares a hearty breakfast. Typical fare includes juice, fresh fruit, homemade muffins and a main course, perhaps an omelet, french toast or scrambled eggs with hash browns. The wooded, 120-acre farm property is laced with walking trails.

Doubles, $60 to $75.

Sarah's Dream, 49 West Main St., Dryden 13053. (607) 844-4321.

Tea service, "Sentimentals," collections and Victoriana are featured at Sarah's Dream, named by innkeeper Judi Williams for her mother, "who always wanted her own business." Her mother never took the plunge, but her daughter realized the dream.

A six-item tea, from cucumber sandwiches and mini-vegetable quiches to scones and walnut pie, is served English style with antique china and linens in the dining room of the 1828 Greek Revival house, which is listed on the National Register of Historic Places. Seven kinds of tea, including the house blend, are offered for $9.50. It's available by reservation at 12:30 and 2:30 Tuesday, Wednesday and Thursday.

Sentimentals is Judi's aptly named nostalgia shop in a rear building, laden with country treasures from tea cozies to vintage dolls, old hats to tender greeting cards.

The collections continue inside the main house, where vintage hats rest on a rack in the front hall. "I collect almost everything," says Judi. Some of her finds are displayed, with restraint, in the five bedrooms. All have private baths and two are two-room suites.

The main-floor suite comes with a queensize brass bed, a fireplaced parlor with a queensize sofa bed, TV and VCR and a side porch. Upstairs is a suite with a kingsize bed and a sitting room with a twin bed and TV. The Rose Room contains wicker chairs and a queensize canopy bed with ornate headboard. Stuffed cats or rabbits are to be found in all the rooms.

Judi serves a breakfast that includes fresh fruit and juices, cereals and a couple of baked items, from scones to quiches. Guests are welcomed at check-in with tea, coffee or soft drinks.

Doubles, $68 to $85; suites, $95 to $120.

Benn Conger Inn, 206 West Cortland St., Groton 13073. (607) 898-5817.

A restaurant of distinction for some time (see Dining Spots), this 1921 classic revival mansion is becoming a destination for inn-goers as well. New innkeepers Peter and Alison van der Meulen have been improving the accommodations and plan eventually to quadruple the number of rooms.

Paintings by chef-owner's wife enhance walls at Dano's On Cayuga.

For the moment, the upstairs of their handsome pillared mansion offers three suites and one small bedroom. Together, they encompass about 3,500 square feet, and guests have been known to comment that the suites are larger than many a small apartment.

Consider the Dutch Schultz suite, named for the infamous bootlegger and racketeer who found it a safe haven following the departure of original owner Benn Conger, a state senator, banker and founder of the Corona Corporation (later Smith-Corona). The brass bed is outfitted with 310-count percale sheets and down or feather pillows, and the TV is hidden in an armoire. You may get lost in the bathroom, surely one of the world's largest – it seemingly goes on forever in assorted rooms and alcoves. Another suite with fireplaced sitting room and queensize brass bed is furnished in Cape May wicker and comes with a clawfoot tub. A smaller suite with a sleeping porch has a bath with a European shower. The Caswell-Massey and Gilchrist & Soames toiletries are stashed in little ceramic bathtubs. Each room contains period furnishings appropriate to the 1920s.

Guests share a small, wicker-furnished common area in the hallway at the head of the stairs. They also can join outside diners in the cozy library/bar with fireplace and piano.

The complimentary breakfast in the pretty conservatory dining room is a five-course feast. Look forward to a choice of juices, fruit (crenshaw melon with mixed berries at our visit) and a pastry course, perhaps Danish aebleskiver, crêpes or blueberry-buttermilk pancakes. Then – can you stand it? – comes the main course. It could be eggs benedict or a frittata with three kinds of wild mushrooms, cheddar and chèvre. The last course is breakfast meats (surely you weren't expecting dessert).

With their renowned dining operation well under control, the van der Meulens were looking to add guest bungalows around their eighteen-acre hilltop property. "We want to get up to fifteen rooms," Alison advised.

Double, $120; suites, $145 to $220. Smoking restricted.

Dining Spots

Dano's On Cayuga, 113 South Cayuga St., Ithaca. (607) 277-8942.

Nearly everyone in Ithaca agrees that Dano's is tops on the city's dining list – for food, value and atmosphere. It's a remarkable accomplishment for a former European ballet dancer who took over a downtown storefront dive in 1990.

Dano (pronounced Dan-yo) Hutnik was born in the Ukraine, grew up in Czechoslovakia and was a ballet dancer for fifteen years in Vienna before entering the restaurant business in New York and San Francisco. A classified ad in the New York Times led him to Ithaca and this old space that he and his wife, artist Karen Gilman, transformed into what they call a French-style bistro in peach and blue-gray. There's seating for 44 at white-linened tables topped with white paper against a backdrop of her striking artworks on the walls. A dramatic vase of gladioli towers over the bar, and desserts are displayed in a nook at the side. Edith Piaf music plays in the background. It's all very crisp, clean and congenial, as Dano table-hops at meal's end and proves to be quite the talker and philosopher.

The short menu of Central European, French and northern Italian fare is handwritten daily. Those in the know go for such specialties as oxtail stew with black and green olives and grilled brine-cured pork chop with spaetzle and braised red cabbage. We shared an appetizer of melted raclette with boiled potatoes, cornichons and pearl onions ($6.50), the classic version and plenty for two.

Main courses are priced from $13.50 for penne with chicken breast, spinach, mushrooms, garlic and feta to $22.95 for rack of lamb in a roasted garlic red wine sauce, served with polenta stuffed with gorgonzola and pinenuts. We found superlative both the sautéed chicken breast with artichokes and sundried tomatoes and served with mouth-watering polenta sticks, and the linguini with shrimp, peas and scallions. We also liked the Hermann J. Weimer dry riesling ($16), the only Finger Lakes choice on a fine little wine list specializing in imported wines and rarely seen Californias. Crème brûlée and a bittersweet chocolate gâteau with raspberry sauce were fantastic endings to one of our more enjoyable meals in a long time.

Dinner, Tuesday-Saturday 5:30 to 9:30, Sunday to 9.

John Thomas Steakhouse, 1152 Danby Road (Route 96B), Ithaca. (607) 273-3464.

A kitchen fire closed the long-popular L'Auberge du Cochon Rouge, a French restaurant of renown, in early 1994. When owner Walter Wiggins rebuilt, he surprised almost everyone by turning the hilltop farmhouse overlooking the Cayuga Lake valley into a New York-style steakhouse. He also surprised local skeptics, some of whom were persuaded that this was even better than its predecessor.

The restaurant's original French theme had run its course and its traditionally masculine decor lent itself to the steakhouse concept, explained manager Mike Kelly, who had overseen a similar venture in Roslyn, Long Island, The interior of the farmhouse remains basically the same, although the interior Red Room was enlarged following the fire. The upstairs L'Auberge Lounge retained links with the past.

Former L'Auberge sous chef William Peterson stayed on as chef, presenting a predictable menu priced from $11.95 for baked scrod to $23.95 for T-bone steak. Prime beef is featured and the house specialty is porterhouse steak, $37.90 for two. There are grilled or blackened tuna, broiled swordfish, broiled salmon, shrimp scampi, a vegetarian platter and a couple of chicken dishes for non-beef eaters. Although all entrées come with a vegetable, the usual salads and side orders cost extra. Appetizers include smoked trout, baked deviled crab, shrimp cocktail and clams casino. Desserts range from old-fashioned bread pudding and assorted ice creams to triple berry strudel.

The fire destroyed L'Auberge's acclaimed wine cellar, but manager Kelly planned to rebuild slowly. At our visit shortly after reopening, there were plenty of good choices priced from the low teens to $60.

Dinner nightly except Monday, 5:30 to 10 or 11; Sunday brunch, 11 to 2.

Renée's, 202 East Falls St., Ithaca. (607) 272-0656.

Within earshot of Ithaca Falls, the highest of the city's many waterfalls. lies this pristine bistro. It's run by Renée Senne, who became known in the area as sous-chef at L'Auberge du Cochon Rouge and chef at the Greystone, upon her return from study-ing at La Varenne in France and teaching at the New York Cooking School.

Bar area at Renee's bistro.

Candles flicker and classical music plays in her intimate dining room and bar area, where the white tablecloths are covered with butcher paper, the windows are shielded by lace cafe curtains, blue lamps hang from the ceilings and posters adorn the walls.

Dinner entrées are priced from $12.50 for lemon chicken served with couscous to $19.75 for lamb chops. Possibilities include grilled Norwegian salmon with roasted new potatoes, pork tenderloin roasted with apples and bacon, roasted game hen provençal and delmonico steak.

Starters could be shrimp cakes served with black beans and roasted pepper sauce, escargots in puff pastry, and Mediterranean vegetables baked in phyllo with goat cheese and sundried tomatoes. One of those plus a hearty salad – say shrimp, artichoke hearts, roasted peppers and olives served on mixed greens – would make a nice summertime supper.

Renée's background as a pastry chef is reflected in such treats as mille-feuille, peach shortcake, apricot genoise with puree, and profiteroles with vanilla ice cream and dark chocolate sauce.

Dinner, Monday-Saturday 5:30 to 10.

Tre Stelle, 120 Third St., Ithaca. (607) 273-8515.

This striking Italian trattoria is the home of wood-fired pizzas and a winning Medi-terranean decor. The owners are designer-architects who did the sculptures in the corners of the dining room, rag-rolled the walls, designed the metal chairs and orchestrated the marble look on the bar. One also is a mushroom expert who picks the chanterelles that turn up in various dishes.

The printed menu is short but sweet: a couple of antipasti, five changing pizzas ($7.50 each), a couple of side dishes and four desserts. At our visit, the chalkboard entrées ($8.50 to $11.50) included lamb shanks with tomatoes and orzo, braciola (flank steak rolled around sausage and egg) and an acclaimed rabbit dish simmered in white wine and bearing a smoky taste from the wood oven. Most folks start with a platter of sweet salami and air-cured ham or the salad of fresh chanterelles on a bed of bibb lettuce, both served with focaccia. The favorite of the pizzas is the della casa (wild mushrooms with sundried tomatoes, caramelized onions and parmesan). Among desserts are ricotta cheesecake with fresh blueberries, polenta cake served with whipped cream and cherry sauce, and almond biscotti.

The excellent all-Italian wine list is priced mostly in the teens.

Dinner, Thursday-Monday 5 to 9:30 or 10:30.

Greystone Inn, 1457 East Shore Drive (Route 34), Ithaca. (607) 273-4096.

Once a bastion of fine dining, this venerable restaurant has risen again in the estimation of local diners. There's no denying the refinement of its several dining rooms with starched white linens, upholstered chairs and a solid, comfortable feeling typical of an expansive fieldstone house built in 1837. And there are few more appealing settings than the rear courtyard, nicely landscaped and outfitted with white wrought-iron tables.

Chef-owner Stephen Dumas is back on track with an updated American/continental menu. Expect main courses ($16.95 to $23.95) like shrimp scampi provençal, grilled swordfish with tomatoes and basil, chicken breast stuffed with spinach and smoked gouda, grilled duck breast framboise, veal piccata and rack of lamb persillade.

Starters could be chilled asparagus dressed with lemon-tarragon vinaigrette or smoked Scottish salmon served with onions, capers and kiev sauce. Desserts include hazelnut-cappuccino torte, bittersweet chocolate chantilly, French chocolate chambord and strawberries romanoff.

Dinner, Monday-Saturday 5:30 to 9 or 9:30.

Coyote Loco, 1876 Judd Falls Road, Ithaca. (607) 277-2806.

A bright blue train depot with yellow stars on the side holds this highly regarded Mexican restaurant and cantina. The depot was moved to the site and nicely transformed with a casual main dining room decked out in Southwestern colors, an upstairs bar and a popular rear deck with an outdoor grill.

The extensive menu embraces the traditional burritos, tacos and enchiladas, most of them done with unusual twists. Witness the puerco pibil burrito (shredded pork in a yucatan sauce of orange and achiote) or the rack of tacos, a sampler of five kinds for $9.75. The "platos unusuales"($10.95 to $14.95) indicate the range of the kitchen. Favorites include ancho chicken, seafood cakes served with an earthy chipotle chile sauce, grilled steak stuffed with black beans and jack cheese, and vegetable molé served with loco beans and a hand-rolled tamale.

Like the menu, the wines and drinks like the frozen house margarita and the piña colada are a cut above the norm. Six Mexican brands are among the beers available.

Open daily, 11:30 to midnight.

Oldport Harbour, 702 West Buffalo St., Ithaca. (607) 272-4868.

The waterside setting is great, but food consistency tends to be a problem at this neat place billed as "a little bit of Europe on the Cayuga inlet." Although there are several interior dining rooms with bentwood chairs at light wood tables with blue mats, we'd dine outside any time we could, on the far garden terrace beside an outdoor bar or on the near deck with the new MV Manhattan tour boat moored beside.

The latter was the setting for a Sunday jazz brunch that brought back memories of New Orleans. One of us tried the clams monte carlo ($5.25) and the pâté maison ($3.75), while the other splurged on poached eggs Oldport with smoked salmon, brie and hollandaise sauce ($9.50), accompanied by roast potatoes, onions and fresh fruit garnish. Everything was adequate, but secondary to the canalside setting and the music.

A few salads and sandwiches are offered, at considerably lower prices, on the daily lunch menu.

Dinner entrées run from $11.95 for chicken mornay to $19.50 for beef wellington or shrimp flambéed in cognac and served over angel-hair pasta. Veal homard, cornish game hen, marinated salmon and steak au poivre are among the offerings. Linzer torte, fresh fruit tarts, cheesecake and German chocolate cake are possible desserts.

Oldport Harbour also runs dinner cruises on the MV Manhattan. A three-hour tour of Cayuga Lake leaves from the restaurant nightly at 6, May-October.

Lunch, Monday-Saturday 11:30 to 2; dinner nightly, 5:30 to 9 or 10; Sunday brunch, 11 to 2:30.

Thai Cuisine, 501 South Meadow St., Ithaca. (607) 273-2031.

Knowledgeable Thai-food lovers consider this the best Thai food in upstate New York. It's served in a serene, white and pink linened dining room in a commercial plaza by a Thai family in the kitchen and a mainly American staff out front.

There's a staggering choice of soups, salads and appetizers at dinner. They range from shrimp chips with special house dip for $2.50 to yum-ta-lay, a salad of shrimp, clams, scallops, squid, mint leaves and fresh chile peppers for $9.95.

It's difficult to choose among such entrées as panang-neur, sliced tender beef simmered in panang sauce with sweet basil and pineapple, served with a side of pickled cauliflower, and gaeng-goong, shrimp simmered in Thai green curry with coconut milk, baby corn, straw mushrooms, chile peppers and kaffir lime. Only a few of the chef's specials cost more than $12.95.

The menu changes daily at lunch, when about six main courses are served with soup or salad for $4.95 to $6.50. The famous Sunday brunch is like a dim sum brunch, offering about 40 little plates for $1.95 each.

Lunch, Tuesday-Friday 11 to 2; dinner Tuesday-Sunday 5 to 9:30 or 10; Sunday brunch, 11:30 to 2.

Moosewood Restaurant, 215 North Cayuga St., Ithaca. (607) 273-9610.

This 1960s-ish establishment on the lower level of the downtown Dewitt Mall is known to vegetarians around the country through the *Moosewood Cookbook,* written by one of the former owners of the co-op operation. Visitors come from all over, some deciding that the cookbook is better than the restaurant. Which is a hazard of a laid-back operation in which chefs rotate in the kitchen and the menu changes twice daily.

Prices are quite modest, entrées at lunch $5 and at dinner, $8.50 to $10. Along with regulars like pita sandwiches, lasagna and tofuburgers, the blackboard menu lists an imaginative selection of casseroles, curries, ragouts, salads and luscious homemade desserts like walnut baklava, chocolate glazed hazelnut cake and a plum tart with whipped cream. At one visit, we liked the sound of tagine, a North African vegetable stew simmered with lemon and saffron on couscous. Moosewood is not strictly vegetarian – varied seafood dishes are offered Thursday through Sunday. Fresh pasta is featured Wednesday or Thursday nights, and Sunday nights are devoted to different ethnic cuisines. Beer and wines are available.

Folks sit in a row of chairs outside to wait for tables inside the recently refurbished dining room. A canopied patio is used for outdoor dining at night.

Lunch, Monday-Saturday 11:30 to 2; dinner nightly, 6 to 9 or 9:30. No credit cards. No smoking.

Benn Conger Inn, 206 West Cortland St., Groton. (607) 898-5817.

The dining operation put this renowned inn on the map, and Ithacans often make the short trip to enjoy special-occasion splurges. Chef-owner Peter van der Meulen mans the kitchen, while his wife Alison does the baking and oversees the front of the house.

The main floor of the Colonial Revival mansion holds a cozy library/lounge and three elegant dining rooms enhanced by fine artworks done by a family friend. Along

the side is a smashing porch/conservatory in white and green, where tables are set with white linens and fresh flowers. The colorful candlesticks and flower pots that grace each table, handpainted by a local artisan, are for sale.

Peter's Mediterranean-inspired cuisine includes appetizers like fish-shaped ravioli filled with smoked salmon and served in a light tomato cream sauce, coquilles St. Jacques and marinated artichoke hearts served hot with gruyère and chèvre. Main courses ($16 to $24) are as varied as shrimp, scallops and mussels in cognac cream, served over black lobster-filled ravioli; smoked chicken ravioli carbonara; grilled flank steak provençal, and rack of lamb with raspberry-mint sauce.

Alison's desserts prove worthy endings, among them an acclaimed crème brûlée with blackberries, a classic French cheesecake with mascarpone and cream cheese, and profiteroles with varied ice creams. The wine list has won the Wine Spectator award of excellence since 1987.

Conservatory at Benn Conger Inn.

Dinner, Wednesday-Sunday 5:30 to 9.

Diversions

The beautiful Cornell University campus and its gorges and Beebe Lake are not to be missed. Pick up a city or a campus map to avoid getting hopelessly lost.

The Gorges. Cascadilla, Fall and Six Mile creeks slice through the city, and Ithaca Falls plummets 150 feet near the Ithaca High School campus. At the edge of town is **Buttermilk Falls State Park.** Buttermilk Creek drops more than 500 feet through dramatic rock formations in a series of cascades and rapids into a swimming hole at the foot of the falls. Nearby, trails in **Robert H. Treman State Park** wind through Enfield Glen for three miles, passing twelve cascades, sink holes and 115-foot-high Lucifer Falls. Just up Cayuga Lake is **Taughannock Falls State Park,** where the 215-foot-high falls are higher than Niagara. All have swimming, picnic areas and hiking trails.

Sapsucker Woods Sanctuary, 159 Sapsucker Woods Road, Ithaca, 254-2473. Home of the famed Cornell Laboratory of Ornithology, the sanctuary has 200 acres and more than four miles of trails through woodlands and over swamps and ponds. Huge picture windows in the Lyman K. Stuart Observatory look onto a garden filled with bird feeders and a ten-acre pond abounding with wildlife. Chairs and telescopes are provided. Original works by renowned artist Louis Agassiz Fuertes are hung in the hallways, and the Crow's Nest Birding Shop has a large selection of bird-related items.

Ithaca Farmers' Market, Steamboat Landing, Ithaca. Ithacans are justly proud of one of the more flourishing farmers' markets in the East. All items for sale are grown, baked or produced by vendors within a 30-mile radius. We've been particularly impressed with the juried crafts and the ethnic foods. Entertainers perform and a festival atmosphere prevails. The market is open seasonally, Saturdays 9 to 2 (April-December), Sundays 11 to 3 (June-October) and Tuesdays 9 to 1 (mid-May to November).

Cayuga Wine Trail. The only Eastern city we know of with a vineyard inside its limits is Ithaca. **Six Mile Creek Vineyard,** one of the region's newest, is nestled on the slope of a valley at 1551 Slaterville Road (Route 79). Picnic tables look across the vineyards and hills, a European-style setting for the sampling of chardonnays, rieslings, seyvals and such, priced in the $6.50 to $10 range. Seven other wineries on the west side of Cayuga Lake, including **Knapp, Hosmer, Swedish Hill, Lucas and Cayuga Ridge** form the Cayuga Wine Trail. A special attraction for lunch and dinner is the fine new **Restaurant at Knapp Vineyards.**

Museums and Galleries. Housed in a stunning eleven-story building designed by I.M. Pei, the **Herbert F. Johnson Museum of Art** at Cornell University is one of the country's leading university art museums. The late Johnson Wax Co. chairman gave the building, best known for its Rockwell Galleries of Asian Art, nicely displayed on the fifth floor where wraparound windows offer awesome views in all directions and visitors can lose sight of the art for the scenery. Other notable collections are those of American art and decorative arts, including 200 pieces of Tiffany glass. Special exhibitions show its diversity and quality; we found one on "American Clothing: Identity in Mass Culture" to be of great interest. Other galleries are scattered about town and downtown. We were particularly impressed by the **Gallery at 15 Steps** and the **State of the Art Gallery.**

Shopping. The Downtown Ithaca Commons, formed by closing a section of State Street to vehicular traffic, is a downtown pedestrian marketplace that works. Trees, landscaping, benches and sidewalk cafes provide a pleasant people place, and plenty of people seem to be around at all hours. The Thursday night Concerts on the Commons are popular in summer. Most of Ithaca's best stores are not in the suburban malls but here. Among our favorites: **Especially in Ithaca** displays handmade footstools resembling a golfer, a lumber jack and a businessman in loafers, suspenders and necktie, so lifelike you'd not want to put your feet on them, among a remarkable array of handcrafted jewelry, fashion accessories and home furnishings by fine artisans. Its sister store, **People's Pottery,** is particularly strong on jewelry. We loved the special cat show at **Handwork,** Ithaca's co-op craft store – crafted cats in all forms from tea cozies to enamel pins to stained glass to a scare cat for the garden. The expanded **Now You're Cooking** offers hard-to-find gadgets, classic cookware and unusual accessories. All kinds of outdoor equipment and clothing are available at **Wildware.**

Extra-Special

Cornell Plantations, One Plantations Road, Ithaca. (607) 255-3020.

The arboretum, botanical garden and natural areas of Cornell University are collectively known as the Plantations. They total nearly 3,000 acres of woodlands, gorges, gardens and lakeside trails bordering the campus. We were quite unprepared for their size or their scope. The Robison York State herb garden, for instance, has sixteen theme beds and 400 species surrounded by antique and shrub roses. Nature lovers could spend hours here. A driving tour past sculptures, ponds, test gardens and tree collections (many of them marked as Cornell class gifts) gives a quick overview, but all the cyclists and walkers have the right idea. If time is short, at least take the self-guided walking tour around Beebe Lake. The Garden Gift Shop in the headquarters building offers all kinds of things from pressed-flower notepaper and magnets to floral glass window hangings. Open daily, dawn to dusk. Free.

Sonnenberg Gardens and Mansion are a major drawing card for visitors to Canandaigua.

Canandaigua/Bristol Hills, N.Y.
The Chosen Place

The Seneca Indians were on the mark when they named this area Kanandagua, "The Chosen Place."

The settlement at the northern end of Canandaigua Lake became the capital of the western frontier. It was the seat of the vast Phelps-Gorham land purchase, the shire town of Ontario, mother of all counties west of Seneca Lake. In 1789 the first office was established here for the sale of land directly to settlers. Leaders of the young nation, four cabinet members among them, lived in stately mansions that still line the broad main street 200 years later.

The westernmost of New York's major Finger Lakes lies cradled between hills. They are particularly majestic at its southern end, an area that has been called "The Switzerland of America." The village there was renamed Naples after a French dignitary said during a visit two centuries ago that the only area of comparable beauty was Naples, Italy. New York's wine industry was born in Naples, and the town paints its fire hydrants purple for the annual Grape Festival in September.

Canandaigua, the western gateway to the Finger Lakes, is a busy summer resort town. Its location beside a lake at the edge of the Rochester metropolitan area makes it the fastest-growing city in New York State (approaching 15,000). The workaday world and the world of summer cottages co-exist side by side. A somewhat tacky lakefront contrasts with the sound of outdoor music at the Finger Lakes Performing Arts Center and the unexpected show of opulence at Sonnenberg Gardens and Mansion.

Just minutes away is the rural tranquility of the Bristol Hills, rising sharply to the south and west of Canandaigua Lake. Here are hidden unspoiled towns, country shops, the highest ski area between the Adirondacks and the Rockies, and a couple of the wineries that help make the Finger Lakes famous. The area holds a fond place in our hearts from our frequent visits when we lived nearby in Geneva and Rochester.

479

Poke along Canandaigua Lake's west shore and the hills and byways above. You'll know, as we do, why the Senecas called this their chosen place.

Inn Spots

Morgan-Samuels Inn, 2920 Smith Road, Canandaigua 14424. (716) 394-9232.

Actor/farmer Judson Morgan, not J.P. Morgan as was originally thought, built this lovely English-style stone house in 1810. A brick wing was added in the early 1900s, and eventually it became the home of Howard Samuels, the plastic-bag inventor and manufacturer who ran unsuccessfully for governor of New York State. Julie and John Sullivan left jobs in Geneseo to buy the house in 1989 and convert it into a masterpiece of a B&B. "We had just visited another B&B," said bubbly Julie, "and knew we were meant to run one." They named it the J.P. Morgan House, only to discover they were in error and, honest to a fault, they renamed it the Morgan-Samuels in 1993.

At the end of a quarter-mile drive lined by maple trees, the house sits like a plantation on a rise with 46 acres of hay fields all around. The scene is truly bucolic. Ducks, turkeys and chickens roam around, and a heifer calf named Kimberly punctuated the tranquility with her mooing as we sat in the slate-floored garden room.

The serenely lovely garden room, a well-furnished living room, a cozy library with TV, a stone-walled and glass-enclosed tea room with potbelly stove, a tennis court and no fewer than four landscaped patios (one with a trickling fountain and another with a lily pond and waterfall) are available for guests. John, who judges livestock shows, plans eventually to add a barn to revive memories of his farming days.

The house contains five guest rooms and the Morgan Suite, a beauty with early 18th-century French furniture, kingsize bed, an extra-long loveseat in front of the TV and a new double jacuzzi in a corner of the bathroom. The Antique Rose Room has a fireplace, a flowered carpet and one of the first kingsize beds ever made. The sunken Garden Room, where the eight Samuels children used to play, has been transformed into a house favorite with a queensize four-poster, a handmade patterned rug from Romania, a cut-lace bedspread from China and a parlor stove in the angled fireplace. The Victorian Room on the third floor, all in burgundies and greens with a tapestry look, has another fireplace, a wonderful bathroom with old stone walls, a kingsize canopy bed, a jacuzzi and lots of Italian marble, not to mention french doors onto a balcony. A fountain sounds like a babbling brook beneath Evy's Chamber, which Julie recently transformed into a Victorian fantasy and named for her mother. It has a rosewood queensize bed, a corner closet ingeniously fashioned from the sideboard of a bed, and a bathroom with raised shower and ceiling in a former closet. Our room on the the third floor, small but exquisitely done, featured a pretty Gothic window beneath a

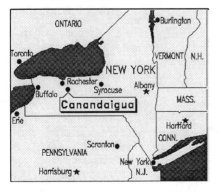

cathedral ceiling. The king bed, awash with fourteen pillows, nearly filled the room. It was neatly tucked into a niche between built-in shelves. The black floral rug matched the wallpaper border. All rooms are air-conditioned, have private baths and are equipped with reproduction radios and tape cassettes.

Breakfast is served in the beamed dining room, in a small breakfast room, in the garden room or on the patio. If the inn is full, all these spaces may be called into use. John is in charge of cooking – he and

Porch-like garden room at Morgan-Samuels Inn looks onto lawns and rural vistas.

five-year-old son Jonathan make an early-morning run to the supermarket to pick out the perfect fruit for the fruit platter, which usually contains two dozen varieties, depending on the season. We counted 26 (and Julie promptly added, "he forgot the blueberries") on the exquisitely put-together silver platter, including local Irondequoit melon, mango, two kinds of grapes, papaya, persimmon, figs, kiwis and prunes sautéed in lemon sauce. With that come fresh orange juice served in delicate etched glasses, a baked apple, muffins (the carrot muffins were huge and delicious) and sticky buns. The main event involves a choice of fluffy buckwheat pancakes with blackberries, blueberries or pecans (or all three), scrambled eggs with herbs, french toast or a six-cheese omelet. We've tried them all but are partial to the omelet, one of the best breakfast treats we've ever had – it looked like a pizza with slices of tomato, scallions, red peppers, onions, jalapeño peppers, mushrooms and lots of herbs and parsley. Monterey jack, mozzarella, parmesan and blue cheeses were on top, and spicy sausage patties and sunflower seed toast (from bread made by Trappist monks) accompanied, as did hazelnut coffee.

Tea (iced or hot) is served in the afternoon, and John will do dinners by advance reservation for six or more guests ($30 to $50 each, depending on number and selection of courses). The birds were chirping, the fountains trickling and classical music playing as we enjoyed dinner by candlelight with fine silver and china in the garden room. Our meal, which John said was typical, produced a procession of whitefish with horseradish sauce, pasta shells in a hot Bahamian sauce, garlic bread, a fabulous chilled peach soup and a mixed salad bearing everything from strawberries and apples to beets, snow peas and artichoke hearts, dressed with raspberry vinaigrette studded with bacon and capers. The main course was filet mignon with a sherry-herb sauce, sided with green beans, mushrooms, cauliflower, potatoes, and broccoli and cheese. Dutch apple pie with ice cream ended a spectacular meal. "I cook the way I like to cook," says John, who has no formal training. He certainly cooks the way we like to eat, although we would have had to be super-human to finish it all.

Music, mostly classical but perhaps New Age in the morning and haunting Gregorian chants at breakfast, is piped throughout the house and across the grounds. The Sullivans display quite a collection of oil paintings, and the bathrooms at their extra-special inn

481

win a prize for the most amenities ever, including toothbrushes. Enchantment, it seems, is in the details.

Doubles, $99 to $150; suite, $195.

The Oliver Phelps Country Inn, 252 North Main St., Canandaigua 14424. (716) 396-1650.

This 19th-century Federal beauty was "the worst-looking house on Main Street" when Joanne and John Sciarratta bought it in 1987. You'd never know it today, such is the transformation the energetic couple have given it. John painted and stenciled every room, his wife decorated with taste, and now it stands out as one of the best-looking houses among many lining the broad main street. The gazebo John built on the wooded side lawn is strategically placed for an advantageous view. The latest addition for guests is a hot tub on the back porch, overlooking the back yard.

The house was once owned by Judge Oliver Phelps, grandson of Oliver Phelps, a Revolutionary War leader who was responsible for the Phelps-Gorham land purchase of 1788. A Tiffany-style lamp with 1,200 pieces of colored glass hangs over the dining-room table. Here Joanne serves a full breakfast of fresh fruit and perhaps a soufflé, omelet, frittata or french toast. Blueberry pancakes and sausages were the fare the morning we visited.

Beyond is an enormous parlor, having been enlarged when a wall was removed during the era when this was a Christian Science church. A group of dolls and teddy bears is ensconced beside one of the sitting areas. Unusual clocks from the couple's collection are located throughout the house.

Upstairs are four air-conditioned guest rooms with private baths. Each bears John's intricate stenciling. Oliver's Suite has a sitting area, a kingsize four-poster bed, a three-quarter brass bed and, for good measure, a cradle. There's a stenciled bench in a bathroom that is as big as many a bedroom, plus stenciling on doors of closets. Geese are the stenciling motif in the Country Duck Room, which has a queensize poster bed and a single bed. Floral stenciling and an Amish painting enhance the Tulip Room. With a daughter off to college, the Sciarrattas have opened a fourth room with a white brass queen bed, stenciling in pinks and blues, a sloping ceiling and the only in-room TV.

Doubles, $75 to $85; suite, $110. Smoking restricted.

Sutherland House, 5285 Bristol St., Canandaigua 14424. (716) 396-0375 or (800) 396-0375.

Diane and Cor Van Der Woude realized a lifelong dream when they opened this B&B in August 1994. Diane, who had been an executive in gourmet food sales with the Wegman's supermarket chain, and her Dutch husband, a carpenter, purchased the deteriorated 1885 Victorian-Gothic summer house, one of five built by Sutherland brothers along Bristol Street in Canandaigua. They undertook a painstaking renovation, knowing exactly what they wanted every step of the way (extra insulation between walls, for instance) and rebuilding accordingly.

The result is four bedrooms, all with new bathrooms. The two largest come with two-person whirlpool baths, kingsize beds and TV/VCRs, and one is a suite with a sitting room. Two smaller bedrooms contain a queensize and double bed, respectively. Guests also enjoy the front parlor, porches and grounds. As you might expect, Diane prepares an elaborate breakfast, which she and her husband partake of with guests. Expect a choice of juices, fresh fruit (baked apple in winter, "which we're tiring of but guests enjoy because they're having it for the first time") and a fancy casserole, french toast or Canadian bacon and eggs. Tea may be offered in the afternoon.

Diane, whose recent business experience had been in human resources, took readily

Oliver Phelps Country Inn occupies Federal house along city's wide main street.

to innkeeping. "I feel like I open a new novel each night as I meet and greet," she reports. "People want to talk and I like to listen."

Doubles, $65 to $115; suite, $135. No smoking.

The Enchanted Rose Inn, 7479 Routes 5 & 20, East Bloomfield 14443. (716) 657-6003.

Her background in the flower business helps explain all the fresh and dried flowers at this new B&B run with TLC by Jan and Howard Buhlmann. "I love flowers," notes Jan, stating the obvious. "So I have them everywhere."

You'll find fresh flowers in the bedrooms and the bathrooms, floral patterns on some of the draperies and bedspreads, garnishes of flowers on the breakfast dishes, a heart-shaped rose garden among the gardens in back, and dried flower arrangements in Everlasting, her gift shop at the rear of the house.

The Buhlmanns share their 1820s Federal-style home with overnight guests in three air-conditioned bedrooms, all with queensize beds and private baths. They're filled with antiques and decorated in an English country style. Each features paintings of local artists. The First Lady's Room offers an antique bed and dresser and two comfy chairs. The Royal Rose Room has a cherry four-poster bed and two antique wicker chairs (one a rocker). The Victoria suite comes with a cherry hand-carved canopy bed draped in lace and awash with pillows, a sofa, a TV with VCR and a small dressing room with another sitting area.

Guests have access to the formal living room but gravitate to a common room that's open to the kitchen. It has a fireplace, TV and a bay window yielding views of the gardens. A handsome display cabinet, obtained from a jewelry store in Rochester, holds quite a collection of bone china and pressed glass in the formal dining room. Breakfast is by candlelight at a table for six. The meal begins with fresh fruit, perhaps fruit salad sprinkled with mint or cantaloupe with raspberries, juice and homemade muffins. The main event could be heart-shaped pecan waffles with brandied peach sauce or an egg soufflé with ham, cheese and mushrooms. Jan garnishes her plates with edible pansies, rose petals and johnny jumpups, and finds that some guests say hers are the first flowers they've ever eaten.

Outside and screened from the highway is a nicely landscaped side and rear yard, full of arbors and gardens. An English garden flanks the rear post-and-beam barn.

Doubles, $95; suite, $125.

The Acorn Inn, 4508 Route 64 South, Box 334, Canandaigua 14424. (716) 229-2834.

Pink impatiens, geraniums and petunias accent the greenery around this handsome, dark brown shingled Federal stagecoach inn built in 1795 in the hamlet of Bristol Center. It's the home and antiques shop of Louis and Joan Clark, he a Canandaigua investment broker and she a specialist in antiques and decorative arts. The grounds include a rear terrace, perennial and rock gardens on two levels, brick walks, mulched nature trails and a creek that meanders into a town park with a jogging track.

The centrally air-conditioned interior is striking as well, appointed in 18th- and early 19th-century English and American formal and country pieces, each priced and for sale. Guests wander through five rooms of antiques shops downstairs before retiring to their rooms, which also are period pieces. The Clarks offer four guest rooms, each with private bath and canopy queen or kingsize bed. All have reading lamps for the side chairs, large closets and thick insulation to muffle noise. The largest is the Bristol (the former ballroom) with king bed, sitting area with TV and a spacious, well-appointed bath with a soaking tub and separate shower. The new Hotchkiss Room comes with floor-to-ceiling windows overlooking the gardens, a sitting area with TV/VCR and a whirlpool tub.

Part of a research library of 5,000 books on art, antiques and architecture enhances the living room. Another common room contains a large 18th-century fireplace ready for hearthside cooking. The attractive dining room and the garden terrace are where the Clarks serve a full breakfast. It might be fresh orange juice, melon garnished with raspberries, french toast and sausages. Pancakes and herb omelets are other favorites.

Tea and sherry are offered in the afternoon. Chocolates and a carafe of ice water accompany nightly turndown service.

Doubles, $95 to $140.

Nottingham Lodge B&B, 5741 Bristol Valley Road, Canandaigua 14424. (716) 374-5355.

The slopes of Bristol Mountain Ski Center across the road are on view from the loft overlooking the soaring great room of this chalet-style lodge that caters to skiers.

But this is no ordinary ski lodge. Bonnie and Bill Robinson have upgraded the creature comforts and decor, providing sprightly furnishings, plush carpeting, floral wallpapers, puffy curtains and queensize brass or canopy beds in three guest rooms, each with private bath.

From the open loft with games, a telescope and a loveseat facing the mountain you can look down on a striking wagonwheel chandelier bearing different colored lanterns. Below is a barnwood-paneled great room with blue sectional sofas, a huge cobblestone fireplace and a dining-room table flanked by ladderback chairs.

Breakfast when we were there included orange juice, cantaloupe slices topped with blueberries and a strawberry sauce, walnut coffee cake, and sausage-cheese strudel or homemade granola. Other main courses might be cheese-filled crêpes with fresh fruit sauce, ham strata, pancakes and sausage quiche. The Robinsons serve cookies and lemonade on summer afternoons and homemade soup or chili during ski season.

Flowers and plants are decorative theme at The Enchanted Rose Inn.

In winter, they offer ski packages with Bristol Mountain and in summer they run bicycle tours.

Doubles, $65. No smoking.

The Maxfield Inn, 105 North Main St., Box 39, Naples 14512. (716) 374-2510.

Only six families have owned this pillared 1841 mansion in the center of Naples. The latest are Russell and Alice Cochran, retirees from the Rochester area who "wanted a big dining room for all our kids and grandchildren."

They bought it as their home, and inherited a recently renovated B&B vacated by local school teachers who had their hands full with three children under 6. The former innkeepers "said we'd love running a B&B, and we do," Alice advised. "The guests are the best part of it."

The Cochrans have seven air-conditioned guest rooms, three with private baths and four sharing two, one of the latter sporting a new jacuzzi. Rooms are outfitted with period pieces in pine, cherry or mahogany and have new wallpaper and carpeting or oriental rugs. A two-bedroom suite with a bathroom between is good for families.

Alice is so fascinated by the heritage of the inn she was writing a book about its original owner, Hiram Maxfield. He owned the area's first winery and had a 2,000-bottle cellar in the basement. He also ran the first bank in town, and its original door leads into the kitchen. The barn was part of the underground railroad.

The high-ceilinged front parlor and library, both light and airy, are full of the Cochrans' diverse collections of glass. Guests relax on the columned front porch or at an umbrella-covered table on the side lawn.

Breakfast, served on a circular porch or in the dining room, starts with fresh fruit — a bowl of blueberries and strawberries with whipped cream (red, white and blue) for the July Fourth holiday when we were there. Next came french toast with sausage. Scrambled eggs, hot breads and popovers are other favorites.

Doubles, $65. No smoking.

The Vagabond Inn, 3300 Sliter Road, Naples 14512. (716) 554-6271.

So you vant to be alone, as Greta Garbo used to say. Here's the place, high on a remote mountaintop in the hills northeast of Naples. Just you and your significant other and up to four more similarly inclined couples cosseted in a luxurious, contemporary house designed for romance. With your own jacuzzi and a TV/VCR with a 250-movie library, and perhaps a fireplace to warm the night air. And a swimming pool, secluded patios and exotic landscaping just outside.

Celeste Stanhope-Wiley started in 1987 with a three-bedroom ranch house in an unconventional location, "alone on a mountain" with a sharp 1,000-foot drop to the Italy Valley below.

Terrace with view at The Vagabond Inn.

Now she shares 7,000 square feet with guests on two floors. You enter a "great room" rich in natural woods with a seating area facing a stone fireplace at one end. At the other end is a dining-room table set for ten beside full-length windows onto a deck with a glorious view beyond. Although it's daytime, the room is dimly lit and little lights simulating candles flicker here and there.

The hostess shows you the well-equipped guest kitchen, employed by fully three-quarters of guests for dinner since the nearest civilization is ten miles away by round-about rural roads. Then she directs you to your room, perhaps the pine-paneled Lodge on the lower level, where the tulips handpainted on the headboard of the kingsize bed match the patterns on the pillows and bedspread. Two plush wing chairs flank the fireplace and a terrace awaits outside. Also in the room is a dining table for four – she had a lot of space to fill, Celeste explains. In the corner alcove beyond the bed is a whirlpool spa, right in the room, beside a bar, mini-fridge and microwave. Once ensconced in the Lodge, you may not be seen again until it's time to leave.

"Everybody needs to run away overnight," says Celeste. She knows. She relates that she was "thrown out of a convent in Greenwich," Conn., as a teenager and ran away from home in nearby Darien. She "went back to my roots" in the Caribbean, settling in Haiti and eventually turning up on her mountaintop. Vagabond, she calls it.

For those of a mind, the finest magazines vie with VCR movies for attention. A collection of recent Bon Appetit issues is in the Shannon (one of two bedrooms named for her grown daughters), newly blessed with a 27-inch TV set. National Geographic Travelers are in the Mahogany Room, where a stuffed gorilla peeks over the double four-poster bed. Architectural Digests grace the Bristol Suite, a grand main-floor space with a kingsize canopy bed, ironwood twig-style furniture on the screened porch, a private deck and an enormous bathroom containing a palm-bedecked hot tub for two, a fourteen-foot mirrored dressing area with twin vanities, and a separate shower and toilet area.

Coffee and tea are available around the clock, as much to satisfy Celeste's needs as those of her guests. She serves "a very full breakfast" between 8 and 11 a.m.; "your arteries start hardening as you sit down." Fresh orange juice and fruits precede such baked goods as homemade muffins and "piña colada sweets," served with winery jams.

Next comes the main course, perhaps crab and vegetable omelet or a 24-egg pie. By then it may be time for a nap.

Next time, Celeste may rent you her new garage suite called Heaven's Gate, into which she had just moved, with privacy screens onto the pool area, walk-in closets and a mirrored bathroom to end all bathrooms, complete with a customized jacuzzi good for all the aches that ail you.

Doubles, $80 to $140; suites, $140 to $175. No smoking.

Thendara Inn and Restaurant, 4356 East Lake Road, Canandaigua 14424. (716) 394-4868.

Although big bucks went into the restoration of this old restaurant in 1987, the inn seems to have been an afterthought. The location is fortuitous – on a rise on a bend in Canandaigua Lake, with water on two sides. But there are no balconies, no decks, no seats, no way to take advantage.

Five guest rooms with private baths on the second floor vary from cramped to one suite with a skylit jacuzzi. Seeking a lake view, we opted for a queen room with what turned out to be a four-poster, a TV and phone, an armoire and one hard dining-room chair for a seat. An air-conditioner blocked the view from one window; curtains that wouldn't pull back screened the other. We opened the window (letting flies in because there were no screens) and finally brought up a plastic lawn chair from the small cocktail terrace so one of us could be semi-comfortable. There was no common room except the bar and only a rickety park bench and a glider-swing on the lawn by the lake.

Between the flies buzzing around our heads and a loud, upsetting domestic dispute taking place in the next room in the middle of the night, this was not one of our more pleasant evenings at an inn. Our letter of complaint to the innkeepers was never acknowledged.

We did like the water view at dinner (see Dining Spots) and the next morning. We asked that our continental breakfast, which was supposed to be eaten in the room (how, we wondered, when there was only one chair and no table), be delivered outdoors. We ate alone on the aforementioned cocktail terrace, enjoying the lakefront over orange juice, strawberries, blueberry muffins and a choice of lox and bagel or sausage biscuit, both quite good.

Doubles, $90 to $125.

Dining Spots

Lincoln Hill Inn, 3365 East Lake Road, Canandaigua. (716) 394-8254.

Everybody's favorite restaurant hereabouts is Lincoln Hill, and with good reason. It has a grand setting on a hillside overlooking Canandaigua Lake within earshot of the outdoor Finger Lakes Performing Arts Center shell. It has tables inside and out. It has an extensive menu. And the food is generally good.

Cheryl and Bill Ward, who were teaching at Monroe Community College in Rochester, bought the 1804 brick homestead and converted it into a large restaurant, opening fortuitously in 1983 on the same day as the FLPAC shell. Inside are several small, cozy dining rooms with pastel linens, antique lace curtains and soft lighting. A lounge contains remarkable modern American primitive paintings of the lake and the area as it was in the latter part of the 19th century by Adelaide Cook Kent, who was influenced by Rufus Porter.

But it was the open front porch with its red oilcloth-covered tables, citronella candles and fresh field flowers to which we were attracted on a summer's evening. It, plus an enclosed side porch and a back patio called the Garden Room, seat 120 outdoors, half again more than the number inside. The scrapbook-size menu, written in calligraphy, is rather daunting. Regulars love it for its range, however. At dinner, you can order an appetizer and a salad or an open-face steak sandwich. Or you can order baked white-fish provençal, chicken and peppers with orzo or mushroom tournedos bordelaise from about two dozen entrées priced from $12.95 to $19.95.

Dinners come with salad, including an excellent one with greens, mandarin oranges, walnuts and a honey-poppyseed dressing, and a garden salad with dijon vinaigrette. We liked the tender calves liver, grilled with onions and bacon, and the prime rib, a thick slab with horseradish sauce. The ample plates, garnished with edible nasturtiums from the gardens out back, yielded potatoes or rice, garlic cloves and zucchini stuffed with vegetables and cheese. French chocolate decadence is one of the good desserts.

Dinner, Tuesday-Sunday 5 to 9 or 10. Closed Sundays in winter.

Thendara Inn & Restaurant, 4356 East Lake Road, Canandaigua. (716) 394-4868.

The 170 seats in three dining rooms offer great views of the lake, especially those in the enclosed wraparound porch decked out in white and mint green, subtly patterned Syracuse china, cut-glass candle holders and chairs with burgundy cushions.

Although known for its food, Thendara was sadly lacking the Monday night we dined. (Perhaps the executive chef, who had made a name at the luxury Lodge at Woodcliff in Pittsford, was off that night.) It took half an hour to get a glass of wine and an hour and a half for the entrées to arrive. By that time, we'd lost our appetite. The hazelnut chicken would have come second in a tasting with chicken McNuggets and the hunter's platter, one of the chef's specialties pairing sautéed pheasant and venison chasseur, was drowned in sauce. The sides of plain cauliflower and broccoli would have been more appropriate for winter than the middle of the summer harvest season. The rolls that helped stave off hunger pangs were quite good; the shared appetizer of almond-coconut shrimp and the salads not so. The glass of house chardonnay was generous but warm; we had to ask for ice cubes for that and the water. Neither of us could finish either our dinners or the bottle of Australian shiraz.

Prices range from $13.95 for stuffed chicken breast or rainbow trout with citrus beurre blanc to $22.95 for steak Thendara, grilled tenderloin and Maine lobster served with two sauces. Although we've heard complaints about the service, they seem to be in the minority. But from the obsequious maître d' who seemed to be taking care of everyone else and totally ignoring us to our laid-back (make that *very*) waitress, we felt the service was abysmal. Comments in the guest book ranged from "excellent" to "always a favorite." Were we on another planet?

Young singles and families tend to gravitate to the **Boathouse,** right on the water – a casual place serving drinks, sandwiches and light fare from 11 a.m. in season.

Dinner nightly, 5 to 9 or 9:30, Sunday 1 to 8. Closed Monday and Tuesday in off-season and January-March.

Casa de Pasta, 125 Bemis St., Canandaigua. (716) 394-3909.

People come from miles around for the pasta in this red brick townhouse at the edge of downtown, we were advised. And the restaurant, established in 1984, received the highest rating from a Rochester Times-Union reviewer.

Owner Bruce Warren's menu is surprisingly bland, however. The pastas ($6.25 to $9.95) include five kinds of spaghettini or ziti with meatballs or mushrooms and such, linguini with garlic and parmesan cheese, lasagna, tortellini alfredo and ricotta stuffed shells. The specials are really special, said the reviewer: pasta puttanesca, gnocchi gorgonzola and veal madeira with pasta the night we were there.

Porch with view of Canandaigua Lake is favored by diners at Lincoln Hill Inn.

Entrées run from $11.95 for whitefish marinara to $17.95 for steak pizzaiola. Scampi, veal parmesan, braciole and chicken cacciatore are menu fixtures. An Italian platter for two ($25.95) brings antipasto, garlic bread and a platter of lasagna, stuffed shells, meatballs and Italian sausage. Pizzas are available except on weekends.

Diners enter through a bar presided over by the convivial owner-host. Beyond are two intimate, noisy dining rooms with pine wainscoting and red and white oilcloths and curtains – a spirited place for regulars who relish homemade Italian cuisine.

Dinner nightly, 5 to 9:30 or 10.

The Peach House, Sonnenberg Gardens, 151 Charlotte St., Canandaigua. (716) 924-5420.

The greenhouse in which Mary Clark Thompson raised peaches and nectarines for her estate gardens is decked out with jaunty tables covered in peach and green. Hanging ferns and white molded chairs add to the summery look, marred only by bud vases containing – horrors, for a place with gardens as its reason for being – fake flowers.

The restaurant is operated by the owners of Thendara. Lunch is served buffet style ($8). The spread includes carved ham, chicken salad, red bliss potato salad, vinaigrette pasta salad, veggie cole slaw, rolls and assorted cakes. A baker's corner offers slices of apple-cranberry or lemon-poppyseed cake, almond-amaretto mousse and mocha swirl cheesecake, soft drinks and coffee. Box lunches ($4.80, with a choice of baked ham or chicken salad sandwich) are available to go.

Lunch daily, 11:30 to 3, mid-May to mid-October.

Mo-Jo's Tacos, 23 Coach St., Canandaigua. (716) 396-2160.

Billed as "Canandaigua's homemade Mexican restaurant," this growing (three-outlet) area chain opened in 1994 in large quarters formerly occupied by the Bristol Deli in the Coach Street Plaza at the edge of downtown.

A wall hanging of a bullfight and red leather booths make up the decor. Tacos and burritos are in the $1.95 to $5.50 range; the "kitchen sink" burrito has everything but.

Chili, nachos, Mexican pizza and quesadillas round out the fare, with a couple of "American" specials each day and sides like chips and salsa, guacamole and cornbread. Portions are generous – we saw an "extra-small" taco salad and it was huge. Start with beef ranchero soup or gazpacho. Finish with flan, sopapillas, fried ice cream, or, a new one on us. a chocolate taco. It's a taco dipped in chocolate with vanilla ice cream, chocolate sauce, whipped topping and chocolate sprinkles.

Open Tuesday-Thursday 11 to 7, Friday and Saturday 11 to 9. No credit cards.

Butch 25's Depot Restaurant, 1 West Main St., Shortsville. (716) 289-3600.

A restored railroad depot has become a favorite culinary destination for Canandaiguans, thanks to "station masters" Butch and Carol Venticinque, a local couple who named it for the anglicized version of their last name, which means 25 in Italian.

For seventeen years, Italian has been the specialty of the house, from $6.95 for spaghetti with sauce to $11.95 for pasta with broccoli and clam sauce. Veal or chicken parmigiana and chicken cacciatore are also available.

Lately, everyone has been talking up the grill side of the menu, which produces marvelous chops and steaks up to two inches thick, priced from $13.50 for prime rib to $19.95 for broiled lamb chops. A 30-ounce New York strip steak for $28.95, billed for those with a hearty appetite, is more than enough for two. Dinner choices also include broiled haddock, scallops, king crab and lobster. All dinners come with salad and choice of potato or pasta.

Appetizers range from zuppa di clams to shrimp cocktail and escargots. Among desserts are New York cheesecake, spumoni and crème de menthe parfait.

Lunch, Tuesday-Friday 11:30 to 2:30; dinner, Tuesday-Sunday, 4 to 11.

The Holloway House, Routes 5 & 20, East Bloomfield. (716) 657-7120.

As it has for years, the green neon sign still glows outside this historic tavern and restaurant dating to 1808 and facing the green in a charming hilltop town. Owners Fred and Doreen Wayne haven't changed the menu much since it bored us to tears in the 1950s. But folks love it, particularly the oldtimers who dress up for lunch and make it their dinner.

There's a ramble of Colonial rooms with ladderback chairs at bare wood tables and frilly sheer curtains on the windows in this landmark on the National Register of Historic Places. The dinner menu runs from $11.45 for roast turkey (our informant said she'd had the best turkey dinner ever the week before) to $16.45 for broiled filet mignon. Complete dinners (add $2.50) start with tomato juice, soup du jour or fruit shrub. Specialties include half a fried chicken with a biscuit, broiled sea scallops with tartar sauce, baked stuffed flounder, seafood newburg en casserole and, on Saturdays, prime rib – ladies' cut or regular cut. They come with au gratin or mashed potatoes, two vegetables that are passed, tossed or fruit salad with French, Russian, Italian or blue cheese dressings, Sally Lunn bread and homemade orange rolls, and desserts like pies, angel food cake, strawberry shortcake and hot fudge sundae.

A Friday night summer buffet packs the crowds in at $15.50 for adults, $8.50 for children, with more than 25 items to choose from. The lunch menu ranges from $5.95 for julienne salad to $9.45 for broiled tenderloin steak. Chicken fricassee, turkey à la king and chicken livers and bacon are featured. Who says the '50s are out of style?

Lunch, Tuesday-Saturday 11:30 to 2; dinner, 5:30 to 9, Sunday noon to 7. Closed December-March.

Benny's, 4233 Route 21 South, Cheshire. (716) 394-9306.

All the tables on the blacktop pavement in front of Benny's and on the side lawn in front of their house next door hint of the informality inside. Tammy and Benny Benziger (she the hostess and he the chef) have won a devoted following for home-cooked food, served inside or out at the little roadhouse restaurant and ice cream parlor they took over in 1993.

All kinds of sandwiches are offered, from $1.75 for grilled cheese to $4.25 for chicken quesadilla. A hot roast beef sandwich with mashed potatoes and gravy goes for a mere $3.75. The all-day menu, already rather prodigious for so small a place, broadens after 4 o'clock, when dinners become available. The menu runs from $4.95 for ham steak to $10.95 for peppercorn steak with a brandy dijon sauce, shrimp scampi and prime rib (Saturday only). Creamed cod is the Friday special. Tammy makes the desserts, perhaps rhubarb upside-down cake, apple crisp or chocolate-chip pie. Wine and beer are available, and the homemade breads, dressings and desserts may be purchased.

Ice cream cones, sodas, floats, milk shakes and sundaes are priced from the past. The most expensive is a banana split, $2.85.

Open daily, 11 to 8 or 9, Memorial Day to Labor Day. Closed Monday and Tuesday rest of year.

Oscars Lakeview Restaurant, 7131 Route 21, South Bristol. (716) 374-6030.

Rochester restaurateur Bill Petos moved his Oscars at Canandaigua Lake venture in 1993 from Bristol Harbor into the former Lakeview Restaurant in the Woodville section of South Bristol. Movie oscars are the theme (an abundance of framed movie posters and advertisements adorn the walls of the dining room and lounge), and a screened, canopied deck overlooks the lake. The result, if not exactly the New York-style restaurant and bar it's advertised as, is the next best thing: an appealing, casual place – the kind that's sadly lacking at the northern end of the lake.

Oscars is ensconced at the lake's quiet southern end beneath sharply rising hillsides; only an occasional boat passes, as opposed to the busier northern end. We enjoyed a light beer and a glass of Heron Hill white wine as we lunched on the deck on a special of marinated flank steak on toast with french fries and a good but messy-to-eat garden pita sandwich ("pick a pita that you're Fonda," the menu advises), both $5.25. The lime meringue pie contained more meringue than lime.

The all-day menu expands at night, when entrées range from $10.95 for garlic chicken and pasta to $16.95 for filet mignon with bordelaise sauce. Grilled swordfish, shrimp sebastian and blackened tenderloin served on a bed of spinach are other possibilities. All kinds of snack foods are billed as sneak previews, short subjects and supporting roles. Frozen drinks and liqueured coffees are the beverages of choice.

Open daily, 11:30 to 10 or 11; Sunday brunch, 11 to 2:30.

Bob's and Ruth's, Route 21 at Route 245, Naples. (716) 374-5122.

A legend in the area, this started in 1950 as a diner and takeout stand, made its name with grape pie, and grew like topsy. The diner and takeout counter remain in front, where you can get a basic American sandwich (starting at $1.95 for egg salad) or a meal of roast chicken or prime rib, $5.70 to $12.95. Eat at the counter or one of the booths or outside at a picnic table in the adjacent Old Town Square Park.

In the rear and reached by a separate entrance is the Vineyard Lounge on one side and on the other, the **Vineyard Room** with two walls of windows looking onto a sea of grapevines. Decor is solid, green and brown, to match a solid menu. Most diners opt for the complete dinner, which includes a locally famous salad bar (homemade preserves, pickled fruits and vegetables, garden vegetables and more). The offerings range from $8.95 for turkey dinner to $18.95 for prime rib, which the menu touts as "the traditional celebrant dinner of this area." Other possibilities include broiled rainbow trout, shrimp scampi, baby back ribs ("a Canadian treat"), broiled ham steak with pineapple and fruited sherry sauce, roast duckling flambéed tableside, veal parmigiana and filet mignon. Grape pie, famous all over the state, is the obligatory dessert in season.

Bob's & Ruth's, open daily from 6 a.m.; The Vineyard, lunch 11:30 to 2:30, lounge to 4:30; dinner from 5, Sunday from noon.

The Redwood, Routes 21 and 53, Naples. (716) 374-6360.

Also starting as a refreshment stand, this oldtimer has been enlarged seven times since 1955 with bar and cocktail lounge and banquet rooms to cater to bus tours. Its heart remains the coffee shop and pub room. Owners Nick and Helen Gerakos offer an extensive menu that's a bit more up to date than many (Buffalo-style chicken wings instead of juice as an appetizer) and broiled chicken for the calorie and cholesterol conscious.

You'll still find the ubiquitous spaghetti and meatballs, lasagna, veal parmigiana, broiled scallops with cheese sauce, open-face steak sandwich, ham steak, golden fried chicken and roast beef, nicely priced in the $10 range. A few items like broiled shrimp, strip steak and beef and reef are priced in the high teens.

Coffee shop, 6 a.m. to 8:30 p.m.; lunch, 11:30 to 1:30; dinner, 4:30 to 8:30 or 9, Sunday noon to 8. Closed Monday and January-March.

Mary Mac's Fish Shanty, 400 Lake Shore Drive, Canandaigua. (716) 394-1171.

This rustic place beside the road is, well, a seafood shanty – the kind the locals think would be at home in New England or the Jersey shore. We don't agree, perhaps because there's no water view and the surroundings are, to say the least, tacky.

But leave preconceived notions aside and enter the tarpaulin-covered area with picnic tables out front, a side alleyway of sorts with a mishmash of tables or a couple of primitive interior rooms. We know folks who come here for the peel-and-eat shrimp dinner for two – $25 buys a plate full of steamed shrimp in the shell with drawn butter, garlic bread, tossed salad and a pitcher of beer or a half carafe of house wine.

The aroma of fried fish nearly overpowered as we studied a rather extensive menu that also yields seafood baked or broiled. Try the Mac's App, a basket full of fried vegetables (from broccoli spears to zucchini), $6.25 for two or more. You'll find cajun shrimp, lake smelt, frogs legs, broiled haddock, surf and turf, crab cakes, even baked lasagna and eggplant parmesan, at prices all over the lot from $5.95 to $16.95.

Captain Yogi, who founded the shanty in 1975 and looked as if he belonged in a Cape Cod fishing village, moved on in 1988, as had Mary and the dog, Mac. The crew carries on.

Open daily from 11:30 in summer, Thursday-Saturday in winter.

Captain Yogi's, 4520 East Lake Road, Canandaigua. (716) 394-1166.

Captain Yogi, it seems, resurfaced down the lake at Crystal Beach. Same format, same style, same character ("dress code: bathing suit to tuxedo, or come as you are"). Owner Dick Howard promotes his as "the inn spot" serving "true New England-style seafood."

The menu is much the same as at Mary Mac's (down to the same "21 shrimp in a basket," $6.25 at both places), with the addition here of submarine sandwiches, Buffalo wings and Boston fries. Dinner prices run from $5.25 for a fish sandwich to $19.95 for twin lobster tails. Here the menu seems to have less seafood and more variation than at the shanty. Prime rib is the specialty on Saturday night.

Open daily from 11 a.m. in summer; Thursday-Saturday in winter. No credit cards.

Hills slope down to Canandaigua Lake, viewed here from the southern end.

Diversions

Finger Lakes Performing Arts Center, Lincoln Hill Road, Canandaigua, 394-7190. Since 1983, the outdoor shell on the Finger Lakes Community College campus has drawn thousands for summertime concerts by the Rochester Philharmonic Orchestra and visiting entertainers. The RPO presents Saturday evening concerts, seating 2,600 in the shell and another 10,000 on the lawn, although financial shortfalls curtailed the orchestra season from the normal twelve to four concerts in 1994. Guest entertainers over the years have ranged from Huey Lewis, Sting and Judy Collins to Steve Lawrence and Eydie Gorme, and Peter, Paul and Mary.

Sonnenberg Gardens and Mansion, 151 Charlotte St., Canandaigua, 394-4922. What a treasure is this – and so unexpected in little old Canandaigua. Restored in 1973 after 40 years of neglect, the Victorian gardens are recognized by the Smithsonian as some of the most magnificent ever created in America. The 50-acre garden estate around their 40-room summer home was planned at the turn of the century by Mary Clark Thompson, a Canandaigua native who married Frederick F. Thompson, a New Yorker whose family started Chase Manhattan and Citibank. Widowed at 67, she traveled the world to create nine formal gardens, an arboretum, a greenhouse complex and more as a memorial to her husband (who, we were told, rather preferred his fishing cottage down Canandaigua Lake to Sonnenberg, German for "Sunny Hill"). Some 75,000 visitors a year admire the Japanese hill garden and tea house, the vast Italian garden with four sunken fleur de lis parterres and the Rose Garden launched with 4,000 bushes from the former Jackson and Perkins Rose Gardens in nearby Newark. Other attractions are Mrs. Thompson's favorite Blue & White Garden, a Pansy Garden in which even the bird bath is shaped like a pansy, and a rock garden entered through a canyon of puddingstone and including 5,500 feet of streams, waterfalls and pools fed by geysers and springs. In the middle of one particularly dry summer, we found the flowers a bit lackluster (not surprising, since a staff of only seven plus volunteers maintain what 75 fulltime gardeners did for their founder). Still we marveled at the accompaniments: belvederes, statues, gazebos, arbors, a temple of Diana, a sitting Buddha, a fountain with a statue of Hercules and even a Roman bath. The vast South Lawn with its rare specimen trees is remarkable: Mrs. Thompson liked to give house parties and asked guests to bring trees to plant, each guest trying to outdo the other. A walking map guides visitors, but more informative are the guided tours of up to two hours in length, offered daily at 10 and 2. The mansion, a testament to the extravagances of the Gilded Age, has its own delights, among them the Lavender and Old Lace gift shop. Sonnenberg also has launched a summer lawn concert series, five Sunday concerts at 6 p.m., and a chamber music series. The new Festival of Lights, in which the mansion is decorated and the gardens are gloriously illuminated with lights and themed figures, extends the season from Thanksgiving to New Year's. Gardens open daily, 9:30 to 5:30, mid-May to mid-October; also nightly in holiday season, 4:30 to 9:30. Adults, $6.

Canandaigua Wine Company Tasting Room, Sonnenberg Gardens. Striking stained glass embellishes the winery tasting room and sales area at the entrance to Sonnenberg Gardens. The largest of the Finger Lakes wineries is located in a plant and showcase headquarters on the western edge of town. This is simply a tasting and sales room, which gets mighty crowded when a bus tour stops by. Open daily, noon to 4, mid-May to mid-October. Free.

Granger Homestead and Carriage Museum, 295 North Main St., Canandaigua, 394-1472. Gideon Granger, who was postmaster general for Thomas Jefferson, moved here in 1813 and resolved to build a homestead that would be "unrivaled in all the nation." This pale yellow Federal mansion is the result and its period rooms with original furnishings are on display. More than 50 horse-drawn vehicles, from coaches and sleighs to an undertaker's hearse, are shown in the Carriage Museum. Open Tuesday-Saturday 1 to 5, May-October; also Sunday 1 to 5, June-August. Adults, $3.

Boat Tours. Canandaigua is known as a summer resort and the best way to experience it is by boat. Town native Gray Hoffman gives enlightening narrated tours five times daily in summer under the auspices of **Captain Gray's Narrated Tour,** from the dock at the Sheraton Inn; adults, $7. He gives the history of the lake and tells who lives in which cottage on an hour-long tour that even natives find informative. The **Canandaigua Lady,** 169 Lake Shore Drive, the only authentic replica of a paddlewheeler in the Finger Lakes, offers lunch, dinner and sightseeing tours daily in summer, $12 to $35.

Shopping. A fun shop to explore in Canandaigua is **Cat's in the Kitchen** at 367 West Ave. Here Laurel Wemett has collected, from tag sales and auctions, all the things our mothers and grandmothers used in the kitchen. She specializes in the Depression era to the 1960s, and it's fun to check the old canisters, cookie jars, china, pots and pans and the corner full of old cookbooks. New items and a few feline gifts, from collectible cat "purrtraits" to figurines, are mixed in. A big stuffed pig wearing sunglasses sits outside on a wicker chair at **Renaissance – the Goodie II Shoppe** at 56 South Main St. Here are all the socially correct gifts, from jewelry to porcelain dolls, bath things, Port Merion china and lovely Christmas ornaments. Teddy bears, cookbooks (we picked up Linda McCarthy's for a vegetarian son) and nifty paper plates and napkins abound. North of town at 1901 Route 332 is **The Five Seasons,** two floors of a log building housing a gift shop to end all gift shops. Owner Sue Ellsworth is known for her handpainted crockery.

Farther afield is **Cheshire,** billed as "a little bit of New England awaiting discovery." **The Cheshire Union,** Route 21, is a renovated schoolhouse containing a gift shop, antiques center, the Schoolhouse Deli and the Company Store. Thousands turn out for its annual folk fair and antique show. "Everything Grape and More" is the theme of **Arbor Hill Grapery,** a delightful place on Route 64 in Bristol Springs. John and Katie Brahm, he a former Widmer's Wine Cellars executive, are proof that wines aren't the only good use for grapes. They sell grape-filled cookies, hot grape sundaes, fillings for grape pies, wine-motif wallpaper, vinegars, gewürztraminer wine jelly and their Arbor Hill Winery wines, eleven varieties from a Niagara for $3.95 to a good little chardonnay for $8.95.

Tiny Naples is the home of some interesting shops around **Old Town Square.** We liked the toys and books at the century-old schoolhouse where **Imagine That** has a fine selection, and picked up a lovely edition of *The Wind in the Willows* for a gift. The new Village Corner complex is the home of **Classics,** an exceptional gift store. Owner Anne Schneider stocks its several rooms with an assortment of sophisticated wares, from linens, pottery and jewelry to cookbooks, candles and Christmas ornaments. Naples offers a Saturday afternoon summer concert series at the Old Town Square park. The year's highlight is the annual **Naples Grape Festival** in late September with arts, crafts, entertainment, food and, of course, those sugary-sweet grape pies.

Widmer's Wine Cellars, 1 Lake Niagara Lane, Naples, 374-6311. Swiss immigrant John Jacob Widmer, whose home is still on view, launched this hillside winery in 1888. We remember it fondly from its days under the aegis of the R.T. French Co. Lately sold to Canandaigua Wine Co., Widmer's is now part of the nation's third largest wine-producing firm. Its winery tour, one of the best in the East, starts with a twelve-minute video shown through the end of a wine barrel. The half-hour guided tour takes you through ancient subterranean passageways where wine is aged in oak barrels, past the famous rooftop sherry barrels and into the fascinating bottling and labeling room. The publicity notes "there are a number of stairs to traverse." The visitor may choose instead to relax in the air-conditioned Widmer's Wine/Food Center for an extensive wine-tasting and sales of wines, juices, jellies and Finger Lakes items. In the adjacent **Manischewitz** cellars, which moved in 1986 from Brooklyn, two rabbis are employed fulltime to oversee the making of kosher wines. Tours are offered Monday-Thursday except Jewish holidays. Widmer's is open Monday-Saturday 10 to 4:30, Sunday 11:30 to 4:30; November-May, daily 1 to 4.

Extra-Special

The Wizard of Clay Pottery, 7851 Route 20A, Bristol. (716) 229-2980.

Out in the middle of nowhere in the Bristol Hills are seven geodesic domes that are home to ex-Rochester teacher Jim Kozlowski's growing pottery empire. Visitors come from across the world – they mark their hometowns with pins on a map in his work-

shop – to see "the workshop where the wizard works wonders." The Wednesday we visited was his afternoon for golf, according to an assistant who called herself a wizette. So we had to be satisfied reading lists of the 29 steps to making a Bristoleaf pot and the twenty most often asked questions and their answers, both garnished with a sense of humor. Jim makes each piece individually, but a staff helps with the decoration. His trademark Bristoleaf pottery is decorated with delicate imprints from all kinds of leaves picked in the surrounding hills. He's most proud of his signed and numbered limited editions, particularly those decorated with leaves handpainted in gold and selling for up to $225 a bowl. Two domes house more than 1,000 pottery lamps with shades; another, bakeware and planters; still another, a zoo craft gallery of arts and crafts reflecting the animal kingdom. There are even a gazebo and a nature trail. It sounds hokey, but isn't really. In 1994, the Wizard opened a store on Newbury Street in Boston. Open daily, 9 to 5.

Index

Also by Wood Pond Press

Inn Spots & Special Places in New England. The first in the series, this book by Nancy and Richard Woodworth tells you where to go, stay, eat and enjoy in New England's choicest areas. Focusing on 32 special places, it details the best inns and B&Bs, restaurants, sights to see and things to do. First published in 1986; fully updated fourth edition in 1995. 488 pages of timely ideas. $16.95.

Getaways for Gourmets in the Northeast. The first book by Nancy Webster Woodworth and Richard Woodworth appeals to the gourmet in all of us. It guides you to the best dining, lodging, specialty food shops and culinary attractions in 22 areas from the Brandywine Valley to Montreal, Cape May to Bar Harbor, the Finger Lakes to Monadnock, the Hudson Valley to Nantucket. First published in 1984; fully revised fourth edition in 1994. 538 pages to read and savor. $16.95.

Waterside Escapes in the Northeast. The latest book by Betsy Wittemann and Nancy Woodworth relates the best lodging, dining, attractions and activities in 35 great waterside vacation spots from Chesapeake Bay to Cape Breton Island, from the Thousand Islands to Martha's Vineyard. Everything you need to know for a day trip, a weekend or a week near the water is told the way you want to know it. Published in 1987; fully revised and expanded in 1996. 474 pages to discover and enjoy. $15.95.

Weekending in New England. The best-selling travel guide by Betsy Wittemann and Nancy Webster details everything you need to know about 24 of New England's most interesting vacation spots: more than 1,000 things to do, sights to see and places to stay, eat and shop year-round. First published in 1980; fully revised and expanded fourth edition in 1993. 394 pages of facts and fun. $12.95.

The Best of Daytripping & Dining. Another book by Betsy Wittemann and Nancy Webster, this is a companion to their original Southern New England and all-New England editions. It pairs 25 featured daytrips with 25 choice restaurants, among 200 other suggestions of sites to visit and places to eat, in Southern New England and nearby New York. Published in 1985; revised third edition in 1989. 210 pages of good ideas. $9.95.

The Restaurants of New England. This book by Nancy and Richard Woodworth is the most comprehensive guide to restaurants throughout New England. The authors detail menu offerings, atmosphere, hours and prices for more than 1,000 restaurants in the same informative style that makes their other books so credible. First published in 1990; revised second edition in 1994. 490 pages of detailed information. $14.95.

The Originals in Their Fields

These books may be ordered from your local bookstore or direct from the publisher, pre-paid, plus $2 shipping for each book. Connecticut residents add sales tax.

Wood Pond Press
365 Ridgewood Road
West Hartford, Conn. 06107
(860) 521-0389